CATEGORIAL GRAMMARS
AND NATURAL LANGUAGE STRUCTURES

STUDIES IN LINGUISTICS AND PHILOSOPHY

formerly *Synthese Language Library*

VOLUME 32

CATEGORIAL GRAMMARS
AND
NATURAL LANGUAGE
STRUCTURES

Edited by

RICHARD T. OEHRLE

Dept. of Linguistics, University of Arizona

EMMON BACH

Dept. of Linguistics, University of Massachusetts at Amherst

and

DEIRDRE WHEELER

English Dept., University of New Hampshire

D. REIDEL PUBLISHING COMPANY

A MEMBER OF THE KLUWER ACADEMIC PUBLISHERS GROUP

DORDRECHT / BOSTON / LANCASTER / TOKYO

Library of Congress Cataloging-in-Publication Data

Categorial grammars and natural language structures.

  (Studies in linguistics and philosophy ; v. 32)
  Bibliography: p.
  Includes indexes.
  1. Categorial grammar. I. Oehrle, Richard T.
II. Bach. Emmon W., 1929-   . III. Wheeler, Deirdre.
IV. Series.
P161.C39 1988   415   88-3052

ISBN 1—55608—030—1

Published by D. Reidel Publishing Company,
P.O. Box 17, 3300 AA Dordrecht, Holland.

Sold and distributed in the U.S.A. and Canada
by Kluwer Academic Publishers,
101 Philip Drive, Norwell, MA 02061, U.S.A.

In all other countries, sold and distributed
by Kluwer Academic Publishers Group,
P.O. Box 322, 3300 AH Dordrecht, Holland.

TABLE OF CONTENTS

EDITORIAL PREFACE

For the most part, the papers collected in this volume stem from presentations given at a conference held in Tucson over the weekend of May 31 through June 2, 1985. We wish to record our gratitude to the participants in that conference, as well as to the National Science Foundation (Grant No. BNS-8418916) and the University of Arizona SBS Research Institute for their financial support. The advice we received from Susan Steele on organizational matters proved invaluable and had many felicitous consequences for the success of the conference. We also would like to thank the staff of the Departments of Linguistics of the University of Arizona and the University of Massachusetts at Amherst for their help, as well as a number of individuals, including Lin Hall, Kathy Todd, and Jiazhen Hu, Sandra Fulmer, Maria Sandoval, Natsuko Tsujimura, Stuart Davis, Mark Lewis, Robin Schafer, Shi Zhang, Olivia Oehrle-Steele, and Paul Saka. Finally, we would like to express our gratitude to Martin Scrivener, our editor, for his patience and his encouragement.

INTRODUCTION

The term 'categorial grammar' was introduced by Bar-Hillel (1964, page 99) as a handy way of grouping together some of his own earlier work (1953) and the work of the Polish logicians and philosophers Leśniewski (1929) and Ajdukiewicz (1935), in contrast to approaches to linguistic analysis based on phrase structure grammars. The most accessible of these earlier works was the paper of Ajdukiewicz, who, under the influence of Husserl's *Bedeutungskategorien* and the type theory that Russell had introduced to fend off foundational problems in set theory, proposed a mode of grammatical analysis in which every element of the vocabulary of a language belongs to one or more categories, and each category is either basic or defined in terms of simpler categories in a way which fixes the combinatorial properties of complex categories.

As an example, consider the language described below:

Basic Categories: s

Recursive Definition of the Full Set of Categories: The set CAT is the smallest set such that (1) if A is a basic category, then A belongs to CAT, and (2) if A and B belong to CAT, then A/B belongs to CAT.

Basic expressions ('$B(A)$' denotes the set of basic expressions of category A):

$$B(s) = \{p_i \mid i \in \mathbb{N}\}$$
$$B(s/s) = \{\sim\}$$
$$B((s/s)/s) = \{\wedge\}$$

Simultaneous recursive definition of the full set of expressions ('$P(A)$' denotes the full set of expressions of category A): if A is a category and x is a member of $B(A)$, then x is a member of $P(A)$; if x is a member of $P(A)$ and y is a member of $P(C/A)$, for some category C, then yx is a member of $P(C)$.

1

Richard T. Oehrle et al. (eds.), Categorial Grammars and Natural Language Structures, 1—16.
© *1988 by D. Reidel Publishing Company.*

While the language defined by these definitions is rich enough to develop a formulation of the propositional calculus, and makes use of the 'Polish' notation introduced by Łukasiewicz, what is most important from a grammatical standpoint is that expressions belonging to complex categories of the form A/C, where A and C are categories that are either simple or derived, may be identified with functions which map expressions of category C into the set of expressions of category A. In fact, it is the systematic use of functions to characterize the compositional properties of grammatical expressions which is most symptomatic of the modern versions of 'categorial grammars' whose investigation is the purpose of this volume. And in this respect, categorial grammars hark back directly to ideas first introduced by Frege in his *Begriffsschrift* (cf. especially §9, pp. 21—23 of the translation in van Heijenoort, 1971).

                                    I

The role that functions play in categorial grammars confers on them a number of properties that make them a focus of interest to linguists, philosophers, logicians, and mathematicians. One way to see this is to consider some of the ways of extending the simple grammar given above. First of all, while it is possible to construct categorial grammars which are purely syntactical systems, it is extremely useful to consider functions and arguments which have non-syntactic, as well as syntactic, properties. The crucial aspect of the enormous impact of Montague's work, for example, is perhaps the deep relation between syntactic properties and semantic properties in the systems he constructed. Other recent work by Bach, Schmerling, and Wheeler has emphasized the applicability of the basic perspective of categorial grammar to the analysis of phonological properties and the phonological composition of expressions. Extended in this way, then, categorial grammars offer a way of studying the composition of grammatical expressions across a variety of phenomenally-accessible domains.

    Second, it is possible to have a richer inventory of basic types. While the grammar above has only one basic type, the system discussed by Ajdukiewicz consists of two types, Bar-Hillel's formulation of bidirectional category systems allows any finite number of basic categories, Lewis (1972) suggests a system with three basic categories (corresponding to sentence, name, and common noun), and the intensional logic of Montague's PTQ (Paper 8 in Thomason, 1974a) is based on the three types *s*, *e*, and *t*.

A third way in which categorial grammars can be enriched is to allow the composition of expressions in ways not directly definable in terms of concatenation. This possibility is explicitly recognized in the writings of Curry (1961) ("A functor is *any* kind of linguistic device which operates on one or more phrases (the argument(s)) to form another phrase" [1961, p. 62]). Lewis (1972), following a suggestion of Lyons (1966) (though with possibly different motives), proposes a categorially-based transformational grammar — that is, a transformational grammar whose base component is a categorial grammar rather than a phrase structure grammar. The syntactic rules in Montague's fragments make it abundantly clear that he felt under no compulsion to restrict syntactic operations to concatenative ones — in fact, he apparently felt no need at all to explicate the notion of possible syntactic operation. One goal of more recent work, typified by an important series of papers by Bach (1979, 1981, 1984), has been to study the properties of categorial systems with basic operations which are not all characterizable in terms of the concatenation of their operands.

Since categorial grammars are based on the algebraic notions *function* and *argument*, there is another way in which extended categorial grammars arise: namely, by exploiting certain natural relations among functions and their arguments. The exploration of these ideas goes back at least to the discovery of the basic principles of combinatory logic by Schönfinkel and Curry in the 1920s. But the first grammatical system in which they play a fundamental role is the associative syntactic calculus of Lambek (1958: cf. also 1961). This system allows operations corresponding to functional composition, type-lifting, and a variety of other rules of type-changing. Rules of functional composition and higher-order types for conjoined terms (as well as for expressions corresponding to quantifiers) can be found in Geach (1972), and a higher order type for all NP's is one of the most characteristic traits of Montague's PTQ. Levin (1976, 1982) also seeks to enrich simple categorial grammars of the type found in the work of Ajdukiewicz and Bar-Hillel with combinatorial operations not restricted to a single type, but raises the problem of which of the various possible operations are desirable in different contexts.

The mathematical rationale of these relations is unlikely to be familiar to those with no background in modern logic or modern algebra. But it is easy to grasp and important in many of the papers which follow. In the next section, we provide enough of an informal exposition of the nature of functions to justify the equivalences among functions appealed to above, such as functional composition and type-lifting. In the following sections, we show how these ideas are relevant to the papers contained in this volume, and how the research reported here bears on current issues in linguistic theory.

II

The terms *function* and *argument* have been used for a long time in linguistics, with various looser and tighter senses. In mathematics and logic, they have an even longer history and in general a much more precise sense. As the above discussion makes clear, categorial grammar can be seen as the result of taking the mathematical notions seriously in the analysis of language structures.

In mathematical contexts, there are a variety of ways in which the notion of a function has been explicated (cf. MacLane, 1986, pp. 126—127). Two of these stand out. In one, a function is thought of as a procedure, operation, or computer program, with a well-defined domain (or ordered set of n domains) of possible arguments, which yields a unique result when it is given an argument (or n arguments) in the domain(s). In the other, a function is thought of more statically as simply a relation between sets (more generally, n sets) such that given any argument (or sequence of arguments) in the first $(n - 1)$ set(s), there is a unique member of the second (or nth) set in the relation. It is necessary to distinguish between *total* functions, where every element in the domain(s) yields a result when the function is applied to it, and *partial* functions, where this is not the case. Easy examples from arithmetic are the functions Square (total) and Divide, a two-argument function, which is a partial function when its domain is the set of all rational numbers, since such things as 'Divide 3 by 0' are illicit. In the latter case, we say that the result is 'undefined'. A partial function from A to a set B can always be extended to a total function from A to $B+$, where $B+$ is gotten from B by adding some new element ('zilch', say) to B and letting that be the element to which the members of A for which the function is undefined correspond. (A familiar kind of example here is the extension of a partial truth function for formulas in a two-valued logic to a total function from the formulas to a set $\{0, 1, \text{zilch}\}$.)

For a long time in mathematics, the concept of a function was used but had no nice representation. This was remedied by Church in the 1930s with the introduction of the lambda operator to create names for functions. Since this notation is fundamental to understanding many of the papers here, let us review it briefly. For a function from a *domain A* to a *range* (or *codomain*) *B*, we write

$\lambda x[P]$, where x ranges over elements in A and P denotes some element in B.

This expression, relative to some assignment g of values to variables, denotes that function f such that for any element a in A, $f(a)$ is the denotation of P in B relative to an assignment g' which is exactly like g, except (possibly) that $g'(x) = a$. The reason for this complicated clause is that P may contain free variables other than x. Notice, by the way, that P may lack free occurrences of x, in which case the lambda expression will be a constant function yielding the denotation of P no matter what argument we feed it.

Students of Montague grammar will be well acquainted with this definition. This notation is probably most often used for giving names to sets by writing the name of a characteristic function from some set (or Cartesian product of several sets), that is, for so-called 'set abstraction'. (A characteristic function is a function into the set of truth values.) However, the lambda notation is completely general: the co-domain itself may be, for example, a set of functions. Easy examples are the arithmetical functions mentioned above, which we may write thus:

$$\text{Square} = \lambda x[x, x]$$
$$\text{Divide} = \lambda x[\lambda y[y/x]]$$

A number of the papers in this volume make use of several results about functions. We will briefly review these ideas here. (In the discussion below, we use the exponential notation 'X^Y' to stand for the set of all functions with domain Y and co-domain X.)

(1) *Currying*: An early result by Schönfinkel (1924) and, independently, by Curry, showed that it is always possible to take an n-ary function and break it down into a series of a 1-ary functions. We have already used this idea in the definition of Divide just given, that is, it is given not as a two-place function but rather as a one-place function which will yield for each argument a another function which we get by setting $x = a$ (thus, Divide (2) is $\lambda y[y/2]$, which applied to 5 yields

5/2). Conversely, any complex function of the curried sort can be 'decurried'. The algebraic basis of this result is the fact that there is an isomorphism between the two function sets:

$$S^{YXZ} \cong (S^Y)^Z$$

given by associating a function f in the first set with a function F in the second just in case $f(y, z) = [F(z)](y)$. Algebraically, then, while f and F are distinguishable, it is both convenient and possible in most contexts to identify them. (The same argument extends easily to n-ary functions with $n > 2$ — take the set Y above to be an $n - 1$ fold Cartesian product.) The linguistic consequence of this result is that theories based on the theory of functions can make use either of many-place or one-place functions (analogous to ideas about 'flat' versus 'hierarchical' structures in phrase-structure grammars).

(2) *Function composition*: Suppose we have a function f from A to B and a function g from B to C. Then there always exists a function h from A to C, where

$$h = \lambda x[g(f(x))], \text{ with } h \text{ usually written as } g \circ f$$

(Strictly, this is true only for total functions: in the case of partial functions, if we want the composite to be a total function, we have to restrict ourselves to cases where the value of f on an argument is defined and within the subdomain of B for which g is also defined.)

(3) *Type-lifting*: Suppose we have an element a in the domain of a function f. Then we can always identify a with a higher-order function g whose domain contains f in such a way that the following equality holds:

$$f(a) = g(f)$$

If a is a member of some set A and f belongs to the function set C^A, this identity characterizes an injection (one-to-one map) from A to the function set

$$C^{(C^A)}$$

Thus, while a and g are distinguishable, it is often convenient to identify them. A well-known example is Montague's treatment of noun-phrases as functions from properties to truth-values (leading to the very fruitful investigations in recent years of generalized quantifiers in natural language).

(4) *Interchange*: Suppose we have a function in the function set

$$(C^B)^A$$

This function can be identified in a natural way with a function in the function set

$$(C^A)^B$$

The requisite correspondence is easily expressed in the lambda notation:

$$\lambda x[\lambda y[f(x, y)]] \rightarrow \lambda y[\lambda x[f(x, y)]]$$

And it is easy to see that this mapping characterizes an isomorphism between the two function sets. As in the cases discussed earlier, this mapping allows us to identify two distinct functions in a way which often proves convenient. Related to this fact in semantically-interpreted directional categorial grammars is the natural identification of a functor f of type $(C/B)/A$, interpreted as f', with that functor g of type $(C/A)/B$, interpreted as g' such that for all arguments a in A and b in B, interpreted as a' and b', respectively, $[f'(a')](b') = [g'(b')](a')$. In this case, however, if f and g share a common phenogrammatical shape — say V —, under the standard interpretation of directional categories, we have two distinct forms — Vab and Vba — associated with a single interpretation. Equivalences of this type which result in the permutation of arguments have obvious syntactic application.

On the other hand, here is a straightforward example from semantics: Montague defines a *proposition* as a function from indices (possible worlds cross times) to truth-values, and a *property* as a function from indices to sets, or rather characteristic functions of sets (see above). So if we let s, e, t be the types for indices, individuals, and truth-values, respectively, we have the types for propositions as $\langle s, t \rangle$, and for properties as $\langle s, \langle e, t \rangle \rangle$. Now given Interchange, we can just as well let properties be functions from individuals to propositions, that is, of type $\langle e, \langle s, t \rangle \rangle$, which will be completely equivalent. This alternative characterization is found in Chierchia (1984), as well as in earlier work by Cresswell (1972) and von Stechow (1974).

III

Even a relatively quick review of the growth of the various strands of 'categorial grammar' found in current work reveals a remarkable historical depth. The work of Ajdukiewicz perhaps represents the earliest attempt to construct a generative grammar of a fragment of a natural language. While this tradition was kept alive within philosophy, because of the possibility it affords of treating the compositional properties of form and interpretation in a common framework, it has been slower to take root in linguistics. It is probably correct to say that the lack of interest in categorial grammar among linguists derived from (1) the early results of Bar-Hillel and his colleagues concerning the equivalence of bidirectional categorial grammars (with a single operation corresponding to functional application) and context-free grammars, together with the then widely-accepted view that natural languages could literally not be described by context-free grammars, as well as from (2) the unfamiliarity of most linguists with model-theoretic approaches to interpretation — approaches which make available the possibility of detailed, explicit, and tractable explorations of the relation between syntax and interpretation.

Montague's papers, particularly PTQ and UG (Paper 7 in Thomason, 1974a), provided a framework in which semantic problems could be (and most certainly have been) profitably pursued. More importantly, perhaps, the emphasis that Montague placed upon the desirability of a homomorphic relation between the properties and composition of syntactic types and the properties and composition of corresponding semantic types exposed to a wider audience the virtues of the categorial grammars he employed. At the same time, the growing sense that transformational analyses were not always appropriate led to the exploration of various non-transformational approaches to grammatical analysis. We suspect that these two converging tendencies were not entirely independent. (For example, R. Thomason's (1974b, 1976) demonstration that coherent alternatives to purely syntactic analyses of certain central grammatical problems existed in a Montague-grammar framework had an impact that has perhaps never been adequately acknowledged.)

The research presented in this volume, much of it interconnected, shows that work in categorial grammar in the broad sense has moved beyond the stage of sporadic rediscovery and reached a critical mass. Broadly construed, categorial grammar allows a much more thorough-going investigation of the foundations of grammatical composition than competing frameworks. The papers that follow make it clear that the attractions of this kind of investigation have already yielded results of interest. And these results in turn imply that there is a great deal more that is within reach.

We turn now to some brief expository remarks concerning the individual papers.

Bach's paper may be read as a general introduction to the use of categorial and near-categorial systems in formulating empirical theories about the structures of natural languages.

Van Benthem's paper explores the properties of the commutative Lambek calculus — a grammatical system which contains expressions of simple type and 1-ary functors which may combine with their arguments in either order, together with certain type-changing rules found in Lambek's (1958) paper. Because of the role that permutation plays in this system, it has interesting properties syntactically — both with respect to other categorial systems, such as the Ajdukiewicz/Bar-Hillel directional system and the directional Lambek calculi, and with respect to the Chomsky hierarchy of re-writing systems. The semantics for this system that van Benthem defines has affinities with the standard interpretation of the intuitionistic logic of implication. The intertwining of logical, mathematical, and linguistic themes in this paper reveals the way in which categorial grammars are especially suited to work along the boundaries between these disciplines.

In 1959, Gaifman obtained a proof of the equivalence of bidirectional categorial grammars and context-free phrase structure grammars (Bar-Hillel 1964, p. 103). As mentioned above, this result led to the general belief in linguistic circles that categorial grammars offered nothing beyond the context-free phrase structure grammars which were generally held to be empirically inadequate. In the intervening years, little has been done to dispel this illusion, in spite of the fact that the categorial grammars introduced by Lambek, Geach, and others go beyond the syntactic devices found in the grammars involved in Gaifman's proof. Recently, however, there has been a revival of interest in the mathematical properties of various categorial grammar, beginning (fittingly enough) with work by Polish logicians. Buszkowski has been at the forefront of this revival, and in his paper here, he reviews these recent results concerning the generative capacity of different types of categorial grammars, particularly the bi-directional grammars of Bar-Hillel (following Ajdukiewicz) and the product-free, associative syntactic calculus of Lambek (1958), and other related systems. These results are formulated within a framework of considerable abstract elegance.

The focus of Casadio's paper is the historically-important relation between categorial grammar and the idea of semantic categories — an idea which goes back at least as far as Aristotle. She discusses the role this theory played in Polish philosophy and logic in the stimulating period between the two World Wars, and shows how these categories are connected with the syntactical properties of categorial grammars. As we emphasized above, the natural relation between semantic categories and syntactic properties is one of the most salient characteristics of categorial grammars.

Chierchia's paper provides a categorial perspective on the binding of anaphoric and pronominal elements whose behavior has been a central concern of work in the Government & Binding (GB) school. Within the GB school, the nearly complementary distribution of reflexive pronouns and ordinary pronouns is accounted for primarily by reference to such notions as c-command, a relation defined over tree structures. There is no structure in categorial grammars which corresponds to this (see Bach, this volume, for example), but a related set of results can be defined over the compositional analysis of an expression in terms of functors and arguments. Chierchia argues for a rapprochement between these somewhat different points of view, in a way which makes use of important insights of Edwin Williams. Apart from the intrinsic interest of his arguments, Chierchia's paper typifies a new kind of maturity in linguistics, especially characteristic of work in which formal standards are high, in which investigations of comparative grammatical theory are carried out with the aim of reconciling differences rather than deepening them.

Dowty's paper is concerned with how recent developments in categorial grammar and GPSG illuminate a classic syntactic problem: the phenomenon of 'non-constituent' conjunction (NCC). The existence of NCC has provided a powerful *prima facie* case in favor of a transformational approach to syntax. The exact character of such rules and, more fundamentally, the motivation of this character has never been exactly clear. Dowty shows in a beautiful way how rules of type-lifting characteristic of extended categorial grammars can be invoked to resolve standard and not-so-standard aspects of 'non-constituent' conjunction.

The contribution of Hoeksema and Janda is devoted to questions of 'word grammar' from a generalized categorial point of view (generalized in the sense that operations other than concatenation are allowed). They attempt to characterize the modes of morphological composition found in the languages of the world and to characterize as well the formal devices which are required to deal with the cases involved. Their results provide both a fruitful foundation to a universal theory of morphological structure and a challenge to the influential recent approaches to morphology by McCarthy, A. Prince, Selkirk, Williams, and others, which attempts to characterize on the basis of weaker premises a proper subset of the data Hoeksema and Janda present.

Huck's paper investigates a variety of ways in which basic categorial grammars of the type discussed by Ajdukiewicz and Bar-Hillel and his colleagues can be extended to deal with the existence of dependencies which are syntactically discontinuous. Such dependencies are a fundamental part of arguments for a transformational approach to syntax. Huck shows that in the case that he investigates (which involves the relative order of noun phrases, particles, and adverbs in English verb phrases), there are alternatives to a fully transformational approach, alternatives which require the existence of non-concatenative but locally defined modes of combination.

Keenan and Timberlake discuss two ways of enriching the categorial structure of a categorial grammar which make it possible to express certain empirical generalizations about natural language in a formally elegant fashion. The first countenances the existence of *n-tuple categories*; the second closes the set of categories under a new unary operation, characterizing a set of *argument categories*. The authors support these innovations in the theory of categories by appealing to a wide variety of cross-linguistic evidence involving empirical properties which can be formulated naturally in this more highly articulated categorial framework.

Lambek's formulation of the calculi of syntactic types has had a profound impact on contemporary research in categorial grammar. In his contribution to this volume, he provides some insight into the origin of this work, discusses the logical consequences of the properties of these calculi when viewed as a deductive system (see also Lambek, 1968, 1969), and explores the connections between this research and algebraic category theory (see also Lambek, 1980), a field whose development has had an invigorating effect on modern logic.

Moortgat discusses how the combinatorial properties of extended categorial grammars resolve apparent morphological conflicts between syntax and semantics. These conflicts arise in a variety of contexts, involving complex affixes, complement inheritance phenomena, and the relative scope of affixes and modifiers. They are not easy to resolve in morphological models which are based on context-free phrase structure associated with a single semantic rule of functional application. Moortgat provides a coherent alternative using properties of functional composition and type-lifting and offers several reasons for preferring this account to theories which are based on rules which re-order syntactic affixes or adjust the scope of their interpretation. The fact that the grammatical operations which Moortgat invokes have interesting consequences with respect to problems of morphology is one sign (among a number in this volume) of the linguistic coming of age of categorial grammar.

Oehrle's paper has several related goals. He first sketches a methodological approach to the investigation of the language capacity which is based on the premise that individuals have partial, but well-defined, access, in a number of different 'dimensions', to linguistic structure. He next suggests that categorial grammars are especially suited to the investigation of the problem of simultaneous composition in these different 'dimensions', for exactly the same reasons that Montague found categorial grammar an appropriate way to study the relation between syntactic composition and semantic composition. One advantage of the resulting grammatical architecture, which is quite powerful, is that it allows the investigation of the relations among the various recognized dimensions to be carried on empirically, rather than fixed on *a priori* grounds; a further advantage is the set of consequences this system has for the formal distribution of linguistic labor among the various dimensions recognized.

Pollard's paper is an explicit comparison of a version of categorial grammar (that of Steedman) with a version of a phrase-structure-like theory (Pollard's own Head Driven Phrase Structure Grammar). In the context of a more general comparison of phrase-structural and categorial theories, Pollard points out the many areas of convergence that have arisen between the two approaches in the last several years. He ends with the judgment that it is perhaps no longer appropriate to think of the various extensions, modifications, and 'generalizations' of the two approaches as distinct theories and also implies that researchers should continue to explore various 'mixes' and 'matches'.

Closely connected to both the lambda-calculus and various realizations of the categorial idea is the study of *combinators* initiated by Schönfinkel (1924) and Curry in the 1920s and introduced to many philosophers and linguists by Quine (1960). Steedman takes up this connection explicitly and tries to answer the question: *why* do natural languages (and some computing languages) make use of just the operations that they do. His tentative answer appeals to the computational advantage of dispensing with variables and variable binding. A novel result of his paper, due in part to joint work with Anna Szabolcsi, is the insight that a number of constructions of extraordinary grammatical interest, such as reflexives, control constructions, and, particularly, parasitic gaps, correspond to simple combinators in combinatory logic. (A *locus classicus* for the study of combinatory logic is Curry and Feys, 1958, together with its companion volume Curry *et al.*, 1972; see also Stenlund, 1972; Stoy, 1977; and Hindley and Seldin, 1986 for succinct and readable expositions of the basic properties of the combinators and their relation to the lambda calculus.)

Steele's paper, which draws upon her longterm studies of the Uto-Aztecan language Luiseño, endorses an abstract notion of functor (of a kind reminiscent of Curry's suggestions in his 1961 paper) and proposes a typology of functors based on a small range of very simple properties. This typology is based on such characteristics as whether a functor of a given type is obligatory in expressions of the type assigned to its co-domain, whether the functor belongs to a small, listable set of elements, and whether the form of the functor is localizable or not in expressions which belong to its co-domain. Steele shows that this typology correlates in interesting ways with the syntactic and morphological characterization of Luiseño expressions. Since the principles on which this typology of functors is based do not depend at all on the particular or idiosyncratic properties of Luiseño but do depend on properties which are universally accessible (including certain semantic types), it is an interesting question whether correlations between functions and their form of the kind that Steele reveals in Luiseño exist elsewhere. Given recent research in such disparate areas as the work in visual cognition that she cites and the extensive role played by rigid, grammatical elements in natural languages, such correlations are extremely likely.

Wheeler's paper is the only paper devoted to questions wholly within the realm of phonology. Categorial approaches to phonology have been few and far between, but categorial ideas have popped up in recent work by Kaye and Vergnaud. Besides the works referred to in his paper, the interested reader should take a look at Schmerling (1982) for a quite different approach to phonology within the general categorial framework. Wheeler's paper contains a detailed analysis of devoicing and voicing assimilation in Russian, with an explicit comparison to a recent study of the same phenomena by B. Hayes (1984) from a more 'standard' point of view.

V

We close with a notational *caveat*: although functor categories hold a place of honor in this book, many of the authors of individual papers refer to them in different and often conflicting ways. This is particularly true of category names in which the category to which a functor belongs consists of some combination of a slash of some kind and the names of the category of the functor's domain and co-domain.

In the bidirectional tradition, if f is a member of the functor category x/y and a is a member of the category y, then fa is a member of the category x; similarly, if f is a member of the functor category $y\backslash x$ and a is a member of the category y, then af is a member of the category x. Within this tradition, to denote the case in which the order of functor and argument commute, it is reasonable to use the fractional notation

$$\frac{x}{y}$$

to indicate the category to which a functor f belongs when a belongs to category y and both fa and af belong to category x. This usage is found in such works as Ajdukiewicz (1967), Flynn (1983), and van Benthem (this volume). Moortgat uses the typographically more convenient form $y \mid x$ to indicate a functor category whose elements have domain y and co-domain x, for cases in which linear order is irrelevant.

These conventions are of course not the only possible ones. Some authors prefer to keep the order in which the co-domain and the domain of a functorial type invariant and to use the direction of the slash to indicate relative order. On this view, if f is a member of category x/y and a is a member of category y, then just as above, fa is a member of category x; but if f belongs to category $x\backslash y$ and a is a member of category y, then af belongs to category x. This convention is found in Dowty's paper.

These conventions for interpreting slash categories are not the only conventions used in the papers that follow to indicate the types of a functors domain and co-domain. But they are the ones most likely to lead to misinterpretation.

The Editors

REFERENCES

Ajdukiewicz, K.: 1935, 'Die syntaktische Konnexität', *Studia Philosophica* **1**, 1—27. (English translation in Storrs McCall, ed., *Polish Logic*, Oxford University Press, 1967.)

Bach, E.: 1979, 'Control in Montague Grammar', *Linguistic Inquiry* **10**, 515—531.

Bach, E.: 1981, 'Discontinuous Constituents in Generalized Categorial Grammar', *NELS* **XI**, 1—12.

Bach, E.: 1984, 'Some Generalizations of Categorial Grammar', in F. Landman and F. Veltman (eds.), *Varieties of Formal Semantics*, Foris, Dordrecht, pp. 1—23.

Bar-Hillel, Y.: 1953, 'A Quasi-Arithmetical Notation for Syntactic Description', *Language* **29**, 47—58; reprinted in Bar-Hillel (1964), pp. 61—74.

Bar-Hillel, Y.: 1964, *Language and Information*, Addison-Wesley, Reading, Mass.

Chierchia, G.: 1984, *Topics in the Syntax and Semantics of Infinitives and Gerunds*, Ph.D. dissertation, Department of Linguistics, University of Massachusetts at Amherst.

Cresswell, M.: 1972, *Logics and Languages*, Methuen, London.

Curry, H.: 1961, 'Some Logical Aspects of Grammatical Structure', in R. O. Jakobson (1961), pp. 56—68.

Curry, H. and R. Feys: 1958, *Combinatory Logic*, Vol. I, North-Holland, Amsterdam.

Curry, H., J. R. Hindley, and J. P. Seldin: 1972, *Combinatory Logic*, Vol. II, North-Holland, Amsterdam.

Flynn, M.: 1983, 'A Categorial Theory of Structure-Building', in G. Gazdar, E. Klein, and G. Pullum (eds.), *Order, Concord and Constituency*, Foris, Dordrecht, pp. 139—174.

Geach, P. T.: 1972, 'A Program for Syntax', in D. Davidson and G. Harman (eds.), *Semantics of Natural Language*, D. Reidel, Dordrecht, pp. 483—497.

Hayes, B.: 1984, 'The Phonetics and Phonology of Russian Voicing Assimilation', in M. Aronoff and R. T. Oehrle (eds.), *Language Sound Structure*, MIT Press, Cambridge, Mass., pp. 318—328.

van Heijenoort, J.: 1971, *From Frege to Gödel: A Sourcebook in Mathematical Logic, 1879—1931*. Harvard University Press, Cambridge, Mass.

Hindley, J. R. and J. P. Seldin: 1986, *Introduction to Combinators and λ-Calculus*, Cambridge University Press, Cambridge.

Jakobson, R. O. (ed.): 1961, *Structure of Language and Its Mathematical Aspects*, Proceedings of Symposia in Applied Mathematics, Vol. XII, American Mathematical Society, Providence.

Lambek, J.: 1958, 'The Mathematics of Sentence Structure', *American Mathematical Monthly* **65**, 154—169.

Lambek, J.: 1961, 'On the Calculus of Syntactic Types', in R. O. Jakobson (1961), pp. 166—178.

Lambek, J.: 1968, 'Deductive Systems and Categories I', *Mathematical Systems Theory* **2**, 278—318.

Lambek, J.: 1969, 'Deductive Systems and Categories II', *Springer Lecture Notes in Mathematics* **86**, 76—122.

Lambek, J.: 1980, 'From λ-calculus to Cartesian Closed Categories', in J. R. Hindley and J. P. Seldin (eds.), *To H. B. Curry: Essays on Combinatory Logic, Lambda Calculus and Formalism*, Academic Press, New York, pp. 375—402.

Leśniewski, St.: 1929, 'Grundzüge eines neuen Systems der Grundlagen der Mathematik', *Fundamenta mathematicae* **14**, 1—81.

Levin, H.: 1976, *First Order Logic as a Formal Language: An Investigation of Categorial Grammar*, Ph.D. dissertation, Department of Philosophy, MIT.

Levin, H.: 1982, *Categorial Grammar and the Logical Form of Quantification*, Bibliopolis, Naples.

Lewis, D.: 1972, 'General Semantics', in D. Davidson and G. Harman (eds.), *Semantics of Natural Language*, D. Reidel, Dordrecht, pp. 169—218.

Lyons, J.: 1966, 'Towards a "Notional" Theory of the "Parts of Speech"', *Journal of Linguistics* **2**, 209—236.

MacLane, S.: 1986, *Mathematics: Form and Function*, Springer Verlag.

Quine, W. V.: 1960, 'Variables Explained Away', in *Selected Logic Papers*, Random House (1966), New York, pp. 227—235.

Schmerling, S.: 1982, 'The Proper Treatment of the Relationship Between Syntax and Phonology', *Texas Linguistic Forum* **19**, 151—166.

Schönfinkel, M.: 1924, 'Über die Bausteine der mathematischen Logik', *Mathematische Annalen* **92**, 305—316, translated as 'On the Building Blocks of Mathematical Logic' in van Heijenoort (1971), pp. 355—366.

Stenlund, S.: 1972, *Combinators, λ-terms and Proof Theory*, D. Reidel, Dordrecht.

Stoy, J.: 1977, *Denotational Semantics*, MIT Press, Cambridge, Mass.

von Stechow, A.: 1974, 'ε-λ kontextfreie Sprachen: Ein Beitrag zu einer natürlichen formalen Semantik', *Linguistische Berichte* **34**, 1—33.

Thomason, R. H. (ed.): 1974a, *Formal Philosophy: Selected Papers of Richard Montague*, Yale Univeresity Press, New Haven.

Thomason, R. H.: 1974b, 'Some Complement Constructions in Montague Grammar', *CLS* **10**, pp. 712—722.

Thomason, R. H.: 1976, 'Some Extensions of Montague Grammar', in B. Partee (ed.), *Montague Grammar*, Academic Press, New York, pp. 77—117.

EMMON BACH

CATEGORIAL GRAMMARS AS THEORIES
OF LANGUAGE

0. GOALS

In recent years, there has been a growing interest in categorial grammar
as a framework for formulating empirical theories about natural language. This conference bears witness to that revival of interest. How
well does this framework fare when used in this way? And how well do
particular theories in what we might call the family of categorial
theories fare when they are put up against the test of natural language
description and explanation? I say 'family' of theories, for there have
been a number of different developments, all of which take off from the
fundamental idea of a categorial grammar as it was first introduced by
Ajdukiewicz and later modified and studied by Bar-Hillel, Curry, and
Lambek. In this paper I would like to discuss these questions, considering a number of different hypotheses that have been put forward within
the broad framework that we may call 'extended categorial grammar'
and making a few comparisons with other theories. In my remarks, I
will take as a general framework the program and set of assumptions
that have been called 'extended Montague grammar' and in particular a
slightly modified version of Montague's 'Universal Grammar' (UG:
Paper 7 in Montague, 1974). From this point of view, the syntax of a
language is looked at as a kind of algebra. Then, the empirical problem
of categorial grammar can be seen as part of a general program that
tries to answer these questions:

(A) What is the set of primitive and derived categories that we need
to describe and explain natural languages in their syntax and semantics
(and phonology, etc.)?

(B) What are the operations that we need to describe and explain
natural languages (in the syntax, semantics, phonology, morphology,
etc.)?

(C) What are the relations that we need in order to hook up with
each other the various categories and operations mentioned or alluded
to in (A) and (B)?

The brief outline just given provides us with a natural breakdown of

17

Richard T. Oehrle et al. (eds.), Categorial Grammars and Natural Language Structures, 17—34.

the kinds of questions I want to take up here: First, we want to ask about the categories of our grammars for natural languages; second, the operations that we allow; third, the relations between the categories and operations on various levels (syntactic, semantic, etc.). And as a second overarching kind of question we want to consider these questions from the classical points of view relating to descriptive and explanatory adequacy, as these terms have been used in the generative literature. We may put these last considerations as two further questions:

(D) Can our theories accommodate facts about natural languages that we know or think that we know?

(E) How well do our theories do in predicting facts about natural languages?

(By the way, I think we need a better term for the general framework in which I am working. 'Montague grammar' seems excessively particular, given the very fundamental changes that have been argued for both in the general outlines of the system, and in the particulars. The same goes for the term 'categorial grammar'. I have no good suggestions.)

There are two dimensions along which we can give a rough characterization of formal linguistic theories these days. By 'formal', I mean explicit, staying somewhat catholic about standards of explicitness. Being explicit is simply a matter of making sure that we can work out just what it is that a theory and the grammatical descriptions carried out within it claim or predict about the data of linguistics: judgments of various sorts by native speakers of the language, crosslinguistic variation, fit with experimental or other evidence about acquisition and processing, etc.

The two dimensions that I have in mind are these: (1) semantic accountability and (2) generativity.

Semantic Accountability

By 'semantic accountability' I mean only this: the acceptance as a reasonable goal to say something explicit about the interpretation or meaning of the abstract syntactic objects posited by your theory. The most prominent approaches to the goal of semantic accountability in the last decades have been model-theoretic in nature, and this is the general approach which I will assume here. But this is not the only possible approach: one may think of meanings as some sort of mental objects or concepts, or one may follow an axiomatic approach, and it may turn out in the end that all of these approaches have something to contribute to our understanding of language. Many linguists do not accept semantic accountability as one of their goals. I don't see much point in arguing about this question. Ultimately, we just have to look at the fruitfulness of the results. I personally believe that the results of a decade and a half of work in the model-theoretic study of natural language semantics amply justify the expectation that continued pursuit of this program is worthwhile.

Generativity

By 'generativity' I mean only this: the goal of a grammatical description is to enumerate or define a set of structural descriptions of the expressions of a language. The acceptance of this goal was the primary turning point in the rise of the kind of linguistics that we associate especially with the work of Chomsky and his coworkers in the fifties.

Closely connected to the last contrast is a difference in style: what we might call the 'constitutional' approach and the 'architectural' approach (I intend 'constitutional' to be reminiscent of its political sense). In the former approach, description operates in a primary way by the statement of principles overlaid on some skeleton of a grammar (usually not explicitly given). The primary work goes into stating constraints or licenses. In the architectural approach, of which I consider various categorial theories to be prime examples, the attempt is made to build into the very structure of a grammar various properties from which will follow principles of the sort stipulated independently in the alternative sort of theory. A noncategorial example of this sort of approach is Kiparsky's model of Lexical Phonology, if I understand it correctly. I will bring up here a number of examples of situations where independently stipulated properties of grammars in other theories simply follow from the design of categorial systems of one sort or another.

Finally, in this initial discussion of the background of my remarks, let me mention a difference of research strategy, where, happily, there seems to me to be no substantive difference to argue about. Some people seem to like to work with systems that overgenerate and then try to figure our how to cut down on the superset of structures that their theories give them, while others like to work in the opposite direction, being careful that their grammars just give what they are sure of. Arguments about these two general approaches often seem to degenerate into discussions of morality. Here, I would make a plea for tolerance. Hopefully, the two approaches will meet somewhere in the middle. More generally, I think it is good when linguists pursue lots of different theories. After all, the only way to argue for the NECESSITY of an empirical theory (strictly impossible) is to show that alternative theories fail, where the one in question succeeds. The reason that this is strictly impossible in an empirical discipline is that to argue for necessity we would have to rule out all possible alternatives. When we deal with the real world we can't do this, of course.

1. WHAT MAKES A GRAMMAR CATEGORIAL?

Let me paraphrase (simplifying somewhat) Montague's definition of a grammar (he calls it a 'language') in UG. We have the following:

A: a set of expressions, together with $\varphi: A \rightarrow Pow(C)$ which assigns each member of A to a set of categories in c.
G: a family of sets of n-place operations, for $n = 1, 2, \ldots$
C: a set of syntactic categories,
R: a set of rules of the form:
$$\langle f; c_1, c_2, \ldots, c_k; c_{k+1} \rangle$$
where f is a k-place operation, and $c_1, \ldots, c_{k+1}$ are syntactic categories

The meaning of such a rule is this: take expressions of category c_1, $c_2, \ldots c_k$, apply the operation f to them and you will get an expression of category c_{k+1}.

If we look at a bidirectional categorial grammar of the familiar sort from the point of view of this general framework, we can see that it does two things: first, it specifies an infinite set of categories starting with a primitive set; second, it confines the operations to just two 2-place operations of concatenation. Moreover, in its fundamental way of dividing expressions into functors and arguments and implicit in the formulations of Bar-Hillel and Lambek, functor categories are distinguished according to the operations that are associated with them. So, for a start, we might set up the basic categorial definition as follows:

GCAT is the smallest set such that:

(1) $\{a_1, a_2, \ldots, a_n\} = \text{PCAT}$,
(2)   GCAT includes PCAT,
(3)   If g is an i-place operation and a_1, a_2, $\ldots$, a_i, b are in GCAT, then $\langle g; a_1, a_2, \ldots, a_i; b \rangle$ is in GCAT.

In a bidirectional sort of categorial grammar, the following choices are made:

in 3 we replace i by 2;
G includes just two operations:
LCON, RCON, where $\text{LCON}(x, y) = \text{RCON}(y, x) = x \,\char"5E\, y$

These two operations both appeal to simple concatenation. The reason for distinguishing them is the hypothesis that functor expressions determine the syntactic operations that combine them with their arguments. This is what is implied by the more familiar notation where we write as follows:

a/b for $\langle \text{RCON}, X, b, a, \rangle$
$b\backslash a$ for $\langle \text{LCON}, X, b, a \rangle$

(where X stands for the functor expression in question). The usual rules for function/argument application may then be schematized as follows:

$a/b\ b \Rightarrow a$
$b\ b\backslash a \Rightarrow a$

Here, the schemata mean this:

For the first, if x is a member of the set of expressions categorized as a/b and y is a member of the class categorized as b then xy is a member of the set categorized as a; similarly for the second.

As I mentioned above, it has been well known for some time that the class of bidirectional categorial grammars is weakly equivalent to the class of context-free grammars. We will consider below some ways in which CG's are not like phrase-structure grammars but let us note for now that any arguments from weak generative capacity against CF grammars are, *a fortiori*, arguments against the weak adequacy of bidirectional categorial grammars, as used and interpreted in the way just outlined.

Let me point out right away that we encounter here one fundamental way in which various categorial theories differ: the treatment of directionality. Recall that Ajdukiewicz's original formalism made use of functor categories that could take arguments on either side (Ajdukiewicz, 1935). Two current theories retain the idea that functors are categorized in this order-free way at a basic level. Flynn (1983) reintroduces directionality for the functors by means of word-order conventions that capture generalizations for a language and across languages, thus offering an interesting set of parameters for Universal Grammar. His approach is quite compatible with the theory just sketched, which was introduced in Bach (1984) as a theoretical proposal in the spirit of Bar-Hillel (1953) and Lambek (1961). Ades and Steedman (1982) handle word-order facts by postulating a separate component of rules of combination for functional application and function composition ('partial combination') in either direction, and allow the possibility of restricting the operation of these rules to particular categories. Either of these approaches has to deal with the fact of exceptions: for example, there are languages that have both prepositions and postpositions (Dutch, German, English: *notwithstanding, ago,* etc.). In a theory like Flynn's, I believe the most natural assumption would be that particular exceptional elements could be specified ad hoc, leaving the general conventions as the unmarked case. The approach of Ades and Steedman would have to incorporate something like exception features determining the applicability of the various rules of combination. In any case, there are interesting puzzles to face. Why, for example, do we have languages that have exceptional 'adpositions' but not, as far as I know, languages that have verbs that are exceptional in the position that their arguments must take? (More on word-order below, under OPERATIONS.)

Another important line of investigation has to do with the arity of our functors. The hypothesis of binarity (built into our definition above) is in no way necessary in a categorial approach. It seems to be a persistent idea in many different theories, however, that the canonical, if not the necessary form of linguistic constructions is binary. This was certainly Montague's practice in PTQ and we see it in a Government-Binding guise in the recent work of Kayne (1984).

One crucial way in which categorial grammars differ from phrase-structure grammars is the fact that the former are built on the notion of function in the strict mathematical sense. Thus, we can carry over into our theories all the things that we know about the general theory of functions in a natural way, that is, without introducing any new concepts, extensions, or special devices. Many of the papers at this conference bear witness to this fundamental point, in particular, with regard to type-lifting, and function composition. Indeed, we seem to be faced here with a certain embarassment of riches. What corresponds in a categorial system to transformational kinds of rules in other theories are the operations that compose functions and change categories, so it is quite expectable that we need to look precisely here for reasonable constraints in our search for explanatory adequacy.

Let me now take up each of the broad areas mentioned above: categories, operations, and relations among different 'components' of our theories.

2. CATEGORIES

There are two sorts of questions to ask here, when we consider the empirical import of our theories. The first has to do with the general structure of the categorial system, the second with the substantive content of the categories. Much recent work in syntax and morphology has been built upon X-bar theory. It is interesting to compare X-bar systems and their attendant concepts with categorial systems, and I shall do so in a moment, but let me first make a historical observation. The ultimate modern sources for the main ideas of X-bar theory are, I believe, the work of Harris in the fifties and an observation by John Lyons (1966; also 1968: pp. 330—332; see Bresnan, 1976, for one of the few explicit acknowledgements of this link), even though some of the ideas are closely related to traditional notions about exocentricity, endocentricity, and the like. Now, what is interesting to me is that Lyons referred explicitly to the categorial tradition and even suggested that it would make a better basis for a transformational system than the then universally used phrase-structure systems! Obviously, this idea was not picked up on (but see Lewis, 1972, and more recently Flynn, 1983).

The primary structural difference between a categorial system of syntactic classes and that of 'some version' of an X-bar system is easy to see. The recursive definitions of syntactic categories in the former projects an infinite set of possible syntactic classes, with a primary split between primitive categories and functor categories. X-bar systems take as primitive a small set of features, and, assuming a binary set of elements in the value space (or possibly ternary, if 'unspecified' is

admitted as a possible value), project a 'very finite' set of possible
syntactic classes. (This statement is actually a little misleading. It is true
that the number of 'major' syntactic classes such as N, V, and so on
is very small but what we should compare to the categorial classes
are really the conjunctions of the major class features and the subcategorization frames.) Now, lots of the categories that we get from the
recursive definition are very nice categories, as we all know, allowing
for example (should I say 'predicting'?) the use of such things as
generalized quantifiers in our theories. But a lot (infinitely many) of the
projected categories seem quite useless if not perverse. For example,
among the possible categories available to languages, and hence the
little language-learner, are ones like these:

$$t/((e\backslash e)/e) \quad t/(t/(t/(t/e)))$$

The first corresponds semantically to a function that maps functions
from individuals to functions from individuals to individuals to truth
values (got it?). Moreover, could we not say that just by virtue of the
finiteness property the X-bar system, being more restrictive, wins hands
down here?

On the other side, an argument for the categorial approach, is that
the categories have a clear content and a built-in semantic import. We
have no idea what the import of such features as Noun or Verb (with $+$
and $-$ values) are (this is a little strong, see Jackendoff, 1977). In
extended Montague grammar and categorial grammar we *must* commit
ourselves on the semantic import of our syntactic categories. In other
theories this is in a sense more a matter of choice than principle. One
way in which we can view the categorial enterprise is as a contribution
to an eventual substantive theory of syntactic and morphological categories.

There are two things to say about the problem of the overabundance
of categories in categorial systems. The first is that we might appeal to
some notion of markedness with respect to the projected categories (or
some constraints on learning theory). In fact, this way of thinking has
some attractions, as it might help us understand something about the
crosslinguistic distribution of systems of 'parts of speech', perhaps also
something about acquisition. Categorial systems have a built-in hierarchical structure that lends itself well to thinking about such matters. The
second thing to remember is the difference in the roles played by the
categories in a grammar, where, as noted already, systems of derived

categories of various sorts, including especially composed categories, take over all or much of the work that is done in other theories by entirely separate sorts of rules. In any event, there are interesting empirical issues involved in these questions (see especially Dowty, this volume).

Let us now consider the actual substance of the categories themselves. It is apparent that an empirical theory must make some choice for the primitive categories on which the structure of the derived categories is built.

Montague followed Ajdukiewicz in taking the categories t and e as primitive (Ajdukiewicz: s and n), quite within the logical tradition, corresponding to the semantic notions of truth values and individuals as they appear in a standard model structure for a first-order language. Most of the initial work in Montague grammar followed him here. But in the last several years we have seen some basic modifications of this system. In particular, Gennaro Chierchia, in arguing for the inclusion of properties as primitive kinds of things in the model, has introduced a radically different kind of model structure which is almost type-free (see Chierchia, 1984). I am sure we will see a number of significant developments in this area in the coming years. I will not enter into a discussion of these possible modifications here, but rather couch my discussion within the more familiar scheme we inherit from Montague and Ajdukiewicz.

What kind of empirical claims are being made by a system of this sort? First of all, as always, we need to ask whether the categorial system is to be interpreted as part of Universal Grammar (in Chomsky's sense rather than Montague's), and if so, whether in a purely formal sense or in a substantive way as well. That is, is it simply claimed that each language will just have *some* list of primitive categories from which the functor categories will be constructed, or are specific categories stipulated as part of the innate human mechanism. It seems that we would want to shoot for the stronger claim and thus build the particular set of primitives into our universal theory. So in the case at hand, we would be claiming that t and e are the universally necessary primitive categories from which each language starts. In effect, then, our theory might be claiming that the syntax of every language contains a category for declarative sentences and for names. You will no doubt note that this is more than Montague claimed (if we make the counterfactual assumption that he was in fact making an empirical claim in his analysis of English in his PTQ (i.e. Paper 8 in Montague, 1974)), for that paper contains no English syntactic category e. Questions about type-shifting become directly relevant here (Partee and Rooth, 1983). Notice that an essential part of testing such claims requires attention to the semantics as well as the syntax (Question C above) and this necessary connection must be treated as one of the most important empirical challenges to the theory and program as a whole.

There is no space here to enter into an extended discussion of this point (or of most of the other points that I will raise). Let me just give one illustration of the kind of question that we are facing here. It seems to me to be true that every language has at least the categories just mentioned, roughly, sentences and names. Further, a minimal syntax would need at least one further category in order to have sentences with any internal structure: t/e or $e\backslash t$. Given type-lifting, we would then expect the category of generalized quantifiers ($t/(t/e)$ etc.), and it has been claimed (Barwise and Cooper, 1981) that this category is also universal. Although I feel in my bones that this is right, it is clearly incumbent on us to look very closely at languages such as Kwakw'ala in which all logical determiner meanings seem to be expressed by auxiliary-like verbal elements. Notice that from the point of view of the logic (and given Schoenfinkel/Curry) we can understand a scheme like $DET(M)(N)$ as exhibiting either one of two structures and in only one of them is there a semantic constituent corresponding to a generalized quantifier.

Before leaving this point, I would like to point to an entirely different kind of evidence that can bear on the question of the empirical support for our syntactic categorizations. Part of practically every syntactic theory is a system of features for dealing with matters of government, agreement, and percolation (i.e. the assignment of feature values to complex expressions as a function of the values of their parts). In Bach (1983b), I have shown one way in which such matters can be dealt with in extensions of categorial theories. Naturally, given the architectural approach of such theories, we would hope that the principles that guide such matters in the morphology/syntax interface would be derivable from independently motivated aspects of the theory, such as basic function/argument structure. The success of such subtheories should then be matched up with that of competing theories. In the case at hand, for example, if we compare the categorial theories to phrase-structure theories of various sorts, at the most general level we are dealing with the theoretical justification for such notions as *head, modifier, specifier* and the like in the latter type of theories and those of categorial grammar such as *functor, argument,* and directly derivable ones such as *endocentric modifier* (for interesting discussion of these points in the context of derivational morphology, see Hoeksema, 1984). I believe that results here are promising. They also throw some light on the question of the theoretical status of various sorts of type-lifting options. It would be a spectacular result, if in some language properties of government or agreement varied according to whether or not some type-lifting option occurred with an attendant flip of the function/argument structure. I'm pretty sure this never happens (so sure, that I would bet some money on it, say $50 — I may have just lost some money, see Moortgat, 1984, for an example that is claimed to illustrate just this point). I conclude that one would want to have a clear theoretical separation between something like a basic functional structure and those relationships that come through type-lifting (see Dowty, this volume, for discussion of this last question). An inspiration for much of the work on principles determining the way features work has been Keenan's Functional Principle (Keenan, 1974; see Bach and Partee, 1980, for an application of the Functional Principle to problems of binding theory).

3. OPERATIONS

Let's now look at some of the questions that arise about the possible operations that we want our theories to provide for natural language grammars. There are three main points that I want to take up here. The first is the question of one-place operations. The second has to do with the *syntactic* side of function compositions of various sorts. The third is the question of operations on categories.

One-Place Operations

From the point of view of Montague's UG, it would be an artificial restriction to disallow one-place operations. Indeed, in the way in which I have laid out the skeleton of the theory above, we can put an upper bound on the arity of the operations, but not a lower bound. In classical categorial theory, on the other hand, there is such a restriction. I believe that this is something of a historical accident which arises from the point of view that we are given a set of expressions in a language and asked to assign pieces of the expressions to categories. This approach then leads naturally to the kind of 'item-and arrangement' view of linguistic structure that has dominated much of American linguistics for the last four decades. As Schmerling (1983) has pointed out, Montague's algebraic approach is much more consonant with the 'item-and-process' model of much earlier descriptive work (this terminology from Hockett, 1954). It is difficult to try to decide between these two approaches at such a general level, and for now, perhaps it must remain a matter of taste. It is obviously always possible, if we have no constraints on the number of different 'inaudibilia' we might posit, to set up an abstract zero morpheme to trigger off any conceivable one-place operation we might want to define. In the other direction, with no constraints on operations, any arbitrary element could be removed from the stock of 'items' and reintroduced by a suitable operation (compare Montague's treatment of determiners in PTQ). I tentatively conclude that categorial and non-categorial theories are on about a par here, with much more research needed, especially on the interactions between morphology and syntax. (Note that Curry, 1961, includes one-place operations as one type of functor. See Bach, 1983c, for some arguments for one-place operations and see Hoeksema and Janda, this volume, for a discussion of the range of morphological operations actually found in natural languages.)

Compositions in Syntax

As I noted above, one of the most attractive features of categorial theories is the potential for composing functions that comes along with the functional basis of the theory. Indeed, the frequent appearance of fusions of categories in natural language can be taken as a kind of confirmation of the validity of the general approach (Bach, 1983a; Hoeksema, 1983). We know what the semantic constraints on compositions must be: given two functions f and g, they can be composed into a new function h with domain A and range C, just in case the domain of g is A, the range of g and domain of f is some set B, and the range of f is C. But what about the syntactic side? Let us take the meaning of our operations of concatenation quite literally. A functor a/b takes expressions of category *b to its right* as its domain. It follows that 'harmonic' functors (that is, functors that are associated with the same concatenation operation) can be combined by composition. So we get free the syntactic compositions of the following two schemata:

$$a/b \ b/c \Rightarrow a/c$$
$$c\backslash b \ b\backslash a \Rightarrow c\backslash a$$

It also follows that *only* harmonic functors can be composed in a perfectly general way. The theory thus provides us with an interesting 'architectural' consequence. Following Ades and Steedman (1982), we can build on this possibility for a treatment of long distance dependencies: an indefinitely long composition of contiguous harmonizing functors will be available to act as arguments for special gap operators such as relative pronouns and particles and question words in languages that have these elements. For example, suppose English *that* is assigned to the category $(CN\backslash CN)/(S/NP)$, then it can take as arguments all of the following sorts of phrases:

> I saw
> I think that Bill saw
> I think that Bill said Sally saw

This treatment enforces the 'adjacency corollary' of Ades and Steedman but with the additional twist provided by the way in which operations are associated with functors rather than provided by independent combination rules. In Ades and Steedman, with no specifications of restrictions to particular categories on the rules of composition (forward and backward partial combination) any two properly related functors can be composed.

Again, this is not the place to enter into an extended discussion of the complicated issues touched on here. Rather I would just like to point out the way in which basic features of the theory can lead to interesting empirical consequences. Notice that there is a further consequence of the treatment of 'gaps' just illustrated. On the assumption that tensed verb-phrases in English are to be treated as members of the category $NP\backslash S$, (internal) subject 'gaps' will have to be treated differently from all other gaps. More generally we will get various 'left branch' effects in English. Notice further that the treatment has built into it a kind of 'empty category principle' (Chomsky, 1982): gaps must be governed, that is, licensed by functor expressions. (It would be interesting to compare these results with approaches such as those of Kayne (1983) and Koster (1984), both of which stipulate something like our harmony principle, or rather its analogue in a phrase-structure system, as a constraint on long distance dependencies.)

Operations on Categories

So far, we have a very nicely constrained way of using syntactic compositions of functors. We might ask whether there are any ways in which we might milk the system for further sorts of operations to be derived from the basic set. In Bach (1981), I suggested a way of looking at local 'reorderings' of constituents as the result of operations on complex categories. Suppose we have a complex category such as $(a/b)/c$. We can now consider the possibility that the same functor be reassigned to a category in which the order of the argument is reversed: $(a/c)/b$. As I show in the paper cited, this provides us with one way of looking at phenomena that have been treated under the heading of 'right-wrap' and the like. Another possible example, but of a slightly different sort, is offered by phenomena such as so-called 'subject-auxiliary inversion' in English (Bach, 1983a). In general, word order problems offer one of the most interesting areas for testing various extended categorial systems, and such systems offer an extremely interesting new perspective for looking at such problems. (Type-lifting operations fall under the general heading of this subsection. They are dealt with in detail in a number of other papers in this volume.)

Long-Distance 'Operations'

A different approach to word-order variation is suggested in Bach (1984). It is a generalization of the system of categories, in which categories are actually sequences of the original categories. Expressions are put together freely and the generalized categories are reduced by rules that make use of the notion of functors that look 'anywhere to the right', 'anywhere to the left', or 'anywhere'. We obtain in this way what I consider to be an interesting class of languages, namely the free permutations of arbitrary CF languages. Since the original note in which I discussed these languages has never been published, let me take this opportunity to present the result.

Let us call the class of grammars, scramble grammars. In the interesting case, where the languages of the grammars are infinite we have the following:

PROPOSITION. The class of languages generated by scramble grammars is a proper subset of the CS languages.

Proof. Consider the language MIX $=$ SCRAMBLE$((abc)^+)$ (the names 'mix' and 'MIX' — pronounced 'little mix' and 'big mix' were the happy invention of Bill Marsh; 'little mix' is the scramble of $(ab)^+$). Intersect MIX with the regular language $R = a^i b^j c^k$. The result is the non-CF language $L = a^n b^n c^n$. By the theorem that says that the intersection of a CFL and a regular language is CF we know that MIX cannot be CF. But there is no scramble grammar that will get exactly L. To see this, note that every scramble grammar of an infinite CFL has an infinite sublanguage which is CF. Clearly L has no such infinite sublanguage.   Q.E.D.

(Geoff Pullum has pointed out to me that this result was obtained in the literature of computer science in the sixties: see Book, 1973, with reference to Sillars, 1968.) It is worth pointing out that we can get L if we add filters to the grammar. What this shows is that Partee's well-formedness constraint actually does have an effect on weak generative capacity.

Before leaving this section, I would like to point out a whole set of problems that have to do with the question of phrase structure. Obviously, phrase structure has an entirely different status within categorial theories than it has in traditional phrase-structure systems. It is sometimes assumed by critics that diagrams showing the way in which categorial resolutions can be carried out are to be interpreted in the same way as phrase-structure diagrams. In fact, they have much more the status of the analysis trees of classical Montague grammar as we see them in PTQ and much subsequent work. It seems to me to be a completely open question whether and how traditional phrase markers or tree diagrams are to play a role in categorial systems. It goes without saying, then, that all of the configurational notions, such as *c*-command and the like, used in Government and Binding theories and related approaches are up for grabs (see Bach and Partee, 1980, and Bach, 1983b, for some discussion).

4. RELATIONS AMONG 'COMPONENTS'

Probably the one most characteristic and essential feature of both Montague grammar and categorial grammar is the tight constraint on the relation between syntax and semantics. *A priori* this must count as a point in its favor in comparison with many other theories. A theory with some constraint on the relationship — say, the homomorphism constraint of Montague's UG — is by definition making stronger claims about possible human languages than one with no constraints whatsoever. I have already touched on this point in the discussion of categories above. But the real empirical force of the theory must come by way of testing its explanatory power. We need to look for places where the theory provides a clear choice among several possible descriptions of some range of facts and then see how well it performs by asking for independent evidence for the correctness of its predictions as to descriptive adequacy. Given the flexibility offered by the possibilities of type-lifting and function composition it is fair to ask the question: isn't it always possible to come up with a compositional semantics for any arbitrary syntactic analysis? So, as always, we want to continue to look for constraints on the parts of the theory and their interconnections.

There has been a substantial amount of work on other parts of categorial theories, especially derivational morphology (see Moortgat, 1984, and especially Hoeksema, 1984, and the literature cited there, now also Hoeksema and Janda, this volume) and phonology (Wheeler, 1981), but relatively little on the interconnections among these subtheories (see Bach, 1983a, b, c for some suggestions about inflectional morphology). If we can take the relations between syntax and semantics as a guide, we would take a homomorphic relation to be the unmarked case, with apparent departures from it providing the most interesting challenges.

5. CONCLUSIONS

I believe that categorial grammar has come of age as a major and interesting approach to empirical linguistic work, again citing as evidence the papers at this conference and much other work presented and published elsewhere, primarily by participants here. Moreover, the influence of this work is beginning to be felt in other camps, especially among our closest cousins, those who are pursuing 'generalized phrase-structure' theories and related approaches (see especially Pollard, this volume, and Gazdar *et al.*, 1985). We can expect the next few years to see much more work along these general lines. The distinguishing characteristic of this work and its most interesting feature is the centrality which it accords to the notion of functions and arguments, an idea that has formed an important core of thinking about language for more than a century.

ACKNOWLEDGEMENTS

I would like to thank Richard Oehrle, Barbara Partee, and Edwin Williams for helpful suggestions about this paper.

REFERENCES

Ades, Anthony E. and Mark J. Steedman: 1982, 'On the Order of Words', *Linguistics and Philosophy* **4**, 517—558.

Ajdukiewicz, Kasimierz: 1935, 'Die syntaktische Konnexität', *Studia Philosophica* **1**, 1—27. Translated as 'Syntactic Connexion' in Storrs McCall (ed.), *Polish Logic: 1920—1939* (Oxford University Press, Oxford, 1967).

Bach, Emmon: 1981, 'Discontinuous Constituents in Generalized Categorial Grammars, *NELS* **11**, 1—12.

Bach, Emmon: 1983a, 'Generalized Categorial Grammars and the English Auxiliary', in Frank Heny and Barry Richards (eds.), *Linguistic Categories: Auxiliaries and Related Puzzles*, Vol. 2, Reidel, Dordrecht, pp. 101—120.

Bach, Emmon: 1983b, 'On the Relationship Between Word-grammar and Phrase-grammar', *Natural Language and Linguistic Theory* **1**, 65—80.

Bach, Emmon: 1983c, 'Semicompositionaliteit', *GLOT* **6**, 113—130.

Bach, Emmon: 1984, 'Some Generalizations of Categorial Grammars', in Fred Landman and Frank Veltman (eds.), *Varieties of Formal Semantics*, Foris, Dordrecht, pp. 1—23.

Bach, Emmon and Barbara Partee: 1980, 'Anaphora and Semantic Structure', in J. Kreiman and A. Ojeda (eds.), *Papers from the Parasession on Pronouns and Anaphora*, CLS, 1—28.

Bar-Hillel, Yehoshua: 1953, 'A Quasi-arithmetical Notation of Syntactic Description', *Language* **19**, 47—58.

Barwise, Jon and Robin Cooper: 1981, 'Generalized Quantifiers and Natural Languages', *Linguistics and Philosophy* **4**, 159—219.

Book, Ronald V.: 1973, 'Topics in Formal Language Theory', in Alfred V. Aho, ed., *Currents in the Theory of Computing*, Prentice-Hall, Englewood Cliffs, pp. 1—34.

Bresnan, Joan W.: 1976, 'On the Form and Functioning of Transformations', *Linguistic Inquiry* **7**, 3—40.

Chierchia, Gennaro: 1984, 'Topics in the Syntax and Semantics of Infinitives and Gerunds', Ph.D. dissertation, The University of Massachusetts, Amherst (G.L.S.A.).

Chomsky, Noam: 1982, *Lectures on Government and Binding*, Foris, Dordrecht.

Curry, Haskell B.: 1961, 'Some Logical Aspects of Grammatical Structure', in Roman Jakobson (ed.), *Structure of Language and Its Mathematical Aspects* (= Proc. of Symposia in Applied Mathematics, XII, American Mathematical Society, Providence), pp. 56—68.

Flynn, Michael: 1983, 'A Categorial Theory of Structure Building', in Gerald Gazdar, Ewan Klein, and Geoffrey K. Pullum (eds.), *Order, Concord, and Constituency*, Foris, Dordrecht, pp. 139—174.

Gazdar, Gerald, Ewan Klein, Geoffrey Pullum, and Ivan Sag: 1985, *Generalized Phrase Structure Grammar*, Harvard University Press, Cambridge, Mass.

Hockett, Charles F.: 1954, 'Two Models of Grammatical Description', *Word* **10**, 210—231.

Hoeksema, Jack: 1983, 'Wanna do Contraction?', *GLOT* **6**, 157—182.

Hoeksema, Jacob [= Jack]: 1984, 'Categorial Morphology', Proefschrift: Rijksuniversiteit te Groningen Drukkerij van Denderingen, Groningen.

Jackendoff, Ray S.: 1977, *X'-Syntax: A Study of Phrase Structure*, MIT, Cambridge, MA.

Kayne, Richard S.: 1983, 'Connectedness', *Linguistic Inquiry* **14**, 233—249.

Kayne, Richard S.: 1984, *Connectedness and Binary Branching*, Foris, Dordrecht.

Koster, Jan: 1984, 'Global Harmony', *Tilburg Papers in Language and Literature* **61**.

Lambek, Joachim: 1961, 'On the Calculus of Syntactic Types', in Roman Jakobson (ed.), *Structure of Language and Its Mathematical Aspects* (= Proc. of Symposia in Applied Mathematics, XII, American Mathematical Society, Providence), pp. 166—178.

Lewis, David: 1972, 'General Semantics', in Donald Davidson and Gilbert Harman (eds.), *Semantics of Natural Language*, Reidel, Dordrecht, pp. 169—218.

Lyons, John: 1966, 'Towards a "Notional" Theory of the "Parts of Speech"', *Journal of Linguistics* **2**, 209—236.

Lyons, John: 1968, *Introduction to Theoretical Linguistics*, University Press, Cambridge.

Montague, Richard: 1974, *Formal Philosophy*, in Richmond Thomason (ed.), Yale, New Haven.

Moortgat, Michael: 1984, 'A Fregean Restriction on Metarules', *NELS* **14**, 306—325.

Partee, Barbara and Mats Rooth: 1983, 'Generalized Conjunction and Type Ambiguity', in Rainer Bäuerle, Christoph Schwarze, and Arnim von Stechow, (eds.), *Meaning, Use, and Interpretation of Language*, de Gruyter, Berlin, pp. 361—383.

Schmerling, Susan: 1983, 'A New Theory of English Auxiliaries', in Frank Heny and Barry Richards (eds.), *Linguistic Categories: Auxiliaries and Related Puzzles*, Vol. 2, Reidel, Dordrecht, pp. 1—53.

Sillars, W.: 1968, *Formal Properties of Essentially Context-Dependent Languages*, Ph.D. dissertation, Pennsylvania State University.

Wheeler, Deirdre W.: 'Aspects of a Categorial Theory of Phonology', Ph.D. dissertation: The University of Massachusetts, Amherst (G.L.S.A.).

Dept. of Linguistics,
University of Massachusetts,
Amherst, MA 01003, U.S.A.

JOHAN VAN BENTHEM

THE LAMBEK CALCULUS

1. FLEXIBLE CATEGORIAL GRAMMAR

There is a noticeable revival of categorial grammar these days, as a vehicle for linguistic description. The systems used differ somewhat from the original calculus of Ajdukiewicz and Bar-Hillel, however. In particular, there is a component of rules for 'type change' of expressions, making for greater flexibility and elegance. One fundamental system of this kind is the so-called 'Lambek Calculus', whose type-change rules show a close analogy with the inference rules of constructive propositional logic. In this paper, we present one calculus of this kind, and survey its theoretical properties as a device in linguistic semantics. Our two main new contributions are a new and complete semantics for this calculus, as well as a modest study of its language-accepting capacity. In this way, we hope to provide a better understanding of the background theory of flexible categorial grammar, in tandem with its descriptive uses.

Before these results are presented, a look at the historical background will be useful. The main idea of Ajdukiewicz was to note the function-argument structure of expressions (following Frege), resulting in the following type-combination rules for adjacent expressions:

$$\frac{B}{A} + A = B \qquad A + \frac{B}{A} = B.$$

Here, the functional type $\frac{B}{A}$ ('from A to B') is undirected, picking up arguments to either left or right. This allows for 'local permutations' in recognition. Later on, Bar-Hillel introduced directed variants, with the usual notations $A \backslash B$ (left-searching), B/A (right-searching), creating additional descriptive power. Nevertheless, the well known equivalence result for such categorial grammars with sets of context-free phrase-structure rules has led to a wide-spread belief in their inadequacy for linguistic purposes. (This belief has been challenged in recent years. For an up-to-date critical survey of the evidence, see Gazdar and Pullum,

Richard T. Oehrle et al. (eds.), Categorial Grammars and Natural Language Structures, 35–68.
© 1988 *by D. Reidel Publishing Company.*

1985.) Still, the mechanism remained attractive to semanticists, as it wears its semantic interpretation upon its sleeves. Thus, for instance, David Lewis has proposed to use the system in combination with transformations — and, of course, Montague Grammar employs a categorial apparatus, be it on top of arbitrary syntactic construction rules (instead of mere concatenation, as in the original enterprise). Such extensions are not our object of study here.

The line of development which is important here is illustrated by Geach (1971), whose main observation is this. Expressions in natural language can occur in many different categories: e.g., 'not' as sentence negation, predicate negation, etc. But, these occurrences are not chaotic: they can be described, starting from a basic category assignment, by some perspicuous rules of generation. Notably, we have the 'Geach Rule'

(G) $(a, b) \Rightarrow (c, a), (c, b),$ for arbitrary c.

That is, if an expression occurs in category (a, b), then it can also occur in $(c, a), (c, b)$ (with an evident transfer of meaning).

Here and henceforth, we shall use the following notation for categories or types (the latter distinction, no matter how valid, will not be important here):

— basic types: e ('entity'), t ('truth value');
— compound types: if a and b are types, so is (a, b) ('from a to b').

Other basic types might be s ('possible world'), etc. Thus, sentence negation has type (t, t), with predicate negation arising through the Geach Rule as follows: $(e, t), (e, t)$. And the same procedure accounts for, e.g., NP-negation: (t, t) also goes to $((e, t), t), ((e, t), t)$. (In these examples of expressions denoting types, outer parentheses have been dropped, for greater readability. This practice will be continued.)

The Geach Rule and its relatives have been used extensively in recent linguistic literature (cf. Ades and Steedman, 1982; Bach, 1984; Moortgat, 1984; Hoeksema, 1984). Of the many arguments to be found in this field, we mention two. First, this set-up makes it easier to capture generalizations across linguistic categories. And also, it opens up new possibilities for reconciling independently motivated syntactic structures with the demands of semantic interpretability.

EXAMPLE (NP-structure): Determiners followed by nouns with attached relative clauses are treated as follows in Montague Grammar:

$$
\begin{array}{ccc}
\text{Det} & N & R \\
p, (p, t) & p & p, p \quad \text{(Here, } p = (e, t).)
\end{array}
$$

$$
\begin{array}{ccc}
& & p \\
& p, t &
\end{array}
$$

But, there is strong syntactic evidence for another mode of combination too, viz. (Det N)R. In ordinary categorial grammar, the latter is hard to get. But, with the Geach Rule, there is an obvious road:

$$
\begin{array}{ccc}
\text{Det} & N & R \\
p, (p, t) & p & p, p \\
p, t & & \\
(p, p), (p, t) & & \\
& p, t &
\end{array}
$$

Nevertheless, this solution is not satisfactory, as we shall see in Section 3, where such diagrams get assigned a 'meaning' for their outcome type. The resulting reading would become

$$
\lambda X \cdot \{[\text{Det}]([N])\}([R](X)).
$$

To obtain the proper reading, viz.

$$
[\text{Det}]([R]([N])),
$$

an additional rule of type change is to be invoked.

As is well known, Montague lifted the type of proper names (e) to that of noun phrases ((e, t), t), for the purposes of co-ordination. Stated more generally, this move becomes the type change rule

(M) $a \Rightarrow (a, b), b,$ for arbitrary b

Now, the above NP-structure can also be analyzed as follows:

$$
\begin{array}{ccc}
\text{Det} & N & R \\
p, (p, t) & p & p, p \\
((p, p), p), ((p, p), (p, t)) & (p, p), p & \\
& (p, p), (p, t) & \\
& p, t &
\end{array}
$$

That this yields the desired interpretation will be shown in Section 3.

Gradually, researchers in this area have become aware that these piece-meal discoveries of useful type change rules are all instances of a more general and perspicuous scheme proposed as early as Lambek (1958). The main insight in that paper is this. The above rules (G) and (M) are instances of *logical validities*, when read as laws about implication:

(G) $a \to b \Rightarrow (c \to a) \to (c \to b)$
(M) $a \Rightarrow ((a \to b) \to b)$.

(The analogy between function application and Modus Ponens was discovered several times in the 1950s.) But then, a general calculus of type change may be set up, on the analogy of logical systems of natural deduction. One version (in a possible family) will be presented in the next Section. Unfortunately, the Lambek calculus fell into oblivion for two decades, for various reasons. Around 1980, linguists started re-discovering it (as indicated above), and also, some Polish logicians (see especially the dissertation Buszkowski, 1982), who were attracted by the mathematical features of the enterprise. Right now, these lines are coming together.

2. A SIMPLE LAMBEK CALCULUS

The general idea behind the system to be presented here can be formulated in two ways. First, think of a sequence of expressions, each with their basic type (or, one of their basic types, if multiple initial assignments are allowed). One starts combining these by application, while allowing type changes along the way, wherever admissible by the rules. This was the spirit of the examples in Section 1, and it leads to a presentation of the calculus as rewriting sequences of types to other sequences (as is done, e.g., in van Benthem, 1983). Another way is to think of a calculus producing only 'sequents' of the forms

$$a_1; \ldots; a_n \Rightarrow b \quad (n \geqslant 1),$$

recognizing sequences of expressions with types $a_1, \ldots, a_n$ as belonging to type b. The latter strategy is followed here, with the following calculus resulting.

Axiom. $a \Rightarrow a$

Rules.
$$a_1; \ldots ; a_i \Rightarrow b \qquad a_{i+1}; \ldots ; a_n \Rightarrow (b, c)$$
$$\overline{}$$
$$a_1; \ldots ; a_n \Rightarrow c \qquad\qquad\qquad ('(,)\text{-elimination'})$$

$$a_1; \ldots ; a_n; b \Rightarrow c$$
$$\overline{}$$
$$a_1; \ldots ; a_n \Rightarrow (b, c) \qquad\qquad\qquad ('(,)\text{-introduction'}).$$

Here, sequences on the left-hand side should always be non-empty.

EXAMPLE (A derivation of M):

$$a \Rightarrow a \quad (a, b) \Rightarrow (a, b)$$
$$\overline{}$$
$$a; (a, b) \Rightarrow b$$
$$\overline{}$$
$$a \Rightarrow ((a, b), b).$$

But, already to derive (G), additional freedom is required in using the rules, countenancing the withdrawal of assumptions from the left-hand side, as well as from the right:

$$c \Rightarrow c \quad (c, a) \Rightarrow (c, a)$$
$$\overline{}$$
$$c; (c, a) \Rightarrow a \qquad (a, b) \Rightarrow (a, b)$$
$$\overline{}$$
$$c; (c, a); (a, b) \Rightarrow b$$
$$\overline{}$$
$$(c, a); (a, b) \Rightarrow (c, b) \qquad (!)$$
$$\overline{}$$
$$(a, b) \Rightarrow ((c, a), (c, b))$$

When such amendments are made, also in the application rules, a calculus results with the following strong property:

if $a_1; \ldots ; a_n \Rightarrow b$ is provable,
then so is $a_{\pi(1)}; \ldots ; a_{\pi(n)} \Rightarrow b$.
for any *permutation* π of $\{1, \ldots, n\}$.

(This is proved in van Benthem 1983.)

This outcome may seem very counter-intuitive from a linguistic point of view; and, therefore, it is important to understand the situation properly. First and foremost, this outcome is a result of our non-directional approach (reflected already in the notation '(a, b)'). Lambek's original formulation of his calculus has the familiar directed slashes /, \; and the resulting calculi do not have the above 'permutation closure'. So, this phenomenon is by no means an essential feature of the enterprise. On the other hand, there are indeed various viewpoints from which permutation closure may not be such a disadvantage after all. On the linguistic side, Bach has pointed at the existence of free word-order languages allowing virtually all permutations of their expressions (cf. Bach, 1984). Also methodologically, Flynn (1983) demonstrates the virtues of having a directionless categorial grammar, supplemented only afterwards by certain 'word-order conventions', acting as linguistic filters. And finally, there is also the more philosophical perspective of van Benthem (1984c), where a flexible categorial grammar is used to capture an independent notion of semantic interpretability, not subordinated to, but parallel with syntactic grammaticality. In that light, a calculus should precisely *account for* the fact that we have so little difficulty in understanding permuted versions of expressions (e.g., when talking to our toddlers).

In any case, here and henceforth, we shall consider a permutation-closed version of the above calculus, adding an explicit Permutation Rule, as formulated above. The resulting calculus is called L; and derivability of sequents will be indicated simply as follows:

$$a_1; \ldots; a_n \Rightarrow_L b.$$

This move makes the system easier to study technically. Thus, one obtains a pilot example for the more complex case of the $/, \backslash$ version, not to be treated here.

For *practical* purposes, however, the above formulation is not quite appropriate yet. A more perspicuous reformulation would be to employ *natural deduction trees* for implicational logic, with rules of Modus Ponens and Conditionalization.

EXAMPLE (Another derivation of (G)):

$$
\cfrac{\cfrac{\cfrac{\dfrac{c \quad (c, a)}{a} \quad (a, b)}{b}}{(c, b)} \text{ (withdraw } c)}{(c, a), (c, b)} \text{ (withdraw } (c, a)).
$$

Notice, however, that there are strong restrictions on Conditionaliza-tion. E.g., one cannot derive $t \Rightarrow (e, t)$, as *empty* withdrawals are forbidden. But also, one cannot derive, say, $e, (e, t) \Rightarrow e, t$ (presumably via $e; e, (e, t) \Rightarrow t?$), as occurrences of 'premises' on the left have to be withdrawn *one at a time*. (Finally, every conclusion always has to remain in the scope of at least one assumption: the empty string is never rewritten to any type.)

$$* \quad \frac{t}{(e, t)} \quad \text{(withdraw } e \text{ vacuously)}$$

$$\frac{\begin{array}{cc} e & e, (e, t) \end{array}}{\begin{array}{cc} e & (e, t) \end{array}}$$

$$* \quad \frac{t}{(e, t)} \quad \text{(withdraw multiple } e\text{'s)}$$

$$\frac{\begin{array}{cc} e & e, t \end{array}}{t}$$

$$\frac{}{(e, t), t} \quad \text{(withdraw } (e, t))$$

$$* \quad \frac{}{e, ((e, t), t)} \quad \text{(withdraw final } e)$$

Viewed like this, L is a calculus with the same 'logical rules' as always, but with different 'structural rules' for book-keeping. In particular, L describes the logic of *occurrences of premises*, rather than premises as equivalence classes of occurrences. This makes L still amenable to general techniques for propositional logic, while also giving it a non-trivially different flavour, as we shall see below. To have a name for its 'traditional' companion, we shall call the latter I: being the constructive or *intuitionistic* logic of implication. (E.g., the above natural deduction system will not derive the non-constructive tautology $((a \to b) \to a) \to a$ ('Peirce's Law').)

Not only from the linguistic viewpoint, but also from the present logical one, our specific calculus L has competitors. For instance, there are obvious modulations of the structural rules concerning Conditional-ization, such as allowing withdrawal of at least one (rather than: exactly one) occurrence of a premise. Or, leaving this particular stipulation as before, there is still the question of admitting successive conditionalizations until no 'assumptions' remain in force.

EXAMPLE (p and $((p, p), p)$): In L, one can derive $p \Rightarrow ((p, p), p)$, but not the converse 'lowering rule' $((p, p), p) \Rightarrow p$. A slight modification would allow the latter, however:

$$\frac{\dfrac{p}{(p,p)} \ {}^{(!)} \ (p,p),p}{p}$$

This particular transition is discussed in Zwarts (1986), in connection with the interaction between intransitive verbs (type p) and adverbial operations of type $(p, p), p$.

Finally, even *directed* slashes \, / might make sense in logic, as distinguishing between the two conditional constructions

$$if \, A, (then) \, B \quad and \quad B, if \, A.$$

There are at least certain anaphoric differences between the two uses, and perhaps even differences of logical import.

Nevertheless, in this paper, we continue with our simple pilot example.

Appendix: Variants of the Combinatorial Mechanism

In practice, there are still various policies for using a calculus of type change. Lambek's approach is an early instance of so-called *parsing as deduction*; and various parsing strategies are possible with the above proof system. In general, Lambek derivations can be highly abstract: Conditionalization manipulates types for 'phantom expressions' not actually occurring in the string to be parsed. On the other hand, our actual linguistic examples mostly exhibited a more conservative strategy, working with application only, and changing *single* types when needed (cf. van Benthem, 1984c).

This raises the question if we can set up the calculus so that all conditionalizations are performed before all instances of Modus Ponens. It turns out that one can go a long way here with the following general forms of G and M (together with Permutation):

(1) G^+: from $(\vec{d}, (a, b))$ to $(\vec{d}, ((c, a), (c, b)))$

(2) M^+: from $(\vec{d}, a)$ to $(\vec{d}, (\vec{c}, (a, b)), (\vec{d}, (\vec{c}, b))))$

(3)   Permutation: from $(\vec{d}, a)$ to $(\pi[\vec{d}], a)$,
         for any permutation π of the type sequence $\vec{d}$.

Here, with $\vec{d} = d_1, \ldots, d_k$, '$(\vec{d}, a)$' stands for '$(d_1, (d_2, \ldots, (d_k, a) \ldots))$'.
As these rules do not decrease complexity, however, they will not
account for such valid cases of type change as 'Argument Lowering':
$(((e, t), t), t) \Rightarrow (e, t)$. This may be remedied again by admitting
categorial axioms; but, we will not pursue the necessary technicalities
here.

3. THEORETICAL QUESTIONS

Now, there are some obvious theoretical questions about the calculus
L. Lambek himself was concerned with *decidability*: by means of a
proof-theoretic 'cut-elimination' argument, he showed that his calculus
was equivalent to one in which all rules add complexity (and hence,
decidability is immediate). For the present formulation, these same
techniques go through (as was observed, amongst others, by W.
Buszkowski (personal communication)); and so we have a

THEOREM. The calculus L is decidable.

For future reference, here is the formulation of an equivalent calculus
with the desired property:

Axiom. $a \Rightarrow a$
Rules: 'Permutation'

$$\frac{a_1; \ldots; a_n; b \Rightarrow c}{a_1; \ldots; a_n \Rightarrow (b, c)}$$

but now rather also a rule of 'left-introduction':

$$\frac{a_1; \ldots; a_i \Rightarrow b \qquad a_{i+1}; \ldots; a_n; c \Rightarrow a}{a_1; \ldots; a_n; (b, c) \Rightarrow a}$$

Note that this calculus has the Subformula Property: one only encounters subformulas of the final types at every node. Hence, proofs can be analyzed quite easily, tracing the history of end-types upward in the proof tree. This method will be used extensively in Section 6.

Another line of enquiry concerns the *recognizing power* of Lambek calculi. In Cohen (1967), an equivalence was claimed in *weak capacity* for Lambek grammars and ordinary directed categorial grammars (and hence context-free grammars). This proof was shown to be defective in Zielonka (1978) and Buszkowski (1985). The situation right now is this. For uni-directional Lambek grammars (only /), the equivalence is valid (Buszkowski, 1985); for the bi-directional variant (with both / and \), the question is open. As for our undirected version, the matter will be studied in Section 5 below. In any case, given the current state of the linguistic debate on the complexity of natural languages (cf. Gazdar and Pullum, 1985), eventual context-freeness of the Lambek calculi would no longer be a sign of fatal weakness — as it was perceived in the 1960s. Times have changed.

In addition, there are also issues of *strong capacity*, a topic which was indeed central in the examples of Section 1. Again, our calculus L has an overabundance of possible combinations (see van Benthem, 1984c), which is to be curbed in the directed variants for linguistic purposes. On this topic, see Zwarts (1986), with applications to the major language types SVO, SOV, etc. For instance, in Zwarts' analysis of the Celtic word order VSO, our calculus L would allow both 'constituents' VS and SO:

$$
\begin{array}{ccc}
\text{V} & \text{S} & \text{O} \\
e,(e,t) & (e,t),t & (e,t),t \\
\underbrace{\hspace{4em}}_{\displaystyle e,t} & & \\
\end{array}
$$

$$
\underbrace{\hspace{12em}}_{\displaystyle t}
$$

$$
\begin{array}{ccc}
\text{V} & \text{S} & \text{O} \\
e,(e,t), & (e,t),t & (e,t),t \\
& \underbrace{\hspace{6em}}_{\displaystyle (e,(e,t)),(e,t)} & \\
& \underbrace{\hspace{9em}}_{\displaystyle (e,(e,t)),t} & \\
\end{array}
$$

$$
t
$$

Once perceived, such unorthodox structures may actually have points in their favour, witness the discussion in the above book.

But, the Lambek approach also generates new questions of its own, having to do, naturally, with the *variety* of type structure which it creates. For instance, one natural question is to describe the total set of 'outcomes' b to which a given set of types $a_1, \ldots, a_n$ can reduce. In general, there will be *infinitely* many of these: if b is derivable, then also (b, c), c, and so on. But, not anything goes. To see this, here is a useful *invariant* of L-derivations. First, define the *e-count* of any type as follows:

e-count $(e) = 1$
e-count $(x) = 0$, for all basic types x, $x \neq e$
e-count $(a, b) = e$-count $(b) - e$-count (a)

And likewise, arbitrary counts may be defined for other basic types. Then, for longer sequences, one merely *adds* individual counts.

EXAMPLE: $(((e, t), t), (e, t))$ has e-count -2, t-count $+1$.

The following result is in van Benthem (1986a):

LEMMA. If $a_1; \ldots ; a_n \Rightarrow_L b$, then b and $a_1; \ldots ; a_n$ have the same counts for all basic types.
The proof is by induction on the length of derivations, and some counting.

One immediate consequence is this: no expression reduces to both the types e and t. Thus, there are limits to the metamorphoses in this categorial grammar. Many further applications are found in Section 6. Here, we just point at a difference with the ordinary logic I, which lacks this invariance. (E.g., it proves $(e \rightarrow (e \rightarrow t)) \Rightarrow (e \rightarrow t)$, with different e-counts on both sides.)

OBSERVATION. L is not faithfully embeddable into I.
Proof. The following are all non-equivalent in L:

$$e, t \quad e, (e, t) \quad e, (e, (e, t)) \ldots ;$$

because of different e-counts. But, I satisfies Diego's Theorem, stating that, on any finite number of atomic formulas, only *finitely* many non-logically equivalent formulas exist. Thus, I lacks the sensitivity needed to embed L. Q.E.D.

Question: Is I faithfully embeddable into L?
Given the above constraint, it might even be thought that the set of all outcomes b for $a_1; \ldots ; a_n$ has the following simple structure:

it contains one simplest type b_0, and all others follow from it, i.e., $b_0 \Rightarrow_L b$. This is not so: (at most) *three* such types may be needed. (For the exact result, see van Benthem, 1983.) For instance, (e, t); (t, e) reduces to both (e, e) and (t, t), none of which L-implies the other. Their counts are identical (as they derive from the same sequence), but a simple proof analysis shows the impossibility of a transition. (That identity of count cannot be all there is to derivability, as evidenced here, follows already from the former relation's being *symmetric*. Obviously, one does not have the same for derivable sequents. For instance, $e \Rightarrow_L ((e, t), t)$, but the converse is not even provable in I, let alone in L.)

There is also a different kind of variety, even for one single outcome $a_1; \ldots; a_n \Rightarrow_L b$. How many different *readings* are there, corresponding to the various proof trees for this sequent? To answer this question, a closer look is needed at systematic connections between L-derivations and their 'meanings'.

4. LAMBDA SEMANTICS FOR TYPE CHANGE

The intuitive motivation of the above type change rules is that they suggest natural ways of lifting denotations from one type to another. For example, in an obvious notation, M corresponds to the transition

$$x_a \mapsto \lambda y_{a,b} \cdot y(x).$$

Likewise, G corresponds to

$$x_{a,b} \mapsto \lambda y_{c,a} \cdot \lambda z_c \cdot x(y(z)).$$

Thus, lambda terms serve as denotational 'recipes' here, for computing a b-value $\tau_b = \tau_b(x_{a_1}, \ldots, x_{a_n})$, for given transitions $a_1; \ldots; a_n \Rightarrow b$.

Upon closer inspection, these terms may be read off from *L-derivations*, rather than final transition sequences. Different proofs for the same sequent may even produce different recipes. In more familiar terms, different categorial sentence structures may correspond to different semantic readings.

The general procedure is described in van Benthem (1983), and need not be repeated here. Its basic idea is simply the following form of *type-driven translation*. For one-step proofs, i.e., axioms $a \Rightarrow a$, the term will be x_a itself. For longer proofs, the following cases arise:

(1) $a_1; \ldots; a_i \Rightarrow b$ (term $\tau_b(x_{a_1}, \ldots, x_{a_i})$) and
$a_{i+1}; \ldots; a_n \Rightarrow (b, c)$ (term $\tau_{b,c}(x_{a_{i+1}}, \ldots, x_{a_n})$) produce
the *application* $\tau_{b,c}(\tau_b)$ for the conclusion
$a_1; \ldots; a_n \Rightarrow c$.

(2) $a_1; \ldots; a_n; b \Rightarrow c$ (term $\tau_c(x_{a_1}, \ldots, x_{a_n}, x_b)$) produces
the *abstraction* $\lambda x_b \cdot \tau_c$ for the conclusion
$a_1; \ldots; a_n \Rightarrow (b, c)$.

(3)   for permutations, perform the appropriate changes among
the free variables.

For instance, when applied to L-derivations corresponding to the two
analyses of the *Det N R* structure mentioned in Section 1, this procedure will yield the two distinct readings mentioned there. (What will be
needed for the purpose of simplification are some *lambda conversions*
of the form

$$\lambda x_a \cdot \tau(B_a) \mapsto [B_a/x_a]\tau,$$

with suitable care as to freedom and bondage.)

Some analysis of the above procedure delimits a special class Λ of
lambda terms serving as recipes (with various restrictions on occurrences of free and bound variables). Conversely, then, every such term
corresponds to an L-derivation, and we have the following result from
van Benthem (1983):

THEOREM. There is an effective correspondence between L-deriva-
tions and Λ-terms expressing their meanings.

This result may be used to solve the earlier question about variety of
readings. By considering associated Λ-terms, and bringing these into
normal form, the above paper proves a further:

THEOREM. For every L-derivable sequent, there are only finitely
many readings, up to logical equivalence.

Actually, the above correspondence is one of a family. A similar connection between the class of *all* lambda terms and derivations in the
intuitionistic implication calculus I plays an important role in logical

Proof Theory. And, as observed in Buszkowski (1984b), there is even a
'continuum' here, with quite a few interesting intermediate steps. The
general picture is this:

lambda-free terms ——————— Λ ——————— full lambda language

Ajdukiewicz calculus — Lambek calculus — Heyting calculus

And indeed, transitions outside of L can still have a very natural
lambda meaning. E.g., the sequent $e; (e, (e, t)) \Rightarrow t$ would come with
the recipe of Reflexivization: $x_{e,(e,t)}(x_e)(x_e)$. (Compare the phrase 'Maia
washes', in the sense of 'Maia washes herself'.)

Finally, returning to the issue of different semantic readings, there
remains a question of empirical adequacy. Often, merely providing a
suitable number of different categorial structures for a single sentence
with various readings is itself taken to constitute an analysis of the
latter. But, of course, the question remains if these different categorial
derivations match up with those readings (via the above procedure).
This is not always straightforward. For instance, to obtain the intuitive
semantic scope-readings for 'Every dog hates some cat', some care is
needed when handling argument positions of the transitive verb (cf. van
Benthem, 1986a, Chapter 7). The lambda algorithm should not be used
blindly.

Digression: Combinatory Logic

Another perspective upon the meaning of type changes arises when
these are described using *combinators* from combinatory logic (cf.
Barendregt, 1981). As Steedman has argued, there is even some evidence for linguistic relevance of the basic combinators S, K, with
definitions

$$Kxy = x$$
$$Sxyz = (xz)yz.$$

As these two form a complete set, defining all lambda terms, the
calculus I would become relevant after all. Be this as it may, it would
also be of interest to have a combinator analysis for the restricted
language Λ. But, as Buszkowski has pointed out (private communication), no finite functional completeness theorem can exist for Λ. (This

follows by an appropriate modification of the argument for non-finite-axiomatizability of the directed Lambek calculus over Ajdukiewicz' system given in Zielonka, 1981.)

Constraints on Type Change

Still, the lambda language is an obedient medium, recording rather than constraining decisions made as to type change rules. How can one arrive at further *constraints*, with some real bite? Here is one proposal. Type changes should not only be feasible in the above sense, but also, they should preserve certain structures on the type domains. One notable case is that of logical implication, or *inclusion*.

Define the relation $\sqsubseteq$ on all type domains as follows:

— on D_e, $\sqsubseteq$ is the identity; on D_t, it is $\leqslant$,
— on $D_{a,b}$, $f \sqsubseteq g$ iff for all $x \in D_a$, $f(x) \sqsubseteq g(x)$.

This relation generalizes, amongst others, truth-functional implication as well as set inclusion. Now, one very reasonable condition to consider is 'preservation of logical consequence':

> if $a_1; \ldots ; a_n \Rightarrow b$ is derivable.
> and $x_1, y_1 \in D_{a_1}, \ldots, x_n, y_n \in D_{a_n}$ such that
> $x_1 \sqsubseteq y_1, \ldots, x_n \sqsubseteq y_n$, then the recipe τ_b should satisfy
> $\tau_b(x_1, \ldots, x_n) \sqsubseteq \tau_b(y_1, \ldots, y_n)$.

(There is some harmless abuse of notation here.) But, not all L-transitions satisfy this condition: G does, but M does not. For instance, even when $x \sqsubseteq y$ in type (e, t), there is no guarantee for the inclusion of the produced $(((e, t), t), t)$-type objects $\{A \subseteq \text{POW}(D_e) \mid x \in A\}$ and $\{A \subseteq \text{POW}(D_e) \mid y \in A\}$. (For trivial reasons, though, Montague's own case $e \Rightarrow (e, t), t$ passes the test.)

Thus, an additional constraint arises on Λ-terms (cf. van Benthem, 1986a). All occurrences of the free variables $x_{a_1}, \ldots, x_{a_n}$ in the term τ_b for $a_1; \ldots ; a_n \Rightarrow_L b$ should be syntactically *positive* in the following sense:

— x_a occurs positively in x_a (but in no other variable),
— if x_a occurs positively in A, then also in $A(B)$, for any (fitting) term B,
— if x_a occurs positively in A, then also in $\lambda y \cdot A$, for any variable y distinct from x_a.

Note that the given recipe for G satisfied this test, whereas that for M did not.

Through the above correspondence between lambda terms and inferences, it can be seen which additional constraint on L-derivations arises in this way:

whenever an inference of the following form takes place:

$$\frac{a_1; \ldots; a_i \Rightarrow b \qquad a_{i+1}; \ldots; a_n \Rightarrow b, c}{a_1; \ldots; a_n \Rightarrow c,}$$

all type occurrences $a_1, \ldots, a_i$ should be transferred to the right-hand side (by (,)-introduction) eventually.

Whether this particular constraint is reasonable, remains a matter of debate. E.g., in Groenendijk and Stokhof (1984), it is claimed that failures of preservation with M, a rule otherwise needed for the purposes of coordination, rather shows that we *need* an L-connected *family* of types for single expressions, with some of their behaviour accounted for at one level, and other aspects elsewhere. Such a viewpoint only reinforces the flexible categorial perspective adopted here.

Encore: Type Change and Inference

The preceding discussion illustrates a more general topic, viz. the interaction of type change rules with already established semantic phenomena. In fact, there is a whole hierarchy of constraints, ensuring certain 'similarities' between old and new meanings (see the discussion of, e.g., the 'homomorphism condition' in van Benthem, 1986a, inspired by Keenan and Faltz, 1985). One particularly important interaction is that between the well-known notion of *monotonicity*, used in various semantic theories, and type changing. We have a systematic theory of (upward or downward) monotone operators, with a complete marking of the syntactic positions they govern (cf. van Benthem, 1986a).

EXAMPLE: 'No girl loves every boy'.

'No' is downward monotone in both its arguments, 'every' has monotonicity type 'left down/right up'. With this information, 'monotonicity markings' can be computed in the phrase structure tree:

The final markings underneath result from obvious algebraic rules of combination.

Now, these markings have been assigned on the usual categorial analysis. What happens to the corresponding inferential behaviour when other constituent structures become available, by our type change mechanism? For instance, on the ordinary reading of an NP with a relative clause 'all (CN R)' (e.g., 'all girls who swim'), both CN and R occur in downward monotone position, supporting the inferences to 'all beautiful girls who swim' and 'all girls who swim professionally'. But what about the non-standard reading "(all CN) R', as given in Section 1 above? A complete solution to this problem may be found in van Benthem (1986b), in terms of the earlier natural deduction calculus for type change, combined with systematic monotonicity marking inter-leaved with all the deduction rules. It turns out that, e.g., the various readings of complex NP structure developed in Section 1 all obtain their correct monotonicity effects.

5. POSSIBLE WORLDS SEMANTICS FOR TYPE CHANGE

The analogy with intuitionistic implication logic I also suggests a more traditional semantics for the calculus L; not for its derivations, but for its sequents as such.

The usual semantics for I has models

$$M = \langle \mathscr{I}, \sqsubseteq, V \rangle,$$

with $\mathscr{I}$ a set of 'forcing conditions' or 'information pieces', $\sqsubseteq$ a partial order ('possible growth of information') and V a valuation giving a truth value to each proposition letter at every $i \in \mathcal{I}$, with *true* persisting along $\sqsubseteq$-successors. Then, evaluation is as follows:

$$M \vDash p[i] \quad \text{iff} \quad V_i(p) = true$$
$$M \vDash \alpha \rightarrow \beta[i] \quad \text{iff} \quad \text{for all } j \sqsupseteq i, M \vDash \alpha[j] \text{ only if } M \vDash \beta[j].$$

Finally, validity for a sequent $\alpha_1, \ldots, \alpha_n / \beta$ ('$\alpha_1, \ldots, \alpha_n \vDash \beta$') means that, in all M, at all $i \in \mathcal{I}$, if $\alpha_1, \ldots, \alpha_n$ hold at i, then so does β. A very straightforward Henkin completeness proof then establishes that always

$$\alpha_1, \ldots, \alpha_n \vDash \beta \quad \text{iff} \quad \alpha_1, \ldots, \alpha_n \Rightarrow_I \beta.$$

The difference in the case of L has to do with one's view of the 'information pieces'. These are now, so to speak, *checks* for verification, that can be cashed only once. This consideration leads to the following new modelling. Models will be of the form

$$M = \langle \mathcal{I}, \oplus, V \rangle,$$

where $\oplus$ is now a binary operation of *addition* of information pieces. Here, $\oplus$ will be required to be

associative: $i \oplus (j \oplus k) = (i \oplus j) \oplus k$, as well as
commutative: $i \oplus j = j \oplus i$;
though not necessarily *idempotent* ('$i \oplus i = i$').

(For directed versions of the Lambek calculus, commutativity will have to be abandoned as well.) This new structure is reflected in the key clause for evaluation of complex types (or formulas):

$$M \vDash (a, b)[i] \text{ iff } \textit{for all } j \in \mathcal{I} \text{ such that } M \vDash a[j], M \vDash b[i \oplus j].$$

One could re-introduce an ordering $\sqsubseteq$ here, by setting

$$i \sqsubseteq j \quad \text{iff} \quad i \oplus j = j.$$

But, this does not make the above clause definable in terms of $\sqsubseteq$ only.

This time, no persistence condition is added for the valuation.

Hence, L-types will lack the *Heredity* enjoyed by all I-formulas (on the former semantics), which, once true at some $i \in \mathscr{I}$, remain true at all $j \sqsupseteq i$. This complicates matters a bit, though not overly so.

Finally, also *semantic consequence* is to be defined with a new twist:

$a_1, \ldots, a_n \vDash b$ if, for all $M = \langle \mathscr{I}, \oplus, V \rangle$, and all
$i_1, \ldots, i_n \in \mathscr{I}$, if $M \vDash a_1[i_1]$ and $\ldots$ and $M \vDash a_n[i_n]$,
then $M \vDash b[i_1 \oplus \cdots \oplus i_n]$.

For instance, it may be checked that all inference rules of L preserve this notion of consequence.

Now, the usual logical topics can be raised with respect to this semantics for the L-language.

First, corresponding to the above truth definition, there is an obvious method of *semantic tableaus* for investigating validity of sequents, searching for possible counter-examples. Its details are messier than with I, because now, one needs to keep track of some finite number of information pieces at each stage (*plus* all their sums), adding new ones to falsify formulas (a, b), while checking truth of formulas (c, d) at others, for ever new combinations. Moreover, in principle, the search can go on *ad infinitum*. For I, this possibility is cut off by using the Heredity of I-formulas: at some suitably large stage, no relevant changes in truth value will occur. Here, no such reasoning is available. But, as in similar arguments for the modal logic S4, judicious 'bending backward' towards pieces already used will result in a *finite* counter-example, if one exists at all. Moreover, the size of that finite model is bounded by the complexity of the formulas involved in an effective way. Thus, filling in details, one obtains a proof for the *decidability* of semantic consequence.

Next, to show that the latter notion is indeed axiomatized by the calculus L, it suffices to show how non-L-derivability leads to counter-examples (i.e., 'completeness'). (Soundness was demonstrated before already.) For this purpose, a simple Henkin model can be constructed. Let $\mathscr{I}$ consist of all finite sets of formulas, viewed typographically as occurrences. The operation $\oplus$ is set-theoretic union. (But note, e.g., that $\{p, q\} \oplus \{p, r\}$ will become $\{p, q, p, r\}$, not $\{p, q, r\}$.) Finally, the valuation V works as follows: $V_i(p) = true$ iff $i \Rightarrow_L p$. Then, a Truth Lemma may be proved, by induction on the complexity of a:

$$M \vDash a[i] \quad \text{iff} \quad i \Rightarrow_L a.$$

Proof. Suppose $i \Rightarrow_L a = (b, c)$. Let $j \in \mathscr{I}$ such that $M \vDash b[j]$. By the inductive hypothesis: $j \Rightarrow_L b$. So, in L, i; $j \Rightarrow c$. Again by the inductive hypothesis: $M \vDash c[i; j]$, i.e., $M \vDash c[i \oplus j]$. In other words, $M \vDash (b, c)[i]$. Conversely, suppose that not $i \Rightarrow_L (b, c)$. Then neither i; $b \Rightarrow_L c$. By the inductive hypothesis: $M \nvDash c[i \oplus b]$. But, by the axiom of L: $b \Rightarrow_L b$, and hence (using the inductive hypothesis once more) $M \vDash b[b]$. Therefore, $M \nvDash (b, c)[i]$.   Q.E.D.

As an immediate consequence, we have a completeness result.

THEOREM. L is complete with respect to the above possible worlds semantics.

As a final topic of interest, there is the issue of *correspondence*. On top of L, there are various further principles, on the road toward the full I, whose semantic content can be established. (For further definitions and background, see van Benthem, 1984a.)

EXAMPLE.

(1)   Thinning: a; $a \Rightarrow a$.

To be unrestrictedly valid, this inference requires that $\oplus$ satisfy, for all i, j,

$$i \oplus j = i \quad \text{or} \quad i \oplus j = j.$$

(Under the earlier definition of $\sqsubseteq$, this expresses 'linearity'.)

(2) a; $a, (a, b) \Rightarrow b$.

Here the equivalent structural condition is a form of idempotence:

$$i \oplus i \oplus j = i \oplus j, \quad \text{for all } i, j.$$

Remark. The correspondence (1) may look surprising, as not even the full I-semantics presupposes linearity of growth patterns. Here again, the Heredity of I-semantics is involved. Once proposition letters have their truth transmitted along $\sqsubseteq$, this phenomenon will extend to all formulas, also in our new semantics. And then, a; $a \Rightarrow a$, or even a; $b \Rightarrow a$, will become valid without any special relational condition at all.

All these themes can be extended to the case where the type change calculus also has an operation $\cdot$ of *concatenation* (as was the case in

Lambek's original paper). The corresponding rules will be

$$\frac{a_1; \ldots; a_i \Rightarrow b \qquad a_{i+1}; \ldots; a_n \Rightarrow c}{a_1; \ldots; a_n \Rightarrow b \cdot c}$$

as well as

$$\frac{a_1; \ldots; a_n; b; c \Rightarrow d}{a_1; \ldots; a_n, b \cdot c \Rightarrow d.}$$

Derivable laws are, e.g., $a, (b, c) \Rightarrow (a \cdot b), c$ and its converse. There is an obvious similarity with the connective $\wedge$ ('and') here. But note that, e.g., the usual natural deduction rule for eliminating conjunction is not available, as $a \cdot b \Rightarrow b$ is invalid.

As for the semantics, the natural clause seems to be the following:

$$M \vDash a \cdot b[i] \text{ iff there exist } j, k \text{ with } i = j \oplus k$$
$$\text{such that } M \vDash a[j] \text{ and } M \vDash b[k]$$

This validates the above rules. Nevertheless, a completeness result is not quite straightforward. (See Došen, 1985; Buszkowski, 1986 for the necessary argument, in somewhat different settings from the present one.)

Despite all these matchings, the present possible worlds semantics stays very close to syntactic analogies (even more than its relative for I; cf. van Benthem, 1984b). In particular, there is a close duality between this approach and the *algebraic* semantics for Lambek calculi developed in Buszkowski (1982, 1986). (This point appears explicitly in Došen, 1986 — which contains an independent discovery of the main results of this section, in the wider setting of a complete generalized propositional calculus. Došen also points out connections with earlier work on the semantics of relevant logics, by Urquhart, Fine, and others.) Indeed, one does not think of the above models as 'ordinary' possible worlds models at all. But then, this may also be a virtue. The present semantics seems to presuppose a more dynamical view of 'evaluation' as 'consuming' an index i to establish the truth of a formula. (For instance, think of i as a counter with registers for proposition letters, lowering the register each time a proposition letter gets verified.) And this metaphor, at least, seems to have some suggestive value beyond the present limited setting.

6. LOCATING THE LAMBEK LANGUAGES

In this section, we return to a more traditional question, summarized in a conjecture found in Buszkowski (1984a):

> The languages recognized by our commutative Lambek grammars are precisely the permutation closures of the context-free languages.

'Recognition' here means the following. We are working with a finite alphabet Σ, assigning one or more initial types to each symbol. One type will be distinguished, say t; and all those sequences of symbols constitute 'the language' of this assignment which have an L-valid derivation to t.

EXAMPLE (propositional logic, Polish):

Let $\Sigma = \{p, \neg, \wedge\}$, and assign $p \mapsto t$, $\neg \mapsto (t, t)$, $\wedge \mapsto (t, (t, t))$, as usual. Evidently, all well-formed formulas will be recognized as t, already on the Ajdukiewicz scheme alone. What the L-apparatus adds are *at least* all permutations of such formulas. And in this case, it recognizes no more. For, suppose that $a_1; \ldots ; a_n \Rightarrow_L t$, with all a_i ($1 \leqslant i \leqslant n$) from among the above three types. Recall the notion of t-*count* (Section 2): the conclusion t has t-count $+1$, and hence so should the premise sequence. Now, t-count$(t, t) = 0$, t-count$(t, (t, t)) = -1$. Therefore, the only sequences reducing to t must have, say,

n occurrences of $\wedge$, $n + 1$ occurrences of p,
and an arbitrary number of occurrences of $\neg$.

But, as is easily seen, any such sequence is a permutation of some propositional formula.

This pattern of argument will be used repeatedly in what follows.

Remarks.

(1) The above class can *not* be recognized if one enriches the calculus from L to I. For, then, since p must be recognized, and hence 'type(p)' $\Rightarrow$ 'distinguished type t', also 'type(p); type(p)' $\Rightarrow$ t, by the I-rules. And so, e.g., the string pp will be recognized, outside of the desired language. Moral: a *stronger* type change calculus may *lose* power of recognition.

(2) Not even all regular languages can be recognized without having to assign more than one type to basic symbols. E.g., $a^* = \{\langle \rangle, a, aa, aaa, \ldots\}$ is recognized by L starting from the assignment $a \mapsto t$ or

t, t. With just one type: $a \mapsto t$, no recognition occurs; as, e.g., $t; t$ does not reduce to t in L (using t-counts). Recognition does become possible, however, with one *complex* distinguished type t, t: as (t, t); $(t, t) \Rightarrow_L (t, t)$. (Compare: we cannot repeat 'She swims she swims . . .' to one single sentence, whereas we can with certain operators: 'The weather is very very very . . . depressing'.)

(3) The examples suggest the following conjecture. Start from any Ajdukiewicz grammar recognizing some language T. Then, its Lambek version will recognize the permutation closure of T.

Counter-example: $\Sigma = \{a, b\}$; $a \mapsto e$, $b \mapsto ((e, t), t)$, $t; t$ is distinguished. The Ajdukiewicz grammar recognizes the empty set, whereas its Lambek variant recognizes $\{ab, ba\}$.

Not all context-free, or even regular languages are permutation-closed. On the other hand, there are permutation closures of context-free languages which are themselves not context-free. For instance, the closure of the regular language $(abc)^*$ is the set of all strings with equal numbers of a, b, c's. And the latter set is not context-free, since its intersection with the regular set $a^*b^*c^*$ is the non-context-free set $\{a^n b^n c^n\}$. An L-grammar recognizing this language has $a \mapsto e$, $b \mapsto (e, s), c \mapsto (s, t)$ or $s, (t, t)$.

Henceforth, we fix some finite alphabet $\Sigma = \{s_1, \ldots, s_k\}$. Now, here is the main result of this section.

THEOREM. All languages consisting of the permutation closure of some context-free language are Lambek recognizable.

(For an outline of an alternative proof to the one to follow, see Buszkowski, 1984a.)

Let T be a permutation closure of some context-free language $T1$. By *Parikh's Theorem* (see Ginsburg, 1966), the set of 'occurrence tuples' for $T1$, i.e.,

$$\{\langle \text{number of } s_1 \text{ in } \varepsilon, \ldots, \text{number of } s_k \text{ in } \varepsilon \rangle \mid \varepsilon \text{ a string in } T1\},$$

is *semi-linear*. That is, this set is a finite union of 'linear' sets generated by one fixed k-tuple of numbers and addition of arbitrary multiples of some finite set of k-tuples ('periods').

Example: The occurrence set for propositional logic ($\Sigma = \{p, \neg, \wedge\}$) is itself linear, being of the form

$$(1, 0, 0) + \lambda(0, 1, 0) + \mu(1, 0, 1).$$

Evidently, T consists of all sequences having an occurrence tuple belonging to the (semi-linear) occurrence set for $T1$.

Now, we can simplify matters. Observe that, for any linear set, there exists already a *regular* language with precisely that occurrence set. The procedure will be clear from the following:

Example: A regular language producing the occurrence set of the propositional formulas is

$$p; \, \neg^*; \, (p \wedge)^*.$$

Hence, any permutation closure of a context-free language is already a permutation closure of some regular language. And to show that the latter can all be L-recognized, it suffices to prove that

(1) every singleton $\{a\}$ is L-recognized;

(2) every union of L-recognized languages is L-recognizable (It is automatically permutation-closed if its components were);

(3) every permutation closure of the concatenation of two L-languages is L-recognizable;

(4) every permutation closure of the Kleene iteration of an L-language is L-recognizable.

All this will be proved, relying heavily on properties of the cut-free version of L presented in Section 2.

SINGLETONS. Let a be assigned t, all other symbols in Σ going to some other type e (say). Among sequences of basic types, only $\langle a \rangle$ itself reduces to t.

UNION. Let $T1$ be recognized via the assignment $G1$, and $T2$ via $G2$, with distinguished types t_1, t_2, respectively. Without changes in recognition, it may be assumed that all types used in the two grammars are different. Now, choose some *new* basic type t^*. Next, assign types to symbols s as follows. Retain all old types. If s has a type of the form $(a_1, (\ldots (a_k, t_1) \ldots))$, with final t_1, then also give it a new type $(a_1, (\ldots (a_k, t^*) \ldots))$. And do likewise for types ending in t_2.

CLAIM. This assignment L-recognizes exactly $T1 \cup T2$.

Proof. If a sequence σ was in $T1$, then it had an L-derivation $a_1; \ldots ; a_n \Rightarrow t_1$ for some distribution of $G1$-basic types over its symbols. Now, let us reflect upon the form of this proof, in the *cut-free* version of L. (This kind of analysis will be repeated throughout this entire argument.) Continuing upward in the proof tree, there will be some branch with always t_1 on the right-hand side (as basic types cannot be reduced). Such a branch must end in an axiom $t_1 \Rightarrow t_1$. Now, replace these two occurrences of t_1 by t^*, and then, going down again, likewise with all their 'offspring' in the derivation. In this fashion, a derivation is obtained for t^* from a sequence of types exactly one of which has a final t^*. (To see this, observe that the left-hand t^* on top can only end up on the *right-hand* side of (,)-introductions.) And such a sequence can be recognized in the new grammar.

The case of $T2$ is symmetric, of course.

Conversely, it is to be shown that any recognized sequence already belongs to $T1$ or $T2$. So, let $a_1; \ldots; a_n \Rightarrow_L t^*$. The t^*-count of t^* itself is $+1$. Now, all types with t^* inserted in final position have t^*-count $+1$. Therefore, exactly one such type must occur among $a_1, \ldots, a_n$.

Case 1: that type is t^* itself.

LEMMA. If $\vec{a}; t^* \Rightarrow_L t^*$ with t^* not occurring in $\vec{a}$, then $\vec{a}$ must be *empty*.

So, in this case, there is just one symbol, which belonged already to $T1$ (t_1) or to $T2$ (t_2).

Case 2: that type also contains subtypes from $G1$.

Then, the whole sequence must consist of $G1$-types, in addition to the starred one, because of the following property of Non-Separability:

LEMMA. If $\vec{a}; \vec{b} \Rightarrow_L c$, then either $\vec{a}, \vec{b}$ share some occurrence of at least one basic type, or $\vec{b}, c$ do.

(The proof of this lemma is by a simple induction on the depth of proof trees in the cut-free calculus.) Then finally, replacing t^* by t_1 in the derivation, the sequence is recognized as being in $T1$.

Case 3: Case 2 with $G2$ instead of $G1$ is symmetric.

CONCATENATION. Let $T1$ be recognized by $G1$ (with t_1) and $T2$ by $G2$ (with t_2), disjoint as before. Again, choose a new distinguished type t^*. This time, admit additional $G1$-types with final t_1 replaced by the type (t_2, t^*).

CLAIM. This assignment L-recognizes the permutation closure of $T1$; $T2$.

Proof. First, to recognize $\sigma_1 \frown \sigma_2$ with $\sigma1 \in T1$, $\sigma_2 \in T2$, recognize σ_1 as in $G1$, but with (t_2, t^*) inserted as in the earlier argument for unions $T1 \cup T2$. Then, recognize σ_2 as before in $G2$, and combine to obtain t^*. This shows one inclusion — further permutation closure being automatic for L.

Next, let some sequence σ be recognized to t^*. As always, t^*-count tells us that exactly one type will occur in σ with (t_2, t^*) in final position. Then, an analysis of the proof tree, using the form of the admissible rules in the cut-free calculus, reveals the following shape:

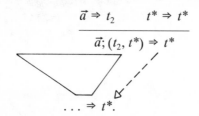

$$\frac{\vec{a} \Rightarrow t_2 \qquad t^* \Rightarrow t^*}{\vec{a}; (t_2, t^*) \Rightarrow t^*}$$

$$\ldots \Rightarrow t^*.$$

Here, $\vec{a}$ consists of $G2$-types only, by the earlier Non-Separability Lemma. In the final sequent, the part (t_2, t^*) occurs inside a type: say, $(x_1, (x_2 \ldots (t_2, t^*) \ldots))$. This must have been brought about by a number of $(,)$-introductions on the left, of the form

$$\frac{\vec{b}_i \Rightarrow x_i \qquad \vec{a}; \vec{c}; \ldots (t_2, t^*) \Rightarrow t^*}{\vec{b}_i; \vec{a}; \vec{c}; (x_i, (\ldots (t_2, t^*) \ldots)) \Rightarrow t^*}$$

Again by Non-Separability, all $\vec{b}_i$-types must belong to $G1$ (as x_i does).

Now, consider the general form of the 't^*-branch'. Its steps are either of the form just indicated, or they introduce some antecedent for another type on the left-hand side, together with enough types for proving that antecedent. Throughout this process, the following holds true, however, at each stage $A \Rightarrow t^*$:

— the totality of all $G2$-types in A derives t_2,
— the totality of all pure $G1$-types in A, being all the non-$G2$-types except for the single one in which t^* occurs, derives all types in the prefix of the latter (preceding its final part (t_2, t^*)).

Applying this to the final sequent, we find that the symbols contributing the $G2$-types form a $T2$-expression, the remaining ones an expression in $T1$ (remember the original form of the special type): the sequence recognized is a permutation of one in $T1; T2$.

FINITE ITERATION. Let T be recognized by G (with t). Again, we choose a new type t^*, and add both t^* and (t^*, t^*) in final positions t. This allows us to recognize all of T^*, by suitable t^*-insertion (for one string in T) and (t^*, t^*)-insertions (for all other strings in T), combining the resulting t^* and (t^*, t^*)'s into one t^*.

The converse again requires a proof analysis. Let any sequence of types reduce to t^*. Following the upward path of the conclusion t^*, there must have been an initial situation of the form

$$\frac{\vec{a} \Rightarrow x \qquad t^* \Rightarrow t^*}{\vec{a}; (x, t^*) \Rightarrow t^*}$$

Case 1: x is not t^*.

In this case, the expression recognized is in T (possibly permuted). This follows from an argument about the remaining form of the derivation, as earlier on for concatenation, using one additional observation:

CLAIM. No symbol t^* occurs in the types of $\vec{a}$.

Proof. As x has t^*-count 0, no T-type in $\vec{a}$ has just one t^* inserted. But, (t^*, t^*)-insertion is impossible too. For, if, say, $(y, (t^*, t^*))$ occurred among $\vec{a}$, then, somewhere up in the tree for $\vec{a} \Rightarrow x$, (t^*, t^*) must have been introduced, resulting in a premise $\vec{b} \Rightarrow t^*$. Consider the first time that this happened: $\vec{b}$ contains no occurrences of t^*, and hence t^*-count($\vec{b}$) $\neq$ t^*-count(t^*): a contradiction.

Case 2: x is itself t^*.

Then, arguing as in previous cases, the final sequent must be of the following form (up to permutation):

$$A_1; A_2; (x_1, (\ldots (x_k, (t^*, t^*)) \ldots)) \Rightarrow t^*,$$

with A_2 a set of types deriving $x_1, \ldots, x_k$, and A_1 deriving t^*. As before, since $x_1, \ldots, x_k$ are pure G-types, the A_2-types cannot contain occurrences of t^*. It follows that the symbols contributing A_2 plus the final type form an expression in T. Applying the same reasoning to the

shorter sequence of symbols contributing A_1 decomposes this eventually into a finite sequence of T-expressions.

Remark. Another way of presenting this, and previous arguments
exists too, relying heavily on the *Subformula Property* of cut-free
derivations.

This concludes the proof that all permutation closures of context-
free languages are Lambek-recognizable.   Q.E.D.

For the converse, one would have to show that the *infinite* variety of
derivations for sequences $\vec{a} \Rightarrow t$ can actually be mimicked using only
changed types up to some finite depth, plus ordinary application and
permutation. (Cf. Proposition 2 in Buszkowski, 1984a.) Another possible strategy would be to show directly that the Lambek calculus leads
to *semi-linear* occurrence sets for its recognized languages. (Cf. the
earlier use of Parikh's Theorem.)

If Buszkowski's conjecture holds, then adopting at least the present
commutative Lambek approach enriches only *strong* linguistic capacity,
without acquiring essentially new *weak* capacity.

In this perspective, it is of interest to see what happens to recognizing power of flexible categorial grammars as we move along the
'Lambda Continuum' of Section 4. For instance, at the furthest extreme,
being the intuitionistic calculus I, a collapse occurs:

THEOREM. The I-recognizable languages are all regular.

More precise information is contained in the following argument.

Let T be a language that is I-recognizable. Then
(1) T is permutation-closed,
(2) if $\vec{a} \in T$, then $\vec{a}\,^\cap\vec{b} \in T$ for all sequences $\vec{b}$ (because of
'Strengthening of Antecedents' in I),
(3) for some fixed number N, if $a^{N+k+1} \in T$, then $a^{N+k} \in T$
(because of 'Thinning', recalling that a single symbol can have received
at most N different basic types, for some suitably large N).

It follows that there exists some *finite* set of sequences $\vec{a}_1, \ldots, \vec{a}_k$,
each with at most N repetitions of symbols, such that an expression
belongs to T if and only if it contains some $\vec{a}_i$ ($1 \leq i \leq k$). Therefore,
T must be a regular language, being a finite union of regular languages.
(E.g., the set of all sequences containing $\langle a\,b\,a \rangle$ is, in Kleene notation,
$\Sigma^*; a; \Sigma^*; b; \Sigma^*; a; \Sigma^*$ — where Σ is the entire alphabet.)

More precisely, the languages obtained here are *existential* in the following sense. The condition for membership is a disjunction of demands of the form

"at least n_1 symbols s_1 occur and . . . and at least n_k symbols s_k occur" (where $\Sigma = \{s_1, \ldots, s_k\}$).

Conversely, all such languages can be I-recognized by a judicious assignment of basic types. Q.E.D.

Obviously, the existential languages are one of the simplest kinds of regular language. (For instance, they can always be recognized by finite state automata without proper loops among states; cf. van Benthem, 1986a, Chapter 8.) So, again, the difference in structural rules between L and I turns out to be crucial for linguistic purposes.

Combining the above results with the well-known fact that the pure Ajdukiewicz calculus recognizes only context-free languages, the following graph of weak recognition arises:

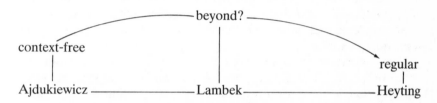

There is much to be pondered in this scheme. For instance, what would be calculi with 'maximum yield'? It should be observed, however, that, once non-I-valid type change rules are admitted, even *all type-0 languages* become recognizable (see Buszkowski's contribution to this volume). (On the other hand, such non-I calculi would not have a natural lambda-semantics, as in Section 4.)

Digression: Linguistic Complexity of Logical Laws

To return to its original motivation, the calculus L produces a kind of logical validities. One question of logical interest may be added here. Linguistic complexity of logical *formal languages* is usually easy to establish. E.g., propositional, or predicate-logical formulas form context-free sets. (Note, though, that relatively minor modifications may affect complexity. E.g., predicate-logical formulas with a ban on 'vacuous' quantification become essentially context-sensitive.) Now, what about the sets of *universally valid* sentences within these formal languages? In particular, given a fixed finite set of proposition letters and logical operators $\rightarrow$, $\wedge$, $\neg$, $\vee$, what is the linguistic complexity of the set of tautologies in this language?

Answer: It is context-free.

Proof. Here, one uses the 'logical finiteness' of propositional logic. In the above vocabulary, there are only finitely many equivalence classes in the Lindenbaum Algebra, say $S_1, \ldots, S_k$. Regarding these as categories in some grammar, write down all valid rules of the form

$$S_i \Rightarrow \neg S_j$$
$$S_i \Rightarrow (S_j \rightarrow S_m), \text{ etc.}$$

Then, with an initial type S ('tautology'), this is a context-free grammar.

Q.E.D.

Remark: This result does not conflict with the known NP-completeness of propositional satisfiability. For, the latter theorem employs a propositional logic with an *infinite* set of proposition letters (encoded in some finitary fashion).

These questions become more interesting for logics without the above property of logical finiteness, such as *intuitionistic* logic in $\rightarrow$, $\wedge$, $\neg$, $\vee$. What is the linguistic complexity of its validities on a finite vocabulary? The latter set is known to be decidable. But, it would certainly correspond to an intuitive feeling if it turned out to be of a higher complexity than its classical counterpart: say context-sensitive.

This completes our investigation of the more traditional aspects of Lambek grammars, viz. their recognizing power. It should be emphasized, however, that traffic is not one-way here. For instance, in the present light, many traditional questions about categorial grammar can be re-thought. To mention one case: usually, one admits *multiple* initial assignments to basic expressions. (Indeed, the equivalence between categorial grammars and context-free grammars depends on this facility.) But, with a calculus of *type change*, many arguments for admitting multiple initial assignment disappear — as multiplicity should preferably be located in the rules, rather than by fiat at the outset. But then, what is the correct 'generative' counterpart to Lambek grammars with *single* initial assignments? The answer appears to be unknown.

The latter type of question may still be too timid, however. After all, if one takes the categorial perspective seriously, then, why should it always have to prove itself by comparison with its generative rival? There are various reasons for turning the tables here. For instance, the categorial grammar format is often just as, or even more convenient for doing some of the basic language theory. Moreover, it suggests many interesting *new* questions for the latter, as abundantly illustrated in this paper. Perhaps, it is time to start changing the text-books.

7. PROSPECTS

The purpose of this paper has been to illustrate the interest of flexible categorial grammars from a technical point of view; thus providing some logical backing for the present-day revival of this approach to natural language.

There remain some obvious open questions, even concerning our basic calculus L — notably, the issue of its recognizing power. Moreover, many of the answers given here remain to be verified for various attractive *variants* of L, which have appeared at several places in the text, with weaker or stronger rules of deduction. More information on the resulting *Categorial Hierarchy* is presented in van Benthem, 1987c. Also, the possible *addition* may be noted of 'co-ordinating' types (such as the conjunction 'and'), over and above the 'subordinating' ones employed here. (For instance, the subordinating binary connective type $(t, (t, t))$ available up to now fits in better with, say, the conditional particle 'if', then with 'and' or 'or'.) This can certainly be done, by adding types having several arguments 'at the same level', and providing suitable application rules for these. (For a more extensive survey, see the editorial Section 'Recent Trends in Categorial Grammar', in Buszkowski *et al.* (eds.), 1986.) Recently also, coordination has been treated using a stronger form of polymorphism, involving *variable types*. For a survey of current developments in the resulting 'categorial unification grammars', see Klein and van Benthem, 1987.

Another important area with many open problems is that of the *directed* Lambek calculi (cf. Buszkowski, 1982). For instance, how should earlier notions (such as type-count) and results be generalized to this setting? Also, new topics arise here, such as the study of dualities between the two slashes \, /, both empirically and theoretically.

Then, the lambda-semantics of Section 4 creates various connections with standard logic, in particular the *Theory of Types*. Many more model-theoretic questions concerning the Lambek Calculus, and the Categorial Hierarchy in general, may be found in van Benthem 1987a, 1987b. Even so, this perspective only gives one example of the various type change mechanisms in natural language. Some of these will actually require a stronger medium of expression for recipes, viz. (at least) the full lambda-language with *identity*. (Cf. van Benthem, 1986a, Chapter 3, for a more systematic discussion.) Examples are 'natural' transitions such as that from an individual to its singleton property:

$$e \Rightarrow (e, t),$$

with associated recipe $\lambda y_e \cdot y \equiv x_e$. And again, there is a famous Montagovian example, viz. his account of the transitive verb 'be' as a type changer from NP-denotations to intransitive verbs:

$$(e, t), t \Rightarrow e, t,$$

with recipe $\lambda y_{(e,\ t),\ t} \cdot \lambda z_e \cdot y(\lambda u_e \cdot u \equiv z)$. (Cf. Partee, 1985.) There is a danger here of diluting the notion of 'type change' too much. As is well known, the lambda language with equality suffices for defining all standard logical constants. But these would not ordinarily be viewed as type changers. Despite this warning, it would still be of interest to extend our original concerns to this wider setting.

Finally, there is the area of *intensional* phenomena, where type change plays a role too (cf. Rooth and Partee, 1983). What is the proper combinatorics behind the various 'intensionalization' strategies in the literature? (For a first attempt, see van Benthem, 1986c.) How much of our present theory will extend beyond the Veil of Opacity?

REFERENCES

Ades, A. and M. Steedman: 1982, 'On the Order of Words', *Linguistics and Philosophy* **4**, 517—558.

Bach, E.: 1984, 'Some Generalizations of Categorial Grammars', in Landman and Veltman (eds.), 1984, pp. 1—23.

Barendregt, H.: 1981, *The Lambda Calculus, Its Syntax and Semantics*, North-Holland, Amsterdam.

Bäuerle, R., C. Schwarze and A. von Stechow (eds.): 1983, *Meaning, Use and Interpretation of Language*, de Gruyter, Berlin.

van Benthem, J.: 1983, *The Semantics of Variety in Categorial Grammar*, report 83—29, department of mathematics, Simon Fraser University, Burnaby (B.C.). Also to appear in Buszkowski *et al.* (eds.), 1986.

van Benthem, J.: 1984a, 'Correspondence Theory', in Gabbay and Guenthner (eds.), 1984, pp. 167—247.

van Benthem, J.: 1984b, *Partiality and Non-Monotonicity in Classical Logic*, report 84—6, Center for the Study of Language and Information, Stanford. Also in *Logique et Analyse* **29**, 225—247.

van Benthem, J.: 1984c, 'The Logic of Semantics', in Landman and Veltman (eds.), pp. 55—80.

van Benthem, J.: 1986a, *Essays in Logical Semantics*, Reidel, Dordrecht (Studies in Linguistics and Philosophy, Vol. 29).

van Benthem, J.: 1986b, 'Meaning: Interpretation and Inference', to appear in *Synthese*.

van Benthem, J.: 1986c, 'Strategies of Intensionalization', to appear in *Filozófiai Figyelö*.

van Benthem, J.: 1987a, 'Categorial Grammar and Lambda Calculus', in D. Skordev (ed.), to appear.

van Benthem, J.: 1987b, 'Categorial Grammar and Type Theory', *Linguistics and Philosophy*, to appear.

van Benthem, J.: 1987c, 'Semantic Type Change and Syntactic Recognition', in Chierchia, Partee and Turner (eds.), to appear.

Buszkowski, W.: 1982, *Lambek's Categorial Grammars*, dissertation, Instytut Matematyki, Adam Mickiewicz University, Poznań.

Buszkowski, W.: 1984a, 'A Note on Lambek—van Benthem Calculus', *Bulletin of the Section of Logic* **13**, 31—37.

Buszkowski, W.: 1984b, 'The Purely Implicational Intuitionistic Propositional Calculus is the Maximal Lambda Complete Type-Change Calculus', manuscript, Instytut Matematyki, Adam Mickiewicz University, Poznań.

Buszkowski, W.: 1985, 'The Equivalence of Unidirectional Lambek Grammars and Context-Free Grammars', *Zeitschrift für mathematische Logik und Grundlagen der Mathematik* **31**, 369—384.

Buszkowski, W.: 1986, 'Completeness Results for Lambek Syntactic Calculus', *Zeitschrift für mathematische Logik und Grundlagen der Mathematik* **32**, 13—28.

Buszkowski, W., W. Marciszewski, and J. van Benthem (eds.): 1986, *Categorial Grammar*, John Benjamin, Amsterdam.

Chierchia, G., B. Partee and R. Turner (eds.): 1988, *Categories, Types, and Semantics*, Reidel, Dordrecht (Studies in Linguistics and Philosophy, to appear).

Cohen, J.: 1967, 'The Equivalence of Two Concepts of Categorial Grammar', *Information and Control* **10**, 475—484.

Došen, K.: 1985, 'A Completeness Theorem for the Lambek Calculus of Syntactic Categories', *Zeitschrift für mathematische Logik und Grundlagen der Mathematik* **31**, 235—241.

Došen, K.: 1986, 'Sequent Systems and Groupoid Models', Matematički Institut, University of Beograd.

Flynn, M.: 1983, 'A Categorial Theory of Structure Building', in Gazdar *et al.* (eds.), 1983, pp. 139—174.

Gabbay, D. and F. Guenthner (eds.): 1984, *Handbook of Philosophical Logic*, Vol. II, Reidel, Dordrecht.

Gazdar, G., E. Klein, and G. Pullum (eds.): 1983, *Order, Concord and Constituency*, Foris, Dordrecht.

Gazdar, G. and G. Pullum: 1985, *Computationally Relevant Properties of Natural*

Languages and Their Grammars, Report 85—24, Center for the Study of Language and Information, Stanford.

Geach, P.: 1971, 'A Program for Syntax', *Synthese* **22**, 3—17.

Ginsburg, S.: 1966, *The Mathematical Theory of Context-Free Languages*, McGraw Hill, New York.

Groenendijk, J. and M. Stokhof: 1984, *Studies on the Semantics of Questions and the Pragmatics of Answers*, dissertation, Filosofisch Instituut, University of Amsterdam. (To appear with Oxford University Press.)

Hoeksema, J.: 1984, *Categorial Morphology*, dissertation, Nederlands Instituut, Rijksuniversiteit, Groningen. Also to appear in the Outstanding Dissertations in Linguistics Series, Garland Press.

Keenan, E. and L. Faltz: 1985, *Boolean Semantics for Natural Language*, Reidel, Dordrecht (Synthese Language Library, Vol. 23).

Klein, E. and J. van Benthem (eds.): 1987, *Categories, Polymorphism and Unification*, Centre for Cognitive Science/Institute for Language, Logic and Information, Edinburgh/Amsterdam.

Lambek, J.: 1958, 'The Mathematics of Sentence Structure', *American Mathematical Monthly* **65**, 154—169.

Landman, F. and F. Veltman (eds.): 1984, *Varieties of Formal Semantics*, Foris, Dordrecht (GRASS, Vol. 3).

Moortgat, M.: 1984, 'Functional Composition and Complement Inheritance', in Hoppenbrouwers, Seuren, and Weijters (eds.), *Meaning and the Lexicon*, Foris, Dordrecht.

Partee, B.: 1985, 'Syntactic Categories and Semantic Types', lecture. CSLI Summer School, Stanford.

Rooth, M. and B. Partee: 1983, 'Generalized Conjunction and Type Ambiguity', in Bäuerle, Schwarze and von Stechow (eds.), *Meaning, Use, and Interpretation of Language*, de Gruyter, Berlin, pp. 361—383.

Skordev, D. (ed.): 1987, *Druzhba Summer School in Applied Logic*, Plenum Press, New York.

Zielonka, W.: 1978, 'A Direct Proof of the Equivalence of Free Categorial Grammars and Simple Phrase Structure Grammars', *Studia Logica* **37**, 41—57.

Zielonka, W.: 1981, 'Axiomatizability of Ajdukiewicz—Lambek Calculus by Means of Cancellation Schemes', *Zeitschrift für mathematische Logik und Grundlagen der Mathematik* **27**, 215—224.

Zwarts, F.: 1986, *Categorial Grammar and Algebraic Semantics*, dissertation, Nederlands Instituut, Rijksuniversiteit, Groningen. Also to appear with Foris, Dordrecht.

Mathematisch Instituut,
Universiteit van Amsterdam,
Roetersstraat 15,
1018 WB Amsterdam,
Holland

WOJCIECH BUSZKOWSKI

GENERATIVE POWER OF CATEGORIAL GRAMMARS

0. INTRODUCTION

This paper surveys the author's results in strong and weak generative capacity of various kinds of categorial grammars. The growing interest of linguists, computer scientists, and linguistically-minded logicians in the domain of categorial grammar calls for a new, more advanced and profound elaboration of its internal mathematics, in which the problems to be discussed here have traditionally been recognized to play a quite fundamental role.

Let us begin with some general remarks. Categorial grammars, literally introduced by Bar-Hillel *et al.* (1960), as a merely slight modification of a parsing algorithm going back to Ajdukiewicz (1935), and further to Frege, Husserl, and Leśniewski, represent the form of grammar that adheres the closest to the very primitives of logical semiotics — functor-argument connection, categorization by types, compositional semantics. (Symptomatically, Hiż, 1967, dubbed the thesis of universality of categorial grammar for the language of mathematics *grammar logicism*.) From the standpoint of formal linguistics, categorial grammars constitute a refinement of Chomsky's phrase structure grammars, since — in opposition to the latter — the former assign an internal structure to category symbols (nonterminals). Consequently categorial grammars fall, essentially, into the genus of so-called metamorphosis grammar (Colmerauer, 1978).

Since the internal category structures involved are provided with a universal interpretation (that is, an interpretation independent of any particular language under consideration), categorial grammars behave more like the formal systems of symbolic logic (e.g. propositional calculi) than the 'one-dimensional' rewriting systems widespread in mathematical linguistics. As a result, besides purely combinatorial techniques, characteristic of the latter discipline, categorial grammar theory also requires a large piece of genuine logical methodology. As striking evidence, let us mention such enterprises as the algebraic semantics for the type calculi of Lambek (1958, 1961) developed by

Richard T. Oehrle et al. (eds.), Categorial Grammars and Natural Language Structures, 69—94.
© 1988 by D. Reidel Publishing Company.

the author (1982, 1985, 1986), the proof-theoretic devices used in those papers, and the lambda-term simulation of type processing, a line coming from Curry (1961), Montague (1974), Cresswell (1973), and recently advanced by van Benthem (1983, 1985).

This methodological difference between categorial grammar and the standards of formal linguistics seems to have been responsible for the relatively small activity of mathematicians in our subject. Actually, not many problems of primary significance have received hitherto a final solution. This explains why the present paper can be essentially original, though it deals with an area belonging for years to the most celebrated branches of mathematical research in categorial grammar. It is hoped that the situation will become more desirable in near future.

The contents to follow are divided into three sections. In Section 1, we consider the classical Ajdukiewicz—Bar-Hillel categorial grammars (ACG's) with emphasis on their strong capacity. We characterize the functorial languages (i.e.: sets of functor-argument structures) generated by ACG's and rigid ACG's. Gaifman's well-known theorem on the weak equivalence of ACG's and context-free grammars (CFG's) will be discussed within this framework.

Section 2 deals with the strong capacity of Lambek categorial grammars (LCG's), introduced by Lambek (1958), and their most interesting variants. These systems enjoy nowadays much appreciation amongst linguists and logicians, due to their relations to the typed lambda calculus, Montague semantics, categorical logic, and universal algebra. After recapitulating some basic properties of those systems, we prove that LCG's are structurally complete, which means that they are able to generate any possible functor-argument structure (in the sense of Section 1) on a string. Similar questions will be examined for several related systems.

Section 3 focuses on the weak capacity of LCG's and their variants. As far back as Bar-Hillel *et al.* (1960) and Chomsky (1963), it was conjectured that LCG's amount to CFG's in generative power on the level of strings. This important hypothesis still remains unproved, however, as an early proof by Cohen (1967) has been shown incorrect (see Buszkowski, 1985a). We sketch the author's positive solution of this conjecture for the restricted case of right-directional LCG's, and an analogous result for nonassociative LCG's (Buszkowski, 1986b). We also report the author's earlier result on the equivalence of Chomsky's type 0 grammars and extended LCG's (ELCG's) — categorial grammars based on finite axiomatic extensions of the Lambek calculus (Buszkowski, 1982a). Some other systems will be regarded, too.

Being intended as a brief survey, not a monograph, this paper abandons details of proofs as well as more thorough linguistic illustrations. The reader is kindly invited to look for them in the quoted literature (e.g. Keenan and Faltz, 1978; Levin, 1982; and Bach, 1984, 1985 provide good logical and linguistic arguments for the extension of classical categorial grammars). Many recent advances are to be found in other contributions to this volume.

1. CLASSICAL CATEGORIAL GRAMMARS

We shall define a number of basic notions, to be extensively used throughout this paper.

The letter V will always stand for a nonempty finite set, being referred to as a *vocabulary*, and its members as *atoms*. By a *string* over V we mean a finite sequence of atoms from V; e denotes the *empty string*. The set $F(V)$, of *functor-argument structures* (*f*-structures) over V, is defined by the following induction:

(F.1) $V \subseteq F(V)$,

(F.2)   if $A_1, \ldots, A_n \in F(V)$, $n \geqslant 2$, then $(A_1 \ldots A_n)_i \in F(V)$, for all $1 \leqslant i \leqslant n$.

Clearly, the symbols '(' and ')$_i$' are supposed not to belong to V, and no atom is of the form $(A_1 \ldots A_n)_i$. Thus, $F(V)$ can be treated as the absolutely free algebra generated by V with the operations $(\ldots)_i$, $1 \leqslant i \leqslant n$, for all $n \geqslant 2$. Equivalently, *f*-structures are simply finite trees with labelled leaves and such that one of the edges coming from each node is marked.

A_i is called the *functor*, and each A_j, $j \neq i$, an *argument* of (in) the *f*-structure $(A_1 \ldots A_n)_i$; we also refer to $A_1, \ldots, A_n$ as the *parts* of that *f*-structure. The *constituents* of $A \in F(V)$ are: A, the parts of A, the parts of those parts, etc. The string over V that results from dropping in $A \in F(V)$ all the symbols not belonging to V is called the *support* of A (supp(A)).

The *size* of $A \in F(V)$ ($s(A)$) equals the maximal number of parts of constituents of A. A sequence $A_0, A_1, \ldots, A_n$ of constituents of A is called a *path* (an *f-path*) in A, of *length* n, if A_{i+1} is a part (the functor) of A_i, all $0 \leqslant i < n$. The end of the longest f-path in A which begins from A is called the *head* of A ($h(A)$). By the *depth* of A ($d(A)$) we mean the maximal length of f-paths in A. By the *rank* of $A \in F(V)$ we mean the length of shortest paths in A which lead from A to some atom from V, and the *degree* of A (deg(A)) equals the maximal rank of constituents of A. The *order* of $A \in F(V)$ ($\circ(A)$) is a non-negative integer, defined by the following recursion:

(∘.1) $\circ(v) = 0$, for $v \in V$,
(∘.2) $\circ((A_1 \ldots A_n)_i) = \max(\circ(A_i), \max_{j \neq i}(\circ(A_j) + 1))$,

and the *complexity* of A equals the number of occurrences of atoms in A.

Thus, for instance, *Joan smiles charmingly* is the support of:

(1)   (*Joan* (*smiles charmingly*)$_2$)$_2$.

One easily checks that $s((1)) = d((1)) = 2$, $\deg((1)) = \circ((1)) = 1$, and $h((1)) = $ *charmingly*.

By a *functorial language* (f-language) we mean any set $L \subseteq F(V)$, for some finite V. Given an f-language L, by CON_L we symbolize the set of constituents of the f-structures from L, by V_L the smallest set V such that $L \subseteq F(V)$, and by supp(L) the set of all supp(A), for $A \in L$. We also define the *size, depth*, and *degree* of $L \subseteq F(V)$($s(L)$, $d(L)$, deg(L)) as the supremum of all $s(A)$, $d(A)$, and deg(A), respectively, for $A \in L$. Notice that $s(L)$, $d(L)$, and deg(L) can be finite or countably infinite.

Each f-language L determines an equivalence relation Int_L on $F(V_L)$, called the *intersubstitutability relation* for L, to be defined as follows:

(Int) $A\mathrm{Int}_L B$ iff, for every $C \in F(\overline{V}_L)$, $C(A/v) \in L$ iff $C(B/v) \in L$,

where $\overline{V}_L = V_L \cup \{v\}$, $v \notin V_L$, and $C(A/v)$ denotes the result of substitution of A for v in C. The equivalence classes of Int_L are called the *intersubstitutability classes* (int-classes) of L, and the total (finite or not) number of them is referred to as the *index* of L (ind(L)). Algebraically, Int_L is the largest congruence on the structure $(F(V_L), L)$ (i.e. an absolutely free algebra with a distinguished monadic predicate).

Types can be identified with the f-structures over a fixed, denumerable set Pr, of so-called *primitive types*. The set of types will be denoted by Tp, and the variables x, y, z are to range over types. We distinguish a primitive type s as the so-called *principal type*. The type $(x_1 \ldots x_n)^i$ (for technical reasons the functor index of a type will be written in the superscript position) is intended to have precisely the same meaning as $x_1 \ldots x_{i-1} \backslash x_i / x_{i+1} \ldots x_n$, the latter notation being traditional. Identifying f-structures and types enables us, after all, to save space, as we need not repeat definitions of many relevant notions. In particular, we have already defined such things, as e.g. $s(x)$, $d(x)$, $\circ(x)$, etc. (caution: we use 'subtypes of x' instead of 'constituents of x'). Following a customary notation, we shall often write x/y and $x \backslash y$ for $(xy)^1$ and $(xy)^2$, respectively.

The variables X, Y, Z will range over finite strings of types. Expressions of the form $X \rightarrow x$ ($X \neq e$) are called *arrows*. The *Ajdukiewicz calculus* (**A**) uses arrows as its only formulas and takes the following axioms and inference rules:

(**A.0**) $x \rightarrow x$,

(**A.1**) $x_1 \ldots x_{i-1}(x_1 \ldots x_n)^i x_{i+1} \ldots x_n \rightarrow x_i$,

(**R.0**) $XyZ \rightarrow z$ and $Y \rightarrow y$ yield $XYZ \rightarrow z$.

We write $\vdash_{\mathbf{A}} X \rightarrow x$ if the arrow $X \rightarrow x$ is derivable in **A**, and similarly for other calculi, to be considered later on. An *Ajdukiewicz–Bar-Hillel categorial grammar* (ACG) can be formally defined as a triple $G = (V_G, I_G, R_G)$, such that: V_G (the *vocabulary* of G) is a non-empty finite set, I_G (the *initial type assignment* of G) is a function which to each $v \in V_G$ assigns a finite set of types, and R_G (the *calculus* of G) equals **A**. Notice that other kinds of categorial grammar will be defined by simply specifying another calculus. The *terminal type assignment* of an ACG G is to be understood as a function $(\cdot)_G$ which to each type assigns a set of strings over V_G, according to the clause: $v_1 \ldots v_n \in (x)_G$ iff $\vdash_{\mathbf{A}} x_1 \ldots x_n \rightarrow x$, for some $x_i \in I_G(v_i)$, $1 \leqslant i \leqslant n$. The set $(x)_G$ will be called the *string-category* of type x determined by G, and we refer to $(s)_G$ as the *language* of G ($L(G)$).

As is easily seen, any **A**-derivation of arrow $X \rightarrow x$ induces a unique f-structure $\overline{X} \in F(Tp)$, such that $\text{supp}(\overline{X}) = X$ (when applying (A.1) one provides the string on the left-hand side with the structure $(x_1 \ldots x_{i-1}(x_1 \ldots x_n)^i x_{i+1} \ldots x_n)_i$). These f-structures can directly be mirrored in the strings from $(x)_G$, G being an ACG. So, for any $x \in Tp$, one also gets a set $(x)^G \subseteq F(V_G)$, called the *structure-category* of type x generated by G, which consists of all the f-structures obtained in the afore-mentioned way from the strings from $(x)_G$. The set $(s)^G$

will be referred to as the *f-language* of G ($FL(G)$). Clearly, $L(G) =$ supp($FL(G)$) and, in general, $(x)_G =$ supp($(x)^G$), for $x \in Tp$.

We state our first theorem, which gives a characterization of the *f*-languages provided by ACG's.

1.1. THEOREM. For any *f*-language L, the following are equivalent:

(i) $L = FL(G)$, for some ACG G,
(ii)   each of the numbers ind(L), $s(L)$, and $d(L)$ is finite.

Proof. To prove the necessity we need some auxiliary notions. Given an ACG G, let $Tp(G)(\overline{Tp}(G))$ denote the set of (all subtypes of) the types involved in I_G, and let $m(G)(\overline{m}(G))$ stand for the cardinality of $Tp(G)(\overline{Tp}(G))$. For $A, B \in F(V_G)$, we set: $A \sim_G B$ (A is *type-equivalent* to B) if A and B belong to precisely the same structure-categories in the sense of G. Evidently, $\sim_G$ is a congruence on $(F(V_G), FL(G))$, hence it is finer than $\mathrm{Int}_{FL(G)}$. Consequently:

(2)   ind$(FL(G)) \leqslant 2^{\overline{m}(G)}$,

since $2^{\overline{m}(G)}$ is the maximum number of equivalence classes of $\sim_G$. An easy argument also yields:

(2') $s(FL(G)) \leqslant s(Tp(G))$, $d(FL(G)) \leqslant d(Tp(G))$.

Now, if L fulfils (i) then L must fulfil (ii), since $Tp(G)$ is a finite set, for every ACG G.

The proof of (ii) $\rightarrow$ (i) requires more sophistication. Assume (ii). Let L^{int} denote the family of all equivalence classes of Int_L. To each $H \in L^{\mathrm{int}}$ we assign a primitive type $p_H \neq s$, and we suppose that $p_{H_1} \neq p_{H_2}$ whenever $H_1 \neq H_2$. We also define functions T_n, $n \geqslant 0$, from $F(V_L)$ into the power-set of Tp, by the following induction:

(3) $T_0(A) = \begin{cases} \varnothing \text{ if } A \notin CON_L, \\ \{p_H\} \text{ if } A \in H \subseteq CON_L - L, \\ \{s, p_H\} \text{ if } A \in H \subseteq L, \end{cases}$

(4) $T_{n+1}(A)$ consists of all types of the form $(x_1 \ldots x_m)^i$, such that $x_i \in T_n((A_1 \ldots A_{i-1}AA_{i+1} \ldots A_m)_i)$, for some $A_j \in F(V_L)$, $j \neq i$, and $x_j = p_{H_j}$ where $A_j \in H_j$, for all $j \neq i$.

We set $T(A) = \bigcup_{n \geqslant 0} T_n(A)$, for all $A \in F(V_L)$. One easily proves that if $T_n(A) \neq \varnothing$ then A is the beginning of an *f*-path of length n

within some $B \in L$. Consequently, $T_n(A) = \emptyset$, for all $n > d(L)$, hence $T(A)$ is finite, for all $A \in F(V_L)$. Define an ACG G by setting: $V_G = V_L$ and $I_G(v) = T(v)$, for all $v \in V_G$. It is not difficult to show that $(x)^G = \overline{T}(x)$, for all $x \in Tp$, hence $FL(G) = \overline{T}(s) = L$ (by $\overline{T}(x)$ we denote the set of all $A \in F(V_L)$, such that $x \in T(A)$). This finishes the proof.

As it happens, the constraints in Theorem 1.1 coincide with the conditions an f-language must satisfy in order to admit a (typed or not) compositional semantics, involving only a finite number of designata (Buszkowski, 1986a). Accordingly, ACG's generate a semantically relevant class of f-languages, viz. those f-languages which can be provided with a finite compositional semantics.

By the *order* of an ACG G ($\circ(G)$) we mean the maximal order of types in $Tp(G)$. Two ACG's G_1 and G_2 are said to be (F-) *equivalent* if $L(G_1) = L(G_2)$ ($FL(G_1) = FL(G_2)$). One often uses 'weak equivalence' instead of 'equivalence'; F-equivalence is a kind of strong equivalence. The ACG constructed in the proof of Theorem 1.1 is of order not greater than 1, which yields:

1.2. THEOREM. Each ACG G is F-equivalent to some ACG G' such that $\circ(G') \leqslant 1$.

Instead of minimizing the order one may pull down $m(G)$, $\overline{m}(G)$, etc. The least value of $m(G)$ is to be attained for the case G is *rigid*, that means, I_G assigns at most one type to one atom. Call an f-language L rigid if $L = FL(G)$, for some rigid ACG G. The class of rigid f-languages, though essentially narrower than that of all f-language of ACG's, certainly deserves close attention, as it embodies some most significant artificial languages of mathematical logic and programming. Natural languages, being typically non-rigid (consider the variety of types of e.g. *and*), can nonetheless be reformed to fulfil rigidity; one simply replaces each type-ambiguous atom by a number of unambiguous copies of that atom (e.g. *and* is to be replaced by and_S of type $(sss)^2$, and_N of type $(xxx)^2$ where $x = (s(ns)^2)^1$, etc.). Algebraically, for any ACG G, $FL(G)$ is a homomorphic image of a rigid f-language, and the homomorphism in question consists in gluing atoms.

To characterize the rigid f-languages we need an auxiliary notion. Given an f-language L and $A, B \in F(V_L)$, we write $A <_L B$ (A is *subordinate* to B with respect to L) if, for some $C \in \mathrm{CON}_L$, B is the functor in C and, either $A\mathrm{Int}_L C$, or A is an argument in C. Recall that a binary relation $<$ on a set W is said to be *well-founded* if, for every non-empty set $U \subseteq W$, there is an element $u \in U$, such that $u' < u$ holds for no $u' \in U$.

1.3. THEOREM. For any f-language L, L is rigid if and only if the following conditions hold true:

(r.1)   the relation $<_L$ is well-founded,

(r.2)   if $A, B \in L$ then $A\mathrm{Int}_L B$,

(r.3)   if $A <_L B$ then $B \notin L$,

(r.4)   if $(A_1 \ldots A_m)_i$, $(B_1 \ldots B_n)_j \in \mathrm{CON}_L$ and $A_i\mathrm{Int}_L B_j$ then $m = n$, $i = j$, and $A_k\mathrm{Int}_L B_k$, for all $1 \leqslant k \leqslant m$,

(r.5)   if $(A_1 \ldots A_n)_i \in \mathrm{CON}_L$, $(A_1 \ldots A_n)_i\mathrm{Int}_L(B_1 \ldots B_n)_i$, and $A_j\mathrm{Int}_L B_j$, for all $j \neq i$, then also $A_i\mathrm{Int}_L B_i$.

For the proof see Buszkowski (1986b). Clearly, (r.1)–(r.5) must entail the constraints of Theorem 1.1. It is however worth noticing that Theorem 1.3 remains true for the case of an infinite vocabulary V_L, and in this case rigidity does not entail finiteness.

An ACG G is said to be *adequate* if $\sim_G = \mathrm{Int}_{FL(G)}$ and the following condition holds:

(5)   if $((x_1 \ldots x_n)^i)^G \neq \varnothing$ then also $(x_j)^G \neq \varnothing$, for all $j \neq i$;

the meaning of (5) is that each 'potential' functor must be an 'actual' functor. In general, for every ACG G, one can effectively find an adequate ACG G', such that $FL(G') = FL(G)$. Interestingly, if L is a rigid f-language then it admits exactly one (up to the shape of primitive types) rigid and adequate ACG G, such that $L = FL(G)$; this unique G may be referred to as *the grammar* of L. Each property of the grammar of L is essentially a property of L itself. In particular, the *order* of a rigid f-language L ($\circ(L)$) can be defined as that of the grammar of L. As a matter of fact, in this sense logicians speak about orders of languages, although they seldom worry about clarifying these things.

As an example, consider an ACG G determined by: $I_G(Joan) = n$,

$I_G(smiles) = n\backslash s$, $I_G(charmingly) = (n\backslash s)\backslash(n\backslash s)$. Clearly, $FL(G)$ contains (1) as well as e.g. $(Joan\ smiles)_2$,

(6) $(Joan\ ((smiles\ charmingly)_2\ charmingly)_2)_2$,

etc. Since G is rigid and adequate (!), it coincides with the grammar of $FL(G)$. Consequently, $FL(G)$ is a rigid f-language of order 2. If one drops $(Joan\ smiles)_2$ from $FL(G)$ the resulting f-language still remains equal to $FL(G')$, for some ACG G', but it fails to be rigid (check that the latter f-language does not fulfil (r.4)).

Phrase-structures (*p*-structures) can be defined as f-structures which lack functor markers; by $P(V)$ we denote the set of all p-structures over V. For $A \in F(V)$, A° denotes the only p-structure whose tree diagram coincides with that of A. For $L \subseteq F(V)$, we set: $L^\circ = \{A^\circ: A \in L\}$ (so, $L^\circ \subseteq P(V)$), and for $L \subseteq P(V)$, by L^f we denote the largest set $K \subseteq F(V)$ such that $K^\circ = L$. Each p-structure can be identified with a *right-directional* f-structure, i.e. an f-structure in which functors always precede their arguments. Accordingly, one may apply to p-structures all the notions introduced above for f-structures, as e.g. order, size, depth, degree, index, etc. We shall characterize the *p-languages* (i.e. sets of p-structures) generated by ACG's.

1.4. THEOREM (Buszkowski, 1986c). For any $L \subseteq P(V)$, the following are equivalent:

(i) $L = FL(G)^\circ$, for some ACG G,
(ii)   each of the numbers $ind(L)$, $s(L)$, and $deg(L)$ is finite.

According to a well known result of Thatcher (1967), a p-language $L \subseteq P(V)$ is the structure language of some CFG if and only if both $ind(L)$ and $s(L)$ are finite. Consequently, for any ACG G, the p-language $FL(G)^\circ$ is the structure language of some CFG, hence the language of G, $L(G)$, is a context-free language. Conversely, each context-free language amounts to $L(G)$, for some ACG G; this is the non-trivial part of Gaifman's theorem on weak equivalence of CFG's and ACG's (Bar-Hillel *et al.*, 1960). For the sake of completeness, we exhibit the key idea of the latter result by applying the framework elaborated above.

Assume L is the string-language of some CFG G. Consequently, $L = supp(\overline{L})$, where $\overline{L}$ stands for the p-language (structure-language) of G. Without any loss of generality we may assume, additionally, $s(\overline{L}) \leqslant 2$ (so, G is to be taken in the so-called Chomsky normal form). As mentioned above, $\overline{L}$ can be regarded as a right-directional f-language. Since $\overline{L}$ is the p-language of G, ind$(\overline{L})$ must be finite, and so is $s(\overline{L})$, as well. We cannot however claim $\overline{L}$ to be the f-language of some ACG, since $d(\overline{L})$ is in general infinite.

Observe that each p-structure of size $\leqslant 2$ admits a unique representation of the form $vA_1 \ldots A_n$, where $v \in V$, $n \geqslant 0$, and parentheses are to be associated to the left (in the same way one represents $A_1, \ldots, A_n$). Thus, for instance, $((ab)(cd))$ is represented by $ab(cd)$. Let us define a transformation $(\quad)^G$ (Gaifman's transformation) of p-structures of size $\leqslant 2$ as follows:

(G) $(vA_1 \ldots A_n)^G = v(A_1^G(A_2^G(\ldots (A_{n-1}^G A_n^G) \ldots)))$.

One easily shows that, for any A, $d(A^G) \leqslant 2$ and $\mathrm{supp}(A^G) = \mathrm{supp}(A)$. Consequently, for $\overline{L}^G = \{A^G \colon A \in \overline{L}\}$, we get $s(\overline{L}^G) \leqslant 2$, $d(\overline{L}^G) \leqslant 2$, and $\mathrm{supp}(\overline{L}^G) = \mathrm{supp}(\overline{L}) = L$. Then, it suffices to prove that ind$(\overline{L}^G)$ is finite. The latter follows from:

1.5. LEMMA. For any $\overline{L} \subseteq P(V)$, if $s(\overline{L}) \leqslant 2$ and ind$(\overline{L})$ is finite then ind$(\overline{L}^G)$ is also finite.

Accordingly, the above lemma captures the very essence of Gaifman's theorem. Incidentally, Gaifman actually proceeded another way: he simply constructed an ACG $\overline{G}$ equivalent to a given CFG G. We shall consider that construction in Section 2. Other proofs can be found in the literature amongst various arguments for the so-called Greibach normal form theorem (cf. Aho and Ullman, 1972), essentially equivalent to 1.5.

In this section we have confined ourselves to languages over the standard algebra of strings with concatenation. It is nonetheless possible to generalize our framework towards arbitrary abstract algebras (Buszkowski, 1984a, 1986b, 1987), which accommodates a quite general concept of language, as suggested in, e.g., Montague (1974), Bach (1984, 1985).

2. LAMBEK CATEGORIAL GRAMMARS: STRONG CAPACITY

Hereafter, we restrict attention to f-structures (also types, p-structures, etc.) of size $\leqslant 2$. Accordingly, each compound type takes one of the forms x/y and $x\backslash y$. The (product-free) *Lambek calculus* (**L**) amounts to the extension of **A** (notice that (A.1) now splits in two schemata: $(x/y)y \to x, x(x\backslash y) \to y)$ by affixing two new rules:

(R.1) $Xy \to x$ yields $X \to x/y$,

(R.1$'$) $xX \to y$ yields $X \to x\backslash y$,

where one demands $X \neq e$. Precisely, **L** constitutes the product-free fragment of the calculus introduced by Lambek (1958). Another axiomatization of **L** consists of:

(A.2) $x/y \to (x/z)/(y/z), x\backslash y \to (z\backslash x)\backslash(z\backslash y)$ (*composition laws*),

(A.3) $x \to y/(x\backslash y), x \to (y/x)\backslash y$ (*conversion laws*),

(R.2) $x \to y$ yields $x/z \to y/z$ and $z\backslash x \to z\backslash y$ and $z/y \to z/x$ and $y\backslash z \to x\backslash z$,

added to the axioms and rules of **A** (cf. Zielonka, 1981). Interestingly the role of (R.2) can be reduced to that of an axiom-forming rule, which means that **L** amounts, in fact, to the extension of **A** by all the new axioms resulting from (A.2) and (A.3) by finitely many (possibly no) applications of (R.2).

The latter axiomatization has the advantage of providing strings of types with f-structures. Assume $\vdash_{\mathbf{L}} x_1 \ldots x_n \to x$. Then, the arrow in question admits the following ('normal') derivation: (i) one finds y_i, $1 \leqslant i \leqslant n$, such that $\vdash_{\mathbf{L}} x_i \to y_i$, by means of (A.0), (A.2), (A.3), (R.2), and (R.0), (ii) one reduces $y_1 \ldots y_n$ to x on the basis of **A**. Evidently the second component is actually an **A**-derivation, hence it induces a unique f-structure on $y_1 \ldots y_n$, and this f-structure is reflected in $x_1 \ldots x_n$.

The arrows derivable in **L** are precisely those valid with respect to a natural algebraic semantics, consisting of so-called residuation semigroups spread over free semigroups (Buszkowski, 1982, 1985, 1986; see also Lambek's contribution in this volume). This semantics possesses a clear linguistic sense: it simply models the algebraic structure of the hierarchy of typed categories in a language. Another important semantics for **L** involves the (directional) typed lambda-calculus. One employs two lambda-abstractors λ^1 and λ^r, and appropriately modified term-forming rules (cf. Buszkowski, 1986d). Let TER_L denote the class of all (directional) terms, satisfying the three constraints: (c.1) each subterm contains a free variable, (c.2) no subterm contains two free occurrences of the same variable, (c.3) each application of $\lambda^r(\lambda^1)$ binds the right-(left-)most free variable in its scope. Then, $\vdash_L x \to y$ holds if and only if there is a term $t \in \text{TER}_L$ of type y, whose only free variable is of type x. This lambda-completeness of L can be proved in a way essentially similar to van Benthem's (1983, 1985) proof of a non-directional variant of this result. The directional typed lambda-calculus calls for a semantics which distinguishes between 'left' and 'right' functions, corresponding to 'left' and 'right' functors, respectively (cf. Buszkowski, 1986a, 1987). Such a semantics can be constructed within the general framework of biclosed monoidal categories (Lambek, 1985). Let us exemplify the terms corresponding to (A.2) and (A.3):

$$(1) \qquad \lambda^r v_{y/z} \cdot \lambda^r w_z \cdot (u_{x/y}(v_{y/z} w_z)), \quad \lambda^1 v_{z\backslash x} \cdot \lambda^1 w_z \cdot ((w_z v_{z\backslash x}) u_{x\backslash y}),$$

$$(2) \qquad \lambda^r u_{x\backslash y} \cdot (v_x u_{x\backslash y}), \quad \lambda^1 u_{y/x} \cdot (u_{y/x} v_x).$$

Interestingly, L admits a third, very significant, Gentzen-style axiomatization (Lambek, 1958; Buszkowski, 1985a; Lambek, 1985). Its application provides a proof-search decision procedure for L.

According to the general pattern from Section 1, an LCG is to be identified with a triple $G = (V_G, I_G, R_G)$ with $R_G = L$. So, all the notions previously defined for ACG's directly apply to LCG's as well.

We aim to show:

2.1. THEOREM. For any LCG G, $FL(G)$ consists of precisely all the f-structures of size $\leqslant 2$ defined on the strings from $L(G)$.

The property being claimed by 2.1 may be referred to as the *structural completeness* of LCG's. Any possible f-structure on the string is allowed, hence in fact types are to be ascribed to strings, not f-structures. Consequently, strong capacity of LCG's reduces, in a sense, to their weak capacity (the latter will be scrutinized in Section 3). The situation looks, of course, quite different if one takes into account typed f-structures, i.e. the terminal type-assignment provided by an LCG; obviously not every typed f-structure can be accepted.

Since the pioneer work of Barbara H. Partee (1975) related to

Montague's writings and Cresswell (1972) linguists have been greatly concerned with comparing category transformations in the sense of categorial grammar with structure transformations celebrated in the realm of transformational grammar. In the light of 2.1 the formalism of **L** is powerful enough to imitate any support-preserving transformation whatever. With other transformations the matter seems more sophisticated. For instance, the transformation leading from:

(3)   *((Joan works) and (Joan smokes))*

to:

(4)   *(Joan (works and smokes))*

cannot be accomplished on the basis of **L**. It however admits a smooth account on the ground of a stronger calculus, corresponding to some class of nondirectional lambda-terms, not limited by (c.2) (see Cresswell, 1973, p. 153, and Buszkowski, 1986d).

To prove 2.1 we first show:

(5) $FL(G) = (FL(G)^\circ)^f$, for any LCG G.

In other words, the *f*-language of any LCG is invariant under arbitrary arrangements of functor-markers. For, assume that $A \in FL(G)$ contains a constituent $(BC)_1$. Thus, the terminal type-assignment of G, which associates s with A, must ascribe some types x, x/y and y to $(BC)_1$, B, and C, respectively. Applying (A.3) one modifies that assignment only in what is ascribed to C: one takes $(x/y)\backslash x$ instead of y. The resulting assignment yields an *f*-structure $A' \in FL(G)$ which differs from A just in containing $(BC)_2$ in the place of $(BC)_1$. For the case in which the initial constituent of A has the form $(BC)_2$ we proceed in a dual way.

Then, to establish 2.1 it suffices to prove:

(6)   for any LCG G, $FL(G)^\circ$ consists of precisely all the *p*-structures of size $\leqslant 2$ defined on the strings from $L(G)$.

We need the following **L**-derivable arrows (which, incidentally, can replace (A.2) in the axiomatization of **L**):

(7) $(x\backslash y)/z \to x\backslash(y/z)$, $x\backslash(y/z) \to (x\backslash y)/z$ *(associativity laws)*.

Assume that $FL(G)^\circ$ contains a *p*-structure A, some of whose constituents have the form $((BC)D)$. Then, $A = \bar{A}^\circ$, for some $\bar{A} \in FL(G)$, and $\bar{A}$ contains a constituent E, such that $E° = ((BC)D)$. By (5), we may assume $E = ((\overline{BC})_2\overline{D})_1$, where $\overline{B}° = B$, $\overline{C}° = C$, and $\overline{D}° = D$. Consequently, the terminal type assignment of G ascribes, say, types x, $x\backslash(y/z)$, z, and y to $\overline{B}$, $\overline{C}$, $\overline{D}$, and E, respectively. We again modify that assignment only in ascribing type $(x\backslash y)/z$ to $\overline{C}$ (use (7)). As a result, we find $\bar{A}' \in FL(G)$ which differs from $\bar{A}$ just in containing $(\overline{B(\overline{CD})_1})_2$ in the place of E. Accordingly, $(\bar{A}')° \in FL(G)°$ arises from A by the substitution of $(B(CD))$ for $((BC)D)$. In a dual way we change any constituent $(B(CD))$ into $((BC)D)$, which yields (6).

To illustrate the strong generative power of $\mathbf{L}$, we show that on the basis of $\mathbf{L}$ one performs the transformations needed in Gaifman's theorem. More precisely, the mechanism of $\mathbf{L}$ allows the transformation of any CFG G (in the Chomsky normal form) into an equivalent ACG $\overline{G}$.

First, we recall Gaifman's construction of an ACG $\overline{G}$, equivalent to a given CFG G (strictly speaking, we follow a simplified method, given in Gladkij, 1973).

Fix a CFG $G = (N_G, V_G, s_G, P_G)$, where N_G and V_G are nonempty finite (not necessarily disjoint) sets, of *nonterminals* and *terminals*, respectively, $s_G \in N_G$ is the *initial symbol*, and P_G is a finite set of *production rules* of the form $p \mapsto qr$ or $p \mapsto v$, where p, q, $r \in N_G$, $v \in V_G$. One chooses a one-one correspondence between pairs $(p, q) \in N_G^2$ and non-principal primitive types, the type corresponding to (p, q) being symbolized by p^q. A function I, ascribing finite sets of types to the nonterminals from N_G, is defined according to the clauses:

(I.1) $s \in I(s_G)$,

(I.2)   if $p \mapsto qr \in P_G$ then q^p, $q^t/p^t \in I(r)$, for all $t \in N_G$,

(I.3)   if p, $q \in N_G$, and x is a type which has been ascribed to q according to (I.1) or (I.2), then $x/p^q \in I(p)$.

Then, $\overline{G}$ is determined by setting: $V_{\overline{G}} = V_G$, and $I_{\overline{G}}(v)$ consisting of all types x, such that, for some $p \in N_G$, $p \mapsto v \in P_G$ and $x \in I(p)$, for all $v \in V_G$. By a tedious induction on derivation trees one proves $L(\overline{G}) = L(G)$ (in fact, $FL(\overline{G}) = \overline{L}^G$, $\overline{L}$ being the p-language of G; see Section 1). The whole proof looks rather cumbersome (Cresswell, 1977, confessed: "I understood it, I think, when I read it but I quickly forgot it"). Presumably the key difficulty lies in the lack of clear intuitive foundations for (I.2) and (I.3). These hard clauses can nonetheless be given such foundations, if one employs the machinery of $\mathbf{L}$.

Let us identify the nonterminals from N_G with distinct primitive types, in particular s_G with s. By $\mathbf{L}'$ we denote the calculus that results from affixing to $\mathbf{L}$ the new axioms $qr \to p$, for every rule $p \mapsto qr \in P_G$. Furthermore, translate p^q into $p\backslash q$.

2.2. FACT. If $x \in I(p)$ then $p \to x$ is derivable in $\mathbf{L}'$.

Proof. The case (I.1) is obvious. For (I.2), since $qr \to p$ is an axiom of $\mathbf{L}'$, (R.1') yields $r \to q\backslash p$, hence we get $r \to (q\backslash t)/(p\backslash t)$ in $\mathbf{L}'$, by (R.0) and the following $\mathbf{L}$-derivable arrow:

(8) $x\backslash y \to (x\backslash z)/(y\backslash z)$.

For (I.3), assume that x has been assigned to $q \in N_G$ according to (I.1) to (I.2). By the above, $q \to x$ is derivable in $\mathbf{L}'$. Now, by (A.3), $\vdash_{\mathbf{L}} p \to q/(p\backslash q)$, hence, using (R.2) and (R.0) we get in $\mathbf{L}'$ $p \to x/(p\backslash q)$, which finishes the proof.

Continuing this line, we might show that Gaifman's proof can be essentially simplified, as some of its steps directly follow from fundamental properties of $\mathbf{L}$ (Buszkowski, 1987). We can draw another interesting consequence from the above observation: for certain purposes it is reasonable to consider systems that result from joining $\mathbf{L}$ with rewriting rules of some CFG. Thus, $\mathbf{L}$ is treated as a kind of transducer which transforms one grammar into another grammar, e.g. a CFG into an ACG, preserving some essential properties of the initial grammar. We return to such extensions of $\mathbf{L}$ in Section 3.

Theorem 2.1 enables us to answer the question of F-equivalence of LCG's and ACG's.

2.3. THEOREM. If G is an LCG, such that $L(G)$ is infinite, then there exists no ACG F-equivalent to G.

Proof. If $v_1 \ldots v_n \in L(G)$, $v_i \in V_G$, then $v_1 \ldots v_n$ being considered as a right-directional f-structure with the parentheses associated to the left belongs to $FL(G)$, because $FL(G)$ contains all possible f-structures on this string. The depth of that f-structure equals $n - 1$. Consequently, if $L(G)$ is infinite then $FL(G)$ must contain f-structures of arbitrarily high depth, which shows that $FL(G)$ cannot be generated by any ACG (use 1.1).

Using 1.4 one can prove the above with P-equivalence (i.e. the coincidence of p-languages) in the place of F-equivalence. Thus, the infinite p-languages generated by LCG's have no common member with those provided by ACG's.

Similar results are to be obtained for various systems related to **L** and LCG's. We shall briefly comment on some more interesting cases.

van Benthem (1983, 1985) (referring to F. Zwarts) considered the so-called *nondirectional* (or: commutative) Lambek calculus (**NL**), which arises from **L** by affixing the *commutativity rule*:

(COM) $XxyY \rightarrow z$ yields $XyxY \rightarrow z$,

that results in the permutation invariance of **NL**-derivable arrows. As shown by van Benthem, **NL** corresponds to the class of non-directional lambda-terms, delimited by (c.1), (c.2), and (c.3'): each lambda-abstractor binds a free variable in its scope. Since we get $\vdash_{NL} x/y \leftrightarrow y\backslash x$ ($\leftrightarrow$ stands for both $\rightarrow$ and $\leftarrow$), there is no reason for differentiating / and \ in **NL**. Being stronger than **L**, **NL** obviously satisfies 2.1 and 2.3 (precisely, the theorems hold for NLCG's, i.e. categorial grammars G with $R_G = $ **NL**).

If one delimits **L** to operate on right-directional types (i.e. those containing no occurrence of \) then he obtains its conservative sub-system, called the *right-directional Lambek calculus* (**RL**). An adequate lambda-semantics arises by banning from TER_L the left lambda-abstractor as well as all types $x\backslash y$. RLCG's do not fulfil 2.1. Precisely, for any RLCG G, $FL(G)$ consists of right-directional f-structures, hence instead of (5) we get simply $FL(G) = FL(G)^\circ$. As concerns (6), $FL(G)$ admits the transformation $(A(BC)) \mapsto ((AB)C)$ (use (A.2)) but not its converse. Nevertheless, 2.3 still holds for RLCG's with essentially the same argument.

Each of these systems possesses its e-variant, to be denoted by $\mathbf{L}_e$, $\mathbf{NL}_e$, and $\mathbf{RL}_e$, respectively, which is produced by simply allowing $X = e$ in (R.1) and (R.1') (thus allowing arrows of the form $e \rightarrow x$ or $\rightarrow x$, for short). From the standpoint of algebraic semantics this move amounts to considering monoids rather than semigroups (Buszkowski, 1985, 1986). In lambda-semantics this leads to dropping (c.1). Interestingly, $\mathbf{L}_e$ properly extends **L**, as, for instance, $x/(y/y) \rightarrow x$ is derivable in $\mathbf{L}_e$ but not in **L**, and similarly for the remaining pairs. As regards our previous results, there is no essential difference between the former (e-free) systems and their e-variants.

Lambek (1961) proposed a weaker calculus, to be called the *non-associative Lambek calculus* (**nL**), which — in the scope of product-free types — amounts to $\mathbf{A}$ + (A.3) + (R.2) (Kandulski, 1985). Algebraically, $\mathbf{nL}$ is to treat p-structures rather than strings. As shown in Buszkowski (1986c), nLCG's are P-equivalent to ACG's (the idea of this proof will be outlined in the next section). On the other hand, since (5) still holds for nLCG's, 2.3 (but not 2.1) remains true for them.

Finally, let us touch on a question of axiomatizability. As mentioned above, $\mathbf{L}$ arises from $\mathbf{A}$ by introducing the axioms that result from applying (R.2) to (A.2) and (A.3); this yields an infinite variety of axiom-schemata. As proved by Zielonka (1981), this variety cannot be replaced by a finite one. Semantically, this means that the transformations definable by terms from TER_L can be generated from no finite family of them by means of functional application as the only operation. The same holds for $\mathbf{RL}$, $\mathbf{NL}$, and $\mathbf{nL}$ but, interestingly, not for $\mathbf{NL}_e$, since the latter calculus possesses a finite axiomatization over $\mathbf{A}$ (Buszkowski, 1986d).

3. LAMBEK CATEGORIAL GRAMMARS: WEAK CAPACITY

That each context-free language (CF-language) can be generated by some LCG appears to be a quite simple consequence of Gaifman's theorem. For, using Gentzen-style techniques one easily shows:

3.1. LEMMA. If $\circ(x_i) \leqslant 1$, for all $1 \leqslant i \leqslant n$, and $p \in Pr$, then $\vdash_L x_1 \dots x_n \to p$ iff $\vdash_A x_1 \dots x_n \to p$.

3.2. COROLLARY. If G_1 and G_2 are an ACG and an LCG, respectively, whose vocabularies and initial type assignments coincide, and their common order is less than 2, then $L(G_1) = L(G_2)$.

Now, according to Gaifman's result, each CFG is equivalent to some ACG $\overline{G}$ with $\circ(\overline{G}) \leqslant 1$ (see (I.1)–(I.3) from Section 2). By 3.2, $\overline{G}$ is equivalent to G', the latter being an LCG whose vocabulary and initial type assignment coincide with those of $\overline{G}$. Consequently:

3.3. PROPOSITION (Cohen, 1967). For any CFG G, there exists an LCG G' (with $\circ(G') \leqslant 1$), such that $L(G) = L(G')$.

Accordingly, the non-trivial claim of Gaifman's equivalence theorem presents us with one half of the equivalence of CFG's and LCG's On the other hand, what corresponds to the trivial part of the former, i.e. that LCG's do not surpass CF-languages, appears to constitute a rather hard and still open question (the positive answer had been predicted as far back, as Bar-Hillel *et al.*, 1960 and Chomsky, 1963; then, Cohen, 1967, published a proof of the equivalence in question but his proof has been shown to be illegitimate — see Buszkowski, 1985a; Zielonka, 1986). The difficulties are caused by the fact that **L** admits the expansion of types. Hence, although the initial type assignment involves a finite collection of types, the process of type transformation may, essentially, make use of an infinite variety of them. We do not know as yet whether this infinite variety can be reduced to a finite one without limiting generative capacity.

An instructive partial result, viz. the equivalence of RLCG's and CFG's, is established in Buszkowski (1985a). Interestingly, the proof goes not by reducing an RLCG to an ACG but by some fine interpretations of the system **RL** in itself. Let us give a brief outline.

First, we define a special family of types, called *simple types*. For $P \subseteq Pr$, the set $Sm(P)$, of *simple types* over P, is the union of the following hierarchy:

(*Sm*.0) $Sm_0(P) = P$,

(*Sm*.1) $Sm_1(P) = P \cup \{p/q: p, q \in P\} \cup \{(p/q)/r: p, q, r \in P\}$,

(*Sm*.3) $Sm_{n+2}(P) = Sm_{n+1}(P) \cup \{p/(q/x): p, q \in P, x \in Sm_n(P)\}$.

One easily shows that, if P is finite, then all sets $Sm_n(P)$, $n \geq 0$, are also finite; furthermore, $Sm_n(P)$ contains precisely those types $x \in Sm(P)$ which fulfil $\circ(x) \leq n$. An important property of simple types is the following:

3.4. CLAIM. If $x_1, \ldots, x_m \in Sm_n(P)$ $(m \geq 2, n \geq 0)$ and $p \in P$ are such that $\vdash_{RL} x_1 \ldots x_m \to p$, then there exist a number $1 \leq i < m$ and a type $y \in Sm_n(P)$, fulfilling the conditions:

(i) $\vdash_{RL} x_i x_{i+1} \to y$,

(ii) $\vdash_{RL} x_1 \ldots x_{i-1} y x_{i+2} \ldots x_m \to p$.

Thus, under the assumptions of 3.4, in order to derive in **RL** the arrow $x_1 \ldots x_m \to p$ it suffices to apply (a finite number of times) reductions of the form $xy \to z$, where $x, y, z \in Sm_n(P)$ and $\vdash_{RL} xy \to z$. By reversing the arrows we obtain a CFG-like derivation. For a finite

$T \subseteq Tp$, and $p \in Pr$, by $L(T, p)$ we denote the set of all strings $x_1 \ldots x_m$, such that $x_1 \ldots x_m \in T$ and $\vdash_{RL} x_1 \ldots x_m \to p$. Using 3.4 one easily proves that $L(Sm_n(P), p)$ is a CF-language, for all $n \geqslant 0$, finite $P \subseteq Pr$, and $p \in P$, hence:

3.5. CLAIM. For any finite $T \subseteq Sm(Pr)$, and all $p \in Pr$, $L(T, p)$ is a CF-language.

As simple types are rather peculiar types (e.g. $(s/s)/(s/s)$ is not simple), the above is far from a final solution. The second step consists in representing each right-directional type as a string of simple types. More precisely, to each right-directional type x (whose primitive sub-types are within $P \subseteq Pr$) we ascribe a nonempty string $str(x)$ of simple types over $P' = P \cup \{\bar{p}\}$, where $\bar{p} \notin P$, fulfilling the following conditions:

(str. 1) if $\circ(x) \leqslant n$ then $str(x)$ consists of types from $Sm_n(P')$,

(str. 2) if $x \neq y$ then $str(x) \neq str(y)$,

(str. 3) $\vdash_{RL} str(x) \to x$.

The details of this construction are rather involved and will be omitted here. It follows from (str. 3) that:

(1) $\vdash_{RL} x_1 \ldots x_m \to p$ entails $\vdash_{RL} str(x_1) \ldots str(x_m) \to p$.

The converse of (1) need not be true, however. Interestingly, it is true for $\mathbf{RL}_e$ in the place of $\mathbf{RL}$ (and (1) holds as well), which yields the equivalence of RL_eCG's and CFG's. For, define $L^e(T, p)$ as $L(T, p)$ but with $\mathbf{RL}_e$ instead of $\mathbf{RL}$. Then, for any finite set T and $p \in Pr$, one gets: $L^e(T, p) = str^{-1}(L^e(str(T), p))$, which means that $L^e(T, p)$ is the counter-image of $L^e(str(T), p)$ given by the homomorphism str. Since $L^e(str(T), p)$ is a CF-language (3.5 holds true also for $\mathbf{RL}_e$), then the well-known closure properties of CF-languages yield:

3.6. CLAIM. For all finite $T \subseteq Tp$, and $p \in Pr$, $L^e(T, p)$ is a CF-language.

Now, given an RL_eCG G, the language $L(G)$ arises from $L^e(Tp(G), s)$ by substitution, hence:

3.7. CLAIM. If G is an RL_eCG then $L(G)$ is a CF-language.

Since 3.3 holds for RL_eCG's as well, we obtain:

3.8. THEOREM. RL_eCG's are equivalent to CFG's.

To establish the above for RLCG's we have an additional task. We define a family *Smt*, of so-called *smart types*, in the following way. For a right-directional type x, the occurrences of subtypes in x can be divided in two disjoint sets, $\text{sub}_1(x)$ and $\text{sub}_2(x)$, defined by induction:

(sub.1) $\text{sub}_1(p) = \{p\}$, $\text{sub}_2(p) = \varnothing$, for $p \in Pr$,

(sub.2) $\text{sub}_1(x/y) = \{x/y\} \cup \text{sub}_1(x) \cup \text{sub}_2(y)$,
$\qquad\quad \text{sub}_2(x/y) = \text{sub}_2(x) \cup \text{sub}_1(y)$.

Given a string X and $p \in Pr$, we also define a type p/X, as follows: (i) $p/e = p$, (ii) $p/(Xy) = (p/y)/X$ (we use induction on the length of X). Each right-directional type is uniquely represented in the form p/X, where $p \in Pr$ is its head and X is a (possibly empty) string of types. A type p/X is said to be *heavy* if $\vdash_{\textbf{RL}} X \to p$. Now, $x \in Smt$ iff (by definition) $\text{sub}_2(x)$ contains no heavy type. To give some examples, $(s/n)/(s/n)$ is smart but $(s/s)/(s/s)$ is not, since $(s/s) \in \text{sub}_2((s/s)/(s/s))$ and $\vdash_{\textbf{RL}} s \to s$.

The significance of smart types follows from the fact that in the scope of those types the systems **RL** and $\textbf{RL}_e$ coincide. Precisely:

3.9. LEMMA. If $X \neq e$ consists of smart types, and $p \in Pr$, then $\vdash_{\textbf{RL}} X \to p$ iff $\vdash_{\textbf{RL}_e} X \to p$.

3.10. COROLLARY. If an RLCG G is such that $Tp(G) \subseteq Smt$ then $L(G)$ is a CF-language.

The final step is to prove:

3.11. CLAIM. Each RLCG is equivalent to some RLCG G', such that $Tp(G') \subseteq Smt$.

Given an RLCG G, we construct an RLCG G', fulfilling the required condition, by 'coloring' primitive subtypes of the types in $Tp(G)$. Again, the construction is rather involved, and we refer the reader to the original paper for details. As a straightforward consequence of 3.3, 3.10 and 3.11, we obtain:

3.12. THEOREM. RLCG's are equivalent to CFG's.

There are still some troubles with adapting this argument for LCG's but, hopefully, they are of a merely technical, not principal, character. On the other hand, one may succeed in following a different way which consists in reducing a given LCG to some ACG, the latter being 'contained' in the former. This idea proved itself fruitful for the case of nLCG's (Buszkowski, 1986c). We sketch the main lines.

As mentioned in Section 2, to axiomatize **nL** it suffices to enrich **A** with all the arrows resulting from (A.3) by an iterated application of (R.2); we call them *new axioms*. A new axiom $x \to y$ is called an *E-axiom* (*R-axiom*) if the complexity of x is less (greater) than that of y. We write $x \overset{*}{\to} y$ if there are types $x_1, \ldots, x_n$ ($n \geqslant 1$), such that $x_1 = x$, $x_n = y$, and $x_i \to x_{i+1}$ is a new axiom, for all $1 \leqslant i < n$. Each arrow $x_1 \ldots x_m \to y$ derivable in **nL** possesses a normal derivation of the following form: (i) for all $1 \leqslant i \leqslant m$, one finds a type y_i, such that $x_i \overset{*}{\to} y_i$, (ii) one reduces the string $y_1 \ldots y_m$ to x on the basis of **A**. The following then holds: if $x \overset{*}{\to} y$ then there exists a sequence $x = x_1 \to x_2 \to \cdots \to x_n = y$ of new axioms in which all R-axioms precede all E-axioms. Take an nLCG G. We construct another nLCG $\overline{G}$ by setting: $V_{\overline{G}} = V_G$ and $I_{\overline{G}}(v)$, $v \in V_G$, consist of all types y such that, for some $x \in I_G(v)$, we get $x \overset{*}{\to} y$ by means of R-axioms only. Due to the above claim, the reduction procedure in $\overline{G}$ need not use R-axioms at all. We show that $\overline{G}$ is equivalent to the ACG G^* with $V_{G^*} = V_G$ and $I_{G^*} = I_{\overline{G}}$. Clearly $L(G^*) \subseteq L(\overline{G})$. Assume $v_1 \ldots v_n \in L(\overline{G})$. Then $\vdash_{\mathbf{nL}} x_1 \ldots x_n \to s$, for some $x_i \in I_{\overline{G}}(v_i)$. A normal derivation of $x_1 \ldots x_n \to s$ uses no R-axiom. An easy induction shows that there are $y_i \in I_{\overline{G}}(v_i)$, $1 \leqslant i \leqslant n$, such that $y_1 \ldots y_n \to s$ is derivable in **nL** without applying new axioms at all, hence $\vdash_{\mathbf{A}} y_1 \ldots y_n \to s$. Accordingly, $L(G^*) = L(\overline{G})$. On the other hand, $L(\overline{G}) = L(G)$ is obvious, hence each nLCG is equivalent to some ACG. The converse is proved as for LCG's, which yields:

3.13. THEOREM. nLCG's are equivalent to ACG's (CFG's).

A closer examination of the above argument shows that it yields, actually, the *P*-equivalence of nLCG's and ACG's.

As concerns NLCG's (i.e. categorial grammars based on **NL** — the nondirectional Lambek calculus), they generate languages invariant under any permutation of strings (since **NL** admits (COM)). In Busz-kowski (1984) and van Benthem (1985) it has been proved that the NLCG's of order not greater than 1 generate precisely the commutative closures of CF-languages (hence they go beyond the scope of CF-languages!). It directly follows from Gaifman's theorem and the lemma:

3.14. LEMMA. If $\circ(x_i) \leqslant 1$, for $1 \leqslant i \leqslant n$, and $p \in Pr$, then, $\vdash_{NL} x_1 \ldots x_n \rightarrow p$ iff $\vdash_A x_{i_1} \ldots x_{i_n} \rightarrow p$, for some permutation $i_1, \ldots, i_n$ of the sequence $1, \ldots, n$.

Whether NLCG's of greater order still yield nothing more than com-mutative closures of CF-languages remains an open problem.

Some authors have considered systems intermediate between **A** and **L** (or **NL**). In particular, Zielonka (1978), Ades and Steedman (1982) and others examined systems resulting from **A** by affixing:

$$(2) \qquad (x/y)(y/z) \rightarrow x/z, \qquad (x\backslash y)(y\backslash z) \rightarrow x\backslash z,$$

and, possibly, some additional arrows. It follows from the non-finite axiomatizability of **L** on the basis of **A** (Zielonka, 1981), and the analogous result for **NL** (Buszkowski, 1986d), that none of these restricted systems can be equivalent to **L** or **NL**. As concerns the weak capacity of the respective categorial grammars, the situation looks as follows. If the system in question is stronger than **A** but weaker than **L** the grammars can generate all CF-languages (Lemma 3.1 and Proposi-tion 3.3 must hold for them with exactly the same arguments); of course, this is so for right-directional as well as bidirectional systems. It is, however, often non-trivial to show that such grammars yield no more than CF-languages (cf. Zielonka, 1978). (Caution: this is trivial if one considers grammars of order less than 2 only.) On the other hand, if one admits a kind of commutativity (e.g. the arrows $y(x/y) \rightarrow x$, as in Ades and Steedman, 1982), then the resulting systems are weaker than **NL** but incomparable with **L**. So, according to 3.14, those of first order can generate no more than commutative closures of CF-languages. Actually, certain rather weak systems of that kind have been proved to generate non-CF-languages (Friedman *et al.*, 1986).

Concluding, the above results enable us to believe that LCG's and some closely akin variants of them, though they strongly increase the capacity of structure generation, on the level of strings do not surpass the paradigm of context-free syntax or lead to a merely slight modification of it (e.g. commutative closure). A quite different situation is observed for systems arising by joining **L** with additional axioms (e.g. the rules of some CFG), as exemplified in our reconstruction of Gaifman's proof (see Section 2). If R is a finite set of arrows, by $L(R)$ we denote the calculus that results from affixing to **L** all the arrows from R as new axioms. Buszkowski, 1982a (see also 1982b for details) proves:

3.15. THEOREM. For any type 0 grammar G, such that $e \notin L(G)$, one effectively can find a finite set R and an $L(R)$CG $\overline{G}$, with $L(\overline{G}) = L(G)$.

Furthermore, the arrows in R can be given one of the forms:

(3) $pq \rightarrow r$,

(3′) $p/q \rightarrow r$, for $p, q, r \in Pr$.

It is noteworthy that to get such strong generative power one needs arrows of both forms. Actually, if R consists of arrows of the form (3) or (3′) but not both, then $L(R)$ is decidable. It should also be mentioned that systems $L(R)$ with R consisting of arrows $p \rightarrow q, p, q \in Pr$, appeared already in Lambek (1968), and their decidability was proved there.

Accordingly, if **L** is used not as a kind of pure tautology system but more as a logic that is to draw consequences from some assumptions (coming from the CFG-framework or anything else), then the resulting generative power becomes incomparably stronger, and attains in fact the maximal level desired in linguistic considerations. Incidentally, algebraic semantics provides another, very convincing motivation for such extended systems. Namely, neither LCG's nor other species of 'tautological' grammar succeed in providing a complete description of the category hierarchies of any language, while this goal can easily be reached with the aid of $L(R)$CG's (Buszkowski, 1982, 1982b, 1985, 1987). Quite probably, extended Lambek grammars deserve recommendation as offering the most promising line of future research in categorial grammar.

Let us also mention another line, initiated by Chytil and Karlgren (1985). These authors consider ACG's with an infinite initial type assignment. One easily checks that such grammars can generate all possible languages. Now, introducing some constraints on the computational complexity of type reduction the authors obtain interesting hierarchies of non-CF-languages, related to so-called degrees of context-sensitivity. In general, the mentioned paper provides a nice connection between categorial grammars and some modern threads of computation theory.

Finally, we wish to formulate a general opinion about the significance of equivalence results on the line categorial-generative grammars. They were sometimes interpreted to shake the value of categorial grammars (as they yield nothing new). The author absolutely disagrees with that standpoint. First, that two kinds of grammar are weakly equivalent does not mean, obviously, that they are simply the same. This means, precisely, that they describe the same reality of string-languages. But they describe it in a different way. Categorial description refers to the algebra of types (and, behind it, logical semantics), while phrase-structure description relies upon the algebra of concatenation (or bracketed concatenation). Approximately, categorial grammar theory can be viewed as a logical meta-theory for the theory of phrase-structure grammar. Hence, second, an equivalence result, say, the equivalence of RLCG's and CFG's, is interesting not only for the former theory but equally for the latter, just providing Chomsky's hierarchy with a kind of representability theorem: CF-languages coincide with those representable (in a sense) in certain logical calculus (**L**, **NL**, etc.). Presumably, the fine deductive structure of type processing systems as well as their relations to lambda-calculi, Cartesian closed categories, propositional logics, and so on, will prove in the future quite fruitful for developing a logically advanced theory of formal grammars.

ACKNOWLEDGEMENTS

The author wishes to express his gratitude to Deirdre Wheeler, Richard T. Oehrle, and Emmon Bach for making it possible for him to participate in the Tucson conference. Special thanks are addressed to Joachim Lambek and Johan van Benthem for helpful comments on many topics concerning categorial grammars.

REFERENCES

Ades, A. E. and M. J. Steedman: 1982, 'On the Order of Words', *Linguistics and Philosophy* **4**, 517—558.

Aho, A. V. and J. D. Ullman: 1972, *The Theory of Parsing, Translation and Compiling*, Prentice-Hall, Englewood Cliffs.

Ajdukiewicz, K.: 1935, 'Die syntaktische Konnexität', *Studia Philosophica* **1**, 1—27.

Bach, E.: 1984, 'Some Generalizations of Categorial Grammars', in F. Landman, F. Veltman (eds.), *Varieties of Formal Semantics*, Foris, Dordrecht.

Bach, E.: 1985, 'Categorial Grammars as Theories of Language', this volume, pp. 17—34.

Bar-Hillel, Y., C. Gaifman, and E. Shamir: 1960, 'On Categorial and Phrase Structure Grammars, *Bull. Res. Council Israel* F **9**, 1—16.

Benthem, J. van: 1983, 'The Semantics of Variety in Categorial Grammar', in W. Buszkowski, W. Marciszewski, and J. van Benthem (eds.), *Categorial Grammar*, Benjamins, Amsterdam/Philadelphia, to appear.

Benthem, J. van: 1985, 'The Lambek Calculus', this volume, pp. 35—68.

Buszkowski, W.: 1982, 'Compatibility of a Categorial Grammar with an Associated Category System', *Zeitschr. f. math. Logik und Grundlagen d. Math.* **28**, 229—238.

Buszkowski, W.: 1982a, 'Some Decision Problems in the Theory of Syntactic Categories', *ibid.* **28**, 539—548.

Buszkowski, W.: 1982b, *Lambek's Categorial Grammars*, Adam Mickiewicz University, Poznań.

Buszkowski, W.: 1984, 'A Note on the Lambek-van Benthem Calculus', *Bull. of the Section of Logic* **13**, 31—37.

Buszkowski, W.: 1984a, 'Fregean Grammar and Residuated semigroups', in G. Wechsung (ed.), *Frege Conference 1984*, Akademie-Verlag, Berlin.

Buszkowski, W.: 1985, 'Algebraic Models of Categorial Grammars', in G. Dorn and P. Weingartner (eds.), *Foundations of Logic and Linguistics: Problems and Their Solutions*, Plenum Press, New York/London.

Buszkowski, W.: 1985a, 'The Equivalence of Unidirectional Lambek Categorial Grammars and Context-free Grammars', *Zeitschr. f. math. Logik und Grundlagen d. Math.* **31**, 369—384.

Buszkowski, W.: 1985b, 'Categorial Grammars in the Eye of Logic', in J. Demetrovics, G. Katona, and A. Salomaa (eds.), *Algebra, Combinatorics and Logic in Computer Science*, Coll. Math. Soc. J. Bolyái, North Holland, Budapest.

Buszkowski, W.: 1986, 'Completeness Results for Lambek Syntactic Calculus', *Zeitschr. f. math. Logik und Grundlagen d. Math.* **32**, 13—28.

Buszkowski, W.: 1986a, 'Three Theories of Categorial Grammar', in *Categorial Grammar*, Benjamins, to appear.

Buszkowski, W.: 1986b, 'Typed Functorial Languages', *Bull. Acad. Pol. Sci.* (Math.), 495—505.

Buszkowski, W.: 1986c, 'Generative Capacity of Nonassociative Lambek Calculus', *ibid.*, 507—516.

Buszkowski, W.: 1986d, 'The Logic of Types', in J. Srzednicki (ed.), *Initiatives in Logic*, Martinus Nijhoff Publishers, to appear.

Buszkowski, W.: 1987, *Categorial Grammar and Its Logic*, Martinus Nijhoff Publishers, forthcoming.

Chomsky, N.: 1963, 'Formal Properties of Grammars', in Duncan-Luce, R. *et al.* (eds.), *Handbook of Mathematical Psychology*, Vol. 2, Wiley, New York.

Chytil, M. and H. Karlgren: 1985, 'Categorial Grammars and List Automata for Strata of Non-CF-languages', in *Categorial Grammar*, Benjamins, to appear.

Cohen, J. M.: 1967, 'The Equivalence of Two Concepts of Categorial Grammar', *Information and Control* **10**, 475—484.

Colmerauer, A.: 1978, 'Metamorphosis Grammars', in L. Bolc (ed.), *Natural Language Communication with Computers*, LNCS, Vol. 63, Springer, Berlin/Heidelberg.

Cresswell, M. J.: 1972, *Logics and Languages*, Methuen, London.

Cresswell, M. J.: 1977, 'Categorial Languages', *Studia Logica* **36**, 257—269, also in: *Categorial Grammar*.

Curry, H. B.: 1961, 'Some Logical Aspects of Grammatical Structure', in R. Jakobson (ed.), *Structure of Language and Its Mathematical Aspects*, AMS, Providence.

Friedman, J., D. Dai, and W. Wang: 1986, *The Weak Generative Capacity of Parenthesis-Free Categorial Grammars*, BUCS Technical Report, Boston.

Gladkij, A. V.: 1973, *Formal Grammars and Languages* (in Russian), Izdat. "Nauka", Moscow.

Hiż, H.: 1967, 'Grammar Logicism', *The Monist* **51**, 110—127; also in: *Categorial Grammar*.

Kandulski, M.: 1985, 'The Non-associative Lambek Calculus', in *Categorial Grammar*, Benjamins, to appear.

Keenan, E. L. and L. Faltz: 1978, *Logical Types for Natural Language*, UCLA Occasional Papers in Linguistics 3, Los Angeles.

Lambek, J.: 1958, 'The Mathematics of Sentence Structure', *American Math. Monthly* **65**, 154—170, also in *Categorial Grammar*.

Lambek, J.: 1961, 'On the Calculus of Syntactic Types', in *Structure of Language and Its Mathematical Aspects*.

Lambek, J.: 1968, 'Deductive Systems and Categories', I. *J. Math. Systems Theory* **2**, 287—318.

Lambek, J.: 1985, 'Categorial and Categorical Grammars', this volume, pp. 297—317.

Levin, H.: 1982, *Categorial Grammar and the Logical Form of Quantification*, Bibliopolis, Naples.

Montague, R.: 1974, *Formal Philosophy* (ed. by R. Thomason), Yale University Press, New Haven.

Partee, H. B.: 1975, 'Montague Grammar and Transformational Grammar', *Linguistic Inquiry* **6**, 203—300.

Thatcher, J. W.: 1967, 'Characterizing Derivation Trees of Context-free Grammars Through a Generalization of Finite Automata Theory', *J. Comput. System Sci.* **1**, 317—322.

Zielonka, W.: 1978, 'A Direct Proof of the Equivalence of Free Categorial Grammars and Simple Phrase-structure Grammars', *Studia Logica* **37**, 41—58.

Zielonka, W.: 1981, 'Axiomatizability of Ajdukiewicz—Lambek Calculus by Means of Cancellation Schemes', *Zeitschr. f. math. Logik und Grundlagen der Math.* **27**, 215—224.

Zielonka, W.: 1986, 'J. M. Cohen's Claim on Categorial Grammars remains Unproved', *Bull. of the Section of Logic*, to appear.

Institute of Mathematics
Adam Mickiewicz University
Matejki 48/49
60-769 Poznań
Poland

CLAUDIA CASADIO

SEMANTIC CATEGORIES AND THE DEVELOPMENT OF CATEGORIAL GRAMMARS*

0. INTRODUCTION

A main claim about Categorial Grammars is that they involve *semantic categories* rather than the standard syntactic categories employed in linguistic description. But, what kind of entities are semantic categories? What relation do they impose between syntactic structure and semantic representation?

The present work will try to give an answer to the above and related questions, reconsidering the theoretical framework supporting the development of Categorial Grammars with particular reference to the theory of semantic categories proposed, at the beginning of the Century, by the philosopher Edmund Husserl and the Polish logicians Stanislaw Leśniewski and Kazimierz Ajdukiewicz.

Notions such as *interchangeability, syntactic connexity*, and *meaningfulness* will be discussed on the basis of the rule system characterizing the original model of a Categorial Grammar and of the extensions put forward by Yehoshua Bar-Hillel and Joachim Lambek. The analysis will conclude with a brief survey of more recent improvements including the generalizations of Categorial Grammar suggested by Emmon Bach and A. Ades and M. Steedman.

As a result of the above developments, Categorial Grammars appear to provide a convincing and powerful framework for the investigation of natural language, overcoming the difficulties confronting them at the end of the Sixties.

1. THE THEORY OF SEMANTIC CATEGORIES

1.1. *Husserl's Meaning Categories*

The basic principles of the theory of semantic categories are due to Edmund Husserl[1]. His *Bedeutungskategorien* represent a significant development of the Aristotelian tradition in which parts of speech are assigned to different classes or *categoriae* on the basis of a cluster of

95

Richard T. Oehrle et al. (eds.), Categorial Grammars and Natural Language Structures, 95—123.
© 1988 *by D. Reidel Publishing Company.*

logico-linguistic properties. In fact, while Aristotelian categories are conceived as mutually exclusive sets, Husserl's categories exhibit a more complex character due to the developments of philosophical logic in the 19th Century, particularly the investigations of Bernard Bolzano and Gottlob Frege[2].

Husserl's *meaning categories*[3] are the formal elements governing what he calls *linguistic articulation*, i.e. the processes by which linguistic expressions of indefinite length and complexity are formed starting from basic or *ultimate* elements. Articulation is not an arbitrary breaking; moreover, it applies at various levels, each represented by a particular form and expressing an appropriate meaning. To give an example, if we consider a conditional sentence of the form **if A then B**, the first level of articulation consists of the antecedent **if** *A* and the consequent **then** *B*, while the constituent parts (subject and predicate) of each sentence *A* and *B* are second level members with respect to the whole and may be represented by the syntactic form: **S is p**[4]; *A* and *B* having been complex sentences, a third or a fourth level of articulation would be possible, but in any case ultimate elements not further divisible would have been reached in a finite number of steps.

The various parts in which a (complex) expression is articulated exhibit a relevant difference with respect to the way they make reference to things in the world, i.e. with respect to their meaning relations. Certain parts, such as sentences, nominal expressions, predicates, have a precise meaning on their own, that is, their meaning is a *matter* in Husserl's terminology. Other parts, on the contrary, are not significant by themselves, although appearing to be indispensable to determine the meaning of the context in which they occur. This is the case of *syncategorematic* words, such as **and, or, is**, etc., whose meaning is dependent on the meaning of the whole proposition they contribute to determine: it is a *form*, in Husserl's words.

The distinction between independent meanings (corresponding to categorematic expressions) and non-independent meanings (corresponding to syncategorematic items) plays a basic role in the characterization of the set of meaning categories. Linguistic expressions of non-independent meanings may occur as parts only of expressions of independent meanings: they appear to the linguistically *incomplete*, i.e. they need to be completed by other parts of speech to produce a significant whole. The modalities of the connection are directly expressed by the meaning of the incomplete expression: a law is associated to each non-independent meaning[5] governing its *integration* with other meanings and indicating the *kind* and the *form* of the contexts where it may be embedded. Consider, for example, the propositional form:

(1)   This S is p

Many exemplifications of this form are possible, such as **This tree is green**, **This gold is green**, or the apparently strange **This algebraic number is green**, but respecting well-defined boundaries. In fact, not any meaning whatsoever may be expressed by the words substituted for the variables S or p. Under the connection law associated to the meaning of the item **is**, any *nominal matter* may be appropriate for S, or any *adjectival matter* for p. We always get a unitary and acceptable meaning, i.e. a proposition of the requested form. But the unitary meaning is lost as soon as we do not conform to the *meaning categories* predicted by the formative item **is**.

A proposition, therefore, appears to be not an arbitrary string of words, but a whole in which each constituent represents a part needing to be integrated with other parts, depending on the meaning categories to which they belong, to form a meaningful unity. On this basis, the above distinction between complete and incomplete expressions is reflected in what Husserl calls the *logical morphology of meanings*, the first and fundamental part of his purely logical grammar[6]. A classification of meanings can be developed starting from the set of the primitive forms, i.e. the forms governing articulation processes. In fact,

each primitive form adheres to a certain *a priori* ... law stating that every meaning connection obeying that form effectively gives rise to a unitary meaning, provided that the terms (the undetermined elements, the variables of the form) belong to certain meaning categories (Husserl, 1913, p. 330).

Therefore, two nominal matters M, N may appropriately be involved in the primitive form M **and** N according to the law stating that such a connection will result in a meaning belonging to the same category; and the same law holds for other meaning categories, e.g. adjectival matters or propositional matters[7].

It is now easy to appreciate the functional character of Husserl's *meaning connection rules* where the outputs may be considered, in a fair analogy to Frege's analysis[8], as the result of the integration of incomplete parts with parts adequate to complete them, in the same way that a function is saturated by its arguments. The mode of composition depends on the set of meaning categories which observe certain universal principles that may be enunciated as follows:

(2) (i) Every linguistic expression must belong to a meaning category.
    (ii) Every meaningful expression is the result of the integration of its parts and the mode of integration depends on the meaning categories to which each part belongs.
   (iii) Replacing a part of a meaningful expression with an expression belonging to a different meaning category will always convert the former into a non-meaningful one.

Having stated that belonging to a meaning category is a necessary feature of linguistic expressions, the principles indicate the conditions of connection and interchangeability. In particular, expressions belonging to the same meaning category may be freely interchanged within a given context[9]; the resulting meaning may be false, as in (3a), or absurd, as it appears to be in (3b), but it is in any case a unitary meaning:

(3) (a) This man is green.
    (b) This quadrilateral is round.

On the other hand, if the boundaries of meaning categories are not observed, the result will be a nonsensical string, as in (4):

(4)   This careless is green (Bar-Hillel, 1957)

So far, *nonsense*, as a lack of a unitary meaning (or ill-formation in syntactic terms) is distinguished from *countersense* or logical emptiness (i.e. the non-existence of a corresponding denotation; e.g. any entity that is a round quadrilateral). While the latter is prevented by the logical rules, the former is prevented by the set of meaning-connection rules that roughly correspond to syntactic formation-rules.

On the basis of this distinction between rules to avoid nonsense and rules to avoid formal countersense, Husserl introduces his conception of a purely logical grammar as a set of analytical laws common to all languages. Meaning categories take on a fundamental role in this framework, since meaningfulness and its mirror counterpart, well-formation, depend on the set of rules to connect meanings through the categories they belong to. The relevant fact, here, is that Husserl's categories are not conceived homogeneously, as the Aristotelian *genera*, but there are categories that form a basis to which other categories apply as *operators*, the result of this application becoming in turn a possible basis for further applications. In this we find *in nuce* the distinction between *basic categories* and *functorial categories* organically defined within the Polish School.

1.2. *The Polish School*

The group of philosophers and logicians referred to as the Polish School developed very intensive investigations in the period between the two world wars. However, their history began in 1895 under the teaching in Łwow of Casimir Twardowski whose interest in science had a great influence on the formation of his Polish students, directing them towards the clarity and precision of scientific method, the rigor and testability of mathematics and logic[10]. Important results were reached both on the syntactic side, with regard to axiomatization and proof theory, and on the semantic side with particular reference to type theory, formalization of interpretation, and development of metalinguistic devices.

The interest for semantics arose mainly in connection with the debate opened by the *Principia Mathematica* of Russell and Whitehead, the crucial question being the discovery within logical systems of syntactic and semantic paradoxes[11]. Russell's solution, founded on the definition of the hierachies of simple and ramified types, was the source of many perplexities because of the complexity of the resulting system and the need for a reducibility axiom to maintain the fundamental properties of mathematics and set theory. The ramified theory of types and the reducibility axiom were considered very unnatural within the Polish School. Different alternatives were pursued, such as Leon Chwistek's theory of constructive types, which avoids the antinomies without having to appeal to remedies like the reducibility axiom[12].

In any case, the question remained open until Stanislaw Leśniewski and Alfred Tarski altered the perspective by developing the relevant distinction between *object language* and *metalanguage*.[13] Leśniewski was the first to emphasize the fact that, in any language containing its semantics, logical laws cannot hold consistently; the ensuing contradictions may be avoided only by reconstructing the language through hierarchical levels, where each further stage has to be enriched by new terms defining and interpreting the terms of the preceding level. Being in agreement with Russell that some hierarchy is necessary in the foundation of interpreted and coherent systems, even if not necessarily identifiable with Russellian type theory, Leśniewski developed a new hierarchy of categories that he called a *grammar of semantic categories* (*semantische Kategorien*).

Compared to Russell's type theory, the grammar of semantic categories is nearer to the intuitive understanding of language, because of its affinity to traditional grammatical analysis of parts of speech and its reference to Husserl's logical grammar, which Leśniewski had known of through the teaching of Twardowski.

1.3. *Leśniewski's Grammar of Semantic Categories*

Leśniewski's system consists of three axiomatic theories that together determine an extensional (or canonical) language *L*. The first two theories, *Protothetic* (a calculus of equivalent propositional functions) and *Ontology* (a calculus of classes developed in terms of a theory of nominal predication), represent a logical system based on the grammar of semantic categories. The third system, *Mereology*, represents an extralogical theory, based on the part-whole relation, containing rules to avoid paradoxes.[14]

The primitive logical basis consists in a set of *directives* which are general prescriptions about the structure of the system[15] and of a single axiom, for each of the above theories, introducing a primitive *constant* on the basis of which all the other constants can be defined. Definitions, logical laws and all the relevant principles are introduced as *theses*: valid logical equivalences, adjoined to the initial axiom, that represent the progressive stages in which the system expands.

The grammar of semantic categories is hierarchically conceived: *functorial categories* of increasing degree may be generated starting from a restricted set of *basic categories*: basic categories are assigned to the primitive constants introduced by the axioms, while functorial categories apply to previously defined categories. Functorial categories, in analogy with Husserl's characterization of incomplete meanings, are intended as categories of functions from certain arguments to appropriate values. The category of each functor, therefore, may be identified by the categories of the arguments together with the category of the function value and may be expressed univocally by a constant of the system under rigorous criteria of contextual determinacy[16].

The following principles hold for constants and expressions of any category (cf. Luschei, 1962, p. 95):

(5) (i) Every variable, constant or expression of the canonical language *L* belongs to a semantic category.

(ii) If functions of the same number of arguments belong to the same category, then so do their functors if and only if all homologous arguments occupy the same respective relative position and belong to the same respective category.

(iii) No expression belongs to more than one semantic category.

(iv) Constants *C* and *C′* belong to the same category if and only if some (and hence every) proposition containing *C* remains significant, though not necessarily of the same sense and truth value, even when *C* is replaced by *C′*.

where (5i), (5ii) and (5iii) express an isomorphic relation between syntax (object language *L*) and semantics (grammar of semantic categories) on the basis of which ambiguous equiform expressions (e.g. the conjunction **and**, which may be either a nominal operator or a propositional operator as in (7) below) are distinguished through category assignment and contextual determinacy. Moreover, on the basis of (5iv), expressions occurring in the same places within equiform propositions will belong to the same meaning category, and may be interchanged within any (extensional) context.

This criterion, with respect to e.g. the propositional contexts in (6):

(6) (a) Socrates is Socrates.

(b) Socrates is human.

(c) Socrates is non-human.

(d) Socrates is identical with Socrates.

(e) Socrates equals Socrates.

has the effect that **Socrates** belongs to the same category as **human** and **non-human** (the category of *nouns*), **is** belongs to the same category as **equals** and **is-identical-with** (the category of propositional functors with two nominal arguments), **non-** belongs to the same category as **identical-with**, etc.

This represents what has been called the *constructive nominalism* of Leśniewski, since subjects and predicates of singular propositions, analyzed with the form *A* **is** *B*, are assigned to the same semantic category. In this respect, Leśniewski's analysis of singular propositions reflects the use of the *copula* in traditional logic, in certain Indo-European languages such as Greek and Latin, or in Slavonic languages such as Polish; the examples above would therefore be better appreciated if words such as the Latin **homo** were employed in place of the English **human**, since the latter cannot appear as a subject (due to its category assignment in English).[17]

1.4. *Functional Categories*

Leśniewski's grammar is able to generate functorial categories of any degree starting from the basic categories of *propositions* (defined by the single axiom of *Protothetic*) and *nouns* (defined by the single axiom of *Ontology*). Notably, the primitive constant of *Protothetic*, the co-implicator (operator of logical equivalence), belongs to the category of functors making a proposition from two propositional arguments, and the primitive constant of *Ontology*, the *copula* of singular predication, belongs to the category of functors forming a proposition from two nominal arguments.

A partial representation of the hierarchy of categories that is generated on this basis[18] may be given by means of the algebraic notation introduced by Kazimierz Ajdukiewicz in his essay of 1935. This notation has the advantage of representing the required category symbols in terms of fractionary indices, more perspicuous than the contextual notation of Leśniewski. A fractionary index, associated to a functorial category, takes as its denominator the indices of the arguments and as its numerator the index of the value of the corresponding function for those arguments, as is shown in the following diagram[19]:

(7)

Category index	Definition	English expressions
s	proposition	Three squared is nine
n	noun	three, nine, three squared
s/s	prop. operator	it is not the case that
s/n	monadic predicate	is nine, is-odd, is-prime
s/nn	diadic predicate	is, equals
s/ss	prop. binary op.	_____ and _____
n/n	nominal operator	squared, halved, tripled
n/nn	nominal binary op.	. . . and . . .
. . .	. . .	. . .

To give some examples, *s/n* is the index of the category of functions from a nominal argument to propositions, *s/nn* is the category of functions from two nominal arguments to propositions (to which the *copula* **is** belongs), *n/n* is the category of functions from a nominal argument to nouns. etc.

Since each of these categories may in turn be taken as argument(s), we obtain functions of increasing degree, e.g. *s/(s/n)* (a function of propositional functions). In each case, the categories of the arguments together with the category of the function value will determine without ambiguity the category to which the new function belongs.

We may ask ourselves if the categories so far defined are actually semantic or if in effect they are syntactical. In fact, the system that Leśniewski develops on this basis is an extensional logical system adequate to express the language of mathematics. On the other hand, the same adequacy does not hold for ordinary language of which the canonical language elaborated by Leśniewski should be a proper representation owing to the 'intuitive' nature of semantic categories and their adherence to parts of speech.

In effect, Leśniewski does not indicate any distinction between syntax and semantics, but formalizes his system in the perspective of the interpretation he intends to give, so that meaningfulness and well-formedness appear to be coextensive, as in Husserl's view. In any event, conceived for an extensional language whose propositions correspond to meaningful indicative sentences, the system does not provide for other kinds of clauses, such as interrogative, imperative, etc., or for non-extensional contexts, just as it does not distinguish among proper nouns, common nouns, adjectives in predicative position and other nominal expressions.

2. SEMANTIC CATEGORIES AND LINGUISTIC DESCRIPTION

2.1. *Ajdukiewicz's Syntactic Connexion*

In 1935, Kazimierz Ajdukiewicz presented in the first number of the review *Studia Philosophica* [20] a reformulation of Leśniewski's grammar of semantic categories in terms of the more economical notation given above.

Although sharing the basic assumptions of Leśniewski's theory,

Ajdukiewicz appears to be more directly interested in the characterization of natural language expressions, saying consequently that the set of (semantic) categories relative to a given language is to be determined on empirical grounds and depends on the particular features of that language. This does not prevent him from maintaining the principles of the grammar of semantic categories, represented in a perspicuous notation. In particular, well-formedness conditions of linguistic expressions are considered dependent on the "specification of the conditions under which a word pattern, constituted of meaningful words, forms an expression which itself has a unitary meaning" (Ajdukiewicz, 1935, p. 207). An expression satisfying such conditions is defined as *syntactically connected.*

On the basis of the algebraic notation, syntactic connexion may be determined by means of an effective procedure that Ajdukiewicz calls *exponent derivation.* The procedure applies the assumption, adopted from Husserl and Leśniewski, of the existence, within each complex meaningful expression, of a basic function-argument(s) order of its constituents. This order does not usually coincide with the external word succession, the surface order we may say, since it depends on the deepest semantic properties of the whole expression. The procedure suggested by Ajdukiewicz is intended to make this structural order explicit: an expression may be analyzed in parts one of which is a functor (the *main* functor) and the other its arguments; all these elements are defined as first level terms and the expression as well-articulated. Since the main functor and its arguments may be in turn complex expressions, the analysis repeatedly applies, generating terms of increasing level. If well-articulated expressions are met at each stage, the complex expression is *well-articulated throughout.*

A well-articulated expression must respect two further conditions in order to be syntactically connected:

(8) (i) To every functor occurring as a main functor of any order, there correspond exactly as many arguments as there are letters in the denominator its index.

(ii) The expression has an exponent consisting of a single index. (Ajdukiewicz, 1935, p. 216)

where (8i) states that at each stage of articulation functors and arguments have to combine in the appropriate way to ensure that the result is a well-formed and meaningful expression, and (8ii) says that such an expression belongs to a meaning category whose index is given by its exponent.

An example of exponent derivation is presented in (9) and (10) on the basis of the categorial lexicon given in (7):

(9) (a) Three squared is nine and nine equals three tripled.

(b) and is   squared three nine equals nine tripled three
    s/ss *s/nn* *n/n*   *n*   *n*   *s/nn*   *n*   *n/n*   *n*

(10)   *s/ss*   *s/nn*   *n/n*   *n*   *n*   *s/nn*   *n*   *n/n*   *n*

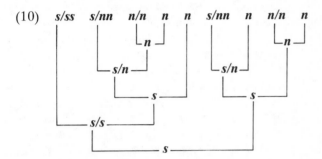

where (9b) gives the *proper sequence* of the categorial indices associated to the words of the complex sentence occurring in (9a): at each stage of articulation, each functor precedes its ordered arguments as required by the procedure. (10) shows the exponent derivation, where each branch (made up of two strokes and a horizontal line[21]) corresponds to the derivation of the categorial index of a proper constituent of the whole expression by means of a *cancellation rule*, performing the operation of functional application, that may be formulated as follows:

(11)   The combination *X/Y Y* cancels to *X*, where *X* and *Y* are indices of any category (or sequences of indices).

2.2. *The PSG Model: Bar-Hillel's Directional Grammar*

Ajdukiewicz's exponent derivation performs an analysis of linguistic expressions whose steps determine the category to which each (proper) constituent belongs. For this reason, Ajdukiewicz's theory may be embedded within an immediate constituent model giving rise to that variant of Phrase Structure Grammar (PSG) that Bar-Hillel first defined as *Categorial Grammar* (see Bar-Hillel *et al.*, 1960, p. 98).

A categorial grammar applies the main principles of the theory of semantic categories so that every sentence is "the result of the operation of one continuous part of it upon the remainder, these two parts being the *immediate constituents* of the sentence, such that these constituents which . . . are phrases, are again the product of the operation of some continuous part upon the remainder, etc." (Bar-Hillel, 1960, p. 76).

The relevant features of a categorial grammar are given within Ajdukiewicz's model, but it appears inadequate in two main respects. A first limitation is represented by the assignment of a single category index to each expression and by the consequent derivation of a single structural anlaysis for each sentence. This may be appropriate for certain formalized languages, such as Propositional Calculus, but it holds neither for more complex formal systems nor for natural language, as Rudolf Carnap pointed out in his *Logical Syntax of Language*, underlining the difference between *substitution* (or full interchangeability) and *replacement*. The former cannot apply without restrictions, as assumed by Husserl and Leśniewski, since in certain formalized languages it is possible for two expression to be mutually interchangeable within some contexts without being interchangeable within every context (see Carnap, 1934). The same holds for natural languages which are characterized by *homonymy*, i.e. the fact that a word belongs to more categories, and by syntactic (or semantic) *ambiguity*, i.e. the fact that different derivations correspond to the same expression [22].

A further inadequacy of Ajdukiewicz's grammar is represented by the way in which categories are specified with respect to *directionality*: the exponent derivation procedure generates sequences of categories rigorously ordered from left to right (see (9b) above) to which word sequences, not immediately corresponding to natural language strings, are assigned. This may work within a logical language since a unique mode of combination of symbols is admitted, but fails to hold for natural languages characterized by several possible word-orders and the problems of homonymy and ambiguity.

Bar-Hillel suggests an improvement to overcome these difficulties based on the following innovations:

(11) (i) Words may be assigned to more than one category.
     (ii) Functor categories are assumed to apply to arguments occurring both on the right and on the left (i.e. are specified with respect to directionality).
    (iii) A combination rule is defined applying from right to left.

Starting from the basic categories *n* (nouns) and *s* (sentences), functorial categories, specified by means of the directional symbols '/' and '\', may be assigned to words and phrases, such as e.g. *n/n* (determiners, adjectives), *n\s* (intransitive verbs, predicates), *n\s/n* (transitive verbs), *(n\s)\(n\s)* (intransitive adverbs).

Assuming that a dictionary lists all the words together with the categories to which they belong, syntactic structure and grammaticality of a given string of words are determinable by an automatic procedure consisting in (i) listing under each word all the category indices to which the word belongs; (ii) performing, everywhere and as far as possible, one of the following operations:

(12) (a) *X/Y Y* → *X*   (right cancellation rule)
　　 (b) *X X\Y* → *Y*   (left cancellation rule)

In analogy to Ajdukiewicz, such a procedure is called a derivation and the last line its exponent. An example of a possible derivation appears in (14) with respect to the category assignment given in (13b):

(13) (a) Paul thought that John slept soundly.
　　　　　　　　　　　(Bar-Hillel, 1960)

(b) Paul　thought　that　John　slept　soundly
　　 n　　*n*　　　*n*　　*n*　　*n\s*　*n\s\n\s*
　　　　　n\s　　*n/n*　　　　　*n\s/n/n\s/n*
　　　　　n\s/n　*n/s*　　　　　　. . .
　　　　　n\s/s　. . .
　　　　　. . .

(14)　**Paul　thought　that　John　slept　soundly**
　　　n　*n\s/n*　*n/s*　*n*　*n\s*　*n\s\n\s*

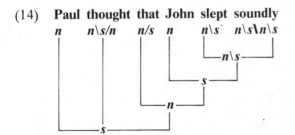

The sequence in (13b) is well formed with respect to the constituent structure determined by the derivation in (14), since its exponent consists of a single category, in this case the category *s* of sentences. The analysis in (14) is one of the four different derivations of the exponent *s* that it is possible to obtain from the very many equivalent derivations allowed by this word sequence, under the given category assignment (which is 'far from being exhaustive'; Bar-Hillel, 1960, p. 77).

So far, the situation appears to be rather difficult: a decision procedure for grammaticality (and other relevant structural relations) involving strings of words of a certain length would require a very high number of derivations; furthermore, to give a complete categorization of the words of a natural language it would be necessary to increase the number of the basic categories, to distinguish e.g. the various kinds of nominal expressions and the different kinds of sentences. This would lead to the procedure's performing an enormous number of operations.

2.3. *The Algebraic Model: Lambek Calculus of Syntactic Types*

The *Calculus of Syntactic Types* proposed by Joachim Lambek[23] represents a more powerful system, reducing the number of operations to be performed. Within this framework, a categorial grammar is viewed as consisting of the *syntactic calculus* generated from a finite set of basic types by means of the three binary operations: *xy* (multiplication), *x/y* (right division), *x\y* (left division).

The syntactic calculus is a deductive system defining a set of *types* closed under the three binary operations. A set of theorems, as those occurring in (17), is inferred on the basis of certain axioms (such as reflexivity and associativity) and of the rules of inference given in (16):

(16) (a) If *A* has type *x* and *B* has type *y*, then *AB* has type *xy*.
     (b) If *AB* has type *x* for all *B* of type *y*, then *A* has type *x/y*.
     (c) If *AB* has type *y* for all *A* of type *x*, then *B* has type *x\y*.

(17) (a) $x/y \; y \rightarrow x$
     (b) $x \; x\backslash y \rightarrow y$
     (c) $(x\backslash y)/z \leftrightarrow x\backslash(y/z)$
     (d) $x \rightarrow y/x\backslash y$
     (e) $x/y \rightarrow x/z/y/z$
     (f) $x/y \; y/z \rightarrow x/z$

On the basis of the statements in (16), the cancellation rules in (17a) and (17b) may be inferred. These are not the unique combination rules admitted by the system, as happens in Bar-Hillel's grammar. Further operations are possible such as that in (17f) which allows two adjacent functorial categories to combine. The content of the rule (later defined as *functional composition* on the analogy of the mathematical operation) is that a function from *x* to *y* combines with a function from *y* to *z*, so that the result is a function from *x* to *z*. The theorems in (17d) and (17e) represent rules to expand types into more complex ones to increase their possibilities of combination[24]. Finally, the rule in (17c) states that, according to associativity, parentheses may be omitted[25].

A powerful and flexible system, able to perform the analysis of a wide range of natural language strings, results from the above assumptions and inferences as can be seen in the following example:

(18) (a) He works for him

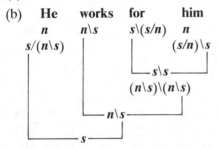

The expansion rule given in (17d) applies at the first stage of the derivation yielding a type appropriate for pronouns in object position; this combines with the type assigned to the preposition **for** by means of the rule of function composition (17f); the resulting type is again lifted (by (17e)) to get an index appropriate to combine with the type of the verb **works**. The resulting type combines with the type of pronouns in subject positions (see Lambek, 1958).

On this basis, the syntactic calculus assigns the type *s* (sentence) to a string of words if and only if the dictionary assigns a type to each word within it and the derivation of the type *s* from such type assignment is a theorem of the system (i.e. type *s* is deducible by means of the admitted set of rules).

3. CATEGORIAL GRAMMARS

3.1. *A Fregean Extension*

The theory of semantic categories, although characterizing the function-argument(s) relation, does not make explicit reference to Frege's theory of functions. However, as Peter Geach maintains[26] a more adequate insight into the meaning of natural language expressions and new generalizations may be achieved if reference is made to that framework.

According to Frege's analysis, a function is an *incomplete* or *unsaturated* expression needing to be saturated by an appropriate argument occupying the argument-place occurring within the function name. As in Husserl's theory, the distinction between complete and incomplete expressions is fundamental, allowing the classification of *names*[27] within two main categories: (i) the category of *proper names* to which complete expressions belong (i.e. the expressions that do not have argument-places); (ii) the category of *function names* to which all those expressions belong that are incomplete (i.e. that have one or more argument-places). The former class includes names of objects, sentences (i.e. names of truth values) etc., while unsaturated expressions belong to the latter class.

On this basis, the notion of function may be extended to every linguistic context: functional expressions may always be obtained by removing one or more occurrences of a complete expression (i.e. a proper name) from a complete expression. A categorial grammar may, therefore, be introduced on the basis of the unique category N of *proper names*; functorial categories may be obtained repeatedly removing one or more occurrences of a category from an expression of category N, by means of the recursive procedure shown in (19):

(19)   Removing from an expression of category N,

   (i) an occurrence of the category N, the result is a first level-one place functor *:NN*;

   (ii) two occurrences of the category N, the result is a first level-two place functor *::NNN*;

   (iii) an occurrence of the functorial category *:NN*, the result is a second level-one place functor *:N:NN*;

   (iv) etc.

where a functorial category is represented by a structure consisting of an initial group of colons ':', to indicate the number of arguments of the functor, and of a sequence of category symbols corresponding to the function value (the first symbol) and to the arguments (the successive symbols in the sequence[28].

This characterization of functorial categories with respect to their level and internal structure is adequate both for formal languages and for natural languages expressions. However, in the latter case, the number of basic categories needs to be implemented as suggested in Geach (1972), where the categories *n* (nouns) and *s* (sentences) are assumed in coherence with the framework of categorial grammars.

On the basis of the procedure in (19), the removal of an expression of category *n* from a sentence produces the functor *:sn* (a sentential functor with a place for a nominal argument), and the removal of an expression of category *:sn* from a sentence results in the functor *:s:sn* (a second level sentential functor with an argument-place for a first level sentential functor). The process may be represented by the rules in (21) which are instances of the rule scheme in (20) (corresponding to the usual cancellation rule):

(20)   *:ab b → a*

(21)   *:sn n → s*
         :s:sn :sn → s

where *:sn* is the category of open sentences such as _____ **flies** that may be saturated by names such as **Socrates** to form sentences such as **Socrates flies**; *:s:sn* is the category of second level functors taking open sentences as arguments, to which quantifiers belong; e.g. **every man** (*:s:sn*) applies to **flies** (*:sn*) to form **every man flies**.

Therefore, an important generalization results from Frege's theory of functions: a relation may be stated between singular propositions such as **Socrates flies** and quantified propositions such as **every man flies**, where the quantifier (quantified NP) is a second level functor. This is an improvement with respect to the preceding models of categorial grammars [29] which do not explain the reason for the existence of different levels of functors. On the contrary, the investigation of the internal structure of categories may help to further understand the combinatorial properties of linguistic expressions and the relationships of apparently independent category assignments.

A good example is given by Geach's analysis of conjunction, which involves expressions of many different categories, as shown in (22):

(22) (a) The boys dance and the girls sing.
     (b) The boys dance and sing.
     (c) All the girls and all the boys dance and sing.

where conjunction applies to sentences in (22a), to verb phrases (category *:sn*) in (22b), to quantified noun phrases (category *:s:sn*) in (22c). In the first case, conjunction takes the category *:s(2s)* (a sentential functor with two sentential argument-places); however, this is not the unique possible category assignment if the recursive rules in (23) are added:

> (23) (a) If $a\ b \to c$, then $a\ :bd \to :cd$
> (b) If $a\ b\ b \to c$, then $a\ :bd\ :bd \to :cd$

Conjunction, being a two argument functor, falls under the rule scheme in (23b) on the basis of which the examples in (22b) and (22c) may be derived from the category assignment of (22a) (assuming $b = :sn$ and $b = :s:sn$, respectively):

> (24) (a) $s(2s)\ s\ s \to s$
> (b) $s(2s)\ :sn\ :sn \to :sn$
> (c) $s(2s)\ :s:sn\ :s:sn \to :s:sn$

A solution is then available for the problem of the proliferation of categories in the analysis of natural language. The number of categories listed in the dictionary may be sensibly reduced by assigning each word to one or a few categories; further category assignments may then be derived through expansion rules such as the rule schemes given in (23). Such rules will increment the combination possibilities of words and expressions ensuring, at the same time, that the new category assignments are related to their sources.

3.2. *A Set of Rules to Derive Categories*

A general definition of a Categorial Grammar may now be given with reference to the different models outlined above.

A (bidirectional) Categorial Grammar is an ordered quintuple characterized as follows [30]:

> (25) $G = \langle V, C, S, R, f \rangle$

where V is a finite set (the vocabulary); C is a finite set of categories which generates a full set C' of categories by the recursive application of the formation rule: if a and b are categories, then so are a/b and

$a\backslash b$; S is a category of C (the category of sentences); R is the set of categorial rules; f is an assignment function of elements of V to finite subsets of C'. On this basis, a sequence $A = B^1, \ldots, B^n$ of elements of V is a sentence, if and only if at least one of the sequences of categories assigned to A cancels to the exponent S under a finite number of application of the rules in R. The set of phrases and sentences so characterized represents the language determined by the categorial grammar G; a language that may be so described is called a *categorial language*.

The set R may contain some or all the rules listed in (26):

(26) (a) $a/b\ b \to a$ **Functional application rules**
$\quad\quad\quad a\ a\backslash b \to b$

(b) $a \to b/(a\backslash b)$ **Expansion rules** (Type raising)
$\quad\quad\quad a \to (b/a)\backslash b$
$\quad\quad\quad a/b \to (a/c)/(b/c)$
$\quad\quad\quad a\backslash b \to (c\backslash a)\backslash(c\backslash b)$

(c) $a/b\ b/c \to a/c$ **Functional composition rules**
$\quad\quad\quad a\backslash b\ b\backslash c \to a\backslash c$

(d) $\dfrac{a/b\ b \to a}{a/b\ b/c \to a/c}$ **Geach inferential schema**

where the rules in (26a) introduce an Ajdukiewicz/Bar-Hillel grammar, the rules in (26b) and (26c) are representative (although not exhaustive) of a Lambek grammar[31], and in (26d) Geach's inferential schema for one-place functors is given. This group of rules, although incomplete with respect to the models from which it derives, allows the analysis of a significant set of natural languages expressions. Some examples are given below, with the aim of briefly showing how a set of categorial rules work:

(27) (a) every number is even (Geach, 1972)
$\quad\quad$ (b) **every   number**
$\quad\quad\quad$ **NP/CNP CNP** $\to$ **NP**
$\quad\quad$ (c) $\quad\quad$ **is   even**
$\quad\quad\quad$ **(NP\S)/AP AP** $\to$ **NP\S**
$\quad\quad$ (d) **NP** $\to$ **S/(NP\S)**
$\quad\quad$ (e) **S/(NP\S) NP\S** $\to$ **S**
$\quad\quad$ (f) **NP NP\S** $\to$ **S**

(28) (a) every number must be even or odd
(b) NP\S = VP
(c) **must be even or odd**
　　VP/VP VP/AP AP AP\AP/AP AP
(d) **even or odd**
　　AP AP\AP/AP AP → AP
(e) **must be**
　　VP/VP VP/AP → VP/AP
(f) **VP/AP AP → VP**

(29) (a) necessarily three is odd
(b) **necessarily (three is odd)**
　　S/S　　　　　　S　　　→ S
(c) three, necessarily, is odd
(d) **necessarily is odd**
　　S/S　　　(NP\S)/AP AP
(e) **S/S → (NP\S)/(NP\S)**
(f) **(NP\S)/(NP\S) (NP\S)/AP → (NP\S)/AP**
(g) **(NP\S)/AP AP → NP\S**

3.3. *Concluding Remarks*

When Bar-Hillel presented his model in the Sixties, categorial grammars were charged with descriptive and explanatory inadequacy. On the one hand, in fact, derivations employed very many steps to obtain the syntactic analysis even of simple sentences; moreover, many different category assignments were necessary to ensure the characterization of natural language contexts. On the other hand, many relevant contexts could not be derived (without assuming very unnatural assignments), such as sentences containing elliptical or discontinuous elements (e.g. he *looked* it *up*), dislocated constituents (e.g. *to Mary* John gave the book) or presenting other long distance dependencies.

Categorial grammars of the Ajdukiewicz/Bar-Hillel format, in fact, are based on a set of cancellation rules i.e. rules of functional application that apply to adjacent constituents one of which, the functor, has to be saturated by the other, its argument. Therefore, distant but related constituents cannot be derived, as it happens within immediate constituent analysis. Effectively, these models of categorial grammars have been proved to be equivalent to context-free phrase structure grammars[32], open, therefore, to the same objections[33].

Extensions of the basic model have been pursued in different directions, such as the introduction of a new primitive, the **lambda** operator, to increase the combinatorial force and the generative capacity of the system (see Cresswell, 1973). An alternative solution is to augment the categorial basis introducing a set of transformation-like rules; this perspective was seen in advance by Bar-Hillel and it is followed in Lewis (1972) and in the extensions of Montague (1974) suggested e.g. by Partee (1975), (1976). Anyway, significant improvements may be obtained even maintaining a simple categorial basis (i.e. a lexicon specified with respect to basic and functorial categories and a set of categorial rules). This goal is reached on the basis of two relevant generalizations: (i) the characterization of categories as complex symbols; (ii) the extension of the set of rules.

The first generalization consists in allowing categories to have internal structures "that pay attention not only to the relative ordering of their arguments, but also to such matters as case, number, person, and the like" (Bach, 1982, p. 103), i.e. to that set of **features** that are relevant to determine lexical and syntactic properties. In this perspective, categories are defined as clusters of features specified with respect to a lexical head and the various levels (bars) in which the category expands[34]. Such a characterization allows, among many other things, the distinction of different kinds of functors (e.g. endocentric modifiers vs. category-switching modifiers) and the employment of devices such as matching of features and feature percolation (see the analysis of English auxiliaries and verbal constructions developed on this basis in Bach, 1983).

The second extension concerns the set of categorial rules. As seen above, a richer set of rules is defined both in Lambek's and in Geach's model allowing the derivation of a wide set of natural language expressions including many cases of long distance dependencies. In any case, no systematic use of these rules occurred before Ades and Steedman (1982). It is within that framework that the crucial cases of dislocation and unbounded dependency are derived on the basis of a set of pure categorial rules including, in addition to functional application, several instances of functional composition defined as recursive combination rules[35]. Moreover, the inclusion of appropriate instances of category expansion rules (or type raising) allows the analysis of a wide range of dependencies and of the relevant facts concerning coordination (see e.g. Partee and Rooth, 1983; Steedman, 1985a; Zwarts, 1985).

Since then, generalizations of categorial grammars have been applied to all the relevant fields of linguistic analysis confirming the adequacy of such a framework with respect to its economy, elegance, and the straightness of the relation it states between syntax and semantics. There is no room here to give detailed information about the many new contributions to the research in this area and the reader is addressed to the bibliography, which is intended to be as full as possible.

NOTES

* This work is part of a research program on Categorial Grammars and Natural Language supported by the Philosophy Department of the University of Bologna and by the Institute of Philosophy of the University of Chieti (Italy). The author was strongly influenced by the Conference on Categorial Grammars in Tucson and she wishes to thanks all the participants and particularly the organizers, Emmon Bach, Richard Oehrle and Deirdre Wheeler. Special thanks are due to Richard Oehrle for his comments and suggestions.

[1] The main reference here is to that part of *Logische Untersuchungen* known as Fourth Logical Research (in the improved version of the second edition of 1913) but the link to Appendix I of Husserl (1929) is also relevant.

[2] For the contribution of Bolzano's and Frege's investigations to Husserl's analysis, see Bar-Hillel (1952) and (1957), and the correspondence to be found in Frege (1891—1906).

[3] The term *meaning category* is employed to mark the contrast to the term *semantic category* relative to the Polish School investigations, since the latter makes explicit reference to a formal theory of meaning, while the former refers to meaning in a more general and intuitive way. See Bar-Hillel (1967).

[4] This form is preferred by Husserl as the more representative of judgments in coherence with the Aristotelian analysis of language that he adopted from his teacher Brentano.

[5] Even if Husserl did not accomplish his intention of giving a complete and formal characterization of the notion of meaning and of the laws governing it, he expressed some very interesting insights on this matter anticipating (and inspiring) the more systematized developments of the Polish logicians and of Rudolf Carnap. The more interesting intuition is perhaps the distinction between the set of rules that he calls pure (analytic) rules of meaning and the set of logical rules. This distinction, as Bar-Hillel points out, corresponds to that stated in Carnap's *Logical Syntax of Language* between *formation rules* and *transformation rules*, where the latter represent the logical rules of deduction and are not to be confused with the set of syntactic rules to which the term refers within standard linguistic literature (Carnap himself, in his successive work, preferred to define these rules as *rules of truth*); see Carnap (1937) and Bar-Hillel (1957).

[6] Husserl's idea of a universal grammar refers back to the rationalist philosophers of the 17th and 18th centuries, but received the right appreciation only after the investigations into logical syntax and semantics were put forward by the Polish School, on the one hand, and Rudolf Carnap, on the other.

[7] Effectively, the way Husserl describes his meaning categories shows that "these categories turn out to be nothing else but the objective counterparts of the grammatical categories that were regarded as standard in Husserl's time (at least for Indo-European languages)! "(Bar-Hillel, 1957, p. 92). The fact is that Husserl's attention was primarily devoted to the analysis of meaning within the framework of his philosophical investigation; however, this does not prevent his understanding of many linguistic facts, as Bar-Hillel points out when he says that "Husserl has got hold of a basic insight into the techniques of language investigation" and "he may well have been the first to see clearly the fundamental role played in linguistic analysis by . . . commutation." (*ibid.*, p. 93)

[8] See Frege (1893).

[9] The substitution law appears to be very strong: in fact it is possible to preserve meaningfulness involving a different meaning category (e.g. a nominal matter instead of an adjectival matter to form instances of (1) such as **This tree is a plant**); on the other hand, many cases admitted by Husserl as significant, such as **This algebraic number is green,** may seem totally meaningless to some speakers.

[10] Within the three main centers of Łwow, Warsaw and Cracow, the investigation was primarily directed towards the foundations of formal logic and mathematics. We may briefly recall J. Łukasiewicz's results with regard to axiomatization of the Propositional Calculus, the axiomatic reductions discovered by J. Łukasiewicz, B. Sobocinski, Wajsberg and A. Tarski, the introduction of a formal notation, known as the Polish notation, rigorously ordered from left to right, offering the advantages of economy and non-ambiguity. For a characterization of these systems see Prior (1955); for a global picture with an historical introduction, see Storrs McCall (ed.) (1967). Finally, some information about the geography of the group: Łukasiewicz worked in Łwow, under the teaching of Twardowski, and among his students we find S. Leśniewski, K. Ajdukiewicz and T. Kotarbinski; everybody went later to Warsaw, except Ajdukiewicz, who remained in Łwow. A new generation of logicians and philosophers then grew up in Warsaw — among them, Lindenbaum, B. Sobocinski, A. Tarski.

[11] A paradox arises when a generalization about all cases of a certain kind (or all members of a set) happens to produce both a case of the same kind and a case not of the same kind, such as the famous Russell antinomy of the class of all classes not belonging to themselves. Generally speaking, paradoxes are caused by circular or self-referential processes and may be avoided, as in the framework of Russell's theory, by means of rules constraining the substitution of variables within an axiomatic system: not any substitution value will be accepted, but only the values admitted with respect to a suitable hierarchy. Within ramified type theory, the hierarchy splits into branches which are specifications of basic ambiguous expression. On the other hand, to express the extensional language of mathematics, the further restrictions of ramified types are virtually annulled by an axiom (or principle) of reducibility. (See, e.g., Russell, 1908, 1924; Church, 1940, 1956.)

[12] Chwistek's theory basically appeals to the notion of function by means of which set theoretical notions may be defined including that of class. See Chwistek (1924/25).

[13] Leśniewski's investigations widely contributed to the development of formal semantics as an adequate and autonomous theory; Tarski himself admitted having been influenced by the theory of semantic categories since it penetrates so deeply into the fundamental intuitions concerning the meaning of linguistic expressions that it is difficult to imagine a scientific language not developed in coherence with that theory (see the Appendix to the German edition of Tarski, 1935).

[14] Leśniewski wrote a lot of articles and essays on the topic, but many have not been translated and several were lost during the second world war. Among those translated into German and English we remember: Leśniewski (1929), (1938), (1930), (1931), (1939). Since he did not publish a systematic synthesis of his work, the technical and fragmentary character of his publications rendered them relatively unknown in Europe with respect to the work of other Polish logicians. A good description and comment on Leśniewski's theory is found in Luschei (1962).

[15] Directives express, in a strictly formal way, the rules for definitions, quantifier-scope assignment, inference of valid formulas from axioms, substitution and extensionality principles. They represent a set of metalinguistic statements, alternative to the postulates and order restrictions of ramified theory of types, to which the simple restrictions of semantic categories correspond within the system.

[16] Within the directives, in fact, principles of contextual determinacy are given such as the employment of parentheses of distinguished form to indicate expressions of different category, an ordered notation (Polish notation) under which a functor always precedes its arguments, delimitation of the scope of functors and operators, etc. Such principles allow the assignment of a semantic category to each linguistic expression and the unambiguous analysis of expressions of the same form but of different category.

[17] For a discussion of Leśniewski's constructive nominalism, see Luschei (1962, pp. 125—128, 144—149); for an application of *Ontology* to Medieval logic see Henry (1972), where Latin expressions and inferential patterns are analyzed on the basis of the assignment to appropriate functional categories.

[18] The grammar of semantic categories appears to be finite at each stage of its development, i.e. embedding a finite number of constants and expressions, but it is potentially infinite, since a further stage may always be introduced and new semantic categories my be defined by means of appropriate theses. (See Luschei, 1962, pp. 84—104.)

[19] Arithmetical expressions have been chosen to represent the English language following a suggestion of Richard Oehrle (personal communication), to avoid some of the difficulties, see above, presented by words such as **human** that in English can never be substituted for terms like **Socrates** in subject position.

[20] The review was founded in Łwow to collect and make known the results of the Polish School to a foreign audience; the articles, therefore, were written in one of the major international languages. The term *connexion* translates the word *Konnexität* employed in the original version of Ajdukiewicz's article; others, such as Bar-Hillel, prefer the translation *connexity* (see Bar-Hillel, 1967).

[21] The representation is derived from Bar-Hillel (1953), (1960).

[22] A string of words is **syntactically ambiguous** if it is assigned the same structural description on the basis of more than one derivation. On the other hand, a string is **semantically ambiguous** if it has different derivations corresponding, within the present framework, to different interpretations. See e.g. Bar-Hillel's analysis of the sentence **Paul thought that John slept soundly**, which is both syntactically ambiguous (many equivalent derivations) and semantically ambiguous (four different derivations).

[23] See Lambek (1958), (1961); Lambek presented a version of his Syntactic Calculus, with more details and comments, in the occasion of the Tucson conference: see Lambek (1985). The category indices in (16) and (17) are as in Lambek (1958).

[24] Different denominations may be found in the literature for these rules, e.g. the term

forward partial combination employed in Ades and Steedman (1982) for the rule in (17f); the term *type raising* is frequently used for the rules in (17d) and (17e). See, e.g., Steedman (1985).

[25] As Lambek points out, the multiplicative system corresponding to his syntactic calculus of types is not necessarily associative (i.e. a semigroup); if the associative law is assumed, a more powerful system results, allowing unbracketed strings and characterizing a stong definition of constituency; if associativity is dropped, then only bracketed strings are allowed corresponding to standard grammatical constituents, but the types must increase in number and complexity (see Lambek, 1985).

[26] The main reference here his Geach (1972); for Frege's theory of functions see Frege (1891), (1893).

[27] The term *name* is taken in a wide sense as a sign (simple or complex) employed to denominate something; therefore, there are names of objects (proper names in the current meaning) just as there are names of truth values (sentences).

[28] The procedure and the notation are introduced in Potts (1973).

[29] Ajdukiewicz tried to develop an analysis of quantifiers, but he confined himself to first level functors suggesting the category *s/s* together with contextual restrictions to distinguish such operators from other sentential functors such as negation. Anyway, this does not explain the relevant fact that quantifiers bind variables; if, following Frege, free occurrences of variables are considered argument-places, open formulas such as $F(x)$ need to be assigned to the category *:sn*. The corresponding quantified formulas will be assigned to the category *:s:sn* of the functors taking as arguments open formulas (see Geach, 1972, p. 494). A detailed analysis of quantification in the framework of categorial grammar and with particular reference to Geach's model is proposed in Levin (1982).

[30] See Bar-Hillel (1962) and Cresswell (1973), (1977). The definition is given for a bidirectional categorial grammar, but, depending on the content of the recursive rules of formation and the members of the set *R*, it may be appropriate also for the unidirectional version (in which only the operator '/' is defined), such as that presented in Ades and Steedman (1982) and for non-directional models as Geach's grammar or the version of the Lambek's system proposed in van Benthem (1984).

[31] The rules of expansion and functional composition are specified with respect to right or left directionality, but functors contrasting in directionality may also occur, as $(x/y)\backslash(x/y)$ for expansion or $x/y\ z\backslash y$ for composition, provided that functions apply in the correct way.

[32] A proof of weak equivalence, known as Gaifman's theorem, is presented in Bar-Hillel *et al.* (1960). The corresponding proof with respect to Lambek's grammar was attempted by Cohen (1967), but, as W. Buszkowski points out, it turns out to be defective; Buszkowski himself derives that result for Unidirectional Lambek Grammars (see Buszkowski, 1985a, 1985b).

[33] See e.g. Chomsky (1956), (1957).

[34] A global analysis of such a characterization with regard to the principles of the *X*-bar theory and within a formal theory of features is developed in Gazdar *et al.* (1985).

[35] These are the rules defined as *Forward Partial Combination* and *Backwards Partial Combination* (see Ades and Steedman, 1982, pp. 527—535).

BIBLIOGRAPHY

Ades, A. E. and M. J. Steedman: 1982, 'On the Order of Words', *Linguistics and Philosophy* **4**, 517—558.
Ajdukiewicz, K.: 1935, 'Die Syntaktische Konnexität', *Studia Philosphica* **1**, pp. 1—27, Engl. transl. 'Syntactic Connexion', in S. McCall (ed.) (1967), pp. 207—231.
Bach, E.: 1979, 'Control in Montague Grammar', *Linguistic Inquiry* **10.4**, 515—531.
Bach, E.: 1983, 'Generalized Categorial Grammars and the English Auxiliary', in F. Heny and B. Richards (eds.), *Linguistic Categories: Auxiliaries and Related Puzzles*, Reidel, Dordrecht, 1983, Vol. II, pp. 101—120.
Bach, E.: 1984, 'Some Generalizations of Categorial Grammars', in F. Landman and F. Veltman (eds.), *Varieties of Formal Semantics*, 1984, Foris Pub., Dordrecht, pp. 1—23.
Bar-Hillel, Y.: 1950, 'On Syntactical Categories', *The Journal of Symbolic Logic* **15**, 1—16; rep. in Bar-Hillel (ed.) (1964).
Bar-Hillel, Y.: 1952, 'Bolzano's Propositional Logic', in Bar-Hillel (ed.) (1970), pp. 33—68.
Bar-Hillel, Y.: 1953, 'A Quasi-arithmetical Notation for Syntactic Description', *Language* **XXIX**, 47—58; rep. in Bar-Hillel (ed.) (1964), pp. 61—74.
Bar-Hillel, Y.: 1957, 'Husserl's Conception of a Purely Logical Grammar', in Bar-Hillel (ed.) (1970), pp. 89—97.
Bar-Hillel, Y.: 1960, 'Some Linguistic Obstacle to Machine Translation', *Advances in Computers I*; rep. in Bar-Hillel (ed.) (1964), pp. 75—86.
Bar-Hillel, Y.: 1962, 'Some Recent Results in Theoretical Linguistics', in E. Nagel *et al.* (eds.), *Logic, Methodology and Philosophy of Science*, Stanford University Press, pp. 551—557.
Bar-Hillel, Y. (ed.): 1964, *Language and Information*, Addison-Wesley.
Bar-Hillel, Y.: 1967, 'Syntactical and Semantical Categories', *The Encyclopedia of Philosophy*, Vol. VIII, pp. 57—61.
Bar-Hillel, Y. (ed.): 1970, *Aspècts of Language*, Jerusalem-Amsterdam.
Bar-Hillel, Y., C. Gaifman, and E. Shamir: 1960, 'On Categorial and Phrase Structure Grammars', *The Bulletin of the Research Council of Israel*, pp. 1—16; rep. in Bar-Hillel (ed.) (1964), pp. 99—115.
van Benthem, J.: 1984, 'The Logic of Semantics', in F. Landman and F. Veltman (eds.), *Varieties of Formal Semantics*, Foris, Dordrecht, 1984, pp. 55—80.
Bocheński, I. M.: 1949, 'On the Syntactical Categories', *The New Scholasticism* **XXIII**, 257—280; rep. in A. Menne (ed.) (1962), *Logico-Philosophical Studies*, Reidel, Dordrecht, pp. 67—88.
Buszkowski, W.: 1985a, 'The Equivalence of Unidirectional Lambek Categorial Grammars and Context Free Gammars', *Zeitschr. f. math. Logik und Grund. d. Math.* **31**, 308—384.
Buszkowski, W.: 1985b, 'Generative Power of Categorial Grammars', this volume, pp. 69—74.
Carnap, R.: 1934, *Logische Syntax der Sprache*, Vienna, transl. *The Logical Syntax of Language*, London—New York, 1937.
Chomsky, N.: 1956, 'Three Models for the Description of Language', in (1956) *Symposium on Information Theory*, MIT Cambridge, Mass., *Readings in Mathematical Psychology*, Vol. 11, Wiley, New York, 1965, pp. 105—124.

Chomsky, N.: 1957, *Syntactic Structures*, Mouton and Co., The Hague.

Church, A.: 1940, 'A Formulation of the Simple Theory of Types', *The Journal of Symbolic Logic* **V**, 56—69.

Church, A.: 1956, *Introduction to Mathematical Logic*, Princeton University Press, Princeton.

Chwistek, L.: 1924/25, 'The Theory of Constructive Types', *Annales de la Societe' Polonaize de Mathematique* **II**, 9—48, **III**, pp. 92—141.

Cohen, J. M.: 1967, 'The Equivalence of Two Concepts of Categorial Grammar', *Information and Control* **X**, 475—484.

Cresswell, M. J.: 1973, *Logics and Languages*, Methuen, London.

Cresswell, M. J.: 1977, *Categorial Languages*, IULC, Bloomington.

Curry, H. B.: 1961, 'Some Logical Aspects of Grammatical Structure', in R. Jakobson (ed.), *Structure of Language and Its Mathematical Aspects*, Proceedings of the 12th Symposium in Applied Mathematics, Providence, 1961.

Curry, H. B., R. Feys, and W. Craig: 1958, *Combinatory Logic*, North Holland, Amsterdam.

Dowty, D.: 1985, 'Type Raising, Functional Composition, and Non-Constituent Conjunction', this volume, pp. 153—198.

Flynn, M.: 1983, 'A Categorial Theory of Structure Building', in G. Gazdar *et al. Order, Concord and Constituency*, Foris, Dordrecht, 1983, pp. 139—174.

Frege, G.: 1891, 'Funktion und Begriff', in G. Patzig (ed.), *Funktion, Begriff, Bedeutung*, Vandenhoeck und Ruprecht, Göttingen, 1975; Engl. transl. 'Function and Concept', in P. Geach and M. Black (eds.), *Translations from the Philosophical Writings of G. Frege*, 1970, pp. 21—41.

Frege, G.: 1893, *Grundgesetze der Arithmetik*, Olms, Hildesheim, 1966; partially transl. in M. Furth (ed.), *The Basic Laws of Arithmetic*, University of California Press, Berkeley and Los Angeles, 1967, and in P. Geach and M. Black (eds.), *Translations from the Philosophical Writings of G. Frege*, 1970, pp. 137—244.

Frege, G.: 1891/1906, *Frege an Husserl, Husserl an Frege*, in G. Gottfried *et al.* (eds.), *Wissenschaftlicher Briefwechsel*, Meiner, Hamburg, 1976; abridged English version in B. McGuinness (ed.), *Philosophical and Mathematical Correspondence*, Blackwell, Oxford, 1980.

Gazdar, G., E. Klein, G. Pullum and I. Sag: 1985, *Generalized Phrase Structure Grammars*, Blackwell, Oxford.

Geach, P. T.: 1972, 'A Program for Syntax', in D. Davidson and G. Harman (eds.), *Semantics of Natural Language*, D. Reidel, Dordrecht and Boston, 1972, pp. 483—497.

Grzegorczyk, A.: 1955, 'The Systems of Leśniewski in Relation to Contemporary Logical Research', *Studia Logica* **3**, 77—95.

Henry, D. P.: 1972, *Medieval Logic and Metaphysics*, Hutchinson & Co., London.

Hoeksema, J. and R. Janda: 1985, 'Implication of Process-Morphology for Categorial Grammar', this volume, pp. 199—248.

Huck, G. J.: 1985, 'Phrasal Verbs and the Categories of Postponement', this volume, pp. 249—264.

Huck, G.: 1984, *Discontinuity and Word Order in Categorial Grammar*, IULC, Bloomington.

Husserl, E.: 1913, *Logische Untersuchungen*, 2nd ed., Max Niemeyer, Halle.

Husserl, E.: 1929, *Formale und Transcendentale Logik*, Max Niemeyer, Halle.

Jordan, Z.: 1967, 'The Development of Mathematical Logic in Poland Between the Two Wars', in S. McCall (ed.) (1967), pp. 346—398.

Kotarbinski, T.: 1967, 'Notes on the Development of Formal Logic in Poland in the Years 1900—1939', in S. McCall (ed.) (1967), pp. 1—15.

Lambek, J.: 1958, 'The Mathematics of Sentence Structure', *American Math. Monthly* LXV, 154—170.

Lambek, J.: 1961, 'On the Calculus of Syntactic Types', in R. Jacobson (ed.), *Structure of Language and its Mathematical Aspects*, Providence, 1961, pp. 166—178.

Lambek, J.: 1985, 'Categorial and Categorial Grammars', this volume, pp. 297—318.

Lejewski, C.: 1954/55, 'A Contribution to Leśniewski's Mereology', *Yearbook V of the Polish Society of Arts and Sciences'*, London, pp. 43—50.

Lejewski, C.: 1958, 'On Leśniewski's Ontology', *Ratio* 1, 150—176.

Leśniewski, S.: 1927/31, 'O podstawach Matematyki', *Przeglad Filozoficzny* XXX (1927), XXXI (1928), XXXII (1929), XXXIII (1930), XXXIV (1931).

Leśniewski, S.: 1930, 'Über die Grundlagen der Ontologie', *Comptes Rendus* XXIII, 111—32.

Leśniewski, S.: 1931, 'Über Definitionen in der Sogenannten Theorie der Deduktion', *Comptes Rendus* XXXIV, Engl. transl. 'On Definitions in the So Called Theory of Deduction', in Storrs McCall (ed.) (1967), pp. 170—188.

Leśniewski, S.: 1939, 'Introductory Remarks to the Continuation of my Article: Grundzuge eines neuen Systems der Grundlagen der Mathematik', in Storrs MacCall (ed.) (1967), pp. 116—170.

Levin, H. D.: 1982, *Categorial Grammar and the Logical Form of Quantification*, Bibliopolis, Naples.

Lewis, D.: 1972, 'General Semantics', in D. Davidson and G. Harman (eds.), *Semantics of Natural Language*, Reidel, Dordrecht, 1972, pp. 169—218.

Łukasiewicz, J.: 1970, *Selected Works*, North Holland, Amsterdam.

Luschei, E. C.: 1962, *The Logical Systems of Leśniewski*, North Holland, Amsterdam.

McCall, S. (ed.): 1967, *Polish Logic*, Clarendon Press, Oxford.

Montague, R.: 1974, *Formal Philosophy*, edited and with an introduction by R. Thomason, Yale University Press, New Haven.

Moortgat, M.: 1984, 'A Fregean Restriction on Metarules', in C. Jones and P. Sells (eds.), *NELS* 14, Amherst, pp. 306—325.

Moortgat, M.: 1985, 'Mixed Composition and Discontinuous Dependencies', this volume, pp. 319—348.

Oehrle, R. T.: 1985, 'Multi-Dimensional Compositional Functions as a Basis for Grammatical Analysis', this volume, pp. 349—390.

Oehrle, R. T.: 1986, 'Boolean Properties in the Analysis of Gapping', manuscript, Dept. of Linguistics, Tucson.

Partee, B. H.: 1975, 'Montague Grammar and Transformational Grammar', *Linguistic Inquiry* 6, 203—300.

Partee, B. H.: 1976, 'Some Transformational Extensions of Montague Grammar', in B. H. Partee (ed.), *Montague Grammar*, Academic Press, New York, 1976, pp. 51—76.

Partee, B. and M. Rooth: 1983, 'Generalized Conjunction and Type Ambiguity', in R. Bäuerle *et al.* (eds.), *Meaning, Use and Interpretation of Language*, W. De Gruyter, Berlin, 1987.

Potts, T. C.: 1973, 'Fregean Categorial Grammar', in R. J. Bogdan and I. Niiniluoto (eds.), *Logic, Language and Probability*, Reidel, Dordrecht, 1973, pp. 245—284.

Prior, A. N.: 1955, *Formal Logic*, Clarendon Press, Oxford.

Russell, B.: 1908, 'Mathematical Logic as Based on the Theory of Types', *American Journal of Mathematics* **XXX**; rep. in Russell (1956), pp. 59—102.

Russell, B.: 1924, 'Logical Atomism', in J. H. Muirehead (ed.), *Contemporary British Philosophy*, London; rep. in Russell (1956), pp. 321—345.

Russell, B.: 1956, *Logic and Knowledge: Essays 1901—1950*, G. Allen & Unwin, London.

Sobocinski, B.: 1934, 'Successive Simplifications of the Axiom System of Leśniewski's Ontology', in Storrs McCall (ed.) (1967), pp. 188—201.

Sobocinski, B.: 1939, 'An Investigation of Prototheic', in Storrs McCall (ed.) (1967), pp. 201—207.

Steedman, M. J.: 1985a, 'Dependency and Coordination in the Grammar of Dutch and English', *Language* **61**, 523—568.

Steedman, M. J.: 1985b, 'Combinators and Grammars', this volume, pp. 417—442.

Steedman, M. J. and A. Szabolcsi: 1985, 'Combinators, Categorial Grammars and Parasitic Gaps', manuscript.

Steele, S.: 1985, 'A Typology of Functors and Categories', this volume, pp. 443—466.

Szabolcsi, A.: 1985, 'Filters versus Combinators', manuscript (to appear in *Festschrift for I. Ruzsa*).

Tarski, A.: 1935, 'Der Wahrheitsbegriff in der Formalisierten Sprachen', *Studia Philosophica* **I**, Engl. trans., 'The Concept of Truth in Formalized Languages', in A. Tarski, *Logic, Semantics and Metamathematics. Papers from 1923 to 1938*, Clarendon Press, Oxford, 1956, pp. 152—279.

Whitehead, A. N. and B. Russell: 1910, *Principia Mathematica*, Cambridge.

Zwarts, F.: 1985, 'Composition Rules in Categorial Grammar', paper presented at the conference "Categorial Grammars and Natural Language Structures", Tucson, 1985.

Institute of Philosophy
University of Chieti
Italy

GENNARO CHIERCHIA

ASPECTS OF A CATEGORIAL THEORY OF BINDING*

1. INTRODUCTION

A great deal of attention has been devoted in recent discussions to the complementary (or nearly complementary) distribution of reflexive and non-reflexive pronouns within certain 'local' domains in languages like English. As is well known, within such domains, non-reflexive pronouns must in some sense not corefer with one another, while reflexives have to have an antecedent. This phenomenon has been called 'opacity' and in what follows we shall refer to it with the term 'anaphoric opacity' (A-opacity for short) to distinguish it from what logicians call opacity. A-opacity is interesting not only in its own right, but also because of the role it plays in determining what kind of structural considerations are relevant in characterizing admissible types of binding in natural language.

In this regard there are two approaches that I would like to contrast. Within current transformational theories (in particular within the Government and Binding (GB) framework) it is assumed that binding, as other aspects of grammar, requires making crucial appeal to tree-theoretic notions such as C-command. These tree-theoretic notions formalize a view of constituent structure that is ultimately rooted in the serial or positional arrangement of expressions. Per contrast, recent versions of categorial grammar contend that binding, as other aspects of grammar, requires making appeal to function-argument structure. The latter structure reflects the process that brings expressions together, which in turn is ultimately rooted in the way things are interpreted. To compute meaning (i.e. truth conditions) one has to analyze expressions into functions and arguments nested in a certain way. The structure that results can of course be represented as a tree, but such a tree has no direct bearing on the serial or positional arrangement of expressions[1].

Even though the underlying assumptions of these two research paradigms appear to be quite different, I think that they can be integrated in ways that are worth pursuing and in what follows I shall investigate one such way. I will develop a categorial theory of binding

125

based on that of Bach and Partee (1980) (BP henceforth). It will be argued, however, that binding is not a purely semantic phenomenon (as BP seem to assume) but has a syntactic counterpart, expressed by coindexing on categorial structure (as in current transformational approaches). In particular, a theory of predication inspired by Williams (1980, 1983) will be defended. Several non-trivial consequences will be seen to follow from the resulting approach.

2. ASSUMPTIONS

I will adopt an extended categorial grammar, as is familiar from much recent work.[2] More specifically, I will assume that each expression is associated with a syntactic category (expressed in a Montagovian notation) and a number of features. Some such features provide information concerning morphosyntax (e.g. case). Other features provide information about what binds what in ways that we shall discuss shortly. A grammar is viewed in the usual (Montagovian) way as a recursive definition that for each category characterizes simultaneously the set of well-formed expressions of that category and their meanings. In particular, the core rule of Universal Grammar is taken to be 'categorial cancellation' in the following format:

(1) (a) If $\alpha \in P_{A/B}$ and $\beta \in P_B$, $\text{Affix}_n(\beta, \alpha) \in P_A$, where $\text{Affix}_n(\beta, \alpha)$ is the result of affixing β after the nth constituent of α.

  (b) If α translates as α' and β translates as β', $\text{Affix}_n(\beta, \alpha)$ translates as $\alpha'(\beta')$.

  (c) The Categorial Theory of Grammatical Relations:

$$\alpha(x_1) \ldots (x_{n-2})(x_{n-1})(x_n)$$
    ind. object —⟋ object —⟑   ⟑— subject

$\text{Affix}_n(\beta, \alpha)$ ought to be regarded as a generalized wrap operation and I would like to maintain that something like it is the sole syntactic operation of UG. I shall not try to settle here what level of constituenthood such rule has access to. For the time being we might simply assume that 'constituent' in (1a) should be understood as 'immediate constituent', although various kinds of generalizations of this assumption might be needed (e.g. to 'words' — see Carlson (1983) and the references mentioned in fn. 3 for relevant discussion). In general, something like $\text{Affix}_n(\beta, \alpha)$ ought to play a role similar to 'move α' in GB and is assumed to be constrained by relatively autonomous sub-systems of principles whose discussion here would take us too far afield.[3] The use of wrap operations seems to be a crucial ingredient of what has come to be known as the categorial theory of grammatical relations (sketchily illustrated in (1c)), that I shall also adopt without discussion.[4] Essentially such a theory defines grammatical relations in terms of the slot that an argument occupies in a function. Such a definition might be regarded as 'configurational', if the semantic nature of the 'configuration' involved is understood. Wrap operations allow for the order of arguments in a function-argument structure (Curry's 'tecto-grammatics') to be different from the surface order of constituents (Curry's 'pheno-grammatics').[5]

Within the framework just sketched how are binding rules and principles to be accommodated? Several proposals have been made. I am familiar with four of them. Perhaps it is worth recalling them briefly.

The oldest proposal goes back to Montague and uses substitution ('quantifier lowering') mechanisms, such as the one illustrated in (2).

(2)   Substitution: every boy thinks that he is a genius

every boy   he₁ thinks that he₁ is a genius

Substitution rules have been advocated and extended by a number of people (e.g. Landman and Moerdijk, 1983; Groenendijk and Stokhof, 1984). As far as I can tell, the arguments in favour of these rules tend to be of a rather unsyntactic nature (an odd circumstance for syntactic rules) and usually boil down to the consideration that they are the most straightforwardly compositional. I will not discuss this approach here in much detail.

The newest proposal concerning binding is the one developed by Steedman and Szabolcsi (1985) based on the use of function composition and type lifting rules. Because of the novelty of this approach and because, by admission of its proponents, it seems to run into problems precisely in connection with A-opacity, I shall not try to discuss this proposal here. Instead, I will concentrate on the following two remaining proposals.

A well-established approach is constituted by Cooper-storage techniques, illustrated in (3).

(3)   Storage   Translation   Q-store

[a man]$_{NP}$	x_3	$\langle \lambda P \exists y[\text{man}'(y) \wedge {}^{\vee}P(y)], 3 \rangle$	store-in
[loves a man]$_{VP}$	love$'(x_3)$	$\langle \lambda P \exists y[\text{man}'(y) \wedge {}^{\vee}P(y)], 3 \rangle$	
every cat loves	$\forall x[\text{cat}'(x)$	$\langle \lambda P \exists y[\text{man}'(y) \wedge {}^{\vee}P(y)], 3 \rangle$	
a man	$\rightarrow$ love$'(x_3)]$		
every cat	$\lambda P \exists y[\text{man}'(y) \wedge {}^{\vee}P(y)]$	$\varnothing$	store-out
loves a man	$({}^{\wedge}\lambda x_3[\forall x[\text{cat}'(x) \rightarrow \text{love}'(x_3)(x)]])$		

Binding on Cooper's approach can be conceived as a discontinuous rule formed of a store-in and a store-out part. On a bottom-up interpretive procedure, the store-in part of the rule corresponds to freezing the NP-interpretation till the point of assigning to it the right scope is reached. At that point the NP-interpretation is used (store-out). It is important to recall that storage is meant by Cooper as a purely interpretive technique that deals with quantification and wh-phenomena by associating multiple readings with semantically ambiguous syntactic structures. Furthermore, for storage to be compositional, meanings have to be things more complex than ordinary intensions. Typically, they will have to be sequences of intensions: the first element of the sequence will correspond to the regular intension, the others to the intension of the stored binders.

Finally, a fourth approach to binding is constituted by the 'slash' notation developed by Gazdar (1982) and illustrated in (4) in connection with relative clauses.

(4)   Slashes:
   (a) $R \rightarrow$ NP S/NP
        +wh

   (b)

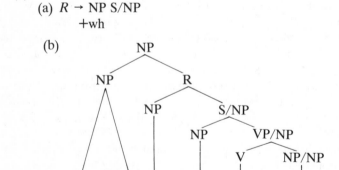

The information that a certain constituent, *who* in (4b) binds something (a gap in (4b)) is encoded locally via the slash-notation in rules like (4a) and propagated in the tree by slash passing conventions till the bindee is recovered. Rules of this kind have been developed just for wh-dependencies and reflexive binding.

The idea upon which the slash-notation is based seems to be that binding relations can be dealt with in terms of a distinguished set of features (or a distinguished 'stack') governed by a set of principles distinct from those that govern categorial (or morphosyntactic) features. In what follows, I shall pursue this view by proposing that *all* binding phenomena (including, that is, quantifier binding) should be treated in terms of (syntactic) binding features, analogous to Gazdar's slashes.[6]

3. THE PROPOSAL

The main motivation for wanting a syntactic representation of binding has to do with the well-known fact that purely interpretive strategies (such as storage) seem to be poorly equipped to deal with a significant number of case marking and agreement phenomena. For example, it has been observed that treating wh-phenomena via storage (as in Cooper, 1983) makes it hard to accommodate case marking on dis-located constituents in languages where it depends on the 'deep structure' position of the constituent. Analogous considerations apply to gender agreement for languages that have grammatical gender. The latter considerations apply to quantifier binding as well as to wh-movement. An exemplification follows.

(5) (a) *ogni tavolo* (m.s.) é stato venduto dallo studente che *lo* (m.s.)
          /*la* (f.s.) ha costruito
     (b) *ogni tavola* (f.s.) é stata venduta dallo studente che *la* (f.s.)
          /*lo* ha costruita
          'every table was sold by the student who built it'
     (c) $\forall x[\text{table}'(x) \rightarrow x$ was sold by the student who built $x]$

Italian has two virtually synonymous words for *table*; one is masculine, the other feminine. (5a—b) illustrate the well-known fact that quantifier binding requires agreement between the binder and the bindee. I see no natural way of extending Cooper's presuppositional treatment of natural gender (or any other purely semantic approach) to cope with the rather widespread phenomena that (5) illustrates.[7]

These considerations suggest that while storage might be a good way of dealing with the (truth conditional) semantics of binding, it has to be integrated by linking conventions in the syntax. Since the slash-notation of Gazdar's has proven to have interesting consequences, it might be worthwhile to see what happens if we treat quantifier scope by means of the same idea.

Let me try to illustrate first informally what I have in mind. Consider the following:

(6) (a)

(a′)

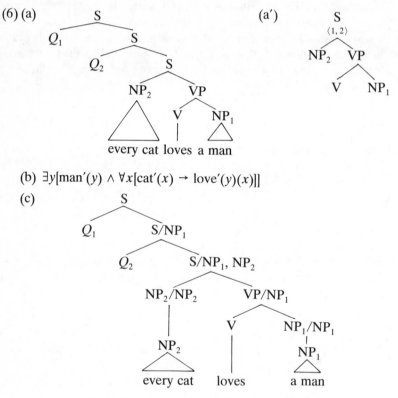

(b) $\exists y[\text{man}'(y) \land \forall x[\text{cat}'(x) \rightarrow \text{love}'(y)(x)]]$

(c)

Q_1 and Q_2 in (6a) act as scope markers. They tell us what the scope of the NPs that they are coindexed with is going to be. So, in (6a) *a man* is assigned wide scope over *every cat*, which means that (6a) will be translated as (6b). One could think of these Q-elements as phonologically null pronouns or one could encode the information that they contain more directly into sequences of indices on S nodes (as shown in (6a′)). I personally find the notation in (6a) more perspicuous.

Evidently, structures like (6a) are very similar to the structures associated with quantifier-lowering substitution rules, only without actual
substitution. They are also very similar to quantifier raising structures,
only without actual raising. In spite of these similarities, I do not think
that my proposal boils down to being a notational variant of either of
the previous techniques, as I will try to argue below.

The S node which is a sister to Q_1 in (6a) will have to contain an NP
coindexed with it. The slash notation is an obvious candidate for the
enforcement of this condition. In fact, (6a) is meant simply as a more
readable short form for (6c). S/NP_1 indicates that that S node contains
an NP_1 somewhere.

The feature *slash* will have at least two values: WH and Q. The
notation to the left in (7a) is the official one; the one to the right is a
variant more readable for certain purposes.

(7) (a) A $A/_Q NP_i$
       Q-SLASH:NP_i

           A $A/_{wh} NP_i$
       wh-SLASH:NP_i

    (b) NP_i/NP_i semantics: x_i, store NP'_i
            |
          NP_i

    (c) $S \rightarrow Q_i \ S/NP_i$ semantics: $NP'_i(^\wedge \lambda x_i [S/NP_i]')$

Furthermore, as more than one NP can be quantified in, the feature
Q-slash can take more than one value, as (6c) illustrates. This extension
of the slash notation appears to be independently needed for languages
that allow for multiple wh-extractions (see, e.g., Gazdar 1982; Engdahl,
1980). The existence of multiple quantifiers (as the existence of multiply
extracted wh-words) requires, in turn, the introduction of multiple
indices (to be regarded as a special kind of feature) in order to keep
track of what binds what. This amounts to a weakening of the strictest
possible form of Partee's (1979) 'well-formedness constraint'.

The slash elimination rule given in (7b) will correspond semantically
to store-in operation in Cooper's sense: i.e. it places a variable (with the
same index) in place of the NP-meaning, stores the interpretation of the
NP and propagates it upwards. Similarly, the rule that introduces the
slash, given in (7c), is interpreted as a store-out operation that does the

actual binding of the relevant variable. In view of the semantics that we
are adopting, the slash notation can be regarded as a syntacticization of
storage. However, it should be borne in mind that the two formalisms
are logically independent of one another. It would be perfectly possible
to adopt the slash-notation with an interpretive procedure different
from storage. For our present purposes, we will, however, stick to a
Cooper-style interpretation of Q-slashes.

The slash notation provides ample means for handling the kind of
long-distance agreement that binding gives rise to. For instance, an
approach that strikes me as particularly straightforward would consist
of assuming that each index is associated or bracketed with morphosyntactic information concerning gender, number, possibly reflexivity,
as illustrated in (8a). This would force items with the same index to
share the same relevant features, as shown in (8b). (8c) introduces a
piece of simple notation that will come in handy later.

(8) (a) $$\begin{bmatrix} n \\ \text{gndr} \\ \text{nmbr} \end{bmatrix}$$

   (b) $_S[Q_1[_S \text{[every student]}_{NP_{\langle 1, m, s\rangle}} \text{ thinks that [he]}_{NP_{\langle 1, m, s\rangle}} \text{ is a genius]]}$
   (c) $FT(n) \approx FT(m)$: the features associated with n are non-
                              distinct from those associated with m.

The right feature matching will be enforced, as usual, by conventions on
feature percolation. In particular, a consequence of the present view is
that we could regard agreement rules in general as rules of coindexing.
Thus, more specifically, we can regard the subject-predicate agreement
as something that coindexes subjects with predicates, and therby forces
them to share the same relevant features (as illustrated in (9b, c)). This
is, of course, very much in the spirit of Williams' approach to predication and indeed can be regarded as a possible way of spelling it out. In
(9d—h), you can see sample lexical entries in the official notation:

(9) (a) For any category A, A_n is also a category
   (b) $IV + NP \Rightarrow S$
        condition: the category index of IV is the same as NP

or

(c) $S/NP_n + NP_n \Rightarrow S$

(d) $\langle he, NP_{\langle 3, m, s \rangle}, \lambda P \, P\{x_3\}, \text{SLASH}: \varnothing \rangle$

(e) $\langle run, S/NP_{\langle 3, m, s \rangle}, run', \text{SLASH}: \varnothing \rangle$

(f) $\langle every \, man, NP_{\langle 4, m, s \rangle}, \lambda P \, \forall x[\text{man}'(x) \rightarrow P(x)], \text{SLASH}: \varnothing \rangle$

(g) $\langle every \, man, NP_{\langle 4, m, s \rangle}, \lambda P \, P\{x_4\}, Q\text{-SLASH}: NP_4, every \, man' \rangle$

(h) $\langle e, NP_{\langle 5, m, s \rangle}, \lambda P \, P\{x_5\}, \text{WH-SLASH}: NP_5 \rangle$

As in BP, each lexical entry is a tuple that contains a phonological representation of the word, an indexed category, an IL-translation, a *slash* feature and possibly more. By general convention, a pronoun associated with the index i translates as $\lambda P \, P\{x_i\}$. A stored NP associated with i translates in the same way. On unstored NPs (and on categories other than NP) an index, in general, will not have semantic effects.[8] The main difference with respect to BP, so far, is that syntax directly generates disambiguated structures where anaphoric links are overtly marked. The interpretive procedure stays essentially the same, except that it is now no longer viewed as a multi-valued function.

What we have described so far is perhaps no more than a mechanics for dealing with quantifier scope, which might legitimately be regarded as a rather scholastic exercise. We haven't said much about the principles that govern binding. We now turn to a consideration of the latter issue.

4. BINDING PRINCIPLES

It is convenient to recall briefly the theory developed by BP, as my proposal stems directly from theirs. BP extend storage in order to cope with A-opacity. In their approach, the index associated with a pronoun is entered into a 'local pronoun store' (LPS). Indices in LPS are passed up and kept disjoint from one another. At NP nodes and S nodes LPS's are emptied, which allows for pronouns in different NP-domains and S-domains to corefer. Similar conditions on stores force reflexive pronouns to be bound to a suitable antecedent in the relevant local domains. 'Suitability' is taken to mean that the antecedent has to come in *later* than the reflexive. If we think of function-argument structure in terms of the categorial tree in which it is syntactically realized, then we can say that the antecedent has to be superior, or 'F-command' the consequent, where F-command is simply C-command at function-argument structure. If we exclude from consideration picture NP reflexives, the F-command requirement restricts the range of possible controllers basically to subjects and objects (with a few qualifications to be detailed shortly). The subject F-commands everything in its domain. The object F-commands arguments that are more internal in its VP (such as indirect objects).

BP's proposal can thus be summed up as in (10). In (11) we provide a formulation of the binding theory within the GB framework, for comparison.

(10)   BP's Categorial Theory of Binding
    (a)   A non-reflexive pronoun must not be coindexed with anything in its minimal NP or S domain
    (b)   A reflexive must be bound to an F-commanding argument in its minimal NP or S domain

(11)   GB
    (a)   an anaphor is bound in its minimal governing category
    (b)   a pronominal is free in its minimal governing category
    (c)   an R-expression is free

(12) (a)   he loves him
    (a') he_1 loves him_1
    (a") $love'(x_1)(x_1)$
    (a''') $love'(x_1)(x_2)$
    (b)   every man loves him
    (b') $\forall x[man'(x) \rightarrow love'(x)(x)]$

The two theories coincide in empirical coverage as far as the core cases are concerned. The main difference is perhaps the truth-conditional explicitness of the categorial approach. To illustrate, in the GB theory (12a') is ruled out by (11b) at S-structure. Only something like he_1 loves him_2 would be grammatical. Nothing is said about the actual model-theoretic interpretation of such structures (e.g. can two non-coindexed pronouns ever refer to the same individual?), although various obvious possibilities come to mind. In the categorial theory, (10a) prevents (12a) from translating as shown in (12a") and forces it to translate as something like (12a''').[9] Principle (10a), coupled with quantifier store, also prevents (12b) from getting the reading in (12b').

The treatment of reflexives is, mutatis mutandis, analogous and also gives parallel results on both approaches.

In spite of these similarities there are some (perhaps non-overwhelming) empirical differences between the two theories (beyond truth-conditional explicitness). I am aware of at least three areas where this is the case.

First, in a categorial framework it is to be expected that some PP's are going to be internal arguments of verbs. Take for instance a verb like *put* that obligatorily subcategorizes for a locative PP. If one were to analyze such PP as a function taking, say, the VP *put the book* as an argument, there would be no way to capture its obligatoriness, while it is easy to do so, if one analyzes the PP in question as an argument. Furthermore, it seems plausible to maintain (indeed, it seems necessary to do so) that in PP's that are internal arguments the preposition is semantically vacuous (say, the identity map), which makes the NP an internal argument of the verb. It becomes then possible for internal PP's to F-command other more internal arguments and hence license a reflexive pronouns in those positions. Thus we should expect to find some PP's (precisely, those that are subcategorized for) that can be antecedents of reflexives. This expectation appears to be warranted, as BP point out. Consider the following example.

(13) (a) Many talked to every student about himself

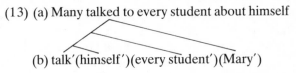

(b) talk′(himself′)(every student′)(Mary′)

Every student in (13a) F-commands *himself* (as illustrated by the categorial tree in (13b)), but does not C-command it. In this case, C-command appears to impose too strong a condition, it appears to rule out too much. One has to resort to a more abstract notion of C-command.

Consider next the examples in (14), which constitute a further area of empirical disagreement between the two theories we are considering.

(14) (a)   Mary showed the men each other

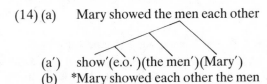

(a′)   show′(e.o.′)(the men′)(Mary′)
(b)   *Mary showed each other the men

In (14a) *the men* F-commands *each other* but not viceversa (as illustrated in (14a′)). On the other hand, given standard assumptions, *the
men* and *each other* do C-command each other. Thus, on the GB
approach both (14a) and (14b) should be good, while on the categorial
approach only (14a) should be good. The facts seem to go with the
latter. Notice that the contrast in (14) cannot be attributed to left-right
asymmetries, as (15) illustrates.

(15) (a) Mary introduced the men to each other
     (b) Mary introduced to each other the men that were standing
         in the corner

(15b) shows that the anaphor can precede its antecedent, if the right
configuration is met. The facts in (14) seem to show that C-command is
also too weak, as it rules out too little. The right structural conditions
seem to be provided by the kind of structure one needs to posit in
order to do semantics.

A third order of considerations concerns languages that have a flat
S-structure (e.g. Chamorro — see Chung, 1983) but may display a
behavior not dissimilar from English. For those languages an underlying
English-like constituent structure will have to be posited within the GB
framework. On the categorial theory such structure comes for free (see
BP and Dowty (1980) for discussion).

For these reasons, I shall incorporate into the framework developed
in Section 3 a version of BP's categorial theory, rather than the GB
approach. I shall argue, furthermore, that incorporating BP's theory in
our framework solves some of the problems that their original proposal
leaves open.

One such problem concerns the specific way of formalizing their
proposal. To put it bluntly: where are the indices that LPS's keep track
of? As BP adopt a strict version of the well-formedness constraint, they
cannot be in the syntax. Hence, if their approach is compositional, such
indices must be in the model.[10] To see what this amounts to, consider
the following:

(16) (a) *he* loves *him*
     (b) love′($\langle i, a \rangle$)($\langle j, b \rangle$)

One is forced to think of the meaning of pronouns as pairs of an index
and a real individual. We cannot require that the actual individuals
denoted by the two pronouns be distinct, for that would be too strong.

So BP's conditions on coreference end up requiring that the indices associated in the model with individuals be distinct. But putting indices in the model and then stating non-coreference as a semantic constraint strikes me as unappealing, since it is hard to believe that those indices are part of what we actually refer to by means of pronouns. So, I think it is worthwhile to consider what other options are available to us.

As we have argued that the treatment of quantification in general requires having indices in the syntax, it seems natural to develop a syntactic theory of A-opacity that exploits function-argument structure. According to the proposal developed above, indices come with number and gender specifications and agreement rules can consequently be viewed as coindexing conventions. Thus, in particular, each verb will carry its feature specifications in the form of an index, as illustrated in the sample lexical entry in (17).

(17) $\langle$love, $(S/NP_n)/NP$, love', SLASH: $\emptyset$, LPS: $n\rangle$

In (17), the slash-feature replaces BP's quantifier store. LPS is the device used to define local domains. We keep for ease of reference BP's name for it, although in our theory it is not a Cooper-store but a syntactic feature. The index associated with the verb *love* in (17) will have to match the index of the subject, by the subject-predicate agreement convention. Thus, we will want to keep such index disjoint from the indices of pronouns in the same local environment. This is why it is entered in LPS. This modification of BP's technique triggers a change in the notion of 'local environment'. BP's approach seems to be based on the classical transformational view, further developed in GB, that opaque domains are, in some sense, the domains of subjects. However, since in (17) the index of the subject is, loosely speaking, already present in the predicate, we can treat predicates as directly determining opaque domains, following, also on this, Williams (1983). We thus replace the theory in (10) with the one below:

(18) The local F-domains of predicates are opaque
where:
F-domain of PRED $(= VP, AP, NP,$ etc.$) =_{df}$ anything
$\qquad\qquad\qquad\qquad_{pred}\qquad\qquad\qquad$ dominated by
$\qquad\qquad\qquad\qquad\qquad\qquad\qquad\qquad$ or taken as an
$\qquad\qquad\qquad\qquad\qquad\qquad\qquad\qquad$ argument by
$\qquad\qquad\qquad\qquad\qquad\qquad\qquad\qquad$ PRED

the local F-domain of $PRED_i$ =df anything in the domain of $PRED_i$ not in the domain of a $PRED_j$ dominated by $PRED_i$

X is A-opaque =df within X non-reflexive pronouns are not coindexed with other arguments and reflexives are coindexed with an F-commanding argument

Notice that according to (18), subjects of tensed clauses are part of the domain of their VP, since they are taken as arguments by the latter. However, VP's can also occur as arguments (e.g. in the form of infinitives or gerunds). In such case, their domain will include only what they dominate. Thus, for example, neither the (matrix) subject nor the (matrix) object will be in the domain of the infinitival VP in (19):

(19)   I promised him_1 [to follow him_1]$_{VP}$

This accounts for the fact that the two occurrences of *him*$_1$ in (19) can corefer, not being in the same local domain. We will have to say something special about the controller, and we shall do so shortly.

I will take no stand here as to how the notion of *A*-opacity should be extended to NP's. Various current proposals could be easily adopted.[11]

4.1. *An Implementation*

For the sake of explicitness, it might be useful to illustrate the crucial rules that a fragment based on the revised categorial theory given in (18) would incorporate.[12] A sample is provided below.

(20) (a)   TV + NP $\Rightarrow$ IV   (here and throughout integers will be used as names for
          0   1   2   the categories mentioned in the rules)

(b)   conditions: (i) $LPS(0) \cap LPS(1) = \emptyset$ non-coreference
                    (ii) $SLASH(2) \cap (LPS(1) \cup LPS(2)) = \emptyset$ crossover
                    (iii) $SLASH(2) = SLASH(0) \cup SLASH(1)$ slash-percolation
                    (iv) $LPS(2) = LPS(0) \cup LPS(1)$ LPS-percolation

(21) (a) $S/NP_n + NP_n \Rightarrow S$
            0   1   2

(b)   conditions: (i) $LPS(2) = \emptyset$ *A*-opacity boundary
                    (ii) same as (20bii)
                    (iii) same as (20biii)
                    (iv) $n \notin LPS(0) \cup LPS(1)$ reflexives
                        +refl

(22)   Reflexives

(a) $\begin{array}{ccc} A & \Rightarrow & A \\ n \in \text{LPS} & & n \notin \text{LPS} \\ +\text{refl} & & \end{array}$

(b)   conditions: (i) $A = \text{IV, TV}$
                             (ii) $\text{FT}(A) \approx \text{FT}(n)$

(c)   translation: $\lambda x_n[A'(x_n)]$

(23) (a) $\text{IV/IV} + \text{IV} \Rightarrow \text{IV}$
                    $\quad\ \ 0 \qquad\ 1 \qquad\ \ 2$

(b)   conditions: (i) $\text{LPS}(2) = \text{LPS}(0)$ A-opacity boundary
                             (ii) same as in (20bii)
                             (iii) same as in (20biii)
                             (iv) $n \notin \text{LPS}(1)$ reflexives
                                  $+\text{refl}$

(20), the verb-object rule, is typical of rules that do not involve the crossing of an A-opacity boundary. All such rules are subject to the same conditions. In particular, condition (i) checks the LPS's of the input for disjointness. We will discuss condition (ii) in a moment. Conditions (iii) and (iv) percolate up information about what is quantified in and what is locally free, respectively. The subject-predicate rule, given in (21), is instead typical of rules that lead from an A-opaque domain into the next. When this happens, LPS's are emptied (condition (i)). Condition (iv) makes sure that reflexives at this point will have been already bound. This rule also has subject-predicate agreement built in.

All this is illustrated in (21a, b).

(24) (a) $\langle$ he loves him, S, $\text{love}'(x_1)(x_2)$, LPS: $\varnothing \rangle$ (ignoring SLASH)

              $\langle$ he, NP_2, x_2, LPS: 2$\rangle\langle$ love him, S/NP_2, $\text{love}'(x_1)$, LPS: 1, 2$\rangle$

                    $\langle$ love, $(\text{S/NP}_2)/\text{NP}$, love', LPS: 2$\rangle\langle$ he, NP_1, x_1, LPS: 1$\rangle$

(b) *he_1 loves him_1 $\Rightarrow \text{love}'(x_1)(x_1)$

(c) *He_1 loves every man_1 $\left.\vphantom{\begin{array}{c}1\\1\end{array}}\right\}$
                                                 $\Rightarrow \forall x_1[\text{man}'(x_1) \rightarrow \text{love}'(x_1)(x_1)]$
(d) *every man_1 loves him_1

(e) *he_1 thinks that every man_1 will come

(f) *who_1 does he_1 think will be hired

The definition of 'locally free' via LPS is furthermore crucial in block-

ing sentences such as those in (24c, d). This is accomplished technically
by condition (ii) in (20)—(23), which we take to be a condition on all
rules. It requires that what is in the slash-feature (i.e. BP's quantifier-
store) of the output be disjoint from what is locally free in the inputs.
Such a condition plays a double duty, it turns out, as it is sufficient to
account for all cases of what is known as strong cross-over (illustrated
in (24e, f)). The reason why this is so is that when, for example, *he* in
(24e) is combined with the rest, its index will already be in the slash-
feature, as it is the same as the index associated with *every man*, and
hence condition (ii) will rule it out. This will happen, of course, only if
every man is 'stored'. Condition (ii) provides us with a way of formalizing the principle that BP, following Keenan, propose to explain crossover.[13] Such a principle maintains that the value of the argument can
never depend on the value of the function, given our understanding of
what functions are. Hence a quantifier contained in a function γ cannot
bind a pronoun which γ takes as an argument, for that would precisely
amount to rendering the argument dependent on the function.

The rule for reflexives (namely (22)) is essentially a notational
variant of the rule proposed by BP. An illustration of its workings is
provided in what follows.

(25)   ⟨he loves himself, S, $love'(x_2)(x_2)$, LPS: ∅⟩   (ignoring slashes)

⟨he, NP_2, x_2, LPS: 2⟩⟨love himself, S/NP_2, $\lambda x_3[love'(x_3)(x_3)]$, LPS: 2⟩

⟨love himself, S/NP_2, $love'(x_3)$, LPS: 2, 3 ⟩
_{+refl}

⟨love, $(S/NP_2)/NP$, $love'$, LPS: 2⟩⟨himself, NP_3, x_3, LPS: 3 ⟩
_{+refl}

Such a rule applies within the VP and binds a reflexive to an F-
commanding argument.[14]

There is one final thing that we need to take care of, namely variable
clashes. In any sentence that contains two quantified NP's we want to
make sure that their indices are distinct, so that no clashes arise. There
are various ways of enforcing this. A straightforward one is provided in
(26) in the form of a general condition on all rules. (26a) avoids
disasters such as translating (26c) as (26d).

(26)   Accidental binding.

   (a) $A + B \Rightarrow C$
       $\quad 0 \quad\ 1 \quad\ 2$

   (b) condition: $Q\text{-SLASH}(1) \cap Q\text{-SLASH}(0) = \emptyset$

   (c) every man$_1$ thinks that a student$_1$ will be late

   (d) $\forall x_1[\text{man}'(x_1) \rightarrow \exists x_1[\text{student}'(x_1) \land x_1 \text{ thinks that } x_1 \text{ will be late}]]$

4.2. *Summary*

We have developed a theory of binding based on the idea that co-indexing is a useful way to encode in the syntax semantic binding (i.e. λ-abstraction), as it ensures agreement between the binder and the bindee. We have proposed a set of principles that govern coindexing which is a revision of the categorial theory developed by BP. The resulting theory dispenses with the use of abstract markers in the interpretation of pronouns (which was necessary on BP's approach), for such 'markers' are argued to be independently needed in the syntax.

These considerations alone might constitute a not unreasonable motivation for the approach we have been developing. However, there are further empirical consequences that follow from it, which are worth discussing.

5. SOME CONSEQUENCES

5.1. *Across-the-board Phenomena*

One of the most interesting results in Generalized Phrase Structure Grammar is the possibility of deriving the Coordinate Structure Constraint (along with the across-the-board exceptions to it) from general principles. In the early times of GPSG (e.g. Gazdar, 1982), the general principle involved was the widely shared opinion that conjunction involves categorial identity. Let us pursue this idea, for the moment. If we adopt (27a) as a conjunction schema, (27b, c) will be well-formed but (27d) will not be.

(27) (a)

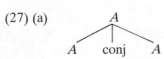

(b)

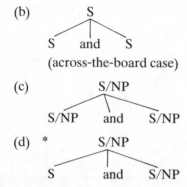

(across-the-board case)

(c)

$$S/NP$$
$$S/NP \quad \text{and} \quad S/NP$$

(d) *

$$S/NP$$
$$S \quad \text{and} \quad S/NP$$

What is interesting about this is the circumstance that a fairly com-plicated array of facts follows at no cost from the simplest possible theory of conjunction.

Now, it is a well-known fact that the coordinate structure constraint is also a constraint on quantifier scope, if we disregard the peculiar behavior of some definite NP's. So, for example, (28a, c) cannot have the readings illustrated in (28b, d) respectively.

(28) (a) *Every man* walked in and *he* had a hat
   (b) $\forall x[\text{man}'(x) \rightarrow x$ walked in and x had a hat]
   (c) One student photographed every boy and every girl
   (d) $\forall x[\text{boy}'(x) \rightarrow \exists y[\text{student}'(y) \wedge \forall z[\text{girl}'(z)$
      $\rightarrow \text{photograph}'(x$ and $z)(y)]]]$

As the reader will have guessed by now, on the view developed here the coordinate structure constraint for quantifiers will follow, just in the way it does for wh-movement, as illustrated below:

(29) (a) *

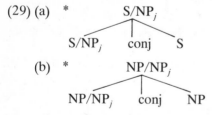

   (b) *

$$NP/NP_j$$
$$NP/NP_j \quad \text{conj} \quad NP$$

(29a) is the structure that would be needed to generate (28a) with reading (28b). (29b) would be needed to generate (28c) with reading (28d). Both these structures cannot possibly be licensed by the con-

junction schema in (27a). This is as it should be, for assuming the
GPSG account of the coordinate structure constraint to be on the right
track, it would be quite odd if the parallel constraint on quantifier
scope should require a separate stipulation.

We may note, furthermore, that while across-the-board exceptions
are predicted to be possible for wh-movement, it is predicted as well
that this is not so for the parallel constructions with quantifiers. To see
why consider

(30) (a)   *every man* came late and *every woman* was punctual

(b)   out by (27a):

(c)   out by condition on accidental binding (i.e. (26)):

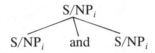

Suppose that the two quantifiers in (30a) have different indices. Then
the identity condition on category labels would not be met. The structure involved would be (30b) and it would not be licensed by the conjunction schema. Suppose, on the other hand, that the two quantified
NP's have the same indices. Such a structure would be well-formed as
far as the conjunction schema is concerned, but it would result in a
variable clash and is thus ruled out by whatever bans variable clashes
(in our terms (26)). The corresponding structure for wh-gaps is not
affected by the ban against variable clashes, as the latter concerns
specifically quantified NP's (i.e. Q-slashes).

Recently, Sag *et al.* (1985) have challenged the traditional view that
conjunction requires categorial identity and developed an alternative
account of the phenomena under discussion. Their account is crucially
based on treating slashes as both foot-features and head-features (and
on the uncontroversial assumption that conjoined structures are multi-
headed). It should be fairly clear that their approach would extend
straightforwardly to the treatment of quantification developed here,
modulo some obvious changes in notation. In fact, treating quantification in terms of a feature akin to Gazdar's slashes, as proposed here,
seems to be a necessary condition for the account in Sag *et al.* (1985)
to extend to coordinate structure effects on quantifier binding.

Thus, in any case the bulk of the properties of coordinate structures follows from the approach we have developed: nothing specific to such properties has to be stipulated. This also shows that while the treatment of quantification proposed here is almost a notational variant of more familiar 'quantifier raising' or 'quantifier lowering' analyses, it is not quite empirically equivalent to them. The present account of the co-ordinate structure phenomenology is not readily available within such alternatives, or, for that matter, within a purely interpretive treatment of binding.

5.2. *Control*

The approach developed here has consequences of some interest in a totally unrelated area, namely the behavior of pronouns in control structures. In the best of all worlds, a theory of A-opacity as defined for simple matrix S's, should automatically extend to embedded clauses, modulo the simplest possible theory of control. The Standard Theory, and its current developments, comes pretty close to this ideal, as the paradigm in (31) will remind us.

(31) (a)   *he* promised *him* to follow *him* $\Box 1 \neq 2, \Box 1 \neq 3, \Diamond 2 = 3$
            1   2   3

    (b)   *he* forced *him* to follow *him* $\Box 1 \neq 2, \Box 2 \neq 3, \Diamond 1 = 3$
            1   2   3

    (c) he_1 promised $him_2[PRO_1$ to follow $him_3]$

    (d) he_1 forced $him_2[PRO_2$ to follow $him_3]$

    (e)   *every man_1 promised him_2 to follow him_1

    (f)   every man_1 forced him_2 to follow him_1

    (g) he_1 promised every man_2 to follow him_2

    (h)   *he_1 forced every man_2 to follow him_2

In (31a) disjoint reference must obtain between the first and the second and between the first and the third occurrence of the pronoun *he*. In (31b), disjoint reference must obtain between the first and the second and between the second and the third occurrence. (31d, e, f, g) illustrate the same pattern with quantifiers. Such a pattern falls into place if one assumes that infinitives really are clauses with a null pronominal subject (PRO) coindexed with an antecedent in the matrix clause. This hypothesis would also account for the apparent violation of clauseboundedness for reflexives in control structures and for the agreement facts. The argument just sketched, a classical one, strikes me as one of the strongest in favour of the clausal analysis of infinitives.

However, on the present approach, there is an alternative to it which seems to be no less insightful and is arguably simpler. What any theory of control minimally has to ensure is agreement between controllers and controllees. As the control relation seems to involve some kind of indirect predication, it seems tempting to view the controller-controllee agreement as a special kind of subject-predicate rule. This is also an idea developed in Williams (1980). Most versions of GPSG incorporate something that plays a role similar to Williams' predication rule, namely the Control Agreement Principle. I will borrow the latter term, bearing in mind that we are dealing here with a generalized form of subject-predicate agreement. In our framework such a process will have to be a form of coindexation between controllers and controllee's, as the latter is the mechanism we are using for agreement in general. What is the consequence of this? Consider again (31a) and (31b). Schematically, their syntactic structure will have to be roughly as shown in (32):

(32) (a) he_1 promised him_2 $_{VP_1}$[to follow him_3]

  (b) he_1 forced him_2 $_{VP_2}$[to follow him_3]

The coreference possibilities illustrated in (31a, b) will then straightforwardly follow from our treatment of A-opacity. The predicate index of the infinitival has to be disjoint from anything in its minimal domain. Control agreement requires that the predicate index be the same as the index of the controller. Thus by the transitivity of identity, the controller will have to bear an index which is different from anything in the domain of the controllee. This is illustrated by means of an example in (33).

(33) (a)   *every man_1 tries to meet him_1

  (b)   every man_2 tries to meet him_1

  (c)   try: $(S/NP_n)/IV_n$

  (d)   force: $((S/NP)/NP_n)/IV_n$

  (e)   promise: $((S/NP_n)/IV)/NP_n$

(33c), in particular, shows how the Control Agreement Principle would be built directly into the category of the relevant verbs. All the ungrammatical sentences in (31) will be ruled out in a similar way.

The point that perhaps is worth emphasizing is the following. Any variant of the Standard Theory (including the GB approach) seems to require at least the following assumptions:

(34) (a) infinitives are clauses with a PRO subject
   (b) PRO carries gender and number specifications
   (c) PRO is coindexed with its controller

Our theory, on the other hand, requires one assumption, namely:

(35)   predicates agree with their controllers

where (35) is just a generalization of the subject-predicate agreement rule. Notice, furthermore, that as (35) is formulated in terms of the notion of predicate, it generalizes straightforwardly also to the control structures that do not involve infinitives, such as those in (36).

(36) (a) every student$_1$ strikes me as proud of himself$_1$/*him$_1$
   (b) I strike every student$_1$ as proud of him$_1$/*himself$_1$
   (c) I consider every student$_1$ proud of himself$_1$/*him$_1$
   (d) Every student considers me proud of him$_1$/*himself$_1$

If one takes the view that opaque domains are the domains of subjects, then the constructions in (36) must all have subjects, either in the syntax or in the semantics. One is virtually forced to a 'small clause' analysis of constructions such as (36c, d). Such line is adopted in most versions of the GB theory. BP would appear to be committed to a similar view (the difference being that the subjects show up in the semantics rather than in the syntax). Several problems associated with this position have been pointed out especially in Bresnan (1982) and Williams (1983).[15]

Thus, it would seem that our approach allows us to inherit the good results of the Standard Theory and its current heirs, without having to posit that all control structures have a null subject. Thus, everything else being equal, Occam's razor should follow its usual course.

5.3. *Other Constraints*

Before concluding, I would like to discuss briefly and without any pretense of completness how the approach developed here stands with respect to various constraints that have been much discussed in recent debates.

In Cooper-style approaches to binding, the most straightforward way of implementing constraints is an island approach, along the lines illustrated below.

(37)   Structures of kind X (e.g. complex NP's, sentential subjects, etc.) may not have a WH (and/or Q) in store.

This approach is, of course, possible in our framework as well. However, our theory has also available the alternative of dealing with islands in a spirit much closer to the GB framework. For example, if it turns out that the best treatment of the Complex NP Constraint, the Sentential Subject Constraint and other related island phenomena is in terms of subjacency, then it is easy to do so in our framework (e.g. along the lines of Gazdar, 1982), while it is impossible on a storage approach (see on this Cooper, 1982). Subjacency seem to require a syntactic treatment of binding.

The same point is evidenced perhaps even more dramatically, by what has come to be known as 'weak crossover', illustrated in what follows.

(38) (a)   *who$_1$ does his$_1$ mother like e_1
             (meaning: for which x (x's mother likes x))
     (b)   *His$_1$ mother loves every Englishman$_1$
             (meaning: $\forall x[\text{Englishman}'(x) \rightarrow x\text{'s mother loves } x])$
     (c)   *... NP$_i$[$_S$ ... pro$_j$ ... NP$_i$/NP$_j$ ...]

The facts concerning weak crossover are complicated and controversial. However, it seems hard to deny that something real is going on and that it cuts across both wh-dependencies and quantifier scope. I, furthermore, tend to believe, with Jacobson (1977), that whatever constraint is involved has to do with both depth of embedding *and* left-right order, which are prototypical unsemantic properties. Trying to state weak crossover directly as a constraint on interpretation would require building into semantics all sort of information that has nothing specifically semantic to it. If, per contra, we have a syntactic representation of scope, we can rule (38a, b) out in a more straightforward way, for example along the lines illustrated in (38c). I am not claiming that (38c) is anything but a compact way of stating the facts, and it might well be that its effects are derivable by some other mean. The point is that it will be hard to derive such effects in theories that do not have a unified syntactic representation of wh- as well as quantifier binding.

6. CONCLUSIONS

It might be useful to flesh out the similarities and differences between the theory developed here and other approaches we have been considering, primarily the GB approach and the categorial one of BP.

The present approach shares with GB the fact that scope is represented syntactically. Furthermore, our theory of agreement and A-opacity is directly inspired by the one of Williams'. The main differences appear to be the following:

(39) (a) full explicitness with respect to the truth conditional import of quantifier binding and A-opacity;
   (b) the binding principles and coindexing mechanisms are factored out in a number of conditions on feature matching and percolation rather than in maps between different levels of syntactic structure;
   (c) there need not be any PRO, as far as A-opacity goes;
   (d) C-command is replaced by F-command.

These differences do appear to be largely conceptual and aesthetic in nature and the two theories appear to have roughly the same empirical coverage and, I think, explanatory force. Limited to the A-opacity phenomenology, the only area in which they seem to make different empirical predictions is in connection with the facts discussed in Section 4 (see especially (13)–(14)).

With previous categorial approaches the theory developed here shares the idea that function-argument structure plays a crucial role in characterizing structural conditions on binding. Its advantages over such proposals, appear to be the following:

(40) (a) it does not require going through a 'reification' of indices;
   (b) it allows for a simple treatment of agreement;
   (c) it yields a treatment of A-opacity that does not involve positing a subject for control structure in the semantics;
   (d) it allows to derive the Coordinate Structure Constraint for quantifiers in a principled manner;
   (e) it simplifies the statement of certain constraints (e.g. weak crossover).

While the proposal we have developed is cast in a transformationless categorial framework (for good reasons, it has been argued), we have also tried to capitalize on ideas that come from the GB theory. To the extent that the results we achieve constitute an improvement over those that the various alternatives taken in isolation achieve, it would seem that some kind of integration between them (which our proposal is meant to approximate), although difficult, might also be rewarding.

NOTES

* I would like to thank the participants to the Tucson Conference on Categorial Grammar and especially Dick Oehrle for their helpful comments.

[1] An interesting discussion of the issues involved can be found in Schmerling (1983).

[2] See for example Bach (1984) and references therein.

[3] For discussion, see e.g. Ades and Steedman (1982), Flynn (1982), Bach (1983), Dowty (1982a), Pollard (1985).

[4] See Dowty (1982a, b).

[5] For more discussion, see Dowty (1982a).

[6] The fact that functional composition and type-lifting might not play any role with respect to binding does not prevent such rules from playing an important role in connection with other phenomena (e.g. 'non-constituent' conjunction — see Dowty, 1985a).

[7] Hoeksema (1983) has convincingly argued that a purely syntactic treatment of number agreement is impossible and has developed a very interesting semantic theory of such phenomenon. However, a *purely* semantic treatment of number agreement strikes me as equally impossible. Consider the following Italian example:

(i)   si é arrivati
        one is (s.) arrived (pl.)

The impersonal subject *si* triggers singular agreement on the auxiliary *essere* and plural agreement on past participle *arrivato*. See Burzio (1986, Ch. 1) for discussion. The point that emerges, then, is that number agreement must have both a syntax and a semantics, none of which can be reduced to the other and whose mode of interaction is as yet not well understood. For a similar point, see Bach (1983).

[8] Apart from the 'intrinsic' semantics associated with features like plurality. See e.g. Hoeksema (1983).

[9] x_1 and x_2 in (12a''') could be mapped into the same model-theoretic entity. The marginality of this interpretation has a plausible pragmatic account. See Dowty (1980) and Reinhart (1983) for discussion.

[10] This point is made rather forcefully in Landman and Moerdijk (1983).

[11] For example, Williams' (1983) proposal that opacity in NP's might be related to definiteness strikes me as promising.

[12] Readers that are turned off by the unfriendly world of 'executions' can safely skip this section.

[13] BP propose a slightly different formalization. They formulate a condition that inserts

everything that is in quantifier store into LPS. The two approaches appear to be interchangeable, as far as our present concerns go.

[14] For this kind of local binding, the combinator-based approach proposed by Steedman and Szabolcsi (1985) might turn out to be right.

[15] For totally independent arguments against a clausal or propositional analysis of control structures, see Chierchia (1984) and Dowty (1985b).

REFERENCES

Ades, A. and M. Steedman: 1982, 'On the Order of Words', *Linguistics and Philosophy* **4**.

Bach, E.: 1983, 'On the Relationship between Word-grammar and Phrase Grammar', *Natural Language and Linguistic Theory* **1**.

Bach, E.: 1984, 'Some Generalizations of Categorial Grammar', in F. Landman and F. Veltman (eds.), *Varieties of Formal Semantics*, Foris, Dordrecht.

Bach, E. and B. H. Partee: 1980, 'Anaphora and Semantic Structure', in K. J. Kreiman and A. E. Ojeda (eds.), *Papers from the Parasession on Pronouns and Anaphora*, Chicago Linguistic Society.

Bresnan, J.: 1982, 'Control and Complementation', *Linguistic Inquiry* **13**.

Burzio, L.: 1986, *Italian Syntax*, D. Reidel, Dordrecht.

Carlson, G.: 1983, 'Marking Constituents', in F. Heny and B. Richards (eds.), *Linguistic Categories: Auxiliaries and Related Puzzles*, Vol. 1, Reidel, Dordrecht.

Chierchia, G.: 1984, 'Anaphoric Properties of Infinitives and Gerunds', in M. Cobbler, S. MacKaye and M. Wescoat (eds.), *Proceedings of the III West Coast Conference on Formal Linguistic*, Stanford Linguistics Association.

Chung, S.: 1983, 'Binding and Coexisting S-structures in Chamorro', in M. Barlow, D. Flickinger and M. Wescoat (eds.), *Proceedings of the II West Coast Conference on Formal Linguistics*, Stanford Linguistics Association.

Cooper, R.: 1982, 'Binding in Wholewheat Syntax', in Jacobson and Pullum (1982).

Cooper, R.: 1983, *Quantification and Syntactic Theory*, D. Reidel, Dordrecht.

Dowty, D.: 1980, 'Comments on the Paper by Bach and Partee', in K. J. Kreiman and A. E. Ojeda (eds.), *Papers from the Parasession on Pronouns and Anaphora*, Chicago Linguistics Society.

Dowty, D.: 1982a, 'The Categorial Theory of Grammatical Relations', in Jacobson and Pullum (1982).

Dowty, D.: 1982b, 'More on the Categorial Theory of Grammatical Relations', in A. Zaenen (ed.), *Subjects and Other Subjects*, Indiana University Linguistic Club.

Dowty, D.: 1985a, 'Type Raising, Functional Composition and Non-costituent Conjunction', paper presented at the Conference on Categorial Grammar, Tucson, Arizona. [This volume.]

Dowty, D.: 1985b, 'On Some Recent Treatments of Control', *Linguistics and Philosophy* **8**.

Engdahl, E.: 1980, *The Syntax and Semantics of Questions in Swedish*, unpublished Ph.D. Dissertation, University of Massachusetts, Amherst, Mass.

Flynn, M.: 1983, 'A Categorial Theory of Structure Building', in G. Gazdar, E. Klein and G. Pullum (eds.), *Order, Concord and Costituency*, Foris, Dordrecht.

Gazdar, G.: 1982, 'Phrase Structure Grammar', in Jacobson and Pullum (1982).

Groenendijk, J. and M. Stokhof: 1984, *The Semantics of Questions and the Pragmatics of Answers*, Jurriaans, Amsterdam.

Hoeksema, J.: 1983, 'Plurality and Conjunction', in A. ter Meulen (ed.), *Studies in Model Theoretic Semantics*, Foris, Dordrecht.

Jacobson, P.: 1977, *The Syntax of Crossing Coreference Sentences*, Garland Press.

Jacobson, P. and G. Pullum (eds.): 1982, *The Nature of Syntactic Representation*, D. Reidel, Dordrecht.

Landman, F. and I. Moerdijk: 1983, 'Anaphora and Compositionality', *Linguistics and Philosophy* **6**.

Partee, B. H.: 1979, 'Montague Grammar and the Wellformedness Constraint', in F. Heny and H. Schnelle (eds.), *Syntax and Semantics*, Vol. 10, Academic Press, New York.

Pollard, C.: 1985, *Generalized Phrase Structure Grammar, Head Grammar and Natural Language*, Ph.D. Dissertation, Stanford, Calif.

Reinhart, T.: 1983, 'Coreference and Bound Anaphora', *Linguistics and Philosophy* **6**.

Sag, I., G. Gazdar, T. Wasow, and S. Weisler: 1985, 'Coordination and How to Distinguish Categories', in *Natural Language and Linguistic Theory* **3**.

Schmerling, S.: 1983, 'Two Theories of Syntactic Categories', *Linguistics and Philosophy* **6**.

Steedman, M. and A. Szabolcsi: 1985, Paper Presented at the Conference on Categorial Grammar, Tucson, Arizona.

Williams, E.: 1980, 'Predication', *Linguistic Inquiry* **11**.

Williams, E.: 1983, 'Against Small Clauses', *Linguistic Inquiry* **14**.

Dept. of Modern Languages & Linguistics,
Morrill Hall, Cornell University,
Ithaca, N.Y. 14853, U.S.A.

DAVID DOWTY

TYPE RAISING, FUNCTIONAL COMPOSITION, AND NON-CONSTITUENT CONJUNCTION

1. INTRODUCTION

A very striking feature of the system of categorial grammar in Ades and Steedman (1982) and Steedman (1985), which differentiates it from most other current work in categorial grammar as well as from related theories like Generalized Phrase Structure Grammar (Gazdar *et al.*, 1985), is its appeal to the operation of *functional composition* as a highly general rule of natural language grammars: Steedman and Ades include in their grammars not only the familiar functional application rule (1) but also the functional composition rule (2) (for which their term is *partial combination*):

(1)   Functional Application: $A/B + B \Rightarrow A$
(2)   Functional Composition[1]: $A/B + B/C \Rightarrow A/C$

Functional composition has two important effects in this theory. First, it is supposed to render the 'slash category' mechanism of GPSG unnecessary for describing long distance (extraction) dependencies, as one can instead analyze a gap-containing constituent such as a relative clause as a constituent missing a NP but otherwise put together, with the aid of functional composition, using the same categories as non-extraction constructions; this kind of analysis is illustrated in (3), where I borrow from Steedman (1985) the analysis of the relative pronoun *which* as of category $R/(S/NP)$ and also the syntactic analysis notation of drawing a line underneath two constituents combined by a syntactic operation and labeling that line with the operation used to combine them (here, either FA for functional application or FC for functional composition):

Richard T. Oehrle et al. (eds.), Categorial Grammars and Natural Language Structures, 153–197.
© 1988 *by D. Reidel Publishing Company.*

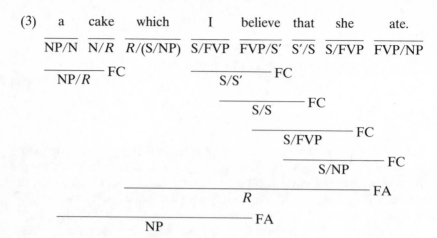

(3)   a   cake   which   I   believe   that   she   ate.

    NP/N   N/R   R/(S/NP)   S/FVP   FVP/S'   S'/S   S/FVP   FVP/NP
    ──────────── FC   ──────────── FC
       NP/R   S/S'
                                       ──────────── FC
                                          S/S
                                       ──────────────── FC
                                          S/FVP
                                       ────────────────── FC
                                          S/NP
                                       ──────────────────────── FA
                                          R
    ── FA
                     NP

The second distinctive effect of functional composition, also illustrated
in this example, is the production of certain highly unorthodox left-
branching constituent structures (here, the S/NP constituent). However,
such peculiar left-branching structures are not limited to extraction
cases but are also produced as alternative constituent structures (along
side the 'normal' constituent structures) for sentences like that in (4)
which involve no extraction:

(4)   I   believe   that   she   ate   those   cakes

    S/FVP   FVP/S'   S'/S   S/FVP   FVP/NP   NP/N   N
    ──────────── FC   ──────────── FA
       S/S'   NP
    ──────────── FC
       S/S
    ──────────────── FC
       S/FVP
    ────────────────── FC
       S/NP
    ──────────────────────── FA
              S

In defense of such unorthodox structures, Steedman and Ades point
out that these analyses do have the interesting property that they would
permit the syntactic parsing of sentences — and indeed their semantic
interpretation as well — to proceed left to right incrementally, almost

word by word, as each new word is encountered. But of course it is known from psycholinguistic studies as well as from common intuitive experience that hearers do in fact interpret sentences in just this way. After caveats about possible competence/performance differences have been made (cf. Ades and Steedman, 1982, pp. 517, 518; Steedman, 1985, pp. 524—525) it is still startling to note that such a syntactic theory would make it possible to mimic this incremental parsing and interpretation phenomenon directly in a competence grammar, suggesting in effect that an 'autonomous syntactic representation' of the familiar sort may not be a necessary part of a linguistic theory at all.

To be sure, it can be objected that there may be linguistic reasons why these 'peculiar' left-branching analyses should be excluded for certain purposes — e.g. correctly describing the domains of agreement and government and of cliticization —, but though Steedman and Ades do not point this out, one might be able to meet these objections by distinguishing in a Steedman-type grammar between a *basic grammar*, including functional application but excluding functional composition, extraction-licensing categories such as $R/(S/NP)$, and a third class of 'exceptional' structures that we will encounter shortly, versus an *extended grammar* containing all these rules and categories. For such a basic grammar would generate all and only the 'normal' constituent structures (for non-extracted constructions, etc.), and linguistic generalizations about 'correct' constituent structures could be stated in terms of the analyses of this basic grammar alone. (To be sure, one would still need to find a way to carry over these correct descriptions of cliticization, etc. from the basic grammar into the extended grammar in some way or other.)

On the other hand, these odd constituent structures have a rather strange status in our linguistic methodology: they are in a sense parasitic on the 'normal' constituents assigned by the grammar, and it is not obvious at all how one might motivate them on independent syntactic grounds, since their existence is supposed to have no effect whatsoever way on the class of strings generated by the grammar, when one compares a Steedman-type grammar with, say, a GPSG-type grammar of the same fragment of English that uses slash-features to generate unbounded dependencies instead of functional composition. In this sense, these odd constituents could be called 'phantom constituents' (to adopt a term introduced in Gazdar and Sag, 1981, and Nerbonne, 1982, for slightly different notion).

To pursue this point a bit further, we might ask whether one could in fact postulate a kind of grammatical theory that used a GPSG-type syntax but appealed to general functional composition only in the semantic interpretation. In this way, one could perhaps forsee a parsing theory that employed a GPSG syntax but still interpreted sentences incrementally, à la Steedman. And interestingly enough, it has been proposed in the most recent version of GPSG (Gazdar *et al.*, 1985) that the semantics of extraction constructions can be done by means of repeated functional composition, just as Steedman and Ades had independently proposed, rather than via variable binding (with the 'trace' interpreted as the variable). Actually, the origin of this idea can be traced to the literature on combinatory logic (e.g. Curry and Feys, 1958), and to Quine (1966), where it is pointed out that variables can be excluded altogether from classical predicate logic, with local but recursive operations such as functional composition replacing variable binding. Given these considerations, is there any hope of distinguishing on empirical grounds a Steedman/Ades type theory from the kind of semantically altered GPSG theory here envisioned? After all, GPSG and categorial grammar have been becoming more and more similar in recent years; witness for example the appeal to function-argument structure in current versions of the control-agreement principle (Gazdar *et al.*, 1985), which is a step in the direction of categorial grammar, or the adoption of agreement features and feature-passing mechanisms of a GPSG sort in Bach (1983). The latest offshoot of GPSG, Pollard (1985), adopts a subcategorization system quite reminiscent of categorial grammar, though with different notation. It is thus relevant to wonder whether GPSG and current categorial grammar are approaching the status of notational variants of the same theory.

To make less hypothetical this question about the syntactic vs semantic status of phantom constituents, let me digress to introduce a concrete example. Consider the case of wide-scope interpretations of NPs, a phenomenon usually handled by some version of 'Cooper Storage' (Cooper, 1982) in current theories. Suppose one were to suggest that the reading of *Everyone loves someone* in which *Someone* has wide scope is to be produced by using functional composition along with 'backwards' functional application as in example (5):

(5)   Everyone   loves   someone.
        ⎯⎯⎯⎯⎯   ⎯⎯⎯⎯⎯⎯   ⎯⎯⎯⎯⎯⎯
         S/FVP   FVP/NP   S/(S/NP)
        ⎯⎯⎯⎯⎯⎯⎯⎯⎯⎯⎯⎯ FC
              S/NP
        ⎯⎯⎯⎯⎯⎯⎯⎯⎯⎯⎯⎯⎯⎯⎯⎯⎯ FA ('backwards')
                   S

(It can be shown that this syntactic analysis does give *someone* wider scope than *everyone*, without any additional Cooper-type storage apparatus.) Bill Ladusaw has suggested to me that there is in fact an interesting reason for pursing this possibility — namely, one might be able to account for the familiar fact (Sag, 1976) that such a wide scope reading for the object NP is impossible in 'VP deletion' sentences like (6):

(6)   Everyone loves someone, and John does too.

The reason, Ladusaw suggests, is that if functional composition as in (5) is the only means of giving the object NP wider scope, then we would expect such a reading to be blocked in (6) because there is literally no syntactic VP in the first conjunct to which the anaphoric form *does* could refer in such an analysis, though of course there is such a VP on the more normal syntactic analysis that gives *Everyone* wide scope.

However, readers familiar with Ades and Steedman (1982) or Steedman (1985) will recognize that if we permit functional application to apply 'backwards' in English (i.e. right-to-left as in (5)), then the grammar is in grave danger of overgenerating, producing, e.g. *Loves everyone someone* and much other such garbage. Indeed, I presently know of no way of incorporating analyses like (5) without drastic overgeneration. Assuming that I have not simply failed to discover the correct way of doing this, I believe the moral of this story is that if indeed we are to capture the scope restriction of (6) via Ladusaw's suggestion, then the phenomenon of wide scope readings of NPs as in (5) is clearly a case where we want to say that functional composition operates only in the semantic interpretation, not in the syntax at all. Then we can describe the scope restriction exhibited in (6) by stipulating that in order for the VP anaphoric form *does* to be interpreted, there must be a complete 'constituent' in the semantic interpretation of the previous conjunct (or previous sentence in the discourse) that is the interpretation *of* a (syntactic) VP in that conjunct (or sentence).

Nevertheless, I want to argue in the rest of this paper that there are indeed cases in English where the Steedman/Ades 'phantom constituents' make their presence manifest in an undisputably syntactic fashion. If, as has been frequently suggested (Gazdar, 1980; von Stechow, 1974; Keenan and Faltz, 1978) natural language conjunction is a process that truly generalizes across all syntactic categories of a language, then we might expect phantom constituents to conjoin and thus to be visible in coordination if anywhere. And in fact I will argue that so-called *non-constituent conjunction* is simply a case of the conjunction of phantom constituents, which arises from the interaction of highly general and independently motivated processes in English. One of these general processes is *type raising*, and I will begin by discussing the type-raising proposals of Partee and Rooth (1983) and presenting a minor but crucial generalization of their analysis (Section 2). Though Steedman (1985) employs type raising in his analyses of both English and Dutch, we will need a slight systematization of his method to insure that only correct word orders can arise from type raising of the sort employed here (Section 3). Section 4 introduces the analysis of non-constituent conjunction, and Section 5 shows this kind of analysis to extend to a peculiar sort of non-constituent conjunction in English that would appear resistant to any possible GPSG-type 'meta-rule' analysis of non-constituent conjunction. Section 6 examines some very interesting predictions that this theory makes for data involving the interaction of conjunction with extraction island constraints. Section 7 compares the present NCC analysis with Steedman's (1985) treatment of Right-Node Raising, and in Section 8, arguments are given that non-constituent conjunction cannot be reduced to constituent conjunction combined with 'ordinary' extraction of a more familiar sort.

Up to this point, I will assume that a Steedman-type analysis of extraction can eventually be made to work properly, at least for languages like English. But since all current versions of this kind of extraction analysis appear to overgenerate somewhat, it is necessary to consider the possibility that functional composition cannot by itself generate extraction constructions successfully, so it will be noted in Section 9 why it is reasonable to retain functional composition for clause-bounded phenomena like non-constituent conjunction while using a feature-passing device (such as the 'slash' feature analysis of GPSG) to handle unbounded extraction; the earlier predictions about the interaction of extraction island constraints and non-constituent conjunction phenomena will need to be reexamined from this point of view. Finally, Section 10 concludes with a comparison of broader predictions about conjunction made by the present framework vs. GPSG.

2. TYPE RAISING

By *type raising* I refer to the process of reanalyzing an argument category as a new functor which takes as its argument the functor that would have applied to it before type raising; a familiar example from Montague Grammar is the reanalysis of 'term phrases' from the category of names (category e) to generalized quantifiers (category $t/(t/e)$), as illustrated by the change from (7a) to (7b):

(7) (a) John walks.   (b) John walks.

$\overline{\quad}$ $\overline{\quad}$ $\overline{\quad}$ $\overline{\quad}$

$\quad e \quad\quad t/e$ $\quad t/(t/e) \quad t/e$

$\dfrac{\quad\quad\quad\quad}{\quad t \quad}$ FA $\dfrac{\quad\quad\quad\quad}{\quad t \quad}$ FA

The general process can be described as in (8):

(8) $\dfrac{A/B + B \quad\quad\quad \Rightarrow A}{A/B + A/(A/B) \Rightarrow A}$

The intended interpretation of (8) is that an expression of category B is to be reanalyzed as an expression of category $A/(A/B)$. Type raising for categorial grammars has been proposed many times, both in logic (e.g. Lambek, 1958, 1961; van Benthem, 1984) and in linguistic analysis (Geach, 1972; Lewis 1972; Partee and Rooth, 1983; Rooth and Partee, 1982; Ades and Steedman, 1982; Steedman, 1985; Hoeksema ms).

The semantics of type raising is likewise generalizable: in 'raising' the category (and therefore the logical type) of the argument β from B to $A/(A/B)$, one maps its interpretation from β' into $\lambda f[f(\beta')]$, where f ranges over functions of the type corresponding to category A/B.

In many cases (for example, 7a, b), type raising has no semantic effect whatsoever. But Partee and Rooth (1983) observe three cases in English where type raising does have a non-vacuous semantic effect that provides a needed reading for some sentences which a grammar without type raising would not easily produce; these cases include (i) a problem with getting all and only the correct readings for both conjoined extensional verbs (*John caught and ate a fish, A fish walked and talked*) and conjoined intensional verbs (*John wants and needs a new car, An easy model theory textbook is badly needed and will surely be written soon*), (ii) 'wide scope *or*' (the reading of *The department is looking for a phonologist or a phonetician* brought out by the continuation '... but I don't know which'), and (iii) the semantics of common noun conjunction as in *Most men and women are happy*, which obviously needs to get the reading 'Most men and .nost women are happy' rather than the incorrect reading 'Most hermaphrodites are happy' which it would receive in straightforward theories of generalized conjunction (Gazdar, 1980; von Stechow, 1974; Keenan and Faltz, 1978) without type raising. What all three cases have in common is that they involve conjunction (or disjunction) in combination with another element whose scope relation to conjunction affects truth conditions, for it is precisely in such cases that type raising gives us readings not obtainable otherwise. I will not discuss these cases here, but refer the reader to Partee and Rooth (1983) for details; the important thing to note here is that type raising is motivated on semantic grounds for at least three different categories in English.

Several linguists (Dowty, 1975, 1982; Bill Ladusaw, pers. com.; and Partee and Rooth, 1983) have pointed out that type raising would seem to offer a very plausible account of how children can acquire names, quantified NPs, and intensional verbs in 'stages' (i.e., in that order) without changing the appearance of the output of their grammars radically and all the while using adult speech as a model: at the earliest stage, children would analyze all NPs as names (i.e., of type e), then reanalyze (some or all) NPs as quantifiers (cf. 7b), then still later reanalyze certain verbs (the intensional ones) as of a higher type than extensional verbs.

2.1. *Type Raising and Word Order*

Before I can introduce the generalized type raising system, it will be necessary to introduce conventions for specifying word order. Both Steedman (1985) and Flynn (1983) have proposed ways for capturing cross-categorial generalizations about the order in which functors combine with their arguments in English, but I will not adopt these for two reasons; first, for my purposes it is not necessary to take a stand on which of these two methods (or other method) is the correct one, and second, it will be easier to follow the analyses below if it is somehow specified in the name of each functor category whether it combines with its arguments to the left or to the right.

One traditional notation for left versus right functor-argument combinations is to use A/B for a functor that combines with an argument of category B on its *right* to form an expression of category A, while using the notation $A\backslash B$ for a functor that combines with an argument of category A on its *left* to form an expression of category B. However, I find it a confusing feature of this system that if the slash leans to the right, as in A/B, B designates the argument category and A the result category, while this relationship is reversed if the slash leans to the left: A is the argument and B is the result category in $A\backslash B$. For complex categories such as $((A\backslash B)/C)\backslash(D/E)$, with multiple slashes of both directions, it becomes very hard to see what is a functor and what is an argument (the final result category is D under this convention, not A). Instead of this notation, I will use A/B for a functor that seeks a B-argument on its right to form an A-expression, and the notation $A\backslash B$ for a functor that seeks a B-argument on its left to form an A; this notation observes the convention that the argument symbol is always to the right of the slash and the result symbol is to the left, no matter which order functor and argument combine in. The proper description of functional application, under this revised convention, is (1'):

(1')   Functional Application in a 'Directional' System:

      (a) $A/B + B \Rightarrow A$ (b) $B + A\backslash B \Rightarrow A$

The general principle about type raising and word order that I will follow here is that (basic grammar) word order should remain unaffected, no matter what instances of type raising are added to a grammar. In a categorial grammar of our kind, the obvious way to do this is to adopt the directional type raising rules in (9):

(9) (a)
$$\frac{A/B + B \Rightarrow A}{A/B + A\backslash(A/B) \Rightarrow A}$$
  (b)
$$\frac{B + A\backslash B \Rightarrow A}{A/(A\backslash B) + A\backslash B \Rightarrow A}$$

Note that the directionality of the slashes acquired by the 'raised' category depends on the direction of the slash in its original functor; as a consequence, the two expressions must combine in the same left-right order after type raising takes place as they did before.

2.2. *Type Raising in 'Stages'*

For what I will call *Stage I* of the grammar, the stage at which the only
noun (phrase) category is *e* (Montague's *entity* category), the categories
and implicit syntactic rules that involve nouns (NPs) are those listed
in (10); here and below, the left column lists combinations with the
(original) functor on the left, and the right column gives the (only)
combination with functor on the right:

(10)   *Stage I Grammar*:

$$(2)\ (t\backslash e)/e\ + e \Rightarrow t\backslash e \qquad (1)\ e + t\backslash e \Rightarrow t$$

$$vp/e \qquad\qquad vp \qquad\qquad vp$$

$$tv$$

$$(3)\ tv/e\ \quad + e \Rightarrow tv$$

$$ttv$$

$$(4)\ (X\backslash X)/e + e \Rightarrow X\backslash X$$

$$pp/e \qquad\qquad pp$$

The symbols written directly beneath other symbols here are abbreviations that will be used for these categories below. The variable X is
used in rule 4 to indicate that prepositional phrases may be used as
modifiers of various categories, such as vp, CN, perhaps tv and ttv, etc.

At what I will call *Stage Ia*, rule (9b) is used to convert category e to
$t/(t\backslash e)$, giving rise to the new subject-predicate rule (11):

$$(11)\quad t/(t\backslash e) + t\backslash e \Rightarrow t$$

$$np_{[S]} \qquad vp$$

Semantically, this step permits subject NPs to become quantifiers.
Along with this step we can now add a new category of common nouns,
CN, and one of determiners, $np/$CN, in order to generate the full range
of NP-meanings. However, note that these NPs can only be used in
subject position (hence the subscript $[s]$), because transitive and ditransitive verbs, and prepositions, are not of the same type as vps,
hence cannot be used in rule (11).

To get the full range of NPs in non-subject position, we must use
rule (9a) to derive three new syntactic rules; these, along with rule (11)
gives us the full *Stage II*, described in (12):

(12) *Stage II*:

  (2) $vp/e + vp\backslash(vp/e) \Rightarrow vp$ (1) $t/(t\backslash e) + t\backslash e \Rightarrow t$
      tv $vp\backslash tv$ t/vp
              $np_{[O]}$ $np_{[S]}$ vp

  (3) $tv/e + tv\backslash(tv/e) \Rightarrow tv$
      ttv $tv\backslash ttv$
              $np_{[O2]}$

  (4) $pp/e + pp\backslash(pp/e) \Rightarrow pp$
              $np_{[OP]}$

But this system looks more than a little bit messy; there are now four distinct categories of noun phrase in the grammar (subject, object, second object, and prepositional object NPs), and they of course have distinct types of semantic interpretations. The category of determiners, too, must be multiplied four-fold. It is probably because of such apparent untidiness that Partee and Rooth (1983, p. 380) do not use their simple type-raising rule to produce NPs in these cases but propose a special, more complex type-raising rule just for non-subject NPs, which gives, in effect, the type assignments from Montague's PTQ to object-taking verbs and prepositions, and this allows all object NPs to have the same type.

I will not follow Partee and Rooth on this point, however, but will instead employ an idea that Steedman (1985) uses in analyzing the Dutch verb raising construction: this is to hypothesize a category of *NP complements* which employs a syntactic variable in its definition[2]:

(13) The NP-complement category:
    $np_{[O]} =_{def} X\backslash(X/e)$, where X ranges over categories that 'result in t' (i.e. $(\ldots (t/x_1) \ldots /x_n)$, for some $x_1 \ldots x_n$)

All the syntactic instances of non-subject NPs in (12) fall under the $X\backslash(X/e)$ schema, which also exploits the fact that all object NPs in English appear on the same side of their functors (i.e., the right side). (Fortunately, the parallel ordering of all object NPs with their functors is a rather consistent typological property across languages.)

Generalizing over the syntax of non-subject NPs would be of no use if it were not possible to generalize over their semantics as well, of course, but this is straightforward too. Let us take first the raising of names (of category e in Stage I) to $X\backslash(X/e)$. For those who prefer to see their semantics explained by translation into a lambda-calculus, the rule is (14):

(14) Where α is an expression of category e translating into α', the result of type raising α to category $X\backslash(X/e)$, as in (13), translates into:

$$\lambda R_{X/e}\lambda x_1 \ldots \lambda x_n[R(\alpha')(x_1) \ldots (x_n)]$$

where category $X = (\ldots (t/X_1)/ \ldots)/X_n$, and each variable x_i in the translation is of the type corresponding to category X_i.

(Equivalently but shorter: the result of type raising α translates into: $\lambda R_{X/e}[R(\alpha')]$.)

And to illustrate the schematized translation of a sample determiner:

(15) Where $a(n)$ is the singular indefinite determiner (of cat $(X\backslash(X/e))/CN$) and β is any CN, then $[a(n)\beta]$ (of cat $X\backslash(X/e)$ translates into:

$$\lambda R_{X/e}\lambda x_1 \ldots \lambda x_n \exists y[\beta'(y) \& R(y)(x_1) \ldots (x_n)]$$

where each variable x_i is as in (14).

For those who prefer to see their semantic interpretation described directly for English, without an intermediate translation, the corresponding rules are:

(14′) If α in cat e has interpretation α', then α in cat $X\backslash(X/e)$ denotes that function f from (X/e)-denotations to X-denotations such that for any (X/e)-denotation b, $f(b)(x_1) \ldots (x_n)$ $= 1$ iff $b(\alpha')(x_1) \ldots (x_n) = 1$, where $x_1 \ldots x_n$ is any sequence of arguments appropriate to an X-denotation.

(Equivalently: that function f such that $f(b) = b(\alpha')$.)

(15′) $[[a(n)]]$ (the denotation of the singular indefinite determiner) is that function f from CN-denotations to $X\backslash(X/e)$-denotations such that for any CN-denotation b and any X/e-denotation c, $f(b)(c)(x_1) \ldots (x_n) = 1$ iff there is some object $a \in b$ such that $c(a)(x_1) \ldots (x_n) = 1$, where $x_1 \ldots x_n$ are as in (14′).

Although I implicitly have in mind Montague's possible-worlds model theory in writing these semantic rules, it should perhaps be pointed out that nothing in this paper prohibits the substitution of a model theory which takes properties and relations as primitives and employs partial functions, as, e.g. Chierchia (1984), Barwise and Perry (1983), Veltman (1980), or Zalta (ms.), or for that matter, a computationally-implemented 'procedural' semantics, as long as one is willing to adopt a 'rule-to-rule' compositional interpretation structured in the form of unary (and where necessary, function-valued) functions, and also a version of generalized quantifier theory for NPs; though not all the authors cited have had this kind of compositional interpretation in mind for their semantics, I know of no reason why this could not be done in each of these cases.

Stage II gives the grammar quantified NPs in all positions, but no intensional verbs or prepositions, where 'intensional' here means 'taking higher-order (or 'non-specific') readings for the verb/preposition's arguments'. (Intensions in the sense of functions on possible worlds are not included here but are compatible with this kind of analysis; cf. Partee and Rooth, 1983.) To get higher-order readings for objects, we can use type lifting rule (10b) again to give us *Stage IIIa*[3]

(16) *Stage IIIa*:

$$(2) \quad vp/(vp\backslash tv) \quad + vp\backslash tv \quad \Rightarrow vp \quad (1) \; t/vp + vp \Rightarrow t$$

$$\text{TV} \qquad\qquad np_{[O1]} \qquad\qquad\qquad np_{[S]}$$

$$(3) \quad tv/(tv\backslash ttv) \quad + tv\backslash ttv \quad \Rightarrow tv$$

$$\text{TTV} \qquad\qquad np_{[O2]}$$

$$(4) \quad pp/(pp\backslash(pp/e)) + pp\backslash(pp/e) \Rightarrow pp$$

$$\text{P} \qquad\qquad np_{[OP]}$$

The last stage, the one in which intensional readings can also be produced in subject position, is achieved by adding the rule in (17) to Stage IIIa:

(17) *Stage IIIb*: $(1) \; t/vp + t\backslash(t/vp) \Rightarrow t$

                                            NP   VP

Since intensional readings will not be involved in the analysis of non-constituent conjunction in this paper, the only stages we need to concern ourselves with from here on are stages I and II.

As observed by Partee and Rooth (1983) and also by Dowty (1982), the dilemma of getting all and only the correct readings for extensional as well as for intensional verbs with conjoined quantifier objects is actually only resolved by assuming that (i) the grammar contains extensional verbs only in their extensional, Stage I type assignments, and (ii) extensional verbs are never raised to higher types except when they must be conjoined with intensional verbs (in e.g. *John sought and found a unicorn*). Type raising therefore differs from functional composition in that the latter is a general syntactic principle applying to *all* syntactic categories bearing the appropriate relation to each other, while this observation about extensional versus intensional verbs implies that we definitely cannot let type raising apply indescriminately to all expressions of a syntactic category fitting the type-raising rule. In other words, type raising is something like a lexical recategorization rule which is used to shift individual lexical items from one category to another. (In this respect, what I am claiming about natural language grammars is very different from the type-raising proposals of Lambek, 1958, and van Benthem, 1984.)

It is unclear how general we want the type raising of NPs to be (i.e. raising from category e to the various generalized quantifier categories). For the present, I assume that noun phrases, too, might be entered lexically only in their lowest possible type and type-raised only when they must be conjoined with a NP of higher type. In other words, names (and perhaps some occurrences of definite and indefinite descriptions[4]) are normally of category e, while only quantified NPs such as *every man* and *no woman* are of types $np_{[S]}$, or $np_{[O]}$. If this view should be correct, it might imply that there is some cognitive processing ecomony in treating sentences as (in some sufficiently abstract sense) strictly first-order whenever possible (e.g. for *John saw Mary*), and using second-order or third-order categories only where absolutely necessary. Yet we will occasionally need to raise proper names to $np_{[S]}$ or $np_{[O]}$ below for syntactic reasons, so the exact extent of this hypothesized type raising seems unclear. (No undesired consequences would arise from putting proper names *only* in $np_{[S]}$ and $np_{[O]}$, as far as I know.)

3. FUNCTIONAL COMPOSITION, TYPE RAISING AND WORD ORDER

I suspect that a very common first reaction to systems like Ades and

Steedman (1982), Steedman (1985), or this one is a serious worry that the addition of functional composition (FC) and type raising (TR) may give rise to numerous overgenerations. Yet if we exclude from consideration the categories that license gaps (e.g. the relative pronoun category $R/(S/NP)$ and Steedman's (1985) 'topicalization' category) and all coordinations, it can be demonstrated by induction over the categorially-defined categories that suitably judicious use of FC and TR does not add any output strings to the grammar that it would not produce anyway. For FC, we need only to insure that the 'main' slashes 'lean' in the same direction, i.e. the only two ways that FC can apply are (18a) and (18b)[5]:

(18) (a) $A/B + B/C \Rightarrow A/C$ (b) $B\backslash C + A\backslash B \Rightarrow A\backslash C$

Considering first the case of (18a), note that without functional composition, an expression of cat B/C could result in an expression of cat B only if there is a C immediately to its right. If there is such a C to the right, then the two will combine by FA to give a B, as in the first tree in (19):

(19)

$$
\begin{array}{cc}
A/B \;\; B/C \;\; C & A/B \;\; B/C \;\;\; C \\
\overline{B}\;\text{FA} & \overline{A/C}\;\text{FC} \\
\overline{A}\;\text{FA} & \overline{A}\;\text{FA}
\end{array}
$$

This A/B can in turn be combined with something to give an A only if there is an A/B to the left of the original B/C; thus in this case there were originally three expressions A/B, B/C, and C, in that order. But if we allow functional composition instead to combine A/B with B/C to form A/C, this can only further combine to give an A if there is a C to the right of the B/C, as in the second tree in (19); the word order must be the same as with FA. Cases where the resulting A/C is not combined with a C to the right by FA but with yet another functor C/D by functional composition can be justified by two successive applications of the process just illustrated that uses only FA; similarly for any n successive uses of FC. The justification for (18b) is the same, except with the order of expressions reversed.

For the two type-raising rules, repeated here,

(10) (a) $\dfrac{A/B + B \Rightarrow A}{A/B + A\backslash(A/B) \Rightarrow A}$ (b) $\dfrac{B + A\backslash B \Rightarrow A}{A/(A\backslash B) + A\backslash B \Rightarrow A}$

it is obvious by parallel reasoning that no new strings will be generated (by the basic grammar) when type raising is added, and I will not pursue the question any further here. Rather, the question I think we should address, when we recall that type raising is to be a lexical recategorization rule, is how *much* proliferation of expressions across categories is going to be needed. But I think we need only a very manageable amount. Note first that we do not need for type raising to apply iteratively to an arbitrary degree (i.e. raising an expression of category B, as in (10a), then type raising the A/B to become functor again, and so on). Instead, I think that interactive type raising of verb and argument never needs to go beyond Stage III (in (16) and (17)). Now if the expression B which is type raised is a lexical expression, then we need at most one new lexical entry for each expression of the category (as in the case of proper nouns). But if B is phrasal, then either (i) B contains no modifiers, in which case it is formed by combining a lexical 'main functor' $B/C_1 \ldots C_n$ with arguments $C_1 \ldots C_n$, so it is only the head $B/C_1 \ldots C_n$ that needs to be raised to category $(A\backslash(A/B))/C_1 \ldots C_n$; else (ii) B is formed by combining a modifier B/B or $B\backslash B$ with a B to form another B, and in this case we will need to raise the modifier B/B to $(A\backslash(A/B))/(A\backslash(B/B))$ (and it either is lexical or will have a lexical head). Altogether, we will need to multiply or change the categories of only (i) proper names, (ii) a few verbs (the intensional ones, and another class to be discussed below), (iii) the adverbs that modify intensional verbs, and (iv) determiners (which are the lexical heads of NPs) — this not directly because of type raising, but indirectly because of the schematization of the *np* category across $np_{[S]}$, $np_{[O]}$, and $np_{[O2]}$ that is a consequence of type raising (and perhaps also the heads of *np/np* modifiers, such as non-restrictive relative pronouns).

Although type raising and functional composition will not add any new strings to the basic grammar (i.e. the grammar without coordination and 'extraction' constructions), this is no longer true when coordination is taken into consideration, as we shall now see.

4. NON-CONSTITUENT CONJUNCTION

4.1. *Non-Constituent Conjunction and Gapping*

Hudson (1982) offers a number of arguments why Gapping should not be considered to be the same grammatical process as non-constituent conjunction (NCC), a term he reserves for cases like (20):

(20) (a) John eats rice quickly and beans slowly.
    (b) Mary eats beans on Tuesday and rice on Thursday.
    (c) John gave a book to Bill and a record to Max.
    (d) Mary gave Susan a book on Monday and Alice a record on Tuesday.
    (e) John persuaded Bill to write a book and Max to write a play.
    (f) Mary painted the chair red and the table blue.

Sag *et al.* (1985) and Russell (1983) have disputed Hudson's arguments. While I concede that the latter authors have shown that the distinction between Gapping and NCC is certainly less clear than Hudson's arguments would superficially suggest, it still seems to me that a few differences remain. For example, Gapping is necessarily associated with a formal register (in my speech at least), while NCC is perfectly natural in all registers. Second, most speakers agree that gapped sentences have a distinctive prosodic contour, while NCC examples do not, a fact that is sometimes acknowledged in writing by placing a comma in the place of the 'gap' in the elliptical gapped clause, though a comma is hardly ever placed within an elliptical NCC phrase. And though Sag *et al.* (1985) do challenge the traditional assumption that Gapping results in exactly two 'remnant' constituents by providing examples like (21) (= their 104) with three remnants (note the commas),

(21)   A businessman will drink a martini to relax, and a health nut, a glass of wine, just to remain healthy.

it seems to me that the naturalness of gapping declines markedly with more than two 'remnants', while NCC examples with three remnants (cf. (20d)) are hardly less natural than examples with only two remnants, and even four remnants seem possible with NCC (*Susan gave Alice a record in the park yesterday and Mary a book at home today*), though definitely not with gapping. Though the relationship between Gapping and NCC remains somewhat unclear, it seems not at all inappropriate at present to pursue analyses of NCC that do not necessarily extend to Gapping as well.

4.2. *Using FC to Produce Non-Constituent Conjunctions*

Though coordination would be most naturally incorporated into a categorial grammar by assigning *and, or,* etc. to a category $(X\backslash X^+)/X$ (i.e. a functor that combines with a member of any category X on the right to give a functor that will then combine with a sequence of one or more Xs on the left to produce an X), I will for simplicity assume here a coordination schema (22), referred to below as C:

(22) $[X^+ \text{ Conj } X] \Rightarrow X$

The simplest examples of NCC can now be produced as in (23), by using the coordination schema to conjoin phantom constituents produced by FC:

(23)   John saw Mary yesterday and Bill today

$$
\begin{array}{ccccccc}
e & tv & vp\backslash tv & vp\backslash vp & \text{Conj} & vp\backslash tv & vp\backslash vp
\end{array}
$$

$$
\underbrace{\qquad\qquad}_{vp\backslash tv}\text{FC} \qquad \underbrace{\qquad\qquad}_{vp\backslash tv}\text{FC}
$$

$$
\underbrace{\qquad\qquad\qquad\qquad}_{vp\backslash tv}\text{C}
$$

$$
\underbrace{\qquad\qquad\qquad\qquad}_{vp}\text{FA}
$$

$$
\underbrace{\qquad\qquad\qquad\qquad}_{t}\text{FA}
$$

(Note that we must assign the names *Mary* and *Bill* to the type-raised cat $vp\backslash tv$ — an instance of the variable cat $np_{[0]}$ — in order for the coordination to be possible, even though their semantics would not otherwise keep them from being of the simpler cat *e*.)

Ditransitive verbs like *give* will have in the simplest case, without coordination, the structure (24):

(24)   John showed Mary Bill

$$
\begin{array}{cccc}
e & tv/e & e & e
\end{array}
$$

$$
\underbrace{\qquad\qquad}_{tv}\text{FA}
$$

$$
\underbrace{\qquad\qquad}_{vp}\text{FA}
$$

$$
\underbrace{\qquad\qquad}_{t}\text{FA}
$$

It might be noted that the ditransitive verb combines first with the NP immediately to its right, then afterward combines with the second NP; this fact is actually forced by the Steedman-type analysis because of what Steedman (1985) calls the *adjacency property* of that theory. This implies that the analysis of Passive in Bach (1980) and Dowty (1978, 1982) — as a rule applying to transitive verb phrases that reinterprets the 'second from outermost' argument as object — must be abandoned, but it is possible to characterize Passive instead, perhaps universally, as an operation that reinterprets a verb's *innermost* NP argument as subject (and likewise, that 'direct object' might be defined universally as the innermost NP argument of a verb). Also, it will now be possible to treat Passive as a lexical rule — as urged by many linguists — rather than as a syntactic rule as required by Bach's analysis of Passive. (For those who prefer to think of interpretation in terms of translation into intensional logic, it should be kept in mind also that the correct translation of (24) will therefore be **showed'**$(m)(b)(j)$, *not* **showed'**$(b)(m)(j)$.)

With quantified NP arguments, a ditransitive can have not only the purely FA-derived structure (25),

(25)   John gave a man a book
$$\frac{\quad}{e} \quad \frac{\quad}{ttv} \quad \frac{\quad}{tv\backslash ttv} \quad \frac{\quad}{vp\backslash tv}$$
$$\frac{\qquad\qquad}{tv}\text{FA}$$
$$\frac{\qquad\qquad\qquad}{vp}\text{FA}$$
$$\frac{\qquad\qquad\qquad}{t}\text{FA}$$

but also the FC-derived structure (26):

(26)   John gave a man a book
$$\frac{\quad}{e} \quad \frac{\quad}{ttv} \quad \frac{\quad}{tv\backslash ttv} \quad \frac{\quad}{vp\backslash tv}$$
$$\frac{\qquad\qquad}{vp\backslash ttv}\text{FC(r-to-l)}$$
$$\frac{\qquad\qquad}{vp}\text{FA(r-to-l)}$$
$$\frac{\qquad\qquad}{t}\text{FA}$$

Note that because the main slash in the two object NP categories is \

rather than /, FC must be performed right-to-left, i.e. we could not switch the category labels on these two NPs and combine them by FC left-to-right (even though there is nothing other than this restriction on FC to determine which NP gets which of the two categories). This is fortunate, because even though permitting the left-to-right FC in this case would not generate any syntactically ill-formed strings, it would get the interpretation wrong, i.e. it would interpret (26) as 'John gave a book a man'. In fact, the analysis in (26) leads to the correct interpretation, as can be confirmed by using the lambda-calculus translations from (15) above and reducing them by lambda conversion. Note, incidentally, that it is the fact that we have assigned the two object NPs to different logical types which permits them to combine by FC in (26).

Given the possibility of (26), where the two objects of the verb form a phantom constituent, we can of course now produce non-constituent conjunctions like (27),

(27)   John gave Mary a book and Susan a record

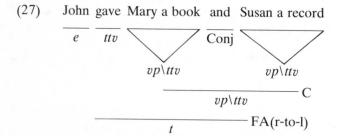

in which the two phantom constituents are analyzed just like *a man a book* in (26).

The rest of the example types in (20) are produced in parallel way: (20d) is simply the combination of the analysis types (22) and (27), (20e) is like (27), with the verb *persuade* in cat $(vp/vp)/e$, and so is (20f), with *paint* in cat $(vp/adj)/e$.

Barbara Partee (per. com.) has pointed out to me that NCC is also to be found in NPs, as well as in VPs:

(28) (a) Gifts of up to $50 to a political candidate by an individual or of up to $100 to a charitable organization by a couple can be deducted.

(b) The excursions through the Alps by bus and from London to Helsinki by boat both sound exciting.

In example (28a), the prepositional phrases might either be argued to be adjuncts (i.e. *gifts* is of category *N* and the prepositional phrases of category *N\N*) or argued to be arguments (i.e. *gifts* is of category $((N/(X\backslash X))/(X\backslash X))$), but in either case these NCCs will be generated by the grammar we now have; in the first case the analysis proceeds like (24) above (but with two rather than one adjunct), and in the second case it proceeds like (27). In (28b), there is one prepositional phrase in the left conjunct (*through the Alps*) where there are two in the right conjunct (*from London to Helsinki*); this does not present a problem, even if the prepositional phrases are analyzed as arguments, if the suggestion in Dowty (1979) is followed that the combination *from NP to NP* is a compound prepositional phrase (thus *from NP* is of a category like PP/PP), rather than two separate arguments.

4.3. *A Morphological Motivation for This Analysis of Non-Constituent Conjunction*

It turns out that type raising within noun phrases can be syntactically motivated — or more accurately, morphologically motivated — even when the conjunction of non-constituents fails to be in evidence. In Corbett (1979) the following example is mentioned:

(29) $\left\{\begin{array}{c}\text{This}\\ \text{*These}\end{array}\right\}$ man and woman $\left\{\begin{array}{c}\text{were}\\ \text{*was}\end{array}\right\}$ squatting in a castle.

This is interesting because a singular determiner, not a plural one, must be used, yet the verb agreement must be plural, not singular. One might at first guess that the singular determiner appears for the same reason that some people accept a singular verb in sentences like *There was a man and two women in the room*, i.e. solely because of its proximity to a singular noun and without regard to the fact that a conjunction is involved. However, this is not the case in (29), because the second as well as the first noun must be singular with *this*, plural with *these*:

(30) (a) This man and $\left\{\begin{array}{c}\text{woman}\\ \text{*women}\end{array}\right\}$ were . . .

(b) These men and $\left\{\begin{array}{c}\text{women}\\ \text{*woman}\end{array}\right\}$ were . . .

(Singular determiners like *one* and *a* behave like *this*, and *these* is paralleled by *few, several*, etc.) If we consider its tree structure, it becomes apparent that (29) is actually a problem for syntactic feature theories of plurality like GPSG:

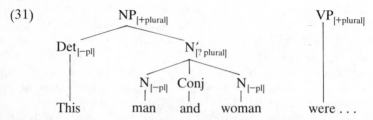

(31)

Presumably, the NP node must be [+plural], to trigger plural agreement on the VP and verb. We have seen that the two nouns and the determiner must all three be singular (or else all plural). So what feature for plurality does the N′ carry? In conjunction of full NPs with *and*, of course, two singular NPs give rise to plural on the mother node (*A man and a woman were here*), so perhaps the N′ here should be plural; as it is the head of the NP, this would explain the NP's and therefore the verb's plurality. But then it is a complete mystery why the determiner should be singular, since by the Control Agreement Principle, it should be plural.

There are of course accounts of plurality and number agreement in English which treat them as a semantic phenomenon, not a syntactic one. In the analysis of Hoeksema (1983), for example, singular determiners, nouns, and verbs are of a different logical type from plural determiners, nouns, and verbs, respectively. When I showed example (29) to Mats Rooth, he immediately noticed that a type raising analysis of the nouns in this example, along the lines of Partee and Rooth (1983), would predict exactly the morphological facts about (29) and (30), given a semantic theory of plurality like Hoeksema's. On the type raising analysis, (29) would have the analysis (32) in our notation:

(32)   This   man   and   woman   were . . .

$$\underline{\quad}\quad\underline{\quad}\quad\underline{\quad}\quad\underline{\quad}\quad\underline{\quad}$$

$np/N \quad np\backslash(np/N) \quad Conj \quad np\backslash(np/N) \quad vp$

$$\frac{\qquad\qquad\qquad\qquad}{np\backslash(np/N)}\;\text{C}$$

$$\frac{\qquad\qquad\qquad\qquad\qquad}{np}\;\text{FA}$$

and according to Partee and Rooth's (1983) analysis, would translate as in (32'), where $\cap$ stands for the conjunction operator, which generalizes across categories, and $\mathscr{D}$ is a variable of the type that determiners translate into:

(32') man $\Rightarrow$ $\lambda \mathscr{D}\mathscr{D}(\text{man}')$
       woman $\Rightarrow$ $\lambda \mathscr{D}\mathscr{D}(\text{woman}')$

   man and woman $\Rightarrow$ $\lambda \mathscr{D}\mathscr{D}(\text{man}') \cap \lambda \mathscr{D}\mathscr{D}(\text{woman}')$
   $= \lambda \mathscr{D}[\mathscr{D}(\text{man}') \cap \mathscr{D}(\text{woman}')]$

   this man and woman $\Rightarrow$ $\lambda \mathscr{D}[\mathscr{D}(\text{man}') \cap \mathscr{D}(\text{woman}')](\text{this}')$
   $= [\text{this}'(\text{man}') \cap \text{this}'(\text{woman}')]$

As the last line demonstrates, the translation of the NP is equivalent to one in which the meaning of the determiner is applied to each noun in turn (as of course we should expect it to be, given that *this man and woman* means the same as *this man and this woman*[6]), and in Hoeksema's semantic account of plurality with its differing type assignment to singulars and plurals of each category, this obviously should work only when determiner and both nouns are singular, or when they are all plural. Given certain further observed semantic properties of the resulting NP — that it is acceptable with collective as well as distributive predicates — it follows that the *and* here must be semantically parallel to what Hoeksema terms the 'collective *and*', which combines with two NPs to give a coordinate NP that is plural and thus takes plural VPs (*John and Mary are a happy couple*). The other thing to note about the odd NP *this man and woman* is that it does not mean *this thing which is both a man and a woman* but, as mentioned, *this man and this woman*; thus it is the kind of NP for which type raising is motivated on independent semantic grounds in the first place (Partee and Rooth, 1983). Not all conjunctions of this general syntactic form have this semantics; as Partee and Rooth note, there are exceptions like *My friend and colleague John Smith*, meaning someone who *is* both a friend and a colleague; significantly, this kind of NP takes singular verb agreement, not plural. And the correct description of this last phrase, in both its [+singular] categorization and its semantics, is still generated by the grammar with the 'unraised' CN-conjunction *and*:

(33)   My   friend   and   colleague

np/N   N   Conj   N

$\overline{\qquad\qquad\qquad}$ C
         N

$\overline{\qquad\qquad\qquad\qquad}$ FA
      np

Jack Hoeksema has called it to my attention that whereas the interpretation *and* has in most contexts permits it to be generalized across categories, as Partee and Rooth have assumed here, Hoeksema's 'collective *and*', which as indicated above, has the kind of collective meaning needed for (32) (cf. Hoeksema, 1983, pp. 74—76), does not have the Boolean properties that permit generalization across categories, so we cannot literally use the semantic analysis in (32′) in Hoeksema's theory. At worst, we would have to specify this interpretation of the *and* that conjoins two type-raised common nouns as in (32″), where '$\&_c$' denotes Hoeksema's collective conjunction that combines with two NP-denotations (generalized quantifiers):

(32″)   [$_{NP\backslash Det}$ NP\Det *and* NP\Det] translates into:
$\lambda \mathscr{P}$[NP\Det′($\mathscr{P}$) $\&_c$ NP\Det′($\mathscr{P}$)],   where $\&_c$ is the 'collective conjunction' of Hoeksema (1983).

This separately stipulated definition actually might not be a bad idea, since Jerry Sadock has pointed out to me that even a language as closely related to English as French does not have the collective interpretation of conjoined common nouns, but only the intersective (Boolean) interpretation:

(33′)   Cette fille et mère
        (= 'this person who is both a daughter and a mother')
        (≠ 'this daughter and this mother')

The same is true of Spanish and Italian, I have been informed.

5. NON-CONSTITUENT CONJUNCTION WITH PARTIAL SUB-CONSTITUENTS

About three years ago I wrote but did not publish a short paper on non-constituent conjunction that used the GPSG-type metarule (34):

(34)   [$_{VP}$ X Y] ⇒ [$_{VP}$ X Y_1 *and* Y_2]

Here, *X* and *Y* are syntactic variables. The metarule says that given any way of dividing up the daughters of a VP into two groups, one can make a second copy of the right-hand group and put a conjunction between the two copies. I won't bother with the semantic part of the rule here; it was awkward and not strictly Montogovian, though it worked otherwise.

I abandoned this approach when Greg Stump pointed out the following kind of counterexamples to me (which can also be found in Sag, 1976):

(35) (a) John went to Chicago on Monday and New York on Tuesday.
    (b) Mary talked about Manet on Wednesday and Renoir on Thursday.
    (c) Rover jumped through the hoop first and the window second.

The property these examples have which makes them resistant to (34) or any other obvious related approach is that the part of the VP which seems to be singled out as the 'conjunct' does not consist just of two or more daughters of VP but rather includes a proper subpart of one daughter; in other words, the underlined portion of the tree in (36):

(36)

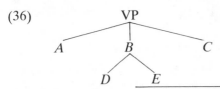

Since metarules by definition deal only with 'adjacent levels' of a tree, no metarule can give us *E* and *C* dominated by VP without also giving us *D*. The only way out of this dilemma that I could imagine would be to suggest that the prepositions left 'outside' the conjunct in (36) are really daughters or perhaps sisters to the verb; though this first possibility sometimes happens, as is evidenced by the acceptability of passives like *This painter is talked about quite a lot*, there is no evidence that this has happened in (35a) or (35c) (*Chicago was gone to by John*, *The hoop was jumped through by Rover*).

It is of some interest, therefore, that the present approach generates such examples without any further modification in the grammar. Before we can see this, we should first ask whether the PP *to Chicago* is an adjunct to the verb *went* in (35a), as in (37a), or an argument of it, as in (37b):

(37) (a) went   to   Chicago   (b)   went   to   Chicago

$$\frac{vp \quad (vp\backslash vp)/e \quad e}{\underline{\hspace{2.5cm}}}\text{FA}$$

$$\frac{vp \quad}{vp\backslash vp}\text{FA}$$

$$\frac{}{vp}\text{FA}$$

$$\frac{vp/(vp\backslash vp) \quad (vp\backslash vp)/e \quad e}{\underline{\hspace{2.5cm}}}\text{FA}$$

$$\frac{}{vp\backslash vp}\text{FA}$$

$$\frac{}{vp}\text{FA}$$

It has been proposed (e.g. McConnell-Ginet, 1982) that many 'VP-adverbs' and, presumably, also VP-modifying PPs, are really arguments of verbs, though on semantic and distributional grounds, there is no reason why at least this PP should not be considered an adjunct (cf. Dowty, 1979), so their status seems unclear. Some cases are known, of course, where an expression that is an adjunct with most verbs apparently must be a subcategorized argument for certain other verbs:

(38) (a)   John read the book.
     (b)   John read the book on the table.
     (c)   *John put the book.
     (d)   John put the book on the table.

     (e)   John wrote the letter.
     (f)   John wrote the letter poorly.
     (g)   *John worded the letter.
     (h)   John worded the letter poorly.

Type raising offers an explanation of how this situation can arise, for type raising would convert a verb taking a certain adjunct *into* a verb taking that adjunct as an argument, e.g., it would convert *went* in (37) from vp to $vp/(vp\backslash vp)$.[7] While *put* and *word* appear only in the raised category, verbs like *go*, I assume, appear in both these categories. We begin with the analysis in (39):

(39)   John   went   to   Chicago   on   Monday

$$\frac{e \quad vp/(vp\backslash vp) \quad (vp\backslash vp)/e \quad e \quad (vp\backslash vp)/e \quad e}{}$$

$$\frac{}{vp\backslash vp}\text{FA} \qquad \frac{}{vp\backslash vp}\text{FA}$$

$$\frac{}{vp}\text{FA}$$

$$\frac{}{vp}\text{FA(r-to-l)}$$

$$\frac{}{t}\text{FA(r-to-l)}$$

With functional composition and type raising of *Chicago*, the VP can be regrouped to make *Chicago on Monday* a constituent,

(40) John   went   to   Chicago   on   Monday

$$e \quad vp/(vp\backslash vp) \quad (vp\backslash vp)/e \quad vp\backslash(vp/e) \quad (vp\backslash vp)/e \quad e$$

$$\underline{\hspace{5cm}}\text{FC}$$
$$vp/e$$

$$\underline{\hspace{5cm}}\text{FA}$$
$$vp\backslash vp$$

$$\underline{\hspace{5cm}}\text{FC(r-to-l)}$$
$$vp\backslash(vp/e)$$

$$\underline{\hspace{5cm}}\text{FA(r-to-l)}$$
$$vp$$

$$\underline{\hspace{5cm}}\text{FA(r-to-l)}$$
$$t$$

and then (35a) is produced as in (41):

(41) John went to Chicago on Monday and Detroit on Tuesday

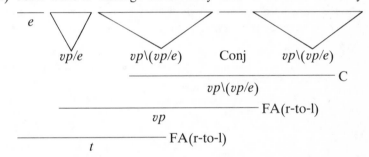

$$e \qquad vp/e \qquad vp\backslash(vp/e) \qquad \text{Conj} \qquad vp\backslash(vp/e)$$

$$\underline{\hspace{6cm}}\text{C}$$
$$vp\backslash(vp/e)$$

$$\underline{\hspace{6cm}}\text{FA(r-to-l)}$$
$$vp$$

$$\underline{\hspace{6cm}}\text{FA(r-to-l)}$$
$$t$$

Although the phrase *went to* can be generated in cat vp/e, the category of transitive verb phrases, there is no reason to suppose that this predicts ungrammatical passives like **Chicago was gone to by John*, because, as noted above, passive can be regarded as a lexical rule in Steedman's approach, and nothing here requires *went to* to appear in the lexical cat vp/e.

6. NON-CONSTITUENT CONJUNCTION AND EXTRACTION ISLAND CONSTRAINTS

In correspondence with Dick Hudson about examples like (35), Hudson pointed out to me that while PPs can in effect be split up by NCC, this does not happen with other, seemingly parallel cases involving NPs:

(42) (a)   *John saw the girl in the evening and boy in the morning.
　　(b) (*)John likes sweet jam at breakfast and coffee at supper. (* on
　　　　reading '. . . likes sweet coffee at supper')

Surprising as it may seem, the present approach may also predict this
fact. Since 'extraction' in Steedman's approach is carried out by means
of the functional composition rule, island constraints on extraction are
stated as constraints on the application of functional composition in his
theory. For example, Steedman (1985) suggests that the NP Constraint
of Horn (1974) and Bach and Horn (1976) be formulated as a prohibi-
tion on functional composition 'into' a NP:

　　(43)　　Functional Composition (with NP-constraint):
　　　　　　$X/Y + Y/Z \Rightarrow X/Z$,　where $Y \neq NP$

But as functional composition is crucially involved in NCC as analyzed
above, the restriction in (43) would automatically block (42a) (type
raising is here used on *saw* to show that the structure might otherwise
be producible in the grammar):

(44)

$$John \quad saw \quad the \quad girl\ in \quad and \quad boy\ in$$

$$e \quad vp/np_{[o]} \quad np_{[o]}/N \quad the\ evening \quad —— \quad the\ morning$$

——————— *FC　N　　Conj　　N
　　　　vp/N　　　　　　　——————— C
　　　　　　　　　　　　　　　　　N

——————————————— FA
　　　　　　　vp

(Actually, it is not clear that (44) is in danger of being produced even
under these assumptions, since I am not sure how phrases like *girl in
the evening* can be generated.)
　　It is also known that the relevant extraction island constraint must
somehow distinguish the structure in (45) from those in (46) and (47)
(cf. Ross, 1967; Horn, 1974):

　　(45)　　Who did John read a book about?
　　(46)　　*Who did Mary read Sue's book about?
　　(47)　　*Who did Mary destroy a/Sue's book about?

There is of course considerable debate over just how the constraint or
constraints involved in (45)—(47) should be formulated, i.e. is the

constraint one against extraction from all NPs or only from complex NPs? The interesting thing about these examples from our point of view is that no matter how the constraint is stated (as a constraint on functional composition), it will correctly distinguish (48) from (49) and (50) if it distinguishes (45) from (46) and (47):

(48)   John read a book about Nixon on Monday and (about) Reagan on Tuesday.

(49)   *Mary read Sue's book about Nixon on Monday and (about) Reagan on Tuesday.

(50)   *John destroyed a book about Nixon on Monday and (about) Reagon on Tuesday.

It has been pointed out to me that there are some examples parallel to (42) which are at least marginally acceptable to some speakers, e.g. (51):

(51) (a) [*]Mary read John's report in the morning and letter in the afternoon.

   (b) [*]Mary saw the president in the morning and vice-president in the afternoon.

I am not sure how these cases might be distinguished from (42); it seems that phonological factors are involved (the length of the common noun in the second conjunct), and also pragmatic factors (the naturalness of referring to the denotations of the two nouns as a class) are involved. But if at least some examples like (51a, b) are acceptable, it is possible that Horn's NP constraint is not the one we should be appealing to here, but rather a complex NP constraint — in our terms, a constraint against functional composition into the *modifier* of a NP, and so should be formulated as (52):

(52)   Complex NP constraint on Functional Composition:
        $A/B + B/C \Rightarrow A/C$, where $B \neq N \backslash N$.

This constraint would still block (49) and (50), as well as (46) and (47) and all extractions from relative clauses (assuming relative clauses are a species of $N \backslash N$), but would not per se rule out (51) or (44).

Somewhat unfortunately, I have not been able to find any other structures where the prediction can be tested that non-constituent conjunction obeys island constraints. The reason is that tests seem to be limited to structures of the form of (36) (repeated here),

(36)

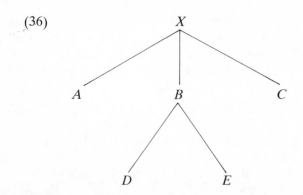

in which (i) node B is an extraction island, and (ii) node C is non-empty (since otherwise conjunction of E alone would be indistinguishable from ordinary constituent conjunction, or, where B has more than two daughters, from NCC *within* a syntactic island, which one would not expect the constraint to block), and preferably (iii) there exists a parallel structure in which B is not an extraction island, so that NCC can be shown possible there.

Thus while the predicted correlation between island constraints and constraints on non-constituent conjunction appears to be evidenced in certain cases (i.e. (48)—(50), in rather striking contrast to (35a—c)), the overall evidence for this correlation is limited and equivocal. In Section 9 below, we will consider a theory in which extraction is handled by a completely different mechanism from non-constituent construction, and in that theory, no such correlation would be predicted between these two domains.

7. STEEDMAN'S ANALYSES OF RIGHT NODE RAISING

Though Steedman (1985) includes no treatment of NCC in English (i.e. with incomplete conjuncts on the right and 'shared' material on the left), he does treat English Right Node Raising [RNR] (i.e. with 'shared' material on the right and incomplete conjuncts on the left), and it will be informative to review this briefly for comparison. The most familiar kind of example is produced as in (53) (using now my categorization rather than Steedman's):

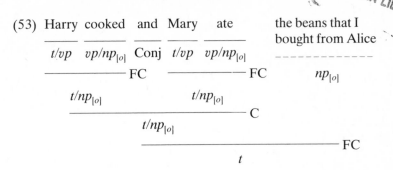

Steedman notes that extraction island constraints will prevent the formation of examples like (54):

(54)   *I know the woman who painted, and you met the man who stole, the picture that Harry was so fond of.

Steedman correctly predicts that constituents can however be right-node-'raised' out of complement clauses when the clause is not an island:

(55)   I believe (that) Harry and know (that) Mary will lend you the money.

But a kind of case which the traditional extraction analysis of RNR cannot account for but which Steedman's analysis can is one where two constituents rather than one are 'shared' on the right:

(56)   [[Joan offered] and [Mary actually gave]]$_{(t/pp)/npo}$ [a gold Cadillac]$_{npo}$ [to Billy Schwartz]$_{pp}$
(57)   John offered, and Mary actually gave, a very heavy policeman a rather pretty flower.

(Incidentally, these do not require type raising to produce an 'argument string' constituent on the right, as did the NCC examples treated earlier, since the conjunction category is one that takes two arguments anyway.)

Especially noteworthy is that sentences can be produced in which both a 'Right Node Raising' and a leftward extraction occur:

(58)   [To which woman]$_{T/(t/PP)}$ [did Harry offer, and will Mary actually give]$_{(t/PP)/NP}$ [an autographed copy of *Syntactic Structures*]$_{NP}$?

Since English does not in general permit multiple extractions, this kind of example is apparently a problem for analyses like GPSG that treat extractions via a slash feature. (This example actually involves the generalized functional application rule of Ades and Steedman, 1982, and Steedman, 1985; cf. Note 1.) See Steedman (ms.) for still other kinds of RNR examples produced by his analysis.

Before leaving this section, I feel obliged to point out that one of Steedman's analyses of parasitic gap sentences in Steedman (ms.), reproduced here as (59),

(59) (a man)   whom   everyone   who   meets   admires

$$\underline{R_s/(S/NP)}\quad \underline{NP/R_s}\quad \underline{R_s/(S/NP)}\quad \underline{(S\backslash NP)/NP}\quad \underline{(S\backslash NP)/NP}$$

$$\underline{\qquad NP/(S\backslash NP)\qquad}\ \text{FC}$$

$$\underline{\qquad\qquad\qquad NP/NP \qquad\qquad}\ \text{FC}$$

$$\underline{\qquad\qquad\qquad\qquad S/NP\qquad\qquad\qquad}\ \text{S}$$

$$\underline{\qquad\qquad\qquad\qquad R_s\qquad\qquad\qquad\qquad}\ \text{FA}$$

violates Steedman's (1985) own formulation of the complex NP-constraint, in that it forms the constituent *everyone who* by functional composition into the relative clause category R_s. But if we relax the formulation of the complex NP constraint to permit (59) to be produced, then as Gerald Gazdar has pointed out to me, we will also predict coordinated NPs such as (60):

(60) (a)   *a man who and robot which can solve this problem
     (b)   *an idea that and man who are much admired

Since the NPs in (60) are manifestly ungrammatical, I conclude that Steedman's formulation of the complex NP constraint is in fact correct, and thus his analysis of subject parasitic gaps in (59) must be wrong.

8. NCC IS NOT HEAD-EXTRACTION (LEFT-NODE RAISING)

One possible kind of phrase-structural and slash-feature analysis of NCC that would not seem to have been ruled out by anything said above is that NCC might be described as the across-the-board leftward extraction of the verbal head from a VP. This analysis has been proposed by Schachter and Mordechay (1983) under the term *Left Node Raising,* and a similar analysis, though for a different class of sentences and for different reasons, was suggested by Jacobson (1983), who used the term *Head Extraction.* Such an analysis is exemplified by (61):

(61)

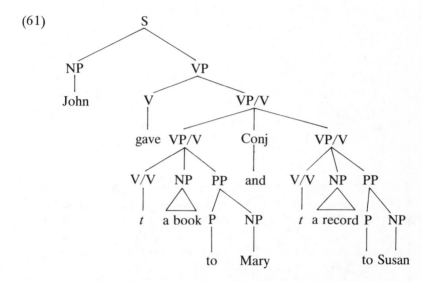

One clear reason why head-extraction cannot suffice to generate all NCC is that examples like (62) exist, in which not only the head but another constituent as well is 'shared' by both conjuncts; i.e. the 'extracted' portion of the VP (in this analysis) is not a constituent, thus the examples are problematic in a way parallel to (56) and (57) for RNR in GPSG:

(62) (a) Susan gave Mary a book on Monday and a record on Tuesday.
    (b) John gave a book to Bill on Monday and to Max on Tuesday.
    (c) Mary caught a fish on Monday with a fly rod and on Tuesday with a spear.
    (d) The portraits of her by Renoir in oils and by Degas in pastels are both in this gallery.

The categorial analysis of course has no difficulty with these:

(62′) S. gave Mary a book on Monday and a record on Tuesday

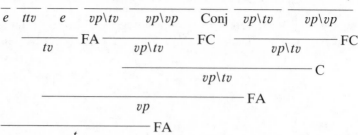

A more interesting problem for this analysis (if ultimately one whose implications are less clear) is provided by the following kind of example, which though awkward, still seems grammatical:

(63)   Bill gave and Max sold a book to Mary and a record to Susan.

This example involves NCC and RNR in the same sentence. The only way I can imagine this example being described at all in a GPSG theory is by treating the right half as a pair of conjoined VPs which have each 'lost' their head verb by head extraction, and the left half as a pair of conjoined sentences that have each lost their VP/V via right-node raising, i.e. (64):

(64)

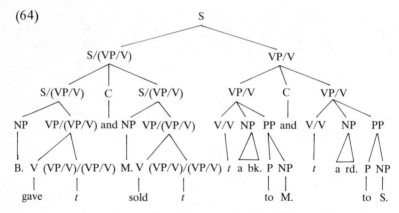

This horror show of course involves multiple slash features, but note that the category VP/(VP/V) is not the 'multiple slash category' suggested by Maling and Zaenen (1982) for the extraction of multiple NPs that occurs in Scandanavian, but rather a category bearing a higher-order slash feature VP/V, i.e. a slash feature that *itself* bears a slash feature. The (VP/V)/(VP/V) would then be a slash-feature-bearing category that bears as feature a slash-feature-bearing category. It would be unfortunate to have to complicate the theory in general and the grammar of English in particular in such a way for this one type of sentence to be produced.

In the present theory, rules generating the two kinds of conjunction involved in this sentence (RNR and NCC) have already been introduced, but they do not quite permit this example to be produced, as they now stand. The left half of the RNR sentence, generated according to Steedman's rules (cf. (56) above), would be of category $(t/pp)/e$:

(65)   Bill   gave   and Max   sold
       ───── ───────── ──── ───── ─────────
       t/vp $(vp/pp)/e$ Conj t/vp $(vp/pp)/e$
       ─────────────── FC   ─────────────── FC (generalized)
           $(t/pp)/e$ $(t/pp)/e$
       ────────────────────────────────────── C
                     $(t/pp)/e$

And the right, as generated above, would be of cat $(vp\backslash pp)/e$:

(66)   a book   to Mary   and a record to Susan
       ────────────────────── ────────── ──── ╲   ╱
       $(vp/pp)\backslash((vp/pp)/e)$ $vp\backslash(vp/pp)$ Conj   ╲   ╱
       ────────────────────────────────── FC   ╲   ╱
              $vp\backslash((vp/pp)/e)$ $vp\backslash((vp/pp)/e)$
       ── C
                            $vp\backslash((vp/pp)/e)$

In each case, these phantom constituents *could* combine with two arguments to form a sentence — a *pp* and an object NP in the first case, and a ditransitive verb and a subject NP in the second case. But obviously, the two categories $(t/pp)/e$ and $vp\backslash((vp/pp)/e)$ cannot combine simply with *each other* to form (63). We can however generate (63) if we first apply the type raising rule (10b) to the ditransitive verbs, as in (67):

(67) $(vp/pp)/e$ $+ \, vp\backslash((vp/pp)/e) \Rightarrow vp$
      ───
      $vp/(vp\backslash((vp/pp)/e)) + vp\backslash((vp/pp)/e) \Rightarrow vp$

The left half of the example in question now proceeds as in (68),

(68)

Bill	gave	and	Max	sold

$$t/vp \quad vp/(vp\backslash((vp/pp)/e)) \quad \text{Conj} \quad t/vp \quad vp/(vp\backslash((vp/pp)/e))$$

$$\underline{\qquad\qquad\qquad\qquad}\text{FC} \qquad \underline{\qquad\qquad\qquad\qquad}\text{FC}$$

$$t/(vp\backslash((vp/pp)/e)) \qquad\qquad t/(vp\backslash((vp/pp)/e))$$

$$\underline{\qquad\qquad\qquad\qquad\qquad\qquad\qquad}\text{C}$$

$$t/(vp\backslash((vp/pp)/e))$$

and now this category will take the expression in (66) as argument to form a sentence.

This is different from type raising as used before, however, in that the input FA rule in (67) is not a rule used by the basic grammar but only one that plays a role in the extended grammar (because its argument cat only has members by virtue of FC). In some abstract sense, perhaps, it might be regarded as a 'higher-order' type raising rule analogous to the higher-order slash feature in (64). The deeper significance of this analogy, if any, cannot be pursed here.

9. NON-CONSTITUENT CONJUNCTION WITHOUT STEEDMAN-STYLE EXTRACTION

The analysis of extraction developed in Ades and Steedman (1982) and Steedman (1985) has been assumed up to this point. While this is a highly interesting theory for several reasons, it must be conceded that it is not yet clear whether all extraction in English, much less in all natural languages, can be successfully treated by this method without over-generating the class of truly well-formed sentences. If Steedman-type extraction is not ultimately successful, does this imply that the treatment of non-constituent conjunction is thereby also rendered unfeasible? The answer, it turns out, is no.

A complete categorial theory of grammar for natural languages will undoubtedly require a fairly elaborate theory of syntactic features, somewhat like that of Generalized Phrase Structure Grammar, to describe morphologically complicated languages in any case (cf., e.g., Bach, 1983), and I am not aware of any reason why a GPSG-style 'slash-feature' analysis of unbounded extraction could not be adopted, in some form, into a categorial grammar of English or other languages. In such a theory, a combinatory operation of functional composition

could still be used, for other syntactic purposes, without danger of
losing the tight 'control' over extraction that GPSG affords by means of
'slash introduction' and 'slash elimination' syntactic rules, where 'slash'
is a syntactic feature quite distinct from the categorial-grammar 'slash
category' that is relevant for defining functional application and composition. For example, relative pronouns in such a theory would not
be assigned to the category $R/(S/NP)$ as suggested above but rather
$R/S_{[+slash]}$, and the further 'propagation' and elimination of the feature
[+slash] would be controlled by feature-passing conventions and slash-
elimination rules, not via functional composition. Barbara Partee has
suggested, in fact, that there may be various reasons for limiting functional composition to the description of 'bounded' syntactic phenomena
while appealing to slash-features and feature-passing conventions for
the description of unbounded phenomena. (The problem of 'clitic
climbing' in French (Finer, 1982)[8] might be a good example of a
motivation for functional composition independent of the motivations
in this paper or in Steedman's work.)

In this envisioned theory, there would be no reason to expect
extraction-island constraints (which would be, in effect, limitations on
the slash-feature-passing conventions) to be reflected in the non-constituent conjunction data (which would involve functional composition)
in the way discussed in Section 6 of this paper.

There is, however, an interesting assymetry here. I believe that it
would *not* be reasonable to maintain a functional-composition analysis
of extraction like Steedman's without also adopting a functional-composition analysis of non-constituent conjunction. The reason for this is
simply that all the ingredients needed for the FC-analysis of non-
constituent conjunction are already present in the FC-analysis of
extraction — functional composition itself, plus the 'floating' type
assignment to NPs, which Steedman (1985) has independently proposed for Dutch to treat the 'verb-raising' construction. In fact, it would
seem difficult if not impossible to avoid this sort of analysis of non-
constituent conjunction, once Steedman's analysis of extraction is
adopted. This seems to imply that a defender of the FC-analysis of
extraction is forced to predict the correlation between extraction island
constraints discussed in Section 6 (because island constraints *are* constraints on FC in that analysis), though the defender of the FC-analysis
of non-constituent conjunction is not necessarily committed to the
prediction that this correlation will be found.

10. CONCLUSION

The two theories of coordination compared here, GPSG and Categorial Grammar *cum* functional composition, make very different predictions about the kinds of coordinate conjuncts we should expect to find in natural languages. The first predicts that conjuncts should essentially consist of constituents — the same constituents that the phrase structural rules produce. The second predicts that not only the 'basic' constituents (in the sense of *basic grammar* mentioned in Section 1) but also any 'extended' constituent can be a conjunct — i.e. any continuous group of words combinable by the basic rules, functional composition, and type raising (with island constraints possibly limiting the options somewhat). In either theory there is of course the possibility of adding a 'patch' to add or exclude further kinds of possible conjuncts, but each such patch detracts from the generality and therefore the appeal of the theory: it is only to the extent that the actual natural language facts come relatively close to the pure kinds of conjunction mentioned above that either theory has its predictive success.

The 'patch' that GPSG currently adds to constituent conjunction is the Gapping schema (69) (cf. Sag, Gazdar, Wasow, Weisler, to appear),

$$(69) \qquad V^2_{[CONJ\ \alpha]} \rightarrow \alpha, X^{2+}$$

where $\alpha \in \{and,\ but,\ nor,\ or\}$

though at the price of an unformalized, non-compositional interpretive procedure that 'matches' constituents in the gapped conjunct with certain ones in the previous clause or VP in as yet unknown ways. But, at the same time, it is claimed that NCC can be reduced to Gapping, and thus (69) is supposed to produce NCC sentences as well. This approach can generate most of the NCC examples discussed here (modulo the unformalized interpretive rule), but it does not predict any interaction between Gapping/NCC and island constraints. Actually, this approach would distinguish between *John drove to Chicago on Monday and Detroit on Tuesday* and the ungrammatical **John saw the girls yesterday and boys today*, because the remnant *Chicago* is an X^2 while *boys* is not. However, it would not predict the contrast in (45)—(47) (i.e. with *read a book about Reagan* vs *read Bill's book about Reagan/ destroy a book about Reagan*). Moreover, it would not obviously distinguish (70a) from the ungrammatical (70b) without further machinery,

(70) (a)   John drove to Chicago in the morning and Detroit in the
           afternoon.
     (b)   *John drove to Chicago in the morning and Detroit the
           afternoon.

because nothing in (69) requires that any of the constituents in the
schema correspond to *adjacent* constituents in the previous conjunct or
sentence. (The present framework does require this, of course.)

Though an analysis of Right Node Raising is a prominent feature of
Gazdar (1981), both Gazdar *et al.* (1985) and Sag *et al.* (1985) are
completely silent on the subject of RNR; perhaps the extraction analysis
of RNR in Gazdar (1981) interferes with some of the later theoretical
developments in GPSG, such as IDLP format. But not even this extraction analysis can account for the examples in (54) and (55), where the
right-node-raised phrase is not a constituent. The categorial functional
composition analysis of NCC in this paper, on the other hand, covers
both NCC and RNR by grammatical processes motivated elsewhere in
the grammar; it interprets all these structures by the very same semantic
rules used everywhere else; it predicts the interaction of both these
processes with extraction island constraints and, in fact, accounts for
all the data discussed in this paper. However, this analysis will not
generate Gapped sentences, because of the *adjacency property* of
Steedman's theory. To generate (71) for example,

(71)   John ate rice, and Mary, beans.

by the methods used in this paper, we would not only have to generate
Mary beans as an 'argument string' constituent, but would also have to
generate *John rice* as an argument string in the left clause so that we
could conjoin it with *Mary beans*, and the adjacency property would
prohibit us from doing this. Thus the present theoretical framework
requires us to conclude that Gapping is a different process from
NCC/RNR in English. An alternative analysis of Gapping (perhaps of
the kind in Sag *et al.*, 1985) is thus the 'patch' that this theory will need
— though (69) is a patch which covers a smaller hole in the grammar's
output than it covers in Gazdar *et al.*'s analysis.

On the matter of Gapping in other languages, it might well be
pointed out that Gapping *could* be analyzed as a species of non-
constituent in VSO and SOV languages in the present approach, as long

as the order of gapped and whole clauses is (72) in the first case and (73) in the second:

(72)   VSO (Conj) SO
(73)   SO (Conj) SOV

But of course, it was pointed out in Ross (1970) that exactly these orders of gapped and whole clauses appears to be universal properties of VSO and SOV languages!

How one views the 'exceptional' status of English Gapping that the present theory forces us to accord it depends on whether one is convinced, via Hudson's (1982) arguments, the considerations mentioned in Section 3, or other reasons, that Gapping should not be collapsed with NCC in English in the first place. If one already believes they are separate processes, then this theoretical result of the present framework merely confirms that view. If one firmly disbelieves this, then it suggests either that alternatives to Steedman's categorial framework should be sought which do not have the adjacency property, or that the whole approach is misguided. If one has no opinion either way, then I suggest that the success of the present approach to NCC and RNR might be one good reason to seek a separate treatment of English Gapping. But these are not questions to be any further pursued here.

ACKNOWLEDGEMENT

This paper has benefitted, to a surprising degree, from timely and appropriate remarks and suggestions from a number of colleagues. When I showed Corbett's example ((29) in this paper) to Jerry Sadock, he suggested it was an instance of non-constituent conjunction; when I showed it to Mats Rooth, he proposed it was derived by type raising. It eventually occurred to me that perhaps both were right, and the present analysis was the result. For other helpful comments, on this analysis and its predecessor, I am indebted to Gerald Gazdar, Jack Hoeksema, Dick Hudson, Geoffrey Huck, John Nerbonne, Richard T. Oehrle, Barbara Partee, Graham Russell, and Greg Stump. This research was supported by a Faculty Professional Leave from Ohio State University, NSF grant no. BNS-8306067, and a grant to the Center for Advanced Study in the Behavioral Sciences from the Alfred P. Sloan Foundation.

NOTES

[1] Actually, these authors require not just the functional composition rule described here, but, for certain kinds of sentences, a generalized version of functional composition which they call *generalized partial combination*. For any categories $X_1 \ldots X_n$, the rule is:

$$A/B + (\ldots (B/X_1)/ \ldots /X_n)/C \Rightarrow (\ldots (A/X_1)/ \ldots /X_n)/C$$

This form of functional composition is not needed for any examples discussed in this paper, except two sentences in Section 7 and Section 8, and will be ignored here; see Ades and Steedman (1982) and Steedman (1985) for details, and Note 10 of the latter for the semantic interpretation of the generalized rule. Functional Composition has been proposed as an enrichment of categorial grammars in a large number of recent papers; see, again, these two works cited for references to many of these.

[2] Steedman's NP-complement category does not appear to be of this type, however, but $X/(X/NP)$, where NP is (I assume) the NP category that appears in Stage IIIb below and X is a 'verbal' category.

[3] This gives the higher-order readings, but it retains the different categories for grammatical functions of NPs. An alternative which uses the same category for all NPs at this stage but does not arise directly from Stage II via a type-lifting rule is the PTQ system Stage IIIa': Here, I introduce the abbreviation NP for the PTQ category common to all NPs:

Stage IIIa':

(2) $vp/(t/vp)$ $+ \ t/vp \Rightarrow vp$ (1) $t/vp + vp \Rightarrow t$
   TVP   NP   NP

(3) $TVP/(t/vp) + t/vp \Rightarrow TVP$
   TTVP   NP

(4) $pp/(t/vp)$ $+ \ t/vp \Rightarrow pp$
   P   NP

I will not pursue the question whether Stage IIIa or Stage IIIa' is the more appropriate next step for the grammar. After adding the rule in (17), the grammar could then be further systematized by replacing vp in the object-taking categories in Stage IIIa or IIIa' by VP; when this is done to Stage IIIa', the result is the so-called 'Universal Grammar' type system, which is also that of Keenan and Faltz (1978).

[4] The reason I suggest including definite and indefinite descriptions at this stage is that I believe such NPs do not have the properties, in their first use by children, that require us to treat them as generalized quantifiers for 'adult' grammars. Also, the proposal below that (adult) grammars actually involve 'floating' types for NPs suggests that a possible way of building a bridge between generalized quantifier theory and Kamp's Discourse Representation Theory (and Heim's File Card Semantics), in which indefinite NPs are treated like names, would be to treat indefinites and definites as of type e in 'Donkey' sentences and cases where they need to establish discourse referents, but of the generalized quantifier types in cases where their quantificational properties become essential.

[5] In Steedman (ms.), directional functional composition rules are proposed which also allow functors to be composed when their slashes lean in different directions. Since only 'unidirectional' functional composition seems to be relevant for the data discussed in this paper, I omit discussion of the more complex possibilities and take no stand as to whether Steedman's additional rules are needed for other problems.

[6] Several people have pointed out to me that the unusual singular construction *this man and woman* only seems appropriate, in their judgment, if the two individuals referred to are a couple or are otherwise naturally associated with each other in some way. Thus Graham Russell (per. com.) finds it very odd to say *This recipe for rhubarb pie and telescope were found in the castle*. Perhaps some of this effect is due to the use of the proximal deictic *this*, which by its normal semantics would in this sentence imply that both objects were in the same proximally indicated place and thus not likely to be together by chance; if so, at least some of the strangeness should vanish in *a telescope and recipe for rhubarb pie were* . . . or *Every telescope and rhubarb pie recipe were.* . . . Any oddness remaining in these last two examples (and I am not a relevant judge here, because in fact *all* these examples sound equally fine to me) is presumably due to implicature, though whether generalized conversational implicature or conventional(ized) implicature attaching to rule (32″) may be hard to determine. In any case, the construction is too productive to be considered simply a list of idioms, so such a rule is necessary in a grammar, and these observations do not so much show that (32″) is wrong as far as it goes (it is truth-conditionally correct), but that it is possibly incomplete in not including conventional implicature. Given the highly language-specific nature of the rule (cf. main text below), it is not surprising that this rule might have an implicature that other English conjunction rules lack.

[7] An interesting question to ask is whether there is semantic motivation for treating the verb as functor to the adverb, as there is for example from intensional verbs for treating the verb as (higher-order) functor to the quantified object NP. One possibility that I know of is the reading of the sentence *John found the money, but he quickly hid it again* which does not entail that John hid the money for a second time but only that the money became 'not readily visible' for a second time; as pointed out in Dowty (1979), this reading seems to require that *again* be treated as an argument of *hide*, or else that some other non-standard analysis of the construction be given.

[8] Finer's own analysis (Finer, 1982) uses functional composition only in the semantics, not in the syntactic analysis (which is rather a GPSG metarule analysis), so a certain amount of work would be necessary to show that a syntactic analysis using functional composition directly would be reasonable here.

REFERENCES

Ades, Anthony E. and Mark J. Steedman: 1982, 'On the Order of Words', *Linguistics and Philosophy* **4**, 517−558.

Bach, Emmon: 1980, 'In Defense of Passive', *Linguistics and Philosophy* **3**, 297−342.

Bach, Emmon: 1983, 'On the Relationship between Word Grammar and Phrase Grammar', *Natural Language and Linguistic Theory* **1**, 65−90.

Bach, Emmon and George M. Horn: 1976, 'Remarks on Conditions on Transformations', *Linguistic Inquiry* **7**, 265−299.

Barwise, Jon and John Perry: 1983, *Situations and Attitudes*, Bradford Books, Cambridge.

Benthem, Johan van: 1985, *The Semantics of Variety in Categorial Grammar, Categorial Grammar*, ed. by W. Buszkowski, W. Marciszewski, and J. van Benthem, John Benjamins, Amsterdam.

Chierchia, Gennaro: 1984, *Topics in the Syntax and Semantics of Infinitives and Gerunds*, University of Massachusetts dissertation.

Cooper, Robin: 1983, *Quantification and Syntactic Theory*, D. Reidel, Dordrecht.

Corbett, Greville G.: 1979, 'The Agreement Hierarchy', *Journal of Linguistics* **15**, 203—224.

Curry, Haskell B. and Robert Feys: 1958, *Combinatory Logic*, Vol. I, North Holland, Amsterdam.

Dowty, David R.: 1975, 'The Montague—Adjukiewicz System of Syntactic-Semantic Categories as a Linguistic Theory of Syntactic Category and Grammatical Relations', unpublished paper, presented at the 1975 annual meeting of the Linguistic Society of America.

Dowty, David R.: 1978, 'Governed Transformations as Lexical Rules in a Montague Grammar', *Linguistic Inquiry* **9**, 393—426.

Dowty, David R.: 1979, *Word Meaning and Montague Grammar*, Reidel, Dordrecht.

Dowty, David R.: 1981, 'Quantification and the Lexicon: A Reply to Fodor and Fodor', *The Scope of Lexical Rules*, ed. by M. Moortgat, H. v. d. Hulst, and T. Hoekstra, Foris Publications, Dordrecht, pp. 79—106.

Dowty, David R.: 1982, 'Grammatical Relations and Montague Grammar', *The Nature of Syntactic Representation*, ed. by Pauline Jacobson and Geoffrey Pullum, Reidel, Dordrecht, pp. 79—130.

Finer, Dan: 1982, 'A Non-Transformational Relation Between Causatives and Non-Causatives in French', *Proceedings of the First West Coast Conference on Formal Linguistics*, ed. by D. Flickinger, M. Macken and N. Wiegand, Stanford University Linguistics Department, Stanford, pp. 47—59.

Flynn, Michael: 1983, 'A Categorial Theory of Structure Building', *Order, Concord, and Constituency*, ed. by Gerald Gazdar, Ewan Klein, and Geoffrey K. Pullum, Foris Publications, Dordrecht, pp. 139—174.

Gazdar, Gerald: 1980, 'A Cross-Categorial Semantics for Conjunction', *Linguistics and Philosophy* **3**, 407—409.

Gazdar, Gerald: 1981, 'Unbounded Dependencies and Coordinate Structure', *Linguistic Inquiry* **12**, 155—184.

Gazdar, Gerald, Ewan Klein, Geoffrey Pullum and Ivan Sag: 1985, *Generalized Phrase Structure Grammar*, Harvard University Press/Blackwell's: Cambridge.

Geach, Peter T.: 1972, 'A Program for Syntax', *Semantics of Natural Language*, ed. by Donald Davidson and Gilbert Harman, Reidel, Dordrecht, pp. 483—497.

Hoeksema, Jack: 1983, 'Plurality and Conjunction', *Studies in Model-Theoretic Semantics* (Groningen-Amsterdam Studies in Semantics, Vol. 1), ed. by Alice G. B. ter Meulen, Foris Publications, Dordrecht, pp. 63—84.

Hoeksema, Jack (ms.): 'On the Structure of English Partitives', unpublished paper, University of Groningen, 1984.

Horn, George M.: 1974, 'The Noun Phrase Constraint', Doctoral dissertation, University of Massachusetts, Amherst, Indiana University Linguistics Club.

Hudson, Richard: 1982, 'Incomplete Conjuncts', *Linguistic Inquiry* **13**, 547—550.

Jacobson, Pauline: 1983, Colloquium Paper presented at the 1983 Annual Meeting of the Linguistic Society of America.

Keenan, Edward L. and Leonard M. Faltz: 1978, *Logical Types for Natural Language*, UCLA Occasional Papers in Semantics, No. 3, UCLA Department of Linguistics, Los Angeles.

Lambek, Joachim: 1958, 'The Mathematics of Sentence Structure', *American Mathematical Monthly* **65**, 154—170.

Lambek, Joachim: 1961, 'On the Calculus of Syntactic Types', *Structure of Language and its Mathematical Aspects*, American Mathematical Society, Providence, pp. 166—178.

Lewis, David K.: 1972, 'General Semantics', *Semantics for Natural Language*, ed. by Donald Davidson and Gilbert Harman, D. Reidel, Dordrecht.

Maling, Joan M. and Annie Zaenen: 1982, 'A Phrase Structure Account of Scandinavian Extraction Phenomena', *The Nature of Syntactic Representation*, ed. by Pauline Jacobson and Geoffrey K. Pullum, D. Reidel, Dordrecht, pp. 229—282.

McConnell-Ginet, Sally: 1982, 'Adverbs and Logical Form: A Linguistically Realistic Theory', *Language* **58**, 144—184.

Nerbonne, John A.: 1982, '"Phantoms" in German Fronting: Poltergeist Constituents?', Paper presented at the 57th Annual Meeting of the Linguistic Society of America.

Partee, Barbara and Mats Rooth: 1983, 'Generalized Conjunction and Type Ambituity', *Meaning, Use and Interpretation of Language*, ed. by R. Baeuerle, Christoph Schwarze, and Arnim von Stechow, Walter de Gruyter, Berlin, pp. 361—383.

Pollard, Carl: 1985, 'Lectures on Head-Driven Phrase Structure Grammars', Lecture notes, Stanford University, February 1985.

Quine, W. V.: 1966, 'Variables Explained Away' (1960), *Selected Logic Papers*, Random House, New York.

Rooth, Mats and Barbara Partee: 1982, 'Conjunction, Type Ambiguity, and Wide Scope "or"', *Proceedings of the 1982 West Coast Conference on Formal Linguistics*, ed. by D. Flickinger, M. Macken and N. Wiegand, Stanford University Linguistics Department, Stanford, pp. 353—362.

Ross, J. R.: 1980, 'Gapping and the Order of Constituents', *Progress in Linguistics*, Mouton, The Hague, pp. 249—259.

Russell, Graham: 1983, 'Constituent Coordination', paper presented at the Spring meeting of the Linguistics Association of Great Britain, University of Sheffield, March 23—25, 1983.

Sag, Ivan: 1976, 'Deletion and Logical Form', Doctoral dissertation, MIT (Published in book form by Garland Publishers, 1980).

Sag, Ivan and Gerald Gazdar: 1981, 'Passives and Reflexives in Phrase Structure Grammar', *Formal Methods in the Study of Language*, ed. by J. A. G. Groenendijk, T. Janssen, and M. Stockhof, Mathematical Centre, University of Amsterdam, Amsterdam, pp. 131—152.

Sag, Ivan, Gerald Gazdar, Thomas Wasow and Steven Weisler: 1985, 'Coordination and How to Distinguish Categories', *Natural Language and Linguistic Theory* **3**, (1985), 117—172.

Schachter, Paul and Susan Mordechay: 1983, 'A Phrase-Structure Account of "Non-Constituent" Conjunction', *Proceedings of the West Coast Conference on Formal Linguistics*, Vol. 2, ed. by M. Barlow, D. Flickenger, and M. Wescoat, Stanford Linguistics Association, Department of Linguistics, Stanford University, Stanford, pp. 260—274.

Steedman, Mark (ms.): 'Combinators, Categorial Grammars, and Parasitic Gaps', unpublished paper, School of Epistemics and Dept. of Artificial Intelligence, University of Edinburgh.

Steedman, Mark J.: 1985, 'Dependency and Coordination in the Grammar of Dutch and English', *Language* **6**, 523—568.

Veltman, Frank: 1981, 'Data Semantics', *Formal Methods in the Study of Language*, ed. by J. Groenendijk *et al.*, Mathematical Center, Amsterdam, pp. 541—566.

von Stechow, Arnim: 1974, 'ε-λ kontextfreie Sprachen: Ein Beitrag zu einer natuerlichen formalen Semantik', *Linguistische Berichte* **34**, 1—33.

Zalta, Ed: 1985, 'A Comparison of Two Intensional Logics', unpublished paper, Center for the Study of Language and Information, Stanford University.

Dept. of Linguistics,
Ohio State University,
Columbus, OH 43210, U.S.A.

JACK HOEKSEMA AND RICHARD D. JANDA

IMPLICATIONS OF PROCESS-MORPHOLOGY FOR CATEGORIAL GRAMMAR

0. INTRODUCTION

0.1. *Preliminaries*

Language can be approached from many points of view. Indeed, its very vastness prevents one from seeing all of it from a single perspective. It is for this reason that the logician H. B. Curry, in his intriguing, though somewhat neglected article 'Some Logical Aspects of Grammatical Structure', compares the study of language with the case of the six blind men and the elephant. According to the story, each blind man touched a different part of the animal, and the one who had it by the tail thought it was like a rope and the one who touched a leg claimed it was like a pillar, and so on. In the study of language, however, it sometimes seems as if the blind men are not really blind: they merely close their eyes to the reality of the elephant. A case in point is the study of morphology, where, after a period of relative neglect, there is now a vigorous ongoing debate about the properties that a restrictive general theory of word-formation and inflection should have. In this paper, we take the position that some recent proposals are restrictive only because they ignore many of the readily available data. This includes most varieties of categorial grammar, insofar as they deal with morphology at all. The main goal of this paper is to propose an extension of categorial grammar in order to enable it to deal with the complexities found in the morphological systems of natural languages.

Notwithstanding the fact that Categorial Grammar is referred to by a proper name, it is not really a single system of syntactic description. Rather, it is a family of related systems which all have in common that they make a primarily semantically-based distinction between functions and arguments. In the simplest such systems, functions and arguments are rigidly and unambiguously associated with particular expressions. In more sophisticated systems, such as the categorial calculus proposed in Lambek (1958, 1961), the number of categories associated with each expression is unlimited and so is the number of possible operations on

199

Richard T. Oehrle et al. (eds.), Categorial Grammars and Natural Language Structures, 199—247.
© 1988 *by D. Reidel Publishing Company.*

these categories (although the categories all derive from a small number of basic categories and the rules from a few basic principles of combination). A fixed function/argument structure is not imposed. Yet, at the same time, concatenation is the only way to combine two expressions in this system. More flexibility in the rules that combine expressions is introduced in some recent variations on the categorial theme, in particular Bach (1984, and elsewhere), as well as Curry (1961) and Lewis (1972), who propose to unleash all the power of transformations on categorial grammar.

The question we address here is: Where between the extremes of the Ajdukiewicz/Bar Hillel systems and the powerful systems envisaged by Curry and Lewis is a theory of categorial grammar located which is both adequate and restrictive? In particular, we want to investigate the possibility of keeping the function/argument structure fixed, while extending the operations on expressions. This means that we will not be looking into the possibilities and problems of adding type-raising operations of various kinds. But before we embark on our mission, let us take a quick look at the history of our topic.

0.2. *Historical Background*

0.2.1. *Item-and-Arrangement versus Item-and-Process*

American structuralist linguistics divided its loyalties between two competing approaches to grammatical description, dubbed by Hockett (1954) 'Item-and-Arrangement' (IA) and 'Item-and-Process' (IP).

In the Item-and-Process approach, the emphasis is on the relation between words in a language — in particular, on the ways in which sets of related words are derived from common bases by the application of certain processes (such as affixation, vowel-replacement, compounding, etc.). In short, the Item-and-Process system of description is designed to model the notion of a derivational relation (where 'derivational' is intended in the sense 'involving a derivation', rather than 'involving derivational, as opposed to inflectional, morphology').

It has been noted many times that there is a straightforward diachronic interpretation of this notion. Indeed, this seems to be one of the reasons why the IP model has been so appealing to many linguists. Yet it must be stressed that there is also a synchronic interpretation of derivation — as a means to describe patterns in the vocabulary of a language at a given point in time.

The Item-and-Arrangement model, on the other hand, is mainly concerned with the formalization and clarification of the constituency-relation — that is, with the ways in which words and phrases can be sliced up into their parts. No attention is thereby paid to the question of what the source of complex words is, and there is no obvious diachronic interpretation for its central notion of constituency.

Interestingly, this very fact has sometimes been used as an argument in favor of the IA model, because it prevents any possible confusion between historical and synchronic interpretations. For example, Hockett (1954, pp. 386—387) writes:

... [I]f it be said that the English past-tense form *baked* is 'formed' from *bake* by a 'process' of 'suffixation', then no matter what disclaimer of historicity is made, it is impossible not to conclude that some kind of priority is being assigned to *bake*, as against either *baked* or the suffix. And if this priority is not historical, what is it?

In the 1940s and 1950s, various ways of formalizing the IA model were considered (cf., e.g., Wells, 1947; Harris, 1951; and Chomsky, 1956). One possible formalization is context-free phrase-structure grammar, but it is not the only one, and in fact it was not the one which influential structuralists such as Wells and Harris preferred. They opted for a system which explicitly allowed discontinuous constituents. As Hockett notes, the very fact that IA was formalized, whereas IP was primarily used by descriptively-oriented linguists (mostly students or followers of Sapir), served to give the former approach credentials that the latter seemed to lack. One of the goals of Hockett's paper was to argue that the IP approach can be formalized quite elegantly in terms of mathematical logic when one views the set of expressions of a language as an algebra and the processes as the operations of that algebra. This, of course, is trivial for present-day Montague grammarians, but it was new and surprising in the early 1950s. To be sure, Hockett cannot be said to have formalized the IP model, since he neither provided a list of the allowed operations nor defined them rigorously.

0.2.2. *Subsequent Developments*

In more recent times, there has been an upsurge of interest in the old debate between the two theories of grammatical description, especially among morphologists. On the one hand, a number of IA theories of morphology have been proposed. These include Williams' (1981) and Selkirk's (1982) arboreal theory of word-structure and McCarthy's (1979, et seqq.) autosegmental or 'prosodic' morphology, to mention just two of the more influential lines of reseach. McCarthy's theory differs from Selkirk's in that it drops the assumption of surface-continuity for constituents in order to account for the type of morpheme-intertwining that one finds in languages like Arabic. Actually, though, despite the fact that McCarthy himself points out similarities between his approach and the 'long-component' analysis of Harris (1951), his descriptions are not cast entirely in IA terms. This is so because he sometimes indulges in rules of 'delinking', 'relinking', and (effectively) metathesis, which can only be viewed as processes, referring as they do to input and output-forms. Due to this and other factors, the generative power of McCarthy's autosegmental system is not at all easy to determine. Clearly, the system is at least as powerful as context-free phrase-structure grammar, since we can view phrase-structure trees as special or degenerate cases of multidimensional autosegmental representations. In contrast to Selkirk and (to some extent) McCarthy, there are proponents of processual statements in morphological descriptions, such as Matthews (1965, 1972), Aronoff (1976), Anderson (1977, 1982, 1984), and Zwicky (1985) — to name just a few — who maintain that IA models, even though they may be quite successful in particular instances (for example in the treatment of agglutinative languages such as Japanese), are not general enough to deal with morphological phenomena overall. None of these authors, however, adopts a categorial approach.

In a recent paper, though, Schmerling (1983a) has contended that Montague's Universal Grammar, which she views as a formalization of the IP model, is superior to the dominant theory in current syntax, X-bar theory, which clearly is a variant of the IA model and in fact has quite a few characteristics in common with Harris' method of syntactic description. In contrast to Montague's general framework, the best-known varieties of categorial grammar, such as Bar-Hillel's bidirectional system (cf. several of the papers in Bar-Hillel, 1964), are strictly IA systems. It is to the more recent variations on the categorial theme (Schmerling's work; cf. also Schmerling, 1983b, along with Dowty, 1978, 1979 and Bach, 1983, 1984) that we must turn for a more processual point of view, as well as to Curry's 1961 paper.

In the following sections, we review some morphological phenomena that make it necessary to extend categorial grammar beyond mere application and concatenation — in other words, that is, beyond the limits of the IA model. When the number of combinatory operations increases considerably, it is no longer convenient to encode them by means of the familiar slashes. Instead, we adopt a notational convention proposed by Bach and represent every function-category as a triple consisting of: (1) the argument or input-category, (2) the value or output-category, and (3) the operation performed. For example, the English determiners have the categorial specification ⟨CN, NP, Pref⟩, since they take common-noun constituents as their arguments, have noun-phrases as their values, and are combined with their arguments by prefixation (that is, by concatenation to the left). As a matter of fact, it is sometimes necessary to refer to more than just the category of an argument-expression. In some cases, we must also specify some of the semantic and even some of the phonological properties of the argument expression in the first element of the triple, as in the case of the English determiner *an*, which combines only with vowel-initial common-noun phrases (cf. the discussion in Section 1.2.1. below).

The further organization of this paper is as follows. We first distinguish four main types of morphological operations: addition, permutation, replacement, and subtraction. (This classification, we should add, is pretheoretical and does not correspond to the actual rules that we introduce below.) Then we demonstrate that all of these operation types figure prominently in the morphology of a significant number of languages, also discussing noteworthy subtypes of each operation. The goal of our investigation is to see just how much we must add to a bidirectional concatenative categorial grammar in the way of descriptive options so as both to keep it linguistically honest and to make it an insightful approach to the analysis of natural language. Of course, most of the data below are neither new nor obscure. However, we feel that it is time for all the relevant facts to be collected in one place so that an assessment can be made of the usefulness of current categorial grammars for purposes of morphology. We begin with the most common morphological operation, addition.

1. ADDITION

Morphological rules of addition include compounding and affixation.

We will say very little in this paper about compounding (but see Dowty, 1979, Fanselow, 1981, Moortgat, 1983, 1984, and Hoeksema, 1984, for fuller discussion of this phenomenon within categorial grammar). Leaving aside compounding, then, we make a distinction between context-free additions, which refer only to the categories of expressions, and context-sensitive additions, which may also refer to the phonological shape of the bases involved. Following recent work in morphology (e.g. Marantz, 1982), we consider reduplication to be a subcase of affixation and so include it here as a special type of context-sensitive addition.

1.1. *Context-free Addition*

Context-free additions are limited to suffixations and prefixations — which we would like to bring together under the rubric 'extrafixations' (based on Latin *extra* 'outside'). In a sense, these constitute the simplest type of addition; in categorial grammar, they can be handled quite elegantly in terms of application and concatenation. Examples of extrafixation include the English inflectional progressive-marker *-ing*, which is productively suffixed to verbal stems, and also the English derivational affix *re-*, which can be prefixed to most transitive verbs. Of course, there are semantic restrictions on *re-* affixation: in particular, the base verb must denote a process, not just a state; cf. the relative unacceptability of **relike the dog* vis-à-vis *rewash the dog*. Such restrictions are probably best dealt with by using partial functions in the interpretation of the affix ('semantic filtering') and will not concern us here.

Clearly, no revision of the categorial model is required by context-free addition. On the other hand, it is quite remarkable that some analysts (e.g., Lieber, 1980; Williams, 1981; Selkirk, 1982; and Strauss, 1982) take this type of operation to be the only normal case and thus propose descriptive models which really apply only to this type of morphology. The wealth of processual morphology to be reviewed below makes such a restrictive theory untenable, however desirable it may seem from a metatheoretical point of view.

1.2. *Context-sensitive Addition*

By 'context-sensitive addition', we understand three distinct types of operations: (a) extrafixations that are sensitive to phonological or morpholexical properties of bases or arguments but that in no sense copy any part of the latter (i.e., that are not assimilatory — or dissimilatory), (b) infixations, regardless of whether or not they involve any copying, and (c) reduplications in a broad sense (by which we mean to include both traditional reduplication and also extrafixations which involve any degree of either assimilation or dissimilation). Each type is problematic for the most restricted type of Item-and-Arrangement (viz., context-free phrase-structure grammar), though not necessarily for the IA approach in general.

1.2.1. *Form-sensitive Extrafixation*

Examples abound of affixes that are particular about the phonological properties of the bases they attach to. For example, the English de-adjectival verb-forming suffix *-en* occurs only after monosyllabic roots ending in an obstruent, preceded optionally by a sonorant — as in, e.g., *blacken, loosen, tighten,* and *worsen* (cf. Siegel, 1974). Likewise, the Dutch plural-affix *-s* is attached productively to nouns ending in a vowel, or in schwa followed by a liquid or nasal, but only sporadically to other nouns (especially borrowed ones; cf. van Haeringen, 1947). Very common are cases where each of several different allomorphs of a single morpheme reflects one out of a number of different classes of arguments on the basis of differing phonological properties found in the latter. For instance, the English indefinite article *a* selects common-noun phrases with an initial consonant, while its variant *an* selects ones with an initial vowel; similar phenomena obtain in many dialects for the English definite article and in a great many languages for articles generally (cf., e.g., French, Italian, Spanish, etc., etc.). Hankamer (1973) and Janda (1987) mention a number of cases where allomorphs are sensitive to the number of syllables in a base. For instance, in the Australian language Dyirbal, the 'transitive verbalizer' suffix *-mal* is attached to a bisyllabic base, but the allomorph *-(m)bal* is attached to bases that are trisyllabic or longer (monosyllabic bases do not occur); similar facts can be found in other Australian languages (cf. Dixon, 1972, especially pp. 85—86).

It is not impossible to handle such facts in a context-free phrase-structure grammar — as long as features are permitted that recapitulate phonological properties of expressions. For example, we could postulate one binary feature distinguishing bisyllabic from other polysyllabic verbs in Dyirbal, and another to distinguish English nouns beginning with a consonant from those beginning with a vowel. Of course, this is really no surprise, because the use of features allows one to do many things that seem to be outside the domain of context-free systems. However, there is an obvious drawback to such uses of features: they repeat information which is available elsewhere, in the phonological specifications of expressions. Such features are completely superfluous once direct reference to the forms of expressions is allowed.

To allow for context-sensitive additions of this type in a categorial system, it is sufficient to add a specification of the phonological requirements made by a functor-expression in the first part of an ordered triple. In this scheme of things, the English article *a* requires an entry like $\langle$/CX/N, NP, Pref$\rangle$, for example, whereas *an* requires $\langle$/VX/N, NP, Pref$\rangle$. (Alternatively, one of these two entries could be simplified and made the default case — in this instance, presumably that for *a*.) We speculate here that, on the segmental level, a prefix may be sensitive only to the initial part of its argument, and a suffix only to the final part of its argument, while both may be sensitive to more global prosodic properties such as the number of syllables, the position of stress, and so on. We return to this issue later on.

1.2.2. *Infixation*

1.2.2.0. Infixation in general. In a series of papers starting in 1979, Bach has proposed a version of categorial grammar that allows the insertion of an argument expression either after the first part or before the last part of a complex phrase. This proposal is motivated by facts like the following. It has frequently been noted that syntactic rules may refer to the margins of expressions. For instance, many languages have clitics that must occur immediately to the right of the first word or constituent in a sentence (this was noted as early as 1892, by Wackernagel). Well-known examples of such clitics are the Latin conjunction *-que*, the Finnish question-marker *-ko/-kö*, the Warlpiri auxiliaries, and so forth. (For the growing literature on this subject, see, e.g., Klavans, 1980; Steele *et al.*, 1981; Kaisse, 1982, 1985; and Nevis, 1985.) Less numerous are instances of elements that must occur in immediate pre-final position, but one example is provided by the English and Dutch conjunctions, which usually precede the last element in a string of like elements (cf. *Tom, Dick, and Harry; signed, sealed, and delivered; the first, second, and third papers*, etc.). Another example concerns certain bound pronouns in the Australian language Ngançara; these encliticize to the element preceding the last constituent, which is the verb (cf. Klavans, 1980). (More rarely, these clitics can also attach to the verb itself, in which case they occur in final position.)

1.2.2.1. *Morphological Infixation.* Morphological data illustrating the same pattern are not hard to find. Many languages have an infix occurring immediately after the first — or before the last — consonant or syllable of a word. Ultan, in his 1975 typological study of infixation, mentions that the position of infixes is almost always defined with reference to a marginal constituent. Consider, for example, the Chamorro verbal infix *-um-*, which occurs with certain intransitive verbs in the non-future tense when their subject is singular. (When the subject is plural, the prefix *man* is used instead; cf. Topping, 1973, pp. 83 ff.)

(1)   *Singular*

    (a) *gumupu yo'*   (Verbal stem: *gupu*)
       'flew'   'I'   = 'I flew'

    (b) *sumaga yo'*
       'stayed' 'I'   = 'I stayed'

    (c) *kumuentos i   lahi*
       'stood up'   'the' 'man' = 'the man stood up'

(2)   *Plural*

    (a) *manggupu siha*
       'flew'   'they' = 'they flew'

    (b) *mañaga siha*   (from *mansaga*, by morphophonemic change)
       'stayed' 'they' = 'they stayed'

    (c) *manguentos siha*
       'stood up'   'they' = 'they stood up'

The infix *-um-*, by the way, is found in many Austronesian languages, including Toba Batak and Tagalog. Another common infix in Austronesian languages is *-in-*, whose use includes, among other things, the nominalization of verbs, as in the following Chamorro examples:

(3)   *Verb*   *Nominalization*
       hasso   'think'   *i hinasso*   'the thought'
       faisen 'ask'   *i finaisen* 'the question'
       sangan 'tell'   *i sinangan* 'the thing told'

The important thing to note about these infixes is that they are found as infixes only in consonant-initial words, where they occur precisely after a word's initial consonant. When there is no initial consonant in a word, they occur with it as prefixes. (In Chamorro, however, according to Topping, vowel-initial words are actually always preceded by a glottal stop, phonetically, so we might in fact just state the rule governing the distribution of the morphemes in question as insertion after the first consonant of a word.) As a matter of fact, it has sometimes been argued that the Austronesian infixes arose through metathesis of prefixes (and Moravcsik, 1977, makes the even stronger crosslinguistic claim that all instances of infixation must be accounted for in this way). For example, Anderson (1972) has argued that the nasalization facts of Sundanese call for underlying forms where the surface-infix *-al-/-ar-* occurs as a prefix (or is at least not underlyingly present as an infix). Now, Stevens (1977) has pointed out some problems for Anderson's account, but Stevens' contention that the plural-infix cannot possibly have started out as a prefix has been refuted by Pullum and Zwicky n.d. We will not take a stand on this issue here, but rather just point out that, since we accept and motivate rules of metathesis later on in this paper, our framework is compatible with Moravcsik's claims.

As expected, there are also infixes that occur before the final element of their hosts. In the Mayan language Tzeltal, a group of numeral classifiers is derived from verbs by infixation of *h* before the final consonant (when the latter is a stop or an affricate; in all other cases, *h* is deleted — cf. Kaufman, 1971). Examples of this phenomenon include the following: *huht* 'holes', from *hut* 'be perforated'; *lihk* 'ropes, cords', from *lik* 'carry', and *peht* 'handfuls of wood', from *pet* 'embrace (below the arms)'.

1.2.2.2. *Formalizing morphological infixation.* Given the above second- and penultimate-position phenomena, both in syntax and in morphology, it is useful to consider extensions of the categorial model that allow a limited type of infixation — viz., infixation in second or prefinal position. Bach's wrapping-rules serve this purpose. To formalize these rules, Bach (1984) introduces the following analytical operations:

(4)   Let x be the string $x_1 \ldots x_n$.
   (a) FIRST(x) = x_1
   (b) RREST(x) = $x_2 \ldots x_n$
   (c) LAST(x) = x_n
   (d) LREST(x) = $x_1 \ldots x_{n-1}$

The operations RWRAP and LWRAP can now be defined in terms of these operations:

(5)   RWRAP(x, y) = FIRST(x) y RREST(x)
      LWRAP(x, y) = LREST(x) y LAST(x).

Bach provides evidence for the usefulness of these rules from a number of languages, including English (cf. especially Bach, 1979), Dutch (cf. Bach, 1984, where the so-called 'verb-raising' structures are derived by infixing an auxiliary verb before the verb-cluster[1]), and Amharic (where the definite article is suffixed to the first word of a noun-phrase; cf. Bach, 1975, 1983, 1984). The Dutch facts are especially interesting because they involve the LWRAP-operation, unlike most of the other examples, and also because they make it necessary to further elaborate the wrapping-operations. In order to make sure that an inserted auxiliary verb forms a syntactic constituent with the other verbs, it must be stipulated that the verb is adjoined to the verbal cluster and not just inserted in front of it. This suggests a division of LWRAP into two distinct operations:

(6) (a) LWRAP-pref(x, y) = (LREST(x) (y LAST(x)))
    (b) LWRAP-suff(x, y) = ((LREST(x) y) LAST(x))

The first operation prefixes the element y to the last element of x, whereas the second one suffixes y to the 'left rest' of x. Both types of rules are needed — the first, for the Dutch verb-clusters; the second, for the description of the Ngançara bound pronouns mentioned earlier. Obviously, we must make similar adjustments for RWRAP:

(7) (a) RWRAP-pref(x, y) = (FIRST(x) (y RREST(x)))
    (b) RWRAP-suff(x, y) = ((FIRST(x) y) RREST(x))

It should be noted that LWRAP-pref, etc. are preferable to simple

LWRAP, etc. in that the latter involve ternary concatenation rather than binary operations of prefixation and suffixation.

The wrapping-operations defined so far do not quite suffice for the description of infixation-phenomena, since they all insert an element y after the first — or before the last — constituent of a phrase x. However, it must also be possible to insert elements immediately after the first or before the last word. For example, Kaisse (1982) (following earlier work by Steele, 1981, and ultimately Wackernagel, 1892) notes that Luiseño and Ancient Greek particles sometimes are inserted after the first word of a sentence, thus often interrupting its initial phrase. To deal with cases like this, it may be useful to introduce the operations FIRST* and LAST*, which look all the way down into a phrase to find, respectively, its first and last individual parts[2] — formally:

(8) (a) FIRST*(x) = FIRST(x') where x' is the result of erasing all phrasal brackets in x
    (b) LAST*(x) = LAST(x').

The corresponding wrapping-operations are just like the ones above, differing solely in involving the operations FIRST* and LAST* instead of FIRST and LAST, respectively.

1.2.2.3. *Parameters for marginality.* So far, we have considered only cases where the relevant margin consists of either a phrase or a word. When we look at morphological data, however, it becomes clear that the notion 'marginal element' may be interpreted in many more different ways. Sometimes, the margin in question is a single consonant, but sometimes it is a consonant-cluster, and sometimes it is a syllable or even a metrical foot.

It is not unlikely that the phonological size (in terms of segments or syllables) of an infix-relevant margin is related to the size of the affix whose positioning is dependent on it. For example, the Austronesian infixes are small, and they are inserted after the first consonant of a word, whereas the so-called 'expletive infixes' of English are foot-sized, and consequently precede the last — or follow the first — metrical foot (according to McCarthy's 1982 analysis).[3] In Dakota, some verbal stems allow infixation of pronominal affixes, all of which are at least syllable-sized, while a few are disyllabic. When inserted, they occur after the first CV (cf. Moravcsik, 1977), as shown by the following forms of the verb *manu* 'to steal':

(9)   *mawanu*   'I steal'
        mayanu   'you steal'
        maungnu 'you and I steal'
        etc.

A clear case of infixation after the initial consonant-cluster of a word is found in the Yurok language of northern California (cf. Robins, 1958). The intensive-infix, whose basic allomorph is *-eg-*, is inserted after the onset of the first syllable in order to express intensity, plurality, or iteration. Examples (from Robins, 1958, pp. 81—82) include:

(10) (a) *cyu · k'ʷen* 'to sit'   *cyegu · k'ʷen* 'to sit often'
     (b) *ho · kʷc*   'to gamble'   *hego · kʷc*   'to gamble often'
     (c) *cwinkep*   'to talk'   *cweginkep*
     (d) *trahk*   'to fetch water' *tregahk*
     (e) *lkyorkʷ*   'to watch'   *lkyegorkʷ* [4]

Alternatively, one might view this as insertion before the first vowel (as Oehrle has suggested to us), perhaps using Vergnaud's 1977 notion of (vowel-)projection. Such an analysis would also be feasible for Austronesian infixation (cf. the Chamorro data discussed above — in fact, Topping (1973) has made exactly this suggestion). We believe, however, that prefixation to the first vowel is not as straightforward an option as one might initially assume. First of all, it is not sufficient to specify the position of the affix with respect to the first element of the vowel projection. One must also specify its position with respect to the consonants. Here, it is not possible to refer to the consonant projection only, since the infix must follow the last consonant to precede the first vowel. Second, the infix itself must be divided up over two projections itself, since it contains a vowel and a consonant. Neither one of these objections is necessarily damning, but they do suggest that prefixation to the first vowel is not obviously going to give a simpler description. At a deeper level, one might worry what other types of 'prefixations' and 'suffixations' would become possible: prefixation to the first nasal sound, suffixation to the last stop? For the present, we feel it is safer to stick to a somewhat more structurally oriented theory of infixation in terms of margins and phonological constituents, although other phenomena discussed later in this paper likewise suggest allowing for a richer set of options.

Another instructive case of infixation is nasal infixation in Atayal, an Austronesian language of Taiwan. The facts are rather complicated (cf. for details Moravcsik, 1977, who cites previous work by Egerod), but it is roughly true to say that *m* and *n* are infixed after the first consonant of a verb to indicate imperfective and perfective animate-actor focus, respectively. For example, cf. *hmop* and *hnop*, both of which are derived from *hop* 'stab'. Interestingly, when there is a word-initial consonant-cluster, the nasals are still inserted after the first consonant, even when this seems to go against universally favored patterns of syllable-structure: cf., e.g., *smpung*, from *spung* 'cut'; *smgagai*, from *sgagai* 'take leave'; *lmpuu*, from *lpuu* 'count', etc. Sometimes, however, clusters are simplified, in which case the infix may come after the second consonant in the base form, but after the first consonant in the resulting surface-form of a word: thus, for example, *kmziap* is derived from *skziap* 'catch', and *rmau* from *prau* 'help'. In other cases, the nasals are prefixed or else replace initial consonants. To some extent, the choice made among these options is lexically governed (cf. the pairs *siunau* 'demand' vs *smiunau* (infixed), on the one hand, and *sina* 'demand' vs *msina* (prefixed), on the other hand). In any case, for the clear instances of infixation in Atayal, we obviously need to say that an infix comes after the first consonant of a word, not after the first onset.

In accounting for such phenomena, we assume that there are a number of levels of analysis simultaneously available for rules to refer to, and we further assume that what counts as a marginal element is different on each level. For a reasonably complete description of all the options, we need levels for at least all of the following:

(11) (a) Segments
    (b) Subsyllabic constituents (onsets, nuclei, and codas)
    (c) Syllables
    (d) Metrical feet
    (e) Words
    (f) Phrases

There is perhaps also a need for a morpheme-level; we discuss this issue briefly below.

The operations FIRST and LAST must be specified for the level-parameter, so that $\text{FIRST}_{seg}(x)$ is the first segment of x, FIRST_{syl} the first syllable of x, and so on (where the subscripts are keyed to the above list). Corresponding to these parametrized versions of FIRST

and LAST, we can define parametric versions of the wrapping opera-
tions — e.g. RWRAP_{seg} for insertion after the first segment, LWRAP_{cod}
for insertion before the last coda, etc.

Sometimes, a rule of combination is not itself a wrapping operation,
but rather one partially specified in terms of wrapping. For instance,
Austronesian infixation is usually restricted to words that begin with a
consonant. When the first segment is a vowel, there is prefixation. We
can describe this state of affairs by the following rule of combination:

(12) $F(x, y) = \text{RWRAP}_{seg}(X, Y)$ if $\text{FIRST}_{seg}(x)$ is a consonant;
        $= \text{PREF}(x, y)$ otherwise

It should be mentioned that such a conditional rule is not needed if we
adopt Oehrle's abovementioned suggestion that Austronesian 'infixation' be treated as immediately prevocalic. Still, the strategy of defining
certain morphological operations in terms of more elementary ones is
very useful, and we rely on it later in this paper. Not all combinations of
operations are found, to be sure, and we could posit some constraints
here. For instance, note that the condition in (12) refers to the first, and
not, e.g. to the last, element of the base. This makes sense, given that
the operation to be performed is RWRAP and not LWRAP. As we
have noted before, affixes seem to be sensitive to the segmental-phono-
logical properties of adjacent material only.

Another thing to note here is that, in general, we expect RWRAP to
alternate with prefixation, since both of them involve left margins, and
we similarly expect LWRAP to alternate with suffixation. We are not
aware of any counterexamples to this claim, so we state it here as a
hypothesis:

(13)   *Hypothesis*
        Rules that combine RWRAP and suffixation and rules that
        combine LWRAP and prefixation do not occur.

An obvious question about infixation concerns whether it is always
defined with respect to margins consisting of a single unit, or whether
there are also infixes that are inserted before or after a string of units.
The literature on infixation does not abound with examples of this type,
but a few candidates can be found in Broselow and McCarthy's 1983/
1984 study of reduplicative infixation. In Nakanai, an Austronesian
language of New Guinea, there is a small set of words with the following pattern (cited from Johnston, 1980, pp. 149):

(14)   *haro*   → *hararo*   'days'
       velo   → *velelo*   'bubbling forth'
       baharu → *baharu*   'widows'

Broselow and McCarthy assume that these cases have a reduplicative infix VC which is inserted before the final VCV-string and copies the first two elements of that string. The VC-string is not a unit; rather, it is a foot minus the initial consonant. Note that there is an alternative account for these facts in which the VC-infix is inserted directly after the final consonant and copies the last elements of the preceding string. This alternative analysis can be implemented by using a wrapping-operation and the machinery for reduplication we develop below. However, Broselow and McCarthy do not opt for this solution, because other infixes may be inserted before the final foot, it appears, and hence they also analyze VC-infixation cases like the following as instances of prefixation to a metrical foot:

(15)   *abi*   *ababi*   'getting'
       kaiamo   *kaiamamo*   'residents of Kaiamo village'

The cases in (14) do not show prefixation to the final foot, but rather infixation in that foot, according to Broselow and McCarthy, because "the extremely restrictive phonotactics of this language would permit no other position . . . [;] we find the infix lodging in the nearest position to foot-initial that is phonotactically permissible, just before the stressed vowel" (*op. cit.*, p. 74). This consideration is suggestive at best, but nothing forces us to give up the alternative suggested above, and so Nakanai does not show that we need a more general set of wrapping operations.

Another possible problem case is internal reduplication in the Salishan language Lushootseed:

(16)   *Plural Reduplication*
       stúbš 'man'   *stúbubš* 'men'
       ʔíbac 'grandchild'   *ʔíbibac* 'grandchildren'

This process involves copying the first VC-substring of the base. According to Broselow and McCarthy, the VC-infix is positioned after the initial CVC-string (which actually should be C_1VC, given the first example above). They claim that, historically, the bases in question were derived from CVC-roots, and so, in principle, we could analyze the data by wrapping the infix between the root and its extension (using the morphemic level). However, Broselow and McCarthy note that borrowings which do not have CVC-roots undergo the same reduplication process. One could take this to be evidence that the optimal analysis involves the insertion of the reduplicative infix after the initial CVC string, and thus make a case for a more powerful version of the wrapping operations. However, as in the Nakanai case, there is an obvious alternative — namely, placing the infix after the initial consonant-cluster and copying the material directly following it. Similar alternatives exist for the other internal reduplications considered by Broselow and McCarthy, and so we tentatively conclude that the wrapping-operations considered here are sufficient for the description of morphological infixation.

1.2.2.4. *Infixes versus circumfixes.* It may be noted here that there are two kinds of functors for every type of wrapping: those that wrap around their arguments (e.g. English complex transitive verb-phrases, on Bach's analysis) and those that are inserted into their arguments. The latter kind of functors, we call infixes; the former, 'circumfixes' (the term 'ambifix' is also used). Morphological examples of circumfixes are rather rare. Dutch has the affix combination *ge-* . . . *-te*, which is used to mark collectives. This combination must be considered a single item, synchronically, since it attaches to nouns, whereas its part *ge-* is attached to verbs and *-te* to adjectives, and also since it is not interpreted compositionally. Examples include:

(17) (a) *gebeente*   'bones' (cf. *been* 'bone')
     (b) *gebergte*   'mountain range' (cf. *berg* 'mountain')
     (c) *geboefte*   'scum' (cf. *boef* 'crook, criminal')
     (d) *geboomte*   'woods' (cf. *boom* 'tree')
     (e) *gedierte*   'animals' (cf. *dier* 'animal')
     (f) *gevogelte* 'birds' (cf. *vogel* 'bird')

Even clearer examples of circumfixes can be found in other, especially Austronesian languages, where it sometimes happens that at least one of the two discontinuous parts does not occur as a prefix or a suffix by itself.

In principle, it is possible to deal with cases like the above in terms of application and concatenation. For instance, let the category of *-te* be $N \backslash X$, where X is some category that is picked up by only one functor — viz., *ge-*, which would have the category *N/X*. Our reasons for not preferring this type of solution are as follows: (1) it is ad hoc, in that it introduces an otherwise unmotivated category *X*, and (2) it fails to recognize the semantic unity of the *ge-. . .-te* combination. In addition, it can be said that, as soon as we admit infixation operations into our armamentarium of descriptive apparatus, we get circumfixes for free, in the sense that we do not need additional operations to handle them.

Nevertheless, it is in fact questionable whether there is any need for circumfixation as a primitive operation in morphology. Rather, that surface-phenomenon can be achieved via simultaneous operations of prefixation and suffixation (which were already introduced here previously and will be discussed again briefly in the next section). That is, just as a semantic value can be associated with a single morphological process (i.e. operation), so such a value can be associated with a conjunction of processes. This situation is independently attested in cases where a morphological category is always marked by a combination of discontinuous elements/operations at least one of which is not a prefix(ation) or suffix(ation). Here, there is no possibility of an analysis with wrapping-circumfixation. For example, the negative of non-future verbs in the Muskogean Amerindian language Chickasaw is marked simultaneously by prefixation of *k-*, infixation of a glottal stop before the last consonant (if it is not part of a cluster), and replacement of the final vowel with *o*. Thus, the non-future negative of e.g. *losa* 'be black' is *-kloʔso* 'not be black' (cf. Janda, 1982a, 1983b, and references there).

Evidence for the correctness of such an approach comes from the fact that the simultaneous operations found in morphological circumfixation — and in other examples of what can be called 'multifixation' — usually also occur by themselves, individually, as the marker of one or more other morphological categories. In other words, the Dutch case discussed above (where the formal extrafix-shapes *ge-* and *-te* occur independently as well as in combination) is the normal one — also reflected, for example, in Chickasaw. On the other hand, the occasional Austronesian situation also previously mentioned (where at least one half of a circumfix does not occur by itself) is relatively rare. Furthermore, there exist numerous complex morphological processes which have no alternative analysis as circumfixation, either because they perform operations at three non-adjacent places in a string (as in the

Chickasaw non-future negative) or because they involve at least one non-additive operation — e.g., prefixation plus replacement, infixation plus permutation, or suffixation plus subtraction (some of which will be illustrated below in later sections).

As pointed out by Janda (1982b) for process-morphology in general and by Schmerling (1983b) for categorial morphology in particular, such instances of single morphological categories marked by combinations of morphological processes can be handled rather elegantly by establishing for the grammar of every natural language a list of semantics-free formal morphological operations which are accessed — alone or in combination — by particular rules (functions) of morphology (each rule consisting, as we also here suggested above, of an ordered triple with argument/input, semantic value/output, and one or more operations). This approach is advantageous not only for operationally-complex morphological rules but especially also for operations that figure in several rules (like Dutch *ge-* and *-te*). Probably the most spectacular example where the same formal operation appears in more than one morphological rule is provided by Modern High German, where Umlaut appears in over sixty rules — sometimes alone and occasionally with prefixes, but usually with suffixes (cf. Janda, 1982a, 1982b, 1982c). For further, discussion of the 'rule-constellations' defined by such recurrent operations in morphology, see Janda and Joseph (1986), Joseph and Janda (1986).

In light of such considerations, then, it is indeed plausible — if not preferable — to analyze morphological circumfixation and other multi-fixations as combinations involving simultaneous prefixation, suffixation, and/or infixation (or reduplication, to be discussed presently), rather than as primitive operations. Consequently, it is not clear that the wrapping-rules discussed earlier need ever be exploited for any other purposes than treating infixation in morphology and e.g. second-position clisis in syntax.

1.2.2.5. *A note on prefixes and suffixes.* Notwithstanding the considerations just mentioned, the parameters for wrapping introduced above are useful, not just for the description of infixes and second-position clitics, but also for suffixation and prefixation. When a functor-expression is attached to the edge of a phrase, it sometimes forms a phonological constituent with a proper part of that phrase. The standard example of this phenomenon is the English phrasal affix *-'s*, as in such examples as *the King of England's crown* (cf. Bloomfield, 1933, and Schmerling, 1983b, for discussion, as well as Janda, 1980, 1981 on diachronic aspects of this affix). We analyze *-'s* as a functor that takes a noun phrase as its argument and combines with it by adjunction to its last word. Formally, *-'s* has the category $\langle$NP, Det, Suff$_{wor}\rangle$, where Det is the category of determiners (defined earlier on in this paper), and *wor* indicates the word-level. Suff$_x$, of course, means suffixation to the last constituent on the *x*-level.

We are now in a position to formulate a constraint on context-sensitive addition — in fact, one hinted at above:

(18)   *Constraint*
Prefixation (suffixation) on level *x* is sensitive only to the properties of the leftmost (rightmost) constituent on that level.

1.2.2.6. *Infixation and generative power.* The addition of wrapping rules to a standard bidirectional categorial grammar with just application affects the generative capacity of the grammar, since it allows it to accept at least some context-sensitive languages as well — such as the *xx*-languages, in which every sentence consists of two identical strings over some alphabet. This increase in power is illustrated by the fact that Bach (1984) has been able to use it to give an adequate characterization of the crossing dependencies in Dutch which, as Bresnan *et al.* (1982) have shown, are beyond the strong generative capacity of context-free phrase-structure grammars. This analysis can be extended to the Swiss German dialect described in Shieber (1985), which is not even weakly context-free. It is likely that the languages which can be characterized by systems with wrapping operations form a proper subset of the context-sensitive languages.

1.2.2.7. *Reference to heads.* Affixes and other bound elements, such as clitics, usually occur next to either marginal constituents or the head of a phrase or word. To account for this phenomenon, Pollard (1984) and Hoeksema (1984) — independently and within somewhat different frameworks — have both proposed to introduce operations on heads into otherwise strictly concatenative systems. As a matter of historical fact, the original formulation of RWRAP in Bach (1979, p. 516) was in terms of heads, not of margins:

(19)   RWRAP: (i) If a is simple, then $\text{RWRAP}(a, b) = ab$;
        (ii) If a has the form $[_{XP} X\ W]$, then
        $\text{RWRAP}(a, b) = X\ b\ W$

Many of the examples that we have so far given of affixation to margins can be reanalyzed as examples of affixation to a head constituent, because in many cases the head is a peripheral element. This is trivially true in binary-branching structures, but even in structures with more than two constituents, the head typically occurs at the periphery. Thus, for example, the insertion of direct objects into English complex transitive verbs can be reanalyzed as a head-adjunction, rather than as a case of RWRAP. This is in fact proposed by Pollard (1984). A similar treatment could be given for the Dutch verb-cluster. On the other hand, most second-position clitics do not submit to such a reanalysis, and it likewise seems that most cases of morphological infixation cannot be dealt with in this manner either. Hence it is clear that at least some facts call for operations which refer to margins. Let us now consider some of the evidence for rules referring to heads.

It has frequently been noted that compounds are inflected in the same way as their heads. In Dutch, for instance, there are several possible plural endings, including *-s*, *-en* and *-eren*. The choice between these alternatives is determined, for non-compound words, to some degree by rhythmical factors (cf. van Haeringen, 1947), but it is nevertheless often quite arbitrary. In the case of nominal compounds, however, the plural-ending is always predictable: it is that of the head-constituent. This is even clearer in German, where there are more ways to form plurals (e.g. *-s, -e, -er, -(e)n*, Umlaut, *-e* plus Umlaut, *-er* plus Umlaut, zero-marking, etc.), but the choice of plural marker for a particular word is again largely lexically-determined. In compounds, the plural-marker is that of the head-constituent; cf. *Vater* 'father' vs *Väter*; *Grossvater* 'grandfather' vs *Grossväter*; *Buch* 'book' vs *Bücher*; *Wörterbuch* vs *Wörterbücher*, and so on. In English, irregular plurals can be used to illustrate the same situation (cf. *tooth/teeth*; *wisdom-tooth/wisdom-teeth*). We can explain these facts if we assume that the plural morphology is expressed on the head in all these cases. Suppose we postulate a general operation PLUR, which puts nouns into their plural forms. Then, we can state the following: If y is the head in $x + y$, then $\text{PLUR}(x + y) = x + \text{PLUR}(y)$.

Head operations come in several varieties. The most common type is affixation to the head component. Other possibilities, such as modification of the head-component (e.g. by vowel-replacement) are also attested; cf., for instance, the above-mentioned case of irregular plural compound nouns in English. We do not claim that all plurals of compounds arise by head-operations, however. For instance, in cases such as *sit-in, push-up, take-over,* and other nouns derived from verb + particle combinations, there is no clear head, and so the English plural-rule has to operate on the whole compound (by default). This might also explain why the exocentric (headless) compound *sabertooth* does not have the plural **saberteeth*, but rather *sabertooths* (cf. Kiparsky, 1982).

For a formalization of head-operations, the notion 'head' must be defined first (see Zwicky, 1984, for a thorough discussion of the literature on heads and some of the problems involved in defining the notion). In recent work in GPSG, the notion 'head' is viewed as a primitive concept (cf. Gazdar and Pullum, 1981). In our view, it is better to consider it a derivative notion, definable in terms of the more basic notions 'function' and 'argument'. Following an idea of Vennemann's (cf., for instance, Vennemann and Harlow, 1977), we define the head of a functor + argument combination $f(a)$ as follows:

$$(20) \quad \text{Head}(f(a)) = a \text{ if } \text{Cat}(a) = \text{Cat}(f(a))$$
$$= f \text{ otherwise}$$

The basic idea behind this definition is that the head-constituent determines the category of the phrase. In general, the output-category is a fixed category specified by the functor category. When the functor is a modifier, on the other hand, one may view it as an operator performing the identity operation on the category of its argument, in which case the argument is the element determining the category of the combination.

Vennemann's definition gives straightforward and largely uncontroversial results in syntax, since it makes the verb the head of a verb-phrase, the noun the head of an adjective + noun combination, the preposition the head of a prepositional phrase, and so on. In English compounds, the head-constituent must clearly be the rightmost one, since the left-hand part functions as a modifier. The right-hand head rule proposed for English compounding by Williams (1981) and others follows automatically from the present definition.

In some cases, it may be necessary to refer, not to the head-constituent of a phrase or a word, but rather to its lexical head. For instance, the lexical head of compounds of the form $[X[YZ]]$ is Z, not

[YZ]. This notion can be defined recursively as follows (cf. Hoeksema, 1984, p. 59):

(21)   *Definition*
   The lexical head of a construction C is:
  (i) C if C is simplex;
  (ii) the lexical head of the head of C otherwise

Cliticization to verbs is a case of adjunction to a lexical head, since verbs are always lexical heads, but not always heads, of sentences. For instance, in *Sue talks*, the verb *talks* is the head, whereas in *I drink 7-UP* the verb is the lexical head, though not the head, of the sentence (the head is the phrase *drink 7-UP*).

1.2.3. *Reduplication*

Yet another type of context-sensitive addition is *reduplication*. Usually, a distinction is made between total and partial reduplication. In the case of total reduplication, a complete word is repeated, as in Latin *quisquis* 'whoever', derived from the pronoun *quis* 'who' by reduplication — or its parallel in Sundanese, *sahasaha* 'whoever', the reduplicated form of *saha* 'who'. A simple way to deal with total reduplication is to introduce an elementary operation *Red* on strings, defined as:

(23) $Red(x) = xx.$

But then, one must also have a retriplication operation for some languages, e.g. Mokilese, where continued action is expressed by retriplication of the verb, as evidenced by examples such as *rikrikrik* 'to continue to gather', from *rik* 'to gather'. We could add another primitive operation here for retriplication, but there is no reason why we should allow just reduplication and retriplication. With Moravcsik (1978), we assume that linguistic theory should not rule out the possibility of there being a language which expresses a morphological feature by repeating a word 5 or even 55 times. To impose an upper limit on the number of times an element may be repeated is entirely artificial — and also unnecessary, since practical reasons already rule out such complicated morphological devices.

  To make arbitrary multiplication possible, we introduce a rather powerful device for multiplying strings, based on the lambda-calculi. The latter are well known in categorial grammar as a means to express complex functions in the translation language. Its usefulness for syntactic purposes, however, has not been exploited much, although Montague's quantifying-in rules come to mind as examples of substitution operations that could be formulated in terms of lambda-reduction. Operations such as reduplication and retriplication can be defined in a very direct manner in terms of lambda-expressions:

(24)   *Definition*
        Red $= \lambda x[xx]$
        Trip $= \lambda x[xxx]$

It is clear that any type of multiplication can be expressed in this formalism.

The reduplication operation is not obviously associated with a lexical item in the same way that affixation is associated with affixes. In a word like *quisquis*, it makes no sense to decide arbitrarily that the first occurrence of *quis* is the functor and the second one the argument, or vice versa. Instead, we assume that some operations are not associated with any expressions at all.

Partial reduplication involves the repetition of a fixed number of segments from a base. Examples of this type of reduplication are found in many Indo-European languages (including Classical Greek, Gothic and Sanskrit), as well as in most other language families.

We analyze partial reduplication in terms of a nonstandard system of lambda-reduction. First of all, however, we need some notational conventions.

We make a distinction between three types of variables: those ranging over consonants (the set VAR-CONS), those ranging of vowels (the set VAR-VOW) and, finally, those ranging over strings of terms, where terms are either variables or constants (the set VAR-STR). The set of all variables, VAR, is the union of the former sets. As for constants, we distinguish between vowels (elements of the set VOW) and consonants (elements of CONS). The rules of substitution will be restricted in such a way that consonants may replace variables that stand for consonants, but not variables that stand for vowels, while vowels may replace variables ranging over vowels, but not variables ranging over consonants. The union of VAR, CONS and VOW is T, and the set of all strings over T is T^*. The set F of wellformed formulas is the smallest set such that:

(25)   *Definition*

    (i) T^* is a subset of F;

    (ii) if f is in F and v in T then $\lambda v[f]$ is in F;

    (iii) if f and g are in F, then $f(g)$, fg and $(f)g$ are in F;

    (iv) if f is in F and g in T^*, then $f(\mathbf{g})$ and $(\mathbf{g})f$ are in F.

The reduction relation '$\Rightarrow$' on F is defined as follows:

(26)   *Definition*

    (i) $\lambda x[f](a) \Rightarrow f[x/a, \mathbf{x}/\mathbf{a}]$ (i.e. the result of substituting a for every occurrence of x in f, and $\mathbf{a}$ for every occurrence of $\mathbf{x}$), provided that x and a have the same type, and x is a variable

    (ii) $\Rightarrow f$, if x is a constant, and

    (iii) $\Rightarrow f[x/\ ](a)$ otherwise, where $f[x/\ ]$ is the result of deleting every occurrence of x.

    (iv) $f(\mathbf{g}) \Rightarrow \lambda f[f](g)$

    (v) $(\mathbf{g})f \Rightarrow \lambda f[f](g^{-1})$, where g^{-1} is the inverse of g.

The first clause is standard. It allows one to substitute a term-argument of a lambda-formula for every variable bound by the lambda-operator — provided that the term and the variable have the same type. This means that, if the variable is taken from VAR-VOW, then the term must be in either VOW or VAR-VOW. Note that bold variables must be replaced by bold forms of the term. The second clause deals with the special case where the lambda-operator binds a constant (a non-standard feature of the present system, adopted solely to facilitate its operation). In such cases, no substitution takes place; rather, the argument is deleted. This is similar to what happens in the case of vacuous binding in standard systems of lambda-conversion. According to the third clause, if a term does not have the same type as the variable, then the variable (as well as the corresponding lambda-operator) is deleted. The last two clauses introduce an abbreviatory mechanism that allows us to drop lambda-prefixes from our formulas. So, e.g., instead of the cumbersome formula $\lambda C_1 C_2 V[C_1 C_2 V](k)(l)(a)$, which in itself already incorporates several abbreviations, we simply write $C_1 C_2 V(\mathbf{kla})$. The bold text is essential in distinguishing arguments from merely concatenated strings.

    To show how all of this works, we turn briefly to Agta plural-reduplication. This process involves prefixation of a reduplicative *CVC*-morpheme. We derive the form *taktakki* (plural of *takki* 'leg') thus:

(27) $\lambda X[C_1 VC_2(X)(X)](takki)$
     $\Rightarrow C_1 VC_2(\boldsymbol{takki})(takki)$ by λ-reduction
     $\Rightarrow tak(\boldsymbol{ki})(takki)$ by λ-reduction
     $\Rightarrow tak(takki)$ by Definition (26ii).

When an Agta noun does not begin with an initial consonant, its plural-prefix has the form *VC*. This follows from Definition (26iii) — in particular, the requirement that, if an argument does not match the variable it is supposed to replace, every occurrence of the variable is deleted. This is illustrated in the following derivation (for *ulu* 'head'):

(28) $\lambda X[C_1 VC_2(X)(X)](ulu)$
     $\Rightarrow C_1 VC_2(\boldsymbol{ulu})(ulu)$ by λ-reduction
     $\Rightarrow VC_2(\boldsymbol{ulu})(ulu)$ by Definition (26iii)
     $\Rightarrow ul(\boldsymbol{u})(ulu)$ by λ-reduction
     $\Rightarrow ul(ulu)$ by Definition (26ii)

The optionality of the initial *C*-slot, then, does not have to be stipulated in the reduplication rule, but follows from Definition (26iii), which resembles Marantz's (1982) principle of phoneme-driven association in autosegmental morphology.

For further illustration, we next give an example of suffixal reduplication:

(29)   Dakota: *hạska* 'be tall', *hạskaska* 'be tall, pl.'
     Derivation:
     $\lambda X[(X)((X)(CCVC))](hạska)$
     $(hạska)((\boldsymbol{hạska})(CCVC))$ by λ-reduction
     $(hạska)((\boldsymbol{hạska})(CCV))$ Definition (26iii)
     $(hạska)((\boldsymbol{hạ})(ska))$ by λ-reduction
     $(hạska)(ska)$ Definition (26ii)

So-called 'marked' prefixation and suffixation, where the segments are not copied from the initial and final parts, respectively, but vice versa, pose no problem for the present system. For instance, Chukchi marked *CVC*-suffixation can be analyzed as below:

(30)   Chukchi: *nute* 'earth', *nute-nut* 'earth, abs. sg.'
       Derivation:
       $\lambda X[X((CVC)(X))](nute)$
       $(nute)((CVC)(\mathbf{nute}))$ λ-reduction
       $(nute)(nut)(e)$ λ-reduction
       $(nute)(nut)$.   Definition (26ii)

The situation becomes slightly more complex when we consider cases where some of the phonological features of an affix are not copied from its base, but instead specified by rule (or 'pre-linked', in autosegmental models). Here, we need to elaborate the system further, viewing segments no longer as units, but as complex symbols. Substitution will now take place on a feature-by-feature basis. This is perfectly straightforward to implement, and so we will not dwell on it here.

Finally, a word should be said about infixal reduplication. Here, an infix is inserted into a base and forms a constituent with either the part preceding it or the part following it. This part is interpreted in our system as the argument of the λ-expression. Once this has been accomplished, everything else is precisely as in ordinary reduplication. As far as we can see, all the facts mentioned in Broselow and McCarthy's 1983/84 survey of this phenomenon can be captured in this scheme (cf. also ter Mors, 1984, and Davis, 1985, for some improvements on the analysis in Broselow and McCarthy 1983/84; our proposals are compatible with ter Mors' work, but not with that of Davis, who suggests template-driven association for internal reduplication).

By way of illustration, we show how to derive the intensified forms of the adjectives *dánkolo* 'big' and *métgot* 'strong' in Chamorro. The intensive form is derived by infixation of a reduplicative *CV*-affix before the final syllable:

(31)   Infix: $\lambda X[CV](X)(X)$, category: $\langle A, A, \text{LWRAP}_{\text{pref, syl}} \rangle$
       Derivation:
   (I) *dánkolo*: *dánko*-$\lambda X[[CV](X)(X)](lo)$
                  dánko-$CV(\mathbf{lo})(lo)$
                  dánko-lo-lo
   (II) *métgot*: *mét*-$\lambda X[[CV](X)(X)](got)$
                  mét-$[CV](\mathbf{got})(got)$
                  mét-go(t)-got
                  mét-go-got

1.3. *The Adequacy of Competing Morphological Theories*

When extended in the ways that we have proposed above, categorial morphology is able to provide an elegant treatment for all varieties of affixation. Infixation, for instance, can be adequately dealt with in some IA theories (e.g. McCarthy's autosegmental framework; cf. his treatment of English expletive infixation in McCarthy, 1982), though, interestingly, not within Selkirk's, 1982, morphological model). Much more difficult to handle for IA are morphological metathesis, replacement, and subtraction. McCarthy's autosegmental framework, which is not a strict IA theory, explicitly allows such surface-effects, since it permits context-sensitive rules of the form $A \rightarrow B/X\_\_\_\_ Y$, where A, B, X and Y are possibly null (and A is at most a single symbol). In this format, as is well known, roundabout ways of doing metathesis can be formulated. However, it is clear that the autosegmental framework was not designed for doing metathesis. It has been denied by its proponents (e.g. McCarthy, 1979, 1982a) that there is such a thing as morphological metathesis. Therefore, we present evidence for the existence of this phenomenon.

2. METATHESIS AS A MORPHOLOGICAL DEVICE

Before we present our evidence for morphological metathesis, a word is in order regarding the question of why there is such a general pre-theoretical disinclination to believe in the existence of morphological metathesis. In a nutshell, the reason is that it seems possible to express actual rules of metathesis only via the transformational format — which is notorious for its capacity to do literally anything to a string. Hence, if metathesis rules are countenanced, one must also accept, along with them, an all-powerful notation which is available for performing a multitude of operations never found in human languages. Of course, this last situation can be avoided in either of two ways: by imposing constraints on the transformational format or by appealing to the general cognitive constraints on human string-processing abilities that the psychological literature has shown to exist. While most linguists have tried to avoid transformational omnipotence by imposing constraints on their formalism, we do not believe that they have been very successful in this respect. For instance, context-sensitive rules are clearly capable of describing metathesis, and hence autosegmental morphology is, too. Furthermore, the existence of phonological metathesis (disputed by no one) clearly indicates that the operation in question must be available to language-users, anyway.

2.1. *Consonant/Vowel Metathesis*

Our first case of morphological metathesis characterizes the so-called 'incomplete phase' in Rotuman, an Eastern Oceanic language within the Austronesian language family. The discussion here is based on Janda (1984) and the references cited there, most importantly Churchward (1940). (The transcriptions, however, are phonetic rather than phonemic.) Every major-category word in Rotuman can appear in either of two forms: the complete phase, which indicates definiteness or emphasis (for nouns) and perfective aspect or emphasis (for verbs and adjectives), and the incomplete phase, which marks a noun as indefinite and nonemphatic (or 'incomplete') and a verb as imperfective and nonemphatic. The incomplete-phase form is derived from that of the complete phase in what appear to be three different ways: sometimes by apocope (as in *fɛʔén* 'zealous', from *fɛʔéni*), sometimes by apocope with a kind of Umlaut (as in *famör* vs *famóri* 'people'), and, finally, by metathesis (as in *ʔépa* vs *ʔɛáp* 'mat'). There are three strong reasons to derive Rotuman incomplete-phase forms from the corresponding complete-phase forms and not vice versa: (1) consonant-final forms of roots almost exclusively occur in the incomplete phase; (2) certain vowels ([ü, ö, ɔ, ö̃]) occur only in incomplete-phase forms, so that, if the latter are taken as basic, four more phonemes must be assumed underlyingly (in addition, the appearance of [æ] in incomplete-phase forms cannot be predicted if these are basic, which would require a fifth additional phoneme); (3) incomplete-phase forms are always predictable from complete-phase ones, but not vice versa — thus, in the complete phase, *ára* 'mole' contrasts with *áro* 'front', but, in the incomplete phase, we have a single form, *ár*.

Such considerations have led most generative analysts to posit for Rotuman at least one incomplete-phase rule for *CVCV* roots whereby the underlyingly final vowel of a word and the preceding consonant switch places. There are differences of opinion about two further issues: first, whether this switch is accomplished by a rule of direct metathesis, and second, if so, whether metathesis applies in all incomplete-phase forms. It appears likely that, historically, metathesis did indeed occur in all such *CVCV*-roots. After this, vowel-coalescence produced rounded vowels in some cases, while in other cases the saltatory vowel was just eliminated, leaving the appearance of apocope in both cases, as well as Umlaut in the first. In the remaining set of cases, apparent metathesis was the result.

Given these facts, all analysts except autosegmental morphologists have posited a morphological metathesis-rule for Rotuman — morphological because the switch in question occurs only in one morphological category and is not accompanied by any affixation. Many accounts essentially recapitulate the presumptive historical sequence of events, positing a completely general metathesis-rule, followed by a rather complicated set of ad-hoc morphological coalescence-processes. However, Cairns (1976) has shown that the coalescence rules needed for Rotuman are not found in a survey of over 200 languages. Furthermore, it turns out to be simpler, overall, to formulate metathesis in a much more restricted way — namely, so that it applies only when the penultimate vowel is higher than the final one. Thus, in our judgment, the optimal rule for Rotuman metathesis is, in standard transformational notation (but omitting the morphological conditions):

$$(32) \quad /X \quad \begin{bmatrix} V \\ m \text{ high} \end{bmatrix} \quad C \quad \begin{bmatrix} V \\ n \text{ high} \end{bmatrix} / \rightarrow /1\ 2\ 4\ 3/, \quad \text{where } m > n$$

The effects of this rule are illustrated below:

(33)   *Complete Phase*   *Incomplete Phase*

aírɛ	'true'	aiér
púrɛ	'rule, decide'	puér
tíkɔ	'flesh'	tiɔ̌k
úlɔ	'seabird'	uɔ̌l
ʔípa	'pigeon'	ʔi̯áp
fúpa	'distribute'	fu̯áp
séma	'left-handed'	sɛ̯ám
fɔ́ra	'tell'	fɔ̯ár

Nevertheless, proponents of autosegmental morphology (AM) have — apparently independently (cf. Saito, 1981; Besnier, 1983; and van der Hulst, 1983) — rejected the suggestion that there is such a rule of metathesis. Rather, they appeal to various mechanisms of their theory that describe the above facts without metathesis. Their approach assumes that Rotuman is like Semitic, in that the vowels and the consonants of a root belong to different morphemes. If this tack is taken, one can analyze Rotuman incomplete-phase formation as the deletion of the final vowel slot in a *CV*-skeleton. The segment previously associated with this slot next attaches to the vowel-slot associated with the prefinal vocalic segment. The two vowels then undergo various rules of coalescence — sometimes involving deletion, sometimes merger (in spite of the findings of Cairns, 1976, mentioned above), and sometimes glide-formation. It should be noted that the linking of two vowels to the same slot is otherwise regarded as highly marked, in AM. Marantz's (1982) treatment of reduplication, for instance, relies heavily on the convention that a vowel already associated with a template-slot deflects, as it were, any association with that slot by an unlinked vowel; segments remaining unlinked at the end of a derivation are either deleted or treated as simply unpronounced. Crucial to this analysis is the claim that Rotuman vowels and consonants belong to different morphemes. There is no semantic basis for such a claim, but McCarthy (1984:14, 1986:214—217) maintains that there are formal arguments for this separation. As evidence (partly following Saito, 1981), he mentions that Umlaut resulting from vowel coalescence appears to propagate leftward through identical vowels, but we do not find this argument convincing. Morphemes based solely on formal criteria have always been controversial, and to dichotomize consonants and vowels in Rotuman simply because they interact more with themselves than with each other is to go out even farther on very thin ice. (For a related view, cf. now also Steriade, 1986.) We believe that vowel-interactions across consonants are more legitimately handled via Vergnaud's (1977) notion of 'projection', which allows one to place all vowels (or consonants) on the same plane without thereby analyzing them as tautomorphemic. We consequently reaffirm our contention that Rotuman incomplete-phase formation involves a morphological rule of consonant/vowel metathesis.

2.2. *Consonant/Consonant Metathesis*

The above-sketched AM reanalysis of metathesis in Rotuman (and similar proposals for Miwok — cf. Smith, 1985; Smith and Hermans, 1982) rely on the separation of vowels and consonants in different morphemic tiers. Such a move is impossible for cases where two consonants change places.

Consider, first, a case of morphological metathesis in the Chawchilla dialect of Yokuts, as described in Newman (1944, pp. 32, 165, 218—219). The so-called 'consequent adjunctive' of the noun stem *xamit* 'scythe' (from the base *xamat* 'mow') has the shape *xamit-haliy̌* in the subjective case, but the metathesized form *xamit-hay̌l* (with a deleted vowel due to a common and very regular phonological rule of Yokuts) in the other, oblique cases. Likewise, the subjective-case form *paṭṭ-ilin* 'one with many body-lice' corresponds to the form *paṭṭ-inl-* (again with vowel deletion) in the other cases. The metathesis in question is clearly not the result of a phonological rule in Chawchilla, since it is restricted to the morphemes *-haliy̌* and *-ilin*. Near-homophonous sequences involving different morphemes never undergo this process.

A parallel example of metathesis from Semitic has been presented by McCarthy himself in some of the seminal works introducing AM. McCarthy (1981, pp. 380—1), for example, discusses a permutation involving the passive/iterative infix *-t-* of Akkadian. This infix occurs in the so-called 'Gt' (passive — and apparently also reciprocal) and 'Gtn' (iterative) verb-classes of Akkadian. Thus, corresponding to the root /mḫs/ 'strike', there are the respective forms *mitḫas* 'be struck' and *mitaḫḫas* 'strike repeatedly'.

Now, when the first root-consonant is a coronal fricative and is directly adjacent to the *-t-* infix, no change occurs in the infix; thus, from the root /ṣbt/ 'seize', the derived form for 'he will seize' is *iṣtabbat*, as would be expected. However, when the passive/iterative infix is separated from a root-initial coronal fricative by a vowel, McCarthy (1981, p. 381) reports that the two consonants "exchange positions by a metathesis rule". Thus, also from the root /ṣbt/ 'seize', the infixed passive/reciprocal form *ṣitbutum* becomes *tiṣbutum* by metathesis, and, from the root /zqr/ 'elevate', the passive form *zitqurum* undergoes the same permutation and becomes *tizqurum*. Following McCarthy (1981, p. 381 [(7)]), the rule in question can be formulated as follows:

$$(34) \quad \begin{bmatrix} -\text{sonorant} \\ +\text{coronal} \\ +\text{continuant} \end{bmatrix} \quad V \quad \underline{+\,t\,+} \quad X/$$

$$ \qquad 1 \qquad\qquad 2 \qquad 3 \quad 4 \;\rightarrow\; /3\,2\,1\,4/$$

Even though this process is described in McCarthy (1981, p. 381) as being "restricted to a particular conjunction of morphological circumstances", he elsewhere (1979, p. 357) surprisingly describes it as a "well-motivated . . . phonological metathesis rule" — although he offers no justification for this claim. Most probably, McCarthy's reason for denying morphological status to the Akkadian (and Hebrew) -*t*- permutation process was that it is not the sole mark of a morphological category. Rather, it affects a segment whose presence in a form already represents the relevant category. Such processes are usually called 'morphophonemic' or 'morpho(pho)nological'. We, however, hold that any process which explicitly refers to a morphological element constitutes a mark or exponent of that element and so arguably belongs to the domain of morphology. (For an extensive exposition and justification of this view, see Janda, 1987.) Consequently, the Akkadian rule just discussed must be counted as yet another morphological metathesis-rule.

2.3. *Metathesis in Categorial Grammar*

Most versions of categorial grammar are not particularly well-equipped to deal with metathesis. Some systems do not allow any permutation (such as the Bar-Hillel systems), while others (e.g. the system discussed in van Benthem, 1984, and this volume) allow every possible permutation of a grammatical string. What we need are one-place operations on expressions that interchange only a few (typically, two) elements in specified positions.

Interestingly, such operations cannot be said to be associated with particular expressions in the same way that suffixation is associated with suffixes and infixation operations are associated with particular infixes. Formally, we characterize morphological metathesis in terms of a triple $\langle A, B, f \rangle$, where A is the input-category, B the output-category, and f the permutation-operation to be performed. The general format for such operations is:

(35) $f(X\,C\,Y\,D\,Z) = X\,D\,Y\,C\,Z$

This is so because, typically, only two elements change positions. Presumably, C and D can be feature-values, segments, or syllables, although we so far have evidence only for segmental permutations. The other types of permutation are attested in speech errors, however, and we do not see what grammatical principles would bar them from acting as morphological operations, as well.

It seems reasonable to require that Y in (35) not be an essential variable, since we do not find cases of long-distance morphological metathesis where, say, the first and the last consonants of a word are interchanged. However, this presumably follows from a much more general theory about action-at-a-distance. (Cf. also Ades and Steedman's (1982) analysis of WH-dependencies for an example of how a long-distance dependency can be analyzed in purely local terms within categorial grammar.)

3. MORPHOLOGICAL REPLACEMENT

3.1. *Frequency and Productivity*

In contrast to metathesis, which is clearly the least common type of morphological process, replacement (substitution) is extremely common. The fact that replacement frequently cooccurs with other morphological processes is partly responsible for its being somewhat neglected. Also relevant may be the fact that most languages have varying numbers of morphological replacements that are not productive.

This is the case in English, for instance. In that language, tense/aspect alternations like *sing/sang/sung* play an important role in the verbal system, while number alternations like *man/men* and *wife/wives* play a minor role in the nominal system. Contrasts like *wreath/wreathe* even help distinguish the verbal and nominal systems from one another. These alternations, however, form a closed system and so represent unproductive morphological processes. Given this lack of productivity, many morphologists prefer a non-processual analysis and treat, for instance the *man/men* alternation in the following way. In the lexicon, there is a single lexical entry which itself contains two allomorphs — marked as singular and plural, respectively. While we recognize the validity of such an approach, we must point out that it still requires some way of relating the two allomorphs, usually by a redundancy or 'via' rule. Such a rule necessarily states a relationship of replacement.

To make the case for rules of replacement as strong as possible, we will give examples of productive cases below.

3.2. *Javanese Elative Adjectives*

A good illustration of a regular and productive morphological replace-ment-rule is provided by the process of elative formation in Javanese. The relevant facts and issues have been discussed at length by Dudas (1974; 1976, pp. 180—201). The elative is an adjectival category which expresses intensity. Thus, the primary adjective *adoh* means 'distant', whereas its elative counterpart *aduh* means 'very distant'. While elative forms like this are usually accompanied by expressive lengthening and pitch-raising of their final vowel, the one constant characteristic of Javanese elative-formation is that the final vowel of an adjective is replaced by *u* if it is rounded and by *i* otherwise. Such replacement is vacuous in the case of final *i* and *u*. Some illustrations are given below:

(36)	*gloss*	*primary*	*elative*
	'bold'	*wani*	*wani*
	'difficult'	*angel*	*angil*
	'easy'	*gampang*	*gamping*
	'heavy'	*abot*	*abut*
	'refined'	*alus*	*alus*

The vowel that is the input to this replacement-rule is not always identical to the final vowel in an underlying form. This is because there is in Javanese a phonological neutralization-rule which raises and rounds word-final *a*, giving rise to alternations such as *dino* 'day' versus *dinane* 'the day'. Similar facts motivate an underlying form /kəmba/ for *kəmbo* 'insipid'. Since the corresponding elative form is *kəmbu*, not *kəmbi*, we have evidence that the abovementioned phonological neutralization-rule applies before the morphological rule of elative formation. This, by the way, constitutes strong support for those frame-works which allow phonological rules to apply in the lexicon before some morphological operations, as in Lexical Phonology, since elative formation in Javanese is a derivational process.

Javanese elative-formation can be formulated as a triple $\langle A_{\text{prim}}, A_{\text{elat}}, f_{\text{elat}} \rangle$, where f_{elat} is defined thus:

(37) $f_{\text{elat}}(X\, V[x \text{ round}]\, C_0) = X\, V[+ \text{high}, x \text{ back}]C_0$

3.3. *Other Cases*

Outside of Javanese, morphological vowel-replacement is familiarly known as 'Ablaut' or 'gradation'. These terms are also sometimes extended to consonantal and tonal replacement-processes. The seemingly-contrastive term 'Umlaut' (or 'mutation', etc.), on the other hand, is often applied to vowel-replacement operations which are phonologically, rather than morphologically, conditioned. However, processes which were originally phonologically-conditioned often are reanalyzed as morphologically-conditioned rules and concomitantly lose their former phonological triggers. This has happened with Umlaut in English, for example, where the former purely-phonological (even phonetic/allophonic) fronting in pre-Old English *mus/müsi* has ultimately given way to purely-morphological replacement in Modern English *mouse/mice*. Since the term 'Umlaut' is still often applied to these alternations, we are left with the rather confusing situation that (as Sapir, 1921, pointed out) some 'Umlaut' is really Ablaut.

The evolution of formerly-phonological vowel-change processes into purely-morphological Ablaut-processes has not by any means been limited to Germanic languages. As mentioned previously, Rotuman morphology involves not only a metathesis rule but also an Umlaut process, and this latter process is a regular and productive operation of morphological replacement.

It might at first seem that Rotuman incomplete-phase Umlaut is not an independent process, since it is always accompanied by deletion of the final front vowel which helps trigger it. However, this apocope rule also occurs separately from Umlaut, and so it makes sense to factor apocope and Umlaut out from each other as separate operations which may but need not be applied in conjunction. The Umlaut operation can be formulated as follows:

(38) $f(X\,V\,C\,V[-\text{back}]) = X\,V[-\text{back}]\,C\,V[-\text{back}]$

Note that the replacement involves only a single feature-value.

The root-and-pattern morphology of Semitic languages such as Arabic is reminiscent of the Ablaut alternations in the Germanic languages. McCarthy's autosegmental analysis of Arabic verbal morphology, which makes no use of replacement rules, raises the question whether it is possible to analyze, say, English strong verbs in a similar way.

In Classical Arabic verb-stem morphology, the vowels mark tense/ aspect and voice, whereas most consonants belong to the verb root (although some represent derivational affixes). In McCarthy's analysis, this situation is reflected in the fact that vowels and consonants belong to different morphemes, which are represented on different morphemic tiers in a multi-layered representation and are linked to a *CV*-skeleton (i.e. an array of consonant- and vowel-timing slots) which itself has morphemic status. Since this account mainly involves the arrangement and linking of independent morphemes, it is essentially an IA theory. It is not likely, however, that this kind of analysis can be extended to cover all cases of vowel- and consonant-alternation. For instance, we could try to analyze the English verb-forms *sing-sang-sung* in terms of a discontinuous morpheme *s ___ ng* and vocalic infixes /I/, /æ/ and /ʌ/ (such proposals have in fact been made by structuralist morphologists; cf. the discussion in Hockett, 1954). However, while one might assign morphemic status to /æ/ and /ʌ/ (because they mark the past tense and the participle, respectively), there is no basis for assigning morphemic status to /I/, as well, since the present tense is not regularly marked in English. Furthermore, it seems to be the case that the vowel associated with the past tense is predictable to some extent (for those alternations that have some degree of regularity) from the complete present-tense form, but not from the root minus the vowel. This follows naturally on a replacement account, but not if the vowels and consonants of the verb roots are taken to be independent morphemes.

Other cases where we cannot do away with morphological replacement involve so-called 'exchange rules' (cf. Janda, 1987, for a review of the literature on this topic and a demonstration that exchange rules are always morphologically conditioned). Perhaps the best-known instance of an exchange rule is one rule of plural formation in the Nilotic language Dinka. As discussed by Anderson (1974) on the basis of Nebel (1948), a large class of Dinka nouns form their plurals by reversing the vowel-length of their corresponding singulars. Thus *nin* 'sleep, slumber' has the plural *niin*, while *čiin* 'hand' has the plural form *čin*. The simplest way to describe this is in terms of a rule changing the length feature-value of the last root-vowel to its opposite. A nearly identical rule functions to mark the plural of verbs in the California-Yuman language Diegueño (cf. Walker, 1970).

We see no straightforward way to deal with such phenomena in IA terms, since there is no constant element that expresses plurality or singularity. Rather, it is the contrast in length with the singular that expresses plurality here.

A final type of replacement operation involves what is also known as 'truncation' (cf. Aronoff, 1976, following earlier work by Isačenko). Sometimes, an affix is not simply attached to a base, but rather appears to replace part of that base. For example, English words like *evacuee* or *nominee* are derived from the corresponding verbs *evacuate* and *nominate* by suffixation of *-ee* and simultaneous deletion of *-ate*. The result, of course, is effectively replacement of *-ate* by *-ee*. This kind of process is probably best analyzed as involving, not direct replacement, but rather affixation plus deletion (so as to allow a maximally simple account of *-ate* affixation). We will therefore discuss truncation more fully in the next section, which is devoted to morphological deletion.

The format for replacement operations is much the same as that for metathesis. The rules in question are characterized in terms of ordered triples $\langle A, B, f \rangle$ indicating the input category, the output category, and the operation performed on the input expression. As a final illustration, consider the operation involved in Dinka plural-formation:

(39)   PLUR($X\ V[x$ long] (glide) [+ seg]) =
$$X\ V[-x \text{ long}] \text{ (glide) } [+\text{seg}]$$

4. MORPHOLOGICAL SUBTRACTION

As in the case of morphological permutation, subtraction often takes place together with other processes — in particular, with addition. Nevertheless, it is possible to defend subtraction as an independent type of morphological process, since there are numerous instances where the most sensible way to relate two items (one of which is longer than the other) is not by deriving the longer one from the shorter by means of addition, but rather the other way around. This is the case, for instance, if the shorter form is predictable from the longer one but not vice versa.

There are several types of morphological deletion: (1) deletion of segments or groups of segments, (2) deletion of morphemes, and (3) combinations of (1) and (2). We will give examples of the first two types of deletion.

4.1. *Morphemic Subtraction*

Aronoff (1976) discusses at some length a phenomenon he dubbed 'truncation' — the reduction of a word to its 'trunk' by subtraction of a morpheme. Thus, for instance, the English adjective *calculable* must apparently be derived by the subtraction of the verb-forming suffix *-ate* from *calculatable* (which is in fact a free variant of *calculable*, for some speakers). This is because there is no English verb **calcul(e)*, whereas the meaning of the word *calculable* requires that it be related to the verb-stem *calculate*. English Latinate morphology abounds with similar cases of truncation, and the phenomenon is well-attested in other languages, as well.

Consider, for instance, *-en* truncation in German derivational morphology (as discussed by van Lessen Kloeke, 1985):

(40)   *Faden*   'thread'   *Fädchen*   'thread (dimimutive)'
        Wagen   'wagon'   *Wäglein*   'wagon (diminutive)'
        Schaden 'damage'   *schädlich* 'damaging'

Van Lessen Kloeke argues that *-en* has morphemic status in Modern High German (expressing inanimateness, at least in masculine nouns), and so the truncation in question involves a full morpheme. Kiparsky (1982) suggests (in an attempt to explain away all rules of truncation) that we are here dealing with a rule deleting phonological material, which then would make it unnecessary to postulate morphemic status for *-en*. However, the fact that certain verbs do not drop the homophonous infinitival ending *-en* in similar derivations (but in fact undergo the insertion of a *t*) seems to indicate that the deletion in question is not phonologically conditioned, as van Lessen Kloeke points out:

(41)   *hoff-en*   'to hope'   *hoffen-t-lich*   'hopefully'
        fleh-en   'to beg'   *flehen-t-lich*   'imploringly'
        wiss-en   'to know'   *wissen-t-lich*   'knowingly'

Yet another case of truncation can be provided here — from Danish, based on Anderson (1975) and references there. The Danish verb generally shows derived vowel- or consonant-lengthening in its infinitival form, and this can be ascribed to the operation of a general phonological rule of Danish which, in the particular case of infinitives, is triggered by the addition of a schwa-suffix that is visible on the surface. Thus, the traditional analysis of the Danish infinitive is that it is formed from verb stems via the operation of a morphological rule of schwa-affixation, following which there applies the phonological lengthening-rule in question. Exactly the same pattern of vowel- and consonant lengthening, though, is also seen in the Danish verbal imperative — despite the fact that it is not marked on the surface by schwa or any other suffix. Rather than view the lengthening in imperative forms as morphologically conditioned, and so just accidentally identical to that found in infinitives, the traditional analysis (adopted by Anderson) reasons that the imperative is derived from the infinitive — or from a shape formally identical to the infinitive — via morphological deletion of the schwa in the latter.

On this view, then, a schwa is first added to Danish verbal stems in order to form infinitives and imperatives, next triggers lengthening in them, and, in the imperative, finally is deleted. Besides the appearance here of a morphological subtraction-operation, another noteworthy issue involved is the fact that a phonological rule (of lengthening) must be ordered before a morphological rule, in a way parallel to the situation already discussed above for Javanese elative-formation.

4.2. *Non-morphemic Subtraction*

The German truncation of *-en* discussed above has a parallel in the formation of Dutch toponymic adjectives. When the adjectival suffixes *-s* and *-er* appear with a place name, the latter's final *-en* is often absent, cf. e.g.:

(42) | *Place-Name*: | *Toponymic Adjective*: |
|---|---|
| *Groningen* | *Gronings* |
| *Kopenhagen* | *Kopenhaags* |
| *Leiden* | *Leids* |
| *Polen* 'Poland' | *Pools* 'Polish' |
| *Scheveningen* | *Schevenings* |
| *Wenen* 'Vienna' | *Weens* 'Viennese' |
| *Zweden* 'Sweden' | *Zweeds* 'Swedish' |
| *Assen* | *Asser* |
| *Bremen* | *Bremer* |
| *Marken* | *Marker* |
| *Muiden* | *Muider* |
| *Zuidlaren* | *Zuidlaarder* (with regular *d*-insertion) |

(The doubled vowels in closed syllables have no phonological import; they reflect only a peculiarity of Dutch orthography.) The above truncation-rule is not completely automatic, as examples such as *Leuvens* (from *Leuven* 'Louvain') show, but it is fairly regular and is presumably productive.

Non-morphemic subtraction without concomitant addition is exemplified by the Rotuman process of final-vowel deletion in the incomplete phase, which was briefly mentioned before. This morphological subtraction-process operates on all (major-class) words of the form . . . *VCV* whose final vowel is not lower than the vowel of the penultimate syllable (whereas words with a lower final vowel undergo the metathesis rule discussed earlier). Sample illustrations are the pairs for the number 'seven', *hífu/híf*, for the verb 'light up', *fúfu/fúf*, and for the adjective 'undercooked', *hála/hál*.

Evidence for the productivity of the morphological rule in question is provided by the fact that it also applies to loanwords from English, such as *kalápa/kaláp* 'club'. As long as incomplete-phase apocope is ordered after incomplete-phase metathesis and before incomplete-phase Umlaut, it can be given the following simple formulation:

(43) $f_{apo}(X C V) = X C$

Here, f is part of a triple $\langle X_c, X_i, f \rangle$, where X ranges over the lexical categories N, A, and V (whatever their proper categorial formulation may be for Rotuman — an issue we will not address here).

The deletion rules described above are relatively well-behaved rules of apocope. Such rules require only operations that analyze a word into a margin and the rest, just like the wrapping-rules mentioned previously. More analytic power may be required for other cases, but there is a definite tendency for morphological subtraction to occur at the edges of a word or stem.

5. CONCLUSIONS

In the preceding sections of this paper, we have presented an overview of the various types of formal operations that are used for morphological purposes by the languages of the world. This body of evidence exemplifies rules of morphology employing addition (including reduplication), permutation, replacement, and subtraction, as well as combinations of these. We have argued against Item-and-Arrangement models — such as most versions of categorial grammar — which treat morphology (and syntax) in terms of general combinatorial schemes allowing only concatenation (or, in the case of autosegmental morphology, linking of elements on various tiers). The untenability of IA models becomes evident even in the case of infixation, where words have to be analyzed into several substrings which do not have an independent morphological status. It is still clearer in the cases of non-additive morphology discussed above.

The fact that simple prefixation and suffixation are so much more common than the more exotic-seeming types of morphological processes discussed here is due to several reasons. First of all, there is a historical explanation. Affixes do not fall from the sky. Via reanalysis, they usually originate from free forms through compounding or cliticization followed by loss of their 'freedom'. Since compounding and cliticization typically involve concatenation, we expect to find the same for affixation. On the other hand, it is correspondingly rare for languages to reach a state whose reanalysis can yield a rule of metathesis (cf. Janda, 1984, for relevant discussion). Second, there is the issue of learnability. Presumably, it is simpler to associate a particular meaning with a constant segmental form than with an operation. For one thing, there is no directionality-problem. In the case of metathesis or subtraction, a child is confronted with pairs of words that can be related in various ways. For instance, when acquiring Rotuman, a child must decide whether to take the incomplete phase or the complete phase as the basic form. This is by no means obvious, since it requires knowledge of the overall patterns in the language. A single pair of words cannot determine the issue. No such problem arises in agglutinative languages with exclusively additive morphology.

Given these considerations, it is hardly surprising that the processes we have been focussing on in this paper are less common than those that have given IA theories their appeal as more constrained descriptive frameworks. This does not mean, however, that 'process morphology' is in some sense less relevant to the theory of morphology, as McCarthy (1981) and Dressler (1985) have suggested. After all, a contention that morphology is concatenative and non-processual is like a claim that all swans are white and none are black. But, in morphology, it seems as if researchers have tried to test this claim by looking for more white swans (and by painting black ones white) rather than by looking for any black swans.

Having accepted an essentially transformational view of morphology (though not necessarily such standard features of transformational theories as abstract underlying structures), we must face the question of whether there are any interesting constraints on these processes. We are convinced that such limitations indeed exist, but we do not believe that they must be direct consequences of one's descriptive framework. For instance, there do not seem to be languages that employ inverse total reduplication. This could be accounted for by invoking some constraint of 'Universal Grammar', but that would hardly explain such a fact. Instead, it seems more attractive to appeal to a psycholinguistic principle here: it is easier to repeat a given string in its original order than in its inverse order. At the same time, it is known that one can train people to invert strings. Thus, in principle, a child could learn a language with inverse reduplication, and hence it appears that, even though this process does not seem very natural, it must be accepted as a possible morphological mechanism. (A close analog is in fact instantiated by such creations in the English technical vocabulary of acoustics as the partial inversions *cepstrum, quefrency,* and *liftering* — from *spectrum, frequency,* and *filtering,* respectively.) In any case, we believe the present uniformly-processual framework provides a useful basis for the psycholinguistic investigation of the relative naturalness of formal operations in morphology.

The implications of process-morphology for categorial grammars are substantial. First of all, it provides evidence for the superiority of the rather liberal models proposed by Curry, Lewis, and Montague over the more parsimonious Ajdukiewicz/Bar-Hillel/Lambek systems. In particular, it indicates the need for operations that are not in any sense associated with overt functor-expressions. Second, process-morphology provides additional motivation for Bach's wrapping-operations and shows how these must be further refined in order to deal with the various kinds of infixation found in natural language.

Allowing more ways of combining two expressions than just concatenation may make it possible to constrain the type-lifting and -lowering operations proposed by various categorial grammarians. For instance, the Dutch verb-clusters referred to previously can be treated in terms of type-raising as well as of wrapping; cf. Steedman (1985), Bach (1984). The use of wrapping, then, may allow one to discard type-lifting for this particular case. The main advantage of using wrapping rather than type-lifting is that the former does not change function/ argument structure. To the extent that a fixed function/argument structure has explanatory power (e.g. for accounts of agreement — cf. Keenan, 1979 — and anaphora — cf. Partee and Bach, 1981), this would be a bonus of fully exploiting the possibilities of wrapping. However, this issue calls for further study before more definite conclusions can be made. Still, the rich possibilities for syntactic description and explanation opened up by extending categorial grammar so as to account for morphological processes demonstrate the promise of a processual-categorial approach for at least these two domains of linguistic investigation, if not for grammar in general.

NOTES

* We would like to thank the following people for help in the preparation of this paper: C. Callaghan, A. Miller, J. Nevis, R. Oehrle, A. Zwicky, and the participants at the Tucson Conference on Categorial Grammars and Natural Language Structures in May-June, 1985.
[1] A rather similar proposal is advanced in Hoeksema 1980, but it is there stated in terms of so-called 'metarules'.
[2] Cf. also Schmerling (1982, n. 5): "I suspect that we want to recognize two such operations, one involving 'first phrase' and one involving 'first word'".
[3] Nevertheless, the fact that all the expletive 'infixes' of English occur as free words in semantically equivalent constructions (e.g. *un-bloody-believable* = *bloody unbelievable*) makes it questionable whether actual affixation is involved, as opposed to a kind of compounding where there is blending (without clipping) via 'sandwiching' (for discussion, cf. Janda, 1985, and references there).
[4] Some of these forms are clearly lexicalized and have special meanings; this one, for instance, means 'to act as a go-between in marriage negotiations'.

BIBLIOGRAPHY

Ades, A. E. and M. Steedman: 1982, 'On the Order of Words', *Linguistics and Philosophy* **4**, 517—558.
Anderson, S. R.: 1972, 'On Nazalization in Sundanese', *Linguistic Inquiry* **3**, 253—268.
Anderson, S. R.: 1974, *The Organization of Phonology*, Academic Press, New York.
Anderson, S. R.: 1975, 'On the Interaction of Phonological Rules of Various Types', *Journal of Linguistics* **11**, 39—62.
Anderson, S. R.: 1977, 'On the Formal Description of Inflection', in W. A. Beach, S. E. Fox, and S. Philosoph (eds.), *Papers from the Thirteenth Regional Meeting of the Chicago Linguistic Society*, Chicago Linguistic Society, Chicago, pp. 15—44.
Anderson, S. R.: 1982, 'Where's Morphology?', *Linguistic Inquiry* **13**, 571—612.
Anderson, S. R.: 1984, 'Rules as "Morphemes" in a Theory of Inflection', in D. S. Rood (ed.), *1983 Mid-America Conference Papers*, Dept. of Linguistics, University of Colorado, Boulder, pp. 3—21.
Aronoff, M.: 1976, *Word Formation in Generative Grammar*, MIT Press, Cambridge, Mass.

Bach, E.: 1975, 'Order in Base Structures', in C. Li (ed.), *Word Order and Word Order Change*, University of Texas Press, Austin, pp. 307—343.

Bach, E.: 1979, 'Control in Montague Grammar', *Linguistic Inquiry* **10**, 515—531.

Bach, E.: 1983, 'On the Relationship between Word-Grammar and Phrase-Grammar', *Natural Language and Linguistic Theory* **1**, 65—89.

Bach, E.: 1984, 'Some Generalizations of Categorial Grammars', in F. Landman and F. Veltman (eds.), *Varieties of Formal Semantics*, Foris Publications, Dordrecht, pp. 1—23.

Bar-Hillel, Y.: 1964, *Language and Information*, Addison-Wesley, Reading.

Benthem, J. F. A. K. van: 1984, 'The Logic of Semantics', in F. Landman and F. Veltman (eds.), *Varieties of Formal Semantics*, Foris Publications, Dordrecht, pp. 55—80.

Benthem, J. F. A. K. van: this volume, 'The Lambek Calculus'.

Besnier, N.: 1983, 'An Autosegmental Approach to Metathesis in Rotuman', unpublished paper, USC.

Bloomfield, L.: 1933, *Language*, Holt, Rinehart and Winston, New York.

Bresnan, J., R. Kaplan, S. Peters, and A. Zaenen: 1982, 'Cross-Serial Dependencies in Dutch', *Linguistic Inquiry* **13**, 613—636.

Broselow, E. and J. J. McCarthy: 1983/1984, 'A Theory of Internal Reduplication', *The Linguistic Review* **3**, 25—88.

Cairns, C.: 1976, 'Universal Properties of Umlaut and Vowel Coalescence Rules: Implications for Rotuman Phonology', in A. Juilland (ed.), *Linguistic Studies Offered to Joseph Greenberg on the Occasion of His Sixtieth Birthday. Second Volume: Phonology*. Anma Libri, Saratoga, California, pp. 271—283.

Chomsky, N.: 1956, 'Three Models for the Description of Language', in *I.R.E. Transactions on Information Theory*, Vol. IT-2.

Churchward, C. M.: 1940, *Rotuman Grammar and Dictionary*, Australasian Medical Publishing Company Limited, for the Methodist Church of Australasia, Dept. of Overseas Missions, Sydney.

Curry, H. B.: 1961, 'Some Logical Aspects of Grammatical Structure', in R. Jakobson (ed.), *Structure of Language and Its Mathematical Aspects. Proceedings of the Twelfth Symposium on Applied Mathematics*, American Mathematical Society, Providence, R.I., pp. 56—68.

Davis, S.: 1985, 'Internal Reduplication and Template-Driven Association', unpublished paper, MIT.

Dixon, R. M. W.: 1972, *The Dyirbal Language of North Queensland*, Cambridge University Press, Cambridge.

Dowty, D. R.: 1978, 'Applying Montague's Views on Linguistic Metatheory to the Structure of the Lexicon', in D. Farkas, W. M. Jacobsen, and K. W. Todrys (eds.), *Papers from the Parasession on the Lexicon*, Chicago Linguistic Society, Chicago, pp. 97—137.

Dowty, D. R.: 1979, *Word Meaning and Montague Grammar. The Semantics of Verbs and Times in Generative Semantics and Montague's PTQ*, Reidel, Dordrecht.

Dressler, W. U.: 1985, 'On the Predictiveness of Natural Morphology', *Journal of Linguistics* **21**, 321—337.

Dudas, K.: 1974, 'A Case of Functional Opacity: Javanese Elative Formation', *Studies in the Linguistic Sciences* **4**, 91—111.

Dudas, K.: 1976, *The Phonology and Morphology of Modern Javanese*, doctoral dissertation, University of Illinois, Urbana-Champaign.

Fanselow, G.: 1981, *Zur Syntax und Semantik der Nominalkomposition*, Niemeyer, Tübingen.

Gazdar, G. and G. K. Pullum: 1981, 'Subcategorization, Constituent Order and the Notion "Head"', in M. Moortgat, H. van der Hulst, and T. Hoekstra (eds.), *The Scope of Lexical Rules*, Foris, Dordrecht, pp. 107—123.

Haeringen, C. B. van: 1947, 'De Meervoudsvorming in het Nederlands', *Mededelingen der Koninklijke Nederlandse Academie van Wetenschappen, afd. Letterkunde*, Nieuwe Reeks, Deel 10, No. 5.

Hankamer, J.: 1973, 'Syllable Counting Rules', paper presented at the LSA Annual Meeting, San Diego, Dec. 28—30, 1973. (Abstract published in *Meeting Handbook*, pp. 51—52.)

Harris, Z.: 1951, *Structural Linguistics*, University of Chicago Press, Chicago.

Hockett, Ch. F.: 1954, 'Two Models of Grammatical Description', *Word* **10**, 210—231.

Hoeksema, J.: 1980, 'Verbale Verstrengeling Ontstrengeld', *Spektator* **10**, 221—249.

Hoeksema, J.: 1984, *Categorial Morphology*, doctoral dissertation, Rijksuniversiteit Groningen, published by Garland Press, New York, 1985.

Hulst, H. van der: 1983, 'Metathesis within the CV-Model', unpublished paper, INL, Leiden.

Janda, R. D.: 1980, 'On a Certain Construction of English's', in B. R. Caron *et al.* (eds.), *Proceedings of the Sixth Annual Meeting of the Berkeley Linguistics Society*, Berkeley Linguistics Society, Berkeley, pp. 324—336.

Janda, R. D.: 1981, 'A Case of Liberation from Morphology into Syntax: The Fate of the English Genitive-Marker -(e)s', in B. Johns and D. Strong (eds.), *Syntactic Change*, pp. 59—114.

Janda, R. D.: 1982a, 'On Limiting the Form of Morphological Rules: German Umlaut, Diacritic Features, and the "Cluster-Constraint"', in J. Pustejovsky and P. Sells (eds.), *Proceedings of NELS 12, 1982, GLSA, UMass/Amherst*, Amherst, MA, pp. 140—152.

Janda, R. D.: 1982b, 'Of Formal Identity and Rule-(Un)Collapsibility: On Lost and Found Generalizations in Morphology', in D. P. Flickinger, M. Macken, and N. Wiegand (eds.), *Proceedings of the First West Coast Conference on Formal Linguistics*, Linguistics Dept., Stanford University, Stanford, California, pp. 179—197.

Janda, R. D.: 1982c, 'High German Umlaut and Morphologization', unpublished paper, University of Arizona.

Janda, R. D.: 1983a, 'Two Umlaut-Heresies and Their Claim to Orthodoxy', in E. Martin-Callejo-Manandise (ed.), *Exploring Language: Linguistic Heresies from the Desert, Coyote Papers: Working Papers in Linguistics from A → Z* **4**, pp. 59—71.

Janda, R. D.: 1983b, '"Morphemes" Aren't Something That Grows on Trees: Morphology as More the Phonology Than the Syntax of Words', in J. F. Richardson, M. Marks, and A. Chukerman (eds.), *Papers from the Parasession on the Interplay of Phonology, Morphology, and Syntax*, Chicago Linguistic Society, Chicago, pp. 79—95.

Janda, R. D.: 1984, 'Why Morphological Metathesis Rules are Rare: On the Possibility of Historical Explanation in Linguistics', in C. Brugman and M. Macaulay (eds.), *Proceedings of the Tenth Annual Meeting of the Berkeley Linguistics Society*, Berkeley Linguistics Society, Berkeley.

Janda, R. D.: 1985, 'An Autosegmental-Morphological Solution to the Problem of Phonesthemes and Blends', paper presented at the 11th Annual Meeting of the Berkeley Linguistics Society, February 16—18, 1985.

Janda, R. D.: 1987, *On the Motivation for an Evolutionary Typology of Sound-Structural Rules*, doctoral dissertation, UCLA.

Janda, R. D. and B. D. Joseph: 1986, "One Rule or Many? Sanskrit Reduplication as Fragmented Affixation", in B. D. Joseph, ed., *Studies on Language Change, OSUWPL* **34**, 84—107.

Johnston, R.: 1980, *Nakanai of New Britain: The Grammar of an Oceanic Language*. The Australian National University, Canberra.

Joseph, B. D. and R. D. Janda: 1986, 'E pluribus unum: The Rule-Constellation as an Expression of Formal Unity Amidst Morphological Fragmentation', paper presented at the Fifteenth Annual Linguistic Symposium, University of Wisconsin-Milwaukee (Milwaukee Morphology Meeting), April 4—6, 1986.

Kaisse, E.: 1982, 'Sentential Clitics and Wackernagel's Law', in D. P. Flickinger, M. Macken, and N. Wiegand (eds.), *Proceedings of the First West Coast Conference on Formal Linguistics*, Linguistics Dept., Stanford University, Stanford, California, pp. 1—14.

Kaisse, E.: 1985, *Connected Speech*, Academic Press, New York.

Kaufman, T.: 1971, *Tzeltal Phonology and Morphology*, University of California Press, Berkeley.

Keenan, E. L.: 1979, 'On Surface Form and Logical Form', L.A.U.T. paper 63, Series A. University of Trier, Trier.

Kiparsky, P.: 1982, 'Lexical Phonology and Morphology', in Linguistic Society of Korea (ed.), *Linguistics in the Morning Calm*, Hanshin, Seoul, pp. 3—91.

Klavans, J.: 1980, *Topics in a Theory of Clitics*, doctoral dissertation, University College London; distributed by the Indiana University Linguistics Club, 1982.

Lambek, J.: 1958, 'The Mathematics of Sentence Structure', *American Mathematical Monthly* **56**, 154—169.

Lambek, J.: 1961, 'The Calculus of Syntactic Types', in R. Jakobson (ed.), *Structure of Language and Its Mathematical Aspects. Proceedings of the Twelfth Symposium on Applied Mathematics*, American Mathematical Society, Providence, R.I.

Lessen Kloeke, W. U. S. van: 'Truncation in German — Morphotactic versus Phonotactic Constraints', in H. Bennis and F. Beukema (eds.), *Linguistics in the Netherlands 1985*, Foris Publications, Dordrecht, pp. 121—128.

Lewis, D.: 1972, 'General Semantics', in D. Davidson and G. Harman (eds.), *Semantics of Natural Language*, Reidel, Dordrecht, pp. 169—218.

Lieber, R.: 1980, *On the Organization of the Lexicon*, doctoral dissertation, MIT; distributed by the Indiana University Linguistics Club, 1981.

Marantz, A.: 1982, 'Re Reduplication', *Linguistic Inquiry* **13**, 435—482.

Matthews, P. H.: 1965, 'The Inflectional Component of a Word-and-Paradigm Grammar', *Journal of Linguistics* **1**, 139—171.

Matthews, P. H.: 1972, *Inflectional Morphology. A Theoretical Study Based on Aspects of Latin Verb Conjugation*, Cambridge University Press, Cambridge.

McCarthy, J. J.: 1979, *Formal Issues in Semitic Phonology and Morphology*, doctoral dissertation, MIT; distributed by the Indiana University Linguistics Club, 1982.

McCarthy, J. J.: 1981, 'A Prosodic Theory of Nonconcatenative Morphology', *Linguistic Inquiry* **12**, 373—418.

McCarthy, J. J.: 1982, 'Prosodic Structure and Expletive Infixation', *Language* **58**, 574—590.

McCarthy, J. J.: 1984, 'Morphological Structure(s)', unpublished paper, University of Texas, Austin.

McCarthy, J. J.: 1986, 'OCP Effects: Gemination and Antigemination', *Linguistic Inquiry* **17**, 207—263.

Montague, R.: 1974 (edited by R. Thomason), *Formal Philosophy. Selected Papers of Richard Montague*, Yale University Press, New Haven.

Moortgat, M.: 1983, 'Synthetic Compounds and Interpretation', unpublished paper, INL, Leiden.

Moortgat, M.: 1984, 'Compositionality and the Syntax of Words', paper presented at the 5th Amsterdam Colloquium, August 29, 1984.

Moravcsik, E. A.: 1977, 'On Rules of Infixing', Indiana University Linguistics Club, Bloomington.

Moravcsik, E. A.: 1978, 'Reduplicative Constructions', in J. H. Greenberg, C. Ferguson, and E. A. Moravcsik (eds.), *Universals of Human Language, Volume 3, Word Structure*, Stanford University Press, Stanford.

Mors, C. ter: 1984, 'Affix to X: Broselow and McCarthy vs Marantz: A Reinterpretation', *The Linguistic Review* **3**, 275—298.

Nebel, A.: 1948, *Dinka Grammar (Rek-Malual Dialect)*, *with Texts and Vocabulary*, Missioni Africane, Verona.

Nevis, J.: 1985, *Finnish Particle Clitics and General Clitic Theory*, unpublished doctoral dissertation, Ohio State University.

Newman, S. S.: 1944, *Yokuts Language of California*, Viking Fund, New York.

Pollard, C.: 1984, *Generalized Phrase Structure Grammars, Head Grammars and Natural Language*, doctoral dissertation, Stanford University.

Pullum, G. K. and A. M. Zwicky: n.d., *The Phonology-Syntax Interface*, unpublished bookdraft.

Robins, R. H.: 1958, *The Yurok Language of Northern California*, University of California Press, Berkeley.

Saito, M.: 1981, 'A Preliminary Account of the Rotuman Vowel System', unpublished paper, MIT.

Sapir, E.: 1921, *Language*, Harcourt, Brace & World, Inc., New York.

Schmerling, S. F.: 1982, 'The Proper Treatment of the Relationship Between Syntax and Phonology', *Texas Linguistic Forum* **19**, 151—166.

Schmerling, S. F.: 1983a, 'Two Theories of Syntactic Categories', *Linguistics and Philosophy* **6**, 393—421.

Schmerling, S. F.: 1983b, 'Montague Morphophonemics', in J. F. Richardson, M. Marks, and A. Chukerman (eds.), *Papers from the Parasession on the Interplay of Phonology, Morphology and Syntax*, Chicago Linguistic Society, Chicago, pp. 222—237.

Selkirk, E. O.: 1982, *The Syntax of Words*, MIT Press, Cambridge, Massachusetts.

Shieber, S.: 1985, 'Evidence Against the Context-Freeness of Natural Language', *Linguistics and Philosophy* **8**, 333—343.

Siegel, D.: 1974, *Topics in English Morphology*, doctoral dissertation, MIT; published by Garland Press, New York, 1979.

Smith, N. S. H.: 1985, 'Spreading, Reduplication and the Default Option in Miwok Nonconcatenative Morphology', in H. van der Hulst and N. S. H. Smith (eds.), *Advances in Nonlinear Phonology: Results of the Amsterdam Workshop on Nonlinear Phonology*, Foris Publications, Dordrecht, pp. 363—380.

Smith, N. S. H. and B. Hermans: 1982, 'Nonconcatenatieve woordvorming in het Sierra Miwok', *GLOT* **5**, 263—284.

Steedman, M. J.: 1985, 'Dependency and Coordination in the Grammar of Dutch and English', *Language* **61**, 523—568.

Steele, S. *et al.*: 1981, *An Encyclopedia of AUX: A Study in Crosslinguistic Equivalence*, MIT Press, Cambridge, Mass.

Steriade, D.: 1986, 'Yokuts and the Vowel Plane', *Linguistic Inquiry* **17**, 129—146.

Stevens, A. M.: 1977, 'On Local Ordering in Sundanese', *Linguistic Inquiry* **8**, 155—162.

Strauss, S. L.: 1982, *Lexicalist Phonology of English and German*, Foris Publications, Dordrecht.

Topping, D. M.: 1973, *Chamorro Reference Grammar*, The University Press of Hawaii, Honolulu.

Ultan, R.: 1975, 'Infixes and Their Origin', in H. Seiler (ed.), *Linguistic Workshop III*, Fink, Munich.

Vennemann, T. and R. T. Harlow: 1977, 'Categorial Grammar and Consistent VX Serialization', *Theoretical Linguistics* **4**, 227—254.

Vergnaud, J.-R.: 1977, 'Formal Properties of Phonological Rules', in R. E. Butts and J. Hintikka (eds.), *Basic Problems in Methodology and Linguistics*, D. Reidel Publishing Company, Dordrecht, pp. 299—318.

Wackernagel, J.: 1892, 'Über ein Gesetz der indogermanischen Wortstellung', *Indogermanische Forschungen* **1**, 333—436.

Walker, C. D.: 1970, 'Diegueño Plural Formation', *Linguistic Notes From La Jolla* **4**, 1—16.

Wells, R. S.: 1947, 'Immediate Constituents', *Language* **23**, 81—117.

Williams, E.: 1981, 'On the Notions "Lexically Related" and "Head of a Word"', *Linguistic Inquiry* **12**, 245—274.

Zwicky, A. M.: 1984, 'Heads', *Journal of Linguistics* **21**, 1—30.

Zwicky, A. M.: 1985, 'How To Describe Inflection', in M. Niepokuj, M. van Clay, V. Nikiforidou, and D. Feder (eds.), *Proceedings of the Eleventh Annual Meeting of the Berkeley Linguistics Society*, Berkeley Linguistics Society, Berkeley, pp. 372—386.

Dept. of Linguistics, 619 Williams Hall,
University of Pennsylvania,
Philadelphia, PA 19104-6305, U.S.A.

Dept. of Linguistics,
526 Humanities Building,
University of New Mexico,
Albuquerque, NM 87131,
U.S.A.

GEOFFREY J. HUCK

PHRASAL VERBS AND THE CATEGORIES
OF POSTPONEMENT

1. THE PROBLEM

It was the existence of sentences like (1), containing phrasal verbs, or verb-particle constructions, which led Bar-Hillel *et al.* (1960) to conclude that categorial grammars were inadequate to analyze natural language ("so long, at least, as the category assignments are natural"):

(1)   He looked it up.

Bar-Hillel assumed that the particle *up* in (1) was a syntactic operator that looked for a complement intransitive verb to its left to form a transitive verb. Although other reasonable category assignments can be imagined, there's no disputing that because *look* is not immediately adjacent to *up* in (1), their categories cannot cancel under functional application as required. The problem is of course general, touching all the discontinuities.

Recently, several proposals have been put forward to extend categorial grammars to deal with discontinuous structures. These proposals may be roughly divided into two classes. In the first class, which consists of what I call *postponement* mechanisms, a syntactic operator is permitted to temporarily postpone combining with its complement in favor of some other element, while at the semantic level a distinguished variable bound by a lambda operator is pushed into the slot of what would be the translation of the complement if it were not postponed. In the second class, the semantics is kept simple, but syntactic trees are permitted whose branches cross.

The various proposals make quite different predictions about the range of discontinuity possible in natural language. In the next section of the paper, I will survey these proposals pretty much in increasing order of power. In the final sections, I will apply the proposals to a number of English constructions containing phrasal verbs, pointing out difficulties for the proposals where they arise.

249

Richard T. Oehrle et al. (eds.), Categorial Grammars and Natural Language Structures, 249–263.
© 1988 *by D. Reidel Publishing Company.*

2. MECHANISMS OF POSTPONEMENT

2.1. *A-Postponements*

The single combinatorial phrase structure rule permitted in traditional categorial grammars (Ajdukiewicz, 1935; Bar-Hillel *et al.*, 1960) is the familiar rule of functional application:

(2) $X/Y + Y = X$

where X and Y are any categories. This rule, which does not specify the direction of the adjunction, may be taken to conflate two subrules in which direction (via the arrow on the denominator) is specified:

(3) (a) $X/\underset{\rightarrow}{Y} + Y = X$
     (b) $Y + X/\underset{\leftarrow}{Y} = X$

To accommodate discontinuity in the grammar, Steedman (1985), among others, has advocated extension of the grammar to include functional composition rules like (4), in which a functor may combine with an argument which is itself an unsatisfied functor:

(4) (a) $X/\underset{\rightarrow}{Y} + Y/\underset{\rightarrow}{Z} = X/\underset{\rightarrow}{Z}$
     (b) $Y/\underset{\leftarrow}{Z} + X/\underset{\leftarrow}{Y} = X/\underset{\leftarrow}{Z}$

I'll call rules of the form of (4) *A-postponements*, where 'A' is meant to suggest that an element of the argument has been postponed. I'll assume that the category X/Z in (4) translates as (5), where z is a distinguished variable that ranges over expressions of the type of the translation of Z:

(5) $\lambda z[(X/Y)'((Y/Z)'(z))]$

We might pictorially represent the effects of A-postponement authorized by a rule like (4a) by the diagram in (6). Here t indicates the position that the argument would have occupied in the diagram had it not been postponed. (This transformational metaphor should not be allowed to obscure the entirely categorial nature of the rules.)

(6)

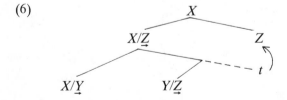

While the rules in (4) clearly affect the structural relationships in which the lexical items participate, they cannot license by themselves the kinds of structures which, in more powerful grammars, wrapping operations are designed to produce. An obvious A-postponement generalization of these rules which simulates wrapping is given in the rules of (7), the effect of the second of which is represented in (8):

(7) (a) $X/\underset{\rightarrow}{Y} + Y/\underset{\leftrightarrow}{Z} = X/\underset{\leftrightarrow}{Z}$
     (b) $Y/\underset{\rightarrow}{Z} + X/\underset{\leftarrow}{Y} = X/\underset{\rightarrow}{Z}$

(8)

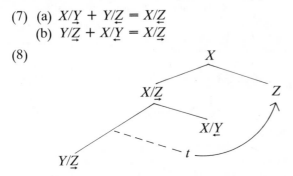

I'll call A-postponement generalizations like (7) *A-wrap postponements*.

2.2. *F-Postponements*

In his extension of categorial grammar, Bach (1981) introduced the possibility of postponing arguments of the main *functor*. Thus, Bach permits rules like (9), where X/Z translates as in (10):

(9) $(X/\underset{\rightarrow}{Y})/\underset{\rightarrow}{Z} + Y = X/\underset{\rightarrow}{Z}$
(10) $\lambda z[(((X/Y/Z)'(z))(Y')]$

The effect of such rules, which I'll call *F-postponements* ('F' to suggest 'functor'), is represented in (11):

(11)

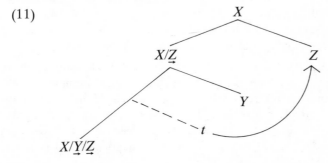

It should be clear when (8) and (11) are compared that F-postponements accomplish essentially what A-wraps do, with different categorization. It is in fact the categorizational indeterminacy so far permitted
in categorial grammars which renders these two extensions equivalent.

The possibility of categorial type-raising (Dowty, 1985), moreover,
greatly improves the power of routine functional application, allowing
the latter to do the work essentially of F-postponement — although at
the significant cost of multiplying categories. For example, type-raising
on the Y argument of (9) yields (12), which is a simple rule of functional application:

(12) $(X/\underrightarrow{Y})/\underrightarrow{Z} + (X/\underrightarrow{Z})/((X/\underrightarrow{Y})/\underrightarrow{Z}) = X/\underrightarrow{Z}$

The effect of (12) is represented in (13), which of course is identical to
(11) up to the type-raising on Y:

(13)

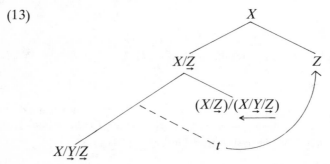

Because type-raising does not alter the form of either the rules or the
categories permissible in the grammar, grammars restricted to just this
kind of postponement will be equivalent to standard categorial grammars, which are of course weakly equivalent to context-free grammars
(Bar-Hillel, 1960).

2.3. $-Postponements

Ades and Steedman (1982) and Steedman (1985) allow an extended
version of A-postponement where more than a single argument of the
main argument is permitted to be postponed. The dollar sign in the
rules of (14), which rules I'll call *A$-postponements*, is a variable
ranging over sets of strings of alternating slash signs and category
symbols: $/Q1/Q2 \dots /Qn$ for Qi = any category and $0 \leqslant i \leqslant n$.

Given the assumption of left association, $A/B/C = (A/B)/C$.

(14) (a) $X/\underset{\rightarrow}{Y} + Y\$ = X\$$
     (b) $Y\$ + X/\underset{\rightarrow}{Y} = X\$$

One possible instantiation of (14a) is given in (15), the effect of which is represented in (16):

(15) $X/\underset{\rightarrow}{Y} + (Y/\underset{\rightarrow}{W})/\underset{\rightarrow}{Z} = (X/\underset{\rightarrow}{W})/\underset{\rightarrow}{Z}$

(16)

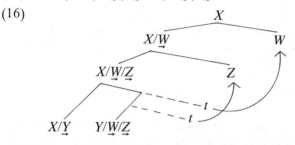

Given the discussion above, we may wish also to extend the $-notation to include the possibility of *A$-wrap postponements*, as in (17):

(17) (a) $X/\underset{\rightarrow}{Y} + Y\$/\underset{\rightarrow}{Z} = X\$/\underset{\rightarrow}{Z}$
     (b) $Y\$/\underset{\rightarrow}{Z} + X/\underset{\rightarrow}{Y} = X\$/\underset{\rightarrow}{Z}$

It's easy to see that, up to the different category assignments, these are equivalent to what we may call *F$-postponements*, as in (18):

(18) (a) $X/\underset{\rightarrow}{Y}\$ + Y = X\$$
     (b) $Y + X/\underset{\leftarrow}{Y}\$ = X\$$

One instantiation of (18) is given in (19), the effect of which is represented in (20):

(19) $X/\underset{\rightarrow}{Y}/\underset{\rightarrow}{Z}/\underset{\rightarrow}{W} + Y = X/\underset{\rightarrow}{Z}/\underset{\rightarrow}{W}$

(20)

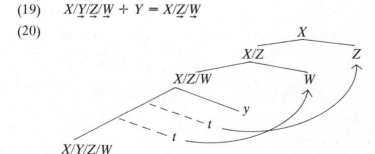

2.4. *Minus-feature Postponements*

Bach, in his 1981 article, offered a second mechanism to handle discontinuity. He assumes the additional rule schemata in (21) and (22), where the feature $[-Y]$ indicates a missing element and is a close relative of Gazdar's (1981) 'slash' categories:

(21) $X/Y = X[-Y]$
(22) $X[-Y] + Y = X$

$X[-Y]$ translates as (23), where y is a distinguished variable that ranges over expressions of the type of the translation of Y. The translation of X in (22) is then (24):

(23) $(X/Y)'(y)$
(24) $\lambda y(X[-Y]')Y'$

Bach apparently intended this mechanism to generate long-distance dependencies, and thus I'll assume the conventions in (25) to percolate the gap up the tree:

(25) (a) $(D/B)[-Y] + B = D[-Y]$
     (b) $D/B + B[-Y] = D[-Y]$

Thus, as shown in (26), an element of the category $(X/Y)/Z$ — recategorized by minus-feature postponement as $(X/Y)[-Z]$ — may combine with an element of category Y to yield an element of category $X[-Z]$:

(26)

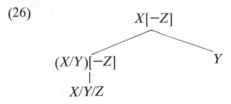

Bach does not say anything about how multiple postponements are to be handled, but we might assume that the minus-feature mechanism operates left-to-right as a first-in/first-out (FIFO) stack. If that's the case, then minus-feature postponement would be exactly equivalent to a combination of A$-wrap and F$-postponement, as in (27):

(27) (a) $X/Y\$ + Y\$' = X\$'\$$
     (b) $Y\$' + X/\underset{\smile}{Y}\$ = X\$'\$$

One instantiation of (27a) is (28), which may be represented by the figure in (29):

(28) $X/\underset{\rightarrow}{Y}/\underset{\rightarrow}{Z}/\underset{\rightarrow}{W} + Y/\underset{\rightarrow}{U}/\underset{\rightarrow}{V} = X/\underset{\rightarrow}{U}/\underset{\rightarrow}{V}/\underset{\rightarrow}{Z}/\underset{\rightarrow}{W}$

(29)

$$
\begin{array}{c}
X \\
X/U \quad U \\
X/U/V \quad V \\
X/U/V/Z \quad Z \\
X/U/V/Z/W \quad W \\
t \quad t \\
X/Y/Z/W \quad t \quad Y/U/V \quad t
\end{array}
$$

Minus-feature under FIFO and A\$-wrap plus F\$-postponements can also be seen to be closely related to Maling and Zaenen's (1982) extension of the theory of slash categories in GPSG to handle multiple gaps. Unlike Maling and Zaenen's devices, however, the postponement mechanisms under consideration here do not generate the transcontext-free language $a^n b^n c^n$.[1]

3. PHRASAL VERBS AND POSTPONEMENT

I'd like now to turn to some facts about phrasal verbs in English to assess the satisfactoriness of the various devices. I will assume that phrasal verbs are of two types. The first type, consisting of combinations like *look up, eke out, while away, chew out, hold up* (rob) and *cover up* (conceal) is idiomatic and calls for a noncompositional semantics. The second type, consisting of combinations like *kick away, put out, nail down, push open,* etc., is semantically compositional and bears some relationship to factitive constructions like *paint the barn red.*

The idiomatic phrasal verbs pose a problem for categorial grammars of the sort under consideration. It should be evident that, because the semantics for these constructions is noncompositional, it will not be possible to routinely F-postpone or A-wrap the particles around the direct objects. That is, where the semantic rule that combines functions and arguments is a rule of functional application, it will not do to posit a semantic translation for *look it up* as indicated in (30), where *a* is a variable of the type of the translation of *up* (whatever that may be), since the meaning of the phrasal verb *look up* is not a function of the meaning of the parts *look* and *up*:

(30)

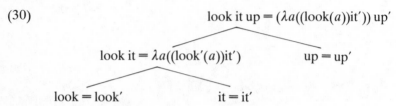

$$\text{look it up} = (\lambda a((\text{look}(a))\text{it}')) \text{ up}'$$

$$\text{look it} = \lambda a((\text{look}'(a))\text{it}') \qquad\qquad \text{up} = \text{up}'$$

$$\text{look} = \text{look}' \qquad\qquad \text{it} = \text{it}'$$

The only obvious solution I see within the general assumptions of the theory incorporating postponement adopted here is to introduce the equivalent of a separate syntactic rule for each idiomatic combination, where each rule has its appropriate noncompositional translation. Thus *look up* might be entered in the lexicon as something like (31), where, e.g., adverbial modification would only be possible on the full vp/e, and not on either of the component parts, which otherwise retain their categorial integrity:

(31) $\langle [[\text{look}]_{\text{vp/e/[up]}_p} [\text{up}]_p]_{\text{vp/e}}, \text{look-up}' \rangle$

It should be clear, however, that neither syntactic functional application without type-raising nor A-postponement will be sufficient to generate the discontinuous verb-particle structures of constructions containing idiomatic phrasal verbs. On the other hand, simple verb-np-particle strings, as in the vp of (1), are generable by A-wrap postponement, under the categorization given in (31). I conjecture that A-wrap postponement will not be sufficient, however, to analyze more complex structures in which particle placement interacts with adverb placement and extraposition from np. For example, given A$-wrap in addition to functional application, the categorization of the lexical items in (32) will account for the data in (33) — see, e.g., (34), which diagrams the vp of (33b):

(32)   throw: vp/$\underset{\rightarrow}{e}$/adv/p

the package: vp/$(\overset{\rightarrow}{vp}/\underset{\leftarrow}{e})$

away: p

quickly: vp/(vp/adv)

(33) (a)   He threw away the package quickly.
    (b)   He threw the package away quickly.
    (c)   He threw the package quickly away.
    (d)   *He threw quickly away the package.
    (e)   *He threw quickly the package away.
    (f)   *He threw away quickly the package.
    (g)   He quickly threw away the package.
    (h)   He quickly threw the package away.

(34)

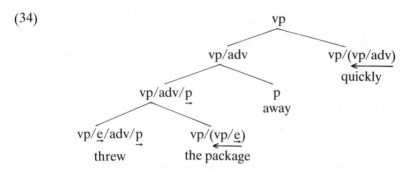

Here *threw* combines with *the package* by A$-wrap to form something
of category vp/adv/p, which can combine successively by functional
application with *away* and *quickly* to form the vp. (I assume here a
theory of adverbs along the lines of McConnell-Ginet, 1982.)

Where the direct object is a pronoun, if it is categorized as something which takes a vp/e/p and delivers a vp/p, this will account (albeit
not revealingly) for the fact that the particle must appear to its right. In
the case of idiomatic phrasal verbs, the categorization suggested in (31)
will similarly permit generation of the sentences (35a, b, g, and h) but
will rule out (35c, d, e, and f):

(35) (a)   He looked up the number quickly.
    (b)   He looked the number up quickly.
    (c)   *He looked the number quickly up.
    (d)   *He looked quickly up the number.
    (e)   *He looked quickly the number up.
    (f)   *He looked up quickly the number.
    (g)   He quickly looked up the number.
    (h)   He quickly looked the number up.

Remember that here the adverb is subcategorized only at the phrasal level — see, e.g., (36) and (37), which represent the vp's of (35a and b), respectively:

(36)

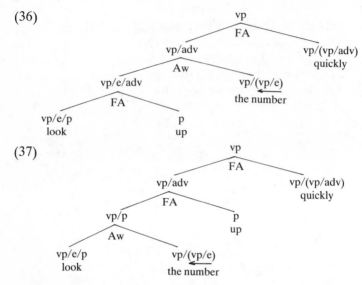

(37)

(I'll ignore here how the translation of *look the number up* in (37) would be determined. Perhaps, as has been suggested, the translation of the predicate in (31) is 'look-up', while the translation of the particle is zero. The unsatisfactoriness of this solution should be quite manifest.)

Now consider the sentences in (38):

(38) (a) He looked up the number that he'd forgotten.
     (b) He looked the number up that he'd forgotten.

While (38a) can be analyzed by straightforward functional application, I believe (38b) will require at least minus-feature postponement or A$-wrap plus F$-postponement as shown in (39):

(39)

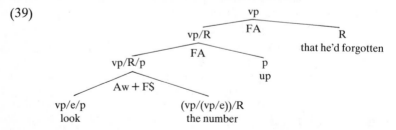

It should be noted that under postponement the relative clause appears to be constrained to be an argument of the np it modifies, *pace* Dowty (1982).

Even with the relatively powerful postponement devices we have employed to accommodate the facts of adverbial placement and extraposition from np, serious questions of adequacy — both syntactic and semantic — remain. Even ignoring the compositional issue — which seems formidable to me — it's not clear how the categorization given in (39) can be maintained when adverb placement is added into the equation. Nor is it clear how heavy np shift can be accommodated by the categorization given in (34).

4. A BRANCH-CROSSING PROPOSAL

Whether or not these problems can be solved within the theory of postponement without significant cost, I'd like to turn to the alternative solution alluded to at the beginning of the paper. Let's say that, in addition to the rules that determine the linear order of sisters, there are also possibly distinct rules that order nonsisters, and that the branches of a tree are permitted under these rules to cross, as specified in Huck (1985). Given the categorization of idiomatic phrasal verbs suggested in (31), we can analyze the vp of (35b) as (40):

(40)

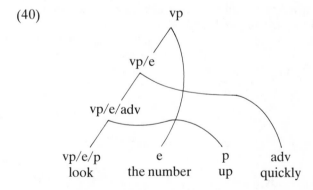

We can simply account for all the facts in (35) and (38) if we assume first a default rule that orders the subcategorized direct object immediately to the right of the transitive verb and, second, an obligatory nonsister rule that pushes focussed or heavy material to the right

periphery of the clause. Note of course that the particle *up* cannot be
heavy, nor can it be focussed, since by itself it has no semantic content.

(35a and b) are distinguished by whether the first rule above picks
out just the verbal element of the verb-particle construction as the
"transitive verb" in question or the combination itself. If the latter, then
(35a) is generated; if the former, then (35b). The categorization given in
(40) does not permit the adverb *quickly* to position between the
elements of the phrasal verb, and there is no nonsister precedence rule
given that will permit that either; hence, (35c, d, and e) are ruled out.
(35f) is similarly not achievable by the categorization without the
crossing of branches, and is not licensed by any nonsister rule which
would effect branch crossing.

Note that this analysis predicts correctly that if the relative clause
"... that he'd forgotten" is added to the right periphery of each of the
sentences of (35), the grammaticality judgments will remain the same,
except in the case of (35f), which is now predicted to be good.

The distinction between the paradigms in (33) and (35) is now a
consequence of the different lexical treatments of the lexical items
involved. If *throw* is assigned the category vp/e/p/adv or vp/e/adv/p^2
as in (41), which diagrams the vp of (33b), the facts given in (33) follow
from that assignment and the object placement and focussing constraints: (33a and b) are again distinguished by whether the particle is
taken to constitute part of the transitive verb, given that *throw* is
categorized as vp/e/adv/p, while (33c) is generated under the category
vp/e/p/adv. (33d, e, and f) are disallowed by the object placement rule.
Where the relative clause "... that Bill brought" is added to the right
side of the sentences, this analysis predicts, again correctly, that (33e)
will remain bad, while the others will be acceptable.

(41)

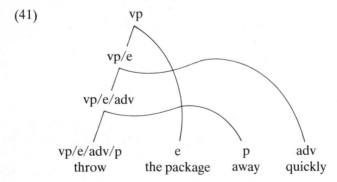

5. SPECULATIONS

It is worth emphasizing that branch-crossing has obviated in (40) and (41) the need for any kind of postponement, which raises the obvious issue of the power of the former. While unconstrained branch-crossing, like unconstrained postponement, will generate the transcontext-free language $a^n b^n c^n$ if unbounded nonsister precedence rules are admitted, I'd argue that crossing is bounded by precedence rules whose domain does not extend beyond the clause (where 'clause' is broadly construed as any sentential constituent whose joint either is also the root node of the full sentence or else is not directly dominated by some other sentential category node). I'd further claim that the precedence relation itself is narrowly defined such that X precedes Y iff the head of X precedes the head of Y, where the 'head of C' is either the daughter C or the daughter C/W where $C \neq W$.

The consequences of these constraints, which I've discussed more fully elsewhere (Huck, 1984, 1985), are rather far-reaching, but I'd like to mention that they suggest a division of labor between branch-crossing and postponement solutions to discontinuity. Branch-crossing is then seen to be essentially bounded and not to disturb the ordering relations among sisters. Thus, particle shift, extraposition from np, and certain adverb placements are prototypical branch-crossing phenomena. In these cases a functor subcategorizes a complement to the right, say, and it remains to the right, although a nonsister may intervene between the two. Importantly, branch-crossing will not permit a functor which subcategorizes a complement to its right to appear to the right of that complement.

In the case of the unbounded dependencies, e.g., topicalization, WH-movement, and relative clause formation, the precedence relation between sisters may be disturbed: what normally appears to the right may now appear to the left. I'd claim these are best handled as minus-feature postponements somewhat in the manner of Gazdar (1981) (see Huck (1984)).

This analysis, incidentally, would provide a partial answer to Ross's (1967, 272) question: "Why should rules which adjoin terms to the right side of a variable be upward bounded, and not those which adjoin terms to the left of a variable?" For those rightward discontinuities to which the presupposition of the first conjunct of this question in fact applies,[3] it is true because these discontinuities are the consequence of branch-crossing, which is clause-bounded by the precedence rules. Ross's question now reduces to the rather less interesting, Why are the postponements involved with topicalization, relative clause formation, and WH-movement invariably leftward?

NOTES

[1] If the minus-feature mechanism is conceived of as an unordered list from which category features may be popped at random, and if linear order rules or filters are permitted in the grammar which apply to nonsisters (see Section 4 below), a particular grammar can be designed which generates the triple-counting language: Assume three lexical items a, b, and c categorized respectively as $(S/C/B)$ or $(S/S/C/B)$, B, and C, which under minus-feature postponement generate all permutations of n a's, n b's, and n c's. Given tree-wide nonsister precedence rules $S/S/C/B < S/C/B < B < C$, just the language $a^n b^n c^n$ will be admitted. I'd speculate, however, that natural language allows only linear precedence rules whose domain is the clause (see Section 5 below). While such a constraint would rule out the triple-counting language, it would allow for the treatment of WH-movement, relative clause formation, and the other unbounded dependencies (see Huck, 1984).

[2] This categorization seems natural given that the adverb in *he quickly led the boy out* can have either wide or narrow scope with respect to the particle. In one reading, it's the leading that was quick, though it may have taken a long while actually to get out. In the other, they arrived outside quickly. Notice no such distinction obtains in sentences with idiomatic phrasal verbs like *look up*, which have only an achievement sense.

[3] Right Node Raising, which produces unbounded rightward dependencies, is accomplished in Gazdar (1981) by minus-feature postponement. It should be noted, however, that McCawley (1982) argues that Right Node Raising involves branch-crossing, as well as multiple motherhood.

REFERENCES

Ades, A., and M. Steedman: 1982, 'On the Order of Words', *Linguistics and Philosophy* **4**, 517—58.

Ajdukiewicz, K.: 1935, 'Die syntaktische Konnexitat', *Studia Philosophica* **1**, 1—27.

Bach, E.: 1981, 'Discontinuous Constituents in Generalized Categorial Grammars', in *NELS XI*, Graduate Linguistics Student Association, University of Massachusetts, Amherst, MA.

Bar-Hillel, Y., C. Gaifman, and E. Shamir: 1960, 'On Categorial and Phrase Structure Grammars', *Bulletin of the Research Council of Israel 9F*, 1—16. (Reprinted in Y. Bar-Hillel (ed.), *Language and Information*, Addison-Wesley, Reading, MA, 1964, pp. 99—114.)

Dowty, D.: 1982, 'Grammatical Relations and Montague Grammar', in P. Jacobson and G. Pullum (eds.), *The Nature of Syntactic Representation*, D. Reidel Publishing Company, Dordrecht and Boston, 1982, pp. 79—130.

Dowty, D.: 1985, 'Type-raising, Functional Composition, and Non-Constituent Conjunction', ms.

Gazdar, G.: 1981, 'Unbounded Dependencies and Coordinate Structure', *Linguistic Inquiry* **12**, 155—84.

Huck, G.: 1984, *Discontinuity and Word Order in Categorial Grammar*, Doctoral dissertation, University of Chicago (Distributed by Indiana University Linguistics Club, Bloomington).

Huck, G.: 1985, 'Exclusivity and Discontinuity in Phrase Structure Grammar', in *Proceedings of the West Coast Conference on Formal Linguistics*, Vol. 4. Stanford Linguistics Association, Stanford, CA.

Maling, J. and A. Zaenen: 1982, 'A Phrase Structure Account of Scandanavian Extraction Phenomena', in P. Jacobson and G. Pullum (eds.), *The Nature of Syntactic Representation*, D. Reidel Publishing Company, Dordrecht and Boston, 1982, pp. 229—82.

McCawley, J.: 1982, 'Parentheticals and Discontinuous Constituent Structure', *Linguistic Inquiry* **13**, 91—106.

McConnell-Ginet, S.: 1982, 'Adverbs and Logical Form: A Linguistically Realistic Theory', *Language* **58**, 144—84.

Ross, J.: 1967, *Constraints on Variables in Syntax*, Doctoral dissertation, Massachusetts Institute of Technology (Distributed by Indiana University Linguistics Club, Bloomington).

Steedman, M.: 1985, 'Dependency and Coordination in the Grammar of Dutch and English', *Language* **61**, 523—68.

The University of Chicago Press,
Chicago, IL 60637, U.S.A.

EDWARD L. KEENAN AND ALAN TIMBERLAKE

NATURAL LANGUAGE MOTIVATIONS FOR EXTENDING CATEGORIAL GRAMMAR

0. INTRODUCTION

The purpose of this paper is to present a variety of linguistically significant generalizations that can naturally be represented within a specific version of categorial grammar we propose below. These generalizations are given in Sections 2—4. Section 1 introduces the specific form of categorial grammar we use, and Section 5 concludes with a tentative suggestion for a formal universal of natural language based on the empirically motivated work of the preceding sections.

1. EXTENDED CATEGORIAL GRAMMAR

We may think of a 'classical' categorial grammar (see Bar-Hillel *et al.*, 1964) as defining a set Cat of *grammatical categories* in two steps:[1] a set of two or more primitive categories is given explicitly, and then this set is closed under a binary function '/' (read 'slash'), from which it follows that C/D is a category whenever both C and D are.

The linguistic insightfulness of classical categorial systems, first realized (to our knowledge) in Montague (1969), lies in the unity of syntactic and semantic analyses it provides. Syntactically, expressions of category C/D combine with ones of category D to form ones of category C. Semantically, such expressions are interpreted by functions from D-type denotations into C-type denotations. In general, for X a category, we write Den_X for the set in which expressions of category X take their denotations (relative to a model), and then for each 'slash' category C/D, $\text{Den}_{C/D}$ is some set of functions from Den_D into Den_C. Modeling natural languages with grammars of this sort yields a principled account of the interpretation of complex expressions as a function of the interpretations of the ones from which they are derived.

The categorial grammars we propose here as models for natural language extend the classical format in two respects. The principal extension is a direct generalization of the 'slash' notation, as follows:

265

Richard T. Oehrle et al. (eds.), Categorial Grammars and Natural Language Structures, 265—295.
© 1988 *by D. Reidel Publishing Company.*

(1)   For some ordinal n, if $\mathscr{C}$ and $\mathscr{D}$ are both n-ary sequences of categories, then $\mathscr{C}/\mathscr{D}$ is a category.

Such categories will be called *n-tuple categories*. When $n = 1$, such a n-tuple category will coincide with a slash category of classical (non-directional) categorial grammar. For $n > 1$, such a category may be called a *proper n-tuple category*, which can be represented explicitly as in (2) (as long as n is finite):

(2) $\langle C_1, \ldots, C_n \rangle / \langle D_1, \ldots, D_n \rangle$

Syntactically, expressions in such categories will combine with ones of category D_i to form expressions of category C_i (for i between 1 and n). As a simple illustration of this notation, consider the category that would be assigned to copular verbs like English *be*. In sentences like *John is the winner, be* combines with an *NP* to form a *VP*, which motivates the category assignment *VP/NP* (using for the moment the informal notation *NP, VP*, and the like, to be replaced shortly by categories stated in a proper categorial format). But in *John is angry, be* combines with an adjective phrase, motivating the category *VP/AP*. In terms of the n-tuple notation English *be* can be assigned the single 2-tuple category $\langle VP, VP \rangle / \langle AP, NP \rangle$. The motivation for introducing n-tuple categories is in fact quite similar to that for floating types introduced in Parsons (1979) (brought to our attention by Richard Oehrle). Indeed, modulo some (not insignificant) differences in notation, most of the specific generalizations presented in, for example, Section 2, can be represented in Parson's notation.

Introducing n-tuple categories into a classical categorial grammar does not appear to affect the generative capacity of such grammars (construed either weakly or strongly). Given a grammar G with n-tuple categories (at least for n finite), it is possible to construct a weakly equivalent grammar G' without n-tuple categories as follows. For each lexical (= basic vocabulary) item e within an n-tuple category $\langle C_1, \ldots, C_n \rangle / \langle D_1, \ldots, D_n \rangle$ in G, assign e in G' to each of the categories C_i/D_i (all i between 1 and n). Thus, the purpose of introducing n-tuple categories is not to increase generative capacity, but rather to provide a level of structure at which syntactic and semantic generalizations concerning items in n-tuple categories may be stated (as we attempt to do in Sections 2—4). To the end of making explicit the notation, we may note the following definition:

(3)   If $\mathscr{C}/\mathscr{D} = \langle C_1, \ldots, C_n \rangle / \langle D_1, \ldots, D_n \rangle$ is an n-tuple category, for each i between 1 and n, the one-tuple category C_i/D_i is the *i-th coordinate* of $\mathscr{C}/\mathscr{D}$.

To define an n-tuple category $\mathscr{C}/\mathscr{D}$, it is necessary and sufficient to state what the coordinates are. In later sections, it will often be convenient to define the category of an expression by saying that it is that n-tuple category all of whose ith coordinates satisfy some specified condition.

Defining possible denotations for expressions in n-tuple categories $\mathscr{C}/\mathscr{D}$ follows the same format as in the syntax. $\text{Den}_{\mathscr{C}/\mathscr{D}}$ will consist of relations R whose domain is the union of the Den_{D_i} (all i between 1 and n) and whose range is included in the union of the Den_{C_i} and which satisfy the following condition:

(4)   For each i between 1 and n, $\{(x, y) \in R: x \in \text{Den}_{D_i}$ and $y \in \text{Den}_{C_i}\} \subseteq \text{Den}_{C_i/D_i}$.

We may write R_i, termed the *i-th coordinate of the relation R*, for the set of pairs (x, y) mentioned in (4). In fact, R_i is a function from Den_{D_i} into Den_{C_i}, and to define some particular element in $\text{Den}_{\mathscr{C}/\mathscr{D}}$, it is sufficient (and necessary) to give its ith coordinates R_i for each i. Parenthetically we may note that by defining the interpretation in terms of relations, we do not limit n-tuple categories $\mathscr{C}/\mathscr{D}$ to ones where $D_i \neq D_j$ whenever $i \neq j$. As discussed in Keenan and Timberlake (1986), for example, the item *break* may be assigned the 2-tuple category $\langle S, VP \rangle / \langle NP, NP \rangle$ with identical D_1 and D_2. Syntactically, an expression of this category combines with NP's to form S's (as in *The toy broke*) and combines with NP's to form VP's (as in [*John*] *broke the toy*). Semantically, *break* is a relation that relates NP denotations both to VP denotations and to S denotations.

A final notational point concerning n-tuple categories. It is frequently convenient to represent the structure of complex expressions in terms of (unordered) tree diagrams of a conventional sort. In particular, given an expression e in a proper n-tuple category $\mathscr{C}/\mathscr{D}$, trees of the form in (5) are acceptable just in case the conditions (5i) and (5ii) are met (Keenan and Timberlake, 1986):

(5)

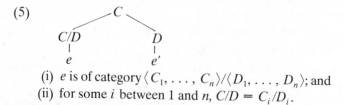

(i) e is of category $\langle C_1, \ldots, C_n \rangle / \langle D_1, \ldots, D_n \rangle$; and
(ii) for some i between 1 and n, $C/D = C_i/D_i$.

For example, if (as above) English *be* is of category $\langle VP, VP \rangle / \langle AP, NP \rangle$, the trees in (6) are acceptable by (5):

(6) (a)

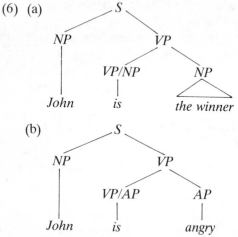

(b)

We turn now to the second enrichment of categorial notation. All approaches to natural language distinguish the category of *student, tall student*, etc., on the one hand, and that of *every student, no tall student*, etc., on the other. While it is not strictly necessary to enrich the categorial notation to make this distinction (see Montague, 1969, 1973), it is convenient and enlightening to do so. The symbol 'N' can be used for the category (*common nounphrase*) to which *student, tall student*, etc. belong, and the symbol '$\overline{N}$' for the category (*full nounphrase*) to which *every student, no tall student*, etc., belong. More generally, we assume that the category formation rules have been enriched as per (7) below:

(7)   If C is a category, then $\overline{C}$ is a category

Categories of the form $\overline{C}$ will be referred to as *argument categories*. In what follows, we will use variables in 'A' (e.g. A, A_1, A_i) as ranging over argument categories. We assume further that N (common nounphrase) and S (sentence) are among the primitive categories, guaranteeing by (7) that $\overline{N}$ and $\overline{S}$ are categories as well — in particular, argument categories. In English, $\overline{N}$'s include expressions like *John, every student, John and every student*, and $\overline{S}$'s will include expressions like *that Fred left* and *that Fred left early but not that Mary stayed late*. Determiners such as *every* and *at least two but not more than ten* will have category $\overline{N}/N$ as they combine with N's to form $\overline{N}$'s. The complementizer *that* in *that Fred left* will have the category $\overline{S}/S$ as it combines with S's to form $\overline{S}$'s. In tree diagrams the category label on the complementizer *that* will be omitted.

Of crucial importance in the examples analyzed later are the various sorts of predicate categories. In general, a one-place predicate ($= P_1$) combines with an expression in an appropriate argument category A_1 to form a zero-place predicate P_0 (or equivalently, S). There are of course various types of P_1 according to the choice of argument category A_1. For example, expressions such as *sleep, hug Arthur, give the book to Mary*, and *believe that Fred left early* are all P_1's of category $S/\overline{N}$, as they combine with $\overline{N}$'s to form S's. Expressions such as *is true, is surprising but true*, etc. are P_1's of category $S/\overline{S}$, as they combine with $\overline{S}$'s to form S's. Similarly, expressions such as *kiss, kiss loudly, hug and kiss* can be identified as two-place predicates ($= P_2$'s) of category $(S/\overline{N})/\overline{N}$ as they combine with $\overline{N}$'s to form P_1's of category $S/\overline{N}$. Expressions such as *believe, incorrectly believe, hope and believe* will have category $(S/\overline{N})/\overline{S}$ as they combine with $\overline{S}$'s to form P_1's of category $S/\overline{N}$. In general, two-place predicates are ones whose categories are of the form:

(8) $\quad (S/A_1)/A_2$, all argument categories A_1, A_2

Even more generally, n-place predicates ($= P_n$'s) are ones whose categories are of the form given in (9a) below, where the A_i range over argument categories. It is often convenient to use the notational variant in (9b):

(9) (a) $(\ldots ((S/A_1)A_2)/ \ldots)/A_n$

$\quad$ (b) $\qquad S$

$\qquad\quad A_1 \ldots A_n$

In giving tree diagrams, we will use the notation style of (9b), in which case we assume that the identity of each A_i can be specified appropriately. For example, in (10), A_1 is $\overline{N}$, and A_2 is $\overline{S}$:

(10)

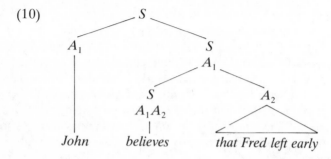

There is a final argument category that will play a significant role in what follows. This is the category of infinitival nominals, such as the A_1 (or subject) category of *is difficult* in (11):

(11)   To swim slowly is difficult.

Given that *swim slowly* is a P_1 (specifically, it is of category $S/\overline{N}$) the infinitive *to swim slowly* is correspondingly $\overline{P_1}$ (more specifically, $\overline{(S/\overline{N})}$). Minimally, then, the infinitival nominalizer *to* will have an n-tuple category whose ith coordinates are of the form $\overline{P_1}/P_1$ (or $\overline{(S/A_1)}/(S/A_1)$, for various values of A_1). Even more generally, *to* can be thought of as creating $\overline{P_n}$ from P_n, for all n. That is, we assign *to* the n-tuple category $\mathscr{C}/\mathscr{D}$ whose ith coordinates are just the categories of the form $\overline{P_n}/P_n$, for $n > 0$. As with *that*, it will be convenient to omit the categorial specification of infinitival *to* in tree diagrams in the following.

We turn now to three class of linguistically interesting generalizations that can be naturally represented in terms of a categorial grammar extended with the n-tuple notation.

2. GENERALIZING OVER THE D_i

The observations in this section, which all involve operators that generalize over predicates of different valence, are among those that provide the primary motivation for the n-tuple notation. They were also among the first to be noted as natural from a categorial perspective. Thus, the essence of the treatment of Passive we give below is already given in Keenan (1980) and Dowty (1982a, 1982b), and the treatment of valency-extending operators discussed below is anticipated in Dowty (1982b). The approach we take here differs from these earlier approaches in the following way. On the earlier approaches, valency-affecting rules such as Passive were in effect treated as a large class of rules. As a consequence, the syntactic, semantic, and morphological similarities among these rules can be guaranteed only by meta-linguistic statements characterizing the rule class. (Equivalently, these approaches might well have treated Passive as an abstract lexical item having many different categories.) On the approach taken here, however, the essential insight of these earlier approaches is incorporated explicitly into the categorial notation. Passive on our approach, then, has a single (n-tuple) category. This provides a more constrained way of expressing the syntactic and semantic unity of the Passive operator. It should be noted, though, that the generative effect of the two approaches is the same; both approaches generate essentially the same class of passive structures.

It is often the case that a functor category will take as argument an expression that itself is a functor category, in particular a predicate; further, that functor will apply to predicates of different valences with the same syntactic, semantic, and morphological results. Generalizations of this sort can be expressed naturally within an extension of categorial grammar that includes n-tuple categories. Formally, this observation can be expressed by the statement in (11):

(11)   For all i, j between 1 and n, c_i differs in form and meaning from the d_i it is derived from in the same way as c_j differs from d_j.

This general formula is most interestingly illustrated by the case where the D_i are predicates in particular. If an operation on predicates has a uniform effect on n-place predicates for different values of n, the regularity can be expressed by specifying that: syntactically, there is a function S such that for all i, $c_i = S(d_i)$; semantically, $\text{int}(c_i) = F(\text{int}(d_i))$, where F is a fixed semantic function associated with the syntactic operation S; and morphologically, there is a fixed morphological function M associated with the syntactic operation S such that $\text{morph}(c_i) = M(\text{morph}(d_i))$.

We illustrate this case with two classes of examples, the large class of what we term valency-affecting rules and the class of modifier operations.

A. *Valency Affecting Rules*

As is well known, many languages (Latin, Totonac, and Bantu languages generally) make productive use of verbal affixing to derived P_m's from P_n's (for the same or especially for different values of m and n). As a familiar example, recall from Latin that P_n's may be affixed with 'prepositions' to form P_{n+1}'s: from the P_1 *ire* 'to go' we get P_2's such as *ad+ire* 'to go-to', *ex+ire* 'to go-from, to exit', etc., and from P_2's such as *ferre* 'to carry' we get P_3's such as *ad+ferre = afferre* 'to carry-to', *ex+ferre = efferre* 'to carry-from', *in+ferre = inferre* 'to carry-into', etc. In general terms, such affixes apply equally to P_1's and P_2's, with transparently the same morphological effect, the same syntactic effect (namely, increasing the valence of the derived predicate by one), and the same semantic effect (the new argument licensed by the rule bears a fixed semantic relation, such as 'goal', 'source', or the like, depending on the specific affix).

More productively used valency-affecting affixes are the so-called 'applied' forms in Bantu languages. Thus Kinyarwanda (Kimenyi, 1978) presents a Benefactive affix /IR/ (appearing in various phonologically conditioned variants) that derives P_{n+1}'s from P_n's in such a way that the new argument is understood to bear a benefactive or recipient relation to the derived $n + 1$-place predicate. Formally, we define the category of /IR/ as an n-place category in the form in (12):

$$(12) \quad \left\langle \frac{S}{A_1A_2}, \frac{S}{A_1A_2A_3}, \frac{S}{A_1A_2A_3A_4} \right\rangle \Big/ \left\langle \frac{S}{A_1}, \frac{S}{A_1A_2}, \frac{S}{A_1A_2A_3} \right\rangle$$

Somewhat more elegantly, we may say /IR/ is that n-tuple category $\mathscr{C}/\mathscr{D}$ whose ith coordinates are of the form:

$$(13) \quad \frac{S}{A_1 \dots A_n A_{n+1}} \Big/ \frac{S}{A_1 \dots A_n}$$

(14) gives an approximate statement of the semantic effect of the Benefactive operation, such that the interpretation *ir* of /IR/ applied to the interpretation p_n of an expression of category P_n with arguments $x_1 \dots x_{n+1}$ is roughly equivalent to the interpretation of the p_n with its original n arguments and the Benefactive relation holding between the individual x_{n+1} and the p_n denotation (as given by the model):

$$(14) \quad ir(p_n)(x_{n+1})(x_n) \dots (x_1) = p_n(x_n) \dots (x_1) \wedge \text{ben}(p_n, x_{n+1})$$

The pairs in (15) and (16) illustrate this suffix on the hoof. In (15), /IR/ derives the P_2 'dance-for' from the P_1 'dance':

(15) (a) Maria y   -a -byin -ye
            she-Pst-dance-Asp

    'Mary danced'

(b) Maria y   -a -byin -i -ye   umugabo
          she-Pst-dance-IR-Asp man

    'Mary danced-for the man'

The Benefactive affix would derive a P_3 'send-for/to' from the lexical P_2 'send', and in (16) the lexical P_3 'give' yields the P_4 'give-on-behalf-of' under the operation of this Benefactive operation:

(16) (a) Umugore a -ra -he   -a   imbwa ibiryo
        woman she-Prs-give -Asp dog   food

    'The woman gives the dog food'

(b) Umugore a   -ra -he -er -a   umugabo imbwa ibiryo
      woman she -Prs-give-IR-Asp man   dog   food

    'The woman gives the dog the food on behalf of the man'

Three points concerning affixes of this sort are worthy of note.

First, Kinyarwanda presents an extensive system of such affixes (Kimenyi, 1978). Thus, in addition to affixes introducing Benefactive arguments, we also find affixes introducing Instrumental, Causee, and various locative arguments. Traditional grammars of Bantu languages typically devote large sections to these affixes and their interaction. Although the combination of affixes is not totally free (a challenge of technical description we will pursue at another time), in principle it is the case that more than one affix can apply to a given predicate, in effect converting a P_n to a P_{n+2}.

Second, Kinyarwanda (as well as other Bantu languages: see Hodges, 1977, for Kimeru and Gary, 1977, for Mashi) does not otherwise present Benefactive arguments as independent prepositional or oblique phrases, the effect of which is that the only way such arguments can occur is through the licensing of verbal affixes; the same is often true for the arguments introduced by other valency-increasing rules. Accordingly, it would be unmotivated in these languages to generate sentences with additional arguments by a rule that manipulated *only* arguments, such as Dative (or any comparable promotion). It is evidently more natural to view the relationship between the pairs of sentences illustrated above as a relationship primarily between *predicates*. This intuition is consistent with the approach of categorial grammar generally, in which the burden of description falls on functor categories.

Third, and this is the point that motivates the n-tuple extension in particular, it is worth emphasizing that the Benefactive affix (and for that matter, other valency-affecting affixes) apply more or less indiscriminately to predicates of different valence. In each case, the new argument bears the same syntactic, morphological, and semantic relation to the derived predicate, regardless of the valence of the predicate. This observation is directly expressed under the n-tuple notation in which each of the ith coordinates are constrained by something like (13) above.

A second and cross-linguistically more visible type of predicate derivation is Passive. Many languages motivate the claim that Passive (or various passives, a point we ignore for the moment) can be represented by a function deriving P_{n-1}'s from P_n's. To take a familiar example, the P_1 *ire* 'to go' of Latin yields a P_0 *itur* '(it) is gone, there is going' (compare Virgil's *sic itur ad astra* 'thus (it) is gone to the stars'). But Latin also derives P_1's from P_2's, as in the P_1 = Pass(P_2) *amatur* 's/he is loved'. While the derivation of P_1's from P_2's via Passive is banal, the direct derivation of P_0's from P_1's is not countenanced by all linguistic theories; the existence of derivations like P_0 = Pass(P_1) illustrated above for Latin then often leads to the formulation of ad hoc mechanisms that have the effect of restricting the derivation of P_0's from P_1's via Passive. To counter this strategy of response, we cite in passing the especially exuberant case of Lithuanian, where the derivation of P_0's via Passive is possible for virtually all P_1's, including many that would not be sanctioned even under revisions of current theories:

(17) (a) Kur   mūsų gimta, kur   augta?
         where by us born   where grown up

         'Where was getting born by us, where getting grown up?'

     (b) Ko   čia degta?
         by what here burned

         'By what did (it) get burned here?'

     (c) Naktį gerokai palyta.
         night goodly rained

         'Last night (it) got rained a goodly amount'

(d) Ar būta tenai langinių?
    been there windows

'And had there really been any existing going on by windows there?'

(e) Jo   būta didelio.
    by him been tall

'By him there had been being tall'

(f) Jo   pasirodyta esant didvyrio
    by him seemed   being hero

'By him (it) was seemed to be a hero'

In all cases the main predicate is the morphologically regular passive form (in these examples, in the nominative neuter singular, the form appropriate for sentences with no subject argument in the nominative case) and the 'agent' (the argument corresponding to the subject argument of the non-passive P_1) is expressed in the genitive case, as it would be for the passive of a P_2.

To describe the derivation of P_0's from P_1's in Latin and Lithuanian as well as the more familiar derivation of P_1's from P_2's, we have minimally that the category of Passive is an n-tuple of the form in (18):

$$(18) \quad \left\langle \begin{matrix} S & S \\ & A_2 \end{matrix} \right\rangle \Big/\Big/ \left\langle \begin{matrix} S & S \\ A_1 & A_1 A_2 \end{matrix} \right\rangle$$

But Passive, viewed cross-linguistically, is even more flexible. To return to Kinyarwanda, Passive can evidently 'promote' (to use the terminology of another approach) any of the three object arguments of a P_4. In our terms, this can be described by formulating Passive as an n-tuple category that reduces the valence of a P_4 to a P_3, as in (19a), of a P_3 to a P_2, as in (19b), or of a P_2 to a P_1, as in (19c):

(19) (a) Umugabo a -ra -he -er -w -a   imbwa ibiryo.
         man   he-Prs-give-IR-Pass-Asp dog   food

'The man has food given to the dog on his behalf'

(b) Imbwa i -ra -he -er -w -a   umugabo ibiryo
    dog   it-Prs-give-IR-Pass-Asp man   food

'The dog is given food on behalf of the man'

(c) Ibiryo bi-ra -he -er -w -a   umugabo imbwa
food   it -Prs-give-IR-Pass-Asp man   dog

'Food is given the dog on behalf of the man'

In (19), the predicate is of course the P_4 'to give-on-behalf-of', derived in turn via Benefactive from the lexical P_3 'give'. (For discussion, see Keenan, 1980, Keenan and Timberlake, 1985.)

Again, in the explicit n-tuple notation Passive in Kinyarwanda would have a category schematically represented as in (20):

$$(20) \quad \left\langle \begin{matrix} S & S & S \\ A_2 & A_3 A_2 & A_4 A_2 A_3 \end{matrix} \right\rangle \Big/\Big/ \left\langle \begin{matrix} S & S & S \\ A_1 A_2 & A_1 A_2 A_3 & A_1 A_2 A_3 A_4 \end{matrix} \right\rangle$$

Combining (18) and (20), Passive universally has the n-tuple category $\mathscr{C}/\mathscr{D}$ where the ith coordinates have the form given in (21a); here we have introduced A as the fixed 'subject' argument:

(21)   Passive in Universal Grammar

$$(a) \quad \frac{S}{A_n A_1 \ldots A_{n-1}} \Big/ \frac{S}{A A_1 \ldots A_n}, \qquad n \in \{0, 1, 2, 3\}$$

(b) $\mathrm{pass}(p_{n+1})(x_{n-1}) \cdots (x_1)(x_n) = (\exists y)(p_{n+1})(x_n) \cdots (x_1)(y)$

Further, the semantic interpretation of each ith coordinate (down to differences in pragmatic and textual functions) can be stated universally as in (21b) (see Keenan, 1980; Dowty, 1982b). Finally, although we have not formalized this in (21), we can expect that for each ith coordinate, the derived P_{n-1} differs in a fixed morphological way from the P_n it is derived from.

B. *Predicate Modifiers*

The preliminary generalization given in (11) above can be illustrated not only by valency-affecting rules but by other structures as well. A larger, more fundamental, and probably more widespread case is given by predicate modifiers. We treat adverbs, prepositional phrases, gerunds (= adverbial participles), and some uses of particles all as ways of forming n-place predicates from n-place predicates, in general preserving the argument structure. Thus, we can think of Modifiers (= Mod's) as having the n-tuple category $\mathscr{C}/\mathscr{D}$ where the ith coordinates are all of the form P_n/P_n, for (in principle) all values of n. While many generative treatments in effect treat Mod's as forming P_1's from P_1's, the n-tuple extension of categorial grammar allows the analogous formation of P_2's from P_2's, P_3's from P_3's, etc. Several semantically based reasons for allowing this greater freedom are discussed in Keenan (1980) and Keenan and Faltz (1985). Here we concentrate on one additional consideration.

Namely, consider prepositional phrases formed with the goal preposition *into*, illustrated by (22) with the relevant tree structure in (23):

(22)   John ran/slipped/fell/dove/plummeted into the pool.

(23)

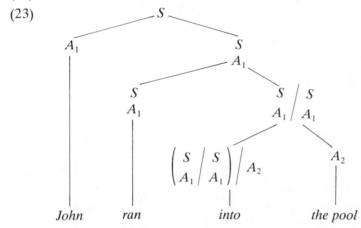

Semantically, the Mod *into the pool* will denote a function f that maps P_1 denotations to P_1 denotations, with the stipulation that the argument of the derived P_1 is understood to change from a location in one domain to a location in another. This fact can be appropriately registered by requiring that such functions satisfy the condition in (24), where $CH(LOC)$ is a property of individuals given by the model:

(24) $f(p_1)(x_1) = p_1(x_1) \wedge CH(LOC)(x_1)$

While more could be said about such functions as $CH(LOC)$, what is important for the present is that Mod's such as *into the pool* determine a property of the argument of the derived P_1.

Next, sentences like (25), with the tree structure in (26), invite us to interpret the second argument (Bill) rather than the first argument (John) as the individual that changed location:

(25)   John threw/shoved/catapulted/knocked Bill into the pool.

(26)

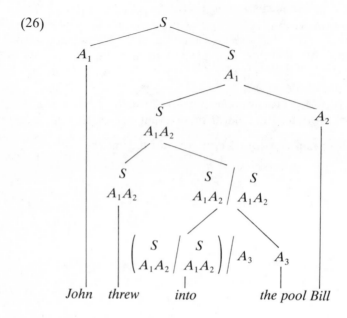

This observation follows naturally in examples like this if the predicate modifier *into the pool* is assigned the *n*-tuple category P_n/P_n given in the text above, and such expressions are interpreted by functions f satisfying (27):

(27) $f(p_n)(x_n \ldots x_1) = p_n(x_n) \ldots (x_1) \wedge CH(LOC)(x_n)$

A similar but semantically richer case involves comitative expressions such as *with Bill* with 'symmetric' predicates:

(28)   John met with Bill

Here we may consider that *meet* is a higher order predicate, as illustrated directly by *John and Bill met (in Chicago)*. In (28), then, it is natural to think of *with Bill* as combining with the higher order predicate *meet* to give a lower order predicate *meet with Bill*. Interestingly, this behavior is not restricted to higher order P_1's like *meet*, but is found as well for higher order P_2's like *compare* (a point that escaped the attention of Lakoff and Peters, 1969). Thus, in (29a), it is natural to think of *compare* as a higher order P_2, while in (29b), *with Bill* combines with the higher order P_2 *compare* to yield a lower order P_2 *compare with Bill*, which can then combine with the individual *Sally* to form the lower order P_1 *compare Sally with Bill*:

(29) (a) John compared Sally and Bill
     (b) John compared Sally with Bill

In terms of the *n*-tuple notation, a comitative expression combines with an *n*-place predicate that is collective on its *n*-th argument to give an *n*-place predicate that is individual on that argument. Using the ad hoc features 'collective' and 'individual' to represent the difference between higher order and lower order predicates, comitative expressions will have an *n*-tuple category $\mathscr{C}/\mathscr{D}$ whose *i*th coordinates have the form:

$$(30) \qquad \left\langle \begin{matrix} S \\ A_1 \ldots A_n \end{matrix} \right\rangle \Big/ \left\langle \begin{matrix} S \\ A_1 \ldots A_n \end{matrix} \right\rangle$$
$$\qquad\qquad \langle \text{ind} \rangle \qquad\quad \langle \text{coll} \rangle$$

Finally, a slightly different (and possibly English-specific) type of predicate operator that is neutral with respect to valence is the so-called 'particles', which can combine either with a P_1 to derive a P_1, in the process determining a property of A_1 (for *out*, 'decrease, loss of existence' or the like):

(31)   The lights went out/His socks wore out/The car spun out

or with a P_2 to derive a P_2, in the process determining the same property of A_2:

(32)   He turned the lights out/He wore his socks out/He spun the car out

Hence these particles will have an *n*-tuple category like that of prepositional modifers, namely the *n*-tuple category $\mathscr{C}/\mathscr{D}$ whose *i*th coordinates satisfy (33):

$$(33) \qquad \left. \begin{matrix} S \\ A_1 \ldots A_n \end{matrix} \right/ \begin{matrix} S \\ A_1 \ldots A_n \end{matrix} \qquad n \in \{1, 2, \ldots\}$$

With this we conclude the discussion of operators that generalize over P_n's for various values of *n* (see Dowty, 1982b, for additional examples).

3. INTERPRETIVE DEPENDENCY

A second class of natural language facts that motivate extending categorial grammar to include n-tuple categories involves what we will call *interpretive dependencies* among coordinates of n-tuples. As noted above in Section 1, we let the relations that interpret n-tuples of the form $\langle C_1 \ldots C_n \rangle / \langle D_1 \ldots D_n \rangle$ be in effect the union of the functions that separately would interpret each coordinate C_i / D_i. Then if f_e is the function that interprets an expression e, and δ_i and δ_j are in the denotation sets of D_i and D_j respectively (for distinct i and j), it is often the case — indeed, generally the case — that the value of f_e at δ_j is dependent on the value of f_e at δ_i.

By assigning such expressions a single category and interpreting them by a single relation, we have available a level of structure at which such interpretive dependencies can naturally be expressed. Without n-tuple categories, such expressions would have to be given as independent, homophonous lexical entries, one for each of the C_i / D_i coordinates. Even if these independent lexical entries were systematically related by lexical rules, there would be no principled reason why the interpretive dependencies among them would be those that are actually observed rather than any other possibility.

We discuss here two examples, both taken from classical cyclic syntax.

A. *Tough*

The sentence in (34) can be represented as in (35):

(34)   To read this book is difficult

(35)

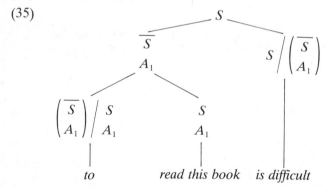

For the Tough sentence of (36), the natural structure is that of (37):

(36)   This book is difficult to read

(37)

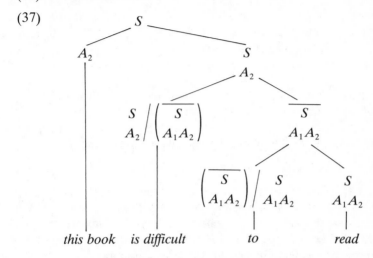

this book   is difficult   to   read

In both structures we have, as announced in Section 1, treated the infinitival complementizer *to* as having an *n*-tuple category; (35) illustrates the coordinate $\overline{P_1}/P_1$, and (37) illustrates the coordinate $\overline{P_2}/P_2$.

If we compare the structures in (35) and (37), we have apparently assigned two (classes of) categories to the predicate *be difficult*, inasmuch as it maps a P_1 infinitive to a P_0 in (35) and a P_2 infinitive to a P_1 in (37). There is a straightforward generalization: *be difficult* maps a $\overline{P_{n+1}}$ (the infinitive of a P_{n+1}) to the appropriate P_n. Formally, *be difficult* is the *n*-tuple category $\mathscr{C}/\mathscr{D}$ whose *i*th coordinates are as in (38). Here (as in the statement of Passive) A is the subject argument.

(38) $$\left. \frac{S}{A_n A_1 \ldots A_{n-1}} \middle/ \left(\frac{\overline{S}}{A A_1 \ldots A_n} \right) \right., \qquad n \in \{0, 1, 2\}$$

Here as elsewhere, it would be possible to specify more fully restrictions on the nature of each argument. In the case at hand, it seems that when $n = 0$, A must be $\overline{N}$ rather than, say, $\overline{S}$. Hence we do not observe, for example, **To entail the Axiom of Choice is difficult.*

We are in effect treating Tough here as a predicate-formation rule (in the sense of Keenan, 1982; Keenan and Timberlake, 1985). We are, of course, aware that Tough is treated in other syntactic theories as a rule of the same type as question formation and relativization (see Chomsky, 1977), on the basis of the observation that Tough, like WH-Movement, is apparently unbounded. Pending an eventual treatment of long distance dependencies in a categorial framework, we will explore here the equally motivated possibility that Tough is rather a predicate-formation rule, by showing that the analysis can account for a variety of cases.[2]

The unique case for a P_1 ($n = 0$) was given in (35) above. One of the possible cases for a P_2 ($n = 1$), when the second argument is $\bar{N}$, was likewise given in (37). (39) illustrates another case of $n = 1$, differing from (37) only in that the relevant argument is $\bar{S}$ rather than $\bar{N}$:

(39)   That Fred took the money is difficult to believe

And finally, to illustrate the case for $n = 2$, let us assume that P_0's like (40) built up from P_3's such as *give-to* have the structure in (41), where in effect the preposition *to* is treated as a case-marking feature of the predicate (other analyses of such prepositions will be compatible with our approach to Tough). In fact, all A_i in (41) are simply $\bar{N}$:

(40)   Mary gives flowers to John

(41)

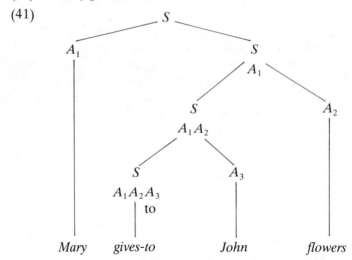

With the P_3 *give-to* safely in hand, we can generate the two possible Tough sentences in (42):

(42) (a) Flowers are difficult to give to John.
     (b) John is difficult to give flowers to.

The variant in (42a) can be generated by allowing Tough to apply to the infinitival nominalization of the complex P_2 *give-to John*. The structure for this, which is given below as (43), is essentially analogous to the earlier structure in (37):

(43)

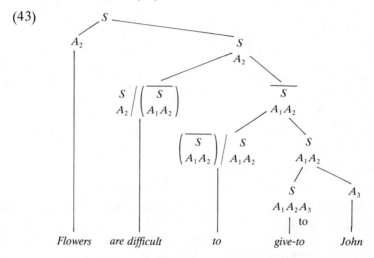

Flowers   are difficult   to   give-to   John

The more interesting Tough structure of (42b) can be represented by the structure in (44). There we have in effect let Tough apply directly to the $\overline{P_3}$ *to give-to* by assigning the matrix predicate *be difficult* the coordinate category $(S/A_3A_2)/(\overline{S/A_1A_2A_3})$.

(44)

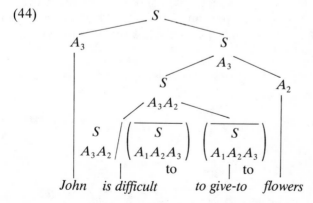

John   is difficult   to give-to   flowers

Thus we can be reasonably confident that a predicate-formation approach to Tough will be able to account for most examples.

Consider now the semantic generalization. We want to guarantee that, for example, *This book is easy to read* and *To read this book is easy* are logically equivalent. This we may do by selecting the functions f which interpret Tough predicates from those that satisfy the condition below:

$$(45) \qquad f(\overline{p_{n+1}})(x_{n-1}) \cdots (x_1)(x_n) = f[\overline{p_{n+1}(x_n) \cdots (x_1)}]$$

Here the x_i range over the individuals in the denotation set for A_i, p_{n+1} is an arbitrary element of the denotation set for an expression of the category P_{n+1}, and in general $\overline{p_{n+1}}$ is the set of properties of p_{n+1} (that is, the set of functions from the denotation set of P_{n+1} into $\{0, 1\}$ that assign 1 to p_n). Note, further, that the expression under the bar in the righthand expression is in fact a possible p_1 denotation. This equation directly guarantees the equivalence in (46):

$$(46) \qquad \text{(is difficult)(to read)(this book)} = \\ \text{(is difficult)[(to(read(this book))]}$$

We have here, then, a case of interpretive dependency where the interpretation of the n-tuple of Tough predicates at most coordinate points (for i greater than 1) is dependent on the interpretation at one specific coordinate point (here, $i = 1$).

B. *Raising-to-Object*

We turn to a second case in which there is an interpretive dependency among the coordinates of an n-tuple. In (47) below, it is reasonable to treat *believe* as a function mapping an $\overline{S}$ to the sort of P_1 that takes an $\overline{N}$ argument to form an S. Thus, (47) has the structure of (48), where A_1 is in particular $\overline{N}$ and A_2 is $\overline{S}$:

(47)   John believes that Fred is a genius

(48)

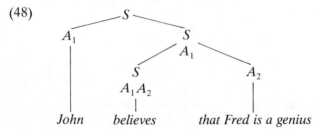

And in (49) below, it is reasonable to treat *believe* as mapping a P_1 infinitive to the sort of P_2 that takes an $\overline{N}$ argument, to form a P_1 that takes an $\overline{N}$ argument (see Bach, 1979). Thus, we assign to (49) the structure in (50), where both A_1 and A_2 are $\overline{N}$ and the third argument of *believe* is the infinitive of a P_1:

(49)   John believes Fred to be a genius

(50)

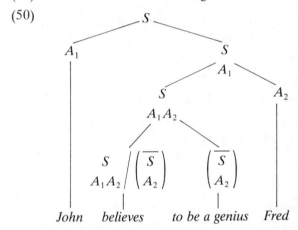

| | John | believes | to be a genius | Fred |

As before, we take it for granted here that the infinitival comple-mentizer has the *n*-tuple category $\mathscr{C}/\mathscr{D}$ with *i*th coordinates satisfying the general formula $\overline{P_n}/P_n$; here the specific coordinate is $\overline{P_1}/P_1$. As elsewhere, the structure in (50) is not intended to account for the linear order of constituents.

   In general, the problem here is analogous to that for Tough pre-dicates. We want to say that *believe* maps a $\overline{P_0}$ to a P_1 and also a $\overline{P_1}$ to a P_2, where in all cases the A_1 argument of the derived P_n is $\overline{N}$. That is, the category of expressions like *believe* will be that *n*-tuple category $\mathscr{C}/\mathscr{D}$ whose *i*th coordinates obey (51):

(51) $$\dfrac{S}{\overline{N}\ A_1 \ldots A_n} \bigg/ \left(\dfrac{\overline{S}}{A_1 \ldots A_n}\right), \qquad n \in \{0, 1\}$$

Merely by choosing the lowest P_1 to be of the appropriate sort, we can generate such examples as (52) and (53) by means of the derivation already given in (50):

(52) John believes $[\underset{(S/\overline{S})}{\rule{1.2em}{0.4pt}}$ to be false] $[\underset{\overline{S}}{\rule{1.2em}{0.4pt}}$ that the earth is flat]

(53) John believes [___ to be difficult] [$\frac{}{(S/\bar{N})}$ to walk and chew gum]
$$\left| \frac{S}{(S/\bar{N})} \right|$$

To return to the issue of interpretive dependency, we note that the interpretation of *believe* and similar predicates with a $\bar{P}_1$ argument is dependent on the interpretation of *believe* with a $\bar{P}_0$ argument. Thus we set the interpretation of *believe* at $\bar{P}_1$ with a further $\bar{N}$ argument to be identical to the interpretation of *believe* at $\bar{P}_0$ with the relevant nominal interpretation as subject of the $\bar{P}_0$. Abstractly, this gives (54), which guarantees the concrete equivalence in (55):

(54) $(f(\overline{P_1}))(Q) = f(\overline{P_1(Q)})$, all $Q \in \text{Den}_{A_1}$

(55) (believes(to(be a genius)))(Fred) = believes($\overline{\text{be a genius(Fred)}}$)

We suspect that a variety of other cases can be treated in equivalent fashion as cases of interpretive dependency.

4. CATEGORIAL OVERLAP

As a third motivation from natural language for the n-tuple extension, we consider cases of what might be termed 'categorial overlap'. In abstract terms, suppose we are given expressions e and e' of the categories $\langle C_1, \ldots, C_n \rangle / \langle D_1, \ldots, D_n \rangle$ and $\langle C'_1, \ldots, C'_m \rangle / \langle D'_1, \ldots, D'_m \rangle$, respectively. Suppose further that for some i between 1 and n and some j between 1 and m, it turns out that $C_i = C'_j$ and $D_i = D'_j$. In this case certain structures containing e and e' (with these values for i and j) will be syntactically isomorphic. It may well be the case, however, that these structures exhibit distinct syntactic, semantic, and/or morphological behavior. While most generative approaches would be obliged to create a certain amount of 'invisible' structure in order to condition the relevant behavioral differences, on our approach we may condition these distinct behaviors in terms of the different n-tuple categories to which the expressions belong, even when the categories overlap at some coordinate. In effect, this means that when an expression with an n-tuple category is interpreted in a particular syntactic context, its interpretation (or morphological behavior) may depend on other possible interpretations of the expression in other syntactic contexts.

We illustrate this type of motivation with two examples.

A. *Raising-to-Object vs Object Control*

Down to certain aspectual differences (which we ignore here), the Raising-to-Object structure in (56a) and the Object Control structure in (56b) are superficially identical in structure, as suggested by the tree in (57):

(56) (a) John believed Fred to have taken the medicine
     (b) John persuaded Fred to take the medicine

(57)

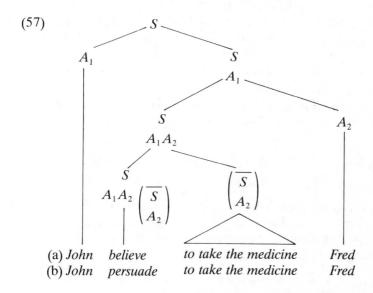

	(a) *John*	*believe*	*to take the medicine*	*Fred*
	(b) *John*	*persuade*	*to take the medicine*	*Fred*

As is well known, however, such structures differ both syntactically and semantically. Syntactically, the second argument can naturally be $\overline{S}$ with a Raising predicate, but not with a Control predicate:

(58)   John believed/*persuaded to be true that Fred left

Conversely, with Control predicates but not with Raising predicates the first argument may be $\overline{S}$:

(59)   That Fred retired early *believed/persuaded John to run for office

These syntactic facts can be directly accounted for by a correct assignment of *n*-tuple categories to *believe* and *persuade*. For predicates like *believe* the *n*-tuple category $\mathscr{C}/\mathscr{D}$ will be one whose *i*th coordinates satisfy:

$$(51) \qquad \frac{S}{\overline{N} \; A_1 \ldots A_n} \Bigg/ \left(\frac{\overline{S}}{A_1 \ldots A_n} \right), \qquad n \in \{0, 1\}$$

It follows from this that the *n*-tuple category of *believe* will include *i*th coordinates of the form $(S/\overline{N})/\overline{S}$, as in *John believes that Fred is a genius*, and corresponding *j*th coordinates of the form $((S/\overline{N})/A_2)/(\overline{S/A_2})$, with A_2 any argument category, as in *John believes Fred to be a genius*. In contrast, *persuade* can be assigned an *n*-tuple category that will have *i*th coordinates of the form $((S/A_1)/\overline{N})/\overline{S}$, with A_1 any argument category, as in *That Fred retired persuaded Bill that life is meaningless*, and corresponding *j*th coordinates of the form $((S/A_1)/\overline{N})/(\overline{S/N})$, as in *That Fred retired persuaded Bill to run for office*. These representative possible *i*th and *j*th coordinates for the two predicates are repeated in (60):

(60) (a) *believe*: $\langle \ldots, S/\overline{N}, (S/\overline{N})/A_2, \ldots \rangle / \langle \ldots, \overline{S}, (\overline{S/A_2}), \ldots \rangle$

  (b) *persuade*: $\langle \ldots, (S/A_1)/\overline{N}, (S/A_1)/\overline{N}, \ldots \rangle / \langle \ldots, \overline{S}, (\overline{S/N}), \ldots \rangle$

Thus, the syntactic facts mentioned above can be accounted for directly by proper specifications on the identity of argument categories.

Semantically, Control but not Raising predicates entail the existence of the relevant (the second) argument:

(61) (a) John believed two students to have kissed the cat
  $\nvDash$ There exist(ed) two students.

  (b) John persuaded two students to kiss the cat
  $\vDash$ There exist(ed) two students.

This semantic fact is, broadly, handled as follows. The relations in the denotation set for the *n*-tuple category of *believe* were given above in (54). The relations in the denotation set for the distinct *n*-tuple category for *persuade* are given in Keenan and Faltz (1985). Specifically, the values of these relations at any $\overline{P}_1$ denotation are functions of the same sort that can interpret ordinary simple P_2's like *kiss*. This requires that the arguments of these functions be individuals, which guarantees the entailment facts for *persuade*. It also requires, in effect, that the syntactic arguments of these predicates be referential. Although some details remain to be worked out, this observation then predicts that non-referential arguments (idiom chunks, dummies) cannot be interpreted as arguments of *persuade* in combination with a $\overline{P_1}$:

(62)   John believed/*persuaded Fred's goose to be cooked
(63)   John believed/*persuaded there to be a danger of fire

In contrast, structures with non-referential arguments are interpretable in *believe* contexts, since the denotations for *believe* plus $\overline{P_1}$ do not require their arguments to be referential.

The evidence for distinguished Raising and Control structures in English is syntactic and semantic. We can also observe systematic morphological differences in languages with a richer system of inflectional morphology. Thus in Lithuanian, for example, we can observe two morphological differences for 'believe' and 'persuade'. First, 'believe' requires a participial form of the $\overline{P_1}$ while 'persuade' requires an infinitive. A second and more interesting fact involves the case marking of the second, $\overline{N}$ argument. Normally, both predicates take an accusative argument when the predicate is not negated. When a predicate is negated, it is a general rule of Lithuanian that the direct object of a P_2 shows up obligatorily in the genitive rather than the accusative. This automatic substitution of the accusative by the genitive under predicate negation holds for 'persuade' but, curiously, not for 'believe', which allows either genitive or accusative. These morphological facts are illustrated in (64):

(64) (a) Jonas netikėjo   jį   /jo   esant kaltu
                            Acc/Gen Prt
              not-believe   him   be   guilty

     'Jonas didn't believe him to be guilty'

     (b) Jonas neprivertė *jį   /jo   būti kaltu
                            Acc/Gen Inf
              not-force   him   be   guilty

     'Jonas didn't force him to be guilty'

Without entering into a detailed analysis of Lithuanian morphology, we can note here that there is a parallelism between the Lithuanian case marking facts and the English semantic observations given earlier. With 'persuade', the second argument behaves in case marking like the second $\overline{N}$ argument of any ordinary P_2; likewise in English, the second argument behaves semantically like the argument of any ordinary P_2. In contrast, with 'believe', the second argument behaves morphologically as if it were not completely an argument of the matrix predicate; this is parallel to the fact that, semantically, that argument is in effect not interpreted directly as an argument of the matrix predicate. In both cases, the difference in behavior between the two predicates is related to *other* coordinates in the n-tuple categories for the predicates: as suggested by (60a), the A_2 of 'persuade' is always there as the second argument in both the ith and jth coordinates, while every jth co-ordinate that has A_2 as the second argument is paired with an ith coordinate in which A_2 is *not* an argument of the matrix predicate. In effect, then, this means that we can condition the behavior of case marking under negation by the distinct n-tuple categories to which the two predicates belong. More generally, our point here is to suggest that, in cases of superficial syntactic isomorphism of two syntactic structures, the structures can in principle be distinguished by referring to the whole n-tuple category to which a given expression belongs.

B. *Arguments vs Predicate Complements*

A second, and cross-linguistically more widespread illustration of categorial overlap involves the overlap between 'true' P_2's (such as *hire, kiss, see*) and 'copular' P_2's (such as *be, seem, become, end up, remain*). These two classes of P_2's can exhibit superficially identical syntactic patterns, as in (65):

>   (65) (a) John hired/kissed/saw an alcoholic
>   (b) John was/became/ended up/remained an alcoholic

If the nominal *an alcoholic* is taken as having the same category (namely, $\overline{N}$) in both cases, then the two classes of predicates must have at least the same coordinate category $((S/\overline{N}))\overline{N}$. As a result, without further mechanisms for distinguishing the two classes of predicates, they might be expected to have identical behavior.

Nevertheless, the two classes of predicates differ systematically in English and in other languages. For English we can cite the obvious fact that only 'true' P_2's are in the domain of Passive:

>   (66) (a)   An alcoholic was hired/kissed/seen by John
>   (b)   *An alcoholic was become/ended up/remained by John

And to take a cross-linguistic example, we may note two differences between 'true' and 'copular' P_2's in Lithuanian. First, although Passive in Lithuanian normally 'promotes' the A_2 of a P_2, the predicate complement with copular P_2's cannot be promoted. This is shown in (67a), where the predicate complement cannot appear in the nominative and control agreement in the passive participle:

(67) (a)   *Didvyris   būtas   Jono
            Nom.m.sg.   Nom.m.sg.   Gen
                         Pass.Prt
            hero   be

            ('A hero was been by Jonas')

    (b)   Jono būta   didvyrio
           Gen Nom.n.sg   Gen
                Pass.Prt
           be   hero

           'There was being a hero by Jonas'

Curiously, though, there is an acceptable passive of copular predicates, in which the predicate complement appears in the genitive (in agreement with the 'agent' of the passive) and the passive participle itself shows 'impersonal' agreement (neuter singular). Evidently in (67b) Passive applies directly to the complex P_1 *būti didvyris* 'be a hero'. This is consistent with the fact, mentioned above, that Lithuanian allows Passive to apply to P_1's.

Second, the case marking patterns of true and copular P_2's differ significantly. Thus, the nominal argument of a true P_2 appears in the accusative if the predicate is *not* negated (68a) and in the genitive if the predicate is negated (68b):

(68) (a) Jonas matė   *didvyris/didvyrį/*didvyriu
                       Nom /Acc   Ins
              see   hero

         'Jonas saw a hero'

    (b) Jonas nematė *didvyrį/didvyrio
                     Acc   /Gen
             not-see hero

        'Jonas didn't see a hero'

The nominal argument of a copular predicate, however, appears either in the nominative case or, under specialized semantic conditions, in the instrumental case; it would never appear in the accusative (69a). Further, negation of the predicate does not trigger genitive case marking (69b):

(69) (a) Jonas buvo didvyris/*didvyrį/didvyriu
             Nom   / Acc   /Ins
        be   hero

     'Jonas was a hero'

   (b) Jonas nebuvo didvyris/*didvyrio/didvyriu
             Nom   / Gen   /Ins
       not-be hero

     'Jonas wasn't a hero'

Both kinds of differences — availability to Passive, case marking — can in principle be stated in terms of restrictions on the domain of operations. Thus, given the analysis that Passive derives P_{n-1}'s from P_n's, we may account for the contrast of (65) above by simply correctly defining the domain of the Passive function so as to include P_2's like *hire, see, kiss* but not *be, seem, remain*. This we may do in a general way, however, only if the categories of the classes of predicates are different.

As it happens, copular predicates combine not only with (apparent) $\bar{N}$'s but typically also with adjective phrases $(= N/N)$ and prepositional phrases $(= P_n/P_n)$, as in (70):

(70) (a) John ended up sick/miserable
   (b) John ended up on the floor/in trouble

True P_2's, however, do not naturally combine with adjective phrases. Thus, true P_2's will have simply the one-tuple category in (71a), while copular predicates will have the proper n-tuple category in (71b):

(71) (a) $\langle S/\bar{N}\rangle/\langle \bar{N}\rangle$
   (b) $\langle S/\bar{N}, S/\bar{N}, S/\bar{N}\rangle/\langle N/N, P_n/P_n, \bar{N}\rangle$

Although the two classes of predicate overlap at one point of their respective n-tuple categories, they nevertheless differ categorially. We can, then, condition the acceptability of passive structures according as the predicate has an n-tuple category like that in (71a) (when the passive will typically be acceptable) or an n-tuple category like that in (71b) (when the passive will be unacceptable).

In principle as well, the category difference between true and copular P_2's can be used to condition the semantic interpretation of the second $\bar{N}$. When an $\bar{N}$ occurs as the complement to a copular predicate (that is, one that also takes a possible N/N complement), it is in some sense assimilated to an adjectival interpretation. It is interpreted essentially as denoting a property rather than a set of properties (see Partee, 1985, for a similar analysis). In this way the n-tuple category for copular predicates indirectly provides another example of interpretive dependency between different coordinates in the n-tuple category.

5. CONCLUSION: A TENTATIVE UNIVERSAL

We have seen above that a categorial grammar with n-tuple categories permits the statement of a certain range of generalizations concerning the syntax, semantics, and morphology of natural language. It is natural, if somewhat premature at this stage of research, to wonder whether it is possible to delimit in terms of the n-tuple notation the class of possible grammatical categories from which the grammars of human languages may draw. Towards this end we offer the following suggestion concerning the class of possible n-tuple categories available to grammars of natural languages:

(72) *The n-Tuple Universal*
      If $\mathscr{C}/\mathscr{D}$ is an n-tuple category in the grammar of a possible natural language, then there is a uniformly definable function g from Cat into Cat such that for all i between 1 and n, $C_i = g(D_i)$.

By 'uniformly definable' here we intend that for all i, j between 1 and n, C_i differs in form from D_i in the same way that C_j differs in form from D_j. The n-tuple categories invoked in Sections 2 and 3 above clearly satisfy this tentative universal. For example, the ith coordinates in the n-tuple category for Passive are all of the form P_n/P_{n+1}. This is to say that the function g needed to satisfy the universal has the form in (73):

$$(73) \qquad g\left(\frac{S}{A A_1 \ldots A_n}\right) = \frac{S}{A_n A_1 \ldots A_{n-1}}$$

For Tough n-tuples, the necessary function (call it $\bar{g}$) would be virtually identical to the g noted above for Passive, the only difference being that C_i is the bar of the corresponding D_i argument for the Passive function. Similarly, the function needed for Raising-to-Object predicates take a $\overline{P_n}$ to a P_{n+1}. And the various functions needed for valency-increasing operators, such as Kinyarwanda's benefactive operator, take P_n's to P_{n+1}'s of various sorts, and so on. It is perhaps less clear that the n-tuple categories invoked for predicates that take predicate complements discussed in Section 4 satisfy this universal in a non-trivial way. We can note, however, the various coordinates of, for example, the predicate *be* can all be described by a constant function that takes various arguments $(N/N, \overline{N},$ etc.$)$ to P_1, and the corresponding transitive *leave* can be characterized by a constant function that gives P_2.

It is obvious that, as the n-Tuple Universal is tested, much will hang on the interpretation of 'uniformly definable'. Pending such work, though, we can nevertheless expect that some variant of the n-Tuple Universal will be able to provide an empirically enlightening constraint on the range of possible categories available to natural languages.

NOTES

[1] Technically, one defines an index set for the grammatical categories, where a category is thought of as a set of expressions.

[2] Indeed, the fact that examples like *To entail the Axiom of Choice is difficult* are ungrammatical might be an argument in favor of a predicate-formation approach. Such examples suggest that it is important what the category of the argument is that is subjected to Tough. On the approach of predicate formation, all that is necessary is to introduce stipulations on the category of the relevant argument, as noted above. On the approach of WH-Movement, it would appear to be necessary to introduce distinctions among different kinds of WH traces, a distinction that is usually not countenanced within that tradition.

REFERENCES

Bach, E.: 1979, 'Control in Montague Grammar', *Linguistic Inquiry* **10**, 515—33.

Bar-Hillel, Y., C. Gaifman, and E. Shamir: 1964, 'On Categorial and Phrase Structure Grammars', in Y. Bar-Hillel, *Language and Information*, Addison-Wesley, Reading, Mass., pp. 99—116.

Chomsky, N.: 1977, 'On WH-Movement', in Peter W. Culicover, Thomas Wasow, and Adrian Akmajian (eds.), *Formal Syntax*, Academic Press, New York, pp. 71—132.

Dowty, D.: 1982a, 'Grammatical Relations and Montague Grammar', in P. Jacobson and G. K. Pullum (eds.), *The Nature of Syntactic Representation*, D. Reidel, Dordrecht, pp. 79–130.

Dowty, D.: 1982b, 'More on the Categorial Analysis of Grammatical Relations', in A. Zaenen (ed.), *Subjects and Other Subjects: Proceedings from the Harvard Conference on the Representation of Grammatical Relations*, Indiana Linguistics Club, Bloomington, Ind., pp. 115–63.

Gary, J. O.: 1977, 'Implications for Universal Grammar of Object-Creating Rules in Luyia and Mashi', *Studies in African Linguistics*, Supplement 7, pp. 85–97.

Hodges, K. S.: 1977, 'Causatives, Transitivity, and Objecthood in Kimeru', *Studies in African Linguistics*, Supplement 7, pp. 113–27.

Keenan, E. L.: 1980, 'Passive is Phrasal (not Sentential or Lexical)', in T. Hoekstra *et al.* (eds.), *Lexical Grammar*, Foris, Dordrecht.

Keenan, E. L.: 1982, 'Parametric Variation in Universal Grammar', in R. Dirven and G. Radden (eds.), *Issues in the Theory of Universal Grammar*, Gunter Narr, Tübingen, pp. 11–74.

Keenan, E. L. and L. Faltz: 1985, *Boolean Semantics for Natural Language*, D. Reidel, Dordrecht.

Keenan, E. L. and A. Timberlake: 1985, 'Predicate Formation Rules in Universal Grammar', in M. Wescoat *et al.* (eds.), *Proceedings of the Fourth West Coast Conference on Formal Linguistics*, Stanford Linguistics Association, Stanford, Calif.

Keenan, E. L.: 1986, 'Polyvalency and Domain Theory', ms.

Kimenyi, A.: 1978, *A Relational Grammar of Kinyarwanda*, University of California, Berkeley, Calif.

Lakoff, G. and S. Peters: 1969, 'Phrasal Conjunction and Symmetric Predicates', in David A. Reidel and Sanford A. Schane (eds.), *Modern Studies in English*, Prentice Hall, Englewood Cliffs, N.J., pp. 113–42.

Montague, R.: 1969, 'English as a Formal Language', in B. Visenti *et al.* (eds.), *Linguaggi nella Societa e nella Tecnica*, Edizioni di Communita, Milan, pp. 99–116.

Montague, R.: 1973, 'The Proper Treatment of Quantification in Ordinary English', in J. Hintikka, J. Moravcsik, and P. Suppes (eds.), *Approaches to Natural Language*, Reidel, Dordrecht, pp. 221–42.

Parsons, T.: 1979, 'Type Theory and Ordinary Language', in S. Davis and Marianne Mithun (eds.), *Linguistics, Philosophy, and Montague Grammar*, University of Texas, Austin, Texas, pp. 127–51.

Partee, B. H.: 1985, 'Syntactic Categories and Semantic Types', presented at *Categorial Grammars and Natural Language Structures Conference*, May 31–June 2, Tucson, Arizona.

Dept. of Linguistics,
UCLA, Los Angeles,
CA 90024, U.S.A.

Dept. of Slavic Languages and Literatures,
University of California at Berkeley,
Berkeley, CA 94720, U.S.A.

J. LAMBEK*

CATEGORIAL AND CATEGORICAL GRAMMARS

0. HISTORICAL INTRODUCTION

Having been under the impression that categorial grammars in general and the so-called syntactic calculus in particular had been swept away by the tide of transformational grammar, I was very surprised to learn of the recent revival of interest in these matters, as, for example, by Buszkowski in Poland and by van Benthem in the Netherlands. Stimulated by the renewed activity in this area, I decided to take another look at it, and in particular, to explore the categorical connection, which had been at the back of my mind all along.

My original motivation stemmed from the observation that a notation which was useful in two branches of algebra, module theory and ideal theory (see, e.g., Lambek, 1966), could also be applied to the study of sentence structure in natural languages (Lambek, 1958). In fact, it was quite apparent that one was dealing with a certain kind of 'closed' category (Lambek, 1969), although this information was suppressed in papers addressed to a linguistic audience.

Perhaps a few reminiscences will be of interest. Having observed the possible application of the algebraic notation to linguistics, I rushed to the library to check whether anyone had had the same idea. There I found a paper in *Language*, only a few volumes back, written by Bar-Hillel, displaying a similar notation, which could be traced back to Ajdukiewicz, Leśniewski and Husserl. Having received a preprint of my paper, Bar-Hillel commented on the carelessness of my typist in writing 'categorical' in place of 'categorial'. I did not dare to tell him that the typist was quite innocent and that I had not realized that these were two distinct words.

It appeared that the word 'categorical' should only refer to the categories introduced by Eilenberg and MacLane in their pioneering article (Eilenberg and MacLane, 1945), while 'categorial' refers to the categories in the sense of types. Sam Eilenberg assures me that their choice of the words 'category' and 'functor' was not influenced by the occurrence of these words in the Polish school of logic. To avoid any

297

Richard T. Oehrle et al. (eds.), Categorial Grammars and Natural Language Structures, 297—317.
© 1988 *by D. Reidel Publishing Company.*

possibility of confusion, I shall here use 'type' in place of 'category' in the latter sense.

While we shall present a definition of 'category' here, albeit somewhat unorthodox, for other elementary definitions the reader is referred to standard texts on category theory (e.g. MacLane, 1971), thus for the definitions of 'functor', 'natural transformation', 'monomorphism' and 'pullback'.

1. SYNTACTIC TYPES

The ideals of a ring and, more generally, the subsets of a semigroup M, are subject to three operations:

(1) $\quad A \cdot B = \{x \cdot y \in M \mid x \in A \wedge y \in B\},$

(2) $\quad C/B = \{x \in M \mid \forall_{y \in B} x \cdot y \in C\},$

(3) $\quad A \backslash C = \{y \in M \mid \forall_{x \in A} x \cdot y \in C\},$

where A, B, C are subsets of M. We read: A *times* B, C *over* B and A *under* C.

It is easily seen that, for all $A, B, C \subseteq M$,

(4) $\quad A \cdot B \subseteq C \quad$ if and only if $\quad A \subseteq C/B,$

(5) $\quad A \cdot B \subseteq C \quad$ if and only if $\quad B \subseteq A \backslash C,$

and of course

(6) $\quad (A \cdot B) \cdot C = A \cdot (B \cdot C).$

The last equation (6) must be dropped if, in place of a semigroup, we are dealing with a multiplicative system which is not necessarily associative. If the semigroup is a monoid with unity element 1, we also have

(7) $\quad I \cdot A = A = A \cdot I,$

where $I = \{1\}$.

When applying this notation to a natural language such as English, we are thinking of the multiplicative system, semigroup or monoid freely generated by the words of the language under concatenation. Which of these three kinds of algebraic system is relevant depends on whether one is interested in bracketed strings (= trees) or unbracketed strings or whether one wants to take the empty string into consideration. I myself have been in two minds about this: I considered unbracketed strings in (Lambek, 1958) and bracketed strings in (Lambek, 1961). Note that Chomsky has even advocated labelled bracketed strings (= phrase markers), but we shall not talk about these here. Whether one wants to include the empty string is probably not a matter of great importance.

Let us then consider the free multiplicative system, semigroup or monoid generated by the words of a language, say English. Sets of strings of English words will be called (*syntactic*) *types*; they will be denoted by capital letters.

To get started, we write S for the type of declarative sentences, and N for the type of names such as *John, Jane*, etc. Now *John works* has type S, and the same is true if *John* is replaced by *Jane* or any other name. Therefore $N \cdot \{works\} \subseteq S$ by (1), hence $\{works\} \subseteq N\backslash S$ by (5), so *works* has type $N\backslash S$. The same is true of *rests* or even of *likes Jane*, as in the bracketed string *John (likes Jane)*. It follows that *likes Jane* has type $N\backslash S$, and this is still true if *Jane* is replaced by any other name. Therefore $\{likes\} \cdot N \subseteq N\backslash S$ by (1), and so *likes* has type $(N\backslash S)/N$ by (4).

Now consider a sentence such as *John works gladly*. If we bracket this as (*John works*) *gladly*, we are led to the type $S\backslash S$ for *gladly*; but, if we bracket it as *John (works gladly)*, we obtain the type $(N\backslash S)\backslash(N\backslash S)$. If we adopt the associative law (6), it is easy to show that

$$S\backslash S \subseteq (N\backslash S)\backslash(N\backslash S).$$

Indeed, this follows from

$$(N\backslash S) \cdot (S\backslash S) \subseteq N\backslash S$$

by (5), which itself is inferred from

$$N \cdot ((N\backslash S) \cdot (S\backslash S)) \subseteq S,$$

an easy consequence of (6). More generally, it was pointed out in (Lambek, 1958) that

$$A\backslash B \subseteq (C\backslash A)\backslash(C\backslash B).$$

According to van Benthem, this rule is now known as Geach's law.

As long as we talk about bracketed strings, we may regard $N\backslash S$ as the type of predicates. When we talk about unbracketed strings, the set $N\backslash S$ will unfortunately contain many strings which are not constituents, for example, *works and Jane rests*. In any case, *and Jane rests* has type

$S\backslash S$, as does any sentence modifying adverb such as *today*. It follows that *and* has type $(S\backslash S)/S$, and so has any so-called conjunction. It also follows that *works and Jane rests* has type $(N\backslash S) \cdot (S\backslash S)$, in addition to the type $N\backslash S$ obtained above. Indeed, it is a consequence of the associative law that

$$(N\backslash S) \cdot (S\backslash S) \subseteq N\backslash S,$$

as we saw above.

Next, consider the sentence *he works*. The pronoun *he* cannot be given type N, since *John likes he* is not a sentence. However, since *he works* has type S and *works* has type $N\backslash S$, we infer that *he* has type $S/(N\backslash S)$. While a pronoun cannot always replace a name, as is seem from the fact that *John likes he* is not a sentence, a name can always replace a pronoun. This is the content of the rule $N \subseteq S/(N\backslash S)$, now called 'type raising', which is derived by (4) from $N \cdot (N\backslash S) \subseteq S$, which itself follows by (5) from $N\backslash S \subseteq N\backslash S$.

Incidentally, if we write N^S for $S/(N\backslash S)$, we easily see that $(N^S)^S = N^S$, so that type raising is a 'closure operation', as mathematicians call it.

Let us now look at the bracketed string *Jane (likes him)*. Since *likes him* has type $N\backslash S$ and *likes* has type $(N\backslash S)/N$, it follows that *him* has type $((N\backslash S)/N)\backslash(N\backslash S)$. If this seems too complicated, we may bracket the same sentence differently as *(Jane likes) him*. Then *Jane likes* has type S/N and *him* will receive the alternative type $(S/N)\backslash S$. Also *likes* will get the new type $N\backslash(S/N)$. If we work with the associative law (6), these type assignments are not independent from the earlier ones. In fact, the following rules are provable with the help of (6):

$$(N\backslash S)/N = N\backslash(S/N), (S/N)\backslash S \subseteq ((N\backslash S)/N)\backslash(N\backslash S).$$

It should now be clear that there are two ways of assigning types to English words, depending on whether we use the associative law or not. If we follow the first approach, unexpected types will be assigned to strings which are not constituents, but we will have a powerful machinery for handling them. If we follow the second approach, types will correspond to meaningful grammatical categories, but will rapidly become fairly complicated.

Whichever of the two approaches we favour, we cannot persist in building up all types from the basic types S and N alone. For instance, we may introduce a type N_c for count nouns such as *man, stone, bean,* etc. Count nouns are usually preceded by articles or determiners, as in *the man works, every man works*, etc. If we regard *the man* as a name, we could assign type N/N_c to *the* and *every*. From a semantic point of view this might be a mistake, as in the story recounted by Bertrand Russell about the people who interpreted the sentence "no man has ascended to heaven" as being about a certain St. Nemo. It would be safer to assign the type $(S/(N\backslash S))/N_c$ to these determiners. Unfortunately, they will have to be given a second type in case *the man* or *every man* appears in place of *him*. In German, this would not be surprising, where 'der' and 'den' are different forms.

In addition to the type N_c for count nouns, one also requires a type N_s for substance nouns, such as *water, rice*, etc., and a type N_p for plurals, such as *men, stones, scissors*, etc. In the sentence *men work*, *work* may then have type $N_p\backslash S$. However, in the sentence *water rises*, *water* must be given the additional type N or $S/(N\backslash S)$. Different determiners go with different kinds of nouns. Thus, *every* goes with N_c, *all* with N_p or N_s, *much* with N_s, *many* with N_p, *the* with N_c, N_s or N_p.

Additional basic types were introduced in (Lambek, 1959) for infinitives, present participles and past participles of intransitive verbs. One may also have to introduce new basic types for sentences which are not declarative, e.g., Q for questions.

One can continue playing this game until every English word has been assigned a finite number of types composed from basic types by the operations $\cdot$, $/$ and $\backslash$. These type assignments should be listed in the dictionary. One hopes that for any string of words it can then be calculated whether it is a sentence. For example, *he* (*likes her*) will have type

$$(S/(N\backslash S)) \cdot ((N\backslash S)/N) \cdot ((S/N)\backslash S)),$$

and the reader should have no difficulty in checking that this set is contained in S.

Let me add a word of caution. If we take such a program seriously, we are not allowed to state a rule such as $N_s \subseteq S/(N\backslash S)$, which, although plausible, is neither listed in the dictionary nor derivable from general principles, that is, from rules (4) to (7).

2. SYNTACTIC CALCULI

In this section we shall investigate the logical consequences of rules (4),

(5), (6) and (7) in Section 1. To this purpose it will be convenient to write $f: A \rightarrow B$ for a proof that $A \subseteq B$. We may also think of this as a *deduction* of B from A, forgetting the particular realization of types as sets of strings.

A *deductive system* consists of two classes, the class of *arrows* (or *proofs*) and the class of *types* (or *formulas*) and two mappings between them:

$$\{\text{arrows}\} \underset{\text{target}}{\overset{\text{source}}{\rightrightarrows}} \{\text{types}\}.$$

In place of

$$\text{source } (f) = A, \text{ target } (f) = B,$$

we usually write $f: A \rightarrow B$ or $A \overset{f}{\rightarrow} B$. Moreover, there is given an arrow

$$1_A: A \rightarrow A,$$

the *identity* arrow, for each type A, and a *composition* of arrows:

$$\frac{f: A \rightarrow B \qquad g: B \rightarrow C}{gf: A \rightarrow C}$$

We may think of $A \rightarrow A$ as an axiom and of $\dfrac{A \rightarrow B \quad B \rightarrow C}{A \rightarrow C}$ as a rule of inference which allows us to manufacture new proofs from old ones.

The *syntactic calculus* (associative, with unity) is a deductive system where the class of types contains a special type I and is closed under the three binary operations $\cdot$, $/$ and $\backslash$, and where the following additional axioms and rules of inference are imposed:

$$\alpha_{A, B, C}: (A \cdot B) \cdot C \rightarrow A \cdot (B \cdot C),$$

$$\alpha_{A, B, C}^{-1}: A \cdot (B \cdot C) \rightarrow (A \cdot B) \cdot C,$$

$$\rho_A: A \cdot I \rightarrow A, \qquad\qquad \lambda_A: I \cdot A \rightarrow A,$$

$$\rho_A^{-1}: A \rightarrow A \cdot I, \qquad\qquad \lambda_A^{-1}: A \rightarrow I \cdot A,$$

$$\frac{f: A \cdot B \rightarrow C}{f^*: A \rightarrow C/B}, \qquad\qquad \frac{f: A \cdot B \rightarrow C}{*f: B \rightarrow A\backslash C},$$

$$\frac{g: A \rightarrow C/B}{g^+: A \cdot B \rightarrow C}, \qquad\qquad \frac{g: B \rightarrow A\backslash C}{{}^+g: A \cdot B \rightarrow C}.$$

Here we have used the abbreviations:

$$f^* \text{ for } \beta_{A, B, C}(f), \qquad {}^*f \text{ for } \gamma_{A, B, C}(f);$$
$$g^+ \text{ for } \beta^{-1}_{A, B, C}(g), \qquad {}^+g \text{ for } \gamma^{-1}_{A, B, C}(g).$$

From these axioms and rules of inference other proofs and derived rules of inference may be obtained. For example, we have

$$\frac{1_{A/B} \colon A/B \to A/B}{\frac{1^+_{A/B} \colon (A/B) \cdot B \to A}{{}^*(1^+_{A/B}) \colon B \to (A/B) \backslash A}}.$$

We may think of ${}^*(1^+_{A/B})$ as a proof of the *theorem* $B \to (A/B) \backslash A$. We list some other theorems whose proofs the reader will easily reconstruct:

$$B \cdot (B \backslash A) \to A,$$
$$B \to A/(B \backslash A),$$
$$I \to A/A, I \to A \backslash A,$$
$$(A \backslash B)/C \leftrightarrow A \backslash (B/C),$$
$$(A/B)/C \leftrightarrow A/(C \cdot B),$$
$$(A/B) \cdot (B/C) \to A/C,$$
$$A/B \to (A/C)/(B/C).$$

The last four of these depend on the associativity axioms α and α^{-1}. The last three have obvious mirror analogues with / replace by \.

We also have the following *derived rules of inference*:

$$\frac{f \colon A \to B \quad g \colon C \to D}{f \cdot g \colon A \cdot C \to B \cdot D}, \qquad \frac{f \colon A \to B \quad g \colon C \to D}{f/g \colon A/D \to B/C},$$

and similarly for $g \backslash f$. For instance, here is a proof of the first in tree form:

$$\frac{\dfrac{\dfrac{A \cdot D \to A \cdot D}{C \to D \quad D \to A \backslash (A \cdot D)}}{\dfrac{C \to A \backslash (A \cdot D)}{A \cdot C \to A \cdot D}} \qquad \dfrac{\dfrac{\dfrac{B \cdot D \to B \cdot D}{A \to B \quad B \to (B \cdot D)/D}}{A \to (B \cdot D)/D}}{A \cdot D \to B \cdot D}}{A \cdot C \to B \cdot D},$$

which means that

$$f \cdot g = ((1^*_{B \cdot D} f)^+)({}^+({}^*1_{A \cdot D} g)).$$

There are many syntactic calculi. For example, the collection of subsets of a monoid is a syntactic calculus if I, $\cdot$, $/$ and $\backslash$ are defined as in Section 1 and there is at most one arrow from a given type A to a given type B, namely precisely when $A \subseteq B$. More interesting for us is the syntactic calculus *freely generated* from a given set $\mathscr{B} = \{S, N, \ldots\}$ of basic types: the set of types is defined inductively from $\mathscr{B} \cup \{I\}$ by the operations $\cdot$, $/$ and $\backslash$, and the set of proofs is freely generated from the axioms by the rules of inference specified above. According to Buszkowski, $A \to B$ is a theorem in this freely generated syntactic calculus if and only if it gives rise to a valid inclusion $A \subseteq B$ under any interpretation of the types by subsets of a monoid.

The program outlined in Section 1 may be made more precise. A *categorial grammar* of a language may be viewed as consisting of the syntactic calculus freely generated from a finite set $\{S, N, \ldots\}$ of basic types together with a dictionary which assigns to each word of the language a finite set of types composed from the basic types and I by the three binary operations.

We say that such a categorial grammar *assigns type S* to a string $A_1 A_2 \ldots A_n$ of words if and only if the dictionary assigns type B_i to A_i ($i = 1, \ldots, n$) and $B_1 B_2 \ldots B_n \to S$ is a theorem in the freely generated syntactic calculus. One may consider the categorial grammar to be *adequate* provided it assigns type S to $A_1 A_2 \ldots A_n$ if and only if the latter is a well-formed declarative sentence according to some other standard.

The reader will note that the dictionary is language specific, while the freely generated syntactic calculus is universal: it is the same for all languages, except perhaps for the number of basic types.

The question now arises, given types A and B, when is $A \to B$ a theorem, that is, when is there a proof $f: A \to B$? In the earlier systems by Ajdukiewicz and Bar-Hillel the corresponding question was easily answered, as there were only the contraction rules $(A/B) \cdot B \to A$ and $A \cdot (A\backslash B) \to B$, not counting the implicit associativity $(A\backslash B)/C \leftrightarrow A\backslash(B/C)$. Our syntactic calculus, on the other hand, contains many expansion rules such as $A \to (B/A)\backslash B$ and $A/B \to (A/C)/(B/C)$. These may even play an important role in the grammar of a natural language, as has most recently been argued by van Benthem. (As was mentioned before, they are now called 'type raising' and 'Geach's rule'.) Nonetheless, there is a decision procedure for the freely generated syntactic calculus, an adaptation of the method used by Gentzen for the intuitionistic propositional calculus. All one has to do is to replace arrows f:

$A \to B$ by *multi-arrows* $f: A_1, A_2, \ldots, A_n \to B$. Leaving out the letter f, we obtain what Gentzen calls a *sequent*. The axioms and rules of inference may be replaced by the following:

$$A \to A,$$

$$\frac{\Gamma, A, B, \Delta \to C}{\Gamma, A \cdot B, \Delta \to C}, \qquad \frac{\Gamma \to A \quad \Delta \to B}{\Gamma, \Delta \to A \cdot B},$$

$$\frac{\Lambda \to B \quad \Gamma, A, \Delta \to C}{\Gamma, A/B, \Lambda, \Delta \to C}, \qquad \frac{\Gamma, B \to A}{\Gamma \to A/B},$$

$$\frac{\Lambda \to B \quad \Gamma, A, \Delta \to C}{\Gamma, \Lambda, B \backslash A, \Delta \to C}, \qquad \frac{B, \Gamma \to A}{\Gamma \to B \backslash A},$$

$$\frac{\Gamma, \Delta \to A}{\Gamma, I, \Delta \to A}, \qquad \to I.$$

Here we have used capital Greek letters to stand for finite sequences $A_1, \ldots, A_n$; but in case $n = 0$ we just left a blank. Note that, with the exception of the axiom $A \to A$, each rule introduces one of the symbols I, $\cdot$, $/$ or $\backslash$ either on the left or on the right of an arrow.

In such a Gentzen style system, it is clear whether a sequent $\Gamma \to S$ is derivable or not: one just forms all possible proof trees with $\Gamma \to S$ at their base. However, to prove that the present formulation is equivalent to our original formulation of a syntactic calculus, it is convenient to have an additional rule, the so-called *cut*:

$$\frac{\Lambda \to A \quad \Gamma, A, \Delta \to B}{\Gamma, \Lambda, \Delta \to B}$$

Fortunately, following Gentzen, one can prove that cuts can be eliminated.

For illustration, here are proofs of $A \cdot 1 \to 1 \cdot A$ with cut and without cut:

$$\frac{\dfrac{\dfrac{A \to A}{A, I \to A}}{A \cdot I \to A} \quad \dfrac{\dfrac{\to I \quad A \to A}{A \to I \cdot A}}{A \to I \cdot A}}{A \cdot I \to I \cdot A} \; ; \qquad \frac{\to I \quad \dfrac{\dfrac{A \to A}{A, I \to A}}{A \cdot I \to A}}{A \cdot I \to I \cdot A}$$

The proof that cuts can be eliminated may be done by induction on $d(\Lambda) + d(\Gamma) + d(\Delta) + d(A) + d(B)$, where $d(\Gamma)$ is the number of occurrences of the symbols I, $\cdot$, $/$ and $\backslash$ in Γ. For systems without the symbol I, this was done in (Lambek, 1958); but the symbol I causes no serious difficulty, as was shown in (Lambek, 1969). The non-associative case was studied in (Lambek, 1961). It may be worth noting that the proof of the cut elimination theorem for the syntactic calculus is easier and, in a sense, purer than the corresponding proof for the intuitionistic propositional calculus, because of the complete absence of Gentzen's so-called structural rules.

We end this section with a brief discussion of *semantic types*, which are even older than syntactic ones. They go back to Bertrand Russell and were used or developed by many people, e.g. Tarski, Church, Husserl and Leśniewski. I wish to single out Haskell Curry, who advocated the application of his 'types of functionality' to natural languages. In modern versions of type theory (e.g. Lambek and Scott, 1986), it is convenient to insist not only on the type B^A of all functions $A \to B$, but also on product types $A \times B$ and, for good measure, on an empty product I.

We may thus define a *semantic calculus* as a deductive system with a specified type I and the class of types closed under two binary operations: $\times$ and exponentiation. Moreover, we impose the following axioms and rules of inference:

$$\circ_A: A \to I; \quad \pi_{A,B}: A \times B \to A, \qquad \varepsilon_{A,B}: A^B \times B \to A,$$

$$\pi'_{A,B}: A \times B \to B,$$

$$\frac{f: C \to A \quad g: C \to B}{\langle f, g \rangle: C \to A \times B}; \quad \frac{f: A \times B \to C}{f^*: A \to C^B}$$

Although Curry himself did not use product types, he had the fundamental insight which here leads us to assert that a semantic calculus is a fragment of intuitionistic propositional logic, which has been called a *positive intuitionistic propositional calculus*. One usually writes:

T for I, $A \wedge B$ for $A \times B$, $A \Rightarrow B$ for B^A.

That this calculus is intuitionistic rather than classical is seen, for example, by realizing that the following is not a consequence of the above axioms and rules of inference:

$$(A \Rightarrow B) \Rightarrow A \rightarrow A.$$

Here is an example of a proof in the semantic calculus:

$$\frac{A \times B \rightarrow B \quad A \times B \rightarrow A}{A \times B \rightarrow B \times A},$$

yielding the *commutativity* arrow

$$\gamma_{A, B} = \langle \pi'_{A, B}, \pi_{A, B} \rangle.$$

3. SEMANTIC AND SYNTACTIC CATEGORIES

From deductive systems to categories is an easy step. A *category* is a deductive system with the following equations between arrows:

$$f1_A = f = 1_B f, \qquad (hg)f = h(gf),$$

for all $f: A \rightarrow B$, $g: B \rightarrow C$ and $h: C \rightarrow D$. There is a switch in terminology: the types are now called *objects* and the arrows are often called *morphisms*.

A *cartesian closed category* is a semantic calculus which satisfies the equations of a category and also the following:

$$f = \circ_A \text{ for all } f: A \rightarrow I;$$
$$\pi_{A, B}\langle f, g \rangle = f \text{ for all } f: C \rightarrow A, g: C \rightarrow B,$$
$$\pi'_{A, B}\langle f, g \rangle = g \text{ similarly,}$$
$$\langle \pi_{A, B}h, \pi'_{A, B}h \rangle = h \text{ for all } h: C \rightarrow A \times B;$$
$$\varepsilon_{A, B}\langle h^* \pi_{C, B}, \pi'_{C, B} \rangle = h \text{ for all } h: C \times B \rightarrow A,$$
$$(\varepsilon_{A, B}\langle k\pi_{C, B}, \pi'_{C, B} \rangle)^* = k \text{ for all } k: C \rightarrow A^B.$$

The first of these equations asserts that

$$\text{Hom}(A, I) = \{\circ_A\},$$

making I into a *terminal* object of the category. The next three equations describe the bijection

$$\text{Hom}(C, A) \times \text{Hom}(C, B) \cong \text{Hom}(C, A \times B),$$

making $A \times B$ the *cartesian product* of A and B with projections $\pi_{A, B}$ and $\pi'_{A, B}$. The last two equations describe the bijection

$$\text{Hom}(C \times B, A) \cong \text{Hom}(C, A^B),$$

making A^B into what is called *exponentiation* with *evaluation* $\varepsilon_{A, B}$.

Many results can be proved about cartesian closed categories. For example, the isomorphism

$$A \times B \cong B \times A$$

is proved by constructing the arrow

$$\gamma_{A, B} = \langle \pi'_{A, B}, \pi_{A, B} \rangle \colon A \times B \to B \times A$$

and checking that

$$\gamma_{A, B} \gamma_{B, A} = 1_{B \times A}, \; \gamma_{B, A} \gamma_{A, B} = 1_{A \times B}$$

as a consequence of the equations of a cartesian closed category. Similarly, another useful isomorphism

$$(A \times B) \times C \cong A \times (B \times C)$$

is given by the arrows

$$\alpha_{A, B, C} = \langle \pi_{A, B} \pi_{A \times B, C}, \langle \pi'_{A, B} \pi_{A \times B, C}, \pi'_{A \times B, C} \rangle \rangle$$

and

$$\alpha^{-1}_{A, B, C} = \langle \langle \pi_{A, B \times C}, \pi_{B, C} \pi'_{A, B \times C} \rangle, \pi'_{B, C} \pi'_{A, B \times C} \rangle.$$

Cartesian closed categories abound in nature. The category Sets, whose objects are sets and whose morphisms are mappings, the category Sets^A, whose objects are functors from a small category A to Sets and whose morphisms are natural transformations, the category Cat, whose objects are small categories and whose morphisms are functors are all cartesian closed categories, and so is any Heyting algebra.

What happens if we raise a syntactic calculus to the level of category by introducing appropriate equations? There does indeed exist such a concept in the literature. A *biclosed monoidal category* $\mathscr{C}$ is a syntactic calculus which satisfies the equations of a category as well as certain additional equations which assure the following conditions:

(a) $\cdot \colon \mathscr{C} \times \mathscr{C} \to \mathscr{C}$, $/ \colon \mathscr{C} \times \mathscr{C}^{\text{op}} \to \mathscr{C}$ and $\backslash \colon \mathscr{C}^{\text{op}} \times \mathscr{C} \to \mathscr{C}$ are bifunctors;

(b) $\rho, \lambda, \alpha, \beta, \gamma$ are natural isomorphisms;

(c) the following composite arrows are identities:

$$A \cdot B \to (A \cdot I) \cdot B \to A \cdot (I \cdot B) \to A \cdot B,$$

$$
\begin{aligned}
((A \cdot B) \cdot C) \cdot D \quad &\to (A \cdot B) \cdot (C \cdot D) \\
&\to A \cdot (B \cdot (C \cdot D)) \\
&\to A \cdot ((B \cdot C) \cdot D) \\
&\to (A \cdot (B \cdot C)) \cdot D \\
&\to ((A \cdot B) \cdot C) \cdot D.
\end{aligned}
$$

The two conditions under (c) are called *coherence* conditions.

While I am not certain of the linguistic significance of all the above equations, I would temporarily like to propose biclosed monoidal categories as being of interest in linguistics.

For readers familiar with rings and modules, I should like to mention an example of biclosed monoidal categories, in fact, the example which originally motivated my interest in them. Let R be an associative ring, we consider R-R-bimodules $_RA_R$, $_RB_R$, and $_RC_R$. From these we define $_R(A \otimes B)_R$, $_R(C \oslash B)_R$ and $_R(A \owedge C)_R$ whose additive groups are given by

$$A \otimes B = A \otimes {_RB}, \text{ the usual tensor product,}$$
$$C \oslash B = \mathrm{Hom}(B_R, C_R),$$
$$A \owedge C = \mathrm{Hom}(_RA, {_RC}).$$

These additive groups are easily turned into R-R-bimodules. Finally, we take $I = {_RR_R}$. In this example, we have written $\otimes$, $\oslash$ and $\owedge$ for $\cdot$, $/$ and $\backslash$ respectively.

As a matter of historical interest, let me point out that Gentzen-type sequents in the context of bimodules are called *multilinear* mappings and that the cut elimination theorem may be used to construct free biclosed monoidal categories without using composition.

What will be of interest here is that cartesian closed categories are biclosed monoidal categories. Indeed, we may write $A \cdot B = A \times B$ and $A/B = A^B = B\backslash A$. We already have the rule

$$\frac{f: A \times B \to C}{f^*: A \to C^B},$$

and its converse

$$\frac{g: A \to C^B}{g^+: A \times B \to C}$$

may be taken to be the derived rule

$$\frac{\begin{array}{cc} A \times B \xrightarrow{\pi_{A,B}} A & A \xrightarrow{g} C^B \end{array}}{\dfrac{\begin{array}{cc} A \times B \to C^B & A \times B \xrightarrow{\pi'_{A,B}} B \end{array}}{\dfrac{\begin{array}{cc} A \times B \to C^B \times B & C^B \times B \xrightarrow{\varepsilon_{C,B}} C \end{array}}{A^{\cdot} \times B \to C}}} ,$$

so

$$g^+ = \varepsilon_{C,B} \langle \pi_{A,B} g, \pi'_{A,B} \rangle.$$

The last two equations in the definition of a cartesian closed category then say

$$(f^*)^+ = f, (g^+)^* = g.$$

What about $*f$ and ^+g? For example, we define the former as follows:

$$\frac{\begin{array}{cc} B \times A \xrightarrow{\gamma_{B,A}} A \times B & A \times B \xrightarrow{f} C \end{array}}{\dfrac{B \times A \to C}{B \to C^A}} ,$$

that is,

$$*f = (f\gamma_{B,A})^*.$$

Finally,

$$\rho_A: A \times I \to A \text{ and } \rho_A^{-1}: A \to A \times I$$

are easily defined by

$$\rho_A = \pi_{A,I}, \rho_A^{-1} = \langle 1_A, \circ_A \rangle,$$

and similarly for λ_A and λ_A^{-1}.

The cartesian closed categories which will most likely be useful in the semantics of natural languages, as they have already proved to be in the semantics of the formal languages called 'type theories', are toposes. A *topos* is a cartesian closed category with a specified object Ω called a 'subobject classifier' (see below). The reader should think of arrows $p: I \to \Omega$ as propositions or truth values. A *subobject classifier* Ω is an object with a specified arrow $T: I \to \Omega$ ($T = true$) such that, to each arrow $h: A \to \Omega$, there corresponds a monomorphism $m: B \to A$ and, to each monomorphism $m: B \to A$, there corresponds a unique arrow $h: A \to \Omega$ so that $m: B \to A$ is an equalizer of the arrows $h: A \to \Omega$ and $A \to I \xrightarrow{T} \Omega$.

For the little use we shall make of this notion here, the reader need not fully absorb this technical definition. The simplest example of a topos is the category of sets, in which $\Omega = \{\top, \perp\}$ consists of precisely two truth-values. More generally, for any small category $\mathcal{T}$, the functor category Sets$^{\mathcal{T}}$ is a topos. For example, let $\mathcal{T} = \{$past, present, future$\}$ (every set may be viewed as a small category), then the objects of Sets$^{\mathcal{T}}$ are triples of sets:

$$(X_{\text{past}}, X_{\text{present}}, X_{\text{future}}).$$

4. LINGUISTIC APPLICATIONS OF CATEGORIES

The possibility of applying categorical methods to linguistics has occurred to many people. The present author has viewed the deductions in a syntactic calculus as arrows in a category in several publications, which were however not addressed to linguists. Perhaps the first to publish on linguistic applications were Hotz and Benson, who considered derivations in a production grammar as arrows in a monoidal category. One of my students, Brian Terry, checked the equivalence between derivations and deductions in an unfinished masters thesis. Christian Houzel of the University of Paris has lectured on applications of category theory to linguistics, without publishing his observations. Michel Eytan discussed such applications in his doctoral thesis at Paris V.

What conceivable applications are there of biclosed monoidal categories to linguistics? Recall that a categorial grammar of a given language has two components: the free syntactic calculus generated by a finite set $\mathcal{B} = \{S, N, \ldots\}$ of basic types and a dictionary assigning a finite number of compound types to each word of the language. From these data, we construct a category, call it SYNTAX, as follows.

We first form the free biclosed monoidal category $F(\mathcal{B})$ generated by $\mathcal{B}$. This is done by imposing on the free syntactic calculus generated by $\mathcal{B}$ all the equations a biclosed monoidal category has to satisfy and only those. Then we adjoin to $F(\mathcal{B})$ the set of all arrows $\mathcal{X} =$

$\{John_N, works_{N \backslash S}, \ldots\}$ determined by the dictionary, where

$$John_N: I \to N, works_{N \backslash S}: I \to N \backslash S, \ldots.$$

Technically, these arrows have the status of indeterminates (see, e.g., Lambek and Scott, 1985). Thus

$$\text{SYNTAX} = F(\mathscr{B})[\mathscr{X}].$$

We shall require a second category to interpret the syntax in, let us call it SEMANTICS. This could be any cartesian closed category with a distinguished object Ω of truth-values, preferably a topos. For good measure, we shall also presuppose a distinguished object $\mathscr{J}$ of individuals. We may think of SEMANTICS as *the* world or rather a composite of all possible worlds.

By an *interpretation* we shall mean a functor

$$\Phi: \text{SYNTAX} \to \text{SEMANTICS}$$

which, first of all, preserves the biclosed monoidal structure. By this we mean:

$$\Phi(I) = I, \Phi(A \cdot B) = \Phi(A) \times \Phi(B),$$
$$\Phi(A/B) = \Phi(B \backslash A) = \Phi(A)^{\Phi(B)},$$
$$\Phi(f^*) = \Phi(f)^*, \Phi(*f) = (f\gamma_{B, A})^*,$$
$$\Phi(\alpha_{A, B, C}) = \alpha_{\Phi(A), \Phi(B), \Phi(C)} = \langle \pi\pi, \langle \pi'\pi, \pi' \rangle \rangle,$$
$$\Phi(\rho_A) = \rho_{\Phi(A)}, \text{ etc.}$$

Furthermore, we require that

$$\Phi(S) = \Omega, \Phi(N) = \mathscr{J}.$$

To interpret the words of the dictionary we must know something about the world. Clearly, we want

$$\Phi(John_N) = \text{John},$$

where it is assumed that John: $I \to \mathscr{J}$ in SEMANTICS. (E.g., if SEMANTICS = Sets, this means John $\in \mathscr{J}$.) It has been suggested (in the American Mathematical Monthly, I don't recall the exact reference) that the functor Φ may be used for catching lions: write the lion's name on a piece of paper and then apply Φ, having first made sure that the paper is inside a cage.

How do we interpret $works_{N\backslash S}$? We take $\Phi(works_{N\backslash S})$ to be the unique arrow $f: I \to \Omega^{\!f}$ in the cartesian closed category SEMANTICS such that, for an indeterminate arrow $x: I \to \!f$, $f^{\lceil}x = \varepsilon_{\Omega, \!f}\langle f, x \rangle$ is the arrow (proposition) [1]

(*) x works: $I \to \Omega$

in SEMANTICS $[x]$. This arrow exists and is uniquely determined by virtue of a property of cartesian closed categories called 'functional completeness' (see, e.g., Lambek and Scott, 1985). It is usually written

$$f = \lambda_{x \in N} (x \text{ works}).$$

Clearly, we must know something about the world before we can calculate

$$\Phi(works_{N\backslash S}) = \lambda_{x \in N} (x \text{ works}).$$

Moreover, the truth-value of the proposition (*) surely depends on time, so the topos in question is not Sets, but more likely Sets$^{\mathscr{T}}$, when $\mathscr{T}$ is the (ordered ?) set of all instances of time.

We are now getting closer to Montague semantics. While Montague may not have known about toposes, his semantics is very similar to a topos Sets$^{\mathscr{T} \times \mathscr{P}}$, where $\mathscr{P}$ is the set of possible worlds [2].

We know that every topos has an internal language, an intuitionistic type theory whose closed formulas are arrows $I \to \Omega$, we call them propositions. This makes it possible to interpret the English words *some, every* and *the* etc. in any topos, at least in the sense in which they are used in elementary logic courses. Thus, writing $D_c = (S/(N\backslash S))/N_c$, we have

$$\Phi(every_{D_c}) = \lambda_{u \in \Omega^{\!f}} \lambda_{v \in \Omega^{\!f}} \forall_{x \in \!f}(u^{\lceil}x \Rightarrow v^{\lceil}x),$$

$$\Phi(some_{D_c}) = \lambda_{u \in \Omega^{\!f}} \lambda_{v \in \Omega^{\!f}} \exists_{x \in \!f}(u^{\lceil}x \wedge v^{\lceil}x),$$

$\Phi(the_{D_c})$ as in Russell's theory of description.

To justify these interpretations, we must first look at the interpretation of count nouns to which these determiners apply (see Example 2 below).

An interpretation of a sentence does not just assign a truth-value or proposition to the sentence, but converts any way of constructing an arrow $I \to S$ from the sentence into a method for calculating its truth-

314   J. LAMBEK

value. This need not be merely true or false, but could depend on time or other circumstances.

We shall look at two examples.

EXAMPLE 1. *John works.*
    We have

$$\frac{John_N: I \to N \quad works_{N\backslash S}: I \to N\backslash S}{John_N \cdot works_{N\backslash S}: I \cdot I \to N \cdot (N\backslash S)}.$$

From this we obtain an arrow $I \to S$ as follows:

$$I \xrightarrow{\rho_I^{-1}} I \cdot I \xrightarrow{John_N \cdot works_{N\backslash S}} N \cdot (N\backslash S) \xrightarrow{+1_{N\backslash S}} S.$$

What does the interpretation Φ do to this? Recalling the meaning of ρ_A and of ^+f in a cartesian closed category and noting that $\circ_I = 1_I$, we obtain:

$$I \xrightarrow{\langle 1_I, 1_I \rangle} I \cdot I \xrightarrow{John \times f} \mathscr{J} \times \Omega^{\mathscr{J}} \xrightarrow{\gamma_{\mathscr{J}, \Omega^{\mathscr{J}}}} \Omega^{\mathscr{J}} \times \mathscr{J} \xrightarrow{\varepsilon_{\Omega, \mathscr{J}}} \Omega,$$

where

$$f = \lambda_{x \in \mathscr{J}} (x \text{ works}), \gamma = \langle \pi', \pi \rangle.$$

Now

$$John \times f = \langle John\,\pi_{I,I}, f\pi'_{I,I} \rangle,$$

so

$$(John \times f)\langle 1_I, 1_I \rangle = \langle John, f \rangle.$$

Moreover

$$\langle John, f \rangle \langle \pi', \pi \rangle = \langle f, John \rangle$$

and

$$\varepsilon_{\Omega, \mathscr{J}} \langle f, John \rangle = f^{\mathfrak{l}} John$$
$$= John \text{ works}.$$

Thus, the given arrow $I \to S$ has been interpreted as the proposition

    John works: $I \to \Omega$.

If this looks as though we have gone in a circle, the reader is invited to translate our argument into French, but letting the object language remain English.

There may be more than one way of constructing a sentence. For example, *time flies* may be analyzed as

$$time_{S/(N \backslash S)} flies_{N \backslash S}$$

or as

$$time_{S/N_p} flies_{N_p},$$

where, for argument's sake, we have ignored the difference between declarative and imperative sentences.[3]

EXAMPLE 2. *Every man works.*

First recall that the count noun *man* has type N_c and the determiner *every* has type $D_c = (S/(N \backslash S))/N_c$ (as well as type $((S/N) \backslash S)/N_c$). Like Montague, we interpret

$$\Phi(N_c) = \Omega^{\mathcal{J}},$$

$$\Phi(man_{N_c}) = \lambda_{x \in \mathcal{J}} (x \text{ is a man}) = m, \text{ say,}$$

$$\Phi(every_{D_c}) = \lambda_{u \in \Omega^{\mathcal{J}}} \lambda_{v \in \Omega^{\mathcal{J}}} \forall_{x \in \mathcal{J}} (u^{\ulcorner} x \Rightarrow v^{\ulcorner} x) = e, \text{ say.}$$

Consider now the arrow

$$I \xrightarrow{\rho_I^{-1}} I \cdot I \xrightarrow{every_{D_c} \cdot man_{N_c}} D_c \cdot (N \backslash S) \xrightarrow{1_{D_c}^+} S/(N \backslash S).$$

Applying Φ to this, we obtain:

$$I \xrightarrow{\langle 1_I, 1_I \rangle} I \times I \xrightarrow{e \times m} (\Omega^{\Omega^{\mathcal{J}}})^{\Omega^{\mathcal{J}}} \times \Omega^{\mathcal{J}} \xrightarrow{\varepsilon} \Omega^{\Omega^{\mathcal{J}}},$$

which is easily calculated to be the arrow

$$e^{\ulcorner} m: I \to \Omega^{\Omega^{\mathcal{J}}},$$

where

$$e^{\ulcorner} m = \lambda_{v \in \Omega^{\mathcal{J}}} \forall_{x \in \mathcal{J}} (x \text{ is a man} \Rightarrow v^{\ulcorner} x).$$

When we apply Φ to the arrow

$$I \to (I \cdot I) \cdot I \xrightarrow{(every_{D_c} \cdot man_{N_c}) \cdot works_{N \backslash S}} (D_c \cdot N_c) \cdot (N \backslash S) \to S,$$

we obtain

$$(e^{\ulcorner} m)^{\ulcorner} f: I \to \Omega,$$

where

$$(e^{\ulcorner} m)^{\ulcorner} f = \forall_{x \in \mathcal{J}} (x \text{ is a man} \Rightarrow x \text{ works}).$$

What we have sketched here is an idea how to interpret sentences in a topos via a categorial grammar. This is, of course, only a beginning; many details have to be worked out and a number of difficulties must be overcome. Moreover, it is only fair to point out that in my present work (Lambek, 1979; Bhargava and Lambek, 1983) I have neglected categorial grammars in favour of production grammars.

NOTES

* The author is indebted to support from the Engineering and Natural Sciences Research Council of Canada and from the Quebec Department of Education.
[1] We have written $f \int x$ (read f *of* x) for $\varepsilon_{\Omega, f}\langle f, x \rangle$ here and later. According to usual mathematical practice, we might have written $x \in f$ instead, thus viewing the arrow $f: I \to \Omega^f$ as a subset of f.
[2] (See, e.g., Thomason, 1974.) We have ignored here Montague's insistence that his underlying logic is intensional. The internal language of a topos is extensional.
[3] This example appears to be the most widely quoted item from (Lambek, 1958).

REFERENCES

Ajdukiewicz, K.: 1935, 'Die syntaktische Konnexität', *Studia Philosophica* **1**, 1—27.
Bar-Hillel, Y.: 1953, 'A Quasiarithmetical Notation for Syntactic Description', *Language* **29**, 47—58.
Benson, D. B.: 1970, 'Syntax and Semantics, a Categorical View', *Information and Control* **17**, 145—160.
van Benthem, J.: 1983, 'The Semantics of Variety in Categorial Grammar', Research report No. 83—29, Simon Fraser University, Burnaby.
Bhargava, M. and Lambek, J.: 1983, 'A Production Grammar for Hindi Kinship Terminology', *Theoretical Linguistics* **10**, 227—245.
Buszkowski, W.: 1982, *Lambek's Categorial Grammars*, Institute of Mathematics, Adam Mickiewicz University, Poznan.
Church, A.: 1940, 'A Foundation for the Simple Theory of Types', *J. Symbolic Logic* **5**, 56—68.
Curry, H. B., and R. Feys: 1958, *Combinatory Logic I*, North Holland, Amsterdam.
Eilenberg, S. and G. M. Kelly: 1966, 'Closed Categories', in S. Eilenberg *et al.* (eds.), *Proceedings of the Conference on Categorical Algebra*, Springer Verlag, La Jolla 1965, pp. 421—562.
Eilenberg, S. and S. MacLane: 1945, 'General Theory of Natural Equivalences', *Trans. Amer. Math. Soc.* **58**, 231—294.
Eytan, M.: 1982, 'Semantique doctrinale appliquée', Thèse, Université René Descartes, Paris.
Hotz, G.: 1966, 'Eindeutigkeit und Mehrdeutigkeit formaler Sprachen', *Elektronische Informationsverarbeitung und Kybernetik* **2**, 235—247.

Lambek, J.: 1958, 'The Mathematics of Sentence Structure', *Amer. Math. Monthly* **65**, 154—170.

Lambek, J.: 1959, 'Contributions to a Mathematical Analysis of the English Verb Phrase', *J. Canad. Linguistic Association* **5**, 183—189.

Lambek, J.: 1961, 'On the Calculus of Syntactic Types', in R. Jakobson (ed.), Studies of Language and Its Mathematical Aspects, Providence, A.M.S., pp. 166—178.

Lambek, J.: 1966, *Lectures on Rings and Modules*, Waltham, New York, 1976.

Lambek, J.: 1968, 'Deductive Systems and Categories I', *Math. Systems Theory* **2**, 278—318.

Lambek, J.: 1969, *Deductive Systems and Categories II*, Springer, L.N.M. 86, pp. 76—122.

Lambek, J.: 1979, 'A Mathematician Looks at Latin Conjugation', *Theoretical Linguistics* **6**, 221—234.

Lambek, J. and P. J. Scott: 1986, *Introduction to Higher Order Categorical Logic*, Cambridge University Press, Cambridge.

MacLane, S.: 1971, *Categories for the Working Mathematician*, Springer Verlag.

Thomason, R. H. (ed.): 1974, *Formal Philosophy*, Selected papers of Richard Montague, Yale University Press, New Haven.

Mathematics Dept., McGill University,
805 Sherbrooke St. West,
Montreal, Canada

MICHAEL MOORTGAT

MIXED COMPOSITION AND DISCONTINUOUS DEPENDENCIES

1. INTRODUCTION

Consider a directional categorial grammar with the rule of functional application **A** and, in addition, the two type-shifting rules below, lifting **L** and division **D**. For obvious reasons I will call this system L after Lambek's (1958) syntactic calculus, where these reduction rules have the status of theorems. I single out lifting and division among the theorems of Lambek's calculus because of their prominent role in linguistic discussion. As will appear from the format, fractional categories are projected from the vertical into the horizontal mode by giving them a quarter turn clockwise. This gives the fractional categories a domain-range structure, which makes it easy to think of them either as syntactic or semantic types: $X \mid Y$ is a functor which combines syntactically with an expression of type X to give an expression of type Y; semantically it is interpreted as a function $f: \mathrm{type}(X) \rightarrow \mathrm{type}(Y)$. (In what follows, I shall refer to the type of a syntactic or semantic object X as '$t(X)$'.) Directionality is encoded in the form of the fraction sign, back-slash standing for left-concatenation, slash for right-concatenation. The vertical slant is used to conflate the modes of concatenation, so that for example one interpretation schema can serve for a pair of directional reduction rules.

(1)　Directional categorial grammar: the system L

$$\mathbf{A}: X\,X\backslash Y \Rightarrow Y \qquad\qquad X/Y\,X \Rightarrow Y \qquad\qquad \text{(application)}$$
$$\mathbf{L}: X \quad\;\; \Rightarrow (X/Y)\backslash Y \quad\; X \quad\;\; \Rightarrow (X\backslash Y)/Y \qquad \text{(lifting)}$$
$$\mathbf{D}: X\backslash Y \;\;\Rightarrow (Z\backslash X)\backslash(Z\backslash Y) \; X/Y \;\;\Rightarrow (Z/X)/(Z/Y) \quad \text{(division)}$$

Interpretation:[1]

$$\mathbf{A}: [Y] = [X \mid Y]([X])$$
$$\mathbf{L}: [(X \mid Y) \mid Y] = \lambda xx([X]) \qquad\qquad x: t(X \mid Y)$$
$$\mathbf{D}: [(Z \mid X) \mid (Z \mid Y)] = \lambda x \lambda y [X \mid Y](x(y)) \quad x: t(Z \mid X),\, y: t(Z)$$

Because L is directional, the rules come in symmetric duals, depending on the choice of the operation.[2] The type-shifting rules respect the directionality of the original types. That is, within the directional system L, $\mathbf{L}$ is valid only if the introduced signs are opposed; $\mathbf{D}$ requires the signs to harmonize. $\mathbf{L}$ allows one to shift the function/argument relations between sisters, preserving the original order, as shown in (2). $\mathbf{D}$ makes it possible to combine two adjacent functors with the same directionality, by dividing the main functor until it can combine with the argument functor by means of $\mathbf{A}$, as shown in (3). It is convenient to have a rule for $\mathbf{A} \circ \mathbf{D}$. The composition rule (4) has this effect.[3]

(2)

$$
\begin{array}{ccc}
& \boxed{\begin{array}{c} Y \end{array}} & \mathbf{A} \\
X & X\backslash Y & \\
(X\backslash Y)/Y & & \mathbf{L} \\
& Y & \mathbf{A}
\end{array}
$$

(3)

$$
\begin{array}{ccc}
& Z & \mathbf{A} \\
& X\backslash Z & \mathbf{C} \\
X \quad X\backslash Y & Y\backslash Z & \\
& (X\backslash Y)\backslash(X\backslash Z) & \mathbf{D} \\
& X\backslash Z & \mathbf{A} \\
& Z & \mathbf{A}
\end{array}
$$

(4) $\mathbf{C}: X\backslash Y \; Y\backslash Z \Rightarrow X\backslash Z \quad Y/Z \; X/Y \Rightarrow X/Z$ (composition)

Interpretation:

$$\mathbf{C}: [X\,|\,Z] = \lambda x [Y\,|\,Z]([X\,|\,Y](x)) \text{ i.e. } [Y\,|\,Z] \circ [X\,|\,Y] \; x{:}\, t(X)$$

The linguistic investigation of categorial grammars of this kind is by now well established. Perhaps the most noticeable (and for some of us disconcerting) property of systems like L is the unconventional notion of constituent structure: if a given sequence of categories $X_1, \ldots, X_n$ reduces to Y, there will be a reduction to Y for any bracketing of $X_1, \ldots, X_n$. The topology of tree structure is the favorite vehicle for explanation in configurational theories, with its notions of c-command, government, etc.; tree-theoretical laws based on these notions do not hold within L. The virtues of this non-standard approach to constituent structure are by now clear: L offers attractive (monostratal) perspectives on the syntax and semantics of non-constituent coordination, restructuring, gapped constituents, and so on. See the contributions to this volume, in particular Dowty and Steedman, and Zwarts (1986).

What L does not give us is a theory of *discontinuous* dependencies: a sequence $X_1, \ldots, X_n \Rightarrow Y$ can be bracketed in any conceivable way, but within the directional calculus it is not possible in general to reduce the permutations of $X_1, \ldots, X_n$ to Y. Non-directional implementations of the categorial calculus have the property that all permutations of a sequence which reduces to Y will themselves reduce to Y, as shown by Van Benthem (1984, 1985). But permutation closure is obtained at a cost: one does not discriminate any more between left- and right-oriented functor expressions. This makes a non-directional version of L the proper tool to analyse non-configurational languages. But the notion of discontinuous dependency makes sense only within a system which is essentially directional, as a disruption of a 'normal' function/argument structure defined on adjacent elements.

In this paper I would like to investigate a number of discontinuous dependencies and bracketing paradoxes in morphology and on the lexicon/syntax boundary. It will turn out that the bracketing paradoxes and the discontinuous constructions can be derived in a uniform way if we are willing to enrich the system L with a mixed version of the composition rule, or equivalently, a non-harmonic version of the division rule. (The interpretation is the same as for the orthodox versions above.)

$$(5) \quad \mathbf{C}^*: X/Y\ Y\backslash Z \Rightarrow X/Z \qquad\qquad Y/Z\ X\backslash Y \Rightarrow X\backslash Z$$
$$ \mathbf{D}^*: X\backslash Y \quad\ \Rightarrow (Z/X)\backslash(Z/Y) \quad X/Y \quad \Rightarrow (Z\backslash X)/(Z\backslash Y)$$

Whereas the L-valid rules in (1) just allow rebracketing of a sequence of categories, the mixed versions in (5) make it possible for a functor to break up the sisterhood relation between head and complement in its domain. I illustrate this impressionistic description in (6). The main functor B/A and the head of its complement $C\backslash B$ govern their arguments in opposed directions. By means of mixed composition B/A can combine with $C\backslash B$ to the right, resulting in a left-oriented composite functor $C\backslash A$. The dependency between $C\backslash B$ and its argument C is now discontinuous.

(6)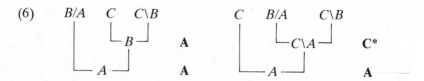

In conjunction with free application of the type-shifting rules, the addition of the non-harmonic rules in (5) is disastrous for the recognizing capacity of the grammar: in non-trivial cases it is enough to make L collapse into a system which is permutation closed. (See the appendix for a demonstration.) So, if we want the grammar to accept the discontinuous constructions without immediately inflating the notion of directionality to the level of triviality, effective constraints on the type-shifting apparatus are needed.

Partee and Rooth (1983) have proposed a type assignment theory and a flexible processing strategy to control the type explosion that would result from free application of the valid shifting rules. Their proposal is to use the lexical type assignment function to constrain type-shifting. In the lexicon, the atoms (the basic expressions) are assigned a minimal type: the most simple type to base an adequate semantics on. As a processing strategy it is posited that all expressions are interpreted at the lowest type possible, invoking derived higher-order types only when needed for type coherence (Partee and Rooth, 1983, p. 368). Type-shifting rules do not apply automatically; they are invoked only to resolve a type-clash: when two types cannot combine because they do not match, the minimal type-shift is applied to achieve type coherence. For example, proper nouns are entered in the lexicon with type e; full NP's require minimally the generalized quantifier type $(e \mid t) \mid t$. Conjunction of a proper noun and a quantified NP leads to a type clash, on the assumption that coordination requires matching types. The clash is resolved by lifting the proper noun from zero-order to second-order type.

(7)   John   but   no girl

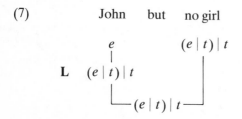

The attraction of the proposal lies in the fact that it locates stipulation entirely in the lexical assignment to atoms. I will adopt the theory of minimal type assignment and investigate the consequences for a strong lexicalist view on the interaction between lexicon and syntax. Strong lexicalism construes the lexicon as an autonomous component: lexical rules cannot be fed by syntactic rules. In Moortgat (1987) I call this position Aronoff's Conjecture, to emphasize the fact that it is a hypothesis which, so far, has withstood empirical challenges. Contrary to this position, it has been argued that certain word-formation processes (to be discussed below) have phrasal scope semantically, hence should be derived from syntactic phrases. The flexible type-shifting theory allows one to reconcile phrasal scope of affixes with the fact that affixation is word-based morphologically.

2. COMPOSITION: LEXICAL EVIDENCE

The evidence for a composition rule in the lexicon is quite solid. I will discuss three seemingly unrelated phenomena in the domain of word-formation that can be unified by means of functional composition: morphological restructuring (metanalysis), complement inheritance, and what I will call the atom condition on verb-raising clusters. Together they exhaust the theoretical possibilities for a composition rule on the morpheme level: they represent composition of two affixes, composition of a stem and an affix, and composition of two free forms. I will show how the appeal to the composition rule is forced by the theory of minimal type assignment, in combination with the theory of word-based morphology. For morphological restructuring, the harmonic form of composition suffices. But in the cases of inheritance and verb-raising, the mixed form of the composition rule can be shown to coexist with the standard harmonic form, without any difference in markedness. In the remainder of this paper, I will use **C** for the strong form of composition, which subsumes the L-valid harmonic case and the non-harmonic case **C***.

2.1. *Morphological Restructuring*

A characteristic property of categorial systems with rules **A** and **C** is the possibility of multiple analyses for one sequence of categories. This property has been exploited in syntactic research as an explanation for restructuring phenomena, e.g. lexicalized P+DET combinations in German and French (Bach, 1983), Dutch postposition incorporation (Hoeksema, 1983), etc. In the traditional German and Dutch morphological literature, one finds extensive discussion of morphological restructuring: the reanalysis of second order derivation as first order derivation.[4]

The motivation for reanalysis is twofold: synchronically, one wants to allow for the one-step derivation by means of a composite affix in cases where the intermediary step is not an existing word; diachronically, reanalysis offers an explanation for the birth of new affixes, by lexicalization of complex (reanalysed) affixes. Morphological reanalysis is straightforwardly derivable by means of the composition rule C and will serve as an introduction to the categorial approach to word formation processes.

Consider the German second-order derivation *Spielerin* ('female person who plays'). The suffix -*er* turns verbs into nouns; its lexical type is V\N. The suffix -*in* forms feminine nouns parallel to masculine personal substantives; it is categorized as N\N. In a standard categorial system with application as the only reduction rule (or, for that matter, in a Selkirkian (1982) word structure grammar) there is only one way to derive the complex form *Spielerin*: the affixes -*er* (V\N) and -*in* (N\N) have to combine successively with a base of the appropriate type, as in the top derivation of (8). When C is part of the combinatory possibilities, the domain of eligible bases for the affix -*in* is extended: the base can be of category N, or it can be a functor with N range, for example the noun-forming affix -*er* (V\N). In the latter case, -*in* can combine directly with the functor by means of partial combination: the type clash for A can be overcome by the valid combinatory rule C (remember that C is shorthand for $A \circ D$). The result of this combination, the composite affix -*erin* (V\N), can now combine with a verbal base by means of A. See the derivation below the line. Notice that the semantics of the two derivations is equivalent, as one can easily verify using the interpretation of composite functions.[5] Now take a derivation such as *Gebärerin* ('female person who gives birth'): it is unlikely, for biological reasons, that this is an -*in* derivation from an -*er* derivation. The composite affix -*erin* allows one to derive *Gebärerin* directly from the verb stem *gebär-*, in accordance with Aronoff's dictum that words are derived from existing words.

(8)

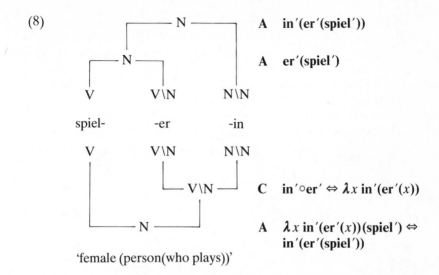

'female (person(who plays))'

This is the synchronic type of evidence for reanalysis. Under the approach defended here, composite affixes have the status of complex lexical entries. Diachronically, then, they are subject to lexicalization processes: they have the potential to acquire idiosyncratic properties, semantically or morphophonologically. Lexicalization may turn a composite affix into a new unanalysable affix. I give an example of semantic and morphophonological lexicalization effects.

A standard Dutch example for the loss of a transparent compositional semantics is given in (9) (cf. Van Marle, 1984). The affix -*ig* (A\A) modifies adjectives ('somewhat A', cf. English -*ish*); the affix -*heid* (A\N) turns adjectives into property denoting nouns ('the property of being A', cf. English -*ness*). In (a) I give the double derivation for a semantically transparent second order derivation: *groenigheid* ('greenishness'). The (b) forms are direct derivations from simplex A's: intermediary -*ig* forms do not exist. But here the composite affix -*igheid* is no longer compositionally transparent: *nieuwigheid* means 'something new', not 'the property of being somewhat new'. In German, this lexicalization process has gone further: -*igkeit* is a pure allomorph of -*heit/-keit* chosen after certain affixes, e.g. -*los* or -*haft*. There is no alternation here with simple -*ig* derivations.

(9)

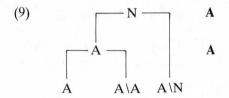

(a)   goed   ig   heid   (b)   nieuw   ig   heid

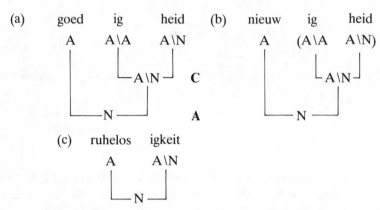

(c)   ruhelos   igkeit

(b) nieuwigheid, fraaiigheid, kleinigheid, vastigheid, vuiligheid, malligheid
   (but: *nieuwig, *fraaiig, *kleinig, *vastig, *vuilig, *mallig)
(c) Schamlosigkeit, Ruhelosigkeit, Leblosigkeit, Kinderlosigkeit
   (but: *schamlosig, *ruhelosig, *leblosig, *kinderlosig)

A composite affix can also acquire phonologically idiosyncratic proper-ties. An example which has not been presented from this perspective is the stress behaviour of the combination -*loosheid* (cf. -*lessness*) in Dutch. Schultink (1979) has remarked that derivations in -*loosheid* are stressed on -*loos* unless the main stress in the simple -*loos* derivation is on the syllable preceding -*loos*. Compare the forms in (10), with the stressed syllables in italic.

(10)   *ra*deloos   rade*loos*heid   *stuur*loos   *stuur*loosheid
      *werk*eloos   werke*loos*heid   be*zit*loos   be*zit*loosheid
      *le*venloos   leven*loos*heid   sys*teem*loos   sys*teem*loosheid

The condition as it is stated above poses a discontinuity puzzle in connection with Siegel's Adjacency Condition. The affixes -*loos* as well as -*heid* are by themselves stress-neutral. On the cycle where -*loos* is attached, one cannot look ahead towards possible further derivation with -*heid*. But when -*heid* is attached, we can no longer refer to the phonological properties of the base of the -*loos* derivation: this violates the locality required by the Adjacency Condition. The problem vanishes as soon as we have in the lexicon a constituent -*loosheid*, which can then locally determine its stress properties. **C** is the way to form this constituent:

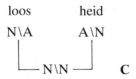

It is crucial to notice in this respect that the stress property of the composite affix -*loosheid* is idiosyncratic, i.e. the effect of lexicalization. This will be clear when one compares -*loosheid* with an affix combination with the same prosodical make-up as -*loosheid*, for example -*baarheid*. The second-order derivations in (11) are stressed on the syllable that is stressed in the simple derivations without -*heid*, as one would expect for a stress-neutral affix.

(11)   *hand*elbaar   *hand*elbaarheid   *handel*baar*heid
        ver*enig*baar   ver*enig*baarheid   *verenig*baar*heid
        ver*wis*selbaar   ver*wis*selbaarheid   *verwissel*baar*heid

Morphological restructuring is problematic for standard generative morphology, i.e. for essentially context-free word structure grammars: it requires rebracketing devices of unclear status, and one has to choose one of the bracketings as 'basic'. Critics of generative morphology have rightly remarked that the constituent structure of complex words is apparently less monolithic than Selkirkian theory would have us believe. **C** allows one to anchor second-order derivations in two ways within the system: the pure **A** derivation has no privileged status. Lexicalization of composite affixes and derivation from possible but non-existent intermediary steps support multiple analysis.

2.2. Complement Inheritance

The derivation of morphological restructuring required composition of the harmonic kind: two left-oriented functors (suffixes) were composed into a complex left-oriented functor. A phenomenon which calls for both harmonic and mixed forms of composition is complement inheritance. Inheritance occurs when an affix is combined with a stem requiring a complement, and the subcategorization for the complement is transmitted from the base to the derived expression. See the examples in (12). Inheritance constructions qualify as relatedness paradoxes in the sense of Williams (1981). Semantically, the affixes have a whole phrase in their scope (stem + complement), but morpho-syntactically they combine with a proper subpart of this phrase (the head): the affix breaks the sisterhood relation between head and complement. Cf. the graphic representation of the conflict between syntactic and semantic architecture below. Because of this mismatch, inheritance has been construed as a challenge to the compositionality principle, and to Aronoff's theory of word-based morphology. Compositionality, in its intuitive form, requires that for the computation of the meaning of a derived word, the meaning of the parts must be sufficient; what we see here is that the affix has scope over the stem plus its complement, not just the stem. The popular strategy to save the principle (recently advocated in e.g. Fabb, 1984) consists in rejecting the restrictive view on the interaction between lexicon and syntax: *believer in magic* would be construed as an -*er* derivation from the phrase *believe in magic*, by means of some affix movement operation which attaches the affix to the verbal head.

(12) (a) belie*ver* in magic, work*ers* in GB, search*ers* after truth, indebted*ness* to the king, reli*ance* on Bill, remo*val* from the board, accessibil*ity* to all students.

(b) tevreden*heid* met de soep, dreig*er* met zelfmoord, *ge*roep om hulp, vergelijk*baar* met wijn, verzak*ing* aan de duivel.

Semantic scope:

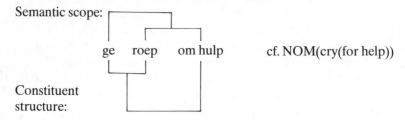

ge   roep   om hulp   cf. NOM(cry(for help))

Constituent
structure:

In a categorial theory with rules **A** and **C**, the properties of inheritance fall out without any relaxation of the compositionality principle or the lexicon/syntax interface. Let us have a look at the left-hand column in (13).[6] These are the basic cases of derivations with the affixes in question. Given the category of the base and the category of the derived expression, we can determine the category of the affixes by solving a simple equation: if $A \cdot$ -*heid* = N, then -*heid* = A\N. The theory of minimal type assignment requires that the affixes get the categories shown in (a) by the lexical assignment function; these categorizations lead to unproblematic **A** derivations as far as the (a) column is concerned. Now, what happens when the base is itself a functor, with the category required by the affixes as range? For the **A** rule these combinations represent a type clash: the **A** rule cannot combine base and affix in the (b) cases. But because **C** is available as an alternative combinatory possibility, the dynamic interpretation strategy allows one to resolve the clash. As a result of the **C** rule, the argument of the base is transmitted to the level of the derived expression. Syntactically, then, **C** allows us to give a surface derivation of inheritance constructions which respects Aronoff's thesis of word-based morphology.

(13) complement inheritance: harmonic and mixed composition[7]

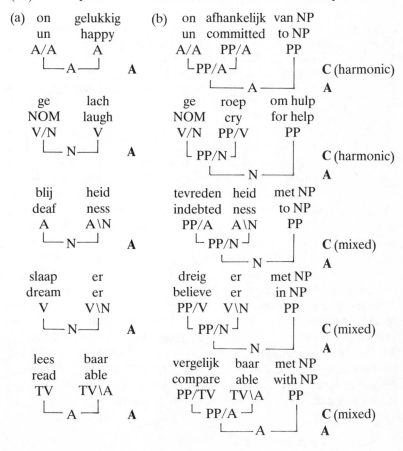

If we want to give a unified analysis to inheritance phenomena, the **C** rule cannot be restricted to the harmonic case, as the examples in (13) show. Prefixation to a right-oriented base (cf. *un-*) is derivable by means of the *L*-valid form of composition, because the composed functors harmonize in their directionality. Suffixation to a right-oriented base is not *L*-derivable, because of the conflicting directionalities of the composed functors, which gives rise to a discontinuous dependency between base and complement. The existence of these discontinuous dependencies is exactly what motivates the addition of mixed composition to *L*: inheritance is insensitive to the distinction between standard and mixed composition.

Table (13) focuses on the syntactic side of inheritance constructions. The interpretations assigned to the composite functors in (b) are displayed in (14).

(14) $(un' \circ committed')(to\ NP') \Leftrightarrow un'(committed'(to\ NP'))$
        $(ge' \circ roep')(om\ NP') \Leftrightarrow ge'(roep'(om\ NP'))$
        $(ness' \circ indebted')(to\ NP') \Leftrightarrow ness'(indebted'(to\ NP'))$
        $(er' \circ believe')(in\ NP') \Leftrightarrow er'(believe'(in\ NP'))$
        $(able' \circ compare')(with\ NP') \Leftrightarrow able'(compare'(with\ NP'))$

The semantics of functional composition resolves the mismatch between morphosyntactic constituent structure and semantic scope that gives the construction the dubious reputation of a 'relatedness paradox'. Although the affixes form a constituent with a lexical base, they are interpreted as having scope over the combination of base plus complement. There is no reason, then, to abandon surface compositionality in the light of complement inheritance constructions. In fact, a stronger claim can be made: there are positive reasons not to abandon surface compositionality.

In general, there are two strategies to deal with discontinuities. The approach defended here enriches the combinatory apparatus with a **C** rule; the operation used by the combinatory rules is just concatenation. This is a Parmenidean approach: affixes do not move; all affix-movement is deception of the senses. Alternatively, one might want to use poor combinatory resources (basically, **A**), and rely on a richer set of operations, including non-concatenative operations (i.e. phrasal infixation moving the affix to the head, cf. Bach, 1984). The movement approach gives up a hard-core assumption of the categorial enterprise, which Steedman has called the Adjacency Property:

the combination rules are unable to combine two non-adjacent items, unless the intervening item(s) can first be combined with one or the other of them (Steedman, 1985, p. 533).

To implement the movement strategy, one can use a variety of methods. I choose here Pollard's (1984) framework of head-wrapping operations, because it is model-theoretically interpreted, and hence easily compared to the approach taken here. But the comments carry over to Pesetsky's (1985) affix-raising in logical form, or Fabb's (1984) syntactic affixation, which are guided by the same idea. A Pollard-style derivation might look like (15). (The constituent nodes are annotated with the corresponding headed string, with the head indicated by a suffixed asterisk, and its interpretation.)

(15)   N: devotedness* to Bill, **ness′(devoted′(to Bill′))**

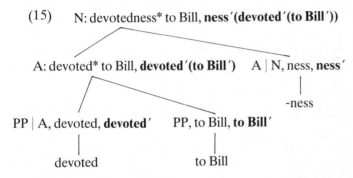

A: devoted* to Bill, **devoted′(to Bill′)**   A | N, ness, **ness′**

|
-ness

PP | A, devoted, **devoted′**   PP, to Bill, **to Bill′**

| |
devoted   to Bill

The first step combines *devoted* with its complement PP by a concatenation operation; the semantic operation is functional application of the head to the complement. The second (crucial) step adds -*ness*, by wrapping the first argument (the complex adjectival phrase) around -*ness*, placing the head of the wrapped argument immediately to the left of -*ness*. Notice that throughout the derivation semantic scope coincides with structural c-command: this is so because surface compositionality is abandoned; the notion of constituent structure (semantic/syntactic) has become abstract — 'parts' for the compositionality principle are no longer 'visible parts': the derivation in (15) contains nowhere a syntactic/semantic constituent *devotedness*.

It is clear that the wrapping approach is equivalent to the use of **C** for simple cases. But wrapping does not generalize to more complex coordination cases, as I will show now. Consider the examples in (16). Given the generalized conjunction theory of Keenan and Faltz (1985),

Gazdar (1982), Partee and Rooth (1983), one may require of an adequate semantic theory that it can interpret any syntactic operation of conjunction/disjunction by means of the generalized semantic operators ⊓ and ⊔. When we combine *-ness* with *devoted* by means of **C**, the result is a syntactic constituent of category PP/N, which corresponds to a semantic category, a function from t(PP) to t(N); in other words, there is a semantic object in the model corresponding to the expression *devotedness*. The category is of a conjoinable type, so given the generalized conjunction hypothesis, one can expect Boolean combinations, which can be straightforwardly interpreted using the generalized coordination operators. These Boolean combinations indeed occur: we see in (16) that composite functions can be conjoined with identical categories, basic or derived, and if derived, derived by the same or by a different rule of morphology. Under the wrapping approach, as we saw above, there is no semantic object corresponding to phrasal infixation. It is impossible, then, to assign a surface interpretation to the conjunctions in (16).

(16)   Boolean combinations

their [preparedness and willingness] to start the fight

(VP/N: *ness+ness*)

John's [reluctance or inability] to accept the offer

(VP/N: *ce+ity*)

his [fidelity and devotedness] to the king

(PP/N: basic+*ness*)

[aansprakelijheid en verantwoordelijkheid] voor schade

(PP/N: *heid+heid*)

[begaanheid en medelijden] met de gewonde

(PP/N: *heid*+basic)

[on voldaan heid en spijt] over de mislukking

(PP/N: *heid*+basic)

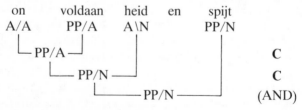

heid′∘(on′∘voldaan′)⊓ spijt′ ⇔
λx[heid′(on′(voldaan′(x)))⊓ spijt′(x)]

Notice in particular the cases where the product of **C** is conjoined with a basic expression. These form crucial evidence against phrasal infixation: one cannot say here that the affix is distributed over the heads in case the base is a conjoined phrase. The same point can be made for the examples in (17): conjunction of the lexical comparative with the syntactic comparative. Fabb (1984, p. 120) uses the construction *unhappier with me* to show that *er*-affixation has to be done in the syntax in order to get the proper scope relations (= more not happy with me). As I have shown, functional composition allows one to reject the correlation between semantic scope and syntactic c-command. The conjunction in (17) moreover shows that we need a syntactic/semantic constituent *unhappier* if we want to be able to derive the Boolean combinations directly. (A′ stands for the type of comparative adjective phrase.)

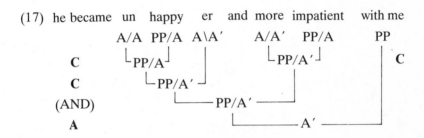

(17) he became un happy er and more impatient with me

2.3. *Verb-raising, Dutch versus German*

Up till now we have seen evidence for the composition of bound morphemes (restructuring), and stem + affix combinations (inheritance). A third type of evidence for functional composition in the lexicon comes from combinations of two free forms: this type is represented by the notorious verb-raising constructions in Dutch and German. In a number of publications, Steedman (1984, 1985) has shown how this type of discontinuous dependency can be derived in a one-level syntax by means of partial combination rules, our **C**.[8] One can compare this approach to Pollard's (1984) proposal to derive the verb-raising clusters by means of head-wrapping operations. And again, generalized conjunction evidence supports the composition approach: verb-raising clusters can appear in Boolean combinations with clusters of the same syntactic category/semantic type.

As with the inheritance construction, it is crucial for our purposes to show that it is not necessary for the conjoined clusters to have the same derivational history: in the examples (18), one conjunct is a basic expression, the other one a product of **C**. These examples show not only that the verb-clusters must be (syntactic/semantic) constituents that can be conjoined with basic expressions of the appropriate category, but also that the complement structure of verb-raising clusters must be identical to the complement structure of basic expressions of the same category. Surface approaches to verb-raising such as Bresnan *et al.* (1982) posit a complement structure for verb-raising clusters in which the NP objects are embedded in VP-complements lacking their verbal head; the headless VP structures are essential to determine the dependencies between the NP's and the verbs in the cluster. This view of the complement structure of verb-raising clusters cannot be reconciled with surface coordination in cases such as (18).

(18)   TTV: basic (*voorlas*) and verb-raising cluster (*liet navertellen*)

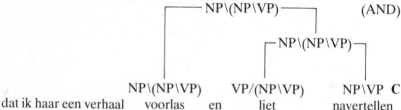

```
                    NP\(NP\VP)      VP/(NP\VP)      NP\VP  C
dat ik haar een verhaal      voorlas      en      liet      navertellen
      that I her a story read and let retell
      'that I read her a story and had her retell it'
```

(TV: basic + VR)
      dat ik een inbreker neerstak maar daarna liet ontsnappen
      that I a burglar knocked-down but then let escape
      'that I knocked down a burglar but let him escape afterwards'

(TV: VR + basic)
      dat hij een meisje zag binnenkomen en meteen omhelsde
      that he a girl saw enter and immediately embraced
      'that he saw a girl come in and embraced her immediately'

A comparison between the Dutch and the German version of the verb-raising construction supports the strong form of **C** advocated here. Abstracting from certain stylistic permutations, the order of the verbs in the German clusters is the mirror-image of the Dutch order, as can be seen from the examples below. That is, in German the verb-raising triggers are left-oriented functors, just like the verbs they form a cluster with. This makes the German construction derivable by means of the L-valid composition rule: the directionalities of the composed functors harmonize. In Dutch, the triggers are right-oriented functors, whereas ordinary verbs take their arguments to the left: hence the crossed dependency in Dutch between arguments and verbs. A unified account of the syntax and semantics of verb-raising clusters in Dutch and German requires the strong form of **C** which allows for harmonic and mixed composition.

(19)   Dutch: German:

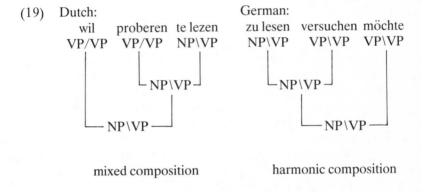

               mixed composition   harmonic composition

The derivation of the verb-raising clusters in the lexicon, as a productive type of verbal compounding, may be controversial, but is unavoidable as soon as the lexical component is equipped with **C**, which is independently motivated on the basis of morphological inheritance and restructuring, as we have seen. The lexical derivation of the clusters is empirically supported: it explains the fact that in Standard Dutch, the cluster has to consist of basic expressions; it is impossible — to use the transformational metaphor — to raise non-maximal projections. On the assumption that the verb clusters are formed in the lexicon, the atom condition follows from Aronoff's Conjecture: lexical rules cannot be fed by syntactic rules. For a syntactic derivation of verb-raising it has to be stipulated (as it is, quite explicitly, in e.g. Houtman's (1984) analysis by means of the feature specification [+L] which requires the complement of a verb-raising trigger to be a lexical expression).

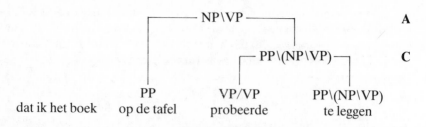

	PP	VP/VP	PP\(NP\VP)
dat ik het boek	op de tafel	probeerde	te leggen

(20)   that I the book on the table tried to put
        'that I tried to put the book on the table'
        *. . . probeerde op de tafel te leggen[9]

3. LEXICAL COMPOSITION AND LIFTING: RELATEDNESS PARADOXES INVOLVING MODIFIER SCOPE

The relatedness paradoxes discussed above provide justification for a calculus of type transitions with (a strong form of) functional composition. I would like to turn now to a set of bracketing paradoxes involving modifier scope. A surface compositional derivation of these constructions requires the full resources of valid type transitions: resources equivalent to the combination of **C** and **L**. When composition and lifting are freely available, the grammar will accept meaningless 'morpheme salads' (cf. Pesetsky, 1985). So these constructions will further illustrate how lexical type assignment can properly constrain the calculus.

Consider the derivations in (21). The synthetic compounds in the bottom row have often been cited in support of phrasal derivation theories. Suppose that the affix -*ed* ('with') is categorized as N\A, on the basis of the simple derivations. Suppose furthermore that derivation from phrases is possible (contrary to Aronoff's Conjecture), and that the grammar contains non-concatenative operations of head-adjunction. Under the phrasal derivation approach, there is a unified explanation for the top and the bottom row: the base of -*ed* affixation can be a basic N, or a syntactically complex one through the combination of an N/N modifier (an adjective) with an N. Affix scope coincides with structural c-command in the abstract constituent structure. The left-branching morphological structure (for example: [[black hair] ed]) is then broken up by the head-adjunction operation which results in the phrasing required by the phonology: ((black)(haired)).

(21)   -ed: basic input (N):
              bearded, stringed, feathered, crested, flavoured
         phrasal input (N/N . N):
              black-haired, narrow-minded, short-lived

Dutch has two affixes corresponding to *-ed*: the suffix *-ig* and the circumfix *ge-· · ·-d*.[10] They both show up in simple denominal derivations, and in synthetic compound doubles, cf. (22). The Boolean evidence which was used above to show the inadequacy of phrasal derivation approaches can be applied to this type of bracketing paradox too: in Dutch (and German), coordination can operate below the word-level on parts of complex words, if they are phonologically independent. Consider the conjoined compound members in (23): given our adequacy criterion for coordination, they should be interpretable by means of the generalized coordination operators; i.e. the right members of these compounds must be constituents syntactically and semantically. But if we want to stick to surface compositionality, we are faced with a double problem: the simple denominal derivations and the synthetic compounds must receive a unified treatment, and the interpretation assigned to the synthetic compounds must be such that the affix has the adjective-noun combination within its scope, although it does not c-command the adjectival left member.

(22)   -ig: hoekig/driehoekig, kleurig/veelkleurig,
                  harig/langharig
         ge...d: gerokt/kortgerokt, gedast/zwartgedast,
                  gespierd/sterkgespierd

(23)   donker-ogig of harig   zwart-geblokt of gestreept
         dark (eye -ed or hair -ed) black (GE-square-D or GE-stripe-D)
         'dark-eyed or dark-haired' 'with black squares or black stripes'

Given a flexible categorial theory with a system of valid type transitions, the relation between the simple *-ig* derivations and the synthetic compound case can be established straightforwardly, if we extend the theory of minimal type assignment in a natural way. Up to now, I assumed that lexical assignment associates an expression with one basic (most simple) type; when the basic type leads to a type clash, type-shifting is triggered to achieve coherence. Assume instead that lexical assignment can associate an expression with a set of types: the basic type (as before), with possibly secondary types derivable from the basic assignment by valid type-shifting schemata. As before, type shifting is not automatic; but shifting can now be triggered by the primary assignment, or a possible secondary assignment. The assignment theory, as presented here, tries to capture in terms of valid type transitions what the possible relations are between different uses/meanings of a basic expression. As such it is part of a characterization of possible lexical rules. From a primary type assignment, a number of secondary assignments can be derived using valid type-shifting schemata, i.e. with completely predictable interpretations. The lexical entry for a basic expression can record which of the potential secondary types are realized. Let me illustrate what I mean. Assume that the affix -*ig* is assigned the following two types by the lexical type assignment.

(24)   Lexical rule for -*ig*

$$-ig: N\backslash A = \mathbf{D} \Rightarrow ((N/N)\backslash N)\backslash((N/N)\backslash A)$$
$$\mathbf{ig}' \qquad\qquad \lambda x \lambda y\, \mathbf{ig}'(x(y)) \qquad x: t((N\,|\,N)\,|\,N),\, y: t(N\,|\,N)$$

The types are related by the valid derivation schema **D**: numerator and denominator of the input fraction are divided by the same type (the type for the missing adjective). The interpretation of the higher-order type is completely determined by the **D** derivation (cf. the semantics of **D** in (1)). The fact that among the infinite number of possible types allowed by the valid type-shifting rules, -*ig* gets the two types indicated, is of course an idiosyncratic fact: not all denominal adjectives have synthetic compound doubles. But it is the only fact we need to stipulate; and indeed the only kind of fact we can stipulate, if it is true that lexical type assignment is the only locus for stipulation.

Given the lexical type-assignment above, the derivation of the synthetic compound construction follows from the dynamics of type-shifting. Let us go through an example. The functor -*ig* looks for an (N/N)\N argument. However, the basic type assignment to *oog* is simply N: a type clash. So we apply the minimal type-shift to get an argument of the appropriate type: **L**, from N to (N/N)\N. Now we can derive the expression -*ogig*, by **A**. The resulting expression is a functor looking for an adjective (N/N), and with range A. The interpretation is completely determined by the type-shifting rules used: it can be read off from the derivation. The adjective *blauw* ends up with only the noun *oog* in its scope: the synthetic compound means 'with blue eyes', not 'in a blue way provided with eyes'.[11]

(25)   blauw   oog   ig   (cf. blue-eyed)

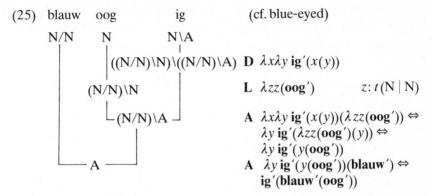

D $\lambda x \lambda y \, \mathbf{ig}'(x(y))$

L $\lambda z z(\mathbf{oog}')$ $z: t(N \mid N)$

A $\lambda x \lambda y \, \mathbf{ig}'(x(y))(\lambda z z(\mathbf{oog}')) \Leftrightarrow$
   $\lambda y \, \mathbf{ig}'(\lambda z z(\mathbf{oog}')(y)) \Leftrightarrow$
   $\lambda y \, \mathbf{ig}'(y(\mathbf{oog}'))$

A $\lambda y \, \mathbf{ig}'(y(\mathbf{oog}'))(\mathbf{blauw}') \Leftrightarrow$
   $\mathbf{ig}'(\mathbf{blauw}'(\mathbf{oog}'))$

Notice that the version of **D** needed for *-ig* synthetic compounds is
valid within *L*: the suffix *-ig* is left-divided by N/N, the operations
harmonize. Operations have to be mixed, however, for the parallel
ge-····-d construction, where the circumfix operator is combined with
left-concatenation, which results in a discontinuous dependency between
the adjectival left member and the noun it applies to: they are separated
by *ge-*. This supports the mixed form of **D**, as inheritance and verb-
raising (German vs Dutch) supported mixed **C**.[12]

4. TYPE-SHIFTING: UNPRODUCTIVE FORMATIONS

The view of the role of the lexical type assignment function defended
here allows one to control local permutations or rebracketings from
the lexicon when they are conditioned by specific lexical items. The
evidence in Section 3 was based on productive constructions. As could
be expected, the phenomenon of lexically governed local permutations
is not restricted to cases of productive word-formation. I mention two
unproductive constructions: they can be interpreted by means of lexical
type shifting, but the kind of formation they represent can not be
generalized.

Consider first the complex prepositional phrases in (26), where a
simple prepositional phrase is closed off by a left-oriented expression of
type PP\PP. There are two realizations for the construction. The (a)
derivation is a pure **A** reduction. But the PP\PP functor can combine
with the prepositional head by means of mixed **C**, resulting in the
permuted construction (b). The prepositional compounds *vanaf* (from
off, 'from', etc.) inherit the directionality of the preposition *van*, as

mixed **C** requires, i.e. they take their NP object to the right. Prepositional compounds such as *vanaf* cannot be productively coined, witness
the ungrammatical examples in (26).[13] But the existing compounds
illustrate the availability of mixed **C** in the lexicon.

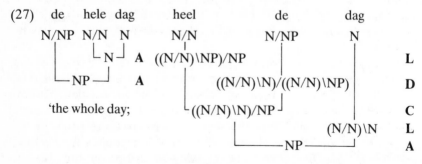

(26)   (a) van   Amsterdam uit   (b) van   uit   Amsterdam
            van   Amsterdam af   van   af   Amsterdam
            door Amsterdam heen   door heen Amsterdam
            naar Amsterdam toe   *naar toe   Amsterdam
            op   Amsterdam af   *op   af   Amsterdam

Another frozen construction that comes to mind is illustrated in (27).
The Dutch adjectives *heel* and *gans* ('whole') can locally permute with
the definite determiner, an idiosyncratic property of these adjectives.
Assume they have a secondary assignment ((N/N)\NP)/NP, validly
derivable from their basic N/N assignment by the lifting rule. The
secondary assignment triggers the type shifts necessary to interpret the
pre-determiner construction with the proper scope relations: type
coherence is achieved by first applying **D** to the determiner (division of
the mixed type); *heel* and *de* can then combine through **C**; the resultant
category in turn triggers **L** for the noun *dag*. Because the construction is
grammatical only with the definite determiner, it seems advisable to
enter *heel de* as a frozen combination in the lexicon. The combination
is interpretable by means of valid type shifting laws, but it does not
generalize to comparable constructions (e.g. *half een dag*, 'half a day').

(27)   de   hele dag   heel   de   dag
       N/NP N/N N   N/N   N/NP   N

       'the whole day;

       translation (reduced): **de′(heel′(dag′))**

5. MIXED COMPOSITION IN SYNTAX: EXTRAPOSITION FROM NP

To close this article we leave the safe borders of the lexicon and enter into the domain of phrasal syntax. The evidence for mixed composition discussed in the preceding paragraphs was based on phenomena from productive and non-productive word formation. This might lead one to conclude that the strong form of **C** could be limited to the domain of the lexicon. One could say that the relaxation of harmonic composition to mixed composition is a way to reconcile Aronoff's Conjecture with the phrasal scope of certain word formation processes. There is evidence from syntax which strongly suggests that the restriction of mixed **C** to the lexicon will not work: extraposition from NP.

To avoid irrelevant complications, I concentrate on the construction in Dutch, and start from the (uncontroversial) assumption that the postnominal modifiers in (28) have the category N\N. In order to allow them to escape from the noun phrase they belong to, they have to be turned from functors into arguments. Lifting of the head noun from N to (N\N)/N is the way to achieve this within the type-shifting calculus. That is, we assume that expressions belonging to the primitive category N automatically also belong to the lifted category of functors looking for a noun modifier and giving an N. The lifted noun type is interpreted as in (29), as dictated by the semantics of **L**.

(28)   omdat hij [een dame met een hondje] bemint
        omdat hij [een dame die een hondje bezit] bemint

        omdat hij [een dame] bemint [met een hondje]
        omdat hij [een dame] bemint [die een hondje bezit]

        'because he loves a lady with a lapdog'
        'because he loves a lady who owns a lapdog'

(29)   dame $\Rightarrow$ **dame**$'$ = **L** $\Rightarrow \lambda x[x(\textbf{dame}')]$ $x: t\,(\text{N} \mid \text{N})$

The derivation of the extraposed construction is unproblematic if the verb can combine with its direct object by mixed composition. The noun phrase *een dame* is of type (N\N)/NP on the lifted reading of dame: that is, it is a functor which is still looking for a nominal modifier. At this point, the derivation blocks in the standard system L: the verb is a left-oriented functor and cannot combine with its object which has to find its N\N argument to the right. There is no L-valid use of **L** or **C** which will accept the extraposed construction, as the reader can check. Mixed composition accepts the combination, and passes on the directionality of the argument functor. The construction is interpreted with the modifier *met een hondje* within the scope of the determiner *een*, as it should be.

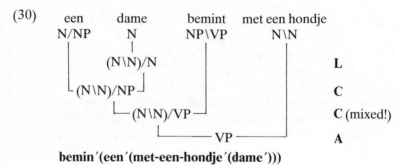

(30)

$$\text{bemin}'(\text{een}'(\text{met-een-hondje}'(\text{dame}')))$$

The extraposition case represents a discontinuity which is structurally reminiscent of the morphological type, but which has different properties with respect to the role of the lexical assignment function. The lifting from N to (N\N)/N, which makes the construction derivable, must be freely available; it is not lexically governed as was the case with the morphological instances of type-shifting we have discussed so far.[14] A proper characterization of the set of completely regular, syntactically available instances of type-shifting falls outside the scope of the present article.

6. CONCLUSION

Morphological bracketing paradoxes and discontinuities represent classic puzzles for context-free word structure grammars, whether they are *X*-bar theories or simple categorial systems. One can react to these puzzles in two ways. One way is to patch up a defective theory locally, each time a new empirical problem arises. The theoretical basis remains more or less intact, but it develops a crust of auxiliary hypotheses. Another approach is to shift to a theory with radically different properties. I have suggested an approach to the syntax of words based on a flexible type-shifting theory. The system *L* was presented as a comprehensive theory of valid type-transitions. A unified treatment of bracketing paradoxes and discontinuities requires a strong form of composition which takes us beyond the power of the directional system

L. With the strong version of composition, the morphological relatedness paradoxes can be resolved without giving up surface compositionality or a restrictive theory of the interaction between lexicon and
syntax. The theory of minimal type assignment allows one to effectively
constrain the application of the type-shifting rules as far as the lexicon
is concerned.

APPENDIX:
MIXED COMPOSITION AND PERMUTATION CLOSURE

We want to show that the addition of mixed composition to the
standard directional system *L* leads to permutation closure, in the
non-trivial case of strings with length > 2. This fact will be obvious
as soon as one realizes that within *L* any tree can be transformed
into a normal form: a uniform (right or left) branching structure headed
by an *n*-ary functor with its *n* arguments: $(\ldots(f\ x_1)x_2)\ldots x_n)$ or
$(x_n(\ldots(x_2(x_1\ f)\ldots).$[15]

```
 B/A         C      C\B
 |               └─ B ─┘        A
 └────── A ──────┘        A
```

Consider the arbitrary tree above, which reduces to A by successive
appeals to the application rule **A**. This tree contains a mixture of right-
and left-oriented functors. In order to transform it into the required
normal form, introduce the desired uniform bracketing (left-branching
or right-branching), and turn the leftmost/rightmost constituent into the
main functor by successive appeals to the Introduction Rule for '/' or '\'
(cf. Lambek 1958, p. 163).

/ Introduction: $X\ Y \Rightarrow Z$	\ Introduction: $X\ Y \Rightarrow Z$
$X \Rightarrow Y/Z$	$Y \Rightarrow X\backslash Z$

Left Normal Form (NF-L)	Right Normal Form (NF-R)
$((B/A\ C)C\backslash B) \Rightarrow A$	$(B/A(C\ C\backslash B)) \Rightarrow A$
$(B/A\ C) \Rightarrow (C\backslash B)/A$ (Intro/)	$(C\ C\backslash B) \Rightarrow (B/A)\backslash A$ (Intro\)
$B/A \Rightarrow C/((C\backslash B)/A)$ (Intro/)	$C\backslash B \Rightarrow C\backslash((B/A)\backslash A)$ (Intro\)

Now consider the normal-form trees below.

$$A/(B/C) \quad A \quad B \qquad\qquad B \quad A \quad A\backslash(B\backslash C)$$

$$\underbrace{\quad B/C \quad}_{\displaystyle C} \Big| \quad \mathbf{A} \qquad\qquad \underbrace{\quad B\backslash C \quad}_{\displaystyle C} \quad \mathbf{A}$$

Permutation of the arguments A, B will also reduce to C, if mixed composition (alternatively, mixed division) is added to **L**: first turn the outer argument B into the main functor by means of **L**, and then combine the lifted B with $A \mid (B \mid C)$ using mixed composition:

$$A/(B/C) \quad B \quad A \qquad\qquad A \quad B \quad A\backslash(B\backslash C)$$

$$\begin{array}{ll} (B/C)\backslash C & \mathbf{L} \\ \underline{\quad A/C \quad} & \mathbf{C}\,(\text{mixed!}) \\ \underline{\qquad C \qquad} & \mathbf{A} \end{array} \qquad \begin{array}{ll} (B\backslash C)/C & \mathbf{L} \\ \underline{\quad A\backslash C \quad} & \mathbf{C}\,(\text{mixed!}) \\ \underline{\qquad C \qquad} & \mathbf{A} \end{array}$$

In this way, all permutations of the sequence can be derived, by switching from left-branching to right-branching normal form, and 'lowering' of the ultimate argument towards the head. See the schematic cycle below, where NF-L/R stands for rebracketing into left/right branching normal form, and P-L/R for left/rightward movement of the non-adjacent argument towards the head, i.e. for the combination $\mathbf{C}\circ\mathbf{L}$ above. Notice that a sequence of length 2 is immune to the effects of mixed composition: there is no constituent to be 'skipped over'.

$$((xy)z)\ \text{P-L}\ ((xz)y)$$
$$\quad \text{NF-L} \qquad (x(zy))\ \text{P-R}\ (z(xy))$$
$$\qquad\qquad \text{NF-R} \qquad ((zx)y)\ \text{P-L}\ ((zy)x)$$
$$\qquad\qquad\qquad \text{NF-L} \qquad (z(yx))\ \text{P-R}\ (y(zx))$$
$$\qquad\qquad\qquad\qquad \text{NF-R} \qquad ((yz)x)\ \text{P-L}\ ((yx)z)$$
$$\qquad\qquad\qquad\qquad\qquad \text{NF-L}$$

NOTES

* Earlier versions of this article were presented at the 5th Jahrestagung der Deutschen Gesellschaft für Sprachwissenschaft (Hamburg, February 1985) and the ZWO Workshop on Morphology (Leiden, April 1985). I thank these audiences for their stimulating comments. All errors are my own.

[1] See Van Benthem (1985) for a rule interpretation procedure which associates L-valid derivations with a lambda-recipe. The type calculus as presented there is an elegant realization of Klein and Sag's (1985) program of 'type-driven translation': it offers at the same time a theory of possible combinatory and type-shifting rules and an algorithm to compute the interpretation of derived types from the interpretations of the basic types.

[2] One can fix the directionality of basic assignments by an appeal to cross-categorial ordering conventions (as in Flynn, 1983, or the GPSG work which separates dominance from precedence, e.g. Gazdar and Pullum, 1981; Gazdar *et al.*, 1985). For the present purposes, I will abstract from ordering defaults, and assume that the type-shifting rules preserve the ordering requirements of the basic assignments.

[3] The composition rule can be generalized to achieve the effect of repeated division (cf. Steedman, 1984, or Moortgat, 1984). But in this paper, the standard form will do.

C (generalized): $X_1\backslash\ldots\backslash X_n\backslash Y \ \ Y\backslash Z \Rightarrow X_1\backslash\ldots\backslash X_n\backslash Z$
$\qquad\qquad\qquad Y/Z \ \ X_1/\ldots/X_n/Y \Rightarrow X_1/\ldots/X_n/Z$

[4] The classic reference is Herman Paul (1920, p. 245): "Sehr häufig ist der Fall, dass eine Ableitung aus einer Ableitung in direkte Beziehung zum Grundworte gesetzt wird, wodurch dann auch wirkliche direkte Ableitungen veranlasst werden mit Verschmelzung von zwei Suffixen zu einem." Discussion of morphological restructuring in Dutch can be found in Sassen (1979, 1980, 1981), Van Marle (1978, 1984), Schultink (1979), among others. I discuss the relevance of morphological restructuring for a lexical composition rule in more detail in Moortgat (1985a).

[5] Trees are annotated with the rules that have formed the derived nodes, and their translation. Basic expressions (stems and affixes alike) translate as unanalysed non-logical constants (**spiel′**, **er′**, etc): the lexical semantics of bound morphemes is irrelevant for the present discussion.

[6] To avoid complications I will limit the attention here to the inheritance of one single complement, a governed prepositional object. The composition analysis can be generalized to multiple inheritance, and to other arguments than PP, as I have demonstrated in Moortgat (1984, 1987). The latter paper also discusses cases of blocked inheritance.

[7] The bases *tevreden, dreig,* and *vergelijk* can be realized either as right-oriented or as left-oriented functors. Harmonic composition leads to ungrammaticality for the nominal derivations *tevredenheid* and *dreiger*: **met NP tevredenheid, *met NP dreiger.* I will assume these are thrown out because they are in conflict with the ordering requirement for basic nouns: arguments to the right. Dutch A's can take their arguments to the left or to the right: the *-baar* derivation is grammatical both as PP/A and as PP\A: *met NP vergelijkbaar, vergelijkbaar met NP.*

[8] Instead of the type-shifting calculus L, Cremers (1985) proposes a 'poor' categorial calculus with just application and mixed composition, in an analysis of the Dutch verb-raising construction.

[9] The atom condition does not hold in Flemish. As the example below shows, Flemish verb-raising can be fed by syntactic rules (the combination of the verb *leggen* with its prepositional object *op de tafel*); hence it must be a syntactic process itself.

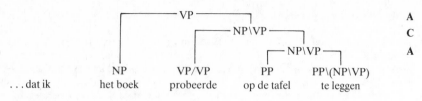

	NP	VP/VP	PP	PP\(NP\VP)
. . . dat ik	het boek	probeerde	op de tafel	te leggen

(Flemish O. K., *Dutch)
that I the book tried on the table to put
'that I tried to put the book on the table'

[10] The circumfix *ge-····-d* can be seen as the combination of a prefixation operation and a suffixation operation which by themselves are meaningless; cf. Schmerling (1983).

[11] Hoeksema (1984) distinguishes two affixes: $-ig_1$ for the simple denominal derivations (N\A), and $-ig_2$ for the synthetic compound derivations (type N\((N/N)\A)). The relationship between the two is captured by stipulation in the translation assigned to the complex type. The virtue of the type-shifting approach is that the two uses of the affix are related by a valid type-transition, which dictates the semantic relationship between the two uses.

[12] The modifier in *blue-eyed* is an adjective. The analysis carries over to deverbal synthetic compounds where the left-hand member is an adverb, which has scope over the verbal base, as in *sharp-shooter, new-comer, langslaper* (long-sleeper, 'person who sleeps long'), etc. By lexical stipulation, the agentive affix *-er* gets a secondary type assignment, derived from the primary type V\N by means of the **D** rule (division by the missing adverb category V/V, this time): V\N $=$ **D** $\Rightarrow$ $((V/V)\V)\((V/V)\N)$. The complex type triggers a type-shifting history parallel to (25). Notice, again, that **D** is not automatically available: otherwise, all deverbal affixes would have synthetic compound doubles with a misbracketed adverb. This is not the case: it has been observed (e.g. Hoeksema, 1984) that the type of synthetic compound illustrated here with *-er* does not exist for *-ing* nominalizations (*foutparkering* 'illegal parking' versus *foutparkeerder* 'illegal parker'), an idiosyncratic fact about these affixes as the *-ing* nominalizations would be perfectly interpretable.

[13] In fact, the prepositional compounds *vanaf*, etc. caused considerable excitement among the defenders of the purity of the Dutch language, when they were still felt as new. Matthias de Vries, in a Johnsonian tirade against the caprices of innovation, calls it an 'absurdity, in flat contradiction with the genius of our tongue' [*Woordenboek der Nederlandsche Taal*, I, 831]. Cf. P. Gerlach Royen (1943, p. 87).

[14] The Extraposition from NP case is similar to Heavy NP Shift in English, which also requires mixed composition, as Steedman and Szabolcsi (1985) have observed. They suggest that a stylistic factor ('heaviness') could be responsible for the relaxation of the harmony requirement on composition.

[15] See Van Benthem (1984, p. 74) for normal-form reduction in the non-directional systems.

REFERENCES

Aronoff, M.: 1976, *Word Formation in Generative Grammar*, MIT Press, Cambridge.

Bach, E.: 1983a, 'On the Relationship Between Word Grammar and Phrase Grammar', *Natural Language and Linguistic Theory* **1**, 65—89.

Bach, E.: 1983b, 'Generalized Categorial Grammars and the English Auxiliary', in Heny and Richards (eds.), *Linguistic Categories*, Vol. 2, Reidel, Dordrecht, pp. 101—120.

Bach, E.: 1984, 'Some Generalizations of Categorial Grammars', in Landman and Veltman (eds.), *Varieties of Formal Semantics*, Foris, Dordrecht, pp. 1—23.

Benthem, J. van: 1984, 'The Logic of Semantics', in Landman and Veltman (eds.), *Varieties of Formal Semantics*, Foris, Dordrecht, pp. 55—80.

Benthem, J. van: 1985, 'The Lambek Calculus', in this volume, pp. 000—000.

Bresnan, J., R. M. Kaplan, S. Peters, and A. Zaenen: 1982, 'Cross-serial Dependencies in Dutch', *Linguistic Inquiry* **13**, 613—635.

Cremers, C.: 1985, 'Een Arme Categorieënrekening voor het Nederlands', Paper presented at the 1985 TIN Meeting.

Dowty, D.: 1979, *Word Meaning and Montague Grammar*, Reidel, Dordrecht.

Fabb, N.: 1984, *Syntactic Affixation*, MIT Dissertation.

Flynn, M.: 1983, 'A Categorial Theory of Structure Building', in Gazdar, Klein and Pullum (eds.), *Order, Concord and Constituency*, Foris, Dordrecht, pp. 139—174.

Gazdar, G.: 1980, 'A Cross-categorial Semantics for Coordination', *Linguistics and Philosophy* **3**, 407—409.

Gazdar, G. and G. Pullum: 1981, 'Subcategorization, Constituent Order, and the Notion "head"', in Moortgat, van der Hulst and Hoekstra (eds.), *The Scope of Lexical Rules.* Foris, Dordrecht, pp. 107—123.

Gazdar, G., E. Klein, G. Pullum, and I. Sag: 1985, *Generalized Phrase Structure Grammar*, Blackwell, Oxford.

Geach, P.: 1972, 'A Program for Syntax', in Davidson and Harman (eds.), *Semantics of Natural Language*, Reidel, Dordrecht, pp. 483—497.

Gerlach Royen, P.: 1943, 'Aanschouwelijkheidsdrang bij Voorzetsels', *Nieuwe Taalgids* **37**, 87—93.

Hoeksema, J.: 1983, 'Wanna Do Contraction?' *GLOT* **6**, 157—182.

Hoeksema, J.: 1984, *Categorial Morphology*. Groningen Dissertation.

Houtman, J.: 1984, 'Een Kategoriale Beschrijving van het Nederlands', *Tabu* **14**, 1—27.

Keenan, E. and L. Faltz: 1985, *Boolean Semantics for Natural Language*, Reidel, Dordrecht.

Klein, E. and I. Sag: 1985, 'Type Driven Translation', *Linguistics and Philosophy* **8**, 163—202.

Lambek, J.: 1958, 'The Mathematics of Sentence Structure', *Am. Math. Monthly* **65**, 154—169.

Marle, J. van: 1978, 'Veranderingen in Woordstructuur', in Koefoed and van Marle (eds.), *Aspecten van Taalverandering*, Wolters-Noordhoff, Groningen, pp. 127—176.

Marle, J. van: 1984, 'Morfologische Veranderingen in Breder Perspectief', in *Vorm en Functie in Tekst en Taal*, Leiden, pp. 131—153.

Moortgat, M.: 1984, 'A Fregean Restriction on Metarules', in Jones and Sells (eds.), *NELS* **14**, Amherst, pp. 306—325.

Moortgat, M.: (1987), 'Compositionality and the Syntax of Words', in Groenendijk, de Jongh and Stokhof (eds.), *Foundations of Pragmatics and Lexical Semantics*, Foris, Dordrecht.

Moortgat, M.: 1985a, 'Complementovererving en Heranalyse in de Morfologie', Paper presented at the 1985 TIN Meeting.

Moortgat, M.: 1985b, 'Functional Composition and Complement Inheritance', in Hoppenbrouwers, Seuren, and Weijters (eds.), *Meaning and the Lexicon*, Foris, Dordrecht.

Partee, B. and M. Rooth: 1983, 'Generalized Conjunction and Type Ambiguity', in Bäuerle *et al.* (eds.), *Meaning, Use, and Interpretation of Language*, De Gruyter, Berlin, pp. 361—383.

Partee, B.: 1984, 'Compositionality', in Landman and Veltman (eds.), *Varieties of Formal Semantics*, Foris, Dordrecht.

Paul, H.: 1920, *Prinzipien der Sprachgeschichte*, Niemeyer, Halle.

Pesetsky, D.: 1985, 'Morphology and Logical Form', *Linguistic Inquiry* **16**, 193—246.

Pollard, C.: 1984, *Generalized Phrase Structure Grammars, Head Grammars, and Natural Language*, Stanford Dissertation.

Sassen, A.: 1979, 'Het Suffix -se: Een Geval van Morfologische Herstructurering (Metanalyse)', *Tabu* **9**, 31—39.

Sassen, A.: 1980, 'Kwesties van Morfologie', in Janssen en Streekstra (eds.), *Grenzen en Domeinen in de Grammatica van het Nederlands*, Groningen.

Sassen, A.: 1981, 'Morfologische Herstructurering (Metanalyse)', in G. R. W. Dibbets e.a. (eds.), *Studies voor Damsteegt*, Leiden, pp. 171—183.

Schmerling, S.: 1983, 'A New Theory of English Auxiliaries', in Heny and Richards (eds.), *Linguistic Categories*, Vol. Two, Reidel, Dordrecht, pp. 1—53.

Schultink, H.: 1979, 'Combinatie van Affixen Binnen Woorden, in het bijzonder in het Nederlands', in Hoekstra and van der Hulst (eds.), *Morfologie in Nederland*, Leiden, pp. 105—116.

Selkirk, L.: 1982, *The Syntax of Words*, MIT Press.

Steedman, M.: 1984, 'A Categorial Theory of Intersecting Dependencies in Dutch Infinitival Complements', in De Geest and Putseys (eds.), *Proceedings of the International Conference on Complementation*, Foris, Dordrecht, pp. 215—226.

Steedman, M.: 1985, 'Dependency and Coordination in the Grammar of Dutch and English', *Language* **61**, 523—568.

Steedman, M. and A. Szabolcsi: 1985, 'Combinators, Categorial Grammars and Parasitic Gaps', draft 5, ms.

Williams, E.: 1981, 'On the Notions "Lexically Related" and "Head of a Word"', *Linguistic Inquiry* **12**, 245—274.

Zwarts, F.: 1986, *Categoriale Grammatica en Algebraische Semantiek*, Groningen Dissertation.

Instituut voor Nederlandse Lexicologie,
P.O. Box 9515,
2300 RA Leiden, The Netherlands

RICHARD T. OEHRLE

MULTI-DIMENSIONAL COMPOSITIONAL FUNCTIONS AS A BASIS FOR GRAMMATICAL ANALYSIS*

In the first part of this paper, I show how one natural methodological approach to linguistic problems leads directly to a framework which emphasizes the generalization of the problem of composition to a number of dimensions. In the second part, I introduce a general notion of *compositional function*, which provides an appropriate abstract setting in which to discuss the problem of multi-dimensional composition. In this general setting, we may think of a grammar G, much as Montague did (1974, Chapter 7, hereafter 'UG'), as the closure of a set of compositional functions over a set of postulated basic expressions (each endowed with properties in the various dimensions under consideration). There are then a number of ways of conceiving of languages associated with G, depending on whether we wish to consider every analysis generated by G, some special class of analyses generated by G (such as those associated with a designated symbol 'S'), the phonological structures definable in the structure G, and so on.

Formally, this point of view is extremely powerful. For example, further assumptions about the domains of composition, their properties, and their interaction yield many familiar theories of grammatical composition, such as the categorial systems of Ajdukiewicz and Bar-Hillel, the syntactic calculi of Lambek, the rule-by-rule treatment of syntactic and semantic composition pioneered by Montague, and more recent work which extends the basic techniques of categorial grammar to the treatment of syntactic discontinuities (Bach, Ades and Steedman) and the treatment of phonological properties of composition (Bach, Schmerling, Wheeler). Moreover, suitable additional assumptions make it possible within this general setting to simulate the analyses of many non-categorial grammatical systems.

Our goal is not to study the properties of the various special cases that arise, but rather to argue that the abstract study of compositional functions and the grammatical systems they give rise to yields a number of consequences of considerable linguistic interest, relating to grammatical architecture and linguistic typology. With respect to gram-

349

matical architecture, we shall argue that the framework advocated here offers an alternative to the division of linguistic labor into grammatical components and that this alternative (a generalization of the 'rule by rule' relation between syntax and semantics in Montague's work) offers insights into this division which are formalizable in theories of language which adopt a strict version of the 'autonomy thesis' only with loss of generality. With respect to linguistic typology, the principal thrust of our results is to show how in two important cases, the space of grammatical possibilities (sometimes characterized with respect to ad hoc 'parameters'), is constrained by the consequences of simple and intuitively-appealing assumptions. While much recent linguistic research has aimed at deriving properties of natural language from as restricted a formal theory as possible, the results obtained here suggest that a great deal can be learned about the intrinsic mathematical properties of natural language structures by thinking about them in a formal framework of considerable flexibility.

1. THE METHODOLOGICAL BACKGROUND

Through language, individuals assign symbolic significance to noises and other physical objects and events. It is evident that in any given case, such an association depends on the existence of an abstract analysis of the (subjective representation of) the physical entity in question: for on the one hand, a single physical entity can be identified in distinct and incompatible ways; on the other hand, distinct physical entities can be identified as symbolically equivalent.

In this situation, then, two obvious questions arise. First, what is the nature of these abstract analyses? Second, what constrains the association of physical event and abstract analysis? Any answer to the second question depends on what answer is provided for the first, together with an account of how the properties of abstract analyses which make contact with physical events interact with the internal state and sampling procedures of the perceiver. For these and other reasons, in what follows, we make no attempt to formulate any theory of linguistic perception which proposes a solution to our second question, important as it is. We may nevertheless gain insight into the first problem by considering how our direct experience of language bears on it.

Identifying a physical entity symbolically immediately gives us access to a number of correlative sub-judgments regarding its analysis. Subjectively, when we hear speech as language (rather than simply as speech, as when we don't quite succeed in eavesdropping on the chatter of people conversing nearby), we inevitably hear it partitioned into (one or more) 'syntactic' parts. We hear a segmental sequence under some prosodic organization (involving pitch, stress, duration, and phrasing). We associate what we hear with symbolic content. While these representative and central aspects of linguistic experience do not exhaust the intuitions one can bring to bear in evaluating a particular speech event, if the sub-judgments in question include both global properties of the subjective analysis (which they must) as well as sets of local properties of various kinds (thus providing at least partial access to different levels of compositional structure), and if we assume that these correlative sub-judgments reflect properties of the abstract analyses we have been forced to postulate, we can exploit these judgments to investigate the properties of the postulated analyses.[1]

This strategy faces one main difficulty. We have access to judgments about properties of abstract analyses, but our intuitions are incomplete; we have no direct insight into the complete structure of the abstract analyses we are compelled to admit; we know that intuitively-based reports about linguistic judgment often disagree with linguistically-based behavior; and — worse yet — we have no intuitive access to the boundary between solid and secure intuition and insecure speculation. The success of our strategy, then, depends on finding a characterization of a large enough set of sub-judgments (large enough so that any theoretical account of linguistic composition makes contact with intuition both at some level which may be considered lexical or basic and at a level which comprehends complex structures), in such a way that they will be inter-subjectively well-defined.[2] If we can fix the limits of judgments to areas in which they are inter-subjectively reliable, however, and if the judgments in question provide a way of characterizing certain global properties as well as a partial decomposition of the analytic structure, we allow the formulation of a natural and central theoretical problem: given an observer, a rich enough set of symbolically-identified physical entities together with the observer's correlative sub-judgments of his or her analyses of each physical entity, how can we model the relations among the observer's judgments, within and across analyses in such a way that our formal model assigns analyses to new cases constructed from the same set of intuitively-accessible parts in a way which agrees with the subjective judgments of the observer.

There are many desiderata that an attractive model of a set of observer judgments must satisfy, but we single out two of them as particularly important. First, such a model will consist of a set of theoretical analyses, each one of which must yield a set of sub-properties that may be matched against the sub-judgments of the observer in question. If we recognize k correlative sub-judgments for each subjective analysis, then it is natural to think of each theoretical analysis as consisting of an n-tuple $\langle a_1, \ldots, a_k, \ldots, a_n \rangle$, whose first k projections (a_1 through a_k) are matched one-to-one against the k sub-judgments provided by the observer.[3]

Our second requirement is that a model of observer judgments make possible, on a finite basis, a characterization of an infinite set of analyses. Under such conditions, of course, only finitely many analyses and sub-analyses can be taken to be simple and the remainder must be taken to be complex and derivable from simpler analyses by means of a finite number of specified operations. We construe this as meaning that the class of phenomenal analyses for any particular sub-judgment, on the one hand, and the class of theoretical analyses corresponding to this sub-judgment, on the other, must both accommodate some set of operations which defines the properties of complex elements in terms of the properties of, and relations among, more basic elements. As a consequence, both phenomenal analyses and theoretical analyses can be thought of as algebras generated over a set of basic structures. In what follows, we will refer to the formal counterpart of each sub-judgment as a 'compositional domain', and we will assume that each compositional domain consists of a set A on which a set of operations is defined.[4]

Compositional domains are in fact thoroughly familiar. As a first example, the syntactic character of a complex expression must be fixed by its mode of composition — otherwise, contrary to fact, complex expressions will be syntactically indistinguishable with respect to further compositional operations. Similarly, the interpretive properties of a complex expression must be characterized compositionally. Third, in view of co-articulation phenomena, sandhi rules, and other properties of 'connected speech', the segmental properties associated with a complex expression must be characterized by rules which clearly cannot be reduced to the concatenation of phonological structures. Fourth, the prosodic properties of complex expressions must be assigned by rule, and the prosodic rules must accommodate both the phonological effects of prosody and their interpretive effects as well.

There are other possible compositional domains, such as those involving the ascription of various pragmatic properties to a given utterance on a given occasion. In what follows, the compositional domains just mentioned form the empirical basis that formal developments are held responsible to.

Thus, we arrive at the following general picture. Linguistic perception requires that physical entities be matched with abstract analyses of some kind. Symbolically identifying a physical entity such as a speech event gives rise to a set of correlative subjectively-accessible sub-judgments. If we can render aspects of a sufficiently rich number of these sub-judgments inter-subjectively well-defined, we can exploit the relations among them in investigating the nature of the abstract analyses associated with a given individual. Since there must be abstract analyses which are complex, we must postulate both a set of basic analyses and a set of modes of composition by which complex analyses can be constructed from simpler ones. In the next section, we shall investigate this problem from a more formal point of view.

2.0. COMPOSITIONAL DOMAINS AND COMPOSITIONAL FUNCTIONS

In this section, we inquire into some of the properties of a set of formal systems which are consistent with the methodological assumptions just discussed. Along with a characterization of compositional functions, we take up a number of examples of rules in various languages which can be formulated naturally in the framework sketched here. We then prove two simple theorems about compositional functions. The first, the Factorization Theorem, shows that there are compositional functions which act on more than one compositional domain which cannot be simulated (on the same vocabulary) by a set of compositional functions which are defined over the structures of a single compositional domain. The second states the conditions under which a set of given compositional functions can be simulated by a single, more general, rule.

We shall assume as given a set of n compositional domains. We assume in addition that each compositional domain has an algebraic structure, so that the ith domain is an algebra $\langle A_i, F_\gamma \rangle_{\gamma \in \Gamma_i}$ where A_i is a set of elements over which a set of operations F_γ, indexed by γ ($\gamma \in \Gamma_i$), is defined. We want to show how we can define a set of categories, a set of basic expressions, and a set of operations whose closure over the set of basic expressions will characterize a language whose well-formed complete expressions have properties corresponding to the sub-judgments discussed in Section 1. The development is a straightforward application of Montague's ideas to an algebraic setting in which every simple object is an n-tuple and every k-ary operation is defined over k n-tuples. The discussion will be facilitated by establishing a few notational conventions, following MacLane and Birkhoff (1967).

2.1. *Notational Matters*

We write $f: D \rightarrow C$ to represent a function f which associates each element of a set D (the domain of f) with a single corresponding element in a set C (the co-domain of f). We may emphasize the fact that f associates an element of C with each element of D by saying that f is a *total* function. In contrast, a *partial* function $g: D \rightarrow C$ associates at most one element of C with each element in D and we say that g is undefined for those members of D which it associates with no element in C. In what follows, we will use the term 'function' to apply to partial functions, since total functions are a special case of this more general concept. When it is necessary to distinguish between the two, we will introduce the appropriate modifiers.

To represent the action of a function f on a particular element d in its domain for which it is defined, we write $f: d \mapsto f(d)$. If $f: D \rightarrow C$ is a function with domain D and codomain C, a function $g: D' \rightarrow C'$ is said to be the restriction of f to D' when D' is a subset of D and C' is a subset of C and for every element d in D', $g(d) = f(d)$. Under these same conditions, we also say that f is an extension of g to D.

Given sets X and Y, we represent the set of all functions from Y to X by means of the exponential notation:

$$X^Y$$

We use the symbol '$\mathbf{k}$' to refer to the set of positive integers from 1 to k ($1 \leqslant k$). We may think of a k-tuple of elements drawn from a set A as the set determined by a member of the function-set A^k. We represent such a k-tuple usually as $\langle a_1, \ldots, a_k \rangle$. When the set $\mathbf{k}$, the set A, and the function from $\mathbf{k}$ to A are contextually clear, we can write simply $\{a_i\}$ ($1 \leqslant i \leqslant k$). Even more simply, we shall use the symbol

'a_i' as a variable over the elements of such a k-tuple. Equally, given a collection of sets E and a function $J: \mathbf{k} \rightarrow E$, we say that E is a family of sets indexed by $\mathbf{k}$ and, for $1 \leqslant i \leqslant k$, we represent $J(i)$ simply as E_i.

When E is a family of sets indexed by $\mathbf{k}$, we use the symbol:

$$\overset{k}{\underset{i=1}{\times}} E_i$$

to represent the k-fold Cartesian product

$$E_1 \times \cdots \times E_k = \{\langle e_1, \ldots, e_k \rangle \mid e_1 \in E_1, \ldots, e_k \in E_k\}.$$

Note that in case each E_i is a singleton $\{e_i\}$, then $\times_{i=1}^{k} E_i$ is simply the k-tuple $\langle e_1, \ldots, e_k \rangle$. Thus, $\langle e_1, \ldots, e_k \rangle = \times_{i=1}^{k} \{e_i\}$. Dropping the braces around 'e_i' simplifies the notation, yielding $\langle e_1, \ldots, e_k \rangle = \times_{i=1}^{x} e_i$, although this introduces an ambiguity when 'e_i' represents a non-singleton set. To avoid this, we use '$\times E_i$' to represent the Cartesian product of the k-sets $E_1, \ldots, E_k$, and '$\times e_i$' to represent the k-tuple $\langle e_1, \ldots, e_k \rangle$. (As in the last sentence, we shall often suppress the superscripts and subscripts of the Cartesian product symbol.)

For any set of k-tuples, with members of the form $\langle a_1, \ldots, a_k \rangle$, we have projection functions $p_1, \ldots, p_k$, which satisfy $(1 \leqslant j \leqslant k)$:

$$p_j : \langle a_1, \ldots, a_k \rangle \mapsto a_j.$$

When the k-tuple is represented as $\times_{i=1}^{k} e_i$, this becomes

$$p_j \left(\overset{k}{\underset{i=1}{\times}} e_i \right) = e_j.$$

Finally, note that there is also a natural way to form the Cartesian product of two or more functions. Given functions $f: A \rightarrow B$ and $g: C \rightarrow D$, for example, define the Cartesian product $f \times g: A \times C \rightarrow B \times D$ by the action $(f \times g): (a, c) \mapsto (f(a), g(c))$. (Note that if f or g is partial, then $(f \times g)(a, c)$ is defined only when $f(a)$ and $g(c)$ are both defined.) This definition extends in the obvious way to k-fold Cartesian products of functions. Given k functions $f_i: A_i \rightarrow B_i$ $(1 \leqslant i \leqslant k)$, then $f_1 \times \cdots \times f_k: \times A_i \rightarrow \times B_i$, in such a way that $(f_1 \times \cdots \times f_k)\langle a_1, \ldots, a_k \rangle = \langle f_1(a_1), \ldots, f_k(a_k) \rangle$.

2.2. *Compositional Functions*

Assume that we have n compositional domains, each of which is an algebra consisting of a set A_i over which a finite set of operations F_i are taken as primitive. We shall assume in addition that each algebra A_i comes equipped with a type structure, whose elements we refer to as '$T(A_i)$'. (Syntactic and semantic type structures are familiar features of categorial grammars. Phonological structures can also be taken to be typed: see Wheeler (1981, this volume), for further discussion.) For each compositional domain A_i, we assume that the set of types $T(A_i)$ is characterized recursively over a finite set of basic types $B\text{-}T(A_i)$. Given these compositional domains, we wish to define an algebraic structure, each of whose elements is an n-tuple whose ith projection $(1 \leqslant i \leqslant n)$ is a polynomial in the algebra A_i, and whose operations are defined over appropriate sets of n-tuples. By identifying a linguistically-analyzed expression with a member of this algebra, then, we ascribe to it properties in each compositional domain — properties which determine its combinatorial properties with other linguistically-analyzed expressions and its contributions to the properties of the results of such combinations.

2.2.1. We begin by specifying a type structure T, which contains a set of basic types and a recursive characterization of the full set of types. Let V_i be a set of variables ranging over $T(A_i)$. We define $V\text{-}T(A_i) = B\text{-}T(A_i) \cup V_i$. We define the set of basic types of T as $\times V\text{-}T(A_i)$. The full set of types is defined recursively to be the smallest superset of the basic types which satisfies the condition that if it contains C and $C_1, \ldots, C_k$ $(1 \leqslant k)$, then it contains the type:

$$C^{C_1 \times \cdots \times C_k}$$

We assume in addition that we have a set of basic expressions, each associated with a type in a way that meets the following two conditions. First, if a basic expression e is associated with a basic type, then $e = \langle a_1, \ldots, a_n \rangle$, where a_i is an element of the compositional domain A_i or is a variable ranging over elements of A_i. Second, if e is associated with a type of the form

$$C^{C_1 \times \cdots \times C_k}$$

then e is a function with domain $C_1 \times \cdots \times C_k$ and co-domain C.

In the simplest case, the function e determines a Cartesian product of functions $f_1 \times \cdots \times f_n$, such that each f_j $(1 \leqslant j \leqslant k)$ in this Cartesian product of functions is a k-ary operation which maps k-tuples of appropriate objects from the jth domains of members of $C_1 \times \cdots \times C_k$ to the jth domain of members of C. But such Cartesian products of functions do not exhaust the functions of this kind. On the one hand, there are functions which assign objects which are identical with respect to one of the k dimensions to elements in C with distinct values in this domain. On the other hand, there are partial functions $f_1 \times \cdots \times f_n$ in which not every f_j $(1 \leqslant j \leqslant k)$ is a total k-ary operation.

As an illustration of a simple case, consider a compositional function $F: A \times B \times C \rightarrow D$, where A, B, C, and D are basic categories. We want F to assign properties in each of the n compositional domains on the basis of the properties of its arguments. If $\langle e_1, e_2, e_3 \rangle$ falls in the domain of F, and $e_1 = \langle a_1, \ldots, a_n \rangle$, $e_2 = \langle b_1, \ldots, b_n \rangle$, and $e_3 = \langle c_1, \ldots, c_n \rangle$, then in simple cases we can characterize the action of F as the action of a Cartesian product of functions:

$$F: \langle e_1, e_2, e_3 \rangle \mapsto \langle f_1 \langle a_1, b_1, c_1 \rangle, \ldots, f_n \langle a_n, b_n, c_n \rangle \rangle$$

where each f_i acts on the Cartesian product of the ith projections of the three respective arguments, namely $\langle a_i, b_i, c_i \rangle$. In this way, $F \langle e_1, e_2, e_3 \rangle = f_1 \times \cdots \times f_n (\times_{j=1}^{n} \times_{i=1}^{3} p_j e_i)$.

In more complex cases, functions which cannot be simulated by the Cartesian product of domain-specific sub-functions can be considered the (disjoint) union of simple functions of this kind.

2.2.2. The method of characterizing the set T of types discussed above is perhaps the approach most nearly in line with the methodological strictures of Section 1: (analyzed) expressions associated with basic types have properties which correspond in each compositional domain with basic types; complex entities are associated with appropriate members of the type hierarchy. On this approach, the type that an entity is associated with fixes its combinatorial properties. But the type of an entity is not (in general) fixed by the properties of a single compositional domain in that entity's structure. There are two alternatives to this view which are worth discussing.

One alternative is to construct the set of types just as we have done here and associate each basic or derived expression with an $n+1$th compositional domain which specifies its type. This is convenient at times, since it localizes information concerning the type of an expression in one place. Yet it is also redundant, since the same information is recoverable from the set of types of the individual compositional domains. As a result, this alternative also violates the effort to localize information in the structure of expressions only on the basis of subjectively-accessible intuitions.

A second alternative erects the set of types in accordance with the type-structure of a single designated compositional domain, which then plays here the role of traditional grammatical categories (construed in the categorial mode, of course). We begin with a set of primitive types, namely, the primitive types of the algebra corresponding to the designated compositional domain and then define the full set of types T recursively in the usual way as the smallest superset of the set of primitive types which is closed under finite exponentiation: that is, if T contains C and $C_1, \ldots, C_k$ ($1 \leqslant k$), then it contains the type

$$C^{C_1 \times \cdots \times C_k}$$

Now, although the non-designated compositional domains play no role in this characterization at all, we will allow them to constrain the properties of basic expressions (and hence, of derived expressions as well). As above, if a basic expression e is associated with a basic type, then we require that $e = \langle a_1, \ldots, a_n \rangle$, where a_i is an element of the compositional domain A_i or is a variable ranging over elements of A_i. However, if e is associated with a type of the form $C^{C_1 \times \cdots \times C_k}$, we require e to be a function with domain $D_1 \times \cdots \times D_k$ and co-domain C, where $D_1 \times \cdots \times D_k$ is a subset of $C_1 \times \cdots \times C_k$ and $e \langle d_1, \ldots, d_k \rangle = f_1 \times \cdots \times f_n(\times_{j=1}^{n} \times_{i=1}^{k} p_j d_i)$. The apparent difference between this approach and the approach discussed earlier in Section 2.2.1. is that here, each f_j ($1 \leqslant j \leqslant k$) in this Cartesian product of functions can be the restriction of a k-ary operation (which maps k-tuples of appropriate objects from the jth domains of members of $C_1 \times \cdots \times C_k$ to the jth domain of members of C) to a smaller domain. Thus, in the earlier case, the constraining influence of more than one compositional domain is built directly into the type structure T: on this alternative account, the set of types is simplified, but the action of functor categories may be constrained by restrictions imposed on its sub-functions.

We need make no definitive choice between this last alternative and the approach of Section 2.2.1. Whether one of these two approaches has advantages not shared by the other is a question we leave to future research.

2.3. *Examples*

The simplest compositional function defined over n compositional domains is the identity function $I_1 \times \cdots \times I_n$: $\langle a_1, \ldots, a_n \rangle \mapsto \langle I_1(a_1), \ldots, I_n(a_n) \rangle = \langle a_1, \ldots, a_n \rangle$. It is convenient to think of the identity function as having rank 0.

The next simplest n-dimensional compositional functions are those which are of rank $(1, 1)$ in the sense that their domain is specifiable with reference to a single compositional domain and their action is confined to this domain, as in a rule of the form $I_1 \times \cdots \times f_j \times \cdots \times I_n$: $\langle a_1, \ldots, a_j, \ldots, a_n \rangle \mapsto \langle a_1, \ldots, f_j(a_j), \ldots, a_n \rangle$. Among the standardly-recognized compositional functions of this type in the linguistics literature are phonological redundancy rules which fill in unspecified information (cf. Wheeler (1981, this volume), and Archangeli (1984) for recent investigations of theories of phonological representation in which 'underspecification' plays a central role) and 'vacuous transformations' — operations which change the hierarchical relations among elements in a string of terminal symbols without changing the order of those elements, such as the operation of raising to object position in English and the restructuring rules proposed most notably by Rizzi (1981).[5] Meaning postulates can be construed as rules of rank $(1, 1)$ which operate in the interpretive domains of certain theories.

Rules which are of rank $(2, 1)$ or $(2, 2)$ make reference to information from two compositional domains. The domain of an operation of rank $(2, 1)$ is fixed by reference to two compositional domains, but it acts on the structure of just one of the two domains in question. An operation of rank $(2, 2)$ acts on both the compositional domains it is defined relative to. As an example of the first type, consider the class of morphologically-governed phonological rules: the domain of such rules is specified at least by reference to both morphological properties and phonological properties, while the effect of such rules is felt in the phonological structure alone (cf. Janda, 1987).

Some interesting examples of the second type can be found in formal language theory. As a first example, suppose that we are given a system S which consists of: (1) a finite set of categories Q; (2) a designated member q_0 of Q; (3) a subset F of Q; (4) a finite vocabulary V; (5) for each element v in V, a function suff-$v \times f_v$: $\langle x, C \rangle \mapsto x + v, f_v(C) \rangle$, where $x + v$ is the suffixation of v to x and $f_v(C)$ is a function from C to C. Thus, $\langle V^* \times C, \text{suff-}v \times f_v \rangle$ is an algebra with elements consisting of pairs drawn from $V^* \times C$ and with a set of operations indexed by V. The sub-algebra A_0 generated by the closure of this set of operations over the single element $\langle e, q_0 \rangle$ determines a subset L of V^*, with $L = \{x \mid \langle x, C \rangle \in A_0 \ \& \ x = p_1(\langle x, C \rangle) \ \& \ p_2(\langle x, C \rangle) F\}$. L is a regular language. (An interesting property of the functions suff-$v \times f_v$ is that while they act in two compositional domains, their action is completely determined by the categorial information of the second co-ordinate of their arguments. This subtlety is not well-represented in our informal notion of rank.)

As a second example, suppose we begin with two disjoint, non-empty, finite sets called Cat and W, and a function C which assigns each element w in W to a member of Cat. We wish to define a subset of $W^* \times Cat$. We begin with a basic set of allowable expressions of the form $(w, C(w))$, with w in W and $C(w)$ in Cat. In addition, we allow a finite number of rules which form non-basic allowable expressions, rules which take the form: $\langle (x_1, C_1), \ldots, (x_n, C_n) \rangle \mapsto (x_1 - \cdots - x_n, \varphi(C_1, \ldots, C_n))$, where x_i $(1 \leq i \leq n)$ is a variable ranging over W^*, C_i $(1 \leq i \leq n)$ is in Cat, (x_i, C_i) is an allowable expression, φ is an n-ary operation over Cat. The value $(x_1 - \cdots - x_n, \varphi(C_1, \ldots, C_n))$ of any such rule belongs to the class of allowable expressions. This schema for an n-ary compositional function is 2-dimensional in the second sense discussed above: its domain makes reference to two dimensions in each argument and its action affects both domains. We note in passing the affinities between such compositional functions and context-free phrase structure rules.

If we provide the above system with a model-theoretic interpretation, we may consider expressions to be triples (x, x', C), with x in W^*, x' the interpretation of the expression, and C the category of the expression. A rule of the form $\langle (x_1, x'_1, C_1), \ldots, (x_n, x'_n, C_n) \rangle \mapsto (x_1 - \cdots - x_n, f(x'_1, \ldots, x'_n), C_{n+1})$, where $f(x'_1, \ldots, x'_n)$ represents the interpretation of the resultant expression, is an n-ary 3-dimensional rule.

We may regard the syntactic rules of functional application in Montague's PTQ as either binary 2-dimensional rules or as unary 2-dimensional rule schemata, depending on whether or not we choose to identify members of 'functor' categories with the compositional functions in question. If we do not, then a rule such as S7 (which reads: 'If $\delta \in P_{IV/t}$ and $\beta \in P_t$, then F6$(\delta, \beta) \in P_{IV}$, where F6$(\delta, \beta) = \delta\beta$') is equivalent to $\langle(\delta,\ IV/t),\ (\beta,\ t)\rangle \mapsto (\delta\beta,\ IV)$. On the other hand, if we identify each member of IV/t with a particular function, we have $(\delta,\ IV/t): (\beta,\ t) \mapsto (\delta\beta,\ IV)$. (These two formulations are related by a function of application, as discussed below.) If we have appropriate model-theoretic values for δ and β, we can add an interpretive dimension to these rules, yielding the following two 3-dimensional alternatives:

$$\langle(\delta, \delta', IV/t), (\beta, \beta', t)\rangle \mapsto (\delta\beta, \delta'(^\wedge \beta'), IV)$$
$$(\delta, \delta', IV/t): (\beta, \beta', t) \mapsto (\delta\beta, \delta'(^\wedge \beta'), IV)$$

Morphological operations are paradigm examples of rank $(3, 3)$ rules, since morphological operations often act simultaneously on phonological form, syntactic category, and interpretation.

Prosodic rules involving pitch and stress often act differently on phonologically-equivalent strings of segments under distinct modes of (syntactic/semantic) composition. Moreover, the effect of prosodic rules is felt both phonologically and interpretively.

Many other examples are available.[6] But the examples already adduced illustrate some of the power and flexibility of 'compositional functions' as characterized above. We have seen that compositional functions arise naturally in the context of the methodological framework sketched earlier. In the sections to follow, we shall argue that interesting grammatical consequences can be derived from compositional functions with reasonable properties.

2.4. *Remarks*

Although we have provided a form for representing k-ary compositional functions, the functions which it is possible and natural to define within this setting vary depending on both the nature of the various compositional domains and the 'sub-functions' available within each domain. For example, among the functions typical of segmental phonology are insertion at a given point, deletion of an element, assimilation of x to y with regard to feature-set F, dissimilation of x from y with regard to feature-set F, and modes of establishing relations among the 'tiers', 'planes', other structures of 'non-linear' phonology. Typical syntactic operations are: left-concatenation, right-concatenation, insertion of x at point y in z (cf. Steele *et al.* (1981) on second-position, Bach (1979, 1981, 1984) on wrapping, Pollard (1984) on head-wrapping), unification (cf. Kay (1979), Gazdar *et al.* (1985), Steele (forthcoming)), and anti-unification (cf. Steele (forthcoming)). Typical interpretive operations are rules of functional application, abstraction, assignment of expressions to values in a model, and inferential rules regarding illocutionary force and other pragmatic matters. While the exact character of these operations is an important problem, I am less concerned here with what operations are allowable than with how they interact, with how they can be organized, and finally, with what consequences these rather abstract issues have for linguistic theory and research.

2.5. *Simple Properties of Compositional Functions*

Some of the properties of compositional functions follow directly from the fact that they are functions. For example, there are natural combinatorial relations among functions which allow the identification of functions which are, strictly speaking, distinct. Among these is the reduction of n-ary functions to 1-ary functions, discovered by Schönfinkel and Curry, based on the isomorphism:

$$X^{Y \times Z} \cong (X^Y)^Z$$

Similarly, given compositional functions $F: A \rightarrow B$, and $G: B \rightarrow C$, there is a composite function $G \circ F: A \rightarrow C$, defined by $G \circ F(a) = G(F(a))$.

Another natural relation among functions which is inherited by compositional functions is the rule of type-shifting, which allows us to identify an argument a of a functor F with a functor h which acts on F and its other arguments in a way non-distinguishable from the action of F on a. The rationale for this rule can be seen by examining a special case: let $a \in D$ and consider the function set:

$$C^D$$

There is only one function h in the function set

$$C^{(C^D)}$$

which, for every G in C^D, satisfies the condition $h(G) = G(a)$.

Consequently, since F falls within the range of this variable, $h(F) = F(a)$.

Finally, it is interesting to consider the possibility of treating a functor F as an argument in another way. Let $F: D \to C$. Then there is a function $h: F \times D \to C$ which satisfies the condition $h\langle F, d \rangle = F(d)$. Under these circumstances, we can call h an applicative function, since it results in the functional application of a functor F to an appropriate argument.

Note that in the case of a multi-dimensional compositional function $\langle f_1, \ldots, f_n \rangle$ over n domains, these properties of functions are applicable equally to the function as a whole and to its individual component parts. For example, following Bach (1983), let the German article *der* be characterized (in part) as a functor which takes as its argument a singular 'feminine' N and constructs a definite, dative NP by adjoining its phonological form to the left of the phonological form of its argument, and let *zu* be characterized (in part) as a functor which makes a locative PP by adjoining its phonological form to the left of the phonological form of a dative NP, then *zur* can be treated as the phonological contraction of *zu* and *der* and the functional composition of the other values associated with *zu* and *der*. There are many other cases in which a given function acts in one compositional domain in a way different from its action in another compositional domain.

2.6. *Factoring*

Certain compositional functions can be 'factored' in such a way that their action can be simulated by a set of simpler functions — simpler in the sense of being of lower rank. For a multi-dimensional function, factorability indicates that at least some of the effects of the function on an object in its domain are independent of each other. When a compositional function cannot be represented as a Cartesian product of domain-specific sub-functions, the barriers posed to such a representation are barriers to factorization as well. For suppose that F is a 1-ary compositional function defined for the two arguments $\langle a_1, \ldots, a_j, \ldots, a_k \rangle$ and $\langle b_1, \ldots, b_j, \ldots, b_k \rangle$ and $a_j = b_j$, but the two k-tuples are otherwise distinct. (In other words, for some $i \neq j$, $a_i \neq b_i$.) If the values for these two arguments under the action of the function F differ in the j-th dimension, then F cannot be completely factored, since its action on the j-th dimension (at least) depends on the properties of its arguments in other components. Thus, compositional functions which do not act invariantly within each dimension cannot be factored. And in our discussion of factorization that follows, we shall henceforth ignore them.

Yet not all functions which do act invariantly can be factored in the relevant sense. In order to explore this question, we need a sharper characterization of the notion factorization. In the interests of simplicity, we will consider the case of 1-ary functions first.

2.6.1. *Factoring 1-ary compositional functions.* Suppose that $F: \times A_i \rightarrow \times A_i$ is 1-ary (and thus acts on a single analysis consisting of n compositional domains) and that we can represent the action of F as:

$$f_1 \times \cdots \times f_n : \langle a_1, \ldots, a_n \rangle \mapsto \langle f_1(a_1), \ldots, f_n(a_n) \rangle$$

Alternatively, assuming that each compositional domain A_i is the domain of the subfunction f_i, we can represent F as:

$$F: \times \mathrm{Dom}(f_i) \rightarrow \times \mathrm{Cod}(f_i)$$

Now, when F is defined over the entire Cartesian product of n compositional domains, there is no difficulty in simulating the action of F by a set of n functions F_i $(1 \leqslant i \leqslant n)$, where:

$$F_i = I_1 \times \cdots \times f_i \times \cdots \times I_n : \times A_i \rightarrow \times A_i.$$

Thus, F_i is the Cartesian product of n subfunctions, the ith of which is the ith subfunction of F and the others of which are the identity functions over the other compositional domains. Applying F to any object for which it is defined has the same effect as applying each of the functions F_i exactly once. Somewhat more technically, applying F to an appropriate argument yields the same result as applying the composition (in any order) of the n functions F_i. This is an instance of factorability, but a very special case, since it depends crucially on the fact that F is a total function. To grasp the more general case, it is necessary to consider partial compositional functions — those which are defined only over a proper subset of $\times A_i$.

Suppose that $G: \times \mathrm{Dom}(g_i) \rightarrow \times A_i$, with $\mathrm{Dom}(g_i)$ a subset of A_i. In other words, the sub-functions g_i need not be total functions on their respective domains A_i. We will say that G is factorable if G can be represented by a set of n functions G_i $(1 \leqslant i \leqslant n)$, with each G_i of the following form:

$$I_1 \times \cdots \times h_i \times \cdots \times I_n : \times A_i \to \times A_i$$

where for all z in A_i

$$h_i(z) = g_i(z) \text{ if } z \in \text{Dom}(g_i)$$
$$h_i(z) = z \text{ if } z \in A_i - \text{Dom}(g_i)$$

In other words, if G is factorable, then the set of functions G_i acts on $\times A_i$, and for any argument $\langle a_1, \ldots, a_n \rangle$, applying each function G_i successively exactly once yields $\langle h_1(a_1), \ldots, h_n(a_n) \rangle$. If $\langle a_1, \ldots, a_n \rangle$ is in the domain of G, we have $\langle h_1(a_1), \ldots, h_n(a_n) \rangle = \langle g_1(a_1), \ldots, g_n(a_n) \rangle = G\langle a_1, \ldots, a_n \rangle$. Otherwise, when $\langle a_1, \ldots, a_n \rangle$ lies outside the domain of G, $\langle h_1(a_1), \ldots, h_n(a_n) \rangle = \langle a_1, \ldots, a_n \rangle$.

1-ARY FACTORIZATION THEOREM. A 1-ary compositional function $G: \times \text{Dom}(g_i) \to \times A_i$ is factorable if and only if either G is of rank $(1, 1)$ or, for every subfunction g_i, $\text{Dom}(g_i) = A_i$.

Proof. If G is of rank $(1, 1)$, then G can be represented as $I_1 \times \cdots \times g_i \times \cdots \times I_n: A_1 \times \cdots \times \text{Dom}(g_i) \times \cdots \times A_n \to \times A_i$. We can factor G into a set of functions G_j as follows: if $j = i$, $G_j = I_1 \times \cdots \times h_i \times \cdots \times I_n: \times A_i \to \times A_i$ (with $h_i(z) = g_i(z)$ when $g(z)$ is defined and $h_i(z) = z$ otherwise, for all $z A_i$); if $j \neq i$, then $G_j = I_1 \times \cdots \times I_n: \times A_i \to \times A_i$. Thus, for any argument $\langle a_1, \ldots, a_n \rangle$, the action of the set of functions $G_j = \langle a_1, \ldots, h_i(a_i), \ldots, a_n \rangle$. When $\langle a_1, \ldots, a_n \rangle$ is in $\text{Dom}(G)$, $\langle a_1, \ldots, h_i(a_i), \ldots, a_n \rangle = \langle a_1, \ldots, g_i(a_i), \ldots, a_n \rangle = G\langle a_1, \ldots, a_n \rangle$. So, if G is of rank $(1, 1)$, G is factorable. Similarly, if G is such that $\text{Dom}(g_i) = A_i$ for every subfunction g_i, then we define a set of functions G_j, each of the form $I_1 \times \cdots \times h_j \times \cdots \times I_n: A_1 \times \cdots \times \text{Dom}(g_j) \times \cdots \times A_n \to \times A_i$. Since $\text{Dom}(g_j) = A_j$, $h_j = g_j$, and thus for every argument $\langle a_1, \ldots, a_n \rangle$ in $\times A_i$, the action of the set of functions G_j yields $\langle g_1(a_1), \ldots, g_n(a_n) \rangle$, agreeing with G. So in this case as well, G is factorable. On the other hand, suppose that the rank of G is greater than 1 and that G has at least one subfunction g_i such that $\text{Dom}(g_i) \neq A_i$. Suppose that we try to represent G as a set of functions G_j, with each function $G_j = I_1 \times \cdots \times h_j \times \cdots \times I_n: \times A_i \to \times A_i$, where as before $h_j(z) = g_j(z)$ when z is in $\text{Dom}(g_j)$ and $h_j(z) = z$ otherwise. Now, if we choose an element $\langle a_1, \ldots, a_i, \ldots, a_n \rangle$ with a_i not in $\text{Dom}(g_i)$ but, for all $j \neq i$, a_j in $\text{Dom}(g_j)$, since $a_i \notin \text{Dom}(g_i)$, then $\langle a_1, \ldots, a_i, \ldots, a_n \rangle \notin \text{Dom}(G)$. But if we apply the set of functions G_j to $\langle a_1, \ldots, a_i, \ldots, a_n \rangle$, we obtain $\langle h_1(a_1), \ldots, h_i(a_i), \ldots, h_n(a_n) \rangle$, which, since G is at least of rank 2 is not equal to $\langle a_1, \ldots, a_i, \ldots, a_n \rangle$. Hence, G is not factorable.

2.6.2. *Factoring k-ary compositional functions.* Factorization also applies to compositional functions which take as arguments more than a single n-tuple. As in the case of 1-ary functions, we restrict our discussion to functions which act invariantly on the respective subdomains of their arguments. Such a k-ary compositional function F can be represented equivalently as $f_1 \times \cdots \times f_n$, where each f_i ($1 < i < n$) is a k-ary subfunction which acts on k arguments from the ith compositional domain. Thus, the following two representations, which differ only in how the domain is represented are equivalent:

$$F: \langle a_{1,1}, \ldots, a_{1,n} \rangle, \ldots, \langle a_{k,1}, \ldots, a_{k,n} \rangle \mapsto$$
$$\langle f_1 \langle a_{1,1}, \ldots, a_{k,1} \rangle, \ldots, f_n \langle a_{1,n}, \ldots, a_{k,n} \rangle \rangle$$
$$f_1 \times \cdots \times f_n : \langle\langle a_{1,1}, \ldots, a_{k,1} \rangle, \ldots, \langle a_{1,n}, \ldots, a_{k,n} \rangle\rangle \mapsto$$
$$\langle f_1 \langle a_{1,1}, \ldots, a_{k,1} \rangle, \ldots, f_n \langle a_{1,n}, \ldots, a_{k,n} \rangle \rangle$$

This equivalence means that we can think of the domain and co-domain of F as follows:

$$F: \underset{j=1}{\overset{k}{\times}} \left(\underset{i=}{\overset{n}{\times}} p_j(\text{Dom} f_i) \right) \to \times A_i.$$

(This formulation leaves open, of course, whether the co-domain of F is an argument category or a functor category. In what follows, this distinction makes no difference.)

The natural extension of factorization to k-ary functions is this: if $F = f_1 \times \cdots \times f_n : \times (\times p_j (\text{Dom} f_i) \to \times A_i$ is a k-ary compositional function, F is factorable means that F can be represented by a set of n functions F_i ($1 \leqslant i \leqslant n$) (with each F_i of the form $I_1 \times \cdots \times h_i \times \cdots \times I_n : \times (\times p_j A_i) \to \times A_i$) in such a way that the restriction of $h_1 \times \cdots \times h_n$ to the domain of $f_1 \times \cdots \times f_n$ equals $f_1 \times \cdots \times f_n$ and $h_1 \times \cdots \times h_n$ acts as an n-place identity otherwise.

Relative to these definitions, the General Factorization Theorem stated below follows at once by adapting the same arguments given earlier to the more general case:

GENERAL FACTORIZATION THEOREM. A k-ary compositional function $G\colon X\,(X\,p_j(\mathrm{Dom}\,g_i)) \rightarrow X\,A_i$ is factorable if and only if either G is of rank $(1, 1)$ or, for every subjunction g_i, $\mathrm{Dom}(g_i) = A_i$.

These results on factorization are not at all deep mathematically. Yet they show how the properties of one dimension in linguistic analysis may influence the action of a function in another domain, in ways that can easily have empirical consequences with respect to the organization of grammars for natural languages: not all possible grammatical rules (from the point of view adopted here) are compatible with all possible architectures (particularly those which minimize the relations between grammatical dimensions for one reason or another).

2.7. *Common Extensions of Compositional Functions*

Factoring a compositional function is a means of representing its action by functions of rank $(1, 1)$. As such, the study of factoring sheds some light on when a paticular set of actions must be represented in a particular way. There is, of course, a corresponding question: when can a set of actions be represented as a single compositional function. In this section, we will consider the conditions under which a set of compositional functions have a common extension. Just as factorability is an indication that a given compositional function can be simplified by representing its sub-functions independently (and perhaps more generally), forming the common extension of two functions means that they can be represented in a single way.

Suppose we have two compositional functions $F\colon C_1 \times \cdots \times C_k \rightarrow C$ and $G\colon D_1 \times \cdots \times D_k \rightarrow C$, each of which sends k-tuples of arguments into C. Suppose as well that $F = f_1 \times \cdots \times f_n\colon \times_{j=1}^{n} \times_{i=1}^{k} p_j C_i \rightarrow C$, and $G = g_1 \times \cdots \times g_n\colon \times_{j=1}^{n} \times_{i=1}^{k} p_j D_i \rightarrow C$. In the first case, we wish to consider, C_i and D_i are disjoint and for each j, $1 \leqslant j \leqslant n$, f_j and g_j are different restrictions of the same k-ary operation h_j^* on the jth compositional domain. In this case, then, it is clear that there is a function H of category $C^{C_1 \times \cdots \times C_k}$, with $H = h_1 \times \cdots \times h_n\colon \times_{j=1}^{n} \times_{i=1}^{k} p_j(C_i \cup D_i)$, where h_j is the restriction of h_j^* to $(C_i \cup D_i)$. This function is obviously a generalization of F and G in the sense that its restriction to the domain of $F = F$ and its restriction to the domain of $G = G$.

Under what conditions do two functions of the same arity generalize

to a common extension? The following obvious theorem answers this
question:

GENERALIZATION THEOREM. Two compositional functions F:
$D_1 \times \cdots \times D_k \to C$ and $G: D'1 \times \cdots \times D'k \to C$ have a common
extension $H: (D_1 \times \cdots \times D_k) \cup (D'1 \times \cdots \times D'k) \to C$ iff for all
e in the intersection of the domain of F and the domain of G, $F(e) =$
$G(e)$.

   Proof. Clearly, if e lies in the intersection of the domain of F and the
domain of G, and it is not the case that $F(e) = G(e)$, then any
generalization H of F and G would have to satisfy $H(e) = F(e) \neq$
$G(e) = H(e)$. This violates the law of identity. On the other hand, if
for all e in the intersection of the domain of F and the domain of
G, $F(e) = G(e)$, then we define H in the obvious way: if e is in the
domain of F, then $H(e) = F(e)$; if e is in the domain of G, then $H(e) =$
$G(e)$.

Whether or not two functions have a common extension depends completely on whether or not the two functions agree on arguments drawn
from the intersection of their domains. Whether or not the union of two
functions expresses an intuitive generalization or not depends as well
on the nature of their respective sub-functions. To see this, it is useful
to examine a few examples.
   Let $F: D \to C$ and let the action of F be represented by $f_1 \times \cdots \times$
$f_n: \langle d_1, \ldots, d_n \rangle \mapsto \langle f_1(d_1), \ldots, f_n(d_n) \rangle$. For every member d of D,
there is a restriction of F to $\{d\}$ which maps it to its value in C. F is the
common extension of all of these restrictions. Even though the domains
of all of these separate restrictions of F are disjoint, F is a generalization of each of the separate restrictions of F to the singleton subsets of
D. An important indication of this fact is the invariance of the operations $f_1, \ldots, f_n$ by which the action of F is characterized: obviously, the
restriction of F to a singleton subset $\{d\}$ of D is simultaneously a
restriction of each operation f_i to the ith compositional domain of $\{d\}$;
by the same token, when we form the common extension of all of these
separate functions, acting on the union of all of these singleton subsets,
we return each f_i to its full domain (relative to the domain of F, of
course). It may seem perverse to decompose a function into its atomic
parts in this way, only to reconstruct it again. But Aronoff (1976)
shows that morphological rules often act more productively over some

sub-domains than over others, and the possibility of considering a given function as the union of its restrictions to a set of sub-domains which covers its domain has interesting applications in the field of learnability (Oehrle, to appear).

As a slightly more complicated example, suppose we have a set F of unary functors and a set Arg of arguments for the members of the set F. We define a relation A of compatibility from F to Arg in such a way that the domain of a functor f in F is the set $\{x \mid x \in Arg$ and $fAx\}$. (This situation holds, for example, in the compatibilities which constrain tensed verbs and nominative noun phrase subjects in languages such as Russian, as well as in a wide variety of other contexts.) The relation A imposes an equivalence relation on F, with two elements f and g of F belonging to the same equivalence class when $\{x \mid x \in Arg$ and $fAx\} = \{x \mid x \in Arg$ and $gAx\}$. There are a number of ways in which we can regard the relation A in this situation. Corresponding to the relation A, for example, there is a function A' defined by the action $(f, arg) \mapsto f(arg)$, if arg is in the domain of f; otherwise the result of applying A' to two arguments blocks their semantic composition (which we can think of as associating the semantic value of the composite with its phonological form). Clearly, the function A' provides a generalization of the various functions which belong to F, and in a way which has affinities with the treatment of agreement by Steele (this volume). There are also a number of ways in which we can impose restrictions on the members of the individual equivalence classes and across these equivalence classes, as well. One powerful restriction is to require that two functors f and g which belong to F may differ only with respect to the role played in their respective actions by constant values in the compositional domains A_i $(1 \leq i \leq n)$. Effectively, this means they can themselves be associated with different phonological forms and different semantical values, but cannot involve different operations over their arguments. On the other hand, if we relax this requirement, we are led to a restricted version of the n-tuple categories of Keenan and Timberlake (this volume).

3. GRAMMATICAL CONSEQUENCES

From the present point of view, a grammar consists of a type structure T over n compositional domains and a set of basic expressions, each associated with one or more types. We identify each functor expression with an operation in this structure. The closure of the operations over the set of basic expressions generates a set of analyses which we may regard as the language associated with the grammar. This general perspective is descriptively a very powerful one. It is all the more remarkable, then, that it also provides an illuminating perspective on a variety of fundamental linguistic problems.

3.1. *Grammatical Architecture*

Compositional functions can act simultaneously on properties in all compositional domains. Thus, there is no *a priori* reason to organize compositional functions into syntactic, semantic, or phonological components. Rather, the natural way to organize a set of compositional functions is by means of the relations formed among their respective domains and co-domains.[7]

In contrast, many current grammatical frameworks — either explicitly or *faute de mieux* — endorse a grammatical architecture based on the properties of individual compositional domains (roughly). In other words, such frameworks impose a division of linguistic labor into 'components' which are intended to deal with the compositional properties of one domain at a time. In general, advocates of this approach to grammatical architecture have assumed the dominance of one component and assigned to the other components they have recognized (when they have recognized other components at all) the task of interpreting the 'creative' efforts of the dominant component. While a cynic might observe that such an architecture is merely the formal result of gluing on 'components' to an abstract system in order to render the result empirically respectable, such observations have often been taken to have been deflected by reference to various 'autonomy theses', particularly the thesis of the autonomy of syntax. The present framework provides a new perspective on this question.

There is a trivial sense in which any two compositional domains are independent: namely, they are independent in virtue of the fact that they are represented by different algebraic structures. On the assumption that the vocabulary in which the structures of a given 'component' are characterized is distinct from the vocabulary of other 'components', then, assertions about autonomy in this sense are hardly surprising.

To consider stronger senses of 'autonomy', it is useful to see what it means to impose various 'architectures' on sets of compositional functions. Let us say that an analysis is 'complete' if it is associated with a non-functor category and is completely specified in each compositional domain. Theoretically, such an analysis is represented as the functional composition of a set of compositional functions applied to an appropriate set of basic expressions. It is quite straightforward in this setting to simulate the architectural structure of such grammatical theories as the 'T-schema' of Chomsky and Lasnik (1977) and Chomsky (1981), for example. First, it is easy to see that the functional product by which any such analysis can be represented is a tree with the final analysis as the root and the basic expressions the leaves. (Compare the 'analysis trees' of Montague.) To impose the structure of the 'T-schema', we require that all the functions which simulate the phrase-structure rules apply first, resulting in a (partial) analysis of category S, say, and then that there be a block of rules (corresponding to the transformational operations) which are operations of rank $(1, 1)$ over the syntactic domain; these functions are followed by a single function (representing the syntax-semantics interface) of rank $(2, 1)$ over the syntactic and semantic domains, whose one operation is in the semantic domain, followed by a finite sequence of operations of rank $(1, 1)$ in the semantic domain; this block of semantic operations is followed by a single function (representing the syntax-phonology interface) of rank $(2, 1)$ over the syntactic and phonological domains, whose single operation is phonological, followed by a finite sequence of phonological rules of rank $(1, 1)$. Clearly, the order between the block of semantic rules and the block of phonological rules can be reversed. In fact, given the information accessible to these rules, they can even be freely interspersed among one another, since the application of a phonological rule is essentially blind to the effects of a semantic rule and vice versa.

As this example suggests, it is possible within the framework of compositional functions (though not necessarily natural on formal grounds alone) to simulate many different modes of grammatical architecture by imposing structure on the composition of compositional functions in any given analysis. Within this framework, moreover, several grades of autonomy are discernible. The extreme of non-autonomy is this: there is a single, non-factorable function which specifies all the properties in one compositional domain on the basis of properties of some other domain. This is extreme in two ways: first, we assume that no information need be taken to be primitive in this domain, since it is all assumed to be predictable from information in the other domain; second, the domain contains no independent operations. The extreme of autonomy is this: the non-empty set of operations within a compositional domain contains only compositional functions of rank $(1, 1)$. That is, the operations which affect structures within an autonomous domain are completely independent of information concerning the properties within other domains. In between these two extremes lies a continuum of possibilities.

While it isn't possible to explore this terrain in detail here, a single example may be instructive. In many current theories, it is assumed that phonological structures are not isomorphic to, but are constructed from, syntactic surface structures. Examples of this kind can be found in Culicover & Rochemont (1983), Selkirk (1984), and Hayes (1984)). While the proposals of these authors differ in various ways, in each case, it is possible to ask what syntactical properties the proposed phonological structures depend on: order, constituency, category, derivational history, and so on. Intuitively, the greater the range of syntactical properties required for the construction of phonological structures, the more dependent phonological representation is on syntactical representation.

Of course, one can equally well ask in such a case whether the 'syntactical' structures involved are properly syntactical. Consider the fact that it is often the case that variations in speech quality that are not segmentally distinctive in English (such as degree of nasalization or laryngealization) have pragmatic consequences (indicating snideness or hesitancy, for instance). Given the grammatical architecture of the 'T-schema', the only way a relation of this kind could be grammatically analyzed would be to introduce an abstract syntactic feature of some kind which is syntactically inert (in the sense that no syntactical rule makes reference to this feature) and whose sole purpose is to facilitate the relation between phonological interpretation and pragmatic interpretation. The abstract feature in question may be considered 'syntactical' in the sense that a certain architecture requires that it be present in the 'syntactic' component. But the necessity of including elements or structures in the 'syntactic' component whose properties are accessible only in non-syntactic domains decreases the degree of 'syntactic' autonomy. The same is true, of course, whenever syntactical rules make reference to structures which are defined with respect to the properties of other compositional domains (such as thematic relations or referential indices, to mention two obvious examples). In all such cases, it is not at all clear how to apply a notion like 'autonomy'. Yet what is clear is that the problem arises as an artifact of theoretical hypotheses about how grammatical architecture constrains the access of operations in one grammatical domain to information coded in another.

It is one virtue of the framework advocated here that the structure of individual compositional domains is determined in part by the nature of the judgments that individuals have access to. This means that certain properties must be taken to be syntactical, others must be taken to be semantical, other must be taken to be phonological, and others must be taken to involve relations across compositional domains. Theoretical constructs not directly linked to particular sub-judgments can of course be associated with any domain. In all these cases, the Factorization Theorem of Section 2 provides a useful link in bringing the formulation of various grammatical rules to bear on the empirical validity of any proposed grammatical architecture (or constraint on the composition of functions). That is, a given architecture will be incompatible with a given compositional function, if the function cannot be factored in a way compatible with the requirements of the architecture.

3.2. *Indexing Functor-argument Relations*

We have assumed thus far that the abstract analysis of a complex linguistic object takes the form of a functional product. This assumption, which we may refer to as the functional representation hypothesis, hardly seems to constrain the properties of languages and the particular analyses they countenance at all. It is compatible with many theoretical claims, in the sense that it is possible to characterize (relative to further assumptions, not necessarily well-justified), the sets of analyses which other theories allow. In this sense, the framework advocated here is formally rather powerful — some might even say over-generous.

Yet formal power has certain advantages. For example, it makes it possible to study the relations among such diverse but decisive influences on language as its growth in the individual, its role in society, its expressive power — in general, the relations between its existence, its form, and its function — without prejudging the character of formal constraints on linguistic structure. At the same time, a rich formal context gives rise to a productive set of interesting problems, problems which take the form: if X is a linguistic structure consistent with our formal premises, do linguistic structures similar to X exist? And such questions often persist, even in the face of theories which are incompatible with X (for no principled reason) or only weakly compatible with X (in the sense that the theory in question offers no reason to expect that X would exist).

It has become usual in linguistics to begin with formal models of a modest character and gradually yield to empirical pressure by adding properties which enrich the class of formally representable languages. This strategy has been enormously productive. In the rest of this paper, I shall try to show (somewhat informally) that something can be learned about the language faculty by following the opposite strategy: namely, starting from an extremely rich (but methodologically well-motivated) formal system and seeking to impose natural restrictions or heuristic biases on analyses with the aim of approximating more and more closely the class of possible human languages on the basis of richer and more exact analyses of known human languages.

The question of what kind of structure can be represented as a functional product is a purely mathematical one. But as a practical matter, certain compositional functions will be better suited to linguistic tasks than others. Consider a function $f: D_1 \times \cdots \times D_k \to C$, where as earlier we shall assume that members of D_i ($1 \leqslant i \leqslant k$) and C have properties in n compositional domains. We now supplement the functional representation hypothesis with two further plausible assumptions. First, we will assume that linguistic communication and acquisition of linguistic structure is enhanced if it is possible to encode in a signal not only a set of meaningful sub-parts but also properties which indicate their relationship to one another. Second, we will assume that the existence of k-ary functions into C ($1 < k$) implies the existence of $(k-1)$-ary functions into C.

3.2.1. *Indexing by relative order.* Suppose we have an expression e whose phonological form e consists of a sequence $\langle a_1, \ldots, a_j \rangle$. If e is complex, then by the functional representation hypothesis, for suitable choice of f and $d_1, \ldots, d_k$, we have $e = f(d_1, \ldots, d_k)$. If the phonological sequence $e = \langle a_1, \ldots, a_j \rangle$ is to represent the functional representation of e, it must represent, in some way, the following facts: (1) e is the product of a functor and k arguments; (2) e is the phonological form of an expression belonging to the co-domain C of the functor f. We cannot discuss how these desiderata can be satisfied in the general case, but in one simple and important special case, $j = k + 1$ and there is a bijection between the sequence $\langle a_1, \ldots, a_{k+1} \rangle$ and a set of phonological forms $\{f, d_1, \ldots, d_k\}$ associated with functor and arguments respectively. We can assume without loss of generality that if the functor is associated with a_f under these conditions, then the bijection which yields the phonological sequence $\langle a_1, \ldots, a_{f-1}, a_{f+1}, \ldots, a_{k+1} \rangle$ is isotonic: that is, the order in which the arguments of f are represented corresponds to the order in which their associated phonological forms occur.

Now, let us assume as well that the functor-argument relations which hold among the functor f and its associated arguments are indicated in the form of any expression compatible with this functional product only by relative order. Clearly, any permutation of the phonological forms associated with the arguments creates needless indeterminacy in identifying the functional product. Thus, we may infer that under conditions in which function argument relations are indicated solely by order, a rigid order of arguments is the optimal system. Consider now where in this order the phonological form a_f associated with the functor might appear. If we restricted ourselves to the case in which f is k-ary, it might seem reasonable to conclude that a_f could occur in any of the $k + 1$ positions before, within, or following the sequence $\langle a_1, \ldots, a_{f-1}, a_{f+1}, \ldots, a_{k+1} \rangle$. But if we require that the position of a functor be determined by a single schema for any functor with co-domain C, and since we have assumed that there are 1-ary functors into C, then only four possible schemata exist, since only the first and last elements of the sequence $\langle a_1, \ldots, a_{f-1}, a_{f+1}, \ldots, a_{k+1} \rangle$ can be assumed to exist for arguments of arbitrary complexity. (I owe this argument to Susan Steele. See Steele *et al.*, 1981.) These are: (1) $a_f, a_2, \ldots$, (2) $a_1, a_f, \ldots$, (3) $\ldots, a_f, a_{k+1}$, and (4) $\ldots, a_k, a_f$. While we cannot enter here into the conditions under which one of these might be favored over another, it is a striking fact that these four positions occur over and over again in syntax (consider the wide-applicability of left- and right-directional categorial systems, the phenomena associated with Wackernagel's Law and other motivation for the wrapping operations introduced by Bach (1979, 1984, and elsewhere)), in the edge-related properties of morphological infixation (see Moravcsik, 1977, and Hoeksema and Janda, this volume), and even in phonology proper with regard to the restriction of extra-metricality to peripheral elements. The point of view considered here raises the intriguing question (brought to my attention by Steele) of whether these diverse phenomena have a common basis.

3.2.2. *Indexing arguments by category.* Many natural language functors can be interpreted as n-place relations on a single set. Expressions which are interpreted as elements of this set may nevertheless differ in their category. Examples of this state of affairs are: (1) the case system of such languages as Latin, Greek, German, and Russian; (2) the 'case' particles of Japanese. If each argument expression of a functional product $f(d_1, \ldots, d_k)$ is associated with a distinct category, then the functor-argument relations of this functional product will be recoverable from any phonological structure which can be partitioned into $k + 1$ sub-expressions in such a way that each sub-expression can be identified either as the phonological form of the functor or as associated with a unique category from the k categories over which f is defined. Indexing arguments by category means that it is unnecessary to index them by order, a fact which is obvious and has long been assumed. But there is no inconsistency between indexing by category and indexing by relative order, and systems which make use of both types of indexing are clearly possible, particularly when one of them is used in the service of pragmatically-oriented systems involving information structure.

We are not able here to enter into a detailed discussion of what it means, morphologically and phonologically, to say that an expression is associated with a particular category or sub-category. But it is worth observing that commonly attested systems of this kind make use of affixation (pre- and post-positional particles), or expression-internal means. From the point of view adopted here, we might expect that the category of a complex expression would be indicated by the form of its functor. The role of complementizer/aux variation in distinguishing different types of subordinate clauses can be interpreted this way. In noun phrases, however, the problem becomes more complicated: if we construe determiners as functors with co-domain a sub-category of NP (such as NP[nom], NP[acc], NP[gen], and so on), then it is natural to expect indications of sub-category to appear on the determiner. This is perfectly fine as long as determiners appear in enough NP's to make the system viable (as in German). But if determiners need not occur (as in Russian), they cannot be the sole morphological means of indicating the sub-category to which an NP belongs. This observation is consistent with the fact that the nominal declension in Russian is more highly-articulated than the German nominal declension. But deeper insight into the interaction of these factors requires more empirical knowledge than I am able to bring to bear on the subject at present.

3.2.3. *Indexing the functor.* In Section 2.7. above, we discussed how a set of functions can have a common extension. The most important example of this is the case in which a set of functors have a common interpretation, defined over the interpretation of a set of arguments $D_1 \times \cdots \times D_k$, but each of the functors is syntactically restricted to apply to a subset of this domain, usually in such a way that the set of arguments $D_1 \times \cdots \times D_k$ is the disjoint union of the domains of the individual functors. In the most common cases, the individual functors constrain the number, person, or gender of one or more arguments. As a result, it is often possible (how often, exactly?) to determine the functor argument relations encoded in an expression from the properties of the functor and the properties of the members of its (set-theoretic) complement in e. And thus this form of agreement is an alternative to relative order and categorization as a means of encoding functor-argument relations.

3.2.4. *Summary.* While we have not tried to characterize exhaustively the ways in which the functor-argument relations of a complex expression can be encoded in its form — in particular, we have neglected the role of suprasegmental information —, we have tried to show that certain formal properties involving syntax and morphology yield, in part, just the sort of information that such an encoding demands. As a result, the very general premises with which we began lead us to expect the existence of a variety of different language types. Although a more rigorous demonstration of the reasoning involved would certainly be welcome, it is worthwhile to contrast this expectation with the typological consequences of many other competing grammatical frameworks. In many such cases, compatibility of expressions is mediated by a set of syntactic relations (for example, case relationships in the case grammar of Fillmore, or properties of linear order and hierarchical relations in phrase structure grammars) which from our point of view represent a rather special case. As recent work (in GPSG, as well as in certain categorial frameworks, much of it stemming from Keenan

(1974)) has shown, it is possible to characterize a variety of naturally-observed agreement relations in an explicit and elegant way. But it nevertheless remains true that from a formal point of view, such grammars would be simplified if agreement relations of the kind discussed here failed to exist. This same point holds for a wide variety of other syntactic theories: the 'government-and-binding' theory of Chomsky (1981), the 'relational grammar' of Perlmutter and Postal, the 'lexical-functional grammar' of Bresnan and Kaplan.

The point of view advocated here suggests how this inadequacy of theory may be overcome.

3.3. *A Typology of Sentential Structures*

This section constitutes a small exercise in the investigation of the relation between form and function from the perspective of multi-dimensional compositional functions. In Steele *et al.* (1981), a rather circumscribed set of grammatical properties was found to be correlated with the instantiations of the cross-linguistically defined AUX. A natural language category is an instantiation of AUX iff it is a constituent which is syntactically made up of a small number of closed class elements and expresses properties of tense and modality. In this definition, the notions 'constituent', 'element', 'tense', and 'modality' are taken as given. Thus, the definition of AUX is both syntactic and semantic. While the coherence of the semantic properties associated with AUX can be construed as evidence of its grammatical reality, a problem arises when we consider the full range of the grammatical realizations of AUX-properties. In many languages, for instance, distinctions among declarative and interrogative sentence types are drawn only intonationally. Although there are languages in which tense and mood depend on properties of a 2nd position AUX constituent, there are others in which tense and mood, for example, are indicated inflectionally. From this situation, we may infer that while a constituent AUX offers one viable solution to the problem of grammatical design that these properties pose, it is a special case of a more general class of solutions. Relative to some assumptions concerning semantical types, on the one hand, and the grammatical realization of functions, on the other, it is possible to propose a more adequate set of solutions to this problem of grammatical design.

3.3.1. *Types and operations.* We shall assume that there is a universally-available set of semantic types relevant to the analysis of syntactically-differentiated sentential categories (such as declarative vs interrogative vs imperative), on the one hand, and mood, modality, and tense, on the other. These types are assumed as well to have internal structure. As in Steele *et al.* (1981, Chapter 4), we shall assume that there is a type corresponding to 'propositional radical', a type corresponding to 'proposition', and a set of types corresponding to various ways of constraining linguistically the set of speech acts that an utterance (on a particular grammatical analysis) may be used to perform. Roughly speaking, the difference betwen these three types is this: a pair consisting of a model and a propositional radical determines a truth value, but a propositional radical in isolation is neither true nor false; a proposition is a function from a possible world w and a set of (contextually-determined) indices into the set of truth values; an assertion is a speech act expressing a relation between a speaker and a proposition evaluated at a given set of arguments. We shall abbreviate these types as '$\sqrt{P}$', 'P', and 'S' in the top line of the diagram below, and refer to this sequence as the *propositional hierarchy.* The arrows represent the actions of compositional functions with domain represented at the tail of the arrow and co-domain represented at the head.

$$\sqrt{P} \rightarrow P \rightarrow S$$
$$2^W \rightarrow 2^{W \times now} \rightarrow 2$$

The bottom line of the diagram assigns each intuitive type of the top line a type consisting of a truth value or a function into the set of truth values. The symbol 2 on the right stands for the two-element Boolean algebra of truth values (cf. Halmos, 1963; Keenan and Faltz, 1985), which we shall assume here is the appropriate type to assign to evaluated propositions (as they occur in assertions). We take (unevaluated) propositions to be entities of the type $2^{W \times now}$, where W represents a set of contextual indices, each one of which specifies a possible world w and a context now which fixes a time and possibly other contextual information. Finally, propositional radicals are interpreted as functions from states of affairs to truth values. (For further details and applications, see Steele *et al.* (1981, Chapter 4), and Oehrle (1987).)

It is useful to decompose these types further into functional products. We consider here, without justification, only two basic types of functional product: in one, a functor V maps a k-tuple of arguments (with respective types $A_1, \ldots, A_k$) directly into the propositional hierarchy; in the other, this mapping is broken up into two steps in such a way that there is a distinguishing argument of type A_1 which combines with a product of other types belong to the category (tenseless) VP. These possibilities are represented in the diagram below (where the symbols '$\sqrt{P}$', 'P', and 'S' are abbreviations for the types associated with them above):

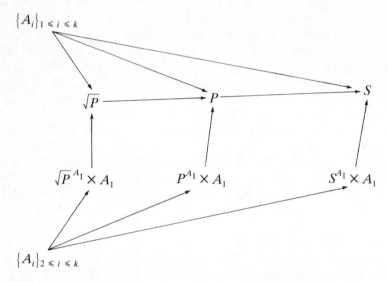

These types need not correspond one-to-one with syntactic types, in the way found in Montague's work. For example, in English, a tenseless verb might be regarded syntactically as a function into an argument category VP, while it is regarded semantically as a function into the functor category $\sqrt{P}^{A_1}$. (We regain Montague's homomorphism property if all complete syntactic categories (that is, non-functor categories) correspond to primitive semantic types. See Chierchia, 1984.) Moreover, while in any particular language we expect to find syntactical expressions which correspond to arguments as well as to expressions of type S, it is not necessary that the other types be syntactically accessible. This is because we may regard many syntactically simple expressions as expressing composite functions with regard to semantical types.

In addition to this set of semantical types, we will suppose that there are three basic ways in which the action of a functor can be overtly indicated: globally (by intonation, for example), as an independent segmental sequence or set of sequences (possibly discontinuous), and morphologically. This is perhaps overly simplified, but relative to this fundamental three-way distinction, we can formulate the problem that interests us: what sets of grammatical structures naturally express the composition of functors which map k-tuples of arguments into linguistically-differentiated speech act types?

3.3.2. *Grammatical domains.* Among the semantic types, there is a natural notion of scope. Any complex member of any type is a functional product and it is natural to say that the functor has scope over its arguments. There is a corresponding notion of scope for the various types of operations we have posited. First, the scope of a global intonation contour may be taken to be the domain over which it is defined — namely, the resulting intonational phrase. Second, a segmental sequence has the same scope as the rule which introduces it. Third, if morphology is independent of syntactic composition (as its heterogeneity suggests), then the domain of any morphological-realized functor is bounded by the domain of the element the functor is applied to. (This means that the interpretation of the morphologically-realized functor may combine by functional composition with the interpretation of the element that it acts on.)

Interesting restrictions on the relations between the semantic action and the grammatical realization of a compositional function associated with any of the arrows in the above diagram exist if we adopt the *Domain Correspondence Hypothesis* that the set of functors of an optimal grammatical system is *domain-harmonic* in the sense of the following definition:

DEFINITION. A set of functors whose co-domains fall in the propositional hierarchy (of the diagram above) is *domain-harmonic* iff the grammatical realization of the arguments in its semantic domain falls within the grammatical domain of its associated operation and the grammatical realization of arguments outside its semantic domain falls outside the grammatical domain of its associated operation.

In particular, grammatical systems which satisfy the Domain Correspondence Hypothesis will have the following properties: (1) if an utterance u is represented by the functional product $f(e)$, then f assigns a global intonation to u; (2) a functor which combines morphologically with an element e to yield an expression e' has scope over an independent word or phrase only if e has scope over that word or phrase. This means that the grammatical realization of functors which act in the propositional hierarchy must take the following form:

$$\{A_i\} \to \cdots \to \cdots \to S$$
morphology . . . segmental sequence . . . intonation

In other words, intonation (which is always present) is associated with the final functor (possibly a composite); morphological properties of V are associated with the functor which maps the set of arguments $\{A_i\}$ into the propositional hierarchy; in between may appear an independent particle sequence.

Apart from intonation, whose presence is always felt, these constraints do not require the existence of an independent particle sequence, since it is possible to mark non-intonationally interpreted functors morphologically, if the morphology is rich enough. (Perhaps Finnish provides an example of this situation.) Nor does it require the existence of morphologically-realized functors within the propositional hierarchy. (English leans in this direction.) Nor does it require that global intonational properties serve a grammatical function in the propositional hierarchy (since these properties may be interpreted in other pragmatic ways not relevant to the distinctions among major speech act types). As a result, a wide variety of formal systems are compatible with the assumptions adopted here. But combination of functors from various attested systems need not result in a set of grammatical functors consistent with the Domain Correspondence Hypothesis. This rules out, for instance, a system in which the mapping from P to S is indicated morphologically on V, while the mapping from $\sqrt{P}$ to P is indicated by a set of independent particles outside the domain of V.

4. CONCLUSION

The methodological issues with which this paper begins lead naturally to an algebraic approach to grammatical composition on which complex expressions, with properties in a number of subjectively-accessible dimensions, are analyzed as a functional product. The multi-dimensional compositional functions by which this point of view can be formally expressed have a number of properties surveyed in Section 2. While grammatical systems based on sets of compositional functions acting on appropriate sets of arguments are formally powerful, the perspective they provide on grammatical issues sheds interesting light on various versions of the 'autonomy thesis'. Moreover, relative to a few natural assumptions, these formal systems suggest the basis for a theoretical typology which has welcome empirical consequences.

APPENDIX

Chomsky's methodological approach to the analysis of language is justifiably famous for the emphasis it puts on the existence of a bridge between the methodological characterization of language and its mathematical characterization. It is primarily because of this dual emphasis that Chomsky's ideas triggered new eras both in the study of formal languages and in psycholinguistics. Yet, as I hope to show, it is possible to offer alternatives to Chomsky's conclusions which are not open to the devastating criticisms he leveled against much previous thinking on the subject, and, at the same time, are much closer to the practice of working grammarians.

Chomsky proceeds as follows (see *Syntactic Structures*, pp. 13f). A language is taken to be a set. Mathematically, of course, this poses no problem; empirically, on the other hand, we take the language of an individual to be characterized by the individual's intuitive (and possibly partial) judgment of well-formedness or grammaticality. A formal grammar of the language of an individual constitutes a model of the individual's intuition of grammaticality, in the sense that the formal grammar and the individual agree on all cases where the individual's judgment is defined.

This is a strikingly bold and simple conception of the problem. Chomsky elaborates on it a good deal in *Syntactic Structures* and later work, specifying for instance some of the things that we should not confuse the grammaticality judgment with, discussing the issue of how to evaluate competing and apparently equally adequate formal grammars, and indicating the critical relations which hold among theories of language structure, theories of language acquisition, and theories of linguistic universals. In *Aspects of the Theory of Syntax.* Chomsky stresses the fact that a grammar is "a description of the ideal speaker-hearer's intrinsic competence" (p. 4). As such, a "fully adequate grammar must assign to each of an infinite range of sentences a structural description indicating how this sentence is understood by the ideal speaker-hearer" (pp. 4f). While it is possible to conflate the notion 'structural description' with the 'abstract analysis' justified above, there are two fundamental differences between them.

First, the thrust of the account suggested above is that well-defined correlative sub-judgments of symbolic identification exist and provide direct but partial evidence concerning the character of the necessary 'abstract analysis' of any given judgment. Chomsky, on the other hand, emphasizes the inadequacies of the reports of individuals concerning their own linguistic competence, in such passages as:

> ... every speaker of a language has mastered and internalized a generative grammar that expresses his knowledge of his language. This is not to say that he is aware of them, or that his statements about his intuitive knowledge of the language are necessarily accurate. Any interesting generative grammar will be dealing, for the most part, with mental processes that are far beyond the level of actual or even potential consciousness; furthermore, it is quite apparent that a speaker's reports and viewpoints about his behavior and his competence may be in error. Thus a generative grammar attempts to specify what the speaker actually knows, not what he may report about his knowledge. (Chomsky, 1965, p. 8)

In particular, there is no attempt to separate the kinds of introspective or intuitive judgments which can be ignored from those which must be respected. Apart from the phonetic level at which judgments of grammaticality are presumably to be tested, the 'levels' of a grammar (organized hierarchically in blocks of components) are added as theoretical conveniences. In contrast, on the view advocated here, the analyses ascribed to sentences by a formal grammar must agree in certain respects with the judgments of individuals whose language capacity the formal grammar is attempting to emulate.

Second, Chomsky apparently considers 'languages' the central focus of investigation rather than individual capacity for language. (Though the emphasis on "an ideal speaker-listener, in a completely homogeneous speech-community" (*Aspects*, p. 3) obliterates the difference between individual linguistic capacity and knowledge and linguistic norms and practice in a social setting.) On the view advocated here, the primary focus is on individual acts of linguistic perception and judgment. 'Languages' in the large, such as 'English', etc., are definable on this view only over the language capacity of populations. As a result there arise new possibilities for the division of labor between individual capacity and social regularity.

The methodological framework sketched earlier shares one important feature with Chomsky's proposal: in each case, the goal is a formal model of properties of the human language capacity. But they differ in a number of respect. First, the notion 'grammatical' is not defined, but simply inculcated by example. (This is not necessarily a defect in itself, since other human skills (e.g., sexing chicks) are apparently transmitted successfully in this way.) Second, grammaticality judgments are notoriously subject to revision in the light of previously unconsidered interpretations or intonations. Third, the notion 'grammatical' is a global judgment only: in contrast to the method of sub-judgments, it gives no information about the relevant properties of the analysis. Fourth, partly as a consequence of the global nature of the grammaticality judgment, decisive evidence for one or another analysis can be found only among increasingly less clear cases. Fifth, the notion 'grammatical (in L)' has no clear meaning in many linguistic contexts, such as those involving code-switching, language mixing, and language invention.

If the method of sub-judgments can be adequately formulated, it has advantages to the approach based on a single, global 'grammaticality' judgment in each of these areas. First, the method of sub-judgments is an attempt to represent aspects of subjective experience in a way accessible to interpersonal scrutiny, and while a similar technique of inculcation may be required relative to each mode of representation, the division of labor actually decreases, rather than increases, the chance of misunderstanding. Second, where the grammaticality judgment is open to revision, often on the discovery of new semantic or phonetic interpretations, this judgmental instability is lessened considerably on the sub-judgments approach, since the fundamental judgment of identification actually gives rise to a set of correlative sub-judgments involving just such properties. Third, while the notion 'grammaticality' is a global judgment and provides no information concerning the properties of the analysis associated with the physical object of judgment, the method of sub-judgments in fact provides a partial decomposition of the analysis. Fourth, while the 'grammaticality' method must rely on increasingly obscure empirical facts to distinguish among theories which agree in weak generative capacity, the method of sub-judgments provides an alternative: if two speakers agree on sub-judgments for a large enough class of important cases (whichever these may be), it doesn't matter very much whether or not they agree on the obscure cases. Fifth, unlike the notion 'grammatical (in L)', the method of sub-judgments is applicable whenever symbolic identification takes place: even in contexts involving radical code-switching, the basic sub-judgments discussed above remain defined, though the notion 'grammatical (in L)' has no meaning. Finally, it should be noted that linguistic practice depends on judgments about the relations among various analytical properties: many of the most interesting linguistic problems involve judgments of consistency between syntactic and interpretative structures, or between syntactic and phonological structures, or between phonological and interpretive structures. It is unlikely that awareness of these problems arises as the result of linguists (or language-learners) sifting through records of grammaticality judgments associated with phoneme sequences. But such observations are completely consistent with the method of sub-judgments advocated here.

NOTES

* Research on this paper was supported in part by a visiting fellowship at the Instituut voor Algemene Taalwetenschap of the Rijksuniversiteit Groningen, sponsored by the ZWO, during 1983, and in part by a summer research grant from the University of Arizona SBS Research Institute during the summer of 1985. I am grateful to these organizations for their support. The methodological point of view which forms the basis of this paper stems from joint work over a period of years with Leon Shiman, the goal of which was to extend to language the analysis of visual stability reported in Shiman (1978). The formal model of Section 2 has affinities with recent work by Bill Ladusaw (1985). Portions of this material have been presented to audiences in the Departments of Mathematics, Linguistics, and Speech & Hearing Sciences at the University of Arizona, in the Instituut voor Algemene Taalwetenschap at the Rijksuniversiteit Groningen, as well as at the Tucson categorial grammar conference. I wish to thank the members of these audiences, especially the last. Conversations with Aryeh Faltz have led to a number of corrections and improvements of earlier drafts, both in regard to content and style. I owe a particular debt to Susan Steele, for her encouragement and support.
[1] These same considerations apply equally well to other temporally-evanescent modes of human articulation, such as the sign languages of the deaf (cf. Klima and Bellugi, 1979). Moreover, we may expect that language that is presented physically in a static way (such as print) will have somewhat different properties.
[2] For some discussion of these issues, see the Appendix, where the views presented here are contrasted with the methodological views advocated by Chomsky in early work. Let me also note in passing the extent to which current linguistic research in phonology, in syntax, in semantics, and in pragmatics relies on detailed and specific

subjective judgments of just the sort required by the research program being advocated here.

[3] One way to ensure that this matching makes sense is to require that the vocabulary of theoretical analysis be an extension of the vocabulary of phenomenal analysis, and moreover, that the language of the ith co-ordinate $(1 \leqslant i \leqslant k)$ of a theoretical analysis be the same as the language in which the corresponding sub-judgment is defined. This requirement would render the notion 'matching' transparent. (But there are alternatives, as we shall see shortly.)

[4] This point of view suggests that we say that a phenomenal analysis and a theoretical analysis match when the algebraic structure of the phenomenal analysis can be embedded in the theoretical analysis in an appropriate way. Compare Note 3.

[5] There are elegant, non-transformational ways of treating both the raising-to-object problem and the restructuring problems of Rizzi using functional composition. On the first, see Pollard (1984); on the second, see Nishida (1987).

[6] Further empirical motivation for multi-dimensional rules may be found in Oehrle (1981).

[7] This 'hand-in-hand' approach is characteristic of Montague's rules of composition. As mentioned earlier in the examples of Section 2.5, if we treat the natural pairs of syntactic and semantic rules of PTQ (say) as single rules, Montague's rules are three dimensional: one dimension is the orthographic line, which consists of sequences of bold-face symbols drawn from the union of the lower case English alphabet and the blank; the third dimension is the model-theoretic constraints placed on the relation between any interpretation of a complex expression and the interpretation of its component parts. Work by Schmerling, Bach, and Wheeler has brought this general approach closer to linguistic reality by substituting phonological structures for the orthographic structures that Montague employed.

REFERENCES

Archangeli, D.: 1984, *Underspecification in Yawelmani Phonology and Morphology*, MIT, Ph.D. dissertation.

Aronoff, M.: 1976, *Word Formation in Generative Grammar*, Linguistic Inquiry Monograph Series # 1, MIT Press, Cambridge, Mass.

Bach, E.: 1979, 'Control in Montague Grammar', *Linguistic Inquiry* **10**, 515—531.

Bach, E.: 1981, 'Discontinuous Constituents in Generalized Categorial Grammar', *NELS XI* Proceedings.

Bach, E.: 1983, 'Generalized Categorial Grammars and the English Auxiliary', in F. Heny and B. Richards (eds.), *Linguistic Categories: Auxiliaries and Related Puzzles*, Vol. Two, Reidel, Dordrecht, pp. 101—120.

Bach, E.: 1984, 'Some Generalizations of Categorial Grammars', in F. Landman and F. Veltman (eds.), *Varieties of Formal Semantics: Proceedings of the fourth Amsterdam Colloquium, September 1982*, Foris, Dordrecht.

Chierchia, G.: 1984, *Topics in the Syntax and Semantics of Infinitives and Gerunds*, Ph.D. dissertation, University of Massachusetts at Amherst.

Chomsky, N.: 1957, *Syntactic Structures*, Mouton, The Hague.

Chomsky, N.: 1965, *Aspects of the Theory of Syntax*, MIT Press, Cambridge, Mass.

Chomsky, N.: 1981, *Lectures on Government and Binding*, Foris, Dordrecht.
Chomsky, N. and H. Lasnik: 1977, 'Filters and Control', *Linguistic Inquiry* **8**, 425—504.
Culicover, P. and M. Rochemont: 1983, 'Stress and Focus in English', *Language* **59**, 123—165.
Gazdar, G., E. Klein, G. Pullum, and I. Sag: 1985, *Generalized Phrase Structure Grammar*, Harvard University Press, Cambridge, Mass.
Halmos, P.: 1963, *Lectures on Boolean Algebras*, van Nostrand Mathematical Studies #1, van Nostrand, Princeton.
Hayes, B.: 1984, 'The Prosodic Hierarchy in Meter', paper presented at the Stanford Metrics Conference.
Hoeksema, J. and R. Janda: (this volume), 'Implications of Process-Morphology for Categorial Grammar'.
Janda, R.: 1987, *On the Motivation for an Evolutionary Typology of Sound-Structural Rules*, Ph.D. dissertation, UCLA.
Kay, M.: 1979, 'Functional Grammar', in C. Chiarello *et al.* (eds.), *Proceedings of the Fifth Annual Meeting of the Berkeley Linguistic Society*, Berkeley Linguistics Society, Berkeley, pp. 142—158.
Keenan, E.: 1974, 'The Functional Principle: Generalizing the Notion of "Subject-of"', in *Papers from the 10th Regional Meeting of the Chicago Linguistic Society*, Chicago Linguistic Society, Chicago, pp. 298—310.
Keenan, E. and L. Faltz: 1985, *Boolean Semantics for Natural Language*, Reidel, Dordrecht.
Keenan, E. and A. Timberlake: (this volume), 'Natural Language Motivations for Extending Categorial Grammar'.
Klima, E. and U. Bellugi: 1979, *The Signs of Language*, Harvard University Press, Cambridge, Mass.
Ladusaw, W.: 1985, 'A Proposed Distinction between *Levels* and *Strata*' (written version of a paper read at the Winter meeting of the LSA in Seattle).
MacLane, S. and G. Birkhoff: 1967, *Algebra*, Macmillan, New York.
Montague, R.: 1974, *Formal Philosophy: Selected Papers of Richard Montague*, edited and with an introduction by Richmond H. Thomason, Yale University Press, New Haven and London.
Moravcsik, E.: 1977, 'On Rules of Infixing', IULC, Bloomington.
Nishida, C.: 1987, *Interplay between Morphology and Syntax in Spanish*, Ph.D. dissertation, University of Arizona.
Oehrle, R. T.: 1981, 'Lexical Justification', in M. Moortgat, H. v.d. Hulst, and T. Hoekstra (eds.), *The Scope of Lexical Rules*, Foris, Dordrecht, pp. 201—228.
Oehrle, R. T.: 1987, 'Boolean Properties in the Analysis of Gapping', in G. Huck and A. Ojeda (eds.), *Syntax & Semantics 20*, Academic Press, New York, pp. 201—240.
Oehrle, R. T.: (to appear), 'Implicit Negative Evidence'.
Pollard, C.: 1984, *Generalized Phrase Structure Grammars, Head Grammars, and Natural Language*, Ph.D. dissertation, Stanford University.
Rizzi, L. G.: 1981, *Issues in Italian Syntax*, Foris, Dordrecht.
Schmerling, S.: 1982, 'The Proper Treatment of the Relationship between Syntax and Phonology', *Texas Linguistic Forum* **19**, 151—166.

Schmerling, S.: 1983, 'Montague Morphophonemics', in ... (ed.), 'Papers from the Parasession on the Interplay of Phonology, Morphology, and Syntax', Chicago Linguistic Society.

Selkirk, E.: 1984, *Phonology and Syntax: The Relation between Sound and Structure*, MIT Press, Cambridge, Mass.

Shiman, L.: 1978, 'The Law of Perceptual Stability', *Proc. Natl. Acad. Sci. USA* **75**, 2049—2053, 2535—2538.

Steele, S. *et al.*: 1981, *An Encyclopedia of AUX: A Study in Cross-Linguistic Equivalence*, Linguistic Inquiry Monograph Series #5, Cambridge, MIT Press, Mass.

Steele, S.: (forthcoming), *A Grammar of Luiseno*, Reidel, Dordrecht.

Wheeler, D.: 1981, *Aspects of a Categorial Theory of Phonology*, Ph.D. dissertation, University of Massachusetts at Amherst.

Wheeler, D.: (this volume), 'Consequences of Some Categorially-Motivated Phonological Assumptions'.

Dept. of Linguistics,
Mathematics Building # 89, Room 209,
University of Arizona,
Tucson, AZ 85721, U.S.A.

CARL J. POLLARD

CATEGORIAL GRAMMAR AND PHRASE STRUCTURE GRAMMAR: AN EXCURSION ON THE SYNTAX-SEMANTICS FRONTIER

1. INTRODUCTION

The notion of a phrase structure grammar first came to the attention of the linguistic community with the publication in 1957 of *Syntactic Structures*, wherein Noam Chomsky asserted that phrase structure grammars were inadequate for linguistic description. He went on to argue for a model of linguistic structure in which the constituent structure trees produced by a phrase structure grammar were subsequently subjected to operations called *transformations* that added, deleted, or moved constituents. Successive versions of Chomsky's transformational grammar came to be accepted as the standard framework for syntactic theory.

At the same time, the notion of the linguistic inadequacy of phrase structure grammar acquired the status of conventional wisdom and persisted among syntacticians of all stripes until the late 1970s, when various proposals for constraining or eliminating the use of transformations were put forward by writers such as Brame, Bresnan, Gazdar, and Peters. The most extreme of these proposals was that advanced by Gerald Gazdar in a series of papers written in 1979 and 1980. In these papers Gazdar adopted the empirical hypothesis that natural language syntax can be adequately described by that subclass of phrase structure grammars which Chomsky called 'Type 2', generally known nowadays as context-free grammars. These papers became the foundation of the phrase-structure-based grammatical framework called Generalized Phrase Structure Grammar (GPSG). One of the milestones in GPSG was the appearance of Pullum and Gazdar (1982), which effectively refuted every published argument that natural languages could not be context-free; a second was the recent publication of Gazdar *et al.* (1985), which sets forth an extensive context-free fragment of English grammar with remarkable attention to matters of syntactic and semantic detail.

Categorial grammar, on the other hand, first came before the

Richard T. Oehrle et al. (eds.), Categorial Grammars and Natural Language Structures, 391—415.
© 1988 *by D. Reidel Publishing Company.*

linguistic community with the 1953 publication in *Language* of Bar-Hillel's 'A Quasi-Arithmetic Notation for Syntactic Description'. Bar-Hillel's notation was a straightforward bidirectional generalization of the symbolic system of *syntactic connection* based upon semantic categories, first proposed by Ajdukiewicz (1935). Unlike phrase structure grammar, though, categorial grammar didn't really begin to take hold among linguists until about a decade ago, when Barbara Partee, Rich Thomason, Robin Cooper, David Dowty and others began to extend the ground-breaking work on natural language semantics begun by Richard Montague in the late 1960s. Now Montague, of course, was a mathematician and philosopher, and had no interest in syntactic theory. This is reflected in the fact that the version of categorial grammar underlying Montague's Universal Grammar was generalized to the point of allowing any specifiable operation whatsoever to combine a functor category with an argument category. So, as might be expected, most linguists who worked on Montague grammar had essentially semantic interests at heart. To the best of my knowledge, the first serious application of categorial grammar to natural language syntax in a spirit akin to Ajdukiewicz's original intentions is found in the work of Emmon Bach and his students at the University of Massachusetts around the beginning of this decade, at just about the same time that interest in phrase structure grammar was becoming renewed.

Now as early as 1958 Bar-Hillel surmised that his bidirectional categorial grammars were closely related to context-free grammars, and the two formalisms were proved to be equivalent in weak generative capacity by Gaifman the following year. A simplified proof, attributed to Shamir, was presented by Bar-Hillel in 1960; this proof first became generally accessible with the publication of Bar-Hillel's *Language and Information* in 1964. This proof, together with the elevation of the doctrine of the inadequacy of phrase structure grammars to an article of faith, no doubt accounts in large part for the general indifference of syntacticians to categorial grammars until recent times.

The proof of Gaifman's theorem consists in providing algorithms for converting a bidirectional categorial grammar (BCG) into a weakly equivalent context-free grammar (CFG), and vice versa. By way of introducing some notation, I will provide a sketch of the easy half of the proof. We assume given a BCG. This means that we are given a finite set of *primitive categories* $\{A1, \ldots, AN\}$. One of the primitive categories, let us say $A1$, is distinguished. From these primitive categories, we form the entire system C of bidirectional categories by recursion, as in (1):

(1)   *The System C of Bidirectional Categories*

      (a) The primitive categories $A1, \ldots, AN$ are all in C;
      (b) if A and B are in C, then so is A/B;
      (c) if A and B are in C, then so is $A\backslash B$.

In addition we are given a finite vocabulary V, together with an assignment function A that maps each symbol x in V to some finite set of categories in C. A string of vocabulary symbols $x1 \ldots xk$ is said to be *reducible* to the category A if there are categories $A1, \ldots, Ak$ assigned to $x1, \ldots, xk$ respectively such that the category sequence $A1, \ldots, Ak$ cancels to A in the usual way, as defined in (2):

(2)   *Reduction of Strings and Cancellation of Categories*

      (a) A category sequence α *cancels* to a category sequence β if there are category sequences $\alpha 1, \ldots, \alpha n$ such that $\alpha 1 = \alpha$, $\alpha n = \beta$, and each $\alpha(i-1)$ cancels directly to αi;
      (b) A category sequence α *cancels directly* to the category sequence β provided either
      (i) $\alpha = \gamma, A/B, B, \delta$ and $\beta = \gamma, A, \delta$ or
      (ii) $\alpha = \gamma, B, A\backslash B, \delta$ and $\beta = \gamma, A, \delta$.

The *language generated* by the BCG is defined to be the set of all strings from V^* reducible to the distinguished category $A1$.

The problem is to produce a CFG that generates the same language. We begin by taking V to be the set of terminals and $A1$ to be the start symbol. Next, we define the set of nonterminals recursively as in (3):

(3)   The set of nonterminals for the equivalent CFG is the least set N such that:

      (a) Each category assigned to some vocabulary item is in N;
      (b) if A/B is in N, so are A and B;
      (c) if $A\backslash B$ is in N, so are A and B.

Finally, the phrase structure rules are defined as in (4):

(4)   The set of phrase structure rules for the equivalent CFG is
        the least set P such that:

    (a) $A \rightarrow x$ is in P for every x in V and every category A
         assigned to x;
    (b) if A/B is in N, then $A \rightarrow A/B\ B$ is in P;
    (c) if $A \backslash B$ is in N, then $A \rightarrow B\ A \backslash B$ is in P.

In a very precise sense, then, categorial grammars and context-free
grammars have been known to be notational variants for over a quarter
of a century. Given this fact, it seems at first blush unaccountable that
distinct linguistic research communities have grown up around the two
formalisms. I think the explanation is that notational variants naturally
suggest different kinds of mathematical variants and generalizations. An
analogy with abstract algebra may help make this point. It is well known
that there is a category isomorphism between the theory of boolean
algebras and the theory of boolean rings. For every theorem of boolean
algebra, there is a corresponding theorem about boolean rings, and
conversely. But the natural extension of boolean algebra is general
lattice theory, while the extension of boolean rings leads to the general
algebra of rings. Neither of these more general theories is in any sense a
notational variant of the other.

In the case at hand, what has happened is something like this: for
one reason or another, both categorial grammar and context-free
phrase structure grammar have proven inadequate to capture certain
kinds of linguistic generalizations. As a result, in the past few years both
formalisms have been extended somewhat, but in different directions.
For example, within categorial grammar, it has been natural to extend
the set of possible syntactic operations beyond the simple concatenation permitted by Ajdukiewicz, to include such operations as wrapping,
scrambling, or case marking (e.g. Bach, 1980; Dowty, 1982). Correspondingly, on the semantic side, there has been a tendency to extend
the permissible semantic operations beyond simple functional application, exemplified by recent proposals of Steedman (this volume) and
others to add functional composition and functional substitution to the
inventory in order to account for certain problems arising in connection
with unbounded dependencies.

Within phrase-structure-oriented research, on the other hand, other extensions have suggested themselves, primarily ones which involve the schematization of rules and the concomitant change in the role played by rules in the building of linguistic structure. This goes hand-in-hand with an increased concern about the internal structure of categories in terms of feature specifications and with the replacement of category-matching by category unification, as in related current frameworks such as the PATR-II of Shieber *et al.* (1984) and Kay's (1979; 1983) 'Functional Unification Grammar'.[1] Under such extensions, the rewriting interpretation of rules is abandoned in favor of an interpretation that treats rules as local well-formedness conditions on trees, which operate in conjunction with a small set of universal constraints that govern the propagation through trees of feature-borne information.

Of course, neither community has had a monopoly on any of these innovations: numerous parallel developments have taken place. For example, Bach's (1983) study of the English auxiliary system was concerned in part with feature-passing conventions in categorial grammar. On the other side of the coin, some of my work (Pollard, 1984) has concerned mild extensions of context-free grammars, such as *head grammars*, where the usual concatenation operation is supplemented with *head-wrapping* operations which insert one constituent inside another at a position adjacent to the latter's lexical head; in this connection I was also led to expand the inventory of semantic operations beyond the functional application inherited by GPSG from Montague. Coincidentally — or perhaps not so coincidentally — the semantic operations I added were functional composition and a third operation called EQUI, which is a slight variant of functional substitution. (Unlike Steedman, however, my motive was to deal with raising and equi control constructions, not unbounded dependencies.)

In addition to parallel developments, there have also been some cases of convergence. For example, at the same time that rules in GPSG have become increasingly schematic, there has been a reverse trend in categorial grammar — again I am drawing from Steedman's work — a trend toward individuating particular instances of combination rules by keying their applicability to the presence of particular categories or even particular features.

In the remainder of this paper, I will try to illustrate some of these developments by taking a closer look at how two different theories

handle the basic facts about subcategorization and so-called extraction
(or long distance dependency) phenomena in English. As the representative of categorial grammar, I have chosen the extension of bidirectional categorial grammar by Steedman and his colleagues alluded to
above.[2] The phrase structure tradition will be represented by Head-
driven Phrase Structure Grammar (HPSG), a framework now under
development at CSLI and elsewhere, which borrows shamelessly from
GPSG, Lexical-Functional Grammar (LFG, Bresnan, 1982), current
unification-based formalisms, and — as I hope will become clear —
categorial grammar. To keep the notation simple, I will usually write
unitary symbols for categories; officially, of course, these symbols stand
for bundles of feature specifications in both theories.

2. SUBCATEGORIZATION AND RULES

2.1. *The Categories of Steedman's System*

The basic categories in the extension of bidirectional categorial grammar proposed by Steedman and his colleagues is as shown in (5):

(5)   *Basic Categories in Steedman's System*

Category	Informal Description
NP	noun phrases
N	nouns
PP	prepositional phrases
AP	adjective phrases
S	finite, nonrelativized, nontopicalized sentences
St = S[+TOP]	topicalized sentences
Sr = S[+REL]	relative clauses
Sing	present participial clauses
Sen	past participial clauses
Sbse	base-form clauses
S′	that-clauses

Of course the various clausal categories are supposed to be distinguished by features of some kind, as for topicalization and relativization. Some typical non-basic categories appear in (6):

(6)   *Some Non-Basic Categories in Steedman's System*

Category	Example	Comments
NP/N	the	determiners seek an N on the right
PP/NP	of	prepositions seek an NP on the right
S\NP (abbr. VP)	ran	verb phrases seek an NP on the left
(S\NP)/NP	ate	transitive verbs first seek the object on the right, then subject on the left
(S\NP)/(Sbse\NP)	must	modal auxiliaries first seek a base-form verb phrase on right, then an NP on left
((S\NP)/NP)/NP	gave	ditransitive verbs first seek 1st object on right, then 2nd object on right, then subject on left
(S\NP)\(S\NP)	quickly	verb phrase modifiers seek the verb phrase on the left

The important thing to note is that the subcategorization requirements for all complements, including subjects, on a word or phrase are directly encoded in its category. This is the property of categorial grammars that Roland Hausser has called 'combinatorial transparency'. To be more specific, in English the complements to the right of a verb are looked for in right-to-left order, and the subject last.

2.2. *The Categories of HPSG*

For comparison, I will next sketch the basic notions of HPSG category structure. Among other things, categories in HPSG contain two distinct kinds of syntactic information, which might be called *inherent* information and *dependency* information; both kinds of information are encoded as the values of features. Inherent features are basically the traditional features, such as part of speech, case, agreement, inflectional form, and so forth. For simplicity, I will write the whole bundle of inherent features as a unitary symbol. Dependency features, on the other hand, encode the various kinds of dependencies inside a phrase which have not yet been discharged. To get started, I will first focus on the feature responsible for local (= lexically governed) dependencies, the *subcategorization* feature (or SUBCAT for short); in Section 3, I turn to the features (called *binding* features) which deal with long-distance dependencies. The value of the SUBCAT feature is just the sequence of categories that the phrase subcategorizes for; to put it another way, the SUBCAT value lists the categories of those grammatical functions governed by the phrase's lexical head which remain to be found. A sampling of HPSG categories is given in (7):

(7)   *HPSG Categories*

Category	Abbrev.	Example	Comments
V[SUBCAT < >]	S	Kim left	Sentences have discharged all subcategorization requirements
N[SUBCAT < >]	NP	Kim	NP's have discharged all subcategorization requirements
V[SUBCAT < NP >]	VP	left	VP's still seek an NP
N[SUBCAT < DET >]	N	cat	N's still seek a DET
DET		the	Not a 'functor' category: we want NP to get agreement & case from the N
V[SUBCAT < NP, NP >]	TVP	ate	Transitive verbs seek 2 NP's
V[SUBCAT < VPbse, NP >]		must	Modals seek a base-form VP and an NP
V[SUBCAT < NP, NP, NP >]			ditransitive verbs seek 3 NP's
A[SUBCAT < NP >]	AP	ready	AP's considered intransitive
P[SUBCAT < NP, NP >]	P	of	Prepositions considered transitive
P[SUBCAT < NP >]	PP	of Bill	

The important point to notice here is that the SUBCAT feature is close to being a notational variant of the slash notation in Steedman's system. There is one significant difference, however. In Steedman's system, the surface order of complements can be read directly off the categories, using the directionality of the slashes. In HPSG, though, the order of categories in the SUBCAT sequence are not directly correlated with surface order. Instead, the order corresponds to an assumed universal hierarchy of grammatical functions (Sag, 1985). The HPSG terminology for grammatical functions is a variant of that proposed by Dowty (1982): the last (= leftmost on the SUBCAT list) complement is the subject, second-last is the direct object, and third-last is the indirect object. The order in which the various complements show up in surface order, though, is mediated by the phrase structure rules, and is not directly represented in the categories themselves. For example, an auxiliary verb has the same SUBCAT value whether it appears in a declarative sentence or an inverted question. This brings us to our next item of comparison, the rules.

2.3. Rules in Steedman's System

In Steedman's categorial grammar, the basic combination rules are just Bar-Hillel's direct cancellation rules, here called *functional application* rules. These are given in (8):

(8)   *Steedman's Functional Application Rules*

Forward Application (>): X/Y: F Y: y ⇒ X: Fy
Backward Application (<): Y: y $X\backslash Y$: F ⇒ X: Fy

The semantic annotations after the colons encode the information that the semantics of the output category is obtained by functional application of the functor category's semantics to the argument category's semantics. By way of illustration, let us consider the structure (9):

(9a)   Kim must leave.

(9b)

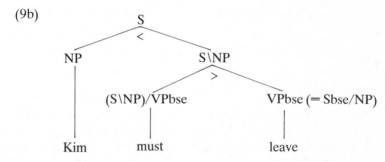

The little notation under each nonterminal node tells which rule was used to construct it. To get the inverted order, an additional lexical entry would evidently be required for *must*, which permutes the order of the arguments (both syntactically and semantically) and also reverses the order of the subject slash. As Bach (1983) has suggested, this might be treated as a lexical rule. This lexical entry would give rise to structures like (10):

(10a)   Must Kim leave?

(10b)

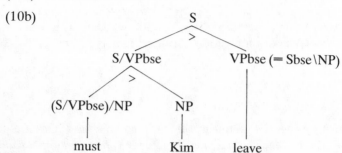

One more example, involving the ditransitive verb *give*, is given in (11):

(11a)   Kim gave Sandy a book.

(11b)

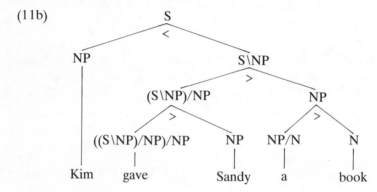

2.4. *Rules in HPSG*

HPSG rules fall into a small number of main types, e.g. head-complement rules, linking rules, coordination rules, etc.; only the first two will
concern us here. In this section I confine my attention to head-complement rules, which combine heads with their subcategorized complements. I will give some examples presently, but first it is necessary to
mention a technical innovation introduced into GPSG by Gazdar and
Pullum (1981). This is the factoring of phrase structure rules into two
distinct components: an *immediate dominance* (or ID) component and
a *linear precedence* (or LP) component. The ID component consists
of rules, called ID rules, that look exactly like conventional phrase
structure rules, except that they make no reference to linear order.

The LP component consists of conditions, called LP statements, that constrain the relative order of sisters within a constituent. To illustrate these notions, Gazdar and Pullum provide the toy grammar (12a):

$$
(12\text{a}) \qquad A \rightarrow \begin{Bmatrix} B & C & D \\ C & B & D \\ C & D & B \end{Bmatrix} \qquad C \rightarrow \begin{Bmatrix} A & B & D \\ A & D & B \\ D & A & B \end{Bmatrix}
$$

$$
B \rightarrow \begin{Bmatrix} A & C & D \\ C & A & D \\ C & D & A \end{Bmatrix} \qquad D \rightarrow \begin{Bmatrix} A & B & C \\ A & C & B \\ C & A & B \end{Bmatrix}
$$

Using the ID/LP format, we can express the same grammar as in (12b):

(12b)   *ID Rules*:   *LP Statements*:

$A \rightarrow B, C, D$ $A < B$

$B \rightarrow A, C, D$ $C < D$

$C \rightarrow A, B, D$

$D \rightarrow C, A, B$

The interpretation of an ID rule, say the first one on the left in (12b), is that A can immediately and exhaustively dominate a B, a C, and a D (with no information given about the order in which they might occur). An LP rule, such as the first one on the right in (12b), says that whenever A and B are sisters, then A must precede B. Although (12b) is equivalent to (12a) in an obvious sense, the ID/LP grammar is more succinct, and also more informative in the sense that it makes explicit some ordering constraints that are only implicit in the conventional grammar.

I am now in a position to exhibit a set of HPSG rules that handle a substantial fragment of English grammar:

(13a) X[SUBCAT EMPTY] $\rightarrow$ COMP, HEAD[SUBCAT $< Y >$]

(13b) X[SUBCAT $< Yn >$] $\rightarrow$
      HEAD[−INV, SUBCAT $< \ldots Y(n-1), Yn >$], COMP*

(13c) X[SUBCAT EMPTY] $\rightarrow$
      HEAD[+INV, SUBCAT $< \ldots, Y >$], COMP*

Rule (13a) is essentially S $\rightarrow$ NP VP: it says that if something is only looking for a subject, then the subject can be a sister. Rule (13b) covers subcategorization for non-subjects: it sanctions the construction of a constituent from a lexical head and all its non-subject complements, as long as the head bears the feature −INV.[3] Rule (13c) sanctions the construction of a constituent from a lexical head that bears the feature +INV (roughly, finite auxiliaries) and *all* its complements, including the subject. Of course this is just the rule for inverted sentences. Notice I haven't said anything here about how the daughters in a constituent get ordered; that task is left to the LP statements, described in detail in Sag (1985).

For a grammar like this to work, a few universal principles are required that tell a rule how to build the mother from the daughters.[4] A simplified version of these principles is given in (14):

(14) *Rule Application Principles*

(1)   Remove symbols from the front of the SUBCAT list one by one, doing one of the following:

   (a) *Subcategorization Principle.* Match the symbol with a complement; or

   (b) *Gap Introduction Principle.* Place the symbol on the head daughter's SLASH list.

(2)   *Binding Inheritance Principle.* For each binding feature *B*, the value of *B* on the mother is obtained by starting with the value on the head daughter and appending (host dependency) or merging (parasitic dependency) into it the values on the other daughters, in the order more-oblique to less-oblique.

(3)   *Head Feature Principle.* For other features, the value on the mother is got from the head daughter.

For the moment the only one of these principles that we will be concerned with is (1a), the Subcategorization Principle, which removes the complement symbols from the SUBCAT sequence on the head as complements are found to match them. Of course this is analogous to cancellation in categorial grammar. Here are the HPSG structures for the forgoing three examples:

(15a) Kim must leave.

(15b)

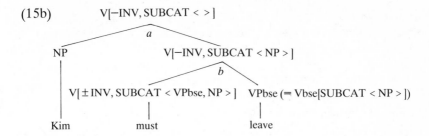

(15) is essentially the same as the structure given by Steedman's grammar.

(16a)   Must Kim leave?

(16b)

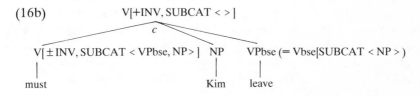

Inverted sentences in HPSG are generated with flat structures, as in (16). Notice that the auxiliary *must* has the same lexical entry as in the declarative sentence (15).

(17a)   Kim gave Sandy a book.

(17b)

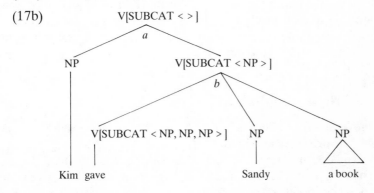

In (17), *a book* counts as the indirect object because it matches the third-last NP that comes off the SUBCAT sequence; *Sandy* counts as the direct object because it matches the second-last.

3. LONG-DISTANCE DEPENDENCIES

3.1. *Topicalization in Steedman's System*

There are two chief mechanisms in Steedman's system for dealing with long-distance dependencies. The first of these is a new family of combination rules, called *functional composition* rules. Like the functional application rules, these come in both forward and backward varieties. But the backward ones are not supposed to play much of a role in English, so I will limit attention to the forward ones. The simplest of the forward composition rules are for the case $n = 1$ (the significance of the parameter n will emerge presently); there are two of these according as the secondary functor category is forward-looking or backward-looking. These are given in (18); the symbol 'B' is the standard symbol for functional composition in combinatory logic.

(18)   *Steedman's Forward Composition Rules* ($> B$)
        (*for the case $n = 1$*)

$$X/Y\!:\!F \ \ Y/Z\!:\!G \ \Rightarrow \ X/Z\!:\lambda x[F(Gx)]$$
$$X/Y\!:\!F \ \ Y\backslash Z\!:\!G \ \Rightarrow \ X\backslash Z\!:\lambda x[F(Gx)]$$

The second mechanism for dealing with extraction is the device of *type-raising rules*, due originally to Lambek. Steedman proposes two such rules, or, to be more precise, one rule and one pair of rule schemata. These are given in (19) and (20):

(19)   *Subject Type-Raising Rule* (↑)

NP: $x \Rightarrow$ S/(S\NP): $\lambda F[Fx]$

The most obvious effect of (19) is to let subjects take VP's as arguments. For sentences without extractions, this is just an option, but as we shall see, in the case of sentences with extractions, it will be the only course open. This rule marks an important departure from the usual practice in categorial grammar, since it is keyed to a particular input category, namely NP.

(20)   *Topic Type-Raising Rules* (↑) *(for the case n = 1)*

For subject extractions: NP: x ⇒ St/(S\NP): $\lambda F[F\,x]$;
For non-subject extractions: X: x ⇒ St/(S/X): $\lambda F[F\,x]$,
where X belongs to {NP, PP, VP, AP, S′}.

Rule (20) marks an even greater departure, for in addition to applying only to certain input categories, it also stamps the feature specification 'plus-topicalized' on the output category. It seems clear that Steedman's type-raising rules are more in the spirit of phrase structure grammar than that of categorial grammar.

Now let us apply this machinery to generate the simplest possible topicalized sentence. The structure is given in (21). Two type-raisings are needed here. The first one is needed because *likes* is unable to look to its left; therefore the subject has to be raised to look for it, by forward composition. The second raising is needed because *Kim likes* is unable to look to *its* left; therefore the nonsubject topic has to be raised to look for *it*, this time by forward application.

(21a)   Bagels, Kim likes.

(21b)

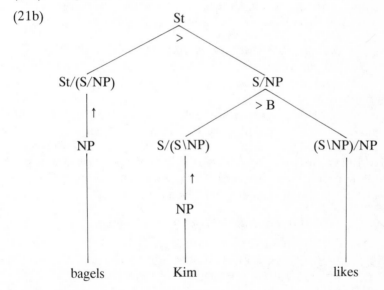

(22a)   Fido, we put downstairs.

(22b)

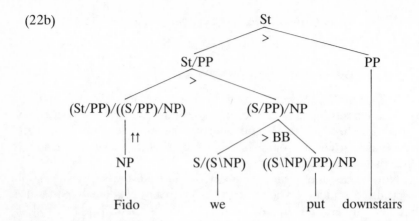

Let us also consider the case where the extraction site is non-final, for this turns out to make a difference. An example is given in (22) above. This example starts out like the last one: we type-raise the subject so it can look for the verb by forward composition. However, as they are stated in (18), the forward composition rules are insufficient, since they work only when the secondary functor is missing *one* argument. We need forward composition for the case $n = 2$, as stated in (23):

(23)   *Steedman's Forward Composition Rules* (> BB)
        (*for the case* $n = 2$)

        $X/Y: F\,(Y/Z1)/Z2: G \Rightarrow (X/Z1)/Z2: \lambda x1 \lambda x2[F(Gx1\ x2)]$

The double forward composition rule given in (23) also has three stablemates for the other possible directionality combinations for the Z's; more generally, for each n, there are 2^n forward composition rules of that order. Next, we have to type-raise the topic. But now it is the topic type-raising rule given in (20) that needs to be extended to the case $n = 2$. The required extension is given in (24):

(24)   *Topic-Raising Rules* (↑↑) (*for the case* $n = 2$)

        For Non-Subject Extractions: $X2: x2 \Rightarrow$
        $St/((S/X1)/X2: \lambda F \lambda x1[F x1\ x2]$,
        where $X1$ and $X2$ belong to $\{NP, PP, VP, AP, S'\}$
        etc.

(This rule has even more stablemates; the calculation of the precise figure is left as an exercise for the reader). Finally, the PP gets taken in, by forward application.

3.2. *Topicalization in HPSG*

Now let us see how the foregoing examples are handled in HPSG. The basic idea is to introduce a second dependency feature in addition to the SUBCAT feature. This feature is called the SLASH feature, and its value will be the sequence of categories that didn't turn up where they were supposed to. This is what I take to be the fundamental difference between Steedman's system and HPSG: HPSG uses two different stacks for local and long-distance dependencies, while Steedman gets by with just one. To see how the two-stack system works, let us first look at the non-topicalized version of (21):

(25a)   Kim likes bagels.

(25b)

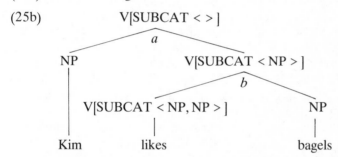

To handle the topicalized version, we first require a rule of a new kind. So far, the only rules we have introduced have been head-complement rules. But topicalization is not a head-complement construction. What we require instead is what is known as a *linking* rule. The linking rule for topicalization is given in (26):

(26)   *HPSG Topicalization Rule (Top)*

$X[+TOP] \rightarrow Y, X[V, SUBCAT < >]$
Linking: SLASH-bind Y to X.

The purpose of the linking instruction on the right will become clear presently. Now the HPSG structure for the topicalized sentence (25) is given in (27):

(27a)   Bagels, Kim likes.

(27b)

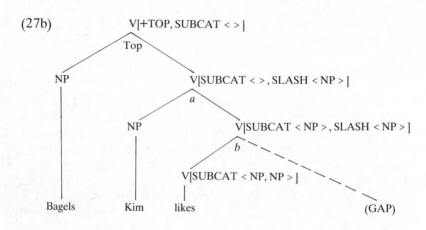

We begin by applying rule (13b) to combine *likes* with its object. Unfortunately, there is no NP for it to combine with. Undaunted, we record this information by moving the NP symbol corresponding to the gap off the SUBCAT list and onto the SLASH list. In other words, instead of using the Subcategorization Principle, we use the Gap Introduction Principle given as item (1b) under (14). This produces the category V[SUBCAT < NP >, SLASH < NP >]. (Gap introduction has a semantic effect too, of course. Essentially, the gap is translated by a variable, and the SLASH category gets indexed by that variable. This is just a variant of Cooper storage.) Next we proceed as if nothing had happened, picking up the subject *Kim* by rule (13a); on this rule application, the SLASH category is passed up to the mother in accordance with the Binding Inheritance Principle, stated as item (2) under (14). This is just the percolation mechanism for binding features. Finally, we pick up *bagels* using the new topicalization rule. Notice the linking instruction attached to this rule: 'SLASH-bind Y to X'. This means: take a category off the top of the SLASH stack of X. If it is consistent with Y, the rule may apply. It follows that this rule never applies when X's SLASH stack is empty. (There is some semantics here too, of course: bind the SLASH variable to the translation of Y.)

Precisely the same strategy works whatever the number or location of gaps. In (28) the HPSG structure for example (22) is given:

(28a)   Fido, we put downstairs.

(28b)

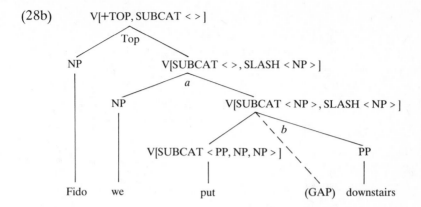

Superficially, the topicalization rule (26) is reminiscent of Steedman's topic type-raising schemata (21), (25), etc. But there are some important differences. For one thing, there is no schematization going on with the topicalization rule, just simple checking of conditions. Secondly, there is no need to limit the range of categories to which the rule can apply, because the only categories that could ever turn up on the SLASH stack are ones that could have been subcategorized for.

With regard to Steedman's treatment, Dowty (this volume) observes that functional composition "is supposed to render the 'slash category' mechanism of GPSG unnecessary for describing long-distance (extraction) dependencies." But we might just as well say that the slash mechanism renders functional composition and type raising of arbitrary complexity unnecessary. I think the questions of whether there are clearcut computational, empirical, or aesthetic wins for either account are still open.

3.3. Relative Clauses in Steedman's System

Let us begin with the simplest cases, where the filler is just the relative word itself, such as *which*. Steedman's account for these cases is parallel to his treatment of topicalization. The difference is that, instead of undergoing type-raising as topics do, relative pronouns are type-raised to start with. Thus the relative pronoun *which* is assigned the categories given in (29):

(29)   *Steedman's Categories for Relative Which*:

$(n = 1)$ Subject: S[+REL]/(S\NP)
             Non-Subject: S[+REL]/(S/NP)
$(n = 2)$ Subject: (S[+REL]/X)/((S/X)\NP)
                             (S[+REL]\$X$)/((S\$X$(\NP)
             Non-Subject: (S[+REL]/X)/((S/X)/NP)
                             (S[+REL]\$X$)/((S\$X$)/NP)

etc.

This gives rise to structures such as (30) below, analogous to the topicalized example (22):

(30a)   [Fido is the dog] which we put downstairs.

(30b)

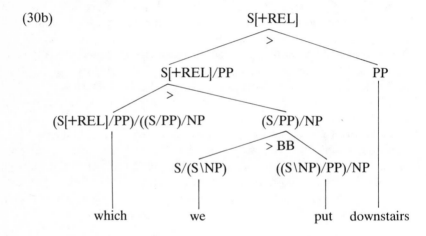

3.4. *Relative Clauses in HPSG*

In HPSG, relatives are treated as binding dependencies. Correspondingly, we introduce a new binding feature REL. The value of REL for any phrase is the list of categories of any unbound relative pronouns that it contains. In particular, the lexical category assignment for relative *which* is simply NP[REL < NP >]; this should be compared with (29). The HPSG analysis corresponding to (30) is given in (31):

(31)

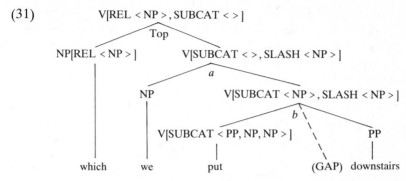

This is precisely like the HPSG analysis (28) for the topicalized example: it even uses the topicalization rule at the top. The only difference is that the REL feature at the top was passed up to it from the relative pronoun by the Binding Inheritance Principle. This point will turn out to be important.

For our final example, let us consider a simple example of pied piping, where the gap filler properly contains the relative. Such an example is given, together with its HPSG analysis, in (32):

(32a)   [I file any reports] the dimensions of which the government prescribes.

(32b)

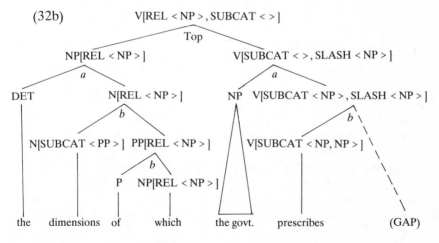

The important point to note here is that the feature specification which encodes the relative dependency, originating from the relative pronoun *which* way down inside the filler, is successively passed by the Binding Inheritance Principle all the way up to the S node at the top. This dependency will eventually get bound when the relative clause combines with a noun or noun phrase higher up (by a linking rule).

Now one of the claims that Steedman makes for his treatment of unbounded dependencies is that he "accounts for the relevant constructions without the invocation of any graph-theoretical notions like 'percolation'". But in the case of sentences like (32) — and this is a relatively tame example — it is unclear how any analysis can be provided within Steedman's system. The problem is that any possible relative gap filler, not just a relative pronoun, has to be made eligible for the type-raising described in (29). But the only thing that identifies a constituent as a potential relative gap filler is the information that it contains an unbound relative pronoun. And in Steedman's system, which lacks any mechanism for transmitting such information, there is no way to make it available. Evidently, there is no principled analysis of pied piping in an extended categorial framework like Steedman's without the addition of a feature-passing mechanism for unbounded dependencies.

4. CONCLUSION

In the past several years, two linguistic research traditions have developed as outgrowths of two interchangeable but notationally distinct mathematical formalisms. The courses followed by the two traditions have at various times converged, diverged, or run parallel; sometimes they have even passed like ships at night. On balance, it seems fair to say that each has come to look more like the other than like the pristine formalism that it grew out of. This being the case, it no longer seems appropriate to characterize such research as distinctly categorial or distinctly phrase-structural. What we are left with is something of a hybrid, then. But just which combination of traits turns out to be optimal remains to be seen.

ACKNOWLEDGEMENTS

This research was supported by NSF grant no. BNS-8511687, and a grant to the Center for the Study of Language and Information from the Systems Development Foundation.

NOTES

[1] For an excellent introduction to the emerging family of unification-based grammar formalisms, see Shieber (1985) and works cited therein.

[2] The system under discussion has been presented in a succession of versions which differ somewhat with respect to certain points of theoretical and notational detail, e.g., Ades and Steedman (1982); Steedman (1983), (1985a), (this volume); Szabolcsi (1983). The description herein is based upon a draft of Steedman (1985b) circulated prior to the conference, subtitled 'Draft 4, March 1, 1985' and described as "aris[ing] in current work with Anna Szabolcsi . . . with whom it is to be jointly authored". As a matter of convenience, I refer to this system as 'Steedman's system', but the cooperative nature of the enterprise should be borne in mind.

[3] Specifications for the feature INV are as follows: finite auxiliaries which must invert (e.g. 1st-sng. *aren't* are +INV; finite auxiliaries which optionally invert are unspecified for INV; all other lexical entries bear the lexical default value −INV.

[4] In spite of the procedural metaphor invoked here for describing principles of rule application, they should not be regarded as essentially procedural rather than declarative in nature. For some discussion of the distinction and its significance, see Shieber (1985); for an explicit formulation in terms of declarative constraints, see Pollard and Sag (in press).

REFERENCES

Ades, Anthony E. and Mark J. Steedman: 1982, 'On the Order of Words', *Linguistics and Philosophy* **4**, 517—558.

Ajdukiewicz, Kazimierz: 1935, 'Die syntaktische Konnexität', *Studia Philosophica* **1**, 1—27. English translation in: Storrs McCall (ed.), *Polish Logic 1920—1939*, Oxford University Press, pp. 207—231.

Bach, Emmon: 1980, 'In Defense of Passive', *Linguistics and Philosophy* **3**, 297—341.

Bach, Emmon: 1983, 'Generalized Categorial Grammars and the English Auxiliary', in Frank Heny and Barry Richards (eds.), *Linguistic Categories*, Vol. 2, Reidel, Dordrecht, pp. 101—120.

Bar-Hillel, Yehoshua: 1953, 'A Quasi-Arithmetic Notation for Syntactic Description', *Language* **29**, 47—58.

Bar-Hillel, Yehoshua (ed.): 1964, *Language and Information*, Addison-Wesley, Reading, Mass.

Bresnan, Joan W.: 1982, *The Mental Representation of Grammatical Relations*, MIT Press, Cambridge, Mass.

Chomsky, Noam A.: 1957, *Syntactic Structures*, Mouton, The Hague.

Dowty, David: 1982, 'Grammatical Relations and Montague Grammar', in P. Jacobson and G. K. Pullum (eds.), pp. 79—130.

Dowty, David: this volume, 'Type Raising, Functional Composition, and Non-Constituent Conjunction'.

Gazdar, Gerald: 1979a, 'Constituent Structures', unpublished manuscript.

Gazdar, Gerald: 1979b, 'English as a Context-Free Language', unpublished manuscript.

Gazdar, Gerald: 1981, 'Unbounded Dependencies and Coordinate Structure', *Linguistic Inquiry 12*, 155—184.

Gazdar, Gerald: 1982, 'Phrase Structure Grammar', in P. Jacobson and G. Pullum (eds.), pp. 131—186.

Gazdar, Gerald, Ewan Klein, Geoffrey K. Pullum, and Ivan A. Sag: 1985, *Generalized Phrase Structure Grammar*, Blackwell's, Oxford, and Harvard University Press, Cambridge, Mass.

Gazdar, Gerald and Geoffrey K. Pullum: 1981, 'Subcategorization, Constituent Order, and the Notion "Head"', in M. Moortgat, H. van der Hulst, and T. Hoekstra (eds.), *The Scope of Lexical Rules*, Foris, Dordrecht.

Jacobson, Pauline and Geoffrey K. Pullum (eds.): 1982, *The Nature of Syntactic Representation*, Reidel, Dordrecht.

Kay, Martin: 1979, 'Functional Grammar', in C. Chiarello *et al.* (eds.), *Proceedings of the Fifth Annual Meeting of the Berkeley Linguistic Society*, Berkeley Linguistic Society, Berkeley, pp. 142—158.

Kay, Martin: 1983, *Unification Grammar*, Technical Report, Xerox Palo Alto Research Center, Palo Alto, Calif.

Pollard, Carl: 1984, 'Head Grammars, Generalized Phrase Structure Grammars, and Natural Language', Ph.D. dissertation, Stanford University, Stanford, Calif.

Pollard, Carl: 1985, 'Phrase Structure Grammar without Metarules', in *Proceedings of the Fourth Annual West Coast Conference on Formal Linguistics*, Stanford University Linguistics Department, Stanford, Calif.

Pollard, Carl and Ivan A. Sag: in press, *Information-Based Syntax and Semantics, Vol. 1: Fundamental Notions*, CSLI Lecture Notes Series, distributed by University of Chicago Press.

Pullum, Geoffrey K. and Gerald Gazdar: 1982, 'Natural Languages and Context-Free Languages', *Linguistics and Philosophy* **4**, 471—504.

Sag, Ivan A.: 1987, 'Grammatical Hierarchy and Linear Precedence', Geoffrey Huck and Almerindo Ojeda (eds.), *Syntax and Semantics, Vol. 20: Discontinuous Constituency*. Also appeared as CSLI Report No. CSLI-86-60.

Shieber, Stuart: 1986, *An Introduction to Unification-based Grammar Formalisms*, CSLI Lecture Notes Series, distributed by University of Chicago Press.

Shieber, Stuart *et al.*: 1984, 'The Formalism and Implementation of PATR-II', in *Research on Interactive Acquisition and Use of Knowledge*, SRI International, Meno Park, Calif.

Steedman, Mark: 1983, 'On the Generality of the Nested Dependency Constraint and the Reason for an Exception in Dutch', Brian Butterworth *et al.* (eds.), *Explanations of Language Universals* (Linguistics, n.s., **21**, p. 1), pp. 35—66. Mouton, The Hague.

Steedman, Mark: 1985a, 'Dependency and Coordination in the Grammar of Dutch and English', *Language* **61**, 523—568.

Steedman, Mark: 1985b, 'Combinators, Categorial Grammars, and Parasitic Gaps', unpublished manuscript, School of Epistemics and Department of Artificial Intelligence, University of Edinburgh, Edinburgh.

Steedman, Mark: this voume, 'Combinators and Categorial Grammars'.
Szabolcsi, Anna: 1983, 'ECP in Categorial Grammar', unpublished manuscript, Max
    Planck Institute, Nijmegen.

Center for the Study of Language
    and Information,
Stanford University, CA 94305, U.S.A.

MARK STEEDMAN

COMBINATORS AND GRAMMARS*

INTRODUCTION

The attraction of Categorial Grammar (CG) as a notation for natural
language grammar has always been the direct relation that it embodies
between the syntax of a language and an applicative semantics. Common sense suggests that just such a relation should hold for natural
languages, just as it does in the systems of logic which gave rise to CG
in the first place. However, the existence of discontinuous constituents,
extractions, and all the other phenomena whose importance was first
and most clearly exposed by Chomsky (1957) makes it clear that
something more is required than the basic ingredients of function
and argument categories, plus functional application, prescribed by
Ajdukiewicz (1935). Those who have attempted to cope with these
phenomena within CG have proposed to 'generalise' (Bach, 1983) or
'extend' (Levin, 1982) the basic context-free apparatus by the addition
of various operations on the functions and arguments, over and above
simple functional application. These additions have included functional
composition and type raising (Lambek, 1958, 1961; Geach, 1972),
'wrapping' (Bach, 1979, 1980), and some others.

The question I try to address here is, what does this *mean*? What
class of operations are we drawing upon, and why does natural
language grammar include them? I will show that the operations that we
have to add bear a striking resemblance to the 'combinators' which
Curry and Feys (1958) use to define the foundations of the lambda
calculus and all applicative systems — that is, systems expressing the
operations of functional application and abstraction. (It therefore seems
appropriate to refer to the class of grammars under discussion here as
'combinatory' grammars.) Crucially, combinators allow the process of
abstraction to be defined without invoking bound variables. The
striking parallel between the particular set of combinators that is
implicit in the grammar of English (and, by implication, other languages), and the systems of combinators that are used in certain highly
efficient compilers for applicative programming languages (Burge,

417

Richard T. Oehrle et al. (eds.), Categorial Grammars and Natural Language Structures, 417—
© 1988 *by D. Reidel Publishing Company.*

1975) suggests that the reason natural language grammars take this form (rather than resembling some other applicative system, such as the lambda calculus itself) may be to do with the computational advantages of avoiding the use of bound variables.

The argument goes as follows. In Part I, I briefly review the varieties of syntactic combinatory rules that are implicit in various constructions in English involving single and multiple dependencies, including extractions, 'across the board' phenomena (Williams, 1978), 'parasitic gaps' (Taraldsen, 1979; Engdahl, 1983), and certain 'raising' phenomena, according to the version of categorial grammar advanced in Ades and Steedman (1982, 'A&S') and Steedman (1985, 'D&C', and 1987a, 'CGPG'). In the second part, I examine the relation to the combinatory systems of Curry and their use in applicative programming languages.

PART I:
COMBINATORY GRAMMARS AND NATURAL LANGUAGE

Any formal grammar for some particular natural language implies a theory of universal grammar. Subject only to principled exceptions that can be explained in terms of other considerations such as the pressures of acquisition or processing, each degree of freedom in the theory that is exploited in order to capture the constructions of a given language constitutes a prediction that some other language may adopt the other alternatives that the theory could allow. The present concern is with the nature of this universal grammatical apparatus, rather than with specific grammars for particular natural languages. Accordingly, I will use a very general form of combinatory categorial grammar here. (As a consequence, while each general class of combinatory rule will be illustrated with examples from English, the rules themselves will over-generalise wildly. For more appropriately restricted grammar fragments for English and Dutch, the reader is referred to the earlier papers.)

1.1. THE CATEGORIAL LEXICON AND THE
RULE OF FUNCTIONAL APPLICATION

For the present purpose, it is convenient to use a *non-directional* categorial lexicon, and *non-directional* combinatory rules. All function categories from a category Y into a category X will be written X/Y, regardless of whether in English they find their arguments to the right or to the left. So for example rightward combining transitive verbs bear the category VP/NP, and leftward-combining VP-adverbials bear the category VP/VP. We shall assume that these categories are semantically transparent.

All combinatory rules will be similarly non-directional. For example, the most basic rule of functional application for a function of the form X/Y with an argument of the appropriate type Y can be written as follows:

(1)   *Functional Application*

A function of category X/Y and interpretation F can combine with an adjacent argument of category Y and interpretation y to yield a result of category X and interpretation Fy, the result of applying F to y.

This basic rule mainly serves to introduce some notation for combinatory rules. X and Y are variables which range over any category, including functions of any order. Since the categories are semantically transparent, the rule can combine syntactic and semantic combination. The application of a semantic function F to an argument y is represented by simple concatenation Fy, and it will later be convenient to employ a convention whereby this operation 'associates to the left', so that 'Fxy' means '$(Fx)y$', '$Fxyz$' means '$((Fx)y)z$', and so on.

In order to write real grammars for strongly configurational languages like English, we clearly need to restrict this basic apparatus. One obvious way to do so is to introduce directional categories, perhaps distinguishing transitive verbs and adverbials in this respect by writing their categories VP/NP and VP\VP, respectively (cf. CGPG). We can also distinguish forward and backward directional 'instances' of the combinatory rules (cf. A&S, D&C, and CGPG). But we will continue to ignore such language-specific details as constituent order here.

Using the rule of functional application and the obvious semantically transparent lexical categories (including the category S/NP for the predicate), we can write derivations for many English sentences, such as the following.

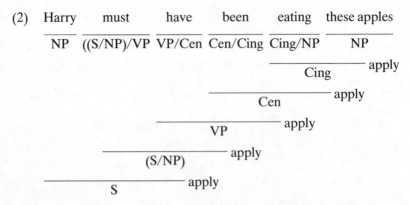

(2) Harry   must   have   been   eating   these apples

(Combination of two entities is indicated by an underline indexed with a mnemonic identifying the rule, with the resulting category written underneath. The nonce symbols Cen, and Cing stand for *-en*-complement and *-ing*-complement, respectively. These very general nondirectional categories and the very general rule of functional application will of course allow a great many other word orders. However, these other word orders are of types that are found in other languages related to English, and it is easy enough to produce more restricted grammars for English (or Dutch, or German), so that is all right.)

The central problem for categorial grammar, as for any theory of grammar, is the presence of discontiguous or 'discontinuous' constructions in natural languages — that is constructions in which elements which belong together in semantics are separated, and it is their existence which has provoked the authors listed earlier to introduce further varieties of combinatory rules.

1.2. EXTRACTION AND FUNCTIONAL COMPOSITION

Consider the following sentence related to (1), in which the object has been 'extracted to the left'.[1]

(3)   These apples Harry   must   have   been   eating

NP	NP	(S/NP)/VP	VP/Cen	Cen/Cing	Cing/NP

The rule of functional application will not do anything for us here, of course. However, A&S proposed to account for such constructions by *composing* the function categories, by the following rule:

(4)   *Functional Composition*:

A 'main' function of category X/Y and interpretation F may combine with an adjacent 'subordinate' function of category Y/Z and interpretation G to yield a function of category X/Z and interpretation $\lambda x [F(Gx)]$, the composition of F and G.

(There is a precedent for such rules in natural language grammar in the work of Lambek, 1958, 1961, and Geach, 1972.) The rule allows the main and subordinate function to be in either left-to-right or right-to-left order, but in a right-branching language like English the predominant pattern of composition is the following 'forward version':[2]

(5)   *Forward Composition*

$$X/Y: F \quad Y/Z: G \Rightarrow X/Z: \lambda x [F(Gx)]$$

Repeated application of this rule in examples like (3) is the main ingredient that is required to achieve extraction, because it allows all the verbs to assemble themselves into a single function requiring the subject and the extracted item as arguments, thus:

(6) These apples Harry   must   have   been   eating

NP	NP	(S/NP)/VP	VP/Cen	Cen/Cing	Cing/NP

$\overline{\hspace{3cm}}$ compose
(S/NP)/Cen

$\overline{\hspace{4cm}}$ compose
(S/NP)/Cing

$\overline{\hspace{5cm}}$ compose
(S/NP)/NP

At this point the grammar still blocks, and will not allow the combination of the composed functor *must have been eating* with *Harry* as its subject and *these apples* as its object, because they are in the wrong linear order.[3] However, one additional device will allow the construction (6), and provide us with a quite general mechanism for unbounded extraction. We introduce a rule of type-raising, which for present purposes we shall assume is confined to subject NPs, but which D&C and Dowty (1985) have argued is very widely implicated in the grammar of Dutch and English. Type-raising (which has also been widely exploited in categorial grammar, again notably by Lambek and Geach, as well as Lewis, 1972, and Montague, 1973), is an operation whereby an argument category, such as NP, is turned into a function mapping functions-which-take-the-original-category-as-arguments into the range of those functions. The semantics of such a raised category is simply to apply the interpretation of the function which it takes as argument to the interpretation of the original NP, so we can write the rule as follows:

(7)   *Subject Type-raising*

        A subject NP with interpretation x must acquire the category S/(S/NP) with the interpretation $\lambda F[Fx]$.

As with all questions relating to language specific constituent order, the present paper ignores the question of how such a rule can distinguish the subject from other NPs.

With the inclusion of type-raising, the extraction can be accepted as follows:[4]

(8) These apples   Harry   must   have   been   eating
    ───────────   ─────   ───────── ─────── ─────── ────────
        NP   NP   (S/NP)/VP VP/Cen Cen/Cing Cing/NP
                  ───────── raise
                  S/(S/NP)
                  ─────────────────────── compose
                          S/VP
                  ──────────────────────────── compose
                            S/Cen
                  ───────────────────────────────── compose
                             S/Cing
                  ── compose
                              S/NP
    ── apply
                          S

Because of the semantics of composition (4) and type raising (7), the result has the same semantics as the corresponding canonical sentence assembled without benefit of the new rule. And the grammar immediately allows unbounded extractions across clause boundaries, a generalisation to which the raised subject category is crucial.[5]

```
(9)  Those cakes    I         can      believe that   she      will      eat
     ─────────  ─────  ──────────  ──────  ────  ─────  ──────────  ──────
        NP        NP    (S/NP)/VP   VP/S′  S′/S    NP    (S/NP)/VP  VP/NP
              ──────────── raise                 ──────────── raise
                S/(S/NP)                           S/(S/NP)
              ─────────────────── compose
                     S/VP
                ─────────────────────── compose
                         S/S′
                    ─────────────────────── compose
                             S/S
                       ─────────────────────── compose
                            S/(S/NP)
                          ─────────────────────── compose
                                   S/VP
                             ─────────────────────── compose
                                       S/NP
     ──────────────────────────────────────────────── apply
                             S
```

Function composition performs here a role very much like slash feature-passing in GPSG. Indeed, in more recent incarnations of GPSG (cf. Gazdar *et al.*, 1985; Pollard, 1985), the semantics of this operation amounts to exactly that. The present proposal simply amounts to the stronger claim that the semantic composition is directly reflected in syntax. In D&C, the rule of functional composition is shown to capture and extend the generalisation of Gazdar (1981) concerning the relation of unbounded dependency and coordinate structure. A number of previously problematic constructions including the multiple crossing dependencies in Dutch infinitival clauses (cf. Bresnan *et al.*, 1982) and so-called 'backward gapping' in Dutch coordinate clauses are shown to be explicable in terms of functional composition and type-raising, and this analysis is considerably extended by Dowty (1987). However, multiple dependencies, whether bounded or unbounded, in which several elements depend upon a single 'moved' item, are *not* explicable in terms of functional composition alone, and it is to these that we turn next.

1.3. MULTIPLE DEPENDENCIES AND FUNCTIONAL SUBSTITUTION

1.3.1. *Parasitic Gaps*

The following construction is of a type which Taraldsen (1979) and

Engdahl (1981) have talked of as including a 'parasitic gap':[6]

(10)   (articles) which I will file _____ without reading _____ $_p$

The term gap (which has nothing to do with the kind of gapping which is found in some coordinate sentences) refers here to what a transformationalist would regard as extraction sites or 'empty categories'. The important properties of the sentence are: (a) that it has more than one gap corresponding to a single extracted item, *which articles*, and (b) that one of these gaps (indicated by subscript p) is in a position from which extraction would not normally be permitted. (That is, (b) below is widely regarded as ungrammatical, although (a) is perfectly all right:)

(11) (a)   (articles) which I will file _____ before reading your instructions
     (b)   *(articles) which I will read your instructions before filing _____

Parasitic gaps are therefore unlike the multiple gaps which are permitted 'across the board' in coordinate structures such as:[7]

(12)   (articles) which Mary will read _____ and Harry will file _____

Neither of these gaps is allowed in the absence of the other, as the following examples show:

(13) (a)   *(articles) which Mary will read _____ and Harry will file letters
     (b)   *(articles) which Mary will read letters and Harry will file _____

The function-composing rule (4) does not offer any promise of handling these multiple gaps. The lexical categories for the example (10) with which the section begins are as follows:

(14) (articles) which I will   file   without   reading
                ——   ——   ——   ————   ——
                NP   S/VP   VP/NP   (VP/VP)/Cing Cing/NP

(Non-subcategorized for adverbials are assumed to be VP/VP: see CGPG for details of how the grammar is to be constrained to only allow English word-order.) We can compose *without* and *reading*, thus:

(15) (articles) which I will   file   without   reading

NP   S/VP VP/NP (VP/VP)/Cing Cing/NP

—————————————————————— compose
(VP/VP)/NP

But there the analysis blocks. The introduction of some further operation or operations appears to be inevitable, if sentences with parasitic
gaps are to be accommodated.

The intuition that sequences like *file without reading* constitute a
semantically coherent entity of some kind in these sentences is very
strong. The fact that such sequences can occur in isolation, in instructions like *shake before opening*, and the fact that they can coordinate
with transitive verbs, as in *file without reading or burn*, suggest that they
are predicates of some kind — more specifically, that they must bear
the category VP/NP (as they do in the GPSG analysis of this construction — cf. Gazdar *et al.*, 1985). Szabolcsi (1983) pointed out that if we
had an additional combinatory rule to construct such predicates,
indexed as 'substitute' in the following derivation, then application and
composition would do the rest:

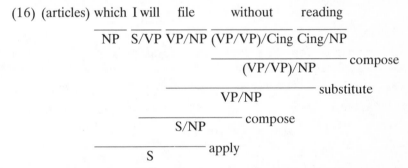

(16) (articles) which I will   file   without   reading

NP   S/VP VP/NP (VP/VP)/Cing Cing/NP

—————————————————————— compose
(VP/VP)/NP

—————————————————————— substitute
VP/NP

—————————————————————— compose
S/NP

—————————————————————— apply
S

The rule in question can be seen as a special case of the following
combinatory rule, which is parallel to the earlier functional application
and composition rules (1) and (4):

(17)   *Functional Substitution:*

A two-argument 'main' function of category $(X/Y)/Z$ and
interpretation F may combine with an adjacent unary subordinate function of category Y/Z and interpretation G, to
yield a function X/Z with interpretation $\lambda x [Fx(Gx)]$

(Function application associates to the left, as usual) This rule allows combinations on the following pattern, as in derivation (16):

(18)   *Backward substitution*

$$Y/Z: G \ (X/Y)/Z: F \Rightarrow X/Z: \lambda x[Fx(Gx)]$$

Extraction of the first gap alone is allowed under the earlier analysis, of course, because the following *backward* version of the composition rule (4) can combine the verb and the adjunct:

(19)   *Backward Composition*

$$Y/Z: G \ X/Y: F \Rightarrow X/Z: \lambda x[F(Gx)]$$

The derivation goes as follows:

(20) *(articles) which I will   file   without reading the contents
          ――― ――― ―――   ――――――――――――
           NP   S/VP VP/NP   VP/VP
                       ――――――――――――――― compose
                                VP/NP
                 ―――――――――――――――――― compose
                            S/NP
                 ―――――――――――――――― apply
                             S

But extraction from the second site alone, as in the illegal (11b), is not allowed by the expanded grammar, because even the new combinatory rule cannot combine *read your instructions*$_{\text{VP}}$ with *before filing*$_{(\text{VP/VP})/\text{NP}}$:

(21) (articles) which I will   read   your instructions before filing
                 ――― ――― ―――   ――――――――――――   ―――――――――
                  NP   S/VP VP/NP   NP   (VP/VP)/NP
                              ―――――――――――――― apply
                                     VP
                        ―――――――――――――――――――――――――――――*

The new rule therefore not only allows the construction, but also captures the 'parasitic' nature of the second gap. At the same time, it will not permit arbitrary double deletions, such as

(22)   *(a man) who(m)   I showed $t \ t_p$
                  ―――   ――――――
                   NP   (S/NP)/NP
                 ―――――――――――――――*

The manner in which this rule can be used in a grammar fragment for English (including subject parasitic gaps), and its further implications are explored more fully in CGPG. But at this point it would be nice to have some independent linguistic support for the introduction of combinatory rules of this sort. Fortunately, there is an obvious constellation of multiple dependency phenomena to turn to for this support.

1.3.2. *Multiple Dependencies in the Lexicon*

'Equi-NP-deleting' verbs, like *want*, together with the related subject- and object-control verbs, are strongly reminiscent of the parasitic construction, in that they assign two thematic roles to a single argument. A number of authors, notably Brame (1976) and Bresnan (1978, 1982), have argued convincingly that these constructions are to be handled in the lexicon, and I shall follow them in this respect. However, I shall also claim that the class of operations that are available in the lexicon is semantically identical to that available to syntax, so it will be easiest to start off talking about equi as if it were in syntax, before changing the notation to transfer the same operations to the lexicon.

The effect of equi-NP deletion can be achieved in the following way. We may assume that infinitival verb phrases like *to leave* have the category Sinf/NP that semantics and their combination with a subject-like NP to the left would suggest, distinguished only from tensed ones like *leaves* by some features distinguishing this argument as accusative and the result as infinitival, indicated by the symbol Sinf. We will also assume for present purposes that verbs like *want* have the straight-forward category VP/Sinf, so that tensed *wants* is (S/NP)/Sinf, a function over infinitival S into the predicate category, with semantics WANT'. On this assumption, one derivation of the non-equi sentence would be as follows:

(23)

Harry	wants	Fred	to leave
S/(S/NP)	(S/NP)/Sinf	NP	Sinf/NP

$$
\begin{array}{c}
\text{Harry} \quad \text{wants} \quad \text{Fred} \quad \text{to leave} \\
\overline{\text{S/(S/NP)}} \quad \overline{\text{(S/NP)/Sinf}} \quad \overline{\text{NP}} \quad \overline{\text{Sinf/NP}} \\
\hline
 \text{Sinf} \text{apply} \\
\hline
 \text{S/NP} \text{apply} \\
\hline
 \text{S} \text{apply}
\end{array}
$$

We could derive the related equi sentence as follows, if we had a rule closely related to functional substitution which we might as well call 'equi' for the moment, and which we will consider as if it were a combinatory rule of syntax.

(24)   Harry   wants   to leave
      ───────   ─────────   ─────────
      S/(S/NP)   (S/NP)/Sinf Sinf/NP
                 ─────────────────── equi
                        S/NP
      ─────────────────────────────── apply
                      S

Recall that functional substitution applies to a main function of the form $(X/Y)/Z$ and interpretation F, and a subordinate function of the form Y/Z and interpretation G to yield a compound function of the form X/Z and interpretation $\lambda x[Fx(Gx)]$. The new operation is strikingly similar, except that it applies to a main function $(X/Z)/Y$ and a subordinate function Y/Z to yield a function X/Z with the interpretation $\lambda x[F(Gx)x]$. (Functional application associates to the left as usual.) Intuitively, this operation looks to be very closely related both to functional substitution, and to functional composition, and in Section 3 this relation will be made explicit.

However, the new combinatory rule cannot be allowed to apply freely in syntax, even to functions composed from appropriate verbs like *want* — otherwise the grammar will overgeneralise wildly. A further problem arises in accounting for the possibility of extraction from the infinitival complement. The following example will block under the proposed analysis:

(25)   (apples) which   Harry   wants   to eat
              ────   ───────   ─────────   ─────────────
              NP   S/(S/NP) (S/NP)/Sinf (Sinf/NP)/NP
                     ────────────────────────────────── *equi

The natural way to allow the extraction and impose the other restrictions is by applying the rule in the lexicon, rather than in productive syntax, as we have already noted is implied by the analyses of Brame, Bresnan and others. Under this assumption, the lexicon would contain the following categories for *wants*, where pred and np are the interpretations of an Sinf/NP and an NP respectively:[8]

(26)   wants: = (S/NP)/Sinf: WANT′
        wants: = (S/NP)/(Sinf/NP):
                    λpred[λnp[WANT′(pred np)np]]

The second of these categories permits the following derivation for (25):

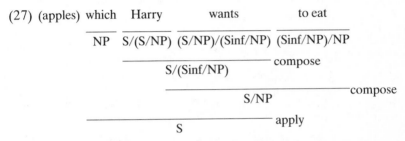

(27) (apples) which   Harry   wants   to eat

It would be natural at this point to extend the analysis to other control verbs, including subject and object control verbs like *promise* and *persuade*. Such an extension (which would also have to consider the passive) goes beyond the scope of the present paper. We will instead briefly note one further case of multiple dependency and the corresponding lexical combinatory rule, before turning to the pressing question of what all this means.

D&C follows Gazdar (1981) in employing the following rule schema to account for a wide range of coordination phenomena:

(28) X conj X ⇒ X

X can be any category, including a function, so the schema not only allows lexical functions like transitive verbs to coordinate, as in *Harry will [cook and eat] the mushrooms*, but also allows functions produced by composition and substitution to coordinate, as in right node-raising (a) and 'across the board' extraction (Williams, 1978, b):

(29) (a) [Harry will cook and Mary will eat], the mushrooms they
             gathered in the dismal orchards behind the Grange
             (articles which) I will [xerox instead of reading and file
             without examining]

D&C applies this schema to some constructions in Dutch which have been argued to involve backward gapping, and Dowty (1987) extends the analysis to a very wide range of non-constituent coordination phenomena in English.

We should really distinguish two schemata of this kind — one where X is an atomic category, like NP, and another where it is a function, as in

(30)   [Harry will cook, and Mary will eat]$_{S/NP}$, the mushrooms which . . . .

We can write the coordination rule for single-argument functions with its semantics in the usual way as follows:

(31) X/Y: F conj: H X/Y: G $\Rightarrow$ $\lambda y[H(Fy)(Gy)]$

Sentence (30) then comes out meaning something we might informally write as:

(32)   AND′ (COOK′ MUSHROOMS′ HARRY′)
             (EAT′ MUSHROOMS′ MARY′)

It begins to look as though the combinatory operations that are available to syntax and the lexicon are an interestingly constrained group of rather closely related operations. To see what their relation is, we shall have to leave linguistics, and turn to combinatory logic.

PART II: COMBINATORY LOGICS AND APPLICATIVE SYSTEMS

What *kind* of operation are we dealing with in the proposal to extend categorial grammar by the addition of functional composition, functional substitution, and the lexical combinatory rules? What *other* operations of this kind might we have chosen, had the data so disposed us? Curry and Feys (1958, esp. Ch. 5) provide a framework for consideration of this question in terms of combinatory logics and the related applicative systems such as the lambda calculus. An applicative system defines the two fundamental processes of *application* of a function, and *abstraction*, or definition of a function. The lambda calculus takes these two operations as primitives, in the guise of functional application itself, and the familiar variable-binding operation of 'lambda abstraction'. However, Curry and Feys define a number of more primitive 'combinators', in terms of which abstraction operators like λ can be defined, without invoking bound variables. (Cf. discussions in: Feys and Fitch, 1969; Hindley *et al.*, 1972; Stenlund, 1972;

Barendregt, 1981). It turns out that the operations of functional composition and substitution, introduced above for purely linguistic reasons, are an interesting subset of the most primitive operations which are required to define the foundations of Combinatory Logic and all applicative systems.

2.1. THE COMBINATORS **B**, **C**, **W**, **I**, **S**, AND **K**

The intuitively most basic set of combinators, in terms of which Curry's first versions of CL were developed, consisted of four combinators called **B**, **C**, **W**, and **I**. The first three of these are intuitively simple. The most important one for present purposes is **B**, which is the combinatory logicians' rather un-mnemonic name for the functional composition combinator. It takes two functions F and G, and yields a composite function of syntactic type X/Z whose semantics is given by the following identity:

$$(33) \quad \mathbf{B}FG = \lambda x[F(Gx)]$$

(Functional application associates to the left as usual, so that the left hand side of (33) is an abbreviation for '$((\mathbf{B}F)G)$'.)

The functional composition rule (4) of the theory presented in Part 1 is simply a typed version of the combinator **B**. We can therefore rewrite the rule of grammar using the equivalence above, as follows:[9]

(34) *Functional Composition*:

A 'main' function of category X/Y and interpretation F may combine with an adjacent subordinate function of category Y/Z and interpretation G to yield a function of category X/Z and interpretation $\mathbf{B}FG$, the composition of F and G.

C is a 'commuting' operator, which maps two-argument functions such as $(X/Y)/Z$ onto the corresponding function $(X/Z)/Y$ with the arguments reversed. Its semantics is expressed in the following equivalence:

$$(35) \quad \mathbf{C}F = \lambda x[\lambda y[Fyx]]$$

No related syntactic combinatory rule is used in the present paper. However, such operations have been widely used in the categorial literature, in the form of rules like Bach's (1979, 1980) 'Right-wrap'.

The 'doubling' combinator **W** takes a function of two arguments to a function of one argument which identifies the two arguments. Its semantics is given by the equivalence:

(36) $\mathbf{W}F = \lambda x[Fxx]$

Again, no related syntactic combinatory rule is used in the present theory, but it too is argued below to be implicated in the lexicon.

A less obvious but immensely useful 'substitution' combinator **S**, (which can be defined in terms of the preceding three), was first proposed by Schönfinkel (1924), and only later incorporated into the combinatory schemes of Curry and his colleagues (see Curry and Feys, 1958, especially the 'historical statement' on p. 184—5). Its semantics is defined by the equivalence

(37) $\mathbf{S}FG = \lambda x[Fx(Gx)]$

This equivalence reveals that the syntactic rule (17) which we have been calling 'Functional Substitution' is merely an incarnation (again typed) of the combinator **S**. We can rewrite the rule as follows:

(38)   *Functional Substitution*:

A two argument 'main' function of category $(X/Y)/Z$ and interpretation F may combine with an adjacent unary subordinate function of category Y/Z and interpretation G, to yield a function X/Z with interpretation $\mathbf{S}FG$.

The 'identity' combinator **I** is rather different from the ones that we have encountered so far. It simply maps an argument onto itself, where

(39) $\mathbf{I}x = x$

This combinator should be considered in relation to another combinator, called **K**, which was also introduced by Schönfinkel, and rapidly adopted by Curry. The 'cancelling' combinator **K** creates a constant function, and its semantics is given by the following equivalence:

(40) $\mathbf{K}xy = x$

Applicative systems up to and including the full generality of the lambda calculus can be constructed from various subsets of these few primitive combinators. A number of results are proved by Curry and Feys (1958, Ch. 5) for various systems of combinators. They note that the combinators fall into two groups. One group includes $\mathbf{I}$ and $\mathbf{K}$, while the other group includes $\mathbf{B}$, $\mathbf{C}$, $\mathbf{W}$, and $\mathbf{S}$, together with a number of other useful combinators which can be defined in terms of these four alone, without the use of $\mathbf{I}$ or $\mathbf{K}$. Curry and Feys show that for a system to be equivalent to the lambda calculus, it must contain at least one combinator from each group. The minimal system equivalent to the full lambda calculus consists of $\mathbf{S}$ and $\mathbf{K}$ alone. (In fact the other combinators that are under discussion here can be considered as special cases of $\mathbf{S}$. In particular, $\mathbf{B}FGx$ is equivalent to $\mathbf{S}(\mathbf{K}F)Gx$. Similarly, $\mathbf{C}Fxy$ is equivalent to $\mathbf{S}F(\mathbf{K}x)y$.[10] It is also important to know that $\mathbf{I}$ is equivalent to $\mathbf{SKK}$.

However, it is also interesting that the combinators that we have invoked in formulating the combinatory grammar of English do *not* include either $\mathbf{K}$ or $\mathbf{I}$, and can, with the important exception of type-raising, be very simply defined in terms of the 'basic' combinators $\mathbf{B}$, $\mathbf{C}$, $\mathbf{W}$ and $\mathbf{S}$. Thus the combinatory rule that was implicit in the lexical semantics of conjunctions like *and*, which Curry and Feys call $\mathbf{\Phi}$, but which we will follow Turner in calling $\mathbf{S}'$, is definable as the following close relative of $\mathbf{S}$:

(41) $\mathbf{S}'HFGx = \mathbf{B}(\mathbf{BS})\mathbf{B}HFGx$

It follows that the coordination schema (31) can be rewritten as[11]

(42) $X/Y\!: F$ conj: H $X/Y\!: G$ $\Rightarrow$ $X/Y\!: \mathbf{S}'HFG$

The lexical combinatory rule 'equi', used in the semantics of equi-NP-deleting verbs does not seem to be recognised in combinatory logic. But its definition in terms of $\mathbf{B}$ and $\mathbf{W}$ is strikingly parallel to that of the combinator $\mathbf{S}'$, except that it includes $\mathbf{W}$ in place of $\mathbf{S}$. It therefore seems reasonable to call it $\mathbf{W}'$:

(43) $\mathbf{W}'Fpx = \mathbf{B}(\mathbf{BW})\mathbf{B}Fpx$

The lexical entry for the verb *want* considered earlier can now be written:[12]

(44)   wants: $= (S/NP)/Sinf\!: \text{WANT}'$
         wants: $= (S/NP)/(Sinf/NP)\!: \mathbf{W}'\text{WANT}'$

The operation of type raising (Section 1.2) can be represented as a further combinator, called '$\mathbf{C}_*$', defined by the following equivalence:

(45) $\mathbf{C}_*xF = Fx$

This operation is related to **I**, and to functional application itself, and cannot be defined in terms of **B, C, S** and **W** alone in a typed system.

2.2. COMBINATORS, FUNCTIONAL PROGRAMMING, AND UNIVERSAL GRAMMAR

The paper began by providing an intuitive and linguistic basis for the introduction into categorial grammar of a small number of function-combining operations. It now appears that these operations correspond closely to the most primitive combinators that are used in combinatory logic in order to define the basis of all applicative systems. There are many gaps in the linguistic account, and many more constructions in many more languages need to be examined before it could be claimed that combinatory grammars constitute an adequate theory of universal grammar. But I hope that the simplicity of the analysis that it offers for the few constructions that have been considered here is striking enough to lend interest to some speculation as to why natural languages might take this form.

The concept of a function is so general as to make it almost hardly worth asking why natural language grammars should look like applicative systems. But the particular combinatory system which we have been led to by the linguistic data poses two more specific questions. The first is: why should it be explicitly combinatory *at all*? Why shouldn't it take the form of some other kind of applicative system such as the lambda calculus? The second is: why does it include these *particular* combinators, and not some others? For example, why doesn't it look like the elegantly minimal **S–K** system?

The whole point of the combinators is that they allow the definition of languages up to the full expressive power of the Lambda calculus — that is, languages in which functions can be defined in terms of other functions — without the use of abstraction and bound variables. In other words, it looks as though natural languages are trying to do without bound variables. But why should they?

The use of variables, via 'environments' embodied in association lists or other data-structures, is a major source of computational overheads in practical programming languages. Turner (1979a, 1979b) has shown that the applicative or functional programming languages (that is, languages closely related to the lambda calculus, lacking assignment and side-effects), can be efficiently evaluated by first compiling them into equivalent expressions using combinators to exclude bound variables, and then evaluating the combinatory 'machine code' by purely substitutive methods.

Turner's proposal is particularly interesting when compared with the system that has been sketched above for natural language.[13] Curry and Feys (1958, Ch. 6A) define the combinatory equivalent of Lambda abstraction as follows. If E is an expression in which functional application is the only operation, then abstraction of the variable x from E, written '$[x]E$' is defined as the inverse of application by the following equivalence:

(46) $([x]E)x = E$

The operation of abstraction can be most elegantly defined in terms of the **S**, **K** and **I** combinators introduced earlier and the following 'bracket abstraction algorithm':

(47) $[x](E1\ E2) \Rightarrow \mathbf{S}([x]E1)\,([x]E2)$
      $[x]x \Rightarrow \mathbf{I}$
      $[x]y \Rightarrow \mathbf{K}y$

where E1, E2 are expressions in which functional application is the only operation, and y is a constant or variable not equal to x. (The left associativity convention is followed, as always. Since **I** is equivalent to **SKK**, we will refer to this as the '**S–K**' algorithm.)

This minimal algorithm is extremely elegant, and quite general: that is, it will remove the variables from any applicative expression. But, as Curry and Feys point out, the combinatory representations that it produces are extremely cumbersome. Turner gives the following examples. Suppose the successor function *succ* is defined as

(48) *succ* $x =$ plus $1x$

Then

(49) *succ* $= [x]$(plus $1x$)

— the trivial bracket abstraction, which should reduce to

(50) *succ* $=$ plus 1

However, the above algorithm produces the following much less terse (though entirely correct) expression:

(51) $[x]$ plus $1x)$ $\Rightarrow$ $\mathbf{S}([x]$ (plus 1)) $([x]x)$
$\Rightarrow$ $\mathbf{S}(\mathbf{S}([x]$ plus) $([x]1))\mathbf{I}$
$\Rightarrow$ $\mathbf{S}(\mathbf{S}(\mathbf{K}$ plus) $(\mathbf{K} 1))\mathbf{I}$

The less trivial factorial function, defined as

(52) $fact = [x]$ (cond (equal $0x$) 1 (times x ($fact$ (minus x 1))))

(where '(cond ABC)' means 'if A then B else C'), yields the following:

(53) $\mathbf{S}(\mathbf{S}(\mathbf{S}(\mathbf{K}$ cond) $(\mathbf{S}(\mathbf{S}(\mathbf{K}$ equal) $(\mathbf{K}$ 0))$\mathbf{I}$)) $(\mathbf{K}$ 1))
$(\mathbf{S}(\mathbf{S}(\mathbf{K}$ times) $\mathbf{I}$) $(\mathbf{S}(\mathbf{K}$ $fact$)
$(\mathbf{S}(\mathbf{S}(\mathbf{K}$ minus) $\mathbf{I}$) $(\mathbf{K}$ 1))))

Such cumbersome expressions do not hold out much hope of being more computationally efficient than lambda abstraction, despite the avoidance of bound variables. Fortunately, algorithms producing much terser output can be formulated using combinator systems other than the minimal **S–K** system. In particular, Curry and Feys (*ibid.*, Ch. 6A.3) show that the algorithm can be greatly improved by the inclusion of the combinators **B** and **C**.

The problem with the minimal **S–K** algorithm is intuitively obvious. **S** is only really necessary when there is an occurrence of the bound variable in *both* subexpressions E1 and E2. If one or other subexpression does not contain the variable, then an extra application of **K** will be needed to 'vacuously' abstract over it. The redundancy of expression is particularly obvious in example (51), in which the vacuous abstraction over the inner expression (plus 1) — in which neither subexpression contains the variable — leads to a redundant application of **S** and two applications of **K**. In fact, this is the pattern of the ill effects of the minimal algorithm, as inspection of example (53) will reveal: it tends to introduce long embeddings of **S**, together with an occurrence of **K** for every constant and **I** for every occurrence of the bound variable itself.

The algorithm can be improved to produce very terse combinatory expressions if the set of combinators used in the algorithm is augmented by others introduced earlier, particularly **B**, or functional composition, and **C**, the commuting combinator. **B** is appropriate when the first subexpression (the operator) does not contain the variable, while **C** is appropriate when the second subexpression (the operand) is variable free. Curry, Burge, and Turner include these combinators in improved algorithms. Turner uses several other combinators, including

S´, defined above, and the related combinators **B**´ and **C**´, and all use some other obvious shortcuts, such as the following rule, which is the equivalent of 'η-conversion':

(54) $[x]\,Ex \Rightarrow E$ (where x is not free in E)

These slight elaborations have two important effects. First the combinatory representations are much terser. Second, the use of the combinators **K** and **I** is reduced to a minimum. For example, the representation of *succ* in example (49) reduces as it should to 'plus 1' (because of the rule of η-conversion above). The combinatory representation of *fact*, example (52), comes out as:

(55)   **S**(**C**(**B** cond (equal 0)) 1) (**S** times (**B** *fact* (**C** minus 1)))

Such expressions are evaluated directly, by 'graph reduction', a technique of literal substitution of expressions by mathematically equivalent, but simpler, expressions. Turner claims on the basis of actual implementations that for certain types of computation, notably ones involving 'lazy' evaluation and the use of higher-order functions, this method of evaluating applicative languages may be considerably more efficient than more orthodox methods. That is, the savings that accrue from avoiding the use of bound variables (and hence avoiding the need to keep track of environments) more than offset the expense of compiling the source language into combinators.[14] For related reasons, Buneman *et al.* (1982) have used combinators including composition to eliminate variables from the functional data-base query language FQL, a technique for which considerable advantages accrue when dealing with very large sets of records.

To say that there is an advantage to minimising the use of bound variables is not to say that they must be entirely excluded, however. Combinator systems, particularly those with small numbers of combinators, tend to make some abstractions much more cumbersome than others, as we have seen in the case of the minimal **S**–**K** system. (Indeed, it is this undesirable property which has made the lambda calculus the preferred mathematical notation for applicative systems.) Natural languages include a variety of explicit bound entities such as 'resumptive' and 'bound variable' pronouns. It would be as perverse to argue that these were *not* realisations of bound variables as it is to argue for 'invisible' bound variables or empty categories in the constructions considered here. It rather seems that the explicit use of variables is retained as a means of last resort for 'difficult' abstractions in natural languages, a proposal which is born out by the general cross-linguistic tendency for pronouns to be free of many of the notorious 'constraints on movement'.

CONCLUSION

These results suggest a reason why natural language grammars should take the particular form that is argued for in the first part of the paper. Applicative or functional programming languages without assignment provide a very general representation for computable functions appropriate to a very wide range of computing machinery. That is, the two notions of abstraction and application offer a general medium for the formulation of rules of all kinds, and for their application to particular cases. It is therefore not too hard to believe that the medium or mechanism of thought should evolve in the form of an applicative system. If so, then the results sketched above make it seem plausible that it would evolve as one keeping the use of variables to a minimum via the use of combinators. (The advantages of eschewing the use of variables seem to be independent of the particular computing machinery involved, so I assume that Turner's results, obtained for von Neumann machinery, generalise to the evaluation of applicative expressions on the undoubtedly non-von Neumann biological machinery.) What is more, a **B, C, S** system looks better in this respect than an **S, K** one. But if natural language at least begins (in both developmental and evolutionary terms) by being hung on to this preexisting applicative system of thought, and if what it is actually *for* is to convey expressions of this system from mind to mind, then it would be entirely unsurprising if the grammar of natural language were transparently to reveal that underlying applicative system.[15] The existence in natural languages of extractions and discontiguous constructions, including those with multiple dependencies, suggests that such is indeed the case.

NOTES

* This paper arises as part of a more ambitious project of work with Anna Szabolcsi, by whom it has been greatly influenced. An earlier version was presented as the first half of a joint presentation with her at the Conference on Categorial Grammar, Tucson Arizona June 1985. It has also benefitted from conversations with Peter Buneman, Kit Fine, Nick Haddock, Einar Jowsey, David McCarty, Remo Pareschi, and Henry Thompson, and from the comments and criticisms of the conference participants.

[1] Such transformationalist terms are of course used with purely descriptive force.

[2] A&S and D&C 'generalise' the rule of functional composition, using a '$' notational device, to include 'higher order' compositions like the following:

Forward Composition'

$$X/Y: F \ (Y/W)/Z: G \ \Rightarrow \ (X/W)/Z: \lambda z \, [\lambda w \, [F(Gzw)]]$$

We shall largely ignore this complication in the present paper merely noting that it is crucial to the analysis of Dutch infinitival clauses in D&C, and that the generalisation is an extremely simple one in the terms of combinatory logic (cf. Section 2.1, Note 9).

[3] The present very unconstrained grammar will of course allow a different and semantically anomalous derivation in which *these apples* is the subject and *Harry* is the object. Such a constituent order is not allowed in English (although it is typical of its first cousin, Dutch) and would have to be excluded in a proper grammar of English. Such a restriction is easy to achieve (see the earlier papers), so we shall just ignore the spurious derivation here.

[4] In D&C and CGPG fronted categories like relative pronouns and topics are also type raised, like subjects, so that they are the function, and the residue of the sentence is their argument. This detail is non-essential (unlike type raising of subjects), and will be ignored in the present paper, as is the related question of how relativised and topicalised clauses are distinguished in the grammar from canonical clauses.

As usual, the completely general rules of application and composition, and an unconstrained type raising rule, give us lots of other word orders. Many are typical of languages closely related to English. Again, the reader is directed to earlier papers for examples of language specific grammars.

[5] The startling implications of this analysis as far as surface structure goes are discussed extensively in D&C, and 1987b. Again many other non-English word orders are allowed, and again many are typical of constructions in related languages. However, some of these overgeneralisations arise from our failure to distinguish subject 'non-A' arguments from other 'A' arguments. For example, the grammar as it stands will allow violations of the Fixed Subject Constraint as in *This woman, I can believe that t will eat those cakes* — see CGPG for a solution to this problem.

[6] As usual, the generative grammarians' vocabulary is used for descriptive purposes only. The example is adapted from Engdahl (1983), replacing a Wh-question by a relative clause, so as to finesse the question of subject aux inversion within the present theory.

[7] See D&C for a discussion of these constructions within the present theory.

[8] Shaumyan (1977), Pollard (1985), and (some drafts of) Keenan and Faltz (1978) present related analyses of equi and related phenomena including formulations equivalent to the present one, to which we return below.

[9] The generalisation of composition referred to in Note 2 corresponds to the combinator $\mathbf{B}^2$, which can be defined as **BBB**. The full generalisation proposed in D&C corresponds to Curry's $\mathbf{B}^n$.

[10] These equivalences are given in their most transparent form. The definitions of **B** and **C** can be reduced to less perspicuous combinatorial expressions not requiring the use of variables — cf. Curry and Feys, Ch. 5.

[11] To coordinate functions with two or more arguments, we need the generalisations $\mathbf{\Phi}^2$ and $\mathbf{\Phi}^n$, parallel to those for composition — cf. notes 2 and 9.

[12] Shaumyan (1977, pp. 94—6) proposes an equivalent analysis of equi to the present one in terms of the combinators **B** and **W**. Pollard (1985) and (some drafts of) Keenan and Faltz (1978) use operations equivalent to **W** ′. Equi can also be analysed as **BSC**.
[13] The following paragraphs follow the argument of Turner (1979a).
[14] See Peyton-Jones (1984); Hughes (1982); Stoye *et al.* (1984) for further discussion and developments.
[15] I am arguing here that natural language grammar directly defines a combinatory system. There is no 'compilation' of natural language structures into combinators, as there is in Turner's proposal for implementing LISP-like programming languages. The proposal is that natural languages already *are* in such a form.

REFERENCES

Ades, Anthony E. and Mark J. Steedman: 1982, 'On the Order of Words', *Linguistics and Philosophy* **4**, 517—558.

Ajdukiewicz, Kazimierz: 1935, 'Die syntaktische Konnexität', *Studia Philosophica* **1**, 1—27. English translation in: *Polish Logic 1920—1939*, ed. by Storrs McCall, Oxford University Press, pp. 207—231.

Bach, Emmon: 1979, 'Control in Montague Grammar', *Linguistic Inquiry* **10**, 515—531.

Bach, Emmon: 1980, 'In Defense of Passive', *Linguistics and Philosophy* **3**, 297—341.

Bach, Emmon: 1983, 'Generalised Categorial Grammars and the English Auxiliary', *Linguistic Categories, Auxiliaries, and Related Puzzles*, II, ed. by Frank Heny and Barry Richards, Reidel, Dordrecht, pp. 101—120.

Barendregt, Hendrik Pieter: 1981, *The Lambda Calculus*, North Holland, Amsterdam.

Bar-Hillel, Yehoshua: 1953, 'A Quasi-arithmetical Notation for Syntactic Description', *Language* **29**, 47—58.

Bar-Hillel, Yehoshua, C. Gaifman, and E. Shamir: 1960, 'On Categorial and Phrase Structure Grammars', *The Bulletin of the Research Council of Israel* **9F**, 1—16. Reprinted in: *Language and Information*, ed. by Yehoshua Bar-Hillel, Addison-Wesley, Reading MA, 1964, pp. 99—115.

Brame, Michael K: 1976, *Conjectures and Refutations in Syntax*, Elsevier North Holland, New York.

Bresnan, Joan W.: 1978, 'A Realistic Transformational Grammar', *Linguistic Structure and Psychological Reality*, ed. by Morris Hall, Joan W. Bresnan, and George A. Miller, MIT Press, Cambridge, MA.

Bresnan, Joan W.: 1982, *The Mental Representation of Grammatical Relations*, MIT Press, Cambridge, Mass.

Buneman, Peter, Robert E. Frankel, and Rishiyur Nikhil: 1982, 'An Implementation Technique for Database Query Languages', *ACM Transactions on Database Systems* **7**(2), 164—186.

Burge, William H.: 1975, *Recursive Programming Techniques*, Addison-Wesley, Reading, MA.

Chomsky, Noam: 1957, *Syntactic Structures*, Mouton, The Hague.

Curry, Haskell B.: 1961, 'Some Logical Aspects of Grammatical Structure. Structure of Language and Its Mathematical Aspects', *Proceedings of the Symposia in Applied Mathematics* **XII**, 56—68, American Mathematical Society, Providence, Rhode Island.

Curry, Haskell B. and Robert Feys: 1958, *Combinatory Logic*, Vol. I, North Holland, Amsterdam.

Dowty, David: 1982, 'Grammatical Relations and Montague Grammar', *The Nature of Syntactic Representation*, ed. by Pauline Jacobson and Geoffrey K. Pullum, Reidel, Dordrecht, pp. 79—130.

Dowty, David: 1987, *Type Raising, Functional Composition, and Non-constituent Coordination*, Paper to the Conference on Categorial Grammar, Tucson, AZ, June 1985. (This volume.)

Engdahl, Elisabet: 1981, 'Multiple Gaps in English and Swedish', *Proceedings of the 6th Scandanavian Conference of Linguistics*, ed. by Torsten Fretheim and Lars Hellan, Tapir, Trondheim.

Engdahl, Elisabet: 1983, 'Parasitic Gaps', *Linguistics and Philosophy* 6, 5—34.

Feys, Robert and Frederic B. Fitch: 1969, *Dictionary of Symbols of Mathematical Logic*, North Holland, Amsterdam.

Gazdar, Gerald: 1981, 'Unbounded Dependencies and Coordinate Structure', *Linguistic Inquiry* 12, 155—184.

Gazdar, Gerald: 1982, 'Phrase Structure Grammar', *The Nature of Syntactic Representation*, ed. by Pauline Jacobson and Geoffrey K. Pullum, Reidel, Dordrecht, pp. 131—186.

Gazdar, Gerald, Ewan Klein, Ivan A. Sag, and Geoffrey K. Pullum: 1985, *Generalised Phrase Structure Grammar*, Blackwell, Oxford.

Geach, Peter T.: 1972, 'A Program for Syntax', *Semantics of Natural Language*, ed. by Donald Davidson and Gilbert Harman, Reidel, Dordrecht, pp. 483—497.

Hindley, J. R., B. Lercher, and J. P. Seldin: 1972, *Introduction to Combinatory Logic*, Cambridge University Press, Cambridge.

Hughes, R. J. M.: 1982, 'Supercombinators: A New Implementation Method for Applicative Languages', *Proceedings of the ACM Conference on Lisp and Functional Programming*, August 1982.

Jowsey, Einar: 1984, *Argument Crossover in Categorial Grammar*, Working paper, Dept. of A. I., University of Edinburgh.

Kaplan, David: 1975, 'How to Russell a Frege—Church', *Journal of Philosophy* 72, 716—729.

Kayne, Richard S.: 1981, 'ECP Extensions', *Linguistic Inquiry* 12, 93—133.

Kayne, Richard S.: 1983, 'Connectedness', *Linguistic Inquiry* 14, 223—249.

Keenan, Edward and Leonard Faltz: 1978, 'Logical Types for Natural Language', *UCLA Occasional Papers in Linguistics* 3.

Klein, Ewan and Ivan A. Sag: 1984, 'Type-driven Translation', *Linguistics and Philosophy*, in press.

Lambek, Joachim: 1958, 'The Mathematics of Sentence Structure', *American Mathematical Monthly* 65, 154—170.

Lambek, Joachim: 1961, 'On the Calculus of Syntactic Types. Structure of Language and Its Mathematical Aspects', *Proceedings of the Symposia in Applied Mathematics* XII, 166—178, American Mathematical Society, Providence, Rhode Island.

Lewis, D.: 1972, 'General Semantics', in D. Davidson and G. Harman (eds.), *Semantics of Natural Language*, Reidel, Dordrecht, pp. 169—218.

Montague, Richard: 1970, 'Universal Grammar', *Theoria* 36, 373—398. Reprinted in: *Formal Philosophy: Papers of Richard Montague*, ed. by Richmond H. Thomason, Yale University Press, New Haven, 1974, pp. 247—279.

Montague, Richard: 1973, 'The Proper Treatment of Qua.:tification in Ordinary English', *Approaches to Natural Language: Proceedings of the 1970 Stanford Workshop on Grammar and Semantics*, ed. by Jaakko Hintikka, J. Moravcsik, and P. Suppes, Reidel, Dordrecht, pp. 221—242. Reprinted in: *Formal Philosophy: Papers of Richard Montague*, ed. by Richmond H. Thomason, Yale University Press, New Haven, 1974, pp. 247—279.

Moortgat, Michael: 1983, 'A Fregean Restriction on Metarules', *Proceedings of the Fourteenth Annual Meeting of the North Eastern Linguistics Society*, ed. by Peter Sells and Charles Jones, Graduate Linguistic Student Association, Amherst, MA, pp. 306—325.

Peyton-Jones, S. L.: 1984, 'Directions in Functional Programming Research', *Distributed Computing Systems Programme*, ed. by D. A. Duce, pp. 220—249.

Pollard, Carl: 1985, *Lectures on HPSG*, Ms, Stanford University.

Shaumyan, S. K.: 1977, *Applicational Grammar as a Semantic Theory of Natural Language*, Edinburgh University Press, Edinburgh.

Schönfinkel, Moses: 1924, 'Über die Bausteine der Mathematischen Logik', *Mathematische Annalen* **92**, 305—316.

Steedman, Mark J.: 1985a, 'Dependency and Coordination in the Grammar of Dutch and English', *Language* **61**, 523—568.

Steedman, Mark J.: 1987a, 'Combinatory Grammars and Parasitic Gaps', *Natural Language and Linguistic Theory* **5.4**.

Steedman, Mark J.: 1987b, 'Combinatory Grammars and Human Language Processing', Paper to conference on Modularity in Knowledge Representation, Amherst June 1985. In J. Garfield (ed.), *Modularity in Knowledge Representation and Natural Language Processing*, MIT Press/Bradford: Cambridge MA, 187—205.

Stenlund, Sören: 1972, *Combinators, λ-terms and Proof Theory*, Reidel, Dordrecht.

Stoye, William R., T. J. W. Clarke, and A. C. Norman: 1984, 'Some Practical Methods for Rapid Combinator Reduction', *Proceedings of the ACM Conference on Lisp and Functional Programming*, Austin TX, August 1984, pp. 159—166.

Szabolcsi, Anna: 1983, *ECP in Categorial Grammar*, Ms, Max Planck Institute, Nijmegen.

Taraldsen, Tarald: 1979, 'The Theoretical Interpretation of a Class of Marked Extractions', *Theory of Markedness in Generative Grammar*, ed. by A. Belletti, L. Brandi, and L. Rizzi, Scuole Normale Superiore di Pisa, Pisa.

Turner, David A.: 1979a, 'A New Implementation Technique for Applicative Languages', *Software — Practice and Experience* **9**, 31—49.

Turner, David A.: 1979b, 'Another Algorithm for Bracket Abstraction', *Journal of Symbolic Logic* **44**, 267—270.

Williams, Edwin, S.: 1978, 'Across-the board Rule Application', *Linguistic Inquiry* **9**, 31—43.

Centre for Cognitive Science and Dept. of Artificial Intelligence,
University of Edinburgh,
2 Buccleuch Place,
Edinburgh, Scotland

SUSAN STEELE

A TYPOLOGY OF FUNCTORS AND CATEGORIES [1]

1. INTRODUCTION

Recent work on visual cognition by Hoffman (e.g. 1983) challenges the
traditional notion that the basic units in visual analysis, the cognitive
primitives, are geometric figures.[2] He argues, rather, that the cognitive
primitives for vision are properties of boundaries. For example, a
region of a planar image will be interpreted in one way if it is analyzed
with a convex edge and in another way if it is analyzed with a concave
edge. Consider Figure 1 (from Hoffman's paper), where the rings can
be taken to trace the trough or the crest of the waves, and the lines
defining the waves are interpreted accordingly.

One consequence of this theory is the possibility of precisely specifying the elements of visual analysis. The problem with geometric figures
as the primitives in a theory of vision is that the range of possibilities

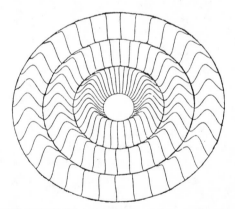

Fig. 1. AMBIGUOUS SURFACE is made by rotating a cosine wave about a vertical
axis. The surface initially appears to be organized into raised concentric rings, with the
. . . circular contours lying in the troughs between the rings. When the page is turned
upside down, however, the organization appears to change: each . . . contour is now
seen to trace the crest of the ring contour is now seen to trace the crest of the ring.
[From 'The Interpretation of Visual Illusions', by Donald D. Hoffman. Copyright ©
1983 by Scientific American, Inc. All rights reserved.]

443

Richard T. Oehrle et al. (eds.), Categorial Grammars and Natural Language Structures, 443–466.
© *1988 by D. Reidel Publishing Company.*

cannot be defined in advance and is, therefore, potentially limitless. On Hoffman's view, simple general properties involving the relation between a region in the visual field and its boundaries can be applied to planar figures of arbitrary complexity.

The problem has a parallel in linguistic theory. A theory which provides an account of linguistic judgements similarly depends on a statement of linguistic primitives. One place where that issue has been particularly obvious is in discussions of categories. Consider, in this light, the following statement from Chomsky's *Logical Structure of Linguistic Theory* (1975).

> To justify the contention that such and such are, e.g. the syntactic categories of the language, it is necessary to give a completely general characterization of the notion of syntactic category, and to show that the chosen categories satisfy this definition, whereas others do not. If the linguist wishes to justify a given assignment of words to syntactic categories in one language by appealing to a certain definition of the notion of syntactic category, formal or otherwise, he must be prepared to set up syntactic categories in every other language by exactly the same definition. (pp. 13—4)

This quotation is embedded in a section expressing considerable pessimism about the possibility of generalizing any definition; that is, according to Chomsky, the justification for assigning elements to syntactic categories varies from language to language. Under the assumption that the justification for assigning elements to syntactic categories varies from language to language, the tack has been to assume that the categories employed in a language have universal applicability. If the definitions do not appear to extend beyond language L_a, but we want a linguistic theory with universal applicability, the assumption has been that we must take as given the categorial labels and the distinctions they presumably name. So, from this perspective, N(oun) is a primitive in the theory — an undefined primitive — and is employed (presumably) in the grammars of all languages.

The equivalent of assuming geometric figures as primitives is, I would propose, the aprioristic linguistic theory sketched above. The same problem arises: the range of possibilities cannot be given in advance. Consider, in this regard, the long-term argument over the category AUX, where one of the arguments presented against the category has been that it expands the list of available categories. (Cf. Pullum and Wilson, 1977, and Pullum, 1981, in particular.)[3]

What I want to do in this paper is sketch out a theory of linguistic categories (actually, category types) which has obvious parallels with

Hoffman's vision theory. The idea depends on the functor/argument relationship basic to categorial grammar, an idea given the best statement in Ajdukiewicz (1967).

In every significant composite expression the relations of functions to their arguments have to be such that the entire expression can be divided into parts, of which one is a functor (possibly itself a composite expression) and the others are its arguments. The functor we call the *main functor* of the expression . . . . When it is possible to divide a composite expression into its main functor and its arguments, we call such an expression *well-articulated*. The main functor of an expression and its arguments we call *first-order parts* of this expression. If the first-order parts of an expression A either consist of single words, or, being composite, are themselves well articulated; and if, descending to the part of parts and to the parts of parts of parts, etc. i.e., to the nth order parts, we always meet with . . . well articulated expressions, we call the expression A *well-articulated throughout*.

Put another way, a functor takes an argument, associated (minimally) with a categorial identification and yields a result, also associated (minimally) with a categorial identification. I find the notation in (1) more perspicuous than other (perhaps more common) categorial notations.

(1)   Functor: argument$_{\text{categorial identification}}$ → result$_{\text{categorial identification}}$

The issue, as I see it, is to enrich the theory of functors with the result that the application of specific kinds of functors to their arguments yields units with a specific kind of linguistic analysis. Thus, functors are the linguistic equivalent of the boundary properties upon which a more adequate theory of visual analysis depends: they impose an interpretation on their argument. Not surprisingly then, this theory of functors affords a solution to the problem of linguistic primitives sketched above. Since the functor types are listable, the theory has the consequence that it can be responsible to language-particular properties — the functors in one language may vary from those in another. But it allows for a statement of similarities across such language-particular properties; all functors of a particular type yield a unit with a particular linguistic identification.

The first three parts of this paper elaborate on these proposals; the last part considers their consequences. Since the language exemplifying the proposals here is Luiseño, a Uto-Aztecan language spoken in Southern California, I will consider the consequences for the analysis of this particular language.[4] But I will take up as well more general consequences, focusing on constituency and the phenomenon commonly termed 'agreement'.

2. FUNCTOR TYPES

The division internal to the class of functors depends on three very simple notions. First, some functors are obligatory to the expression type in which they occur, while others are not.

(2)   Functors
            +obligatory
            −obligatory

In Luiseño, for example, there exists an element in a sentence which controls the number and form of arguments; this element is a functor that takes an Argument Structure and yields a Propositional Radical. (I will refer to this functor, as in (3), as the *Argument-Categorizing Element.*[5])[6]

(3)   Argument-Categorizing Element: Argument Structure →
            Propositional Radical

Consider, for example, that the Argument-Categorizing Element *'ooviquš* in (4) is accompanied by two elements, one of which has object-marking (generally, the suffix -*i*) and the other of which has the Postposition -*ik*.[7]

(4)   'ooviquš: ⟨. . .i . . .ik⟩ → Propositional Radical

            as in: 'ooviquš nil   potaana-y   'o-yk
                       ACE   Prt:Cmplx his:blanket-I you-IK

            'I was giving his blanket to you.'

In contrast, *'ariquš* as in (5) is accompanied by one element with object marking:

(5)   'ariquš: ⟨. . .i⟩ → Propositional Radical

            as in: 'ariquš nil   potaana-y
                       ACE   Prt:Cmplx his:blanket-I

            'I was kicking his blanket.'

and *miyquš* is accompanied by one element with number marking, the simplest instantiation of which is the plural suffix -*um*.

(6)   miyquš: ⟨. . . number⟩ → Propositional Radical

as in: miyquš mil   yawaywich-um
       ACE   Prt:Cmplx beautiful-UM

'They were beautiful.'

The Argument-Categorizing Element is obligatory to the result; a Propositional Radical which does not include an Argument-Categorizing Element is impossible.

On the other hand, there is a set of forms whose members include the equivalent of English 'try', each of which takes as its argument a Propositional Radical and yields a modified element of the same type. I refer to the members of this set as the P-Functor.

(7)   P-Functor: Propositional Radical → Propositional Radical

(8)   noyaax: 'ooviquš potaanay 'oyk → Propositional Radical

as in: 'ooviquš nil   noyaax potaanay   'oyk
       ACE   Prt:Cmplx TRY   his:blanket:obj you:to

'I was trying to give his blanket to you.'

As a comparison of (4) and (8) will readily reveal, the P-Functor is obviously not obligatory to a Propositional Radical. A functor which is obligatory to its expression will be termed a *Domain-Defining Element*.

(9)   Functor
        + obligatory = Domain-Defining Element
        −obligatory

So, in Luiseño, the Argument-Categorizing Element is a Domain-Defining Element; the P-Functor is not, although it is still a functor.

Now, internal to the set of obligatory functors — the set of Domain-Defining Elements — is yet a second division. Some Domain-Defining Elements belong to open classes of elements; some Domain-Defining Elements do not.

(10)   Domain-Defining Element
            +obligatory
            +listable

            +obligatory
            −listable

In Luiseño, for example, every Domain of Analysis that is a sentence contains one of a set of elements, the most obvious instantiation of which is the Particle Complex argued in Steele *et al.* (1981) to belong to the category AUX. One example, *nil*, is found in the examples in (4) and (8). The set is a closed class; hence, the instantiations of the functor at issue, the Sentence-Defining Element, are listable.

(11)   Sentence-Defining Element: Proposition → Sentence

On the other hand, the instantiations of the Argument-Categorizing Element, the functor from Argument Structure to Propositional Radical, cannot be listed; *'ooviquš*, *'ariquš*, and *miyquš* in the examples in (4) through (6) are just three members of an open class of lexical items.

A Domain-Defining Element (i.e. an obligatory functor) which is also instantiated by members of a closed class will be termed a *Rigid Domain-Defining Element* — rigid in that its membership can be listed and rigid in that the presence of one such is required in a particular Domain of Analysis.

(12)   Functors

    +obligatory = Rigid Domain-Defining Element
    +listable

    +obligatory = non-Rigid Domain-Defining Element
    −listable

    −obligatory

So, in Luiseño, the Argument-Categorizing Element is not a Rigid Domain Defining Element, but the Sentence-Defining Element is.

Finally, internal to the set of Rigid Domain-Defining Elements is another bifurcation. Some such functors are localizable; any of their instantiations have a fixed position in the resulting expression. Some functors are not localizable; their instantiations are distributed throughout the expression.[8]

(13)   Rigid Domain-Defining Elements

    +obligatory
    +listable
    +localizable

    +obligatory
    +listable
    −localizable

For example, in Luiseño, the instantiations of the Sentence-Defining Element have one of three (mutually exclusive) positional possibilities, varying with the form at issue; so, the Sentence-Defining Element may occur in sentential second position as with *nil* in (4) and (8), sentence initially as *wuśkapi* in (14) below, or it may be a particular kind of affix.

(14) wuśkapi 'oovique potaanay 'oyk
      WUŚKAPI was:giving his:blanket:obj you:to

'I wonder if he was giving his blanket to you.'

On the other hand, the argument to this localizable Rigid Functor — what I termed in (11) the Proposition — is itself analyzable into a functor (the Propositional Functor) and its argument, the Propositional Radical.

(15) Propositional Functor: Propositional Radical → Proposition

The Propositional Functor is a Rigid Functor whose instantiations are not localizable; they are, rather, conditions on properties of the Propositional Radical, properties which occur in no fixed position nor necessarily in any particular part of the Propositional Radical. Recall that a Proposition contains an Argument-Categorizing Element, an Argument Structure, and, sometimes, the elements instantiating the P-Functor. Let me represent, therefore, a Propositional Radical as a triple, as in (16).

(16) ACE; Argument Structure; *try*

For any such collection to form a Proposition, two things must hold. First, there is a sort of 'agreement' across these parts. All three of these parts can mark person and number; when more than one part does the person and number properties must be compatible. The examples in (17) through (20) are illustrative. The first member of each of these pairs is fine and the person/number values are identical; the second member of each of these pairs is unacceptable and the person/number values are different.

(17) (a) $ACE_{pl}; \langle \ldots number_{pl} \rangle; -$

miyx-wun pum yawaywich-um
ace-near:non:future:PL sde beautiful-PL

'They are beautiful.'

(b) ACE_{sg}; $\langle$ . . . number$_{pl}$ $\rangle$; —

    *miy-q   pum   yawaywich-um
    ace-near:non:future:SG   sde   beautiful-PL

(18) (a) ACE_{sg}; $\langle$ . . . object . . . ik $\rangle$; try$_{1st\ sg}$

    'oovi-q   up noyaax
    ace-near:non:future:SG   sde 1ST:SG:try

        potaanay   'oyk
        his:blanket:obj you:to

'I am trying to give his blanket to you.'

(b) ACE_{pl}; $\langle$ . . . object . . . ik $\rangle$; try$_{1st\ sg}$

    *'oovi-wun   up noyaax
    ace-near:non:future:PL sde 1ST:SG:try
    potaanay   'oyk
    his:blanket:obj you:to

(19) (a) $ACE_{no\ number}$; $\langle$ . . . reflexive$_{1st\ sg}$ . . . ik $\rangle$; try$_{1st\ sg}$

    'oovi-quš   nil noyaax
    ace-distant:non:future:NO:NUMBER sde 1ST:SG:try

      notaax   'oyk
      refl:1ST:SG you:to

'I am trying to give myself to you.'

(b) $ACE_{no\ number}$; $\langle$ . . . reflexive$_{1st\ sg}$ . . . ik $\rangle$; try$_{3rd\ pl}$

    *'ooviquš   nil
    ace-distant:non:future:NO:NUMBER sde

    pomyaax   notaax   'oyk
    3RD:PL:try refl:1ST:SG you:to

(20) (a) ACE_{sg}; $\langle$ . . . reflexive$_{3rd\ sg}$ . . . ik $\rangle$; try$_{3rd\ sg}$

    'oovi-q   up poyaax
    ace-near:non:future:SG   sde 3RD:SG:try

      potaax   'oyk
      refl:3RD:SG you:to

'He is trying to give himself to you.'

(b) ACE_{pl}; $\langle \ldots reflexive_{3rd\,sg} \ldots ik \rangle$; $try_{3rd\,sg}$

    *'oovi-wun   up   poyaax
    ace-near:non:future:PL   sde 3RD:SG:try

      potaax   'oyk
      refl:3RD:SG you:to

Second, and somewhat more complicated, there is a sort of 'anti-agreement'. Each of the three parts at issue can include a form with a Possessive prefix.

(21) (a) $ACE_{Possessive}$; . . .

      noo p   'oy   no-ma'max
      I   sde you:obj POSSESSIVE-like
    'I like you.'

(b) . . . $\langle Possessive \ldots \rangle$ . . .

      noo p   no-toonav   qala
      I   sde POSSESSIVE-basket:Number is:setting
    'I have a basket.'

(c) . . . $try_{Possessive}$

      noo p   no-yaax   tooyaq
      I   sde POSSESSIVE-try is:laughing
    'I am trying to laugh.'

But, with certain complications that I can't go into here, it is impossible to have two such Possessive-marked parts.[9]

(22)   *noo p   no-yaax   'oy   no-ma'max
       I   sde POSSESSIVE-try you:obj POSSESSIVE-like

(Note that what would be the gloss of this impossible sentence seems to be fine — 'I am trying to like you.'.) These two conditions together comprise what is called in (15) the Propositional Functor; that is, the Propositional Functor takes a collection as in (18a) and, because the parts satisfy its conditions (i.e. exhibit compatible person and number and include a single Possessive among them), the result is a Proposition.

(23)   'agreement' condition and 'anti-agreement' condition:

        ACE_{sg}; $\langle \ldots object \ldots ik \rangle$; $try_{1st\,sg} \rightarrow$ Proposition

The Propositional Functor is thus a partial function: not all Propositional Radicals (as e.g. (18b)) can be mapped to Propositions. The important point for our purposes here is that the properties to which the functor is sensitive cannot be localized to any particular place in the argument; the person, number and Possessive properties are distributed throughout the argument. Thus, the Propositional Functor is a non-localizable functor.[10]

I've proposed, then, a four-way division among functors based on three very simple attributes — their necessity, their listability, and their localizability.[11]

(24)   +obligatory
         +listable
         +localizable

         +obligatory
         +listable
         −localizable

         +obligatory
         −listable

         −obligatory

(25) summarizes this division as it applies to the functors we have discussed in Luiseño.

(25) (a) +obligatory
         +listable
         +localizable

         Sentence-Defining Element

    (b) +obligatory
         +listable
         −localizable

         Propositional Functor

    (c) +obligatory
         −listable

         Argument-Categorizing Element

    (d) −obligatory

         P-Functor

3. DOMAINS OF ANALYSIS

I stated above that an argument to a functor is associated with a categorial identification, as is the result of the application of a functor to an argument. Let me refer to a unit with a categorial identification as a *Domain of Analysis*. So, Luiseño has at least the three Domains of Analysis listed in (25) — Sentence, Proposition, and Propositional Radical. Every Domain of Analysis in a language, but one, obligatorily includes a functor: Since there has to be a beginning point in an analysis, there must be one Domain lacking a functor.[12] (This is presumably the distinction made by Ajdukiewicz between composite expressions and non-composite expressions.) Thus, a functor takes a Domain of Analysis and yields a Domain of Analysis, but a Domain of Analysis can exist in the absence of a functor. (26) is a revision of the rule schema in (1) along these lines.

(26)   Functor: Domain of Analysis → Domain of Analysis

Every Domain of Analysis has, as its name suggests, an analysis. In particular, every instantiation of a Domain of Analysis has a semantic value (its meaning), a formal value (its formal type), and a phonological value (its phonological form). Thus, (26) is an abbreviation for (27).

(27)   Functor: $\langle$phonological value$^i\rangle$
                  $\langle$formal value$^a\rangle$
                  $\langle$semantic value$^r\rangle$

        → $\langle$phonological value$^j\rangle$
            $\langle$formal value$^b\rangle$
            $\langle$semantic value$^s\rangle$

The proposal of this section is that such analyses can be classified into different types.

Every Domain of Analysis (hence, every categorial type) is associated with a semantic evaluation. The semantic evaluation of an element is simply a (semantic) generalization relating it to other elements of the same categorial type. For the most obvious example, consider lexical items (arguably a Domain of Analysis), each of which has a particular semantic content. The semantic evaluation of a lexical item is a generalization relating it to other lexical items. For example, the Luiseño lexical items can be divided, on formal grounds, into four subtypes, each of which subtypes has a clear and obvious semantic coherence. The generalization across the members of a subtype is the semantic evaluation of each member.[13]

(28) (a) Set A 'Naturally occurring and maximally free objects

  hunwu-t 'bear'
  hengeema-l 'boy'
  ku'aa-l 'fly'
  muu-ta 'owl'
  tuupa-sh 'cloud'
  teme-t 'sun'

(b) Set B 'Objects defined in a system'

  po-na 'his father'
  po-yo 'his mother'
  po-ma 'his hand'
  po-'e 'his foot'

(c) Set C 'Manmade and/or portable objects'

  kii-cha 'house'
  kuu-la 'arrow'
  too-ta 'rock'
  'eng-la 'salt'
  wiiwi-sh 'wiwish'

(d) Set D 'Events/states'

  'ari-quʃ 'was kicking'
  xiima-quʃ 'was smiling'
  xilla-quʃ 'was raining'
  yawaywi-quʃ 'was beautiful'
  ʃe'-quʃ 'was standing'

A semantic evaluation does not replace the semantic value of an element, as the examples in (28) suggest. It is, as stated, a generalization across related elements.

Some Domains of Analysis (hence, some categorial types) are, in addition, syntactically evaluated. Every Domain of Analysis has a formal value, but Domains of Analysis can be distinguished from one another according to whether the Domain is a single expression, as opposed to a collection of expressions. The former is syntactically evaluated; the latter is not. A syntactically evaluated Domain of Analysis may have an internal analysis, may include sub-expressions, but the whole has a syntactic integrity. The point here is to distinguish between Domains which are 'constituents' and Domains which are not — that is, to define 'constituent'. A Domain which is a 'constituent' is syntactically evaluated; a Domain which is syntactically evaluated is one to which the syntactic rules of the language refer (and not to its subparts). There are two possibilities in this regard. On the one hand, a 'constituent' (syntactically evaluated Domain) can behave as a unit for the purposes of some rule; on the other, a 'constituent' (syntactically evaluated Domain) can define the domain of some rule. A simple example of a syntactically evaluated domain — of a 'constituent' — is an English NP. An NP can include a number of parts, but there are clear conditions across these parts, conditions having to do with order and agreement; further, as seen in most generative analyses of English, NP defines the domain of the application of many rules. An English NP, thus, is semantically evaluated, but it is also syntactically evaluated. Similarly, in Luiseño, the Domain of Analysis termed *Proposition* above is syntactically evaluated. Such a Domain has a number of different parts — minimally, given the rules above, an Argument-Categorizing Element and an Argument Structure. Yet, the whole has a syntactic integrity: Most obviously, the Propositional Functor insures a global consistency for person and number values, the result of which is that the unit can be assigned a single such value. So, (23) can be revised as in (29).

(29)   'agreement' condition and 'anti-agreement' condition:

$$(ACE_{sg}; \langle \ldots object \ldots ik \rangle; try_{1st\ sg}) \rightarrow [1st\ sg]$$

The identification [1st sg] in (29) identifies the formal value of the Proposition. The important point here is that the Proposition behaves as a single unit with this value for the purposes of rules which act upon it; thus, the Proposition is syntactically evaluated. The Propositional Radical, on the other hand, lacks a syntactic evaluation. As indicated in (29), a Propositional Radical, the argument in (29), is simply a collection of parts. As noted above, not all such collections have the properties requisite to a Proposition: Not all of them would yield a single person/number value.[14]

Finally, some Domains of Analysis (some categorial types) which are semantically and syntactically evaluated are, in addition, phonologically evaluated. A phonological evaluation is not the phonological form of a Domain; every (instantiation of a) Domain has a phonological form. Rather, the phonological evaluation of a Domain is an identification of the Domain as 'connected'. The weakest condition for a phonological evaluation is contiguity; i.e. no Domain of Analysis which has a phonological evaluation can be interrupted. Consider, in this regard, Luiseño sentences. I noted above that some instantiations of the Sentence-Defining Element in Luiseño occur in second position in their argument. So, given the Proposition in (29) we have the sentence in (18a), but none of those in (30).

(30) (a) *'ooviq   noyaax up   potaanay   'oyk
        is:giving I:try   sde his:blanket:obj you:to

  (b) *up 'ooviq   noyaax potaanay   'oyk
        sde is:giving I:try   his:blanket:obj you:to

  (c) *'ooviq   noyaax potaanay   up 'oyk
        is:giving I:try   his:blanket:obj sde you:to

  (d) *'ooviq   noyaax potaanay   'oyk   up
        is:giving I:try   his:blanket:obj you:to sde

And this even though none of the members of the Proposition have a fixed position relative to one another and even though the members of these parts can be intermingled. All of the sentences in (31) are good and all mean 'I am trying to give his blanket to you.'

(31) (a) noyaax up   'ooviq   potaanay   'oyk
       I:try   sde is:giving his:blanket:obj you:to

  (b) potaanay   up   noyaax 'ooviq   'oyk
      his:blanket:obj sde I:try   is:giving you:to

  (c) potaanay   up   'ooviq   noyaax 'oyk
      his:blanket:obj sde is:giving I:try   you:to

The important point is that the members of a Proposition need not be contiguous to one another, while all the members of a Sentence must be. Hence, a Luiseño Sentence is a phonologically evaluated Domain, but a Proposition is not. A slightly stronger condition for connectedness has to do specifically with intonational properties, a condition that probably applies in languages in which order is a functor yielding syntactically evaluated Domains. Consider, in this regard, the fact that the differences among English sentence types turns (at least in part) on their intonational contour.

The three-way division among Domains of Analysis just proposed is summarized in (32).

(32)   Domain of Analysis, type A: Semantic Evaluation

        Domain of Analysis, type B: Semantic Evaluation
                                    Syntactic Evaluation

        Domain of Analysis, type C: Semantic Evaluation
                                    Syntactic Evaluation
                                    Phonological Evaluation

4. THE PROPOSAL

I've introduced a classification of functors, as well as a classification of Domain types. The proposal is that the two are connected. Whether a Domain of Analysis is to be assigned a syntactic evaluation or a syntactic and a phonological evaluation, in addition to the obligatory semantic evaluation, depends on — and can be predicted from — its functor. So, among Domains of Analysis dependent on functors which are Domain-Defining Elements (i.e. obligatory to the Domain of Analysis) there is a three-way division.

(33)   +obligatory
        −listable

        +obligatory
        +listable
        −localizable

        +obligatory
        +listable
        +localizable

This three-way division corresponds to the three-way division in (32). That is, I propose that Rigid Domain-Defining Elements (i.e. functors which are both obligatory and listable) yield Domains of Analysis that are syntactically evaluated. If the Domain-Defining Element in a Domain of Analysis is not rigid, the Domain of Analysis will be semantically evaluated only. Further, the distinction (within Rigid Domain-Defining Elements) between localizable and non-localizable functors differentiates among syntactically evaluated Domains of Analysis that are also phonologically evaluated and those that are not.

(34)   *Functor*   *Domain of Analysis*

  (a) +obligatory   Semantic Evaluation
       −listable

  (b) +obligatory   Semantic Evaluation
       +listable   Syntactic Evaluation
       −localizable

  (c) +obligatory   Semantic Evaluation
       +listable   Syntactic Evaluation
       +localizable   Phonological Evaluation

That is, a Domain of Analysis which is a result of the application of an obligatory, listable, but non-localizable functor is a 'constituent', while a Domain of Analysis which is the result of the application of an obligatory, listable, and localizable functor is not only a 'constituent' but is also 'connected'.

(35) shows its application to the three Domains of Analysis discussed for Luiseño as summarized in (25), given the divisions in (24).[15]

(35) (a) Semantic Evaluation only: Propositional Radical

    (b) Semantic and Syntactic Evaluations: Proposition

    (c) Semantic, Syntactic and Phonological Evaluations: Sentence

The claim made in regard to Luiseño by (35), then, is that the Proposition is a 'constituent' and the Sentence is a connected 'constituent'.

(34) allows us to return to the issue raised at the beginning of this paper. The problem with geometric figures in a theory of vision is that the range of possibilities cannot be defined in advance and is, hence, potentially limitless; similarly, the assumption of universally applicable categorial labels in linguistic theory follows from the problem of providing them with a definition which has cross-linguistic application. In contrast, functors — and, in particular, Rigid Domain-Defining Elements — are the linguistic equivalent of the boundary properties proposed by Hoffman upon which a more adequate theory of visual analysis depends: they can be listed; they impose an interpretation on their argument; the interpretation varies with the boundary property (or functor).

It is important to point out in this regard that the Domain type of the result is not predictable from the Domain type of the argument. The Propositional Functor in Luiseño takes a semantically evaluated Domain (the Propositional Radical) and yields a syntactically (and semantically) evaluated Domain (the Proposition). But there is another Rigid Domain-Defining Functor which takes a phonologically evaluated Domain as its argument and still another which takes a syntactically evaluated Domain as its argument. The first takes words, which I can't analyze here but which are phonologically evaluated Domains, and yields a single syntactic unit usually termed a constituent, but since we have used the term more broadly here we will call the result a simple constituent. The second takes simple constituents and yields Argument Structures.[16]

(36) (a) Constituent Functor: Word*
      → Simple Constituent

(b) Argument Functor: Simple Constituent*
      → Argument Structure

Both these functors, like the Propositional Functor, are conditions across their arguments — i.e. non-localizable. The Constituent Functor requires that, if a sequence of words is to be a simple constituent, the members of the sequence must share formal properties — i.e. the Constituent Functor is like the Propositional Functor in requiring 'agreement'. For a simple example, consider the two words in (37).

(37)   yuvaataant-um tapashmal-um
         black-PL   mouse-PL

         'black mice'

Both words in (37) have the plural suffix *um*. In contrast, the words in (38) — which lack compatible number — cannot be a simple constituent.

(38)   yuvaataant-um tapashmal
         black-PL   mouse

(39) makes this explicit.

(39)   Agreement: Word* → Simple Constituent

The Argument Functor requires 'anti-agreement' across its arguments.

For example, a simple constituent whose members are identified with the plural affix, as in (37), may serve as a member of an argument structure. The sentence in (40) is illustrative.

(40)   yuvaataant-um tapashmal-um pum nokunnga qalwun
       black-PL   mouse-PL   sde my:sack:in are:sitting

       'I have black mice in the sack.'

But two such number-marked constituents may not occur in any argument structure. (41) makes this explicit.

(41)   Anti-agreement: Simple Constituent* → Argument Structure

In short, the functor in both (36a) and (36b) is, like the Propositional Functor, obligatory, listable, but not localizable.

Therefore, the results in both (36a) and (36b) — the simple constituent and the argument structure — are, like the Proposition, syntactically evaluated Domains, are 'constituents'. Independent evidence to this effect is far beyond the scope of this discussion. I note here simply that each of these provides the domain within which different kinds of embedding are defined. The analysis of relative clauses depends on reference to the constituent; the analysis of complements, on reference to the argument structure; and the analysis of adjuncts, on reference to Propositions. (Cf. Steele (forthcoming (a)) and (forthcoming (b)) for details.)

The crucial point for the purposes of this paper is quite simple: the Domain type of the result is fixed by the functor type alone — not by the argument type, thus reinforcing the parallel with the proposed primitives of theories of vision.

5. CONSEQUENCES

I have argued here for a theory of functors by which each yields identifiable Domain types. And I have drawn on the parallel to Hoffman's theory of vision, whereby the interpretation of a region of planar image depends on its boundary properties. The discussion has been necessarily abstract, although the shape of the Luiseño analysis done within the theory should be clear. In conclusion, I consider some more concrete consequences of the adoption of the theory advanced here.

5.1. *Consequences for Luiseño*

This proposal has the interesting consequence for the analysis of Luiseño of allowing the statement of regularities across categories. I take up here only one example of this result. Given the rules upon which I have focused, it is clear that a sentence has three 'levels of analysis' — the Propositional Radical, the Proposition, and the Sentence. And, the 'levels' have a hierarchical relationship of sorts; that is, the first is a semantically evaluated domain, the second is semantically and syntactically evaluated, and the third is semantically, syntactically, and phonologically evaluated. Although I can't discuss it here in any detail, the word in Luiseño has the same type of internal analysis. There is the lexical item — a semantically evaluated Domain, as illustrated in (27); a structure built on that which (because of its functor) is semantically and syntactically evaluated; and a structure built on that structure which (because of its functor) is semantically, syntactically, and phonologically evaluated.

(42) Lexical Item

Functor: Lexical Item → Left-Occurring String
Functor: Left-Occurring String → Word

(43) gives a simple illustration of these three.[17]

(43) (a) (taana)

(b) po: (taana) → [potaana]

(c) i: [potaana] → [potaanay] 'his blanket (object)'

Such regularities are entirely within the spirit of linguistic theories which expect parallels across category types, although the parallels proposed here are closer to the relatively abstract ones of Wheeler (1981) than they are to those of $\bar{x}$-theory.

5.2. *More General Consequences*

More generally, the three-way distinction that I have proposed has interesting consequences for constituency — or at least what is apparently presumed to be constituency. On the one hand, some units which have been taken to be constituents would not be constituents, or at least would not be constituents given certain identifications of the functor. One obvious example is the English VP. If the V in a VP is taken to be the functor, under the proposals here the VP would not be a syntactically evaluated Domain: The functor does not belong to a closed class of elements. It may be that this is the right result; it may be, rather, that the functor is not the V.[18] On the other hand, some units which have been identified as semantically evaluated Domains would be better analyzed as syntactically evaluated. Consider, for example, Hale's (1981) analysis of discontinuous elements in Warlpiri. The issue is the relationship between the first and the last word in sentences such as (44) (= Hale's (2).)

(44)   kurdu-jarra-rlu   kapala maliki wajilipinyi
         child-DUAL-ERG aux   dog   chase:non:past
         wita-jarra-rlu
         small-DUAL-ERG

'The two small children are chasing the dog.'

One possibility is to generate these as a single unit, as indicated in (45), ignoring (for our purposes) extraneous details:

(45) $[[\text{kurdu-jarra-rlu}]_n [\text{wita-jarra-rlu}]_n]_{np}$

and then have rules which break this constituent up. (Carlson (1983) presents an elegant possibility in this regard, one which doesn't depend on scrambling.) Another possibility — the one which Hale opts for — is to generate the two words at issue as separate constituents and to have an operation merge them into a single *semantic* expression. The basic problem is the fact that the elements of what is clearly a semantically evaluated Domain are not contiguous. The proposals of this paper argue that contiguity is not the critical consideration for syntactic constituency. Only phonologically evaluated expressions are necessarily connected; hence, it is possible to have syntactic units which are discontinuous. The crucial property of any such unit is not the place of its members relative to each other and other units, but rather the functor type.

NOTES

[1] This paper lays out the framework within which the analysis of Luiseño in *A Syntax of Luiseño* is done. For the details of the analysis, I refer to the interested reader to that work.

Thanks are due to the students of the Linguistics Department at the University of Arizona who have listened to earlier versions and to Richard Oehrle for his encouragement.

The following abbreviations and symbols are used in this paper: obj = object; Prt:Cmplx = Particle Complex; sde = Sentence-Defining Element; ace = Argument-Categorizing Element; ( ) enclose semantically evaluated Domains; [ ] enclose syntactically evaluated Domains; and { } enclose phonologically evaluated Domains.

[2] Similar proposals along these lines have been made also by Shiman (1978).

[3] The issue arises whether categorial labels are taken to lack further analysis or whether they are taken to be abbreviations for a set of features. In the latter case, the issue is what, if any, limits are to be imposed on the list of features. (Cf. in particular Gazdar *et al.*, 1985.)

[4] The Luiseño data is drawn from my work with Mrs. Villiana Hyde, a native speaker of the Rincon dialect of Luiseño. The data is presented in the orthography introduced in Hyde (1971).

[5] The term *Argument-Categorizing Element* is neutral as to the category of the element so identified, since, in Luiseño, a number of different category types can serve in this function. The *Argument Structure* is the full complement of arguments required by the Argument-Categorizing Element and the form in which each must occur.

[6] Most rules in this paper are actually rule schemas. Consider, for example, the rule in (3). The label *Argument-Categorizing Element* subsumes a number of different possibilities, as does *Argument Structure*. Hence, the result is not a single possibility. A more specific example of this rule schema is offered in (i):

(i) ⟨'ooviquš⟩ : ⟨potaanay 'oyk⟩
⟨distant non-future⟩ ⟨...object...to⟩
⟨give⟩ ⟨his blanket to you⟩

→ ⟨'ooviquš potaanay 'oyk or
potaanay 'ooviquš 'oyk or
'ooviquš 'oyk potaanay or
potaanay 'oyk 'ooviquš or
'oyk 'ooviquš potaanay or
'oyk potaanay 'ooviquš⟩
⟨⟨distant non-future⟩; ⟨...object...to⟩⟩
⟨give his blanket to you⟩

The functor, the argument, and the result are each given as a value triple — the first representing the phonological value; the second, the formal value; and the third the semantic value. Because the order of functor and members of the argument is entirely free, the phonological value of the result is a set of possibilities. These various properties are a crucial part of the Luiseño analysis, but they are beyond the scope of this paper.

[7] These two suffixes have the shape *y* and *yk* respectively in the example sentence (4), since the forms to which they attach end in vowels. More importantly, note that the Argument Structure in (4), (5), and (6) appears to be lacking one of the arguments required by *'ooviquš, 'ariquš,* and *miyquš* respectively. The 'missing' argument has no obligatory lexical form, but rather is a person/number value dependent on the

properties of the obligatory lexical items. For discussion of this point, see Steele (forthcoming (a)).

[8] Actually, I require two slightly different definitions of localizability, one to apply to words and one to units larger than words. In the first case, a functor is localizable if all its instantiations occur in the same place as one another in the Domain; in the second case, a functor is localizable if each of its instantiations occurs in a fixed place. This distinction is necessary because the parts of words are rigidly ordered relative to one another, while the order of words relative to one another lacks such absolute rigidity.

[9] A Possessive-marked form is one which bears an obligatory Possessive. The contrast between *'ariquś* in the (a) examples below and *yawquś* in the (b) examples is instructive in this regard.

(i) (a)   po-toonav-i   pil   'ariquś
           POSSESSIVE-basket-obj   sde   was:kicking

           'She was kicking his basket.'

     (b)   po-toonav-i   pil   yawquś
           POSSESSIVE-basket-obj   sde   had

           'She had his basket.'

(ii) (a)   paa'ila-y   pil   'ariquś
           turtle-obj   sde   was:kicking

           'She was kicking the turtle.'

     (b)   *paa'ila-y   pil   yawquś
           turtle-obj   sde   had

'ariquś is clearly not sensitive to the presence or absence of a Possessive in the Argument Structure, while *yawquś* clearly is — hence, the contrast between (ib) and (iib). The Possessive in the Argument Structure in (ib) is, therefore, obligatory, while that in (ia) is not.

[10] The treatment of 'agreement' as a condition across the members of the Proposition, as opposed to making one member of the Proposition that which predicts the number and person properties of the other, is supported by the existence of 'anti-agreement'. The treatment of agreement here is, thus, to be distinguished from that of Bach (1983). In fact, insofar as it is assumed that functors must be expressions, the treatment of agreement here must be taken to be an extension of categorial grammar.

[11] The combinations of these three properties yields more than the four types identified in (24), obviously. The following are not found there.

     (i)   +obligatory
           −listable
           +localizable

           +obligatory
           −listable
           −localizable

−obligatory
+listable
+localizable

−obligatory
+listable
−localizable

−obligatory
−listable
+localizable

−obligatory
−listable
−localizable

It may be that there are functors which fall in each of these classes. However, I have weighted the three properties with the result that such distinctions are predicted to have no consequences. That is, if a functor is not obligatory, its other properties are simply unimportant; similarly, if a functor is obligatory but not listable, its localizability or lack thereof is without consequence.

[12] An alternative is to treat the members of this Domain as 0-ary functors. The result would be that all Domains involve functors and arguments.

[13] The division in (28) is a simplification. There is another set — formally distinct in certain respects from those in (28) and formally identical in others — which has certain other (equally predictable) semantic properties. See Steele (forthcoming (b)) for discussion.

[14] However, a Propositional Radical would have, by the classification of functors and Domain types proposed in this paper, a semantic evaluation.

[15] The three-way distinction among Propositional Radical, Proposition, and Sentence is adopted from Steele *et al.* (Chapter Four). The identification of a Proposition here is, however, not entirely identical to that in the earlier work, since here all Sentences involve a Proposition.

[16] The *-notation in the rule (36a) is not identical to that in rule (36b): In the absence of a word, there will be no simple constituent; in the absence of a simple constituent, there may be an argument structure. This distinction follows from the difference between the functors at issue and need not be incorporated otherwise in the rules.

[17] (43) is a simplification. *potaana* can be argued to have number added before the object suffix, e.g. *potaana-m-i* 'his blankets (objects)'. In fact, number behaves in the Left-Occurring String like the P-functor behaves in the Propositional Radical. That is, number is a functor from Left-Occurring String to Left-Occurring String.

[18] Fixing linear order can be treated as a functor. If this were the functor in English that took a V and the arguments to its right, then the VP would count as a syntactically evaluated Domain under the classification offered here.

REFERENCES

Ajdukiewicz, K.: 1967, 'Syntactic Connexion', in S. McCall (ed.), *Polish Logic 1920—39*, Clarendon Press, Oxford.
Bach, E.: 1983, 'On the Relationship between Word-grammar and Phrase-grammar', *NLLT* **1**, 65—90.
Carlson, G. N.: 1983, 'Marking Constituents', in F. Heny and B. Richards (eds.), *Linguistic Categories: Auxiliaries and Related Puzzles*, D. Reidel Publishing Co., Dordrecht, pp. 66—98.
Chomsky, N.: 1975, *Logical Structure of Linguistic Theory*, Plenum Press, New York.
Gazdar, G., E. Klein, G. Pullum, and I. Sag: 1985, *Generalized Phrase Structure Grammar*, Harvard University Press, Cambridge.
Hale, K.: 1981, 'On the Position of Walbiri in a Typology of the Base', IULC, Bloomington.
Hoffman, D.: 1983, 'The Interpretation of Visual Illusions', *Scientific American* **249**, 154—162.
Hyde, V.: 1971, *An Introduction to the Luiseño Language*, R. W. Langacker *et al.* (eds.), Malki Museum Press, Morongo.
Pullum, G.: 1981, 'Evidence Against the 'AUX' Node in Luiseño and English', *Linguistic Inquiry* **12**, 435—463.
Pullum, G. and D. Wilson: 1977, 'Autonomous Syntax and the Analysis of Auxiliaries', *Language* **53**, 741—788.
Shiman, L. G.: 1978, 'The Law of Perceptual Stability', *Proc. of Nat. Acad. of Sci. USA* **75**, 2049—2053, 2535—2538.
Steele, S.: (forthcoming (a)), 'Constituency and Luiseño Argument Structure'.
Steele, S.: (forthcoming (b)), *A Syntax of Luiseño*, D. Reidel Publishing Co., Dordrecht.
Steele, S., A. Akmajian, R. Demers, E. Jelinek, C. Kitagawa, R. T. Oehrle, and T. Wasow: *An Encyclopedia of AUX: A Study in Cross-Linguistic Equivalence Linguistic Inquiry* Monograph 5. MIT Press, Cambridge.
Wheeler, D.: 1981, *Aspects of a Categorial Theory of Phonology*, UMass dissertation.

Dept. of Linguistics,
University of Arizona,
Tucson, AZ 85721, U.S.A.

DEIRDRE WHEELER

CONSEQUENCES OF SOME CATEGORIALLY-MOTIVATED PHONOLOGICAL ASSUMPTIONS*

1. INTRODUCTION

Most of the recent work within the broadly defined framework of 'Categorial Grammar' has focused on problems relating to the syntax and semantics of natural languages. In this paper, I will address the question of what a phonological component would be like which is compatible with the basic tenets of categorial theories. That is, I will make the assumption that the phonological component is categorial in nature and then examine some of the consequences. As a case study, I will focus on the analysis of final devoicing and voicing assimilation in Russian.

In Section 2 I will briefly review what I see to be the essential properties of a categorial grammar and show how these properties motivate an alternative view of the nature of phonological rules and representations. Section 3 contains a discussion of Hayes' (1984) analysis of the voicing assimilation facts in Russian. His analysis is developed within the standard theory of segmental phonology, and many of his assumptions are incompatible with basic assumptions of categorial grammars. I will present an alternative analysis of the data, as reported by Hayes, in Section 4. Concluding remarks follow in Section 5.

2. CATEGORIAL PHONOLOGY

Standard generative phonology is basically transformational in character. Phonological rules apply to underlying representations to derive surface phonetic representations. Since Chomsky and Halle (1968), phonologists have been concerned with the nature of underlying representations, the form and interactions of rules, and, more recently, with the organization of segments into suprasegmental constituents. Again, the standard assumption is that there are phonological rules, of one form or another, which apply to underlying representations to yield the derived phonetic representation. With the advent of hierarchical struc-

467

Richard T. Oehrle et al. (eds.), Categorial Grammars and Natural Language Structures, 467—488.
© 1988 *by D. Reidel Publishing Company.*

tures, the debate in the literature has focused on questions relating to the internal structure of syllables, the form and application of syllabification rules, and on determining what higher domains are relevant for the description of phonological processes.

Categorial theories of grammatical description, on the other hand, are non-transformational in character. In the syntax, words (basic expressions) which are associated with the appropriate function and argument categories may be combined by rules of functional application to form larger derived expressions which are simultaneously given a semantic interpretation. The grammar provides a direct recursive definition of the set of well-formed sentences of the language. The theory is compositional in the sense that well-formed strings are combined to form larger and larger well-formed strings. Recent research has focused on extending the theory to account for syntactic examples which appear to involve discontinuous dependencies. At the moment, I do not see that there are similar violations of strict concatenation in the phonological syntax.

Following Bach and Wheeler (1981) and Wheeler (1981) I will be assuming the two general principles stated in (1) below.

(1)   *Compositionality*: the interpretation of the whole is a function of the interpretation of the parts.

       Invariance: once a feature or set of features has been specified in the phonetic interpretation of a string, the value (interpretation) of the feature(s) may not subsequently be changed.

The principle of compositionality is 'borrowed' from the other interpretive component: semantic interpretation. As far as possible, the goal is to have general principles apply uniformly to all syntactic rules and rules of interpretation. Thus, the phonetic interpretation of a segment (or larger constituent) may vary depending on the context it is in. This simply means that there may be phonetically conditioned alternations in the phonological systems of languages. The principle of invariance is also related to properties of semantic interpretation, though perhaps not so obviously given its statement above. The general idea is that once an interpretation has been established for a constituent, that interpretation cannot be changed. However, there is nothing to prevent leaving aspects of the interpretation unspecified and filling in the interpretation later. Semantic interpretations in the categorial grammar literature are consistent with the principle of invariance, though I have never seen it stated as such. As required by compositionality, the semantic interpretation of the derived constituent is a function of the interpretations of the parts relative to their mode of composition. The key notion is that the interpretations of the parts remain intact. An example of a violation of invariance in the syntax/semantics component would be if we were to change the interpretation of 'man' (i.e. *man'*) into *boy'* in the course of a syntactic derivation.

So, let us assume that segments are the basic expressions of our phonological grammar. These segments will be associated with specific categories to encode the various phonotactic constraints of the language, in much the same way that words belong to different categories depending on their syntactic/semantic properties. The first step is to define the set of well-formed syllables of the language in question. Languages often have different restrictions on the set of possible initial and final consonants in syllables. For example [ŋ] may only occur syllable-finally in English, while [h] may never occur in that position. Such restrictions are accounted for through the assignment of segments to specific categories depending on their distribution and phonotactic constraints. In the most general case, we would have the following grammar for generating the set of well-formed syllables.

(2)   Category   Basic Expressions

Category	Basic Expressions
N	{Vowels}
$N\backslash N$	{Consonants} (syllable final)
S/N	{Consonants} (syllable initial)

Rules of Functional Application:

(i)   If $\alpha \in N\backslash N$ and $\beta \in N$ then $\beta\alpha \in N$.
(ii)   If $\alpha \in S/N$ and $\beta \in N$ then $\alpha\beta \in S$.

I have adopted the convention of using 'directional slashes' in function categories to make it easier to keep track of the linear order of functions and arguments in the derived string. Nothing crucially depends on this assumption, nor on my choice of category labels. The set of vowels is associated with the category N, and they form the Nucleus of the syllable. Syllable final consonants (codas) are associated with the leftward looking function category labelled $N\backslash N$. Thus, they combine with a preceding nucleus and the derived constituent is of category N. Syllable initial consonants (onsets) are associated with the rightward looking category S/N, encoding the fact that they precede their arguments in the derived constituent. The derived Syllable is of category S. The rules of the phonological syntax in (2) above will yield the following derivational tree, assuming that each of the segments is in fact in the set of basic expressions of the specified category.

(3)

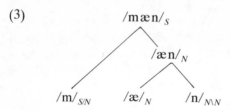

There are several features of the analysis tree in (3) which are worth noting. First of all, as I mentioned before, there is nothing sacred about the particular set of category labels I have chosen. The right branching structure in (3) roughly corresponds to the internal structure of syllables advocated by phonologists working within the metrical theory (Kiparsky, 1979; Selkirk, 1980; among others). There is an important difference between metrical structures and (3), however. In metrical theory, and other hierarchical and/or autosegmental theories of the syllable (Clements and Keyser, 1981, and related work), syllabification rules apply to linear strings and structure the underlying representation into syllables (and possibly larger constituents). Phonological rules typically refer to these structures, conditioning the application of the rules. In addition, the structures themselves may be altered through the application of various types of restructuring rules (e.g. resyllabification rules). The categorial theory that I am proposing here is more restrictive. It is important to recognize that (3) is an analysis tree which encodes the derivational history of the derived syllable, it is not a structure which has been assigned to the string by rules. There is no sense in which the 'tree' exists as an independent entity which can be manipulated by rules. So, for example, it would be theoretically impossible to have resyllabification rules which 'move' segments from one syllable to another.

Second, I am assuming that there are phonetic interpretation rules which apply in conjunction with the rules of the phonological syntax. If, for example, we were talking about a language which nasalizes vowels before nasal consonants in the same syllable, that would be part of the phonetic interpretation rule which applies in conjunction with the syntactic rule combining the nucleus (N) and coda ($N\backslash N$). Thus, larger constituents are built up out of smaller, well-formed, phonetically interpreted parts. I will encode this in the analysis tree as follows. Following standard conventions in phonology, slashes are used to designate phonemic representations and square brackets indicate phonetic representations.

(4)

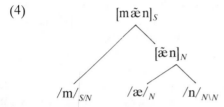

Here again, there are significant differences between standard metrical theory and categorial phonology. In metrical theory, constituents within hierarchical structures (onset, nucleus, coda, rhyme, syllable, etc.) may be referred to in phonological rules to limit the application of the rule to a particular domain. In categorial phonology restrictions on the domain of application of rules are a consequence of the fact that the phonetic interpretation rules apply in conjunction with the rules of the phonological syntax. Rules apply within restricted domains not because that domain is specified in the statement of the rule but rather because the interpretation rule applies at the time when the segments are combined to form the constituent.

Finally, notice that I have not made a distinction between the nucleus and the rhyme in terms on the category label associated with them — they are both of category N. This has several interesting consequences. Basically, it means that the rules of the phonological syntax will not be able to distinguish rhymes which contain only vowels from those which contain a coda in addition to the vowel in the nucleus. At first, this may seem absurd to phonologists, but the claim is merely that the phonotactic rules of the language will not place restrictions on the onset which are dependent on whether or not the syllable is open or closed. To the best of my knowledge, this is a true prediction. Additionally, since onsets are of the category S/N, they combine with constituents of category N to form syllables, regardless of whether the argument is a

basic expression of category N (i.e. vowels) or a derived expression of
category N (i.e. complex rhyme). Thus, it is possible to give a straightforward account for the observed universal that all languages with
heavy syllables (CVC) also have light syllables (CV). The converse is
not true: there are languages with only light syllables. It is, of course,
possible that a language will not have any basic expressions of category
$N\backslash N$, in which case it will not have any closed syllables, only open ones.
Thus, syllable markedness is directly related to the number of basic
categories which need to be posited in the phonological grammar.[1]

To summarize, I am assuming that the phonological component is
modelled on the syntactic and semantic components. Specifically, I take
segments to be the basic expressions which are associated with various
categories depending on their phonotactic distribution. Elements of
appropriate categories are combined by rules of functional application
to form larger and larger constituents. Rules of phonetic interpretation
apply in conjunction with the rules of the phonological syntax and
specify how particular segments are to be interpreted. Generally
speaking, the rules of the phonological syntax are responsible for
capturing the phonotactic constraints of the language in question, while
the rules of phonetic interpretation account for the phonological
alternations.

3. RUSSIAN VOICING ASSIMILATION —
A STANDARD GENERATIVE ACCOUNT

In this section I will present the data relating to Russian voicing
assimilation by discussing the analysis presented in Hayes (1984).[2] All
of the data and rules discussed in this section are taken from that work.
In the following section I will present an alternative analysis of the facts,
as they are summarized here.

Russian exhibits both word-final devoicing and voicing assimilation
in consonant clusters, as is illustrated below in (5a) and (5b), respectively.

(5a)   klub [p]   'club'   (cf. gen. sg. kluba [b])

(5b)   Mcensk # že [zgž]   'Mcensk, though'
        zub + ki   [pk]   'little teeth'

Derivations such as the one in (6) below show that final devoicing feeds
voicing assimilation.

(6)   /vizg/   'scream'
        k   final devoicing
        [sk]   voicing assimilation

The analysis seems quite straightforward, but becomes rather more complicated when sonorant clusters and the behavior of the phoneme /v/ are taken into account. It is necessary to make a distinction between obstruents and sonorants since sonorant consonants do not trigger voicing assimilation, as illustrated in (7).

(7)   pesn′ [s′n′]   'song'
        tr′i   [t′r′]   'three'

According to Hayes, the analysis is further complicated by the fact that sonorants may allow Assimilation to propagate through them, as in:

(8)   iz Mcenska [smc]   'from Mcensk'
        ot mzdy   [dmzd] 'from the bribe'

That is, sonorants do not block the application of voicing assimilation in clusters. At the surface, it appears as though the assimilation process proceeds as if the sonorants were not there.

The labiodental fricative /v/ has extremely strange properties, given the general patterns described above. With respect to final devoicing, /v/ patterns together with the other obstruents, as might be expected. An example is given below in (9a). Furthermore, it devoices, again as expected, when it is the target of voicing assimilation, as seen in (9b).

(9a)   zdorov [f]   'healthy'

(9b)   korov+ka [fk]   'cow (dimin.)'
        krivd   [ft]   'falsehood (gen. pl.)'

In all other respects, however, /v/ patterns like a sonorant. It fails to trigger voicing assimilation, as shown in (10a) and, according to Hayes' account, it permits voicing assimilation to propagate across it, as in (10b).

(10a)   s vami [sv]   'with you'

(10b)   ot vdovy   [dvd] 'from the widow'
        bez vpuska [sfp] 'without admission'

Furthermore, and this is the hardest to explain, devoiced word-final /v/s fail to trigger voicing assimilation.

(11)   trezv   [zf]   'sober'
        xorugv′ [gf′]   'banner'

So, the pattern seems to be that when /v/ is the target of a rule it acts like an obstruent, but it behaves like a sonorant when it is the trigger of the rule. Hayes (1984, p. 319) says: "Given this split behavior, a reasonable guess is that /v/ should be derived from underlying /w/, a segment that is in fact absent on the surface in most dialects of Russian." Deriving /v/s from underlying /w/s explains why they behave like sonorants with respect to the application of the rules in question. The rules Hayes proposes are given below in (12). Some sample derivations follow in (13).

(12)   Final Devoicing
        $C \rightarrow [-\text{voice}] / \_\_\_ \#$

        Voicing Assimilation
        In a consonant cluster, assign the voicing of the last obstruent to all consonants on its left.

        W Strengthening
        $$\begin{bmatrix} C \\ -\text{cons} \\ +\text{labial} \end{bmatrix} \rightarrow [-\text{son}]$$

        Sonorant Revoicing
        $[+\text{son}] \rightarrow [+\text{voice}]$

(13) (a) /w skwažine/   (b) /tolst # li/
          w̥ skw   lst̥ l   Voicing Assimilation
          f̥ skv   —   W Strengthening
          —   lst l   Sonorant Revoicing

     (c) /s wami/   (d) /jazw/
          —   zw̥   Final Devoicing
          —   —   Voicing Assimilation
          s v   zf   W Strengthening

     (e) /iz mcenska/   (f) /bez wpuska/
          s m̥c   s w̥p   Voicing Assimilation
          —   s f̥p   W Strengthening
          s mc   —   Sonorant Revoicing

Hayes' Voicing Assimilation rule applies to all consonants. That is, it applies to both obstruents and sonorants, as can be seen in (13a, b, e, and f). His rule of W Strengthening then applies to convert /w̥/ and /w/ into [f] and [v] respectively. 'True' sonorants which have been devoiced by voicing assimilation are revoiced by the Sonorant Revoicing rule (cf. 13b, 13e).[3] The reason why /v/ (/w/ in Hayes' terms) does not trigger voicing assimilation in examples like (13a) is that it is a sonorant at the time Voicing Assimilation applies. The rule of W Strengthening is crucially ordered after Voicing Assimilation. The derivation in (13d) shows how Hayes accounts for the fact that word-final /v/s undergo final devoicing but then do not trigger voicing assimilation. The final devoiced /w/ does not trigger the application of voicing assimilation since it is a sonorant and the rule specifies that consonant clusters agree in voicing with the last obstruent. W Strengthening then applies to convert the /w̥/ into an [f].

Within the generative framework, Hayes' analysis is quite appealing in that he is able to provide a fairly simple analysis of a complex array of facts. The rules in (12) are crucially ordered, as is generally the case in standard segmental analyses. Positing an abstract underlying segment (i.e. /w/) provides the basis for an account of the fact that /v/s behave like sonorants with respect to the application of the Voicing Assimilation rule. Devoiced word-final /w/s, for example, do not trigger devoicing of a preceding obstruent because W Strengthening is crucially ordered after Voicing Assimilation. Hayes assumes that all sonorants may undergo devoicing through voicing assimilation, even though all sonorants are reported to be voiced phonetically (cf. 13b and 13e). This is not problematic for his analysis, but does require him to posit an additional rule: Sonorant Revoicing.

As mentioned in the preceding section, analyses like Hayes' are not in keeping with the spirit of categorial grammars in that they are transformational in character. Underlying representations are mapped onto phonetic representations through the application of the rules in (12). In addition, rules like Sonorant Revoicing violate the Invariance principle in that sonorants which have been devoiced by voicing assimilation are then subsequently revoiced by Sonorant Revoicing. In the following section I will propose an alternative analysis — one which is consistent with categorial theories of linguistic analysis.

4. A CATEGORIAL ANALYSIS OF
RUSSIAN VOICING ASSIMILATION

In this section I will apply the categorial theory of phonology which I
outlined in Section 2 to the analysis of voicing alternations in Russian.
In keeping with the spirit of the categorial framework, I will assume that
the basic expressions, in this case phonemes, are associated with
particular categories. The rules of the phonological syntax stipulate how
expressions belonging to specified categories may be combined to
derive larger and larger phonological constituents. Rules of phonetic
interpretation apply in conjunction with the rules of the phonological
syntax. In keeping with the principle of compositionality, the interpretation of the whole will be a function of the interpretation of the parts.
That is, as expressions are combined, the interpretation of the derived
constituent is determined with reference to the interpretations of the
constituents which were combined.

The principle of invariance prohibits changing the interpretation of
features which have been specified in the phonetic interpretation. This
would appear to eliminate any phonological alternation, a consequence
which would clearly be undesirable, given what we know about phonological systems. Features which are involved in phonological alternations are initially left unspecified in the phonetic representation. During
the course of a 'derivation', unspecified features may be filled in
(interpreted) through the application of phonetically conditioned interpretation rules. Any features which have not received an interpretation
by the end of the derivation are assigned the (universally defined)
unmarked value for that feature. I am assuming that the unmarked
value for voicing is [−voice] in obstruents and [+voice] in sonorants. I
will use upper case letters to represent partially specified segments in
the phonetic interpretation. That is, a /b/ which is unspecified (uninterpreted) for [voice] will be represented as [B].[4]

As in Section 2, I am assuming that S/N is the category associated
with the set of possible syllable onsets, N is the category of vowels
(syllable nuclei), and that the possible codas are in the set of basic
expressions of category $N\backslash N$. At this point, I will not attempt to further
analyze consonant clusters which can occur in onset and coda positions.
That is, I will assume, for example, that /kl/ is an element of category
S/N, without trying to derive the constituent through functional application. To begin with, we minimally need the following:

(14)   Category   Basic Expressions

N (nucleus) $\{$i, e, a, o, u, . . .$\}$
$N\backslash N$ (codas) $\{$p, t, k, b, d, g, sk, zg, v, vd, . . .$\}$
S/N (onsets) $\{$p, t, k, b, d, g, kl, mc, mzd, v, . . .$\}$

Rules of Functional Application and Phonetic Interpretation:

(i) If $\alpha \in N\backslash N$ and $\beta \in N$ then $\beta\alpha \in N$.
$PI(\beta\alpha) = PI(\beta)\frown PI(\alpha)$, with the value for [voice] left uninterpreted for all segments in $PI(\alpha)$.

(ii) If $\alpha \in S/N$ and $\beta \in N$ then $\alpha\beta \in S$.
$PI(\alpha\beta) = PI(a)\frown PI(\beta)$.

In the rules above, $PI(\gamma)$ is intended to refer to the P̲honetic I̲nterpretation of γ. Segments within the coda of syllables are not interpreted for the feature [voice]. Invariance prohibits us from assigning an interpretation for this feature since we observe alternations in the voicing of segments in this position, depending on the voicing of the onset of the following syllable (if in fact there is one). Since the theory is compositional in nature, as syllables are constructed we don't, in principle, know what the larger environment is going to include. So, no decision can be made about how to interpret the feature [voice] until later in the derivation. Onsets may be interpreted for [voice] since alternations are not observed in this position.

Given the rules in (14), we would have the following analysis tree for a word like 'klub' ([klup]). Again, I assume that any features whose values are left unspecified at the end of a derivation are interpreted as having the unmarked value by Universal Marking Conventions (UMC). The UMC will specify obstruents as [−voice], and sonorants will be interpreted as [+voice].

(15)   klub 'club'

$[kluB]_S \Rightarrow [klup]$ by UMC.

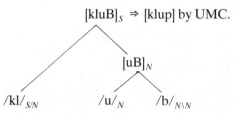

$/kl/_{S/N}$ $\qquad$ $/u/_N$ $\quad$ $/b/_{N\backslash N}$

$[uB]_N$

The final obstruent remains uninterpreted for [voice], in accord with (14i). Since there are no further rules which apply to the string, the final obstruent is interpreted as [−voice], the unmarked value of the feature for obstruents. In the analysis I am proposing here, there is no need for an independent rule of final devoicing — it is an automatic consequence of the fact that consonants are not interpreted for voice in the coda of syllables and receive the unmarked specification.

Furthermore, the apparent feeding relation between final devoicing and voicing assimilation which we see in examples like 'vizg' ([visk]) follows automatically from this analysis. In this case, both obstruents in the final cluster are uninterpreted for voice and are subsequently interpreted as voiceless by the universal marking conventions. Nothing more needs to be said.

(16)   vizg 'scream'

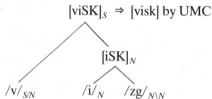

$$[viSK]_S \Rightarrow [visk] \text{ by UMC}$$

$$[iSK]_N$$

$$/v/_{S/N} \qquad /i/_N \qquad /zg/_{N \backslash N}$$

Additional rules of functional application are needed to derive polysyllabic words. It is in these words where we will see the effects of voicing assimilation. First of all, let the category of derived phonological words be W. The rules in (17a) are intended to account for the fact that words in Russian may be monosyllabic, or that syllables may be interpreted as belonging to function categories such that they may combine with other syllables to form words. Here again, nothing hinges on the precise choice of category labels. The rule of functional application in (17b) applies to generate polysyllable words. A function, which I have referred to as VA (i.e. voicing assimilation), applies to the phonetic interpretations of the expressions which are combined to form the derived constituent.

(17a)   If $\alpha \in S$ then α may be a member of W or W/W.

(17b)   If $\alpha \in W/W$ and $\beta \in W$ then $\alpha\beta \in W$, where $PI(\alpha\beta) = VA(PI(\alpha) \frown PI(\beta))$.

For now, I will assume that the Voicing Assimilation rule/function is stated as follows, and that it applies iteratively from right to left to fill in the feature [+voice] for any consonants which are in the appropriate environment.[5]

(18)   Voicing Assimilation (VA (x)) — Iterative.

$$[+\text{cons}] \rightarrow [+\text{voice}]/\underline{\hspace{1cm}}\begin{bmatrix} +\text{cons} \\ +\text{voice} \end{bmatrix}$$

In standard segmental analyses, the voicing assimilation rule usually employs the so-called α-notation. That is, consonants become [+voice] if the following consonant is [+voice], and [−voice] if the following consonant is [−voice]. I am assuming here that the rule has the simpler form, and that it is only the feature [+voice] which spreads through consonant clusters. It is not necessary to have the 'devoicing' component of the voicing assimilation process incorporated into the rule. 'Devoicing' follows from the independent assumption that the unmarked value for [voice] is [−voice] for obstruents. Some derivations follow to illustrate the application of (17) and (18).

(19a)   zubki 'little teeth'

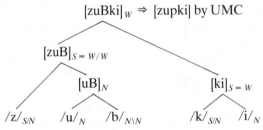

(19b)   ot vdovy 'from the bribe'

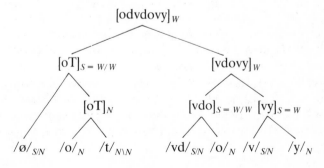

Voicing assimilation does not apply in (19a) since there is no voiced consonant to trigger the rule. The unspecified [T] in example (19b) is interpreted as [+voice] through the phonetic interpretation rule of Voicing Assimilation (18) which applies in conjunction with the rule of functional application combining syllables to form words.[6]

I will now turn to the analysis of voicing assimilation in consonant clusters containing sonorants. In a standard generative analysis like Hayes', it is necessary to assume that voicing assimilation 'propagates' through nasal consonants in order to derive the correct phonetic form for examples such as: 'iz mcenska' ([smc]). Sonorant Revoicing then applies to voice the nasal, since all sonorants are phonetically voiced (cf. the derivations in (13)). The categorial analysis I am proposing needs to be modified slightly in order to account for the fact that sonorants do not, in general, trigger voicing assimilation. In examples like 'iz mcenska', if the nasal were fully specified, then it would incorrectly trigger voicing assimilation (e.g. *[zmc]). There is a straightforward explanation for the behavior of sonorants in the analysis I am proposing. It is possible to account for the fact that sonorants do not trigger voicing assimilation in Russian by assuming that they are uninterpreted for [voice] when the voicing assimilation process applies. I have not explicitly stated that sonorants are uninterpreted for [voice] as part of the phonetic interpretation rule (14ii). The key to the analysis is that voicing is not a distinctive feature for sonorants in Russian, and so it could be argued that [voice] is simply not included among the set of features for sonorants in phonemic representations. If this is the case, then it automatically follows that sonorants will not be interpreted for [voice] until late in the derivation when the Universal Marking Conventions apply to fill in unmarked feature values. As a consequence, sonorants can not trigger voicing assimilation in the present analysis since that rule is only triggered by segments which are [+cons, +voice]. Leaving [voice] uninterpreted in sonorants correctly predicts that the derived cluster in 'iz Mcenska' will be interpreted as [smc] by the Universal Marking Conventions, as is shown in (20a) below. If the sonorant has itself undergone voicing assimilation and is marked [+voice] by (18), then we would expect it to act as a trigger for the voicing of a preceding obstruent. This is in fact the correct prediction, as can be seen in (20b). From now on, all sonorant consonants will be represented with upper-case letters (e.g. /M/) to indicate that they are unmarked for the feature [voice] in phonemic (and phonetic) representations.[7]

(20a) iz mcenska 'from Mcenska'

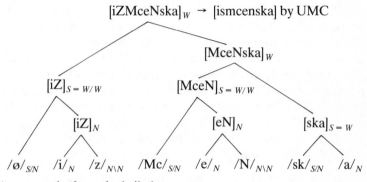

(20b) ot mzdy 'from the bribe'

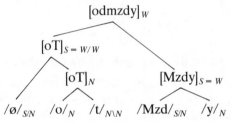

The analysis of words like 'pesn'' ([pes´n´]) suggests that we need to look more carefully at the internal structure of consonant clusters in the codas of syllables. At first, it appears as though the analysis is making the correct predictions, as is shown in the following derivation.

(21) pesn' 'song'

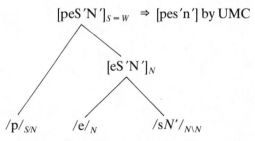

However, examples like 'žizn'' ([žiz'n']) suggest that the situation is more complicated. In general, sonorants do not trigger voicing assimilation, as was pointed out earlier. The problem here is how to insure that the obstruent preceding the final sonorant surfaces as voiced, since we would expect it to be voiceless by the Universal Marking Conventions (*[žis'n']). The solution, within the proposed theory, is to assume that there is an additional rule of functional application which derives obstruent-sonorant clusters in codas, and that the obstruent is fully interpreted phonetically. Assuming that $N \backslash N$ is the general category for codas, we need only assume that sonorants are associated with the category $(N\backslash N)\backslash(N\backslash N)$. That is, they are functions which combine with preceding expressions of category $N\backslash N$ to derive an expression of category $N\backslash N$. As part of the phonetic interpretation of the derived expression, the obstruent will be interpreted for [voice].

(22)   Category   Basic Expressions

$N\backslash N$ $\{s, z, \ldots\}$
$(N\backslash N)\backslash(N\backslash N)$ $\{M, N, \ldots\}$

Rule of Functional Application and Phonetic Interpretation:

If $\alpha \in (N\backslash N)\backslash(N\backslash N)$ and $\beta \in N\backslash N$ then $\gamma \in N\backslash N$.
$PI(\gamma) = PI(\beta)^\frown PI(\alpha)$, with the value for [voice] left uninterpreted in $PI(\alpha)$.

Given the additional rules in (22), words like 'pesn'' and 'žizn'' would have the following derivations. Again, I am assuming that all features of phonemic representations not specifically left uninterpreted are phonetically interpreted.

(23a)   pesn' 'song'

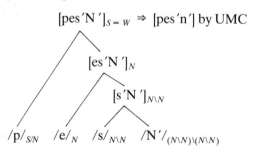

(23b)   žizn´ 'life'

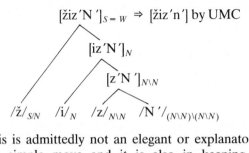

$$[\text{žiz}´\text{N}´]_{S\,=\,W} \;\Rightarrow\; [\text{žiz}´\text{n}´] \text{ by UMC}$$

$$[\text{iz}´\text{N}´]_N$$

$$[\text{z}´\text{N}´]_{N\backslash N}$$

$$/\text{ž}/_{S/N} \quad /\text{i}/_N \quad /\text{z}/_{N\backslash N} \quad /\text{N}´/_{(N\backslash N)\backslash(N\backslash N)}$$

While this is admittedly not an elegant or explanatory solution, it is a relatively simple move and it is also in keeping with the general approach being advocated here. It is curious that final obstruent-sonorant clusters like [s´n´] and [z´n´] which seem to require a special rule of functional application are clusters which violate sonority sequencing constraints within syllables (Hooper, 1976; Kiparsky, 1979; Selkirk, 1984; etc.). The general pattern in languages is that the relative sonority of segments decreases towards the margins of syllables. Since sonorants are more sonorous than obstruents, final obstruent-nasal clusters are highly marked. Perhaps the marked nature of these clusters correlates with the necessity of having an additional rule of functional application.

Finally, we are in a position to consider the problem of /v/ and all of its peculiar properties. Recall that, in traditional terms, /v/ undergoes voicing assimilation just like other obstruents. This is predicted, given the analysis presented here, as is shown in the derivations in (24a) and (24b) below. Voicing is not specified for obstruents in the coda of syllables and they will ultimately be realized as voiceless unless there is a voiced obstruent in the onset of the following syllable.

(24a)   korovka 'cow (dimin.)'

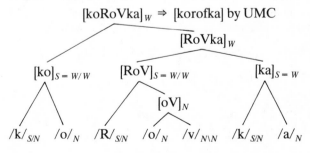

$$[\text{koRoVka}]_W \;\Rightarrow\; [\text{korofka}] \text{ by UMC}$$

$$[\text{RoVka}]_W$$

$$[\text{ko}]_{S\,=\,W/W} \qquad [\text{RoV}]_{S\,=\,W/W} \qquad [\text{ka}]_{S\,=\,W}$$

$$[\text{oV}]_N$$

$$/\text{k}/_{S/N} \quad /\text{o}/_N \quad /\text{R}/_{S/N} \quad /\text{o}/_N \quad /\text{v}/_{N\backslash N} \quad /\text{k}/_{S/N} \quad /\text{a}/_N$$

(24b)   krivd 'falsehood (gen. pl.)'

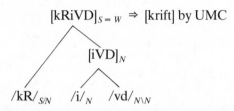

$[kRiVD]_{S=W} \Rightarrow$ [krift] by UMC

The traditionally problematic examples are where /v/ apparently behaves as though it were a sonorant. In words like 'svami' ([svami]), the /v/ does not trigger voicing assimilation. Also, a /v/ which has undergone final devoicing does not trigger devoicing of preceding obstruents in the cluster, as in 'trezv' ([trezf]). Such examples are truly problematic for standard segmental analyses, and force phonologists like Hayes to posit abstract underlying representations. But, given the analysis I am proposing here, the derivation of words like 'svami' is perfectly straightforward. As I pointed out earlier, we do not find voicing alternations within the onsets of syllables. Through the rule of phonetic interpretation in (14ii), all obstruents in the onsets of syllables will be interpreted for [voice]. Invariance prevents voicing assimilation from applying in initial clusters like [sv].

(25)   svami 'with you'

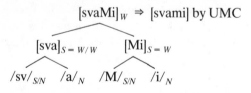

$[svaMi]_W \Rightarrow$ [svami] by UMC

Now, consider examples where a 'devoiced' word-final /v/ fails to trigger voicing assimilation in the final cluster. Given the analysis presented here, we would expect to have the following derivation.

(26) $[tReZV]_{S=W} \Rightarrow$ *[tresf] by UMC

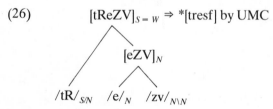

The correct surface phonetic representation is [trezf]. In essence, the final /v/ is behaving as we would expect — it is phonetically devoiced, just like any other obstruent in that position. What is peculiar is the fact that the preceding obstruent is voiced, since all other obstruents in that position (i.e. in the coda of a word-final syllable) are voiceless. Thus, in our terms, the problem is to ensure that the phonemic value of the voicing feature is interpreted for obstruents like /z/ in words like 'trezv'. That is, voicing needs to be phonetically interpreted in word-final obstruent clusters where the final segment is /v/ since the universal marking conventions are not sufficient to guarantee the correct result. We already have the rules needed to ensure the correct result. All we need to do is assume that /v/, together with the class of sonorants, is a member of the set of basic expressions of category $(N \backslash N) \backslash (N \backslash N)$. Rather than assume that syllable final clusters like /zv/ and /sv/ are basic expressions of category $N \backslash N$, then, let us assume that they are derived through the rule of functional application in (22). As a result, any obstruent preceding /v/ will be interpreted for [voice], and we will be able to predict the correct phonetic realizations. A derivation is given below to illustrate.

(27)   trezv 'sober'

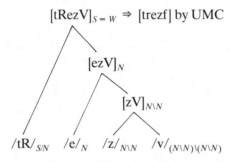

$$[\text{tRezV}]_{S = W} \Rightarrow [\text{trezf}] \text{ by UMC}$$

$$[\text{ezV}]_N$$

$$[\text{zV}]_{N \backslash N}$$

$$/\text{tR}/_{S/N} \quad /\text{e}/_N \quad /\text{z}/_{N \backslash N} \quad /\text{v}/_{(N \backslash N) \backslash (N \backslash N)}$$

In the categorial analysis proposed here, then, there is no need to posit abstract /w/s in underlying representations in order to account for how [v] patterns with respect to Voicing Assimilation. The curious properties of [v] follow from the simple assumption that it belongs to the same (syntactic) category as the set of sonorants. While it appears that historically [v] does derive from /w/, it is neither necessary nor useful in the present synchronic analysis to recapitulate that diachronic process. Instead, [v]s pattern with sonorants with respect to the rules of the phonological syntax, but, unlike true sonorants, [v]s are interpreted as [−voice] by the Universal Marking Conventions since this is the unmarked value for [voice] in obstruents. Despite the shift in the phonetic quality of /w/ to /v/, historically, the category assignment of the segment has remained unchanged.

5. CONCLUSION

The analysis of Russian final devoicing and voicing assimilation which I have proposed is based on fundamental assumptions of categorial theories of linguistic analysis. Investigating the phonological component from a categorial point of view raises many interesting questions with respect to the form and application of phonological rules.

In the proposed analysis, there is no independently stipulated rule of final devoicing. Failure to specify voicing automatically results in voice-lessness for final obstruents by the Universal Marking Conventions. Voicing Assimilation is literally just that — it results in clusters being interpreted as voiced if there is a voiced obstruent in the cluster. There is no need for a devoicing component to the rule since, again, any obstruents which are uninterpreted for [voice] are realized as voiceless. Furthermore, Voicing Assimilation does not need to be restricted so that it is only triggered by obstruents. Since voicing is not a distinctive feature for sonorants the feature [voice] is not specified in phonemic representations. Consequently, sonorants may never trigger Voicing Assimilation because the rule requires the triggering segment to be [+cons, +voice].

The general approach to phonological analysis advocated here makes a very interesting — and strong — prediction. Given the constraints imposed on phonological derivations by the Invariance Principle, leaving the feature [voice] uninterpreted in the phonetic interpretation of segments is a necessary precondition for there being a voicing assimilation process in the language. If all segments were fully interpreted, then Voicing Assimilation would be prohibited from applying by the Invariance Principle, and consequently could not actually be a rule of the grammar. So, the prediction is that languages which have a regressive voicing assimilation process operating between syllables, like in Russian, must also have final devoicing.

The behavior of /v/ is not as exceptional as it appears to be in standard generative analyses of Russian. The reason it does not trigger voicing assimilation (cf. [svami]) is a consequence of the fact that Invariance prohibits feature values from being reinterpreted once they have received a phonetic interpretation. The peculiar behavior of /v/ word-finally is viewed as the result of a special category assignment for /v/. That is, it is necessary to assume that /v/ is a basic expression of category $(N\backslash N)\backslash(N\backslash N)$. This category and the rule of functional application are independently needed in the grammar to account for final clusters with sonorants. Within the categorial analysis I am proposing here, it is not necessary to derive [v]s from underlying sonorants, as Hayes does. We do not need to posit abstract underlying representations to account for the observed array of facts. With respect to the rules of the phonological syntax, /v/s pattern like sonorants because they are all associated with the category $(N\backslash N)\backslash(N\backslash N)$. Phonetically, syllable final /v/s behave just like other obstruents — they are interpreted as voiceless by the Universal Marking Conventions.

NOTES

* I would like to thank Emmon Bach, Jim Cathey, Greg Iverson, and especially Dick Oehrle for both their continued encouragement and their comments on earlier versions of this paper. All remaining errors are, of course, my own.

[1] Current work (Wheeler and Iverson (in preparation)) explores these topics in further detail.

[2] According to Lunt (1958), the traditional phonemic inventory of Russian includes:

   (i) five stressed vowels /í, é, á, ó, ú/
   (ii) three unstressed vowels /i, a, u/
   (iii) one glide /j/
   (iv) four liquids /l, l', r, r'/
   (v) four nasals /m, m', n, n'/
   (vi) eleven spirants /f, f', v, v', s, s', z, z', s, z, x/
   (vii) thirteen stops /p, p', b, b', t, t', d, d', c, c, k, k', g/

I am using /C'/ to represent palatalized consonants. The spreading of palatalization within consonant clusters will not be discussed.

[3] Ultimately, Hayes attempts to 'explain away' Sonorant Revoicing in terms of phonetic implementation and claims that it is not actually a rule of the phonology.

[4] The present paper was prepared for publication before I had seen the account of Russian Voicing Assimilation presented in Kiparsky (1986). Though housed within the otherwise quite different theory of Lexical Phonology, Kiparsky's analysis also makes crucial use of feature underspecification. Like Hayes, Kiparsky assumes that [v]s are derived from underlying /w/s.

[5] The problem Hayes discusses with respect to iterative application of segmental rules does not arise in the analysis being proposed here. There are independent reasons, to

488 DEIRDRE WHEELER

be discussed below, for why sonorants do not trigger the voicing assimilation process. Neither is it necessary to adopt a prosodic or autosegmental analysis as Hayes argues (following Halle and Vergnaud (1981)).

[6] In (19b) I have chosen to represent the onset of the initial syllable as $/ø/_{S/N}$ rather than complicate the grammar to allow for syllables without onsets (i.e. constituents of category N) to be syllables on their own. Nothing hinges on this assumption.

[7] In principle, since voicing is not distinctive in vowels either, they should be represented as /I, A, U, etc./. For clarity and ease of exposition, however, I will not do so here.

REFERENCES

Bach, E. and D. Wheeler: 1981, 'Montague Phonology: A Preliminary Account', in W. Chao and D. Wheeler (eds.), *University of Massachusetts Occasional Papers in Linguistics*, Vol. VII, pp. 27—45.
Chomsky, N. and M. Halle: 1968, *The Sound Pattern of English*, Harper and Row, New York.
Clements, G. N. and S. J. Keyser: 1981, *CV Phonology: A Generative Theory of Syllable Structure*, MIT Press, Cambridge, Mass.
Halle, M. and J.-R. Vergnaud: 1981, 'Harmony Processes', in W. Klein and W. Levelt (eds.), *Crossing the Boundaries in Linguistics*, D. Reidel Publishing Company, Dordrecht, pp. 1—22.
Hayes, B.: 1984, 'The Phonetics and Phonology of Russian Voicing Assimilation', in M. Aronoff and R. T. Oehrle (eds.), *Language Sound Structure*, MIT Press, Cambridge, Mass., pp. 318—328.
Hooper, J.: 1976, *An Introduction to Natural Generative Phonology*, Academic Press, New York.
Kiparsky, P.: 1979, 'Metrical Structure Assignment is Cyclic', *Linguistic Inquiry* **10**, 421—441.
Kiparsky, P.: 1986, 'Some Consequences of Lexical Phonology', in C. Ewin and J. Anderson (eds.), *Phonology Yearbook*, Vol. 2, Cambridge University Press, Cambridge, pp. 85—138.
Lunt, H.: 1958, *Fundamentals of Russian*, Mouton, The Hague.
Selkirk, E. O.: 1980, 'The Role of Prosodic Categories in English Word Stress', *Linguistic Inquiry* **11**, 563—606.
Selkirk, E. O.: 1984, 'On the Major Class Features and Syllable Theory', in M. Aronoff and R. T. Oehrle (eds.), *Language Sound Structure*, MIT Press, Cambridge, Mass., pp. 107—136.
Wheeler, D.: 1981, *Aspects of a Categorial Theory of Phonology*, Ph.D. dissertation, University of Massachusetts, Amherst. Distributed by the Graduate Linguistic Student Association, University of Massachusetts, Amherst.
Wheeler, D. and G. Iverson: (in preparation), 'Phonological Constituents and Categories'.

Dept. of Linguistics,
University of Iowa,
Iowa City, Iowa 52242, U.S.A.

INDEX OF NAMES

INDEX OF SUBJECTS

510   INDEX OF SUBJECTS

INDEX OF CATEGORIES AND FUNCTORS

STUDIES IN LINGUISTICS AND PHILOSOPHY

formerly *Synthese Language Library*

1. Henry Hiż (ed.), *Questions.*1978.
2. William S. Cooper, *Foundations of Logico-Linguistics. A Unified Theory of Information, Language, and Logic.* 1978.
3. Avishai Margalit (ed.), *Meaning and Use.* 1979.
4. F. Guenthner and S. J. Schmidt (eds.), *Formal Semantics and Pragmatics for Natural Languages.* 1978.
5. Esa Saarinen (ed.), *Game-Theoretical Semantics.* 1978.
6. F. J. Pelletier (ed.), *Mass Terms: Some Philosophical Problems.* 1979.
7. David R. Dowty, *Word Meaning and Montague Grammar. The Semantics of Verbs and Times in Generative Semantics and in Montague's PTQ.* 1979.
9. James McCloskey, *Transformational Syntax and Model Theoretic Semantics: A Case Study in Modern Irish.* 1979.
10. John R. Searle, Ferenc Kiefer, and Manfred Bierwisch (ed.), *Speech Act Theory and Pragmatics.* 1980.
11. David R. Dowty, Robert E. Wall, and Stanley Peters, *Introduction to Montague Semantics.* 1981.
12. Frank Heny (ed.), *Ambiguities in Intensional Contexts.*
13. Wolfgang Klein and Willem Levelt (eds.), *Crossing the Boundaries in Linguistics: Studies Presented to Manfred Bierwisch.* 1981.
14. Zellig S. harris, *Papers on Syntax,* edited by Henry Hiż. 1981.
15. Pauline Jacobson and Geoffrey K. Pullum (eds.), *The Nature of Syntactic Representation.* 1982.
16. Stanley Peters and Esa Saarinen (eds.), *Processes, Beliefs, and Questions.* 1982.
17. Lauri Carlson, *Dialogue Games. An Approach to Discourse Analysis.* 1983.
18. Lucia Vaina and Jaakko Hintikka (eds.), *Cognitive Constraints on Communication.* 1983.
19. Frank Heny and Barry Richards (eds.), *Linguistic Categories: Auxiliaries and Related Puzzles. Volume One: Categories.*
20. Frank Heny and Barry Richards (eds.), *Linguistic Categories: Auxiliaries and Related Puzzles. Volume Two: The Scope, Order, and Distribution of English Auxiliary Verbs.* 1983.
21. Robin Cooper, *Quantification and Syntactic Theory.* 1983.
22. Jaakko Hintikka and Jack Kulas, *The Game of Language.* 1983.
23. Edward L. Keenan and Leonard M. Faltz, *Bolean Semantics for Natural Language.* 1985.
24. Victor Raskin, *Semantic Mechanics of Humor,* 1985.
25. Gregory T. Stump, *The Semantic Variability of Absolute Constructions.* 1985.
26. Jaakko Hintikka and Jack Kulas, *Anaphora and Definite Descriptions.* 1985.
27. Elisabet Engdahl, *Constituent Questions,* 1985.

28. M. J. Cresswell, *Adverbial Modification*, 1985.
29. Johan van Benthem, *Essays in Logical Semantics*.
30. Barbara Partee, Alice ter Meulen, and Robert Wall (eds.), *Mathematical Methods in Linguistics*, 1987.
31. Peter Gärdenfors, *Generalized Quantifiers*, 1987
32. Richard T. Oehrle et al. (eds.), *Categorial Grammars and Natural Language Structures*, 1988.
33. Walter J. Savitch et al. (eds.), *The Formal Complexity of Natural Language*, 1987.
34. Jens Erik Fenstad et al., *Situations, Language and Logic*, 1987.
35. U. Reyle and C. Rohrer (eds.), *Natural Language Parsing and Linguistic Theories*, 1988.